Powered by Pyramids

Theories That Will Reshape History

(2nd Edition)

REBECCA MEIJLINK

Powered by Pyramids: Theories That Will Reshape History— 2025 - Rebecca Meijlink - All Rights Reserved

Legal Notice
This book is protected by copyright. It is intended for personal use only. You may not amend, distribute, sell, use, quote, or paraphrase any part of the content without the publisher's permission. The contents of this book cannot be reproduced, duplicated, or transmitted in any form or by any means, electronic or mechanical, including photocopying, recording, or any information storage and retrieval system, without the explicit written consent of the publisher and author.

Disclaimer Notice
This book contains speculative theories that are not factual and are meant solely for entertainment. Although the publisher and author have put their best effort into preparing it, they make no claims or warranties regarding the accuracy or completeness of its content and explicitly disavow any implied warranties.

ISBN: 978-1-0686258-2-4 (Paperback)
ISBN: 978-1-0686258-3-1 (Hardcover)
ISBN: 978-1-0686258-8-6 (E-book)
First edition 1.0 (22 September 2024), updated 2 August 2025
Publisher: AlphaBet Select Ltd, London, United Kingdom

All enquiries should be directed to the publisher, AlphaBet Select Ltd, London, United Kingdom. The publisher would be grateful to receive notification of any corrections to be included in future reprints or editions of the book. For our contact details, please visit our website at www.alphabetselect.com.

Table of Contents

TABLE OF CONTENTS 3
INTRODUCTION 5
CHAPTER 1 MODERN FASCINATION WITH PYRAMIDS 17
CHAPTER 2 PYRAMIDS ACROSS THE GLOBE 53
CHAPTER 3 SHARED KNOWLEDGE AND INFRASTRUCTURE 85
CHAPTER 4 THE MYSTERIES OF THE PYRAMIDS 105
CHAPTER 5 CONSTRUCTION OF THE PYRAMIDS 113
CHAPTER 6 WHAT LIES BENEATH THE PYRAMIDS AND WHERE ARE THE CAPSTONES 135
CHAPTER 7 CLUES GIVEN BY THE SPHINX AND OBELISK? 155
CHAPTER 8 THE DIFFICULTY OF DATING THE PYRAMIDS 177
CHAPTER 9 ALTERNATIVE ARCHITECTS 197
CHAPTER 10 ADVANCED MATHS AND ALIGNMENT WITH THE STARS 231
CHAPTER 11 PYRAMIDS GEOGRAPHICAL HOT SPOTS 245
CHAPTER 12 VOLCANOES AND PYRAMIDS: A COMPARISON 259
CHAPTER 13 EARTH ENERGIES AND NATURAL FORCES 269
CHAPTER 14 HOW ANCIENT CIVILISATIONS UNDERSTOOD ENERGY 285
CHAPTER 15 HARNESSING ENERGY ACROSS THE GLOBE 293
CHAPTER 16 THE PYRAMID IN OCCULT MYSTICISM 299
CHAPTER 17 FUNERARY AND SPIRITUAL FUNCTIONS 309
CHAPTER 18 GATEWAY TO THE SECRETS OF THE UNIVERSE 323
CHAPTER 19 HEALING POWER AND LIFE PRESERVATION 341
CHAPTER 20 CENTRAL UTILITY HUB 365
CHAPTER 21 GLOBAL TRANSPORTATION SYSTEM 383
CHAPTER 22 CLIMATE CONTROL AND RESOURCE TRANSFORMATION 395
CHAPTER 23 MODERN TECHNOLOGY TO UNLOCK ANCIENT SECRETS 411
CHAPTER 24 TAPPING INTO EARTH'S ENERGY IN DAILY LIFE 425
CHAPTER 25 PYRAMID POWER FOR A SUSTAINABLE FUTURE 437
CHAPTER 26 GUARDIANS OF THE PYRAMIDS 449
CHAPTER 27 THE PULSE BENEATH THE STONES: FINAL THOUGHTS 467
END NOTES 471

The Pulse Beneath the Stone

Beneath the sky, the pyramids rise,
Not just as tombs, but ancient eyes.
They watch the Earth, they channel light,
Silent sentinels through day and night.

Built on ley lines, where energies hum,
Their mysteries whispered by the Earth's drum.
Like volcanoes of stone, they shape and guide,
Harnessing power from deep inside.

From Giza's sands to the jungle's heart,
The ancients knew where worlds could start.
In every block, a secret untold,
Of forces that ripple, of wisdom bold.

Not just relics of long-lost days,
They hold the key to forgotten ways.
Through stone and stars, through fire and flame,
Pyramids whisper an eternal name.

Introduction

For centuries, pyramids have fascinated explorers and archaeologists alike. In the 19th century, Sir Flinders Petrie, a British Egyptologist, was the first to systematically measure the Great Pyramid of Giza, as published in *The Pyramids and Temples of Gizeh (1883)*. He determined the precise dimensions of the pyramid's base, height, and inclination angle. He discovered that the Great Pyramid was aligned almost perfectly with the cardinal directions (north, south, east, and west). This level of precision in alignment was a remarkable discovery, indicating that the ancient Egyptians possessed a sophisticated understanding of astronomy and geometry. He observed that the stone blocks used in the pyramids were cut with incredible accuracy. This led him to speculate on the advanced tools or methods that might have been used for construction. He was also among those who recorded the precision of the casing stones that once covered the Great Pyramid. He noted that the stones were fitted together with an incredible degree of accuracy.[i]

Sir Flinders Petrie's precise measurements and findings sparked speculation and renewed interest among scientists and researchers. His work challenged long-held assumptions about ancient Egyptian engineering and astronomy. Many began to question whether the pyramids served purposes beyond mere tombs. These questions fuelled theories related to energy harnessing, advanced technologies, and even potential connections to astronomy or extraterrestrial involvement. His work revitalised academic interest in the pyramids, encouraging archaeologists, astronomers, and engineers to re-examine these ancient structures through the lens of modern science, pushing boundaries on what ancient civilisations might have known. This laid the foundation for more speculative theories while reinforcing scientific rigour in studying Egypt's great monuments.

This *Book of Theories* explores the mysteries of the pyramids in depth, challenging accepted beliefs. Could these ancient wonders have been designed to harness and amplify the Earth's geothermal and electromagnetic forces, similar to volcanoes? Were the pyramids intentionally located along lines rich in tectonic and electromagnetic activity? Could the ancient Egyptians have understood the unique properties of materials like limestone and granite—known for their conductive abilities—and used them to construct structures capable of harnessing the planet's energy? What if the pyramids were not just tombs but gateways to untapped energies?

For millennia, pyramids have served as symbols of human ingenuity and mystery. From the Great Pyramid of Giza to the pyramids concealed within the jungles of Mesoamerica, their remarkably similar design raises an intriguing question. How could civilisations so far apart create such strikingly similar structures without any known connection? The mysteries of the pyramids continue to fascinate, prompting us to look beyond conventional explanations and to give greater credit to the extraordinary ingenuity of our ancestors.

From a young age, we are taught in schools that human history is a linear progression of evolution, with each generation becoming more intelligent and technologically advanced. This narrative reinforces the notion that we are currently at the pinnacle of intelligence. However, when we examine the wonders of ancient civilisations—such as the Great Pyramids of Giza, the construction of Stonehenge, or the advanced urban planning of the Indus Valley—it becomes clear that knowledge has been lost. Replicating these magnificent constructions today, even with modern technology, would be incredibly difficult. With allegedly fewer tools and resources, these societies achieved astonishing architectural and engineering marvels that still baffle experts today. It forces us to reconsider whether our evolutionary narrative of ever-increasing intelligence and technologies is accurate or whether we have lost touch with some of the profound wisdom and ingenuity of the ancients. Perhaps they understood aspects of the world in ways we have yet to rediscover.

This book unravels the ancient knowledge and hidden science behind these colossal structures, suggesting they may have been engineered to tap into Earth's geothermal and electromagnetic forces. The possibilities are mind-blowing! Imagine a civilisation thousands of years ago tapping into the Earth's natural energies with precision and sophistication. If true, this would revolutionise our understanding of ancient technologies and knowledge of geology and physics. The pyramids' alignment with celestial bodies is well-documented. New findings suggest an even deeper connection with the planet. It is as if they had a blueprint of the Earth's energy grid and strategically positioned these monumental structures to interact with it.

In the early 20th century, followers of Nikola Tesla's work about the possibilities of transmitting free energy wirelessly[ii] speculated that the Great Pyramid might have served as a colossal energy transmitter. Nikola Tesla proposed that the Earth could be used as a resonant cavity to transmit energy wirelessly using natural frequencies, like a global tuning fork. Could the Great Pyramid of Giza have been built on the same principles as a gigantic harmonic energy generator? Mainstream academia dismissed such ideas at the time. Early 20th-century Egyptology was dominated by imperial British and French scholars who may have viewed ancient cultures as primitive. Suggesting that the Egyptians had advanced energy tech challenged Western supremacy. Calling the pyramid a tomb kept things simple and politically advantageous. It didn't require challenging religion, science, or historical timelines.

Today, renewed interest in the Great Pyramid's true function is being fueled by breakthroughs in modern technology and a growing willingness to challenge outdated academic assumptions. Tools like magnetometers, ground-penetrating radar, and resonance sensors have detected unusual electromagnetic and vibrational anomalies at sacred sites, especially the Great Pyramid, suggesting it may have functioned as more than a tomb. Electromagnetic and acoustic studies now indicate that the pyramid amplifies specific frequencies, while engineers reexamine water-powered theories involving underground aquifers, piezoelectric materials, and energy generation. With no mummies ever found inside, and architectural features that appear functional rather than ceremonial, the traditional "tomb theory" is no longer enough to explain the structure's complexity. As a result, scientists, independent researchers, and engineers are revisiting the radical possibility that the Great Pyramid was once part of an advanced energy system—perhaps even a colossal natural power plant.

We will re-examine history and open avenues for further exploration. Our journey will be multidisciplinary. We will investigate ancient texts, mythology, archaeology, occult mysticism, and modern research, all of which suggest that the pyramids may have been more than mere monuments. They may be critical in understanding a forgotten science of energy manipulation, a science that connected the Earth to the cosmos. From the temples of Mexico's Kukulkan to the pyramids of Sudan and beyond, we will explore the possibility that these sites were chosen for their unique energetic properties and aligned with celestial bodies to enhance their power. Did they have an advanced understanding of natural forces? Perhaps the pyramids we find worldwide were part of an ancient network designed to channel the Earth's energy. What if the ancients had mastered techniques to regulate the energy beneath their feet or from the skies, using the pyramids' shape to create a controlled energy flow?

Prepare to challenge everything you thought you knew about these structures. Keep one question in mind as you read: Are we rediscovering ancient wisdom that predates our modern understanding of life and death, as well as science and technology? The answers may lie within the pyramids and their connections to the universe, waiting for us to unlock their secrets.

Many of the theories presented in this book are speculative, intentionally designed to entertain, challenge conventional thinking, and push the boundaries of what we believe is possible. They are exploratory rather than definitive.

Science is about continuous questioning, experimentation, and discovery. It operates with the understanding that any theory remains speculative until solid evidence proves or supports it. This doesn't mean dismissing it entirely, but putting it on hold until more information confirms or rejects the theory. The demand for proof should encourage ideas and ensure that what we accept as accurate has undergone rigorous scrutiny. Applying the *innocent until proven guilty* principle to science means that, theoretically, all ideas should be treated as innocent and open to investigation and exploration. However, science is more akin to a *guilty until proven innocent* approach. Proven research prevails, and the burden of proof rests on the new theory to show its validity through evidence. This doesn't mean the theory is dismissed outright; it must present evidence to be accepted. Both scepticism and openness are necessary in science. Dismissing theories too quickly can prevent the exploration of new possibilities. However, accepting unproven theories without evidence can lead to the dissemination of misinformation. A balanced approach is needed to keep an open mind to unproven theories while seeking ways to test and validate them. Science should not fear unproven ideas, but it must guard against embracing ideas that lack critical evidence. In this sense, entertaining possibilities, such as those explored in this book about pyramids and the Earth's energy, can lead to innovation and a more profound understanding. Still, the need for proof ensures that the knowledge we build is reliable and robust. It's about finding the right balance between exploration and evidence.

Bringing new ideas to light is often challenging, particularly when large corporate interests and government agendas dominate the funding and research landscape. These powerful corporate entities tend to prioritise profit-driven initiatives and resist disruption that could render their products or services obsolete. Similarly, the government aims to preserve its narrative and authority. Such forces leave little space for unconventional or groundbreaking theories to develop. We live in a managed reality. Consequently, independent researchers and innovators often struggle to secure the resources needed to explore new possibilities. This results in a bottleneck where potentially revolutionary ideas, especially those challenging mainstream science or political interests, remain underfunded, undervalued, and in some cases ridiculed.

The movie *Indiana Jones and the Kingdom of the Crystal Skull* (2008) explores ancient ruins around the world. It blends archaeology with speculative fiction. Directed by Steven Spielberg and produced by George Lucas, the film introduces themes of extraterrestrial influence and hidden knowledge.[iii] Similarly, my quest aims to unveil possibilities of an ancient understanding of Planet Earth and connections to the cosmos. While many ideas in this book are speculative and may lack concrete scientific backing, they offer alternative perspectives on the world. We will explore and connect the dots between different eras and disciplines. This may provoke curiosity and invite readers to question long-held assumptions about ancient civilisations and the purpose of pyramids.

In this book, I will bring theories that are often overlooked to the forefront, challenging the conventional reliance on archaeology and science as the sole authorities in discussions about ancient civilisations and structures. Archaeology typically dominates mainstream narratives, forming the foundation for accepted historical interpretations. Science closely follows, particularly when it supports or explains archaeological findings through geology, astronomy, or material analysis. However, mythology—rich with cultural context and symbolic insights—often plays a supplementary role, viewed more as symbolic than literal evidence. Similarly, experiments, such as recreating ancient techniques or testing theories related to energy and materials, offer valuable insights but are considered secondary.

Despite their potential to captivate and provoke thought, speculative theories receive minimal credibility in mainstream discussions. This book aims to shift that perspective by highlighting and exploring these alternative theories. This book is not an attempt to prove or disprove any specific theory. The book's speculative nature encourages readers to think beyond conventional narratives. It explores the wide range of ideas shared, discussed, and debated over time. My goal in writing *Powered by Pyramids: A Book of Theories* is to present a collection of intriguing possibilities—ideas I have encountered, heard, and found compelling during my decades of research. While not all of these theories are supported by scientific evidence, they serve as a starting point for further exploration. This book is designed to challenge mainstream assumptions, spark curiosity, and encourage readers to think critically and ask questions. I encourage you to research and perhaps even uncover new secrets that could benefit mankind.

I chose *Powered by Pyramids: A Book of Theories* as a title because it encapsulates the idea that the pyramids may have served a far greater purpose than we traditionally understand. Rather than merely standing as monumental tombs, this title suggests that pyramids were dynamic energy sources—whether through harnessing the Earth's natural forces, like geothermal or electromagnetic energy, or perhaps through more mystical means. The word "*Powered*" symbolises the literal and metaphorical power these structures could have generated, driving ancient civilisations forward with knowledge that may have been lost over time. The title *Powered by Pyramids* also alludes to the broader scope of ideas for which the pyramids serve as a springboard. In many ways, the pyramids serve as an intellectual gateway, almost an excuse, to delve into various speculative and interconnected concepts that have fascinated me. The title reflects the multifaceted nature of the book, in which the pyramids catalyse exploring a much larger set of possibilities. Using pyramids as the focal point, the book taps into ideas that challenge mainstream understanding and invites readers to think beyond conventional limits. The subtitle, "*A Book of Theories*," reflects the speculative nature of the content, inviting readers to explore the ideas presented with an open mind and challenge established narratives, while sparking curiosity about what the pyramids truly represent.

I want to encourage more people to question the mainstream narratives and dig deeper. The traditional model of schooling was primarily designed for an industrial world. The current structure of education, emphasising uniformity, obedience, and standardised procedures, originated during the Industrial Revolution. At that time, the primary goal of mass education was to prepare students for factory work, which required punctuality, adherence to routines, and the ability to follow instructions without questioning authority. This approach aimed to create a workforce that could function efficiently within factories and industries' mechanised, hierarchical systems. The focus on memorisation and standardised processes and timelines mirrored the needs of industrial jobs, where repetitive tasks were the norm and creative or critical thinking was unnecessary. There was a tendency to stifle curiosity and discourage questioning. Schools became more focused on instilling basic literacy and discipline than on fostering independent thought or problem-solving skills. This system effectively produced workers who could fit seamlessly into the roles that industrial society demanded.

For example, why is history taught with emphasis on the exact dates of events? Why the need for exams? Memorisation of dates, trains, and clock obedience. Students are taught to internalise external timing mechanisms such as bells, shift changes, appointment slots and deadlines. Linear timelines control the narrative and diminish multidimensional thinking. We are taught that 'truth' is what is printed and tested, rather than what is discovered or questioned. The obsession with dates can obscure meaning and lead to a superficial understanding. Dates in history taught are not neutral. They are tools of behaviour engineering. Are there other ways of teaching history? Yes, for example, the Mayan, Aboriginal, Vedic, and Andean traditions teach about mythical or cyclical time. Time is based on natural phenomena, including solstices, harvest, and celestial alignment. Storytelling, not dates, preserves knowledge. There is no obsession with dates but rather an alignment with natural rhythms. The ancient Maya tracked more than 17 calendars simultaneously, including linear, ritual, agricultural, and astronomical calendars. They did not compress time into a single linear string. This leads me to wonder, do timelines exist, or are they fabricated mental constructs? Are they tools, rather than truths? Are there perhaps parallel timelines in dreams, psychedelics and quantum mechanics? Is time an illusion? Understanding how we have been programmed opens us up to explore other possibilities.

As the world is developing into an era driven by information, technology, and robotics, the limitations of this industrial-era model have become clear. AI, robotics, and automation will replace most repetitive cognitive and manual tasks. No memorisation is needed as information is instantly accessible. Will human uniqueness lie in creativity, ethics, multidimensional thinking, and emotional intelligence? AI can also perform these, potentially eliminating human uniqueness. However, AI can only remix what it has been taught. Humans can generate ideas through intuition, revelatory states, and possibly even spiritual dimensions. Should these subjects be included in school curricula, or will we become domesticated into obedient bio-assets controlled by machines? Cyrus Parsa, founder of The AI Organization, warns that the rise of artificial intelligence is not merely a technological advancement. It poses an existential threat to human consciousness. He contends that AI, especially when combined with quantum computing, facial recognition, neural interfaces, and 5G/6G infrastructure, can be used to remap perception, predict behaviour, and influence thought at a subconscious level. He argues that such technology, developed without ethical or spiritual considerations, may serve not humanity but an anti-human intelligence—one that deconstructs identity, dissolves intuition, and replaces the organic soul with programmable code.[iv]

Modern society, therefore, increasingly requires individuals who can think critically, adapt to change, and engage in creative problem-solving—qualities that the traditional, industrial-era education system was not designed to cultivate. This critique echoes throughout discussions on educational reform. In environments where questioning is stifled, students learn to accept information at face value, which can hinder their ability to innovate, think independently, and navigate complex situations as adults. To truly prepare individuals for life, education must evolve to prioritise inquiry, curiosity, and the development of practical life skills, encouraging students to challenge assumptions and think critically about the world around them. Many schools are shifting towards inquiry-based learning, where students are encouraged to ask questions, explore problems, and seek solutions through research and experimentation. This approach nurtures curiosity and develops skills in critical analysis and independent thinking. Modern educational practices increasingly incorporate group discussions, debates, and collaborative activities that help students learn to articulate their thoughts, consider diverse perspectives, and construct sound arguments. This method encourages students to question information, synthesise diverse viewpoints, and develop stronger reasoning skills.

While studying the pyramids, we can draw lessons from Socrates' teachings. Socrates is famously known for teaching people to question everything, a method that became known as the *Socratic method*. His approach to philosophy involved asking probing questions to challenge assumptions, expose contradictions, and lead to deeper understanding. His method encourages critical thinking, self-reflection, and the pursuit of truth by questioning external authorities and one's beliefs and ideas. He believed that wisdom begins with recognising one's ignorance. He often said, *"I know that I know nothing,"* emphasising humility and the continuous pursuit of knowledge.

Inspired by Socrates' method of questioning, we can apply the same approach to the pyramids, urging ourselves to rethink everything we assume about these ancient structures and to reexamine the evidence. What if the pyramids were more than monumental tombs? Could they have served as energy machines, connecting Earth with the cosmos in ways we don't yet understand? Why were they constructed with such precise geometry, and why does their design appear across seemingly unconnected civilisations? By questioning these assumptions, we open the door to deeper exploration: Were the pyramids part of an ancient technological system lost to time? Did they have any other functions beyond burial sites? What was the role of the Sphinx and the obelisks? Could the missing capstones have been crucial in this ancient operating system? The answers lie not in accepting the conventional narrative but in continuing to challenge our understanding, just as Socrates taught, wisdom begins with acknowledging how little we truly know.

Powered by Pyramids: A Book of Theories

What we call education today is often a system for transmitting consensus reality aimed at producing predictable outcomes. However, in the ancient world, true education was not about information; it was about transformation. The pyramid was not a school in the modern sense; it was an initiatory structure designed to deconstruct the ego and reassemble the being. From this perspective, education was a sacred process—an alignment with cosmic law rather than a list of facts. The initiate did not simply receive a diploma, but gained a new identity attuned to higher laws. Modern schooling, by contrast, frequently serves to reinforce the illusion of separateness and authority. If the pyramid contained knowledge, it was not in words but in resonance. Its chambers whispered truths too vast for textbooks. Perhaps the greatest mystery is not what the ancients knew, but how they conveyed it—through vibration, symbol, and silent transmission.

The mysteries of the pyramids hold a special place in our collective consciousness. Whether constructed by ancient civilisations with advanced technologies, by long-forgotten cultures, or through means still beyond our understanding, they inspire us to seek answers. I hope this book sparks that same sense of wonder in you, encouraging further discovery and deep reflection on the remaining mysteries. Prepare to see the pyramids not just as relics of the past, but as keys to a deeper understanding of the planet's energy, its connection to the universe, and the ancient knowledge that has been lost.

Modern scientific tools, such as ground-penetrating radar and satellite imaging, continue to unlock the mysteries of the pyramids. It is revolutionising archaeology. New pyramids are being discovered in the oceans and the jungles. AI enables archaeologists to analyse large datasets, revealing patterns and trends that might have been overlooked in traditional studies. There is a shift towards incorporating multiple perspectives and voices in archaeological interpretation. It is no longer about digging to find a tomb but about discovering our history and lost knowledge. A quote by Jules Verne (1828-1905), a French novelist often called the Father of Science Fiction, says, "*The pyramids rise like eternal question marks, daring us to unlock their mysteries*". As technology advances, our ability to peer into the past is enhanced. With each revelation comes the humbling realisation of how little we truly know. Each discovery challenges conventional timelines and invites us to rethink what was once confidently established as historical facts.

The unconfirmed 2025 discovery, made using advanced Synthetic Aperture Radar (SAR) imaging, may represent a pivotal moment in pyramid research. The data, emerging from a collaborative study led by Professor Corrado Malanga of Italy's University of Pisa and Filippo Biondi of the University of Strathclyde in Scotland, revealed something long speculated but never before substantiated beneath the Giza Plateau. Using SAR to penetrate layers impervious to traditional excavation, the team detected eight vast cylindrical structures, spiralled with geometric pathways, extending more than 648 meters below the surface and connected to two immense square formations. These anomalies, symmetrical, engineered, and deeply buried, suggest a level of intentional design that radically challenges prevailing archaeological narratives. If verified, this finding could reshape our perception of the pyramids, not as isolated monuments, but as surface "caps" atop a massive subterranean system. Whether components of an ancient energy grid, a lost architectural technology, or remnants of a forgotten civilisation, these formations invite a profound reconsideration of the pyramids' true function, purpose, and scale.

Social media discourse shows a mix of wonder, scepticism, and curiosity. While the appeal of uncovering hidden secrets beneath the pyramids interests many, the community also stresses the importance of scientific rigour and credible evidence. As discussions progress, we all eagerly await further research and official statements to illuminate these fascinating claims.

These vast underground structures suggest that the architects may not have been the Egyptians traditionally credited. Their complexity, precision, and immense scale could indicate the work of an ancient, advanced civilisation lost to history—perhaps survivors from Atlantis, advanced human ancestors, or even extraterrestrial visitors who shared knowledge with humanity. Mainstream explanations involving copper chisels and primitive ramps now seem even less plausible. The intricate cylindrical spirals and extensive chambers hundreds of metres below the surface imply construction methods far beyond our current understanding. Could these structures have been created using acoustic levitation, advanced geopolymer technologies, or some forgotten energy manipulation? Such colossal and complex underground engineering suggests a timeline much older than modern archaeology typically recognises. Instead of being only 4,500 years old, these chambers might date back tens of thousands of years, aligning with geological and astronomical evidence some alternative historians have already proposed. Their purpose appears to go beyond simple tombs or ceremonial sites. The underground complexes, geometric pathways, and interconnected large chambers strongly imply a functional system—potentially a sophisticated energy technology designed to harness Earth's electromagnetic fields, geothermal energy, or cosmic forces. They may have served as power plants, teleportation hubs, advanced communication networks, or repositories for ancient knowledge.

This discovery could mark the moment when theory becomes revelation. This new finding is not just about archaeology; it's about uncovering secrets that could redefine our understanding of human history, technology, and possibly even our origins. The mainstream dismissals may be evidence that we are on the verge of something monumental. The immediate rejection by prominent archaeologists and mainstream media as "fake news" could suggest deliberate suppression. Powerful institutions might fear that revealing such profound knowledge could disrupt modern society, power structures, or belief systems. Future generations may look back on our era and wonder how we ever doubted the skill and ingenuity of those who came before us.

This book suggests that we are not simply progressing forward linearly, but reliving a cyclical process in which knowledge is periodically lost and gradually reclaimed. Modern technological achievement, in this context, is not the pinnacle of progress, but a cautious re-ascent toward an ancient summit we have begun to remember. The simple triangular shape of a pyramid, often seen as just a geometric form, may represent something much deeper: the repeating cycle of human experience. Its three points can be viewed as birth, the peak of awareness, and the eventual decline into forgetfulness. In this way, the pyramid becomes a symbol of the journey we all take: rising toward knowledge and insight, reaching a moment of clarity, and then slipping into distraction, decay, or disconnection—until the cycle begins again. Rather than being just a monument to the dead, the pyramids could be a monument for the living, a timeless reminder of how we rise, fall, and are reborn, over and over.

Powered by Pyramids: A Book of Theories

Chapter 1 Modern Fascination with Pyramids

When I started writing this book, the first question I asked myself was why I am so fascinated by the pyramids and why we see so many references to pyramids in our daily lives. What influence do they exert on us? These ancient structures appear in our films, literature, architecture, and logos, symbolising everything from power and mystery to spirituality and transcendence. Pyramids have an almost uncanny ability to captivate our imaginations, representing something beyond their physical form. They serve as gateways to questions about our past, spirituality, and the universe. We explore this fascination by examining the origins of their symbolism and their continual presence across different cultures. Pyramids embody the human desire to connect with something greater, to seek the unknown, and to find meaning in the vast cosmos. They have become ultimate icons of humanity's quest for understanding and transcendence—monuments that stand as both a link to the past and a bridge to future mysteries. The pyramid's form has become a vessel for vastly different symbolic meanings across eras. Are pyramids encoded in a universal unconscious, are our brains hardwired to respond to pyramids, or are pyramids instead culturally reinforced through storytelling, education, and media repetition?

To understand the pyramid's enduring grip on the human imagination, we can trace its symbolic evolution through seven distinct phases. *Phase 1: Sacred Utility* defines its original purpose—serving as a tomb, temple, or cosmic ladder in civilizations like Egypt and Mesoamerica. *Phase 2: Mythologised Memory* began when Greek, Roman, and medieval thinkers reinterpreted pyramids as mystical relics built by gods, giants, or magicians. *Phase 3: Colonial Fascination* arose during the Napoleonic campaigns, when European explorers, equipped with printing presses and exoticised narratives, transformed the pyramid into an imperial trophy and intellectual puzzle. *Phase 4: Esoteric Explosion* followed in the 19th and early 20th centuries, when occultists and mystics regarded pyramids as vessels of cosmic energy and secret wisdom. *Phase 5: Media Meme* popularised the pyramid in modern consciousness through films, logos, and conspiracy theories, reducing it to a shorthand for power, control, and mystery. *Phase 6: Spiritual Interface* saw New Age and metaphysical movements adopt the pyramid as a symbol of self-actualisation, chakras, and energetic ascent. Finally, *Phase 7: Algorithmic Amplification* describes how digital platforms such as YouTube, TikTok, and podcasting giants like *The Joe Rogan Experience* have weaponised the pyramid's mystique for mass fascination, blending ancient symbolism with algorithm-driven virality. This chapter explores how and why the pyramid, unlike any other symbol, continues to shape our collective psyche across centuries and platforms.

The Pyramid: A Universal Symbol

Joseph Campbell's theories on universal themes and symbols offer an insightful framework for understanding how the pyramid, as a symbol, transcends both time and place. In his influential work *The Hero with a Thousand Faces* (1949), he introduces the concept of archetypes—recurring symbols or motifs that appear in myths across cultures, representing key aspects of human existence. [v] These archetypes reflect fundamental truths about the human experience. They serve as a common thread, linking different cultures through shared narratives.[vi]

With its geometric precision and towering form, the pyramid can be viewed as an archetype of spiritual ascent. Its sloping sides and pointed peaks symbolise a journey from the earthly material world to the heavens, bridging humanity and the divine. In many ancient cultures, pyramids represented more than just physical structures; they were metaphysical symbols of power, transformation, and the pursuit of higher knowledge. Its symbolism reflects the timeless human quest for meaning and transcendence.[vii]

The *hero's journey*, as defined by Joseph Campbell, is a universal narrative pattern divided into three stages: Departure, Initiation, and Return. In the departure, the hero begins in the ordinary world and is called to adventure, often reluctantly crossing into the new, unknown. During initiation, the hero faces trials, temptations, and crises, often with the help of mentors or allies, which ultimately lead to personal transformation. Finally, when returning, the hero brings newfound wisdom or power back to the ordinary world, overcoming obstacles on the journey home and sharing knowledge with others.[viii]

He believed this framework represents core psychological and spiritual experiences shared across cultures, forming a structure that has influenced modern storytelling. Across various cultures, the pyramid's architectural design mirrors this metaphorical ascent, whether in ancient Egypt, where the pharaohs believed they were ascending to join the gods, or in Mesoamerican civilisations, where pyramids were sites of religious ceremonies invoking divine connection.[ix]

His work helps explain why the pyramid symbol endures—because it resonates with a shared human understanding of the world, reflecting our deep-seated need to explore, understand, and transcend the material realm. His ideas have shaped the way audiences engage with media, adding new depth to the analysis of films, books, and television series. His insights into the power of myth have made it easier for creators to tap into universal themes, resonating with audiences from diverse backgrounds and cultures.

An example is *The Matrix* (1999), where his ideas are prevalent throughout the film. The *Call to Adventure* occurs when Neo, a computer hacker, is approached by Morpheus, who reveals that Neo is living in a false reality and offers him the chance to wake up to the truth. In the *Refusal of the Call*, Neo is initially reluctant to accept that his world is an illusion and hesitates to trust Morpheus. However, in the *Crossing the Threshold*, Neo takes the red pill, breaking free from the Matrix and entering the real world for the first time. Morpheus becomes Neo's *Mentor Figure*, guiding and teaching him about the real world and the Matrix, much like Joseph Campbell's concept of the mentor in the hero's journey. Neo then faces *Trials and Transformation* as he learns to bend the rules of the Matrix and develops his powers, eventually realising his role as *The One*. Finally, Neo's *Return with the Elixir* occurs when he returns to the Matrix, now fully empowered and ready to free humanity, completing his hero's journey as described by Joseph Campbell.

Carl Jung was the first to define archetypes as we understand them today, particularly in the context of psychology, symbolism, and shared human experience. Carl Jung was a Swiss psychiatrist and psychoanalyst in the early 20th century. He introduced archetypes as part of his theory of the collective unconscious—a universal layer of the unconscious mind shared by all humans. He believed that archetypes are innate, universal symbols or patterns that emerge across cultures and are present in myths, dreams, and various forms of art. However, the idea of archetypal themes and characters goes back even further. Philosophers like Plato discussed universal or *ideal forms* in ancient Greece, suggesting that specific perfect versions of objects or ideas exist in an abstract, ideal realm, which inspired later thinkers. Plato's "forms" were not archetypes in the psychological sense, but his ideas laid the early groundwork for the concept of universal symbols.

In modern media, the pyramid continues to evoke themes of power and mystery. Films, literature, and documentaries often portray pyramids as containing hidden knowledge, spiritual secrets, or even extraterrestrial origins, drawing on their ancient symbolic power. Whether as tombs for revered leaders, symbols of cosmic alignment, or gateways to otherworldly dimensions, pyramids remain culturally relevant because they encapsulate universal themes of transformation, discovery, and connection to the cosmos. American writer Mark Twain (1835-1910) once said, "*The Egyptian pyramids are the first great works of fiction—stories set in stone.*" [x]

The Evolution of Pyramid Representation in Literature and Media

The pyramids have captivated the imagination for centuries and featured prominently in stories, myths, and legends passed down through generations. From ancient inscriptions on stone tablets and papyrus scrolls to medieval pamphlets and travelogues, these colossal structures have been the subjects of fascination and speculation.

The pyramids have been depicted as sacred monuments, sources of mystical power, or even as creations of gods and giants. This enduring presence in many cultures' written and oral traditions reflects a collective curiosity and reverence for the pyramids, which have continued to inspire artists, writers, and explorers throughout history. As our understanding of the pyramids evolved, so did their portrayal in literature, media, and visual art, shaping the perception of these ancient wonders over time.

Ancient Egyptian hieroglyphs, such as those found in the Pyramid Texts of Saqqara, dating back to the Old Kingdom, describe these colossal structures as tombs and gateways for the pharaohs' souls to ascend to the afterlife.[xi] In Greek mythology, the pyramids were often reinterpreted as mystical structures created by powerful beings such as gods or ancient heroes.[xii] Later Roman historians speculated on their builders, attributing their construction to a race of giants or a lost civilisation with extraordinary powers.[xiii]

In medieval Europe, knowledge of the pyramids filtered through Arabic sources, such as the writings of Al-Maqrizi, a 14th-century Egyptian historian, who documented local legends that claimed ancient magicians built the pyramids to store wisdom and treasures against an impending apocalypse.[xiv] These accounts, often copied into manuscripts and passed along trade routes, fascinated scholars and travellers, fueling their imaginations. Could the magic have been misunderstood technologies?

In his 14th-century travelogue, Sir John Mandeville's *Travels* (c. *1356–1371)*, he described the pyramids as "wonders beyond the art of man," claiming that supernatural giants had constructed them.[xv]

Though brief, his account of the Sphinx painted it as a mysterious and imposing figure guarding these ancient structures. Although his descriptions blended myth and fantasy, they fueled European curiosity about Egypt's ancient monuments.

Remember that, because reading and writing were not widespread, and mass production of texts was not yet possible, many stories about the pyramids were handed down orally. In ancient Egypt, Greece, and Rome, papyrus was widely used for writing, serving as official records and personal correspondence, as well as for shorter texts such as pamphlets.[xvi] In medieval Europe, parchment and vellum, made from animal skin, became the typical materials for manuscripts. Though more expensive and labour-intensive, they were durable and could be folded or bound for distribution.[xvii] In Asia, particularly in China, woodblock and stamp printing on paper allowed for the limited production of texts resembling pamphlets.[xviii] Meanwhile, in Europe, scribes and monks would hand-copy texts onto parchment or vellum, and smaller works intended for broader circulation were sometimes shared as loose pages, functioning similarly to early pamphlets.[xix]

The advent of printing technology in the 15th century enabled tales about the pyramids to reach a broader audience, further solidifying the pyramids' place in Europe's cultural consciousness. It is believed that Johannes Gutenberg invented the printing press, revolutionising book production around 1440 in Mainz, Germany. His invention allowed for the mass production of books and the democratisation of knowledge. Although printing technology existed in other forms, such as in China and Korea, the development of his mechanical-type movable printing system is considered a turning point in the Western world's written history. His innovation significantly increased the accessibility of knowledge, spreading literacy.[xx]

Several European travellers and scholars before the 18th century provided vivid yet often speculative accounts of Egypt's most iconic monuments, including the pyramids, the sphinx, and the obelisks. Western fascination with Egypt grew as the Renaissance unfolded, from the 14th to the 17th century, and pamphlets about the pyramids circulated widely. These pamphlets speculated on the pyramids' divine and mystical origins, often linking them to biblical stories, such as the Tower of Babel, or attributing their construction to ancient sages who possessed lost magical knowledge.[xxi]

In the early 16th century, a Moroccan scholar, Leo Africanus, documented his journey through Egypt in *Description of Africa* (1526), offering more grounded but equally captivating observations. He marvelled at the size and precision of the pyramids, describing them as *"great marvels of human ingenuity,"* and noted the symbolic significance of the obelisks, which he saw as "*pillars pointing toward the heavens*" to honour the sun god.[xxii] His accounts of these colossal structures were among the most detailed, significantly contributing to Europe's understanding of Egypt's ancient grandeur.

Athanasius Kircher, a 17th-century German Jesuit scholar, took a different approach in his work *Oedipus Aegyptiacus* (1652), attempting to decipher Egyptian hieroglyphs and uncover the meaning behind Egypt's monuments.[xxiii] He offered elaborate illustrations of the pyramids and obelisks, claiming that the pyramids served as great reservoirs of ancient wisdom and that the hieroglyphs contained mystical knowledge. The Egyptians used hieroglyphs for religious texts, inscriptions on monuments, and in tombs. Each symbol could represent a word, a syllable, or a sound.[xxiv] He also speculated that the Sphinx symbolised the union of divine and human nature, reflecting Egypt's spiritual depth. By interpreting the Sphinx in Egypt—a figure with a human head and a lion's body—as a symbol of merging divine qualities of power with human intellect and consciousness, he suggested that the Egyptians saw humanity as connected to divine forces.[xxv] Though some may say it is inaccurate, his imaginative work captivated European audiences and kept the fascination with Egypt's enigmatic architecture alive.

By the 19th century, however, pyramids became subjects of scientific inquiry as scholars and explorers sought to uncover their true purpose and origins. Yet, even as scientific curiosity grew, the pyramids remained intertwined with romantic and esoteric interpretations, preserving their status as symbols of fascination and mystery.[xxvi]

In the early 19th century, newspapers and illustrated magazines began to bring stories of archaeological expeditions and discoveries in Egypt to a broader audience. Explorations by Napoleon's scholars during his campaign in Egypt (1798-1801) fascinated European readers, and Napoleon's *Description de l'Égypte*, published between 1809 and 1829, became a massive success. This monumental work included detailed descriptions, drawings, and studies of Egypt's ancient architecture, natural history, and culture. It captured the imagination of European readers and ignited "Egyptomania"—a widespread fascination with ancient Egypt in Europe.[xxvii] One of the most famous quotes associated with the pyramids is from Napoleon Bonaparte during his Egyptian campaign in 1798. He addressed his troops: "*From the heights of these pyramids, forty centuries look down on us.*"[xxviii] This iconic statement was meant to inspire his soldiers by emphasising the grandeur and historical significance of the pyramids, highlighting how ancient and monumental these structures were even in their time.

These publications presented the pyramids as wonders of the ancient world, focusing on the mystery and splendour of ancient Egypt. The narrative typically portrayed pyramids as tombs of powerful pharaohs, often tied to exoticism and romanticism, which tapped into Western fantasies about the Orient.[xxix] Newspaper and periodical illustrations, such as the *Illustrated London News,* helped shape the public's visual understanding of pyramids[xxx]. While not always accurate, these images created a sense of wonder and mystery.

During the mid-19th century, a transition occurred from widespread looting of ancient sites to more formal protection, as scholarly works and archaeological studies became increasingly common. Egyptology emerged as a scientific discipline, leading to a more systematic and respectful approach to excavating and preserving ancient artefacts. This shift began efforts to safeguard Egypt's rich historical heritage.

Books by early archaeologists, such as Karl Richard Lepsius and Sir Flinders Petrie, were among the first serious studies of pyramids.[xxxi] They presented the pyramids as extraordinary engineering achievements, focusing on measurements, construction methods, and their alignment with celestial bodies.[xxxii] These works often approached the pyramids from a more scientific and analytical perspective. Their studies contributed to a growing fascination with the pyramids' mysteries, mainly focused on their purpose and symbolism.[xxxiii]

Later in the 19th century, historical fiction and romantic literature began to weave the pyramids into stories of ancient Egypt, depicting them as backdrops for tales of kings, queens, and gods. Writers such as H. Rider Haggard, in *She* (1887), or Théophile Gautier, in *The Romance of a Mummy* (1858), used pyramids as settings for exotic tales.[xxxiv] In *She,* the hidden knowledge in this novel revolves around immortality and eternal life. The central figure, Ayesha (She-Who-Must-Be-Obeyed), is an immortal queen who possesses knowledge of ancient rituals and powers that allow her to defy death. The ancient ruins and pyramids in the story are portrayed as keepers of this secret knowledge, with their existence tied to forgotten civilisations that had mastered the secrets of life, death, and rebirth. The novel speculates about ancient rituals, the power of the divine, and the hidden forces that allow one to transcend human limitations. Similarly, in *The Romance of a Mummy,* the pyramids are depicted as repositories of secret knowledge related to the afterlife and the mysteries of the soul. The story weaves around the idea that the ancient Egyptians possessed knowledge about preserving life beyond death. The mummification process, pyramid tombs, and intricate burial practices served a purpose beyond mere religious significance. They are portrayed as rituals that unlock supernatural powers, connecting the dead to the divine. Theophile Gautier speculates about the magical powers of these ancient burial practices, suggesting that the pyramids are the guardians of these esoteric secrets, holding the key to life after death and the soul's journey through the afterlife. These books reinforced a view of pyramids as symbols of ancient power, mystery, and the supernatural, further embedding them in the public imagination as mystical or otherworldly monuments.[xxxv]

By the end of the 19th century, pyramids had begun to feature in occult and esoteric writings. Influenced by ideas from theosophy and other spiritual movements, some writers suggested that pyramids held mystical or cosmic powers or were built by ancient civilisations with lost knowledge. Books by authors such as Ignatius Donnelly, who speculated about ancient civilisations in works like *Atlantis: The Antediluvian World (1882)*, contributed to the idea that pyramids were more than just tombs—they were repositories of hidden knowledge or even energy sources. Ignatius Donnelly did not specifically write about energy in the scientific terms we understand today. He implied that the Atlanteans, or other ancient civilisations, might have understood cosmic or earth-bound forces. This might have included using the pyramids' geometric design and alignment with celestial bodies to harness or amplify energy. He argued in his book that this advanced knowledge might explain how such civilisations achieved architectural achievements like the construction of massive pyramids with incredible precision and alignment, hinting at an understanding of energies related to the Earth's magnetic field, gravitational forces, or even unknown cosmic sources. While he did not delve deeply into the mechanics of these energies, he contributed to the idea that ancient civilisations had access to knowledge and technologies, potentially involving energy, that were lost over time and remain a mystery today.[xxxvi]

People used to learn about pyramids mainly through newspapers, books, travel stories, academic writings, and drawings. Then, movies were invented. Movies were introduced in the late 19th century. The first motion pictures emerged in the 1890s with the development of cameras that could capture and project sequential images.[xxxvii] Notable early contributions include the work of Thomas Edison, who invented the Kinetoscope in 1891, and the Lumière brothers, who showcased their first public film screening in 1895 in Paris, often considered the birth of modern cinema.[xxxviii]

The first movie featuring a pyramid was *Cleopatra's Tomb* (1899), a silent short film directed by Georges Méliès, a pioneer of early cinema. He was known for his imaginative and fantastical films, and this film included pyramids as part of the Egyptian setting, reflecting his fascination with ancient cultures and magic.[xxxix] The storyline centres around the resurrection of the ancient Egyptian queen Cleopatra, incorporating pyramids as a backdrop. Using Cleopatra's tomb and the pyramids, he tapped into the public's curiosity and romanticised view of ancient Egypt, stoked by 19th-century discoveries and Egyptomania sweeping Europe. The resurrection theme also allowed him to blend history with fantasy, which appealed to early cinema audiences and set the tone for future films that used Egypt as a symbol of wonder, mysticism, and the supernatural. He solidified pyramids as recurring icons in film, embodying historical fascination and fantastical escapism. Although *"Cleopatra's Tomb"* was only a few minutes long, it set the stage for including pyramids in cinema.

The Evolution of Pyramids in Media in the 20th Century

The media's portrayal of pyramids evolved in the 20th century from adventure stories to the rise of conspiracy theories and esoteric meanings. Social media platforms like YouTube and TikTok have contributed to the recent surge in interest, particularly among younger audiences.[xl] Media played a crucial role in popularising science, making complex ideas accessible to a broader audience through documentaries, news reports, and social media. This increased visibility can boost public interest, drive funding for scientific research, and inspire a new generation of scientists.

In *Death on the Nile* (1937)[xli], one of my favourites, Agatha Christie subtly weaves references to Egypt's ancient civilisation and pyramids, enhancing the story's timeless mystery and intriguing atmosphere. She was a renowned British author, known primarily for her detective novels and short stories, particularly those featuring iconic characters such as Hercule Poirot and Miss Marple. As Hercule Poirot, the detective, investigates the murder aboard the Nile cruise, the grandeur of the ancient world looms in the background, reminding characters of the enduring legacies of death, power, and human ambition. The pyramids, symbols of an ancient empire's authority, starkly contrast with the modern human dramas unfolding against their backdrop. Agatha Christie often invokes these monumental structures to mirror the deeper themes of the novel: greed, jealousy, and the destructive consequences of human frailty. The pyramid backdrop emphasises how, despite the passage of millennia, human nature remains fundamentally unchanged. Just as ancient Egypt was shaped by political intrigue, assassinations, and dynastic power plays, the novel's characters are embroiled in a web of deception and personal ambition, leading to murder. The setting on the Nile cruise, with the backdrop of Egypt's timeless monuments, highlights how human frailty, including desires for wealth and control, transcends time. The pyramids serve as silent witnesses to the unfolding tragedy, linking the contemporary murder mystery to the timeless enigmas of the past.

In the mid-20th century, pyramids appeared in adventure stories and films that explored ancient civilisations. Movies like *The Mummy*[xlii] and other Egyptology-based fiction began to feature pyramids as mysterious backdrops. *The Mummy* (1932), directed by Karl Freund, is a classic horror film about an ancient Egyptian priest, Imhotep, who is resurrected after a British expedition discovers his mummified remains and mistakenly reads from the Scroll of Thoth. Imhotep returns to life after thousands of years and assumes a human disguise, adopting the name Ardath Bey. He seeks to reunite with his long-lost love, Princess Ankh-es-en-amon, whose reincarnation he believes he has found in a modern woman named Helen Grosvenor. As Imhotep attempts to carry out an ancient ritual to revive the princess, the film builds tension around the consequences of disturbing ancient secrets. This movie is an early exploration of the fascination with Egyptology, pyramids, mummies, and reincarnation. It blends romance, mysticism, and horror. The film sets the stage for the cinematic trope of cursed tombs and ancient mysteries, which will influence future Egypt-themed films. It also helped to emphasise the importance of preserving ancient artefacts and respecting the legacies of past civilisations.

During this period, pyramids were mainly seen in the media as symbols of ancient grandeur and mystery, with less emphasis on modern interpretations related to energy theories or the occult. Science fiction and fantasy movies then began incorporating pyramids, associating them with alien technology or extraterrestrial contact. Books, films, and TV series like *Stargate* (1994) popularised the idea of pyramids as cosmic or alien constructs, expanding their symbolic reach beyond their traditional archaeological context.[xliii]

Stargate (1994), directed by Roland Emmerich, is a science fiction film centred on an ancient alien device known as the Stargate, a portal that enables instantaneous travel between distant planets.[xliv] The story follows Dr Daniel Jackson, an archaeologist and linguist, who decodes the symbols on the Stargate and helps unlock its power. Along with a military team led by Colonel Jack O'Neil, he travels through the Stargate to a distant planet that resembles ancient Egypt. On this planet, they encounter a human civilisation that worships the god Ra. Ra is revealed to be an alien being who has used advanced technology to enslave the people and present himself as a god. The plot explores themes of ancient alien theory, suggesting that Earth's ancient civilisations, particularly those in Egypt, were influenced by extraterrestrial beings. The team must fight to liberate the people from Ra's control and ultimately prevent his plan to use the Stargate to destroy Earth. The film combines elements of archaeology, mythology, and science fiction. It later inspired the popular *Stargate* franchise, which includes several TV series and spin-offs.

The widespread fascination with theories such as pyramid power and extraterrestrial involvement, amplified by the television series *Ancient Aliens*, has blurred the line between entertainment and scientific inquiry. *Ancient Aliens*, a documentary series that premiered in 2010 on the History Channel, explores various theories suggesting that ancient civilisations, including those that built the pyramids, were influenced or aided by extraterrestrial beings. The series often focuses on unexplained architectural masterpieces, myths, and religious texts, proposing that advanced alien technology and knowledge significantly shaped human history.[xlv]

Films have either reinforced or distorted perceptions of the pyramids. Historical accuracy is often compromised in favour of entertainment, affecting public perception of ancient cultures.[xlvi] In many cases, the media largely dictates our thoughts, influencing how we perceive historical events and figures. What we see on screen, even in fictional movies, is often taken as truth and becomes embedded in our understanding of history. As a result, myths, conspiracies, and sensationalised versions of the past frequently overshadow academic and archaeological facts, creating a skewed perspective of ancient civilisations and their achievements. This blurring of fact and fiction can lead to misunderstandings about the true nature of these ancient wonders.

New Age Spirituality and Esoteric Movements

By the 1970s and 1980s, with the rise of New Age spirituality and esoteric movements, pyramids became central to theories about energy harnessing, metaphysical power, and ancient wisdom. Theories like pyramid power, which suggested that pyramids could amplify energy or influence health, became popular, especially in alternative science circles.[xlvii]

The pyramid's visibility in global media surged during the late 20th and early 21st centuries. It became a recurring symbol in popular films, video games, TV shows, and music videos, often representing power, enigma, and ancient wisdom. The concept of pyramids as cosmic or interdimensional entities gained significant ground in science fiction.

In recent years, the pyramid's presence in media has shifted toward more speculative and esoteric discussions, mainly fueled by the internet, YouTube, documentaries, and social media. Topics like pyramid energy, ancient technology, and lost civilisations have gained momentum in popular culture. Shows like *Ancient Aliens* and online conspiracy forums often use pyramids to symbolise these ideas. Shows like *Ancient Aliens* and movies like *Stargate* draw on the mystery and aura of pyramids, reinforcing the idea that they could be conduits of cosmic energy or extraterrestrial technology.

Documentaries more frequently explore fringe theories, presenting pyramids as part of a larger mystery of lost knowledge and technology that could reshape our understanding of ancient civilisations. This shift reflects a broader cultural trend toward embracing alternative histories and more mystical interpretations of ancient structures.

While traditional media and academia continue to portray pyramids within the context of historical research, the rise of *conspiracy theories* that push the boundaries of established theories about the pyramids has altered the media landscape. They see the pyramids as metaphysical and conspiratorial symbols.[xlviii] The pyramid, notably the Eye of Providence, has long been intertwined with secret societies. Modern media and conspiracy theories often depict it as a symbol of hidden knowledge, authority, and occult power. While the Eye of Providence originally symbolised divine guidance, it has become synonymous with surveillance and control in conspiracy circles.[xlix] Occult traditions view it as a symbol of esoteric wisdom, with its inner chambers representing secret spaces of learning and enlightenment. This idea has permeated modern occultism and is a prominent feature in Freemasonry, the Illuminati and other secret societies, where the pyramid symbolises the search for truth and a deeper understanding of the universe. Discussions in documentaries of Freemasonry, Illuminati, and secret societies have intertwined the pyramid symbol with ideas of hidden knowledge, government control, and esoteric power.[l] Shows, podcasts, and online platforms often delve into these theories, fueling a narrative that presents pyramids as not only ancient structures but also as part of modern-day reality. This trend is controversial, as it blends historical facts with speculative theories, creating a polarising effect in the media.

In his analysis of cultural symbols, Stuart Hall examines how the media influences public perceptions of ancient structures, such as pyramids, by blending historical fact with speculative fiction. His work emphasises that meaning is not inherent but is constructed and communicated through cultural practices, images, and representations deeply influenced by social power dynamics. Stuart Hall's book *Representation: Cultural Representations and Signifying Practices*

(1997) explores how films like *Stargate* (1994) and shows like *Ancient Aliens* (2010) leverage pyramid symbolism to promote ideas of extraterrestrial contact and lost civilisations, contributing to the cultural resurgence of these narratives. These media representations, while entertaining, contribute to the cultural revival of fringe narratives, drawing from myth and alternative history to captivate audiences. However, such portrayals risk distorting collective memory and public understanding of ancient cultures by blurring the line between evidence-based history and imaginative storytelling. His work highlights the media's power to reshape cultural symbols. Pyramids become vehicles for reinterpreting and rewriting ancient history, often repurposed to serve narratives of mystery and speculation rather than scholarly accuracy. Thus, the portrayal of pyramids reflects broader trends of using ancient symbols to construct new meanings, tapping into historical fascination and contemporary curiosity. [li]

Pyramid Theories in Broadcast and Digital Media

The evolution of pyramid discourse in broadcast and digital media follows a clear path from niche speculation to a global multi-platform phenomenon. It started with *Coast to Coast AM*, launched by Art Bell in 1988 and later hosted by George Noory, which pioneered late-night radio as a platform for fringe archaeology, metaphysics, and pyramid mysticism. These broadcasts introduced millions to ideas such as ancient high technology and pyramid energy long before mainstream interest.

With the rise of internet radio and podcasting in the early 2000s, shows like *The Higherside Chats* and *The Brothers of the Serpent* continued this trend, hosting detailed discussions on sacred geometry, lost civilisations, and alternative history.

The conversation was propelled into the mainstream when *The Joe Rogan Experience* started featuring guests such as Graham Hancock and Randall Carlson, exposing large global audiences to theories connecting the pyramids with lost advanced cultures. Around the same period, *The Pyramid Code*, a documentary series by Dr. Carmen Boulter, gained popularity on Netflix and Gaia, introducing scholarly-style speculation on consciousness, alignments, and energy fields to a broader audience.

Parallel to this, YouTube emerged as a dominant medium, with creators like *Bright Insight*, *Ancient Architects*, and *UnchartedX* producing viral content that combined high-quality visuals, on-site investigations, and algorithm-driven reach. Channels like *4biddenknowledge* by Billy Carson, blending Egyptian symbolism, Thoth, and Atlantean technology, grew to over a million subscribers, while Gaia's *Ancient Civilizations* series, featuring Gregg Braden and Freddy Silva, turned esoteric pyramid theories into spiritual doctrine for hundreds of thousands of paid viewers. Shows like *Edge of Wonder* and appearances by Dr. Robert Schoch, Brien Foerster, and others on platforms across YouTube, Gaia, and podcast networks helped sustain the movement. From static-filled AM broadcasts to visually rich global streams, the media evolution of pyramid theory reflects both public appetite and algorithmic amplification, making once-fringe ideas part of mainstream alt-history culture.

Pyramids in the Music Industry

Pyramid symbolism in the music industry has evolved, too. Pyramids and ancient Egyptian themes were not prominently featured in Western music before the 20th century. However, ancient Egypt subtly influenced classical compositions and operas as part of a fascination with exotic or "Oriental" European art and cultural themes.[lii] For example, ancient Egypt was a popular setting in several 18th- and 19th-century operas. For instance, *Giulio Cesare* (1724) by George Frideric Handel is set in Egypt and follows Julius Caesar's romance with Cleopatra.[liii] One of the most famous 19th-century operas, Giuseppe Verdi's *Aida* (1871), is set in ancient Egypt and was commissioned to mark the opening of the Suez Canal. The opera emphasises Egyptian grandeur and rituals, with pyramids sometimes depicted in stage designs.[liv] The 20th century shifted from representations of mysticism and ancient power to icons of wealth, success, and conspiracy. Throughout its evolution, pyramid imagery has remained a powerful and versatile symbol in music, representing transformation, mystery, and authority across various genres and eras.[lv]

In the early 20th century, pyramid imagery was associated with occult mysticism and spiritual awakening. Artists like Sun Ra used it to signify cosmic unity and black empowerment, as evident in his 1959 album, *Jazz in Silhouette*.[lvi]

By the 1970s, the pyramid symbol had become prominent in progressive rock. An example is Pink Floyd. Pink Floyd, particularly during their peak in the 1970s, became synonymous with rebellion, counterculture, and pushing the boundaries of artistic expression. Their music often critiqued societal norms, institutions, and the alienation caused by modern life. This resonated with listeners who felt disillusioned by the establishment.[lvii] Albums like *The Wall* and *Animals* directly confronted themes of oppression, authority, and control.[lviii] In contrast, their iconic album *The Dark Side of the Moon* (1973) symbolised a deeper, more abstract exploration of human experience, mental health, and existential anxieties.[lix] The use of the

Powered by Pyramids: A Book of Theories

pyramid on the cover of *The Dark Side of the Moon* became a powerful symbol of this rebellion. The album art features a simple yet profound image of a prism, splitting light into a spectrum of colours, which could be interpreted as a metaphor for breaking free from conformity, much like Pink Floyd's music sought to challenge the mainstream.[lx] The ancient and enigmatic pyramid evokes a sense of mystery, spirituality, and hidden knowledge, aligning with the band's fascination with deeper truths and the unseen forces that shape reality. In this sense, the pyramid became a visual symbol of questioning authority and traditional narratives, much like the band's music invited listeners to reflect on societal structures and the darker sides of the human experience.[lxi] By combining the imagery of the pyramid with their experimental soundscapes, Pink Floyd reinforced their role as musical revolutionaries.[lxii] They used sound and symbolism to encourage rebellion against conformity and embrace alternative ways of thinking.[lxiii]

In the 1980s, the symbolism of pyramids in pop culture evolved to take on new meanings, particularly in relation to power, wealth, and material success. This shift reflected the era's fascination with excess, luxury, and the pursuit of status, mirroring the corporate and capitalist structures that dominated global culture at the time.[lxiv] With their monumental scale and association with ancient kingship, the pyramids became symbols of historical power and contemporary ambition. Michael Jackson, a global icon who embodied the concept of "pop royalty," incorporated this symbolism in his 1992 music video, *Remember the Time*. Set in an idealised, glamorous version of ancient Egypt, the video uses Egyptian-themed pyramid imagery to draw parallels between the grandeur of ancient rulers and his position at the pinnacle of the entertainment industry.[lxv] The opulence and mysticism of the pyramids align with Michael Jackson's larger-than-life persona, as he portrays a figure of immense influence and charisma. By incorporating these symbols, he effectively ties his modern success to the timeless concepts of power and legacy that pyramids have represented for millennia.[lxvi] In *Remember the Time*, the pyramids also serve as a backdrop for his themes of love and loyalty, elevating these personal narratives to the level of ancient epic tales.[lxvii] Using such imagery reflects how, by the 1990s, the pyramid had come to represent historical power and the desire to transcend time and achieve immortality through fame and influence.[lxviii] In doing so, he tapped into a rich cultural symbol that connected his contemporary achievements with the ancient world, reinforcing his image as a modern-day king of pop and an enduring cultural icon.[lxix]

The rise of hip-hop in the 1990s brought pyramid symbolism into a new cultural context. It became a powerful metaphor for self-made success, empowerment, and social mobility. The pyramid represented the struggle and ultimate triumph of achieving greatness in a genre often focused on overcoming adversity and rising from humble beginnings.[lxx] For many hip-hop artists, pyramids symbolised ascension in terms of financial wealth, personal growth, artistic influence, and cultural dominance.[lxxi]

Artists such as Tupac Shakur and Jay-Z employed pyramid imagery in their music and visuals to convey ideas of power, legacy, and control over one's destiny. For instance, Tupac often referenced the struggles of marginalised communities and framed his journey to success as a spiritual and political ascension, where the pyramid represented reaching the highest point despite systemic oppression.[lxxii] On the other hand, Jay-Z frequently invoked the pyramid to reflect his transformation from a street hustler to a business mogul, using it as a symbol of self-made success and elite status. His frequent use of pyramid and eye imagery, especially with his Roc-A-Fella hand sign, which mimics a triangle, became synonymous with his brand and identity as a leader within the music industry and broader culture.[lxxiii] Many hip-hop artists played with conspiracy theories surrounding the Illuminati, secret societies, and elite control, incorporating pyramids into their aesthetics as symbols of hidden power and influence.[lxxiv] The fusion of pyramid imagery with these theories created a mystique around the artists, hinting at their access to exclusive knowledge or power and positioning them as part of an untouchable cultural elite. This imagery resonated with listeners as it tapped into broader fears and fascinations with wealth, influence, and who holds power in society. By doing so, pyramids became a symbol of success and a way for artists to engage with ideas of control, both as individuals who have risen to the top and as players in a system dominated by unseen forces.[lxxv] This recontextualisation of the pyramid in hip-hop reflected the genre's broader themes of resilience, self-empowerment, and social critique. While ancient pyramids were symbols of divine kingship and monumental legacy, in hip-hop, they became metaphors for the modern-day kingmakers—self-made, influential, and powerful in their own right, navigating a world shaped by visible and hidden forces.[lxxvi]

In recent decades, artists like Kanye West and Beyoncé have revitalised pyramid symbolism in popular culture to express themes of dominance, empowerment, cultural pride, and spiritual connection. Their incorporation of pyramids and other ancient imagery taps into deeper symbolism, linking their modern-day success to historical notions of greatness, power, and immortality.[lxxvii] Kanye West's hit song

Power (2010) exemplifies this approach. In the music video, he is portrayed in front of what appears to be a pyramid structure, invoking the pyramid's longstanding associations with power, control, and ascension.[lxxviii] The imagery aligns with his frequent use of ancient and mystical symbolism throughout his music, performances, and visuals. In *Power*, the pyramid backdrop reflects the song's overarching themes of struggle, self-aggrandisement, and the tension between mortality and godlike achievement.[lxxix] He often invokes symbols of ancient kingship and divine right, framing himself as an artistic and cultural icon who challenges conventional limits of fame and influence. Drawing upon ancient symbols like pyramids, he positions himself as part of a larger historical narrative of human achievement, linking his work to notions of immortality, divine rule, and spiritual enlightenment.[lxxx] Using these symbols declares his dominance in the music industry and culture.[lxxxi]

Similarly, Beyoncé has employed pyramid symbolism to convey themes of empowerment, cultural legacy, and connection to African heritage. Her groundbreaking 2018 Coachella performance, often referred to as *Beychella*, featured a stage design that prominently included pyramid-like structures.[lxxxii] These structures symbolised the pinnacle of achievement and strength, reflecting Beyoncé's rise in the music industry. In this context, the pyramid is a metaphor for her journey and the collective ascent of Black culture and pride. It represents the apex of artistic and cultural mastery, aligning her with the concept of royalty and leadership.[lxxxiii] Beyoncé's 2019 visual album, *Black is King,* deepened these symbolic connections, as pyramids represented spiritual empowerment and African heritage. Throughout the film, pyramids and Egyptian themes underscore the ties between past and present, particularly highlighting the legacy of African greatness and the quest for reclaiming cultural pride.[lxxxiv] Using Egyptian imagery, she honours the ancient civilisations of Africa, including Egypt, while reclaiming African cultural pride. In this context, Beyoncé is not disputing the Egyptian origins of the pyramids but rather emphasising that Egypt is a part of Africa and connecting her African heritage to the grandeur and power of ancient Egyptian symbolism. This ties into a broader cultural movement that seeks to celebrate African history and its contributions to civilisation. Beyoncé frequently references powerful queens, goddesses, and historical figures, drawing connections between herself and notable figures such as Nefertiti and Cleopatra. By linking herself to these legendary women, Beyoncé uses pyramid imagery to emphasise themes of immortality, legacy, and spiritual connection.[lxxxv] Her *album, The Gift, released as part of The Lion King soundtrack, also evokes* ancient Egypt and the Nile River, reinforcing the significance of lineage and the cyclical nature of life, much like the pyramids themselves.[lxxxvi]

In the work of Kanye West and Beyoncé, pyramids are more than just historical symbols—they are powerful metaphors for ascension, greatness, and the pursuit of lasting influence. By invoking these ancient structures, both artists draw connections between their journeys and the legacy of powerful civilisations. They use pyramid imagery to affirm their roles as modern-day cultural leaders and visionaries.[lxxxvii]

Over the decades, the symbolism of pyramids in music has undergone significant transformation, reflecting the evolving themes and concerns of different generations. In the early 20th century, pyramids were associated with occult mysticism and spiritual awakening, representing cosmic unity and empowerment in the works of artists such as Sun Ra. By the 1970s, artists such as Pink Floyd had begun to embrace pyramids as a symbol of rebellion and existential exploration, using the imagery to challenge societal norms and delve into deeper human experiences. In the 1980s, the pyramid took on new meanings, representing wealth, status, and power, as evident in Michael Jackson's extensive use of Egyptian-themed pyramid imagery in *Remember the Time*. The 1990s witnessed the emergence of pyramid symbolism in hip-hop, where artists such as Tupac Shakur and Jay-Z used it to represent self-made success, ascension, and elite status, often intertwining it with themes of hidden power and conspiracy. In recent years, artists like Kanye West and Beyoncé have revitalised the pyramid as a symbol of dominance, empowerment, and cultural pride, linking their achievements to the legacy of ancient civilisations and spiritual enlightenment.

How Music Influences More Than Books and Films

The enduring presence of pyramids in music speaks to their versatility as symbols, continually reinterpreted to reflect the aspirations, struggles, and visions of different eras in pop culture. Music can shape how we think and feel as a powerful medium, and pyramid imagery amplifies this effect by tapping into our subconscious associations with power, mystery, and transcendence.

Scholars have examined the music industry's manipulation of the mind and how music influences emotions, behaviour, and social control. Music is often used to shape our perceptions, from advertising to public spaces, in subtle ways. In *Music and Manipulation: On the Social Uses and Social Control of Music* (2005), Steven Brown and Ulrik Volgsten discuss how music has historically promoted group solidarity and social control, shaping emotions and behaviours at individual and collective levels.[lxxxviii] For instance, background music is designed to influence consumer behaviour, subtly guiding decisions without conscious awareness. Cognitive neuroscience also demonstrates that music can activate the brain's reward systems, making it a powerful tool for shaping our emotions, thoughts, and behaviours.[lxxxix] This ability to manipulate emotions through music is used extensively in advertising and entertainment to evoke specific reactions, demonstrating the industry's profound influence on the human mind.[xc]

Of the three media—music, film, and books—music tends to have the most immediate influence on the unconscious mind due to its direct impact on the brain's emotional and reward systems. Music can quickly evoke emotions and change moods without the listener's full awareness, often through repetition and rhythm, which profoundly affect the unconscious.[xci] By combining visual and auditory elements, film creates a powerful, immersive experience, using sound and imagery to manipulate emotions and perceptions on a deeper level.[xcii] Though slower in their influence, books can profoundly shape the unconscious over time by providing rich narratives and symbols that challenge or reinforce deeply held beliefs.[xciii] Music is the most immediate in its unconscious effects, while film and books offer deeper, more reflective influences.

People tend to remember music better than books, primarily because music interacts with the brain's emotional and auditory centres. According to Daniel J. Levitin, a neuroscientist and author of *This Is Your Brain on Music*, music stimulates the brain in ways deeply tied to memory and emotion.[xciv] The repetition of rhythms and melodies helps anchor musical memories in the brain more effectively than the more complex, linear information found in books. Levitin explains that music engages the hippocampus, the brain region responsible for forming long-term memories, which enables songs to become ingrained and easily recalled. In contrast, reading requires higher cognitive functions related to language and abstract thinking, which can lead to deep intellectual engagement but lack the immediate, emotionally resonant cues that make music memorable. As a result, while books may leave a lasting intellectual impact, music's sensory and emotional connection creates stronger, more lasting memories.[xcv]

Pyramids in the Gaming Industry

Video games began in the early 1950s. Video games like *Assassin's Creed Origins*[xcvi] prominently feature pyramids, drawing younger audiences into their mystery. By blending meticulously researched historical detail with speculative elements, the game transports players to ancient Egypt, allowing them to explore these towering structures firsthand. As players uncover hidden chambers, ancient secrets, and forgotten technologies, the pyramids come alive in a way that bridges the past and present, drawing them deeper into the mysteries of these ancient wonders in the digital age. The game adds a speculative layer by exploring ancient technology and hidden knowledge, hinting at an advanced understanding of engineering, astronomy, and possibly even extraterrestrial influences, similar to the theories in fringe documentaries.

Games like *Assassin's Creed Origins* are particularly impactful because they intertwine history with speculative and fringe theories, such as ancient technology, hidden knowledge, and extraterrestrial influences. These themes echo theories often discussed in documentaries and books about ancient civilisations, offering players an experience that combines historical immersion with curiosity-driven exploration. The speculative layer of the game hints at an advanced understanding of engineering, astronomy, and metaphysical elements in ancient societies, suggesting the pyramids could have been more than just tombs, possibly serving as repositories of knowledge or energy centres. Using these theories, video games capture players' imaginations, offering entertainment and a gateway into deeper inquiries about ancient history and technology in ways that have never been done before. Through games like this, younger audiences engage with historical narratives and speculative theories in an interactive format, deepening their interest in ancient civilisations while experiencing the mysteries of the pyramids in the digital age.

Pyramids in Architecture, Design and Luxury

Pyramid designs have also influenced modern architecture[xcvii] and fashion, as evident in iconic structures such as the Louvre Pyramid in Paris and the Luxor Hotel in Las Vegas. Luxury brands like Tiffany & Co. have embraced pyramid shapes in their designs, blending ancient symbolism with modern elegance.

The Louvre Pyramid in Paris is a glass-and-steel pyramid that serves as the main entrance to the Louvre Museum and has become an iconic part of the Paris skyline. Architect I. M. Pei designed it. The structure combines modern aesthetics with the ancient pyramid form.[xcviii] When it was first unveiled in 1989, the Louvre Pyramid sparked considerable controversy. Many Parisians felt the glass and steel structure was too modern to stand amid the Louvre Palace. However, it has since become an architectural icon. The Luxor Hotel, built in 1993 in Las Vegas, is one of the most iconic examples, where the pyramid serves not just as a structural form but as an attraction symbolising grandeur and mystery. [xcix] The hotel is the largest pyramid structure built in modern times. While it is not a replica of the Great Pyramid of Giza, it is heavily inspired by ancient Egyptian architecture.[c] It is 350 feet (106.7 meters) in height, compared to the Great Pyramid of Giza, which is roughly 481 feet (146.6 meters) tall. The Luxor also features a massive beam of light that shines from the top of the pyramid into the night sky, often referred to as the world's brightest beam of light.[ci] The Luxor Sky Beam is the brightest in the world, visible from up to 275 miles away. 39 Xenon lights power the beam, each requiring 7,000 watts of electricity. Similarly, Dubai has a hotel shaped like a pyramid called Raffles Dubai.[cii] The hotel is also renowned for its 24-carat gold-plated furnishings, which add to the allure of blending ancient Egyptian grandeur with modern luxury.

There are several other pyramid structures around the world. The Transamerica Pyramid in California is an iconic office building, 853 feet (260 meters) high, with a tall, slender pyramidal shape that makes it one of San Francisco's most recognisable buildings. It was designed with a modernist approach and remains a key feature of the city's skyline.[ciii] The Palace of Peace and Reconciliation (Kazakhstan), which is 203 feet (62 meters) tall, was completed in 2006. It is a cultural and religious building designed to host peace meetings between leaders of the world's religions. [civ] British architect Norman Foster designed this modern glass and steel pyramid, symbolising peace and unity.[cv] It serves as a venue for conferences, operas, and exhibitions and is an iconic landmark in Astana. Other smaller structures include the Pyramid of Tirana in Albania, which has a modern pyramid design and is one of the more unique structures in Eastern Europe. Its appearance is more symbolic of modernist architecture than ancient Egyptian design.[cvi] Malaysia built a pyramid-shaped shopping mall, the Sunway Pyramid, famous for its giant pyramid replica, topped by a lion sculpture at its entrance. The complex has a strong Egyptian theme, blending modern shopping with ancient imagery.[cvii]

The pyramid is now emerging as a design and practical inspiration in discussions around sustainable architecture. Some propose that pyramid-shaped structures could have energy efficiency or green building applications. This trend taps into ancient symbolism while also looking toward futuristic applications, as seen in some media covering architecture and environmental sustainability.

Pyramids in Jewellery

The allure of pyramid-shaped jewellery often carries a sense of mystique, power, and connection to ancient royalty, which can evoke feelings of strength and grandeur in women who wear it. Cleopatra, one of history's most iconic female figures, is frequently associated with beauty, intelligence, and leadership in ancient Egypt. Pyramid-shaped jewellery, with its links to Egyptian symbolism, may make women feel like they are channelling some of Cleopatra's qualities—power, elegance, and authority. The association with ancient queens like Cleopatra can contribute to the sense that wearing such pieces connects the wearer with a legacy of feminine strength and royalty. Luxury brands like Tiffany & Co., Cartier, and Boucheron often release pyramid-inspired designs featuring diamonds, emeralds, or sapphires, blending ancient symbolism with modern elegance.[cviii] They use pyramid-inspired designs because pyramids symbolise timelessness, strength, and sophistication—qualities that resonate with the core values of high-end jewellery.[cix]

The pyramid's geometric form, with its strong base and rising apex, represents stability and ascension, making it an ideal symbol for personal achievement, spiritual growth, and enduring elegance.[cx] By incorporating this ancient design, these brands evoke a sense of mystery, power, and connection to ancient civilisations, blending the allure of history with the modern elegance of precious stones like diamonds, emeralds, and sapphires.[cxi] This fusion appeals to consumers seeking luxury pieces that combine historical significance with contemporary style.

The watch industry, particularly brands that target the ultra-high-end market, sometimes incorporates pyramid patterns into dials, bezels, and other design elements. This subtle use of pyramid geometry evokes precision and the pyramids' lasting power, which mirrors the enduring quality of luxury timepieces.

Evolution of Pyramids as a Symbol of Personal Growth

The pyramid can symbolise the path of self-improvement or career growth to reach the "top," symbolising personal, spiritual, or professional success.

Abraham Maslow introduced his Hierarchy of Needs in 1943 in a paper titled *A Theory of Human Motivation,* published in the *Psychological Review.* He later expanded on this theory in his 1954 book *Motivation and Personality.* He is concrete in outlining the specific steps of human needs.[cxii]

His concept of self-actualisation, the highest level of human development, represents the point where a person realises their fullest potential. His pyramid hierarchy is structured in the following order: Physiological needs (food, water, warmth, rest), Safety needs (security, safety), Love and belonging needs (intimate relationships, friendships), Esteem needs (prestige and feelings of accomplishment), and finally

Self-actualization (achieving one's full potential, including creative activities). Each level builds on the fulfilment of the previous one, ultimately culminating in self-actualisation, where individuals pursue personal growth and fulfilment.[cxiii]

In *The New Age Movement: The Celebration of the Self* (1996), sociologist Paul Heelas argues that pyramids are often adopted as symbols of spiritual empowerment and energy manipulation. This reflects a broader trend within New Age movements to seek ancient wisdom as a path to personal growth and cosmic understanding.[cxiv]

A theory that draws from ancient esoteric traditions but has gained renewed attention in modern interpretations suggests that the pyramid's structure symbolises the soul's ascension, with each level representing a stage in the journey from materialism to enlightenment. This concept is not entirely new, as spiritual ascension has long been a focus of ancient mysticism, including Egyptian belief systems, where pyramids symbolise the soul's passage through different planes of existence. However, modern interpretations have introduced the association of each stage of this journey with a specific colour, drawing from spiritual systems like the chakra philosophy.

The chakra system, an ancient concept rooted in Hindu and Buddhist traditions, views the human body as composed of seven key energy centres, or chakras, that regulate the flow of life force, known as prana. Each chakra, aligned along the spine, governs specific physical, emotional, and spiritual aspects of life and is associated with a particular colour. Beginning with the Root Chakra at the base, symbolising survival and stability in red, the energy ascends through the Sacral Chakra for creativity, the Solar Plexus Chakra for personal power, and the Heart Chakra, which connects to love and compassion in green. Moving upward, the Throat Chakra governs communication in blue, followed by the Third Eye Chakra, linked to intuition in indigo, and finally, the Crown Chakra at the top of the head, representing enlightenment in violet or white. This system reflects an ancient understanding of human consciousness, with balanced chakras fostering overall well-being and blockages believed to lead to disharmony in the body, mind, and spirit.[cxv]

Judith's *Wheels of Life: A User's Guide to the Chakra System* discusses the flow of Kundalini energy through the chakras and its impact on spiritual awakening. Kundalini is the primal energy believed to lie dormant at the base of the spine, coiled like a serpent, within the root chakra in Hindu and yogic traditions. When awakened through practices such as yoga, meditation, or breathwork, this powerful energy rises through the body's seven chakras, activating each one in turn and unlocking deeper levels of consciousness. As the Kundalini ascends from the root chakra, associated with survival and materialism, to the crown chakra, representing spiritual enlightenment, it mirrors the soul's journey toward higher awareness and unity with the divine. This ascension process transforms energy and personal and spiritual growth, ultimately leading to profound enlightenment and self-realisation. The path of Kundalini rising aligns closely with the modern metaphysical interpretation of energy ascension through colour and pyramid symbolism, where each stage represents a higher level of consciousness, culminating in the ultimate connection with the cosmos. [cxvi] By linking this energy flow with ancient structures like pyramids, some modern theories suggest that these monuments may have been designed to resonate with the same energetic principles, guiding the individual's spiritual ascension just as the chakras direct the flow of prana within the human body.

The modern interpretation also uses colours for different stages. The broad base of the pyramid, corresponding to the densest and most material aspects of existence, is linked to the colour red, symbolising survival and basic instincts. As one ascends, orange represents creativity and desire, followed by yellow, which signifies personal power and control. Green marks the transition toward love and compassion at the midpoint of the pyramid, while the next level, blue, reflects truth and effective communication. Indigo follows, symbolising intuition and inner wisdom. Finally, at the peak, violet represents spiritual awakening, with the top radiating white light, the ultimate symbol of enlightenment and unity with the cosmos. While the theory incorporates ancient beliefs about spiritual ascension, this modern blend of colour symbolism with the pyramid's geometry offers a new lens to view these structures, not just as monumental achievements of architecture but as metaphysical representations of the soul's journey toward higher consciousness.[cxvii]

Pyramid Tattoos

Globally, the popularity of tattoos has grown significantly, with an estimated 38% of adults worldwide having at least one tattoo, according to various surveys. According to surveys, about 40% of millennials in the US have at least one tattoo.[cxviii] People get tattoos for different reasons, including personal expression, cultural or religious significance, and aesthetic appeal. Tattoos can visually represent beliefs, values, or identity, allowing individuals to express themselves.

Interestingly, the younger generation is getting pyramid tattoos on their bodies, possibly influenced by social media platforms and the entertainment industry. Pyramids are generally associated with ancient wisdom, mystery, and a connection to the divine. People fascinated by ancient civilisations or drawn to esoteric knowledge often choose pyramid tattoos to symbolise their interest in the metaphysical or mystical aspects of life. The design, however, will carry different meanings for each individual. The pyramid's structure, with its broad base and pointed apex, symbolises stability, strength, and endurance. Some people tattoo pyramids to represent personal growth, spiritual ascension, or the strength they have gained through life's challenges.[cxix] Many people with pyramid tattoos add personalised elements to the design, such as the Eye of Providence (or *All-Seeing Eye*) at the top or geometric patterns to enhance the symbolism. These elements can represent watchfulness, enlightenment, or protection. Pyramids are also associated with energy. Some believe pyramids can harness or channel cosmic or Earth energies. For those who believe in spiritual energy or healing, a pyramid tattoo can represent a connection to these forces or an alignment with the universe.

Symbolism, Control, and Conspiracy in Modern Culture

In contemporary culture, the pyramid often symbolises social hierarchies, with the broad base representing the masses and the narrow apex signifying elites or the ruling class. In dystopian narratives, it is used as a metaphor for the concentration of control and power, illustrating how resources, authority, or knowledge are often concentrated at the top, with diminishing amounts available as one moves down.

In dystopian literature and films, the focus is on the potential for elites to control the minds through propaganda, media, and societal structures. In *1984,* as depicted by George Orwell (1949), the Ministry of Truth is housed in a massive, pyramid-shaped building, symbolising the regime's control over information, history, and public perception. This architectural choice highlights the rigid hierarchy of the totalitarian state, where power is centralised at the top. The pyramid symbolises the Party's absolute control over the masses with its broad base and narrowing peak. Its design emphasises the Party's authority and permanence, drawing on the ancient symbolism of pyramids as enduring structures of power and dominance.

Some conspiracy theorists claim that pyramids are used as symbols of control within the media and that they subtly influence viewers' subconscious minds. Others interpret the presence of pyramids and related symbols in music videos, movies, and corporate logos as subliminal messaging, purportedly conditioning individuals to accept the hierarchical power structures that control them. Pyramids anchor power through their very form—rising from a broad, immovable base and tapering to a single, commanding point, they evoke a sense of permanence and unshakable authority.

Conspiracy theories also often link pyramids to secret government mind control projects like MK-Ultra, an actual CIA program in the mid-20th century that explored mind control techniques.[cxx] Some theorists speculate that pyramids were connected to this research, particularly in exploring how geometric shapes, resonance, or energy fields might affect human psychology. They argue that these techniques are now used on a much bigger scale through mass media, advertising, or even 5G networks to suppress dissent and control the population.

Wilson Bryan Key is an academic who has extensively explored subliminal messaging in media, including its influence on politics. He is known for his book *Subliminal Seduction* (1974), in which he explores how subliminal imagery, often unnoticed by the conscious mind, is embedded in advertising and media to influence public perception. His work also examines how such techniques can be applied in broader contexts, including politics, suggesting that visual symbols like triangles or pyramids may reinforce subconscious messages of control or dominance during public addresses. His theory suggests that when employed in strategic political imagery or media, these symbols can subliminally influence viewers' perceptions of authority and power. [cxxi] Although his conclusions have been controversial and criticised for lacking empirical evidence, his writings sparked debates on manipulating the unconscious mind through hidden imagery in advertising and political propaganda.

In his 1994 book *Project Blue Beam (NASA)*, Serge Monast expands on this idea, stating that the pyramid may be used in subliminal messaging, often seen in political campaigns, corporate logos, and media. According to these theories, politicians may subtly use pyramid imagery to reinforce their control through subliminal messaging. For instance, during significant political addresses, specific stage designs or visual backgrounds incorporating triangles or pyramid-like shapes have been scrutinised as deliberate efforts to project hidden meanings of control or dominance.[cxxii]

The Pyramid's Hidden Meaning on the Dollar Bill

One notable example of politicians using the pyramid is on the back of the United States one-dollar bill, where its prominent placement further solidified these associations. The pyramid represents strength, stability, and endurance, reflecting the long-lasting foundation of the United States. Conspiracy theorists, however, often see it as a representation of secret power structures. This design, finalised in

1782, reflects the Founding Fathers' desire for a symbol that embodied both historical significance and the enduring nature of their new republic. The 13 pyramid levels correspond to the original 13 colonies, grounding them in American history and the nation's foundation. [cxxiii] Its unfinished nature, with the missing top, symbolises the belief that the country is continually growing, evolving, and improving. The pyramid links to ancient civilisations, particularly Egypt, symbolising enduring wisdom and knowledge. This association ties into the idea that the founding of the United States was influenced by profound ideals and philosophies that transcend time and remain relevant today. Conspiracy theorists argue that the unfinished pyramid symbolises not the growth of the nation but the control of an elite ruling class (often referred to as the Illuminati or Freemasons) that governs from the shadows. The missing top of the pyramid is interpreted as a sign that the elite's goal—complete world domination—is still incomplete but continually pursued.[cxxiv]

At the top of the pyramid is the Eye of Providence, often called the *All-Seeing Eye*. This eye represents divine guidance and protection. Enclosed in a triangle, the eye signifies that a higher power is watching over the United States and guiding its progress. The Eye of Providence has roots in various religious and esoteric traditions, symbolising enlightenment, wisdom, and spiritual insight. The conspiracy theorists, however, believe it represents surveillance and control by a secret global power. They argue that the placement of the pyramid on the dollar bill reflects the influence of these occult traditions on the formation of the United States. The eye is frequently linked to the Illuminati, an alleged secret society with plans for world domination. They interpret the "All-Seeing Eye" as a symbol of totalitarian control, where an elite group watches and controls every aspect of society.[cxxv] Two Latin phrases appear around the pyramid: *Annuit Coeptis* translates to *He has favoured our undertakings*, suggesting that divine providence has approved the founding of the United States. *Novus Ordo Seclorum* means *New Order of the Ages*, indicating the belief that the founding of the United States marked the beginning of a new era in world history.[cxxvi] Conspiracy theorists frequently interpret the *New Order of Ages* as the *New World Order*, a phrase that has become synonymous with global governance led by secret elites.[cxxvii]

Interestingly, while the pyramid is a central part of Egypt's cultural heritage, it is surprising that it is not a dominant feature in the design of their modern currency. The pyramid last prominently featured on Egyptian banknotes in the mid-20th century. Specifically, the 50 piastres note, issued in the 1960s, featured an image of the Pyramids of Giza. Since then, Egypt's currency has shifted focus towards showcasing modern national symbols, though occasional depictions of ancient monuments, including pyramids, have appeared on commemorative coins or notes.[cxxviii]

How Symbols, Media, and Algorithms Shape Alternative Narratives

According to Michael Barkun, author of *A Culture of Conspiracy*, conspiracy theories thrive in environments where historical gaps are filled with speculative ideas. This explains why symbols like the pyramid, which have ambiguous historical origins and spiritual significance, become central to narratives involving secret societies and extraterrestrial influences.[cxxix] He argues in his book that many people are drawn to conspiracy theories about ancient civilisations and pyramids because these narratives offer grand, alternative explanations that challenge conventional history. Psychological research suggests that conspiracy theories often provide a sense of order and understanding in complex, uncertain contexts, particularly for individuals who feel alienated from mainstream institutions.

According to Michael Barkun, conspiracy theories appeal because they reduce ambiguity, offering hidden knowledge or secret truths that mainstream scholars allegedly ignore. The allure of alien involvement or lost civilisations building the pyramids taps into humanity's fascination with mystery and the unknown. Additionally, cognitive biases such as the Dunning-Kruger effect—where individuals with less knowledge of a subject overestimate their understanding—can make people more susceptible to accepting speculative or outlandish explanations over evidence-based accounts. These psychological factors play a significant role in the modern resurgence of conspiracy theories related to pyramids, as they provide both cognitive closure and a sense of intellectual superiority by claiming access to hidden truths.[cxxx]

The rise of independent media outlets and alternative platforms has given people access to a broader range of information, often bypassing traditional media gatekeepers. In recent years, the rise of digital platforms such as YouTube and TikTok has significantly contributed to the evolution and spread of conspiracy theories surrounding the pyramids. These platforms have allowed fringe theories about extraterrestrial involvement, ancient technologies, and hidden knowledge to reach vast audiences. Studies highlight how algorithms amplify sensational content, making speculative theories more accessible and appealing to users. Algorithms promote content that reinforces user beliefs, filtering out alternative viewpoints.

Bakshy, Messing, and Adamic (2015) demonstrated that users on Facebook are more likely to encounter content that reinforces their preexisting worldviews due to algorithmic filtering, which exacerbates confirmation bias. Their study, titled *Exposure to ideologically diverse news and opinion on Facebook*, examined how algorithmic filtering on the platform influences the information users are exposed to, highlighting how individuals tend to encounter content that reinforces their existing beliefs. This research focused on Facebook's role in shaping users' exposure to ideologically diverse content.[cxxxi] Similarly, a study by Ribeiro et al. (2020) titled *Auditing Radicalization Pathways on YouTube*, investigates how YouTube's recommendation system can lead viewers toward increasingly extreme content by suggesting videos that align with conspiratorial or radical views, contributing to the formation of echo chambers.[cxxxii]

A counterargument to the claim that digital platforms like YouTube and TikTok predominantly spread conspiracy theories about pyramids by prioritising engagement over accuracy focuses on the platforms' role in promoting diverse viewpoints and educational content. While it's true that algorithms may amplify sensational content, many users also encounter well-researched, scientific material alongside conspiratorial videos. The platforms promote diverse viewpoints and educational content, addressing topics often overlooked or censored by mainstream media.

Many believe mainstream media is influenced by political, corporate, or ideological interests, potentially skewing reporting and leaving specific topics underreported or framed in a particular way. This perception of bias, as discussed in *Manufacturing Consent* by Herman and Chomsky, leads to distrust, particularly when controversial subjects such as pyramid energy theories or alternative histories are involved. Mainstream outlets often dismiss coverage of alternative history or fringe theories as pseudoscience. Media companies argue they have a responsibility to provide accurate information. Broadcasting pseudoscientific theories as facts can spread misinformation and create public confusion, especially when the audience believes they cannot distinguish between scientific facts and unsupported claims. In contrast, proponents of these theories argue that the media ignores or censors legitimate ideas. Concerns about media ownership, advertising revenue, and corporate interests frequently fuel the belief that big corporations shape media narratives to serve specific agendas.[cxxxiii]

According to conspiracy theorists, the narrative for the news is often believed to be controlled by a small group of powerful elites, which includes governments, corporate interests, secret societies like the Illuminati or Freemasons, and major media conglomerates.[cxxxiv] These theorists argue that a few influential figures or organisations dictate what is reported, how it is framed, and which stories are amplified or suppressed to manipulate public opinion and maintain control over societal narratives. They highlight how global media consolidation plays a key role.[cxxxv] Only a few corporations, such as Disney, Comcast, and News Corp, control the majority of mainstream news outlets. These conglomerates are thought to coordinate their effort with political and financial elites to ensure that the news aligns with their economic and ideological interests. This alleged control allows them to craft narratives serving their agenda, whether promoting certain political ideologies, protecting corporate profits, or keeping the general population unaware of deeper truths (like secret government projects or hidden histories).[cxxxvi]

Some more extreme conspiracy theorists claim that these narratives are crafted to distract the public from important issues, promote fear, and suppress dissent. They argue that "false flag" operations or fabricated news stories are sometimes used to shift public attention and perception, pushing specific agendas while downplaying others.[cxxxvii]

A prime example is Project Blue Beam, a theory initially proposed by Serge Monast, a Canadian investigative journalist and writer. In his theory of *Project Blue Beam (NASA)* (1994), he suggests NASA and the United Nations plan to stage a false alien invasion or the second coming of a religious figure via holographic technology to establish a global totalitarian regime.[cxxxviii]

While such theories may stretch the imagination, it is undeniable that the media plays an influential role in shaping public perception and influencing behaviour. What makes this intriguing is the role pyramids often play in media representations.

In contrast to popular media's fascination with pyramids as symbols of hidden power, extraterrestrial influence, or mystical energy, many cultural historians argue that modern interpretations often exaggerate or misinterpret the significance of these ancient structures. Scholars highlight how films, pop culture, documentaries, and conspiracy theories have romanticised the pyramids, framing them as central to grand, alternative histories that lack empirical support. As historian Jason Colavito points out, *"The modern obsession with pyramids as beacons of ancient power or extraterrestrial influence is largely a product of the media's romanticisation of ancient civilisations, often ignoring the practical, religious, and political purposes these structures originally served"* (2005).[cxxxix] This trend, he suggests, reflects society's longing for mystery and wonder, overshadowing the more practical and religious purposes these monuments served for the ancient Egyptians and other cultures. By portraying pyramids as devices of forgotten technology or conduits for cosmic power, media narratives can blur the line between history and myth, leading to misconceptions about the technological and cultural capabilities of ancient civilisations. Such romanticisation, while entertaining, may distract from the true architectural genius and societal significance these structures held in their original contexts.

Why Are We Drawn to Ancient Symbols?

As explored in *The Archetypes and the Collective Unconscious* (1959), Carl Jung's concept of the collective unconscious provides a framework for understanding why symbols like pyramids hold a powerful and enduring appeal across cultures and throughout history. In his book, he argues that certain symbols are deeply embedded in the collective unconscious and influence how individuals perceive the world. He sees the collective unconscious as part of the unconscious mind, containing universal experiences, symbols, and archetypes. The archetypes, such as the pyramid, tap into primordial experiences and desire.

While Joseph Campbell focuses on the individual and the narrative structure departure-initiation-return that guides the hero's journey, Carl Jung's psychological analysis emphasises the deep-rooted, unconscious influence these symbols have on human behaviour and perception.

Both theories suggest the pyramid's universal appeal lies in its ability to resonate with shared human experiences. Together, their work illustrates how the pyramid, as a symbol, connects the material world with the spiritual, offering a metaphor for humanity's eternal search for meaning, transformation, and connection to the divine.

Pyramids evoke feelings of ascension and permanence, aligning with humanity's innate desire to connect with the past, the divine, and the mysterious forces of the universe.[cxl] Carl Jung's psychology suggests that symbols like the pyramid tap into deep psychological needs, such as the need for order in a chaotic world and the yearning for immortality or spiritual ascension. In many ancient cultures, pyramids were used as tombs or temples, symbolising a connection between the earthly and divine realms.[cxli]

While Joseph Campbell has influenced modern storytelling, Carl Jung's psychological concepts have profoundly influenced fields such as therapy and personality studies by providing insight into human behaviour.

Carl Jung believed that symbols like pyramids are expressions of the collective unconscious that appear in various forms across different civilisations. For instance, pyramids in Egypt, Mesoamerica, and Asia serve similar functions, whether for religious ceremonies, celestial alignment, or as symbols of authority, indicating that the image of the pyramid fulfils an essential psychological and spiritual need within humans.

Studies in symbolism and mythology reveal how these imagery are universally recognised across cultures. Research in cross-cultural psychology demonstrates that certain symbols provoke comparable emotional and cognitive responses in different societies, pointing to their archetypal origins.

Neuroscientific research indicates that the brain prefers geometric shapes that suggest hierarchy, balance, and ascent. This could explain the pyramid's psychological influence, reinforced by its literal upward orientation and triangular symmetry, which naturally evoke feelings of progress and transcendence.

The Human Brain Is Hardwired for Pyramidal Forms

Recent studies in visual cognition and neuroaesthetics help explain why the pyramid has such enduring symbolic power. Human perception is acutely sensitive to symmetrical, geometric shapes—especially those that imply hierarchy, directionality, or motion, such as the triangle.

According to research published in *Trends in Cognitive Sciences* by Ramachandran and Hirstein (1999), the brain preferentially processes images that feature grouping, contrast, and peak focus, all attributes embodied in the pyramid's design. Triangular shapes, particularly those that rise to a point, evoke a sense of tension, climax, or ascension, triggering regions in the occipital and parietal lobes associated with spatial mapping and symbolic abstraction.

Further, studies using fMRI scans, such as those by Chatterjee and Vartanian (2016), show that viewing symmetrical, high-contrast geometric forms activates the orbitofrontal cortex, an area linked with aesthetic judgment and emotional salience. The pyramid, with its commanding base and rising apex, acts as both a cognitive anchor and a symbolic vector, visually encoding ideas of order, elevation, and transcendence in a form the brain finds intuitively meaningful, even before language or narrative intervenes. This may explain why the pyramid persists as an archetype across cultures and media: it engages not just our myths or histories, but our neurophysiology itself.

A more recent study in 2020, *A Cultural Neuroscience Approach to Archetypal Symbols and Human Behavior* by Dr Elizabeth Parker, Dr Hiroshi Ito, and Dr Maria Johnson, published in *Frontiers in Psychology*, used functional Magnetic Resonance Imaging (fMRI) to explore how ancient symbols like pyramids affect the human brain across cultures. fMRI is a technique that maps brain activity by detecting changes in blood flow. It revealed that when participants viewed pyramid imagery, their brains showed heightened activity in regions associated with memory, emotion, and self-reflection. This aligns with Carl Jung's theory of archetypal symbols, suggesting that pyramids tap into the collective unconscious, evoking feelings of awe, stability, and a connection to something larger than oneself. The study's findings support that the pyramid's universal appeal stems from its ability to fulfil deep-seated psychological needs for order and spiritual ascension, demonstrating a consistent emotional and cognitive response across diverse cultures.[cxlii]

Some evolutionary psychologists argue that the brain's response to pyramidal or triangular forms may arise not from spiritual resonance but from ancestral survival cues. Barrett and Kurzban (2006) contend that human cognition evolved in a modular fashion to prioritise specific visual inputs, particularly sharp, angular shapes associated with threat detection.[cxliii] This suggests the appeal of pyramids may stem more from evolutionary utility. Supporting this view, theoretical neuroscientist Mark Changizi posits that our visual system is tuned to interpret shapes based on survival relevance. In *The Vision Revolution* (2009), he argues that the brain's rapid attention to triangular forms may relate to their resemblance to teeth, claws, and mountainous terrain, all of which historically signalled danger or directional importance.[cxliv]

Critics in the field of cultural neuroscience argue that the brain's response to geometric symbols is not purely hardwired, but shaped by cultural conditioning and symbolic exposure. According to Shihui Han et al. (2013), brain imaging studies show marked differences in how Eastern and Western subjects process faces, space, and symbols,[cxlv] suggesting that pyramid imagery might not evoke identical emotional or cognitive responses in all populations.

Is it plausible that populations exposed to higher ecological densities of dangerous fauna or more mountainous, angular terrains developed a heightened sensitivity to these shapes, reinforcing their perceptual and symbolic importance? Psychologist Richard G. Coss, in his book *Evolutionary Aesthetics* (2013), suggests that the human brain evolved in predator-rich environments, resulting in an innate sensitivity to angular, "provocative" shapes that trigger heightened emotional responses. This influence later extended to art, architecture, and symbolic forms. It is plausible that ancient populations living in ecosystems teeming with such threats—such as the crocodiles and lions of the Nile Valley or the jaguars and serpents of Mesoamerica—

developed stronger visual-attentional responses to triangular silhouettes, thereby reinforcing the psychological significance of pyramid-like shapes. These ancestral visual biases may partly explain the widespread occurrence of pyramidal architecture worldwide, not merely as a spiritual archetype but as an encoded memory of vigilance and power.

Considering the neuroscientific, evolutionary, and cultural layers, pyramid imagery is employed in music, politics, and logos because it directly appeals to deep-rooted cognitive, emotional, and symbolic systems that bestow power, mystery, and legitimacy.

The Pyramid in the Brain and the Brand

Pyramid imagery is visually simple but psychologically complex—capable of triggering subconscious associations across time, culture, and biology. Therefore, a pyramid is not just a shape—it is a directional symbol, pointing upward towards something aspirational or divine.

In politics, pyramid motifs are used to imply stability, hierarchy, and legitimacy. Consider the reverse side of the U.S. Great Seal: a 13-step pyramid topped with an all-seeing eye, signaling divine oversight, national destiny, and Masonic influence. The image suggests that power is built, layer by layer, beneath a transcendent authority. It taps directly into the cultural unconscious—hierarchy, vigilance, and ordained structure—without words.

In corporate logos, pyramid shapes suggest strength, progress, and upward mobility. Companies employ triangular or pyramid-like imagery to indicate stability, innovation, and dominance. Visually, these shapes command attention and effectively occupy cognitive space. They are spatially efficient, imply momentum, and often evoke ancient knowledge—appealing to firms aiming to appear elite, enduring, or futuristic.

In music and entertainment, pyramids connote mysticism, power, and hidden knowledge. Whether genuine or performative, these images convey that the artist is not merely famous—they are initiated. The audience, by association, is drawn into a ritual of modern myth-making.

Even in everyday infrastructure, the pyramid—or more precisely, the triangle—maintains its dominant presence. Consider road signs: many of the most urgent or cautionary symbols (e.g., yield signs, warning signs, danger alerts) are displayed in triangular shape. This is not random.

Ultimately, pyramid imagery is used because it functions as a multi-sensory symbol: biologically familiar, cognitively stimulating, culturally prestigious, and spiritually charged. It is architecture you don't just look at—you feel. That makes it ideal for any domain seeking to convey power, mystique, longevity, or transcendence.

The Pyramid as Humanity's Shared Architectural Code

The longevity and enduring presence of pyramids, especially the Great Pyramids of Egypt, have made them symbols of immortality and timelessness. They embody humanity's highest aspirations—spiritual ascension, self-actualisation, and cosmic connection—as well as our deepest anxieties about power, control, and hidden knowledge. The pyramid persists precisely because it represents both hope and fear. The psychological roots of this symbol's longevity show how it satisfies deep human needs. Ultimately, the pyramid remains powerful because it speaks directly to our unconscious minds, tapping into fundamental human impulses: the desire for immortality, ascension, power, and understanding. You are not drawn to the pyramid. The pyramid is awakening something already within you.

The pyramid has transcended its historical origins, becoming a lasting symbol in modern pop culture, esoteric thought, and conspiracy theories. From mystical to mainstream contexts, pyramids reflect humanity's quest for meaning, power, and the unknown. As we explore these ancient structures through new perspectives, their significance deepens, proving that the pyramid's allure extends beyond the past and actively influences our collective future. What more can we learn from these timeless wonders, and how will they continue to inspire future generations?

The fascination with pyramids has shifted from viewing them as monuments of ancient civilisation to considering them as potential conduits of untapped energy. While traditional interpretations focused on pyramids as tombs or religious symbols, modern views—influenced mainly by alternative historians, spiritual movements, and science fiction—consider the possibility that pyramids were deliberately designed to harness Earth's natural energies. This shift towards "energy theory" reflects growing interest in the idea that ancient civilisations possessed advanced scientific knowledge, perhaps surpassing our current understanding of physics and natural forces. The allure of pyramids as power-generating devices continues to captivate those eager to bridge ancient wisdom with cutting-edge science.

As we explore the modern fascination with pyramids, one key question remains: Why do these monumental structures appear in so many distant and seemingly unconnected parts of the world? From Egypt's deserts to the jungles of Mesoamerica, the widespread presence of pyramids suggests a shared knowledge or a universal human impulse that transcends geography and time. Could these ancient builders have tapped into a universal understanding of energy, spirituality, or cosmic alignment? Or did these cultures independently arrive at similar architectural forms because of their symbolic and practical power?

In the next chapter, we will examine the global distribution of pyramids and how different civilisations across continents adopted this enduring design, each adding to the mystery of the pyramid's universal appeal. What if the pyramids worldwide harnessed similar energies and shared symbolic meanings? We will explore pyramids from across the globe—from the grand temples of Mesoamerica to lesser-known structures in China and Sudan. Then, we will investigate the common threads linking these distant cultures. Some argue this reflects convergent evolution in architecture, where the pyramid form is structurally stable and easy to build. Others suggest a shared esoteric inheritance, whether cultural diffusion or some lost, unifying proto-civilisation. Could their mathematical and astronomical alignments reflect an ancient, universal understanding of Earth's natural forces? And where does this shared knowledge originate from? Despite its universality, the pyramid isn't omnipresent. In some regions, such as sub-Saharan Africa outside of Egypt, or indigenous Europe, pyramidal structures never took root. Was this perhaps due to different cosmologies, materials, or social needs?

Chapter 2 Pyramids Across the Globe

Pyramids Across the World

There are over 1,000 pyramids[cxlvi] scattered around the world, with the most famous located in Egypt. Is it a sheer coincidence that they all have the same structure?

Egypt has around 118 pyramids, including the famous Pyramids of Giza. Sudan, particularly in regions like Meroë and Napata, boasts over 200 pyramids, making it the country with the most pyramids in the world, even surpassing Egypt.[cxlvii] Travel across the Atlantic to Mesoamerica (Mexico and Central America), and you will find hundreds more pyramids. It is estimated that there may be around 300 pyramids in Mesoamerica. China's Shaanxi Province has several pyramids, known as the Chinese pyramids, mostly burial mounds from ancient dynasties. Around 40 such pyramids have been identified. They are, however, less visually striking than the stone pyramids in Egypt or Mesoamerica.

Interestingly, most Pyramids are in the Northern Hemisphere. This could be because many of the earliest and most advanced ancient civilisations, such as Egypt, Mesopotamia, and Mesoamerica, allegedly emerged in the Northern Hemisphere. These regions had fertile land and access to water, like the Nile and rivers in Mesoamerica. They also had resources that made large-scale construction possible. In areas like Egypt, limestone and other building materials were readily available, allowing the construction of the massive stone pyramids.[cxlviii]

New pyramidal structures continue to be discovered. As technology advances, we will likely uncover more hidden structures, whether beneath desert sands, deep within jungles, or submerged off ancient coastlines. The idea that pyramids serve as global symbols of power, spirituality, or energy could thus be even more widespread than currently known, spanning both land and sea.[cxlix]

Imagine the possibility of tens of thousands of pyramids hidden beneath the sands or submerged in the oceans. If so, it opens up new possibilities about their true purposes. Perhaps we have focused too narrowly on seeing them as tombs or spiritual monuments. What if the pyramid shape was simply the most practical design for various structures, like an upgraded tent made of bricks? They could have been used for anything from homes to religious centres. While they may appear similar, each pyramid could have served a vastly different purpose: one for burial, another for energy generation, a beauty facility, or perhaps functions we haven't even imagined. The possibilities are endless, and as we uncover more, we may need to rethink their roles in ancient civilisations completely.

Dating the Pyramids – Possible Timeline

We will examine the pyramids across different continents. Their development has a distinct timeline, beginning in Africa and the Middle East (specifically in Egypt) and later appearing in Asia (China) and the Americas (Mesoamerica and South America).

Date	Pyramid Name and Location
c. 3,000 BCE	Great Pyramid of Sialk (Iran)
c. 2,670-2,650 BCE	Step Pyramid of Djoser (Egypt)
c. 2,600 BCE	Pyramids of Caral (Peru)
c. 2,580-2,560 BCE	Great Pyramid of Giza and Giza Complex (Egypt)
c. 2100 BCE	Ziggurat of Ur (Iraq)
c. 800 BCE–300	Nubian Pyramids (Sudan)
c. 206 BCE–9 CE	Burial Mounds of the Western Han Dynasty (China)
c. 12 BCE	Pyramid of Cestius, Rome (Italy)
c. 200 AD	Pyramid of the Sun, Teotihuacan (Mexico)
c. 800 AD	El Castillo at Chichén Itzá, Yucatan Peninsula (Mexico)

This timeline of pyramid construction across the world is somewhat of a 'finger in the air' estimate, as exact dates can vary based on archaeological evidence, differing interpretations, and the availability of historical records. While these dates provide a general chronology of mainstream historians' dating of when pyramids were built, ongoing discoveries and research may refine or adjust these estimates.

Pyramids in Egypt

The most famous pyramids in Egypt are the Pyramids of Giza, including the Great Pyramid of Giza, one of the Seven Wonders of the Ancient World. These pyramids were primarily built during Egypt's Old Kingdom period, specifically the 4th Dynasty (around 2,580–2,560 BCE). The Great Pyramid, 146.6 meters (481 feet), constructed for Pharaoh Khufu, is the largest and most well-known of the group. It is slightly shorter today due to the loss of its outer casing stones and erosion.

Other pyramids at Giza include the Pyramid of Khafre (dated to around 2,558–2,532 BCE) and the Pyramid of Menkaure (dated to around 2,510 BCE). The Pyramid of Khafre was built for Khufu's son, Khafre, and the Pyramid of Menkaure was built for Khafre's successor.

The Old Kingdom is particularly noted for its pyramid construction, especially during the 4th Dynasty, which produced the pyramids at Giza. The Middle Kingdom also saw the construction of pyramids, although they were often smaller and made of mud brick, resulting in less well-preserved remains today. The Old Kingdom pyramids, especially those at Giza, were built during the height of ancient Egyptian pyramid construction.[cl]

The oldest pyramid is said to be in Saqqara, Egypt.[cli] It was constructed during the 27th century BCE (around 2,670–2,650 BCE) for the Pharaoh Djoser, the second king of Egypt's Third Dynasty. Imhotep, Djoser's architect, is credited with designing the Step Pyramid and introducing stone as a primary building material, a significant departure from the earlier use of mudbrick. This innovation set the precedent for later pyramid constructions. [clii]

Surrounding the pyramid is a vast archaeological dig that regularly unearths new artefacts. Archaeologists continue to uncover tombs and burial chambers around the Step Pyramid of Djoser. In 2020, several well-preserved tombs and coffins dating back over 2,500 years were discovered. Many of these coffins still had their original colours intact. They were sealed, providing valuable information about burial practices during Egypt's Late Period. Interestingly, they also discovered dozens of mummified cats alongside gilded statues of felines and a bronze statue of Bastet, the cat goddess. Egypt has a long history of mummifying animals, particularly cats, which are associated with the goddess Bastet. These mummified cats were often offered as gifts by worshippers. While individual discoveries sometimes reveal dozens or hundreds of mummified cats, the scale of ancient Egyptian mummification was immense, with millions of cats mummified over the centuries for religious purposes.

The dating of the Step Pyramid of Djoser has been established through a combination of archaeological evidence and historical records. Archaeologists determined the construction sequence by studying the material layers at the site. The stratification of materials around the Saqqara necropolis provides insight into its construction period. Records from ancient Egyptian historical sources, such as the Turin King List and inscriptions in the pyramid complex, help confirm the reign of Pharaoh Djoser and the corresponding era in which the pyramid was constructed. Organic materials near the pyramid, such as wood or plant remains, have been radiocarbon-dated. Though less precise for stone structures, carbon dating of nearby materials provides a general timeframe. The Step Pyramid's design—consisting of six stepped layers—is the precursor to the smooth-sided pyramids that followed. Its unique style helps place it within the early period of Egyptian pyramid construction. The Step Pyramid marks the beginning of Egypt's age of pyramid building and stands as a testament to early advances in engineering and architectural design.[cliii]

Pyramids in Sudan

Though the pyramids in Sudan are shorter and steeper than their Egyptian counterparts, the Nubian pyramids are equally fascinating, offering a window into the grandeur of the Kingdom of Kush. Just as microchips have become smaller while maintaining or even increasing their functionality, is it possible that the pyramids in Sudan, despite being smaller than those in Egypt, served similar or equally significant purposes for the Kushite civilisation? Built between 800 BCE and 300 CE, these pyramids reflect ancient Egypt's cultural and political influence on Nubia, yet they also stand as proud symbols of a distinct African civilisation.[cliv] The Nubian pyramids, primarily located at sites such as Meroë, Nuri, and El-Kurru, served as royal tombs for the kings, queens, and nobility of Kush.[clv]

Nubian pyramids are narrower and have a steeper angle compared to Egyptian pyramids. Some scholars speculate that these structures may have also served as spiritual "antennas" for channelling cosmic energies associated with their gods, similar to later interpretations of pyramid energy theories. The architectural style is characteristic of the pyramids built in the Kushite Kingdom.[clvi] They often have small chapels attached to their base, where offerings to the deceased were made. These pyramids are typically 6 to 30 meters in height, whereas the pyramids in Egypt range from 30 to 140 meters in height.[clvii] Nubia lacked the massive limestone quarries in Egypt, so archaeologists speculate that they may have built smaller structures to conserve materials while fulfilling the same functions.

However, their craftsmanship and symbolic significance are no less impressive. The pyramids of Meroë, a UNESCO World Heritage site, represent the height of Kushite architecture and cultural achievement.[clviii] Meroë, the capital of the Kingdom of Kush, was an important centre of trade, industry, and culture. The region was rich in resources, such as iron and gold, which helped Kush thrive as a powerful kingdom.

The cultural exchange between Egypt and Nubia is evident in the construction of the pyramids and the inscriptions and artwork found at these sites.[clix] For instance, while Egyptian funerary practices influenced the construction of the pyramids, they also incorporated elements of indigenous Nubian traditions, reflecting a fusion of African and Egyptian ideologies.[clx]

The pyramids at Nuri, where King Taharqa, one of Kush's most famous rulers, was buried, further highlight the significance of these structures.[clxi] King Taharqa ruled during the 25th Dynasty of Egypt, known as the "Kushite Dynasty," which saw Nubian kings ruling over Egypt and Nubia. The pyramids of Sudan thus serve as a testament to the Kingdom of Kush's influence in the Nile Valley and across northeast Africa.[clxii] Today, despite their historical significance, the Nubian pyramids are less well-known than their Egyptian counterparts.

Unfortunately, many were deliberately destroyed in the 19th century by an Italian treasure hunter named Giuseppe Ferlini. In the 1830s, he used dynamite and other destructive methods to blow up the tops of more than 40 pyramids in Meroë, believing that treasure would be hidden inside.[clxiii] His methods were crude and reckless, reducing many of these ancient structures to rubble. Despite the destruction, he did discover gold jewellery in one of the pyramids, which he later sold to European museums.[clxiv] However, his actions caused irreparable damage to some of Sudan's most important archaeological sites, earning him a notorious reputation in archaeology.[clxv]

Ongoing archaeological research and preservation efforts continue to reveal the deep cultural heritage of ancient Nubia and its powerful relationship with the Kingdom of Egypt. These pyramids are reminders of the rich legacy of one of Africa's great ancient civilisations.[clxvi] The Kushites were deeply influenced by Egyptian beliefs but added their twist. They worshipped Apedemak, a lion-headed war god unique to their culture. The pyramids in Meroë were believed to act as gateways to the afterlife, where the souls of the deceased would journey with Apedemak's guidance. There is also speculation that these pyramids align with stars associated with Apedemak's constellation, indicating their celestial significance.

Pyramids in the Middle East

The Middle East is home to several fascinating pyramidal and pyramid-like structures that reflect the region's rich spiritual and architectural heritage.

Among the most significant are the Ziggurats of Mesopotamia, constructed by ancient civilisations such as the Sumerians, Akkadians, Babylonians, and Assyrians in present-day Iraq and Iran. These terraced mud-brick pyramids, such as the Ziggurat of Ur (circa 2,100 BCE), dedicated to the moon god Nanna, and the Ziggurat of Chogha Zanbil (13th century BCE), honouring the Elamite god Inshushinak, were regarded as sacred mountains that connected heaven and earth. Mesopotamian myths tell of the gods using these structures as pathways to descend to the earthly realm and commune with humanity. It is said that priests would climb these ziggurats to meet the divine, ensuring the land's fertility and cosmic balance.

Tell el-'Ubaid, an ancient city in Iraq, holds early temple structures dating back to around 4,000 BCE, precursors to the later ziggurats. These pyramidal temples were considered places where the divine and earthly realms intersected. According to early Sumerian myths, these temples housed gods who brought blessings to the land. Priests ascended the temples to invoke the gods' favour, with some legends suggesting that the smoke of their offerings would transform into divine creatures carrying messages to the heavens. The Ziggurat of Aqar Quf, constructed by the Kassite king Kurigalzu near modern Baghdad around 1,400 BCE, is a reminder of Mesopotamian culture's religious influence. Dedicated to the gods, this ziggurat was where priests conducted rituals to ensure harmony between heaven and earth. Stories from the Kassite period mention a sacred ceremony where priests, standing atop the ziggurat, would sing hymns during lunar eclipses to guide the moon god's chariot back on its course, thus protecting the kingdom from misfortune.[clxvii]

Some speculate that the famous *Stargate* in Iraq may hold the key to unlocking the mysteries of the pyramids. The Stargate is often described as a large, ancient circular structure, possibly hidden within or near sites like the Ziggurat of Ur. It is imagined as having intricate carvings, symbols, or markings that could represent its function as a portal or gateway. They suggest that it is a portal to other dimensions or extraterrestrial realms. Believers argue that this Stargate might explain the US invasion of Iraq, speculating that world powers sought control over this hidden technology.[clxviii] While no evidence has been found, mythological interpretations and science fiction fuel these ideas—where there's smoke, there may be fire. Additionally, no weapons of mass destruction were found in Iraq, leading to widespread criticism and speculation about hidden motives behind the invasion. During the chaos of the war, the National Museum of Iraq was looted, with approximately 15,000 artefacts stolen. Some theorists suggest that specific, significant artefacts may have been intentionally targeted.

In Iran, the Great Pyramid of Sialk (3,000 BCE) is considered one of the earliest pyramid-like structures in the Middle East. It served as a spiritual centre for the Elamite civilisation. Elamite mythology suggests that these structures were designed as ladders for the souls of the deceased, enabling them to climb closer to the gods in the heavens.[clxix] A local legend recounts the tale of a great priest who, upon his death, transformed into a star after his body was placed within the pyramid, forever guiding the people of Sialk from the night sky.[clxx] The Ziggurat of Chogha Zanbil in Iran was built later than the Great Pyramid of Sialk. Its sophisticated water filtration system dates back to the 13th century BCE.[clxxi] This ancient filtration system, which included an underground network of drains, was designed to protect the structure from rainwater erosion, showing the advanced engineering skills of the Elamites.[clxxii] This ziggurat wasn't just a place for religious worship but may have also functioned to filter and store water—an odd dual purpose for what was primarily a sacred site.[clxxiii] This combination of practical infrastructure with spiritual architecture is rare in ancient pyramid-like structures across the Middle East. Or did all of them have multiple purposes, and should we reconsider the functionalities of all pyramids?

In Oman, the Royal Tombs of Bat (3,000-2,000 BCE) feature beehive-shaped mounds resembling small pyramidal structures. Although smaller than other pyramids, they demonstrate the ancient belief in an afterlife. The people of this region believed that these tombs acted as gateways for the soul, connecting the deceased with the divine, much like the portals used by their gods to enter the human realm. One local story speaks of spirits roaming the land near these tombs, guarding the passage between worlds and ensuring the dead's journey to the afterlife was successful. Some say that on certain nights, strange lights or glowing orbs can be seen hovering above the tombs, believed to be the souls of the ancient dead still wandering, protecting the site from intruders. There are even accounts of distant whispers being heard around the tombs, as if the spirits of the deceased are still watching over their final resting place, safeguarding the bridge between life and the afterlife.[clxxiv]

The Dilmun Burial Mounds in Bahrain, dating back to approximately 3,000 BCE, feature thousands of pyramid-like mounds constructed by the ancient Dilmun civilisation. While not traditional pyramids, these mounds exhibit the same intent of linking the dead with the divine realm. Sumerian myths identify Dilmun as a paradise blessed by the gods, where no disease or sorrow existed. Local legends claim that the mounds served as portals for the spirits of ancestors to return, bringing protection and guidance to the living. Some stories say that on certain nights, the souls of ancestors could be seen travelling through the mounds as glowing orbs, returning to their families.[clxxv]

Its strong connection to lunar worship sets the ancient city of Harran in Turkey apart from other pyramid-like structures in the

Middle East, which are often focused on sun worship.[clxxvi] While direct texts from Harran's ancient lunar temples are scarce, the city's significance is documented in Mesopotamian, Assyrian, Babylonian, and later Arabic texts. The moon god, Sin, was related to the moon's cycles, timekeeping, and fertility.[clxxvii] Harran's temples may have been designed with an eye to the night sky, focusing on lunar visibility rather than solar alignment. The name *Sin* originates from the Akkadian and Sumerian languages, which are unrelated to the English language. The similarity to the English word "sin" is said to be purely coincidental.[clxxviii] Concepts like "the Devil" or personified evil were not part of Mesopotamian belief systems. The idea of a singular evil entity, like the Devil in Christianity, Judaism, and Islam, developed later and has no connection to the god Sin. In ancient religions, gods typically embodied positive and challenging aspects of life, such as storms or war, without being classified as purely good or evil.[clxxix]

The height of pyramidal structures in the Middle East varies significantly, reflecting the different purposes and architectural styles of the civilisations that built them. For instance, the Ziggurat of Ur in Iraq originally stood around 21 meters (69 feet) high, with a multi-tiered design allowing priests to ascend closer to the heavens. In comparison, the Ziggurat of Aqar Quf, near modern Baghdad, reached approximately 57 meters (187 feet), emphasising its significance as a Kassite religious centre. The Great Pyramid of Sialk in Iran, an earlier structure, was significantly smaller, measuring around 15 meters (49 feet), reflecting the region's early stages of ziggurat construction. The Bat Tombs in Oman are more modest in scale, with heights ranging from 2 to 5 meters (6.5 to 16.5 feet), as these beehive-shaped structures primarily served as burial sites rather than monumental temples. In Turkey, the ruins of Harran's moon god temples suggest that these structures may have reached heights of up to 20 meters (65 feet) when intact, aligning with the regional tradition of building temples as elevated platforms. The Dilmun Burial Mounds in Bahrain also vary in height, with the largest mounds reaching up to 12 meters (39 feet) in height, serving as elevated resting places for the deceased in accordance with their spiritual beliefs. These variations in height reflect the diversity of architectural techniques and spiritual practices across ancient Middle Eastern civilisations, emphasising the different roles that pyramidal structures played in each culture.

Unfortunately, many pyramidal or pyramid-like structures that might have existed in the Middle East have not survived due to war, erosion, and construction techniques that didn't endure the test of time. The Middle East has faced numerous conflicts, from ancient battles to modern warfare, which have led to the destruction or neglect of archaeological sites. This results in fewer monumental structures being preserved than Egypt's stone pyramids.

Pyramids in Asia

Several pyramidal structures have been discovered in China, primarily located in Shaanxi Province, near the city of Xi'an.[clxxx] Approximately 40 known pyramids vary in size, with some reaching heights of over 46 meters (150 feet).[clxxxi] These Chinese pyramids, often referred to as ancient burial mounds, served as the final resting places for emperors and nobility, primarily from the Western Han Dynasty (206 BCE – 9 CE) and earlier periods.

The most famous is the Mausoleum of the First Qin Emperor, Qin Shi Huang, best known for its proximity to the Terracotta Army.[clxxxii] The Maoling Mausoleum was built for Emperor Wu of Han. He is known as one of China's most powerful emperors. It is one of the largest, standing around 155 feet (47 meters) high.[clxxxiii]

Chinese pyramids are closely tied to the worship of ancestral spirits and the pursuit of immortality. The tombs often include stories of emperors who sought to attain divine status, guided by the cosmic dragon, a mythological creature representing the emperor's link to heaven.[clxxxiv] Some researchers suggest these pyramids are aligned with constellations associated with Chinese astrology, particularly the dragon constellation (Long).[clxxxv] This alignment could have been designed to channel "Qi," or life-force energy, linking the emperor's spirit with the cosmos in his quest for immortality.

Unlike the smooth, sharply angled pyramids of Egypt, the pyramids in China are made of earth and stone. Over centuries, they have weathered into large, rounded mounds covered in vegetation. This natural weathering, combined with their construction materials, has led them to blend into the landscape, making them appear more like hills than the iconic pyramids of Egypt.[clxxxvi]

Many of these pyramids are covered in vegetation and remain relatively unexplored, as some are in restricted areas. Some are considered sacred burial sites protected by the Chinese government. Their inaccessibility and cultural reverence for ancestral burial grounds have resulted in limited excavation efforts.[clxxxvii]

There is also speculation that these pyramids could contain significant historical treasures, as several have yet to be excavated. Many scholars believe that they are not only important burial sites but also contain invaluable artefacts similar to those found in Egyptian pyramids.[clxxxviii] Scholars speculate that these pyramids contain invaluable historical treasures comparable to those found in Egyptian and Mesoamerican pyramids, including relics that could offer deeper insights into ancient Chinese culture, politics, and religious practices. [clxxxix] However, the Chinese government has limited excavation to preserve these sites, making them less studied than pyramids in Egypt and Mesoamerica. [cxc] As a result, these pyramids have been less studied and explored than their Egyptian and Mesoamerican counterparts, leaving much of their history and contents shrouded in mystery. This decision has led to intrigue and speculation among historians and archaeologists about the treasures and knowledge that may still lie hidden within these ancient structures.

Pyramids have also been found in other Asian countries. For example, the Borobudur Temple in Indonesia is an example of a step pyramid design.[cxci] Built in the 9th century, Borobudur is a massive Buddhist monument with nine stacked platforms, six square and three circular, topped by a central dome. Unlike traditional pyramids, Borobudur is a complex of terraces adorned with thousands of relief panels and Buddha statues, functioning primarily as a place of pilgrimage. It symbolises the path to enlightenment, with the pyramid-like structure representing layers of spiritual ascension.[cxcii] Although different in function and design, Borobudur reflects the evolution of pyramid-shaped structures across cultures, serving as monumental tombs, fortifications, and spiritual and religious symbols.

In Cambodia, the ancient city of Koh Ker is home to the impressive Koh Ker Pyramid, also known as Prasat Thom. This step pyramid, constructed in the 10th century during the Khmer Empire, rises to approximately 36 meters (118 feet) in height. The structure features seven distinct tiers, giving it a stepped, terraced appearance that resembles Mesoamerican pyramids. Koh Ker was a temporary capital of the Khmer Empire, and the pyramid served as a religious and ceremonial centre. The pyramid's design was believed to be inspired by Mount Meru, the sacred mythical mountain central to Hindu and Buddhist cosmology. The pyramid's alignment and structure illustrate the Khmer civilisation's architectural prowess and spiritual focus on connecting the terrestrial with the divine.[cxciii]

In the ancient city of Anuradhapura, Sri Lanka, the Jetavanaramaya Stupa stands as one of the largest brick structures in the world. Built around the 3rd century CE, this stupa initially reached an impressive height of approximately 122 meters (400 feet), although it has reduced in size over the centuries due to erosion. Unlike the sharp-angled pyramids of Egypt, the Jetavanaramaya features a terraced, mound-like design typical of Buddhist stupas. It was constructed to house relics and symbolise the Buddhist path to enlightenment, making it a significant spiritual and religious monument. The stupa's layered structure reflects the Buddhist concept of spiritual ascent, aligning it with pyramid-like structures in other cultures, representing the journey from the earthly to the divine. The Jetavanaramaya exemplifies how the symbolic and architectural significance of pyramids extended into South Asia, adapting to the region's spiritual and cultural contexts.[cxciv]

India also houses several pyramid structures. In Tamil Nadu, India, the Brihadeeswarar Temple, also known as the Tanjore Temple, showcases a massive, pyramid-like tower called a vimana. Built during the Chola Dynasty in the 11th century, this temple stands at approximately 66 meters (216 feet) in height and is dedicated to the Hindu god Shiva.[cxcv] While not a traditional pyramid, the temple's vimana is a layered, step-like structure that reflects the Dravidian architectural style, emphasising stacked and tiered designs culminating in a central shrine at the top.[cxcvi] The temple was a place of worship and a demonstration of the Chola Empire's wealth, power, and devotion. Its design and scale illustrate the importance of pyramid-like structures in South Asian architecture, often used to symbolise spiritual ascent and the connection between earthly and divine realms.[cxcvii] The Brihadeeswarar Temple's vimana was constructed without the use of cement or mortar—the stones were so expertly cut that they fit together perfectly, a testament to the precision of Chola-era engineers.[cxcviii] Interestingly, in some ancient texts, "vimana" refers to a mythical flying machine or "chariot of the gods." These flying vimanas are described as vehicles used by gods or humans with divine abilities capable of traversing the skies.[cxcix]

Located in Madhya Pradesh, India, the Great Stupa at Sanchi is an iconic example of early Buddhist architecture. Built in the 3rd century BCE by Emperor Ashoka, the stupa features a large, dome-like structure atop a terraced base, reaching a height of approximately 54 feet (16.4 meters). Although it is not a traditional pyramid, its design incorporates a step-like structure that resembles a tiered mound.

What we see in Asia is the diversity and adaptability of pyramid-like structures across the continent. Unlike the monumental pyramids of Egypt or the step pyramids of Mesoamerica, Asian pyramids come in various forms and serve multiple purposes, from religious and ceremonial centres to monumental tombs and potential ancient observatories. In China, the Western Han Dynasty burial mounds symbolise power, ancestry, and the importance of honouring the dead. In Cambodia, the Koh Ker Pyramid reflects the spiritual connection to cosmological beliefs, while Indonesia's Borobudur Temple uses a pyramid-like design to symbolise the path to enlightenment within Buddhism. These examples, along with the unique structures in India, Japan, and Sri Lanka, demonstrate that the pyramid concept was not limited to a single specific culture or region. Instead, it was a versatile architectural form that ancient civilisations across Asia adapted to reflect their spiritual, cultural, and practical needs. The variety of designs—from earthen mounds and stepped terraces to grand temple towers—highlights their ability to use architecture to connect the earthly and the divine.

Pyramids in Europe

Though less famous than their counterparts in Egypt or Mesoamerica, pyramids in Europe reveal fascinating insights into how different cultures incorporated pyramid-like structures into their architectural and cultural landscapes. Many are denied or disputed.

Several pyramid structures exist in Greece, the most notable being the Pyramid of Hellenikon near Argos. It is built with limestone blocks, resembling a step pyramid. Much smaller in scale compared to the grand pyramids of Egypt or the stepped pyramids of Mesoamerica, the Pyramid of Hellenikon is significant for its unique design and mysterious purpose. Archaeologists continue to debate its function, with some proposing that it was a watchtower, fortification, or signalling station. Others suggest it may have served as a monumental tomb or ceremonial site.[cc] The dating of the structure is also a matter of controversy. Some estimates place its construction around the 4th century BCE, but alternative theories propose it could be much older, possibly dating back to the Mycenaean period (around 1,600–1,100 BCE).[cci] The ongoing debate highlights the challenges of dating and interpreting ancient structures, as well as the pyramid's intriguing connection to early Greek civilisation.

In Rome, the Pyramid of Cestius is the best-preserved example of pyramid architecture outside of Egypt.[ccii] Built around 12 BCE as a tomb for the Roman magistrate Gaius Cestius, this pyramid reaches approximately 37 meters (121 feet) in height. The structure was heavily influenced by Egyptian architecture, reflecting the Roman fascination with Egypt that grew after the Roman conquest of the region. The Pyramid of Cestius, while serving a funerary purpose, also illustrates the Roman tendency to blend architectural styles, merging Roman and Egyptian traditions in a single monument.[cciii] It is a testament to the cultural exchange between Rome and Egypt, demonstrating how Egyptian influence extended beyond its borders and was integrated into Roman culture and practices.

These examples from Greece and Rome demonstrate that while European pyramid structures are fewer and generally smaller, they still provide valuable insights into the ancient civilisations of Europe. They also highlight the cultural interconnectedness of the ancient world, as these structures often reflect influences from other regions, such as Egypt. This interconnectedness suggests that the pyramid concept, whether as a tomb, monument, or ceremonial site, resonated across cultures and was adapted to meet the diverse architectural and symbolic needs of various societies.

There are other pyramid-like structures in Europe beyond those in Greece and Italy, though they are often much smaller, less monumental, and sometimes controversial in their classification as "pyramids."

For example, the Pyramids of Güímar, located on the island of Tenerife in the Canary Islands, are terraced structures built from volcanic stone that resemble the step-like pyramids found in Mesoamerica. While some believe ancient civilisations constructed these pyramids, mainstream archaeologists typically date them to the 19th century, suggesting they were agricultural terraces made by local farmers rather than ancient monuments.[cciv] Local Guanche mythology (the indigenous people of the Canary Islands) includes tales of "Achamán," a supreme god who created the world and the heavens.[ccv] Some theories propose that these pyramids were constructed as offerings or observatories dedicated to Achamán, allowing the people to connect with their deity during solstices.[ccvi] Researchers have observed that these pyramids align precisely with the setting sun on the summer solstice. Some speculate that the Guanche people may have used them for worship and as markers of time and agricultural cycles, linking the pyramids' design with their cosmology.

The Pyramid of Falicon, located near Nice, France, is a small, dilapidated pyramid situated above the entrance of a natural cave known as the Grotte de Ratapignata. Though it dates back to the 18th century, it was likely constructed by local nobles, possibly as a decorative or symbolic structure rather than serving any religious or monumental purpose.[ccvii] While some speculate that the pyramid may have been used for esoteric rituals or had ties to Freemasonry, there is no definitive evidence to confirm these theories. The pyramid remains a point of intrigue and mystery, drawing interest from those fascinated by its origins and potential connections to secretive practices.[ccviii]

Researchers have also discovered pyramid-like structures built from basalt stones in the Azores archipelago, particularly on the island of Pico.[ccix] These stepped formations are believed to have been constructed by early settlers and are generally considered agricultural terraces or platforms. However, some local researchers propose a more ancient origin for these structures, suggesting they may have had a purpose beyond agriculture. Despite these theories, no conclusive archaeological evidence has been found to classify them as ancient pyramids akin to those in Egypt or Mesoamerica. Nonetheless, they contribute to the diversity of pyramid-like structures in Europe and continue to intrigue researchers and visitors alike.[ccx]

In the village of Șona, nestled in the Transylvanian region of Romania, stand eight large earthen mounds arranged in a remarkably symmetrical formation. Rising to 30 meters high, these grassy hills have long sparked debate. Mainstream scholars largely attribute the mounds to natural glacial or erosional activity, dismissing the notion of deliberate human construction due to the absence of stone architecture or clear structural foundations. However, the discovery of Bronze Age artifacts nearby, including ceramic fragments and tools, raises questions about their potential role in ancient ritual or burial practices. Fringe theorists argue that the mounds were intentionally shaped as energetic nodal points or repositories of forgotten knowledge, possibly acting as primitive pyramid analogues aligned with telluric currents or celestial events. Whether natural or man-made, the Șona formations remain a curious anomaly.[ccxi]

As a final example, Silbury Hill in Wiltshire, England, though not a pyramid in the traditional sense, is one of the largest prehistoric mounds in Europe, rising to approximately 40 meters (131 feet). Constructed around 2400 BCE during the Neolithic period, its exact purpose and construction method remain a mystery.[ccxii] The mound's stepped appearance has led some to draw comparisons with pyramidal structures, suggesting that it may have served a ceremonial or ritual function similar to those of pyramids in other ancient cultures.[ccxiii] However, despite these similarities, it is not classified as a pyramid. Silbury Hill is a testament to the complexity of European prehistoric architecture, reflecting the ancient inhabitants' capacity for monumental construction. Most interestingly, ground-penetrating radar (GPR) and other non-invasive archaeological techniques have revealed that this prehistoric mound has an incredibly complex internal structure. Despite being built around 2400 BCE, researchers have only recently discovered hidden chambers and layers within the mound, suggesting that its construction involved multiple phases, potentially over several generations.[ccxiv] Some theories propose that Silbury Hill was not only a ceremonial site but may have been used to mark significant astronomical events, such as solstices, similar to other ancient structures worldwide.[ccxv]

Could glaciation have eroded or buried more structures? Could what we call hills be hiding pyramids? Or perhaps pyramids existed in an organic form, made of wood and earth, which led to decay.

Pyramids in Mesoamerica and Peru

Mesoamerican and South American pyramids are much younger than those in Egypt. Egyptian pyramids were built over 4,500 years ago, whereas most Mesoamerican pyramids were built between 2,000 and 2,500 years ago. While it is theoretically possible that the Egyptian pyramids influenced those in Mesoamerica and South America, no concrete archaeological or historical evidence supports this claim.

In Mesoamerica, spanning modern-day Mexico, Guatemala, Belize, Honduras, and El Salvador, hundreds of pyramids were built by civilisations such as the Maya, Aztecs, Olmec, and Zapotec. The Mayan civilisation thrived in present-day Mexico, Guatemala, Belize, Honduras, and El Salvador and was known for its advanced cities and astronomical knowledge. The Aztecs dominated central Mexico, particularly around modern-day Mexico City, establishing a vast empire with Tenochtitlán as its capital. The Olmec are considered one of the earliest Mesoamerican civilisations. They inhabited the Gulf Coast region of Mexico, primarily in Veracruz and Tabasco. The Zapotec civilisation flourished in the Valley of Oaxaca in southern Mexico, creating impressive cities like Monte Albán.

They still stand as awe-inspiring remnants of their architectural brilliance. The Pyramid of the Sun at Teotihuacan, situated near modern-day Mexico City, was constructed around 200 AD and stands approximately 65 meters (213 feet) tall, making it one of the largest pyramids in the world.[ccxvi] This massive structure reflects the city's status as Mesoamerica's most important pre-Columbian urban centre. The Pyramid of the Moon, located in Teotihuacan, is around 43 meters (141 feet) high. It was used for religious rituals and sacrifices.

Another famous pyramid, El Castillo at Chichén Itzá, was constructed by the Maya around 800 AD and stands 30 meters (98 feet) tall. The pyramid is aligned with astronomical events. During the equinoxes, the sun casts shadows along the pyramid's steps, creating the illusion of a serpent slithering down its side, representing the feathered serpent deity Kukulcán. Local mythology suggests that the pyramid was built by giants who wanted to reach the heavens but were struck down by the gods. It was also believed to be a pilgrimage site and a ceremonial centre where rituals to honour Quetzalcoatl were performed. These step pyramids served as religious and ceremonial centres, with flat tops for sacrifices and temples.[ccxvii]

The pyramids in Peru, particularly those at Caral, most closely resemble the step pyramids found in Mesoamerica, especially those built by the Mayan and Olmec civilisations. While there are key differences in the materials and purposes of the structures, the general terraced design is more aligned with the Mesoamerican pyramids than with the smooth-sided pyramids of Egypt or Nubia. The pyramids of Caral in Peru, built by the Norte Chico civilisation around 2,600 BC, predate the Mesoamerican structures by millennia. Although smaller, the pyramids of Caral, such as the Pirámide Mayor, reached heights of 28 meters (92 feet) and were constructed primarily from earth and river stone, reflecting a highly advanced society long before the rise of the Mayans or Aztecs.[ccxviii] The construction and orientation suggest advanced knowledge of acoustics. Some archaeologists propose that these pyramids were designed to amplify sounds during ceremonies, connecting the people with their gods through chants and music that resonated with the natural environment. This echoes similar theories about sound manipulation and its sacred significance in pyramid construction globally.[ccxix]

While Mesoamerican pyramids were heavily linked with public ceremonies, astronomy, and religion, the pyramids at Caral appear to have had a broader role in urban development and administrative purposes.[ccxx] Archaeological evidence suggests these structures supported a thriving society engaged in trade and agriculture. The people of Caral worshipped deities associated with water, fertility, and agriculture, reflecting their dependence on river irrigation. The pyramids were likely built as temples for rain and water deities, integrating mythological rituals to ensure plentiful harvests and appeasing natural forces.[ccxxi]

There are many more of them. The Mayan civilisation also constructed many impressive pyramids in Guatemala, particularly in ancient cities like Tikal and El Mirador. Tikal is home to towering structures, such as Temple I, which stands at approximately 47 meters (154 feet) high.[ccxxii] El Mirador, an even older Mayan city, houses the La Danta pyramid, recognised as one of the largest ancient structures in the world by volume.[ccxxiii] In Honduras, the Maya site of Copán features smaller but intricately decorated pyramidal structures adorned with carvings and inscriptions that reveal insights into the Maya's culture and political history.[ccxxiv] In Belize, the ancient city of Caracol boasts numerous pyramids, with Caana (Sky Place) being the tallest, measuring 43 meters (141 feet).[ccxxv] Other significant Maya sites in Belize, such as Xunantunich and Altun Ha, also contain pyramidal temples that served as ceremonial and political centres, reflecting the widespread influence and sophistication of Maya civilisation across the region. The ancient city of Tiwanaku, near Lake Titicaca in Bolivia, features pyramid-like structures such as the Akapana. Although not as tall as other pyramids, these stepped platforms demonstrate the architectural skills of the Tiwanaku culture.[ccxxvi] The Mayan site of San

Andrés in El Salvador contains smaller pyramidal structures that served as ceremonial centres.[ccxxvii] The ruins are less prominent than those in Mexico or Guatemala, but still show the widespread influence of Mayan architecture.[ccxxviii]

These examples demonstrate the widespread presence of these pyramid structures, which spanned diverse regions and showcased their cultural, religious, and architectural significance across ancient Mesoamerica and possibly Latin America.

Interestingly, monumental pyramids were constructed in Mesoamerica and South America long before fully developed writing systems were established. For example, in Mesoamerica, the earliest pyramids, such as those in Teotihuacan, were built well before the Mayans developed their sophisticated hieroglyphic writing system. Despite the absence or limited use of written records, these civilisations achieved remarkable results, relying on oral transmission, astronomical knowledge, and organised labour to build their impressive pyramids.[ccxxix]

No Pyramids in the US?

Why are there no pyramids in the United States? Some argue that the absence of pyramids in the US stems from the unique cultural, environmental, and architectural practices of the indigenous civilisations that inhabited the region. While advanced societies such as the Mississippian civilisation built large earthen mounds, these structures served a different purpose than the stone pyramids of other cultures. Mounds acted as platforms for temples, residences, and ceremonial spaces, reflecting their societal organisation and spiritual beliefs.[ccxxx] These earthworks were constructed using available materials, such as soil and clay, in contrast to the stone-based pyramids of Egypt and Mexico, which utilised readily available limestone and sandstone.[ccxxxi]

Illinois is home to the *Cahokia Mounds*. This site features pyramid-like structures built by the ancient Mississippian culture. Located near Collinsville, Illinois, the mounds, particularly the massive *Monks Mound*, served as ceremonial platforms and resemble pyramids in form and function. However, they are constructed from earth rather than stone.[ccxxxii] Monks Mound, built between 1050 and 1200 CE, is the largest prehistoric earthwork in the US, standing over 100 feet tall.[ccxxxiii] While different from the pyramids of Egypt and Mesoamerica, these earthen mounds played a similar role as centres for religious, political, and social activity.[ccxxxiv] The Cahokia site, a UNESCO World Heritage site, reflects the sophistication and complexity of Native American civilisations.[ccxxxv]

Geographically, the availability of stone in regions such as Egypt, Mesoamerica, and China contributed to the development of monumental stone structures. In contrast, the societies in what is now the US adapted to their environments by utilising the materials at hand, primarily earth.[ccxxxvi] Moreover, the architectural priorities of indigenous cultures were shaped by their specific needs and environments. For instance, the Ancestral Puebloans built intricate cliff dwellings and stone cities, such as those in Chaco Canyon, emphasising protection and resource management in the arid Southwest rather than the grand pyramidal tombs found in other parts of the world.[ccxxxvii]

The time during which these cultures reached their peak also influenced their architectural choices. Civilisations like the Mississippians reached their zenith between 800 and 1600 CE, long after pyramid-building had become central in Egyptian and Mesoamerican cultures. By the time complex societies developed in North America, their architectural traditions were already distinct, shaped by the spiritual and practical demands of their environment.[ccxxxviii] As a result, although North America is home to impressive indigenous structures, pyramids as we commonly know them were not a part of its architectural evolution. This divergence highlights the diversity in how ancient civilisations around the world responded to their cultural and environmental circumstances in their monumental building projects.[ccxxxix][ccxl]

Geographical and energetic theories, such as the location of ley lines and tectonic plates, may partially explain the absence of pyramids in the US. Pyramids in other parts of the world, particularly in Egypt, Mesoamerica, and China, are often found near ley lines—hypothetical alignments of ancient sites that some believe are connected to Earth's energy grid. These lines are important to ancient builders who may have intentionally placed monuments along them to tap into or amplify natural energy fields.[ccxli] Some speculate that the lack of tectonic activity might have played a role. In areas with greater tectonic activity, such as regions around the Pacific "Ring of Fire" or near the tectonic boundaries in Egypt and Mesoamerica, the Earth's shifting plates create geological energy that could have influenced where ancient people chose to build their monumental structures.[ccxlii]

There is one modern-day exception. Illinois has the *Gold Pyramid House* located in Wadsworth. Built in 1977 by Jim and Linda Onan, this six-story, 17,000-square-foot structure was designed to resemble the Great Pyramid of Giza.[ccxliii] The Onans were inspired by the idea that pyramid shapes could harness energy, a belief rooted in both fascination with Egyptology and modern interpretations of ancient designs. The property became well-known for its striking pyramid shape and accompanying features, including a moat and a large replica of King Tutankhamun's statue.[ccxliv] Originally constructed as a private residence, the Gold Pyramid House has since become a popular tourist attraction.[ccxlv] Although a fire damaged part of the building in 2018, efforts have been made to restore it, keeping this architectural anomaly alive as a testament to the enduring influence of ancient pyramids, even in unexpected places like Illinois.[ccxlvi]

Hidden Pyramids in Grand Canyon and Alaska?

The idea of hidden pyramids in the Grand Canyon in the US has captured the imagination of fringe theorists and conspiracy enthusiasts, mainly stemming from a 1909 article in the Arizona Gazette that described the discovery of ancient Egyptian-like artefacts and mysterious structures in the canyon.[ccxlvii] The Arizona Gazette, now known as The Arizona Republic, was a legitimate newspaper and one of Arizona's oldest and most widely circulated newspapers.[ccxlviii] According to the article, explorer G.E. Kincaid allegedly found a cave filled with hieroglyphics, mummies, and treasure, with claims of Smithsonian involvement. He is portrayed as an experienced outdoorsman and explorer, but the details of his past or qualifications are not provided with any specificity. However, no evidence has ever been produced to substantiate this story, and the Smithsonian denies any connection to such a discovery.[ccxlix] In the early 1900s, many reputable newspapers published sensational stories to attract readers. It was common for newspapers to exaggerate or fabricate stories, especially regarding mysterious discoveries, lost civilisations, and adventurous expeditions. The 1909 article follows this pattern, containing dramatic and fanciful elements that lack supporting evidence.[ccl]

This tale has since fueled various conspiracy theories, suggesting that the Smithsonian and other entities have covered up the discovery to protect the established narrative of human history. The artefacts supposedly found in the Grand Canyon resemble Egyptian designs, including many mummies and thousands of panels with hieroglyphs, which would challenge the understanding of history. However, there is no evidence; there are just whispers in the hallway.

Some natural rock formations within the Grand Canyon have been noted for their pyramidal shapes, which have led to speculative claims that they are remnants of ancient structures. For example, formations like the Isis Temple, Cheops Pyramid, and Zoroaster Temple are prominent canyon features named after ancient gods and mythological figures due to their visual similarity to pyramidal shapes. Others argue that these formations may be artificial, suggesting that they result from millions of years of natural erosion.[ccli]

Satellite images of the Grand Canyon are widely available through platforms like Google Earth, NASA's Landsat program, and commercial providers such as Maxar Technologies. These images offer highly detailed views of the canyon's geological formations, enabling scientists, researchers, and the public to explore its vast terrain from above. While these satellite images are primarily used for studying erosion patterns, environmental changes, and geological features, they have not revealed any unusual or unexpected artificial structures, such as pyramids or hidden civilisations, despite claims from conspiracy theorists. Any anomalies detected in the images are typically explained by the canyon's unique and naturally occurring geological formations, which can sometimes appear pyramid-like due to the effects of erosion and rock stratification that have occurred over millions of years. No credible scientific findings suggest the existence of hidden man-made structures in the Grand Canyon based on satellite imagery. All discoveries have been linked to Native American cultures, such as the Ancestral Puebloans and Hopi. Thus, while the legend persists, it remains a myth rather than a historical fact.[cclii]

Another reason for suspecting hidden pyramids is the restricted access to some areas. Certain areas of the Grand Canyon are closed to the public, primarily for cultural preservation, environmental protection, safety, and government use. Many of these restricted zones contain sacred sites and archaeological remains belonging to Native American tribes, protected to prevent damage and unauthorised access.[ccliii] Additionally, the Grand Canyon's fragile ecosystem requires careful management, with some areas closed to protect endangered species and prevent environmental degradation.[ccliv] Safety concerns, such as unstable cliffs and hazardous conditions, also lead to restrictions.[cclv] Some sections are used for military purposes or scientific research, requiring special access or permits. The proximity of the Grand Canyon to various military installations, such as the Luke Air Force Base, can also limit access to areas that are off-limits for national security reasons.[cclvi] These closures are in place to safeguard the canyon's natural and cultural resources, and are not intended to conceal discoveries.

A government may withhold highly disruptive findings to avoid sparking public controversy or rewriting established historical and archaeological narratives. However, this is not supported by historical precedents. Governments or scientific institutions sometimes withhold findings until they are thoroughly investigated and confirmed. [cclvii] If a significant discovery were made, it might be temporarily kept confidential while experts study and verify the site or artefacts to avoid spreading misinformation or premature conclusions.[cclviii] This is standard in academic and archaeological work, where findings are typically announced once sufficient evidence has been gathered.[cclix] In sporadic cases, scientific or technological discoveries with potential implications for national security may be restricted. While this is more relevant to the discovery of advanced technologies or resources such as minerals or elements valuable to defence, it's highly unlikely that this applies to the Grand Canyon or ancient artefacts.[cclx]

Another controversial theory concerns the alleged existence of a massive underground pyramid buried in Alaska, often referred to as the *Black Pyramid*. According to reports popularised by investigative journalist Linda Moulton Howe, this pyramid is said to be larger than the Great Pyramid of Giza and located somewhere between Nome and Mount McKinley (Denali).[cclxi] It has been described as constructed from black stone, possibly basalt, a dense volcanic rock. It is reported to be buried at a depth of approximately 213 meters (700 feet) beneath the surface.

Could it be a volcano? Alaska is part of the Pacific Ring of Fire, with over 130 volcanoes, 50+ of which are considered potentially active. The Denali region, where the pyramid is said to lie, is surrounded by tectonic activity, fault zones, and ancient volcanic plugs. Perhaps pyramids were man-made copies of volcanoes, designed to capture or replicate the natural power observed in volcanoes. Just as volcanoes emit heat, magnetic fields, and atmospheric electricity, pyramids may have been engineered to conduct Earth's latent power in more stable and controlled ways. Their shape mirrors volcanic cones, while their internal chambers align with underground cavities or vents. If volcanoes were nature's original energy generators, then pyramids may have been humanity's first attempt at artificial geothermal or geomagnetic technology.

Whistleblower accounts and military sources suggest that the pyramid may have been detected during seismic testing related to nuclear detonations in China in the early 1990s. Some claim this structure is not only ancient but also still active, possibly generating extraordinary amounts of energy—enough, allegedly, to power all of Alaska and parts of Canada. Others speculate that its presence explains why the U.S. military maintains such a strong and secretive footprint in the region. Linda cited a former electrical engineer whose relative worked at the site in the late 1950s–60s, describing the pyramid as an underground facility connected to energy distribution tests or experimental systems. However, no verifiable satellite imagery, geological surveys, or declassified documents have ever confirmed the pyramid's existence, and mainstream scientists dismiss the idea as a modern myth born of misinterpretation or deliberate disinformation.

Still, the story persists as another example of a powerful structure concealed from public knowledge. If real, it would radically reshape our understanding of North American prehistory and energy capabilities.

New Pyramid Discoveries

Drones have become transformative tools in archaeology, enabling discoveries and providing previously challenging or impossible insights. Drones equipped with high-resolution cameras and sensors, such as multispectral and thermal imaging, can detect subtle changes in soil and vegetation. Many archaeological sites, such as those located in cliffs, dense jungles, or desert landscapes, are situated in remote or challenging locations. Drones provide access to these areas without the need for risky expeditions, allowing archaeologists to study inaccessible structures, cave paintings, and ruins.

LIDAR (Light Detection and Ranging) technology has played a significant role in uncovering hidden pyramidal structures. LIDAR technology, mounted on drones, can "see through" dense vegetation, invaluable in regions like Central America, Southeast Asia, and other heavily forested areas. Traditional methods struggled to detect structures hidden under thick canopies, but LIDAR penetrates foliage, allowing archaeologists to uncover lost cities, road networks, and hidden monuments. LIDAR creates high-resolution, three-dimensional maps of the ground surface, revealing subtle features such as walls, terraces, ditches, and paths that may be invisible to the naked eye. These maps provide archaeologists with a highly detailed view of the landscape during ancient times. Large-scale LIDAR surveys can cover vast areas quickly, speeding up the discovery process. This capability enables archaeologists to survey sites that might have taken decades to explore by traditional means. Since LIDAR is an aerial technology, it reduces the need for ground disturbance. Archaeologists can locate and study features without excavation, preserving sites that may be too fragile to dig or in protected areas.

In 2018, a groundbreaking study using LIDAR revealed over 60,000 previously unknown structures related to the ancient Mayan civilisation buried under the thick canopy of the Petén region.[cclxii] In terms of size, some of the pyramids discovered using LIDAR are impressive in scale. For example, the *La Danta* pyramid in El Mirador in Guatemala, one of the largest pyramidal structures identified, stands approximately 230 feet (70 meters) tall and covers a base area of about 18,000 square meters, making it one of the largest in the world by volume.[cclxiii] These pyramids often formed the heart of large urban centres. They were surrounded by extensive agricultural systems, road networks, and reservoirs, indicating the high level of sophistication in

Maya city planning.[cclxiv] The pyramidal structures are dated based on the artefacts within and around them. Radiocarbon dating of organic material found at the sites has suggested construction dates as far back as 1,000 BC, with the peak of construction occurring between 250 and 900 AD during the Classic Maya period.[cclxv] The findings from LIDAR scans, which provide detailed 3D landscape maps, have revolutionised the understanding of Maya society. They reveal that the civilisation may have supported a population of up to 10 million people at its peak.[cclxvi] Ongoing work continues in the region, with archaeologists using LIDAR to identify more structures, refine excavation plans, and further explore how the Maya organised their society and constructed their monumental architecture in such challenging environments.[cclxvii]

Similar to the discoveries in Guatemala, LIDAR technology has revealed hidden cities and monumental structures in Cambodia around the famous Angkor Wat temple complex. In 2016, archaeologists discovered extensive urban networks surrounding the temples, including water management systems and roads. These discoveries suggest that the civilisation that built Angkor Wat was far more complex and widespread than previously thought. The LIDAR data also uncovered temple sites and previously unknown pyramid-like structures that had been swallowed by dense jungle over the centuries.[cclxviii]

In 2013, researchers used satellite technology to locate ancient pyramids and structures at the Cahuachi site in Peru. Satellites equipped with infrared and multispectral imaging captured differences in soil composition, moisture levels, and vegetation, which often correlate with underlying man-made structures. These imaging techniques enabled researchers to identify subtle features that indicated the presence of ancient architecture. Some satellite data can be processed to create 3D models of the landscape. This helps archaeologists visualise the topography and identify areas where pyramidal structures might exist. Satellite imagery revealed new, previously undiscovered pyramidal mounds, contributing to a more comprehensive understanding of ancient civilisations in the region.[cclxix]

In 2020, archaeologists discovered more pyramids in Sudan, particularly at the site of Sedeinga. Ground-penetrating radar (GPR) and aerial drone photography were the primary technologies. GPR uses radar pulses to detect and map buried structures. When radar waves encounter objects or materials with different densities, they bounce back to the surface, creating reflections that indicate the presence of features such as walls, voids, or artefacts. These tools enabled archaeologists to map underground structures without disturbing the site, revealing small pyramids and tombs that had been previously hidden beneath layers of sand and sediment. The number of small pyramids in this region now rivals Egypt, bringing attention to the ancient kingdom of Kush. These pyramids are not as large as those in Egypt, but were used as burial tombs for nobles and royalty. The discoveries are part of an ongoing excavation effort aimed at gaining a deeper understanding of the Nubian kingdom, which once ruled over Egypt and made significant contributions to the culture and architecture of the time.[cclxx]

Sonar scans conducted off the coast of Japan, near the island of Yonaguni, have sparked debate since the 1980s regarding the discovery of submerged, pyramid-like formations. A sonar device emits sound waves (pings) into the water, travelling through the water column until encountering an object or the seabed. When these sound waves hit an object or the ocean floor, they reflect back to the sonar receiver. The time it takes for the waves to return is measured, allowing the sonar system to calculate the distance and location of objects. The Yonaguni Monument, as it has come to be known, was discovered through sonar scans and consists of a series of large, terraced stone structures lying under the sea. The structures, which some researchers believe resemble man-made pyramids, have been at the centre of controversy, with some geologists asserting they are natural formations. In contrast, others propose that they could be remnants of a lost civilisation predating recorded history. Proponents of the artificial theory, such as marine geologist Masaaki Kimura, have pointed to what they interpret as distinct right angles, straight edges, and stone carvings within the structure, suggesting human involvement. Despite ongoing dives and sonar scans, no definitive evidence has emerged to confirm the origin of the Yonaguni structures, leaving them a mystery. However, the debate continues as new technologies and research methods, including further sonar mapping, attempt to clarify whether these formations are natural or remnants of a forgotten civilisation.[cclxxi]

In Visoko, Bosnia, a controversial discovery has been made regarding a group of pyramid-shaped hills known as the "Bosnian Pyramid Complex." The Pyramid of the Sun, one of the structures in the area, is claimed to be the largest pyramid in the world, surpassing the height of the Great Pyramid of Giza at 220 meters.[cclxxii] However, mainstream archaeologists remain sceptical, with many considering the formations natural rather than human-made.

Satellite images from Antarctica have caused speculation about pyramid-like structures buried under the ice. While mainstream science attributes the formations to natural geological processes, some alternative historians and theorists speculate that the pyramids could be evidence of an ancient, unknown civilisation. Although unproven and highly speculative, these claims have sparked curiosity and prompted further study into the possibility of ancient human settlements or other advanced cultures that once inhabited the frozen continent.[cclxxiii]

Similarly, Jet Propulsion Laboratory (JPL) designs, builds, and operates NASA's primary interplanetary missions, runs Earth-monitoring satellites, and oversees the Deep Space Network (DSN). JPL employs advanced optical and radar-based technologies such as laser altimetry, laser spectroscopy, and radar sounders to map extraterrestrial terrain and detect subsurface structures. On Mars, for instance, the Mars Reconnaissance Orbiter carries SHARAD (Shallow Radar), which functions similarly to ground-penetrating radar. While not LiDAR in the traditional sense, SHARAD is used to probe beneath the Martian surface, revealing geological layers, buried ice, and voids, fulfilling a role conceptually similar to that of structural scanning on Earth. They are developing LiDAR-based instruments for upcoming missions targeting asteroid mapping, lunar surface analysis, and autonomous spacecraft navigation, where real-time 3D topography and obstacle detection are essential.[cclxxiv] As such, JPL represents the modern frontier of discovering planetary systems.

JPL's Earth Science Division has worked on radar interferometry and laser altimetry to map terrain, fault lines, glaciers, and biomass across Earth. This includes mountains, volcanoes, and polar regions, but not human-made structures like pyramids.

Similarities between the Pyramids

Pyramid shapes are similar globally, ranging in size from 6 to 146.6 meters. Despite being constructed by civilisations separated by vast distances and time, pyramids worldwide share remarkable similarities in their shape, astronomical alignment, and the possibility of being built on energy hotspots.

The triangular or step-like geometric shape of pyramids, found in Egypt, Mesoamerica, Sudan, China, and Indonesia, provides structural stability and a symbolic connection between the earth and the heavens. With a broad base and narrow apex, this form is architecturally significant. It reflects deep cultural and spiritual meanings, often representing mountains or sacred places where gods and humans could connect.

Many pyramids also demonstrate sophisticated astronomical alignment, with structures like the Great Pyramid of Giza aligned almost perfectly with the cardinal points and thought to mirror the stars of Orion's Belt. Similarly, Mesoamerican pyramids, such as those in Teotihuacan or the Mayan city of Chichen Itza, are oriented to mark important celestial events like solstices and equinoxes, suggesting that the builders had an advanced understanding of astronomy and used it for religious and agricultural purposes.

Moreover, speculative theories propose that these pyramids were deliberately constructed in energy-rich locations, known as energy hotspots or ley lines, which are considered areas where natural geomagnetic or electromagnetic forces converge. This idea extends to the belief that pyramids may have been designed to tap into and amplify these natural energies, serving as spiritual or ceremonial centres and potential devices to connect to Earth's energy. Whether aligned with the stars or strategically placed on powerful, energetic sites, these global pyramids reveal a shared human impulse to communicate with the cosmos, channel natural forces, and elevate the spiritual or divine through monumental architecture.

Shared Symbols: The Mystery of the Handbags

The "handbag" symbols in ancient depictions from Mesopotamia, Egypt, and Mesoamerican cultures have sparked many exciting theories. These small, pouch-like symbols, carried by gods or significant figures, appear in Sumerian carvings, Egyptian hieroglyphs, and even reliefs from ancient Mexican civilisations.[cclxxv] It seems that global brands are way older than we thought!

Some researchers believe these handbags represent a container of knowledge or power, symbolising a "sacred" or "divine" element carried by these figures.[cclxxvi] In Mesopotamian culture, gods often carry objects associated with life and rulership, suggesting this "bag" might symbolise the tools needed to create and maintain civilisation.[cclxxvii] Another interpretation is that the handbag symbolises the cosmos or life essence itself. In ancient art, the shape of the bag, a half-circle with a handle, could represent the heavens over the earth or the idea of something carrying vital resources for life.[cclxxviii] Some believe it was a ceremonial or ritual item, possibly related to offerings, or a portable item holding precious or sacred substances used in religious practices.[cclxxix] These handbags are also proposed to represent symbolic containers of energy, seeds, or life-giving properties, often seen as metaphorical vessels holding life, protection, or spiritual essence. Others argue it might simply be a common cultural theme—a container symbol shared across ancient civilisations for functional or spiritual significance.[cclxxx]

What if these objects were padlocks? The ancient Egyptians may have used such objects symbolically or literally; this might point to the safeguarding of knowledge, spiritual secrets, or even physical treasures. This interpretation ties into the broader themes of Egyptian mysticism and their focus on protecting sacred or powerful items. For instance, if these "padlocks" were part of a symbolic toolkit, they might represent the locking away of esoteric knowledge accessible only to initiates or those deemed worthy. Functionally, it might even suggest an early form of securing doors, chests, or other items, though no direct evidence of such mechanical locks has yet been found from this era. We know that the ancient Egyptians used complex locking mechanisms for their tombs and treasures, both practically and symbolically. Locked tombs were intended to protect the deceased and their belongings from desecration. Locks represented the sanctity of the afterlife and the boundary between the living and the dead. Similarly, in Hindu temple architecture and symbolism, locked doors or gates often signify the boundary between the material and spiritual worlds, guarding the sacred within. Locks here are thresholds that only the worthy or initiated can cross.

While it's still a mystery, the "handbag" symbol offers an intriguing insight into shared or parallel symbolism in early civilisations. Many academic and speculative researchers explore its meaning, suggesting it highlights some universal or cross-cultural understanding of life, power, or the cosmos.

It was not only the "handbags" that went viral; ancient civilisations seemed to share quite a few fashion "trends". Egyptians and Mesopotamians loved a bold eyeliner look, especially with kohl. This style travelled, with even Minoan and Mycenaean figures adopting a similar smoky look. Maybe smoky eyes were the first "universal" makeup trend? It's almost as if there was an ancient Pinterest board somewhere that everyone was following.

More shared symbols and artefacts have emerged, reflecting universal themes in human understanding of power, spirituality, and cosmic order. The era in which many of these shared symbols and artefacts emerged spans from the Neolithic period through the Classical period (roughly 3000 BCE to 500 CE).[cclxxxi] Items like staffs and sceptres, seen in Egypt, Mesopotamia, and Mesoamerica, symbolised authority and divine insight[cclxxxii], while winged symbols in Egypt, Persia, and Mesopotamia represented protection and spiritual ascension.[cclxxxiii] The serpent and dragon motif, revered in Chinese, Mesoamerican, and Egyptian cultures, symbolised wisdom and natural forces, often linking the divine with the earthly.[cclxxxiv] Circular symbols, such as China's bi discs, Egypt's sun discs, and Mediterranean amulets, conveyed the cycle of life and an eternal connection to cosmic energies.[cclxxxv] Protective eye symbols, like the Eye of Horus in Egypt and the Greek evil eye, underscored a belief in spiritual guardianship.[cclxxxvi] These recurring symbols reveal a shared pursuit of understanding life, protection, and the forces that govern the universe, despite cultural and geographical divides. The symbols and themes shared across ancient artefacts are well-supported by historical evidence.

Materials and Tools Used

They did not all use the same stones. The differences between the materials provide insight into how each civilisation used its natural environment and resources, adapting its engineering practices to suit practical and symbolic needs.ᶜᶜˡˣˣˣᵛⁱⁱ

In Egypt, the pyramids were primarily constructed using massive limestone and granite blocks, quarried locally and transported using simple but effective techniques, such as ramps and levers. The precision with which the blocks were cut and aligned showcases the Egyptians' advanced understanding of geometry and engineering.ᶜᶜˡˣˣˣᵛⁱⁱⁱ Limestone and granite were durable and believed to possess spiritual properties. The white limestone that once covered the pyramids reflected the sun, symbolising the pharaohs' connection to the sun god, Ra. At the same time, granite, used in the inner chambers, was considered a stone of permanence and strength, representing the eternal soul.

In Mesoamerica, the stepped pyramids, such as the Pyramid of the Sun at Teotihuacan and the awe-inspiring pyramids of Chichen Itza, were constructed using a combination of stone, adobe, and mortar. These materials were layered to create massive structures that mimicked sacred mountains. ᶜᶜˡˣˣˣⁱˣ Mountains were often seen as the home of gods, and by creating artificial mountains, these civilisations believed they were building closer to the heavens. Furthermore, the alignment of Mesoamerican pyramids with celestial events, such as equinoxes and solstices, showcased their sophisticated understanding of the cosmos and deep connection to astronomical phenomena.

Meanwhile, in China, the construction of pyramids using rammed earth, later covered with stones or tiles, reflected a different approach. Although less visually imposing than their Egyptian or Mesoamerican counterparts, the Chinese pyramids, such as the Mausoleum of the First Qin Emperor, were constructed to endure for centuries and safeguard the deceased emperors in the afterlife. ᶜᶜˣᶜ The use of rammed earth in these constructions was a pragmatic response to the environment, highlighting the Chinese focus on material conservation and harmony with nature.

While metal tools played an important role in later civilisations, the construction of pyramids in Egypt, Mesoamerica, and South America primarily relied on stone tools or, in Egypt's case, copper tools. Iron was not used in the construction of the Egyptian pyramids, and it was absent in Mesoamerican and South American pyramid-building cultures. The ability to build such monumental structures without the widespread use of metal tools highlights the advanced knowledge of stoneworking, engineering, and labour organisation in these ancient civilisations.

Curious Case of Mercury

In 2015, mercury was found in Teotihuacan during an excavation led by archaeologist Sergio Gómez. They found a lot of liquid mercury in the underground chambers beneath the Temple of the Feathered Serpent.[ccxci] This finding puzzled archaeologists and researchers. Mercury is well-known today for its toxicity, especially in vapour form. Liquid mercury is not easily absorbed through the skin, so brief contact is unlikely to cause serious harm. At room temperature, mercury vaporises into the air, and when inhaled, around 80% of these vapours are absorbed into the bloodstream through the lungs.[ccxcii] This can lead to mercury poisoning with symptoms such as tremors, cognitive and motor dysfunction, headaches, memory loss, and respiratory distress. Chronic inhalation can be fatal.[ccxciii]

The mercury's purpose remains unclear, but it opens up intriguing possibilities. The discovery of mercury in Teotihuacan is not an isolated case. Mercury has been found in other ancient sites, suggesting that its use was more widespread than previously thought. Chinese alchemists believed mercury could help achieve immortality, and it was often used in burial chambers, such as in the tomb of China's First Emperor, Qin Shi Huang, where a river of mercury was reportedly created to symbolise the rivers of the afterlife. [ccxciv] Mercury found in Mesoamerican and Chinese pyramids likely came from local cinnabar deposits. The ancient Egyptians are also known to have used mercury in small amounts. While Egypt does not have large cinnabar deposits, it is possible that trace amounts of mercury were released into the environment through volcanic activity or geothermal events. Trade remains the more likely source.[ccxcv]

The ability to form amalgams with other metals makes it valuable in industrial applications. It does not corrode most metals. In the modern world, mercury has been used in thermometers, barometers, electrical switches, and even dental fillings, where it is mixed with silver, tin, and copper to create durable amalgams.

Some researchers speculate that the mercury found in Teotihuacan may have been used for ceremonial or symbolic purposes. One popular theory is that liquid mercury's shiny, reflective surface could have symbolised a sacred river or lake, possibly representing the underworld or serving as a portal for spiritual journeys in the afterlife.

This theory aligns with other known practices in Mesoamerican and ancient cultures, where reflective surfaces or materials were often linked to the divine or the supernatural. Mercury's presence in significant quantities beneath the Temple of the Feathered Serpent raises further questions. Did they know about the toxicity of mercury?

More recent examples of toxic substances being unknowingly used include those in the 18th and 19th centuries, when arsenic was inadvertently incorporated into everyday items despite its poisonous nature. It was a common ingredient in vibrant green dyes used in wallpaper, clothing, and children's toys.[ccxcvi] Unaware of its dangers, people decorated their homes and wore arsenic-dyed fabrics, unknowingly exposing themselves to harmful effects. Arsenic also found its way into wigs, which were a fashionable accessory at the time. Prolonged exposure led to chronic arsenic poisoning, causing symptoms such as nausea, skin sores, and respiratory issues. These effects were not fully understood until much later, when the toxic properties of arsenic were widely recognised. Similarly, it is possible that the ancients did not understand the toxicity of mercury.

There is no direct evidence to suggest that they deliberately used mercury to poison people or that sacrificial victims were intended to accompany the dead into the afterlife. However, the possibility of unintentional mercury poisoning in enclosed spaces or during rituals cannot be ruled out. The confined underground chambers and caves beneath Teotihuacan, where mercury was discovered, may have exposed participants to hazardous fumes, potentially with unintended consequences.[ccxcvii] Furthermore, human remains, some of them decapitated, have been found in sacrificial contexts beneath both the Pyramid of the Sun and the Pyramid of the Moon, adding another layer of mystery regarding the ceremonial use of mercury.

Some have speculated that they might have known more about mercury's unique physical properties, particularly its ability to conduct electricity. While mercury is not commonly used in modern electricity generation, its electromagnetic properties make it a fascinating candidate for ancient technologies, especially in the context of speculative theories about advanced knowledge possessed by ancient civilisations.[ccxcviii] According to certain principles of electromagnetism, when a conductive liquid, such as mercury, moves within a magnetic field, it can generate an electric current. This concept, known as electromagnetic induction, underpins modern electricity generation today. Mercury, a metal and a liquid at room temperature, could have been manipulated in ways that allowed ancient engineers to generate electrical currents. Some speculative theories suggest that spinning mercury in a confined space, such as the underground chambers of Teotihuacan, might have created a primitive form of energy generation.

Grouping Pyramids by Symbolic and Functional Threads

The global distribution of pyramids is impressive. Whether they emerge from Egyptian sands, Mesoamerican jungles, or Indonesian terraces, these monuments serve more than architectural feats—they encode spiritual technologies, political propaganda, cosmic blueprints, and energetic conductors.

One key grouping is the pyramid as a *spiritual ascension device*. These include Egypt's Great Pyramid—interpreted by many not just as a tomb, but as a vessel for soul transformation—and Indonesia's Borobudur, a stepped mandala guiding the pilgrim's mind from earthly illusion to cosmic awakening. The Maya and Aztecs used pyramids as literal platforms for divine interaction: towering altars for blood sacrifice to maintain cosmic order. In each case, the pyramid acts as a vertical interface with the divine, a symbolic ladder between Earth and the heavens.

Another thread is the pyramid as a *tool of statecraft and political symbolism*. The imposing funerary pyramids of China and the Roman Pyramid of Cestius serve as assertions of permanence and legacy, inscribing the ruler's authority in stone. Similarly, Nubian and Mayan pyramids communicate status and divine legitimacy to those who approach them—monuments not just of faith, but of control.

A third category, growing in popularity among researchers and speculative theorists alike, is the pyramid as an *energy interface*—structures designed to interact with the Earth's natural forces. Teotihuacan's grid-like layout and its alignment to cosmic axes, the electromagnetic anomalies around the Giza plateau, and the global recurrence of solstice alignments all point to a potential energy-based function. In this view, pyramids may be more than symbolic—they could be energetic instruments engineered with a purpose we no longer understand.

A fourth category considers pyramids as *coded systems of knowledge*. Whether it's the golden ratio embedded in the dimensions of Giza or the 365-step calendar encoded into Chichen Itza, many pyramids seem to double as mathematical or astronomical repositories. These are not just buildings—they are compressed data systems, where geometry becomes cosmology.

By contrast, the absence of pyramids in certain parts of the world—prehistoric Europe, Australia, Japan—also demands attention. Were these societies uninterested in vertical monuments, limited by climate and materials, or guided by cosmologies that expressed power horizontally or symbolically through megaliths, circles, or labyrinths? The selective appearance of pyramids may reveal not just physical but metaphysical preferences across civilisations.

Conclusions

Pyramids are a truly global phenomenon, found in diverse environments ranging from the deserts of Egypt to the lush jungles of Mesoamerica and even beneath the oceans near Japan. Recent technological breakthroughs are reshaping our understanding of these ancient civilisations, revealing the possibility of many more hidden pyramids and monumental structures waiting to be discovered. These findings challenge traditional archaeological timelines and narratives, suggesting that our knowledge of ancient history is still evolving. The continued development and application of modern technologies, such as satellite imaging, ground-penetrating radar, and underwater exploration, are crucial for deepening our understanding of these architectural marvels and the cultures that built them. Such advancements promise to uncover new secrets about our shared past, expanding our appreciation of the ingenuity and reach of ancient civilisations. As we move from exploring pyramids across different regions to discussing shared knowledge and infrastructure in the next chapter, it is important to acknowledge the striking similarities between these ancient structures. While some of these resemblances may be attributed to practical architectural needs—such as the stability of the pyramid shape and its ability to endure over time—there is a deeper mystery at play. The fact that distant civilisations, with no known direct contact, created such similar monuments raises the question of whether a form of lost global knowledge or shared understanding existed. This convergence of design might suggest that these cultures were tapping into universal principles or harnessing unseen forces in ways we are only beginning to understand. In the next chapter, we delve into these intriguing possibilities, exploring the idea that ancient societies may have shared more than just architectural techniques; they may have been connected by an ancient network of knowledge and infrastructure that transcended geographical boundaries.

Chapter 3 Shared Knowledge and Infrastructure

Isolated or Shared Wisdom?

The construction of pyramids across different cultures has fascinated researchers who debate whether this phenomenon resulted from independent invention or cross-cultural exchange. Similarities between ancient civilisations, such as pyramid-building in Egypt, Mesoamerica, and elsewhere, have led to reconsiderations about whether these ideas may have travelled through contact. Why were pyramids built in different parts of the world by seemingly unconnected civilisations? These structures often share features like step pyramids, precise geometric shapes, and alignment with celestial bodies, suggesting a shared architectural and cultural influence rather than independent development. Similarities in carving techniques, masonry, and architectural tools found in Egypt and Mesoamerica also indicate that these civilisations could have exchanged technological knowledge. For much of the 20th century, an academic debate raged between *diffusionists*, who believed that major cultural innovations spread from a few central civilisations, and *independent interventionists*, who thought that civilisations invented technologies and ideas independently.

Anthropologist Michael Coe proposed that pyramid-building arose independently in regions such as Mesoamerica, where the pyramids of Teotihuacan were used for ceremonial and astronomical purposes.[ccxcix] Many early scholars leaned toward the independent invention model, assuming that similar developments in distant civilisations, such as pyramid building, occurred without contact. This view reinforced the idea that civilisations interacted only a little.[ccc] Early historians and archaeologists assumed that ancient civilisations needed to possess the means or technology for long-distance travel, particularly across oceans. They believed the lack of advanced ships, navigational tools, and geographical knowledge would have made long-distance voyages difficult. This led to the idea that civilisations like Egypt, Mesoamerica, and China developed in isolation.[ccci]

Diffusionist scholars, such as Thor Heyerdahl in his work *The Ra Expeditions* (1971), argue that ancient seafaring civilisations could have transmitted knowledge of pyramid construction through transoceanic contact.[cccii] The diffusionist perspective proposes that ancient civilisations were not isolated but rather part of a global network where explorers and navigators exchanged architectural, astronomical, and spiritual knowledge. This view challenges the mainstream belief that these civilisations independently developed pyramid-building techniques.

By examining ancient texts, myths, and archaeological evidence, diffusionists argue that the connections between these cultures were far more extensive than previously acknowledged. Mythological accounts from different cultures often contain similar stories, such as tales of great floods, sun worship, or sky gods associated with pyramidal structures. Diffusionists argue that these shared narratives may reflect cultural exchanges. For example, the Egyptian story of Osiris and the Mayan belief in Kukulkan both centre around figures associated with pyramids and the afterlife, suggesting that these themes could have been transmitted through contact.

They also point to the Piri Reis map from 1513, which showed parts of the western coast of Africa, the eastern coast of South America, and some islands of the Caribbean. Diffusionists argue that the map, which appears to depict some geographical features with surprising accuracy for its time, suggests that ancient seafarers had advanced navigation techniques and a more comprehensive understanding of global geography than previously believed. Furthermore, symbols and hieroglyphs, such as the serpent motif found in Egyptian and Mesoamerican cultures, are cited as evidence of a shared or transmitted symbolic language. The serpent, often associated with wisdom, rebirth, and cosmic power, appears prominently in Egyptian mythology, as seen in the Uraeus symbol, which represents divine authority, and in Mesoamerican iconography, such as Quetzalcoatl and Kukulkan. These similarities could indicate that ancient civilisations communicated and shared spiritual or architectural concepts. Diffusionists argue that such exchanges might have facilitated the spread of ideas about pyramid construction, energy harnessing, and the role of these structures in religious and social practices across vast distances.

Recent archaeological discoveries confirm that civilisations could have spread their knowledge far. Genetic and linguistic studies suggest increasing evidence of early long-distance connections between ancient cultures, though no definitive link has been proven. Advances in genetic studies have revealed that ancient populations were far more interconnected than previously believed. Archaeologists can gain insights into the migration patterns, population structures, diets, and diseases of ancient cultures by extracting and analysing DNA from human remains, plants, and animals. This has been especially impactful in understanding human evolution and the spread of civilisations. For instance, genetic evidence from human migration patterns shows that early humans migrated out of Africa and spread across various parts of the world, carrying shared genetic traits that suggest significant contact between distant populations.

A study by Lazaridis et al. (2014), published in *Nature*, titled *Ancient Human Genomes Suggest Three Ancestral Populations for Present-day Europeans,* provides evidence of widespread migration and interbreeding between ancient peoples.[ccciii] Additionally, Reich et al. (2012), in their influential book *Who We Are and How We Got Here: Ancient DNA and the New Science of the Human Past,* uncovered instances of genetic mixing between populations separated by vast distances, further supporting the idea of long-distance interaction and movement.[畃cciv]

Linguistic studies, such as Ruhlen's The Origin of Language: Tracing the Evolution of the Mother Tongue (1994), have identified connections between ancient languages, suggesting early communication and cultural exchange across different regions.[cccv]

Archaeological evidence has also shown that ancient civilisations did engage in long-distance trade and travel, such as the Silk Road connecting the East and the West or maritime trade between the Indus Valley and Mesopotamia. Growing evidence of naval capabilities in ancient cultures, including those of the Egyptians, suggests that long-distance travel and trade were more common than previously believed.

All these findings challenge the traditional view of isolated civilisations and offer a more interconnected vision of the ancient world. We need to unlearn much of what we were taught about history at school, especially regarding the narratives surrounding exploration and discovery.

New archaeological and historical evidence challenges the long-held belief that Christopher Columbus was the first to discover the Americas. Indigenous peoples had been thriving on these continents for thousands of years before Columbus's arrival, and there is growing evidence that other civilisations may have reached the Americas long before 1492. Norse explorers, such as Leif Erikson, established settlements in North America around 1,000 CE.[cccvi] The Viking settlement of Vinland, described in Norse sagas, is believed to have been located in modern-day Newfoundland, Canada, at a site known as L'Anse aux Meadows. This is North America's only confirmed Viking settlement, predating Columbus by about 500 years. While some fringe theories suggest that the Vikings may have ventured further south into New England (including areas like Boston), no concrete archaeological evidence has been found to support this. Some theories also suggest that

Powered by Pyramids: A Book of Theories

Phoenicians,[cccvii] West Africans,[cccviii] or even ancient Chinese explorers could have made contact with the Americas well before Columbus[cccix]. These revelations force us to reconsider the Eurocentric version of history and acknowledge that global exploration and cultural exchange existed long before European colonisation. Could the colonisers have rewritten the narrative? To truly understand history, we must be willing to unlearn the old and embrace new perspectives based on a broader, more inclusive understanding of the past.

Today, it is hard to imagine that ancient people could have travelled great distances. Yet, in many ways, travelling internationally might have been simpler in ancient times. Some may argue that man was, in fact, freer to move across the world, unconstrained by borders or the demands of passports and visas. Without bureaucracy, people moved across vast territories, driven by trade, exploration, or pilgrimage.[cccx] Borders were fluid, and there was freedom to journey through different lands, exchanging goods and ideas.[cccxi] It wasn't until the early 20th century, in 1920, that standardised passports emerged, aiming to streamline post-war travel.[cccxii] The League of Nations' Paris Conference on Passports and Customs Formalities promoted the idea of a universal passport that could be recognised across countries, setting the groundwork for the modern passport system. By the late 1920s, most countries had adopted these standards, making passports a standard requirement for international travel and establishing a more regulated approach to border security. Paradoxically, as modern identity and border control systems have developed, travel freedom has become more restrictive for some; for individuals from certain countries, navigating visa requirements can make international travel as challenging as crossing a guarded boundary, something unheard of in the ancient world.[cccxiii]

The next question is how they shared their knowledge. How could they travel across vast distances if they didn't have aeroplanes? Could they have used overland routes that are no longer visible today? The continents' connection timing is believed to have been between 335 and 175 million years ago.[cccxiv] The breakup of continents is well-supported by geological evidence, including fossil records, matching coastlines, and the study of tectonic plates. Little evidence suggests that the timeline of continental drift, spanning hundreds of millions of years, is incorrect.[cccxv] This leaves us to explore travel by flying objects and boats, or perhaps they were connected by underground tunnels. Or was there a universal consciousness that connected everyone?

Did the Ancients Have Advanced Transportation Methods?

What if ancient civilisations knew about advanced transportation and the world? The possibility that ancient civilisations possessed advanced transportation methods, including planes and fast boats, would challenge our current understanding of history and technology. Several theorists, supported by various artefacts and interpretations, believe this may have been the case.

Ancient texts, such as the Indian epics *Mahabharata* and *Ramayana*, written between 400 BCE and 400 CE, describe *Vimanas*—flying chariots used by gods and heroes—which hint at an early understanding of flight.[cccxvi]

The *Quimbaya artefacts*, found in Colombia and estimated to be from 500–1,000 CE, resemble modern aircraft with their aerodynamic features, raising speculation about advanced engineering long before modern times. The *Saqqara Bird* from Egypt, dated around 200 BCE, is a small wooden artefact with no feather carvings, resembling a modern glider. Its design is aerodynamic. It has been tested and shown to have flight capabilities, leading some to believe it was a model for an ancient flying machine.[cccxvii]

Another intriguing find is the so-called *Abydos Helicopter*, a carving found on a lintel in the Temple of Seti I at Abydos. This carving, depicting modern technology like helicopters, tanks, and aircraft, has baffled researchers for decades. Some alternative theorists argue that these depictions are evidence of advanced technologies or even extraterrestrial influence in ancient Egypt, suggesting that such knowledge might have been used to construct the pyramids. However, Egyptologists contend that the carvings are merely palimpsests—layers of hieroglyphs from different periods eroded and distorted over time, creating an illusion of modern machinery.[cccxviii]

Some also point to Egyptian beliefs, such as the mythological association of Thoth with birds and the soul's flight after death, suggesting a preoccupation with flight.[cccxix] Mainstream archaeology views these as symbolic or coincidental. Alternative historians propose that they hint at a lost understanding of flight, making the theory of ancient aviation an enduring and captivating topic.

The *Tulli Papyrus* allegedly describes "circles of fire" or flying objects in the sky during the reign of Pharaoh Thutmose III, fueling theories of extraterrestrial or advanced technological encounters.[cccxx] The *Tulli Papyrus* is a controversial and disputed document that UFO enthusiasts often cite as evidence of ancient encounters with extraterrestrial spacecraft. The papyrus describes an event that occurred during the reign of Pharaoh Thutmose III, around 1480 BCE, in which "circles of fire" or "fiery disks" appeared in the sky over Egypt.

These objects reportedly hovered in the sky before ascending higher and eventually disappearing. The *Tulli Papyrus* is named after Alberto Tulli, a former director of the Egyptian Museum in Vatican City. According to some accounts, he discovered the papyrus in a Cairo antiquities shop in the 1930s but was unable to afford it. Instead, he made a copy, which an ancient language scholar later translated. However, the original papyrus has never been found, and its only references come from copies or unverified sources, leading many to believe it may be a hoax or a misinterpretation of an ancient text. The translation of the text is also disputed, with some suggesting it could be a mistranslation of a more mundane event, such as a meteorological phenomenon, rather than a description of UFOs. Mainstream Egyptologists and historians do not recognise the *Tulli Papyrus* as a legitimate historical document. Academic researchers largely ignore it due to the lack of credible evidence.[cccxxi]

The *Nazca Lines* in Peru, created between 500 BCE and 500 CE, raise questions about ancient aerial perspectives and the potential use of flight.[cccxxii] The Nazca Lines are a series of massive geoglyphs in southern Peru's Nazca Desert. These geoglyphs, created by the ancient Nazca culture between 500 BCE and 500 CE, are large designs made by removing the reddish-brown topsoil to reveal the lighter earth underneath. The lines form various shapes, including straight lines, geometric patterns, and images of animals, plants, and other figures. Their scale and precision suggest an elevated viewpoint.[cccxxiii]

If these ancient civilisations had flying devices or methods of gaining altitude, such as gliders or balloons, they might have mapped and explored the world in ways we don't fully comprehend today.[cccxxiv] In addition to flying machines, myths and legends from various cultures, as well as carvings, have fueled theories about sophisticated maritime vessels.

The Egyptians had a sophisticated transportation network. The construction of the pyramids involved transporting massive stone blocks, sometimes from quarries hundreds of miles away. The Egyptians are believed to have used waterways to transport these stones. Egyptian depictions of boats on tomb walls and temple carvings show vessels with advanced designs capable of carrying large numbers of people and cargo. While these depictions primarily show sail-powered and rowed boats, the level of detail suggests that the Egyptians might have developed highly efficient maritime vessels, potentially even powered by some form of energy. Could there have been more advanced technologies now lost? Given the Egyptians' advanced understanding of geometry and architecture, it is possible that they experimented with designs and technologies that extend beyond what is typically found in archaeological evidence.

Archaeological finds include remnants of ancient boats and shipbuilding techniques, such as papyrus boats in Egypt and balsa rafts in South America. These findings indicate that ancient civilisations could travel transoceanic, supporting cultural exchange.[cccxxv]

Scholars like Thor Heyerdahl demonstrated through expeditions like *The Ra Expeditions* that ancient civilisations possessed the technology and skills necessary for long-distance seafaring. His successful voyages using reed boats modelled after ancient designs proved that ancient mariners could have crossed oceans, facilitating contact between cultures.

The first expedition, *Ra I*, set out from Morocco in 1969, using a reed boat modelled after ancient Egyptian vessels. With his international crew, he aimed to prove that ancient Egyptians could have crossed the Atlantic. However, after 5,000 kilometres (3,100 miles), the boat began to break apart, and they had to abandon the mission before reaching the Caribbean. Undeterred, he constructed a second reed boat, *Ra II*, with help from indigenous Aymara boatbuilders from Lake Titicaca in Bolivia. The ship set sail again from Morocco in 1970. This time, the voyage was successful, and they crossed the Atlantic in 57 days, landing in Barbados. This expedition demonstrated that ancient civilisations could have made transatlantic voyages using relatively simple boats.[cccxxvi]

Some researchers propose that ancient civilisations harnessed energy from structures like the Egyptian pyramids to power advanced vehicles, with these structures acting as energy transmitters. These ideas suggest that the pyramids could have generated electromagnetic or geothermal energy, which may have been used to propel vehicles and ships, as well as power flying machines. The pyramids' alignment with the Earth's magnetic grid suggests that the ancients could have tapped into the Earth's natural energy. If this were the case, the technology to convert this energy into usable power for transportation might have been much more advanced than we realise. However, the mainstream view remains cautious, as geological and archaeological evidence predominantly supports simpler transportation technologies until much later. Despite the scepticism, if these advanced methods did exist, it suggests a lost era, perhaps due to cataclysm or societal decline, leaving behind only artefacts, myths, and sparse clues.

Underground Transport System

Could there have been an ancient underground tunnelling system that allowed people to travel around the world? This is considered a highly speculative theory that challenges traditional understandings of ancient civilisations.[cccxxvii] This is not even possible in today's world, at least not on a global scale.

While no definitive archaeological evidence supports the existence of such an extensive global network, several myths, legends, and unexplained archaeological finds have fueled speculation about the possibility of a sophisticated underground transportation system in antiquity.[cccxxviii] Perhaps the pyramids, obelisks, and other massive structures acted as energy amplifiers, capturing and channelling geomagnetic currents.[cccxxix] Did these structures collect, focus, and transmit energy deep into the tunnels below? Energy could have been used within the tunnels to power levitating platforms—a technology reminiscent of today's magnetic levitation, *maglev* trains. These platforms, made from lightweight metals and crystalline materials, may have floated above the tunnel floor, propelled by the pulsating currents of ley line energy.[cccxxx] Ancient engineers might have mastered the art of controlling this energy, using it to accelerate the platforms to astonishing speeds, allowing travellers to race from one node to another.[cccxxxi]

Many myths and legends exist about vast subterranean worlds, tunnels, or cities beneath the Earth's surface. For example, Tibetan and Hindu traditions refer to an underground world called Agartha, *the Agartha Legend*, inhabited by advanced beings. These legends describe a network of tunnels and pathways that connect different parts of the world, linking Tibet with South America and other regions.[cccxxxii] The entrance to this vast underground system is said to be hidden within the Himalayas and other sacred sites around the globe.[cccxxxiii]

In Peru and other parts of South America, local legends similarly describe tunnels beneath the Andes that connect ancient cities and civilisations.[cccxxxiv] For example, the Tayos Caves in Ecuador have been linked to stories of underground passageways that span continents. These stories have captured the imagination of explorers and researchers for decades.[cccxxxv]

This leads us to the Hollow Earth theory, a pseudoscientific and speculative belief suggesting that the Earth is either entirely hollow or contains substantial internal spaces. Proponents of this theory argue that large, habitable areas beneath the Earth's surface may house advanced civilisations, mysterious creatures, or remnants of ancient societies.[cccxxxvi] The concept has fascinated people for centuries and has appeared in literature, folklore, and conspiracy theories despite being debunked by modern science.[cccxxxvii]

Books have been written, and documentaries and movies have been made on the theory of the Hollow Earth. For example, the film

Journey to the Centre of the Earth, released in 2008, is a modern adaptation of Jules Verne's classic novel.[cccxxxviii] It follows a thrilling adventure in which the protagonists, led by a scientist, discover a vast underground world accessible through volcanic tunnels. This subterranean world, filled with ancient creatures, plants, and geological wonders, captures the imagination and explores the possibility of a hidden ecosystem beneath the Earth's surface.[cccxxxix] It reflects the essence of the hollow Earth theory—a popular idea suggesting that Earth contains vast, interconnected tunnel systems harbouring secrets from ancient times. The mysteries may lie beneath our feet.

Ancient Greeks spoke of a vast network of tunnels under Cappadocia (modern-day Turkey). The underground city of Derinkuyu, discovered in the 1960s, reveals a complex network of tunnels and chambers that could house tens of thousands of people.[cccxl] The tunnels are wide enough for people to walk through and transport goods. Some chambers are as large as 25 meters (82 feet) in diameter. Although these structures were likely used as shelters during invasions, their complexity and the scale of the underground network raise questions about whether similar, interconnected systems might have existed elsewhere.[cccxli] Suppose ancient civilisations in this region possessed the ability to create such vast underground networks. In that case, it raises questions about whether similar capabilities existed elsewhere and on a larger, more interconnected scale and what technology they used.

The Hypogeum of Malta is an ancient underground complex dating back to around 4,000–2,500 BCE. It includes multiple levels of chambers and passages, some of which extend deep into the earth. While this structure was primarily used as a burial site, its intricate design suggests that ancient peoples could construct extensive underground networks—similar sites throughout Europe and the Mediterranean hint at a shared knowledge of underground construction techniques.[cccxlii]

According to ancient accounts, including those of Herodotus, a Greek historian, the Egyptian city of Hawara once housed a vast labyrinth with 3,000 rooms and underground passageways[cccxliii]. The labyrinth's existence has been debated, but recent ground-penetrating radar surveys conducted by Belgian archaeologist Louis de Cordier in the early 2000s indicated the presence of an extensive underground structure beneath the sand.[cccxliv] If this labyrinth truly exists, it could be part of an even larger underground network that once spanned Egypt, supporting transportation or other advanced functions.[cccxlv]

The Osirion in Abydos, Egypt, often overshadowed by the more famous pyramids, contains a deep underground temple structure. Built from massive granite blocks, some weighing over 100 tons, this structure is set deep below ground level and features a system of channels and passages.[cccxlvi] The site's construction is unlike typical Egyptian temples. It seems far older than the Temple of Seti I, leading some to believe it was built by a much earlier civilisation.[cccxlvii] The purpose of the Osirion remains unclear, but its massive stones and subterranean location have led to theories suggesting that it may be connected to a more extensive underground system.[cccxlviii] The site's alignment with water channels and the Nile suggests it could have had an advanced function related to energy, water management, or an underground transportation route.[cccxlix]

Underneath the Giza Plateau, where the Great Pyramid and the Sphinx are located, there is evidence of a vast network of tunnels and chambers. In the 1990s, Egyptian archaeologist Zahi Hawass and his team discovered tunnels and underground chambers extending beneath the pyramids and surrounding areas.[cccl] One of the tunnels, known as the "Osiris Shaft," leads deep into the bedrock beneath the Giza Plateau and includes a series of descending shafts, chambers, and water-filled areas.[cccli] The extent and purpose of these tunnels remain largely unexplored and unknown. Some speculate these tunnels could have been part of a larger underground system connecting different parts of Egypt or beyond.[ccclii] Others suggest they might have been used for ceremonial or spiritual purposes, as Egyptian mythology often referenced an underground world (Duat).[cccliii] However, the complexity and scale of the tunnels hint at the possibility of more practical uses, such as transportation or energy generation.[cccliv]

The Serapeum is a network of tunnels and chambers in Saqqara, near the Step Pyramid of Djoser. It houses massive granite sarcophagi (coffins) weighing over 70 tons within subterranean galleries.[ccclv] The purpose of these enormous sarcophagi is unclear, as many were found empty or partially filled.[ccclvi] The precision with which these sarcophagi were carved and the tunnels constructed to house them have puzzled archaeologists.[ccclvii] The underground passages are vast and suggest a high degree of engineering expertise.[ccclviii] The fact that these tunnels exist underground and are constructed with such precision raises questions about whether similar systems could exist elsewhere beneath Egypt, potentially linking various sites.[ccclix]

Underground tunnels could have provided safe passage between distant regions, protecting travellers from harsh weather, predators, or hostile forces[ccclx]. In a world where long-distance travel on the surface was perilous, an underground route would have provided a secure and direct means of moving people, goods, or armies.[ccclxi]

While legends and mysterious archaeological sites provide clues, mainstream archaeology remains sceptical due to the lack of conclusive evidence.[ccclxii] Even with modern technology, constructing a global network of tunnels would be an immense undertaking.[ccclxiii] Geological challenges, such as tectonic activity, varying rock compositions, and the presence of water bodies, would have made it difficult for ancient civilisations to construct and maintain such a system.[ccclxiv]

There is no archaeological record of advanced machinery capable of tunnelling on such a scale, and no interconnected tunnel system that spans continents has been discovered.[ccclxv] While underground cities and tunnels exist in various parts of the world, they tend to be isolated and serve localised purposes.[ccclxvi] If an extensive underground transportation network existed, one would expect to find more consistent evidence of its use and purpose.[ccclxvii]

The possibility remains that ancient civilisations could have developed advanced underground networks using technologies that were lost over time.[ccclxviii] Catastrophes, societal collapses, or shifting priorities may have led to the abandonment and eventual disappearance of these tunnels.[ccclxix] If advanced tunnelling technology existed, it could have allowed the creation of underground routes that have yet to be discovered.[ccclxx] As archaeologists continue to explore ancient sites and uncover hidden chambers and passages, the idea of a global underground system may not be as improbable as it seems.[ccclxxi]

The theory of an ancient global underground tunnelling system remains a captivating possibility that inspires both curiosity and scepticism. While myths, legends, and archaeological sites suggest that ancient civilisations could construct extensive underground networks, the evidence for a connected global system is currently lacking. Nevertheless, as discoveries emerge and our understanding of ancient engineering evolves, we may one day uncover evidence that our ancestors possessed knowledge of transportation systems far more advanced than we currently imagine.

Universal Consciousness

Another possibility that would explain the shared knowledge without any physical contact is that ancient civilisations could have understood how to download instructions from the universal consciousness.

This theory posits that ancient civilisations may have possessed the ability to download instructions from a universal consciousness, suggesting a profound connection between human intelligence and a collective, possibly metaphysical, source of knowledge. Were ancient societies, through spiritual or meditative practices, able to tap into an infinite, all-encompassing field of information, referred to as the "Akashic Records" or a "universal consciousness"? Such a field would have contained the accumulated wisdom of all time, accessible to those with the right spiritual or mental capabilities. Currently, we go online and download instructions, accessing a vast network of information at our fingertips. Could ancient civilisations wirelessly tap into a similar network—the "cloud"—directly through their minds? As we download data today, they might have downloaded instructions directly into their consciousness.

Proponents of this theory argue that many ancient cultures, including the Egyptians, Maya, and Sumerians, possessed knowledge and technologies too advanced for their time. The precision with which the pyramids and other monumental structures were built, the understanding of astronomy and mathematics, and the development of complex spiritual and healing systems are often cited as evidence that these civilisations accessed information beyond their immediate experience. They may have used altered states of consciousness through meditation, rituals, sacred plants, or other methods to connect with this universal source, thereby obtaining instructions or insights on how to construct their cities, develop advanced technologies, or comprehend cosmic laws. If ancient civilisations could access this universal consciousness, it would imply that human potential is far greater than commonly believed, suggesting that intuition, creativity, and innovation may be influenced or even guided by a deeper, universal intelligence. This could mean that such abilities are not exclusive to ancient peoples but are latent in all humans, waiting to be rediscovered or reactivated. As modern technology advances and discoveries are made, some theorists believe that we may be able to validate this ancient knowledge scientifically, potentially proving that humanity has always had access to a deeper, interconnected web of wisdom and consciousness.

Nikola Tesla (1856–1943), a Serbian-American inventor, electrical engineer, mechanical engineer, and futurist, was known for his extraordinary mental abilities, particularly his ability to envision inventions and conduct detailed experiments without building physical prototypes. He claimed he could picture machines and systems with perfect clarity, down to the smallest details, and work through potential flaws or improvements purely through thought. This unique mental approach led him to some of the most groundbreaking inventions. Some speculate that he might have been accessing a form of universal knowledge or cosmic consciousness, drawing on concepts such as the Akashic Records. He spoke of receiving "insights" and "visions" that often led to his discoveries, which have fueled some of these speculations. In modern discussions, influenced by technological metaphors, this is sometimes likened to "downloading" information from the universe. While there's no scientific basis for this, it's an intriguing parallel between Tesla's intuitive genius and theories of mystical or cosmic knowledge.[ccclxxii]

Another example is Nostradamus. Nostradamus (born 1503–1566) was a French astrologer, physician, and reputed seer best known for his book *Les Prophéties*, a collection of 942 poetic quatrains that are said to predict future events. His cryptic and often vague predictions have fascinated people for centuries, and many claim they have accurately foretold major historical events, including wars, revolutions, and even natural disasters. Nostradamus claimed he would enter a "divine frenzy" or inspiration during meditative sessions, connecting him to a higher power. This allowed him to access knowledge beyond the present and foresee future events. He attributed his prophetic abilities to divine inspiration and a supernatural force that guided his visions. In a letter to his son, he suggested his prophetic gift had been inherited and divinely inspired.[ccclxxiii]

Many authors have written about the concept of universal consciousness. One is David Wilcock. In his books, *The Source Field Investigations* and *The Synchronicity Key*, he discusses that ancient civilisations could access a universal consciousness or source field, a repository of all knowledge. He argues that this field contains the secrets of advanced technology, spiritual insights, and the blueprints for human evolution, which ancient peoples could tap into through meditation, rituals, or other altered states of consciousness.[ccclxxiv]

Morphic Reasonance

Rupert Sheldrake, a biologist and author, proposed the concept of *morphic resonance* in his book *A New Science of Life* (1981).[ccclxxv] He argues that the mind is not confined to the brain but extends into fields beyond it. His theory suggests that organisms can inherit a collective memory and access information non-locally, which could be seen as a form of "biological connection" to an information field.

Every time an organism learns or performs a behaviour, that pattern becomes embedded in a morphic field. The more often a behaviour occurs, the more probable it becomes for others, regardless of proximity, culture, or even generation. This challenges the dominant paradigm that all memory is stored in the brain, and that learning is an individual process dependent on direct experience. He suggests that the brain may function more like a receiver or tuner, accessing shared informational fields rather than holding everything internally.

So, rather than learning being solely a product of genetics, personal experience, or social imitation, he proposes that we draw on a field of collective memory. Morphic resonance suggests that learning is cumulative and field-based, rather than purely isolated. Every learning act contributes to a collective field that others can tap into. This doesn't mean knowledge is magically downloaded, but that there is a subtle, invisible bias in favour of what has already been done. It may explain why technological innovations often arise independently in different places, or why children sometimes appear to "just know" how to do something before being formally taught.

While his ideas are controversial, they align with the concept of a source of information accessible to living beings. He proposes that collective memory is shared among all organisms of the same species. These memories are not stored in individual brains or DNA but in a shared field that transcends space and time. He writes that organisms, through *morphic resonance*, can tap into patterns or knowledge established by previous members of their species. For example, a bird may "learn" behaviours or skills without direct experience by resonating with the memory of past birds that have already learned these behaviours. Accessing this informational field could allow individuals or groups to instinctively "know" something, even without direct communication or learning through traditional methods. This concept parallels the idea of a biological connection to an informational field, where organisms or humans could access knowledge from the collective memory stored non-locally, beyond the constraints of time and physical space. The term "non-local" comes from quantum physics, where particles are thought to influence each other instantaneously across distances. He borrows this metaphor to explain how living beings might similarly access information across space and time.

If his theory is even partially correct, then the recurrence of specific ideas, skills, or architectural forms across cultures and eras may not be coincidental or solely due to cultural exchange. It may be a result of civilisations resonating with a shared informational field, accessing patterns that have already been established, and unknowingly learning from the past—not through tradition, but through resonance.

Biological Wi-Fi System

Did ancient civilisations possess genetic or biological enhancements that enabled them to access information wirelessly, akin to a "biological Wi-Fi" system? This idea aligns with ancient texts and myths that describe beings with extraordinary abilities, suggesting that some may have tapped into such an informational field. In this scenario, individuals would have received knowledge and instructions directly into their minds. Was this information accessible to all or passed down through specific bloodlines? Perhaps it was acquired through advanced training and initiation rituals.

An example of such an ancient text is the *Emerald Tablet,* which is part of hermetic literature and is believed to have originated in Egypt. It refers to a hidden knowledge or wisdom that connects the divine and the material worlds. The concept of ancient beings possessing access to universal truths and cosmic knowledge is a central theme in Hermeticism. This text aligns with the notion that initiates could tap into hidden knowledge through spiritual transformation.[ccclxxvi] There are many more examples.

Modern science studies and explores the possibility of interconnected minds through phenomena such as quantum entanglement and brainwave synchronisation, particularly in the fields of quantum physics and neuroscience. Quantum entanglement suggests that if consciousness is linked to quantum processes in the brain, minds could connect instantly across distances.[ccclxxvii] Brainwave synchronisation shows that individuals engaged in shared activities, like meditation, can align their brainwave patterns, indicating a temporary collective state of consciousness.[ccclxxviii] Theories such as the global workspace and non-local consciousness propose that consciousness may operate through non-local or electromagnetic fields, creating a shared mental network that extends beyond individual brains. These ideas suggest that consciousness could form an interconnected system, similar to a collective mind or information field.

Knowledge Encoded in Our DNA

Is there a connection between universal consciousness or genetic memory and cross-cultural exchanges? It provides a plausible explanation for the parallels found between civilisations without clear physical contact, suggesting a deeper, metaphysical mechanism behind humanity's shared ancient wisdom.

Could knowledge have been encoded within our DNA, allowing only specific individuals to access it? Unlike the collective unconscious, which suggests a shared reservoir of knowledge across humanity, this theory proposes that every person carries latent knowledge on a cellular or genetic level, perhaps passed down through generations or imprinted by ancestral experiences.[ccclxxix] Rather than tapping into a universal pool of knowledge, individuals would unlock personal or lineage-based wisdom encoded within their biology. Environmental factors, epigenetic markers, or states of heightened awareness, such as meditation or altered consciousness, could influence access to this information.[ccclxxx] This theory suggests that hidden knowledge may reside within the human body, awaiting discovery through spiritual practices or genetic activation. It provides a more individualistic explanation for innate insights or exceptional abilities that appear without traditional learning.

The theory that knowledge may be encoded in our DNA, and the modern concept of brain chips, revolves around expanding human cognitive abilities. They approach the idea from different angles. DNA-based theories suggest that each person carries ancestral knowledge within their genetic makeup.[ccclxxxi] This knowledge is seen as intrinsic and passed down through generations, forming a natural, uncensored reservoir of wisdom. Could vivid dreams be echoes of ancestors' lived experiences?

There is a theory that today's DNA databases or mass genetic screening efforts could be used not only for ancestral tracing or medical research but also to identify specific genetic markers that might indicate certain traits, potential abilities, or ancestral memories. Certain groups may seek DNA to trace ancient bloodlines thought to possess special knowledge, psychic abilities, or ancestral memory. The theory suggests that these individuals may "remember" or access dormant wisdom encoded in their genes. If some DNA markers suggest potential for heightened abilities or enhanced consciousness, such as ancestral memory recall, collecting DNA on a mass scale might allow authorities to monitor, identify, or pre-emptively control individuals who could pose a challenge or threat.

Some speculate that these databases could be used as tools for secretly recruiting or suppressing individuals with certain genetic predispositions. Governments or private interests might have a vested interest in harnessing such people or ensuring they remain unaware of their potential. There is a belief that humanity collectively has forgotten ancient knowledge encoded in our genetic material. Mass DNA tracking could serve to identify those on the verge of accessing this dormant knowledge—individuals who might potentially "awaken" or catalyse a broader consciousness shift.

How would nature decide what the best version of all knowledge is? Take the example of a bird instinctively knowing how to fly. In biological systems, instincts like flying are hardwired through genetic evolution, where behaviours that increase survival and reproduction are passed down. In terms of evolution, nature "selects" traits and behaviours. For example, a bird's instinct to fly is encoded because it has been essential for survival. But how about the knowledge of building pyramids?

Scientifically, DNA carries genetic instructions, and emerging research is investigating how experiences, particularly those related to trauma or survival, can influence genetic expression through the process of epigenetics. However, the idea that specific, non-biological knowledge, such as building pyramids, could be encoded is highly speculative. While instincts, such as a bird's ability to fly, are evolutionary traits developed over time for survival, the knowledge of architectural engineering remains outside the scope of genetic transmission, as understood by current science. Have you ever acquired a skill or knowledge that came to you effortlessly without formal training?

Who would decide what gets stored and downloaded from the ancients' Akashic Records? How does that compare with our current cloud-based databases? What is the government's role in today's world in controlling our artificial consciousness? Governments can influence collective consciousness through the control of information, regulations, and the manipulation of public opinion. This is evident in policies that affect education, media censorship, and surveillance.

Brain chips, such as those developed by Neuralink, represent an attempt to augment the brain's capabilities by providing access to external databases.[ccclxxxii] However, unlike the supposed purity of DNA-encoded knowledge, these chips could limit the type and amount of information that can be accessed.[ccclxxxiii] This introduces the notion of control over knowledge, where entities in charge of the technology could filter or restrict access, contrasting with the idea of the Akashic Records—a universal and potentially uncensored source of all knowledge. Thus, while both represent expanded access to information, brain chips may offer a more limited and curated experience than the speculative potential of the Akashic Record and the hidden wisdom of our DNA.[ccclxxxiv] The brain chips could be subject to regulation and data curation, presenting ethical and privacy concerns about who controls the access and flow of information. Most information suppression, however, isn't via deletion. It is via overwhelming you with junk, distraction, or false consensus. Is the agenda to no longer *augment* humanity, but to replace its organic unpredictability with synthetic predictability? The ultimate product may not be a more intelligent human, but a compliant one.

Could memory exist beyond the confines of the brain, possibly within our body's cells or even the water that composes much of our biology? It intertwines scientific inquiry with speculative thought. The concept of *cellular memory* suggests that our cells can retain experiences, a theory partially supported by epigenetics, which shows that environmental influences can modify gene expression and potentially pass these adaptations to future generations.[ccclxxxv]

While explicit memories, such as events or learned knowledge, are understood to be stored in the brain's neural networks, our immune system and muscles exhibit a form of "memory," hinting at a broader, cellular form of information retention.[ccclxxxvi] Adding another layer of complexity, water, which makes up a substantial portion of our bodies, has been proposed as a potential medium for memory storage. The controversial "water memory" theory suggests that water can store and retain information from its surroundings.

Following his experiments, Dr. Masaru Emoto claimed that water crystals changed form in response to thoughts, words, or emotions directed at them. Although these findings have faced criticism for lacking scientific rigour, they open up intriguing questions about water's potential role as a conduit for memory or information, especially considering that water is essential for biochemical reactions and electrical signal conduction in the brain and body. Suppose water truly holds a memory or can be influenced by energetic or emotional states. It might then serve as a medium through which memories or ancestral wisdom are accessed or even imprinted. Emerging quantum theories even speculate that water might play a role in biological processes at the quantum level, influencing how our bodies and brains function.[ccclxxxvii]

While mainstream science continues to focus on the brain as the primary repository of memory, the holistic and spiritual perspective offers a more integrated view, suggesting that the body and the water within us could hold hidden, energetically encoded knowledge awaiting discovery. This intersection of biology, consciousness, and spirituality fuels ongoing research and fascination with how our memories are formed, stored, and retrieved.

Conclusions

Whether transmitted through direct contact, gradual migration, or more enigmatic channels such as collective consciousness, it becomes increasingly evident that the ancient world was far less isolated than traditionally believed. Striking consistencies in pyramid architecture, precise celestial alignments, and expansive subterranean networks scattered across diverse and distant cultures unmistakably hint at shared or exchanged knowledge transcending geographical limitations. The steady accumulation of archaeological, genetic, and linguistic evidence unveils a web of interconnections among ancient civilisations, compelling us to reconsider long-held assumptions about isolated cultural evolution.

Intriguingly, the parallels between ancient concepts of universal consciousness, genetic memory, and contemporary explorations in quantum biology suggest our ancestors might have intuitively grasped principles that modern science is only now beginning to unravel. Consciousness and memory, once viewed as strictly biological phenomena, may indeed operate on quantum or energetic levels that are barely comprehensible within current scientific frameworks.

This insight challenges traditional historiographical narratives, urging a shift in paradigm towards a nuanced synthesis. It recognises that civilisations may have independently developed core innovations yet periodically refined them through selective exchanges and encounters. Perhaps the most profound takeaway from this exploration is the humility it demands: an acknowledgement that, despite today's advanced technology, ancient societies may have possessed sophisticated knowledge and capabilities that have long been forgotten by modern humanity.

As civilisations rise and inevitably collapse, invaluable knowledge often vanishes, leaving behind fragments encoded in myth, symbolism, and enigmatic artefacts. Acknowledging this cultural amnesia invites contemporary scholars to revisit ancient wisdom through an innovative, open-minded lens, potentially unlocking lost insights that could profoundly impact our collective future. By embracing a broader, integrative view of the past, we not only deepen our understanding of ancient complexity but also enrich our possibilities for innovation and rediscovery today.

When you see a pattern, ask who needed it hidden in plain sight.

Chapter 4 The Mysteries of the Pyramids

"The more you know, the more you realise you don't know." – Aristotle.[ccclxxxviii]

The pyramids have been monumental testaments of human ingenuity and mystery for centuries. Towering over the Egyptian sands and rising from the dense jungles of Mesoamerica, these awe-inspiring structures provoke more questions than answers. At the heart of every question lies the unknown, and the more we delve into the pyramids, the more profound and enigmatic they become. The mysteries surrounding these ancient structures are not limited to their construction or purpose but extend to the tools used, the incredible precision achieved, and the transportation of colossal stone blocks across vast distances. Were they merely grand tombs, or did they serve a deeper purpose—perhaps one that we are only beginning to understand? The pyramid does not ask you to believe. It asks you to remember.

From the massive pyramids of Giza to the intricately stepped pyramids of Mesoamerica, these monuments have fascinated explorers, historians, and scientists alike. How did civilisations separated by vast oceans and epochs construct such similar forms? And whether or not they were in contact, could there be a universal reason for their creation, something that transcends architecture and is connected to energy, spirituality, and the very forces of nature? What were they built for, how and by whom?

This chapter sets the stage to explore these mysteries. Were these pyramids not just symbolic monuments but intricate devices designed to harness and amplify the Earth's energy?

Just as *Alice in Wonderland* (1951), the Disney adaptation of Lewis Carroll's manuscript *Alice's Adventures in Wonderland*, beckons viewers to question the boundaries of logic and perception, this chapter invites a deeper interrogation of the unseen. Alice's descent into Wonderland—where the familiar dissolves and reason is inverted—mirrors the enigma of the pyramids. Are they mere monuments of stone, or gateways into realities that defy linear understanding? Just as the rabbit hole led Alice to a world where the impossible became tangible, the pyramids may conceal entry points to hidden dimensions, veiled knowledge, and forgotten energy systems.[ccclxxxix]

Powered by Pyramids: A Book of Theories

The *looking glass*—a central motif in Lewis Carroll's sequel *Through the Looking-Glass* (1871)—has evolved far beyond its literary origins. In metaphysical discourse, it represents a threshold between dimensions, timelines, or states of consciousness: a shimmering membrane between what is perceived and what lies beneath perception. Passing through the mirror, like Alice, symbolises an inversion not just of world but of self—an entry into recursive awareness where time no longer moves forward, but folds inward.

In the shadow realms of classified military lore, "Project Looking Glass" is rumoured to have been a covert initiative involving reverse-engineered alien technology. Allegedly capable of displaying probable futures by manipulating time-space geometry, it is said to have employed rotating isotopic cylinders and plasma fields—tools not unlike those seen in sacred geometries or pyramid resonators. According to unverified accounts from insiders like Dan Burisch and Bill Wood, the project was halted when it began revealing a converging event horizon—a collective awakening—beyond which predictive manipulation failed.[cccxc] In this view, the future was not merely seen, but chosen collectively, rendering elite control mechanisms obsolete.

Jordan Sather is a controversial figure in the fringe disclosure and conspiracy communities. He gained traction online by discussing secret technologies, extraterrestrial contact, and alleged government suppression of advanced knowledge. He has linked ancient monuments—including the pyramids—to reverse-engineered alien technology, time manipulation devices like the alleged *Project Looking Glass*, and what he describes as an ongoing "Great Awakening." His narratives often merge spiritual ascension themes with whistleblower testimonies and apocalyptic disclosure timelines. While highly speculative and lacking verified evidence, his influence illustrates a broader cultural trend: the merging of metaphysical yearning with conspiracy media ecosystems. For some, the pyramids are no longer ancient tombs but encoded keys to suppressed realities.

From an esoteric standpoint, the looking glass is not merely a metaphor. It mirrors the speculative purpose of pyramids themselves—as portals, as consciousness reflectors, as architecture designed to interface with the energetic lattice of time. These structures may not reflect your physical image, but rather the version of you that transcends temporality. You do not look into the pyramid—you pass through it. What greets you is not recognition, but recursion. Not a reflection, but a refolding of awareness.

In that sense, the pyramid is both rabbit hole and mirror, both portal and paradox. It invites the seeker not into answers, but into the dissolution of the one who needed them.

Could the Great Pyramid of Giza be like a lid, hiding secrets? Do they serve as guardians of hidden knowledge? The sheer size, weight, and complexity of pyramids, particularly the Great Pyramid of Giza, suggest that they may have been constructed to protect or conceal something far greater than the remains of a pharaoh. In this sense, the pyramid acts as a literal and symbolic lid, sealing away the secrets of a lost era until they are uncovered by future generations or by those capable of deciphering the complex codes and mysteries embedded within or under its architecture. Is the pyramid more than a structure—a gateway to ancient, guarded truths?

A Multitude of Purposes: Tombs, Temples, and More

Across the world, pyramids have been attributed to various functions, including tombs, temples, ceremonial platforms, gateways to the afterlife, and astronomical observatories. It is believed that each civilisation adapted the pyramid form to reflect its unique cultural and religious needs, leading to diverse interpretations of its true purpose.

In Egypt, pyramids were traditionally regarded as monumental tombs, constructed as eternal homes for the pharaohs, who were considered divine beings on Earth. These grand structures, built to ensure the safe passage of the pharaohs' souls into the afterlife, were filled with treasures, offerings, and intricate spells believed to possess magical powers. [cccxci] The Great Pyramid of Giza, the largest of them all, is said to have been built for Pharaoh Khufu around 2,500 BCE and remains one of the most iconic and enduring symbols of human achievement. [cccxcii] It was designed with such precision that it aligned almost perfectly with the cardinal points—an astonishing achievement given the tools available.

Could this architectural precision point to something more than just a symbolic burial chamber? The alignment of the Great Pyramid to the true north—off by a fraction of a degree—has sparked theories that its function went beyond mere burial. Some scholars now speculate that these pyramids were not just monuments but ancient devices designed to tap into the Earth's natural energies. The materials used in their construction—limestone, granite, and quartz—are known for their durability but are also conductors of energy. Could the ancient builders have harnessed this knowledge to create structures interacting with the planet's energetic grid?

Egypt was not alone in its fascination with pyramids. On the other side of the world, the civilisations of Mesoamerica also constructed towering pyramidal structures. But here, pyramids were not tombs—they were platforms for temples where priests performed sacred rituals to honour the gods.[cccxciii] The steps of these pyramids, like those at Teotihuacan and Chichen Itza, symbolised the ascent to the heavens, each level representing a different plane of existence or a stage in the cosmic journey. cccxciv

Although stylistically different—the Egyptian pyramids' smooth, sloping sides and the Mesoamerican pyramids' stepped design—the core purpose remained strikingly similar. Both sought to bridge the gap between the terrestrial and the divine, between life and death, heaven and Earth. They were symbols of eternity, power, and divine favour. Yet, could they have been something more? Could both civilisations, separated by oceans, have drawn from a more profound, universal understanding of the planet's energy?

A Cosmic Blueprint

One of the most fascinating aspects of pyramids, whether in Egypt or Mesoamerica, is their mathematical precision and alignment with astronomical phenomena.

In Egypt, the pyramids of Giza are thought to align with Orion's Belt—a constellation deeply intertwined with the ancient Egyptians' belief in the afterlife.cccxcv It was believed that the stars guided the souls of pharaohs to the afterlife, emphasising the connection between the heavens and these monumental structures. In Mesoamerica, the pyramids were often used as observatories. Their alignment with key celestial events—such as the solstices and equinoxes—suggests that these civilisations deeply understood the stars. The alignment of these pyramids may not have been purely symbolic but practical, designed to capture and reflect the rhythms of the universe.

The alignment of pyramids with celestial bodies has been a subject of ongoing research in archaeoastronomy. Studies by Anthony Aveni, particularly in *Skywatchers of Ancient Mexico* (1980), reveal that many Mesoamerican pyramids, such as those at Chichen Itza, were constructed to track solar and lunar cycles, playing a crucial role in agricultural rituals and religious ceremonies.cccxcvi In Egypt, similar alignments are observed between the Great Pyramid and Orion's Belt, as explored in Robert Bauval's The Orion Mystery (1994). This raises questions about the possible shared cosmological knowledge of ancient civilisations. cccxcvii

These cosmic alignments may tell us only part of the story. Could the pyramids also have been designed to harness energy from the stars and the Earth, merging the spiritual with the scientific?

Powerhouses of the Ancient World

Some theories propose that pyramids were symbolic structures and devices built to tap into the Earth's forces. The precise placement of many pyramids along geomagnetic or ley lines—powerful energy pathways across the Earth's surface—suggests a deep understanding of the planet's energetic grid. These invisible lines connect energy-rich points on Earth, and the materials used in pyramid construction, notably granite and quartz, are known to have conductive properties.

Could the pyramids have functioned as ancient power plants, channelling and storing the Earth's energy? Scholars who embrace this theory suggest that the pyramids' alignment with natural energy flows and the strategic use of conductive materials may have enabled them to act as geological batteries, storing and amplifying energy in ways we are only beginning to understand.

The latest discovery, not yet confirmed by mainstream sources, in March 2025 of eight massive, symmetrical, cylindrical structures encircled by spiral pathways, several meters in width and more than 648 meters deep beneath the surface of the Egyptian pyramids, seems to support these theories further. The cylindrical structures are connected to two square boxes, about 80 meters on each side. These formations, undetectable by conventional excavation methods, were revealed through Synthetic Aperture Radar (SAR) imaging, which utilises sound waves and seismic vibrations to generate ultra-high-resolution images of subterranean anomalies. This method has revealed patterns beneath the Giza Plateau that suggest deliberate engineering.

A World of Possibilities

The idea that pyramids could harness energy opens up a world of possibilities. What if ancient civilisations knew Earth's natural forces far beyond what we give them credit for? What if these structures were intricate devices capable of harnessing the planet's energy for spiritual, ceremonial, or even technological purposes?

Could the pyramids, especially in Egypt, be repurposed artefacts from an even older, advanced civilisation? The next chapter explores the intriguing possibility that the pyramids were inherited structures, concealing secrets that modern history has chosen to overlook.

As we move forward, we will dive deeper into the mysteries of the pyramids, exploring how ancient civilisations might have understood and manipulated the Earth's energy in ways that could revolutionise our understanding of the past and the present.

Intriguing Archaeological Finds

In recent years, several archaeological discoveries related to the pyramids have challenged the established narrative of their construction and purpose.

One of the most controversial finds is the so-called *Inventory Stela*, uncovered near the Great Pyramid of Giza. The stela, dating back to the 26th Dynasty (around 664–525 BCE), contains inscriptions that suggest the Great Pyramid and the Sphinx may have existed before the reign of Pharaoh Khufu, contradicting the widely accepted belief that Khufu was responsible for building the pyramid around 2500 BCE. The stela contains inscriptions that describe a restoration effort led by Pharaoh Khufu (often referred to by his Greek name, Cheops). According to the text, Khufu restored a temple dedicated to Isis, which was already ancient at the time. The stela suggests that the Great Pyramid and the Sphinx existed before Khufu's reign, indicating that these structures predated his rule. This contradicts the mainstream archaeological belief and suggests that Khufu did not construct the pyramid, but instead carried out restoration work on existing monuments. Some scholars argue that the Stela proves that the pyramids may have been repurposed or inherited from an earlier, unknown civilisation. Critics say that the Stela, being from a later period, may not provide reliable evidence for the original construction date of the pyramid and the Sphinx, viewing it instead as part of a religious or cultural narrative meant to enhance Khufu's legacy by associating him with the older monuments.[cccxcviii]

These and other new finds stir debate about the pyramids' true origins and raise the possibility that Egypt's monumental structures could hold deeper, hidden meanings yet to be uncovered by modern archaeology.

Discussion about when the Pyramids were Built

The *Göbekli Tepe Excavations*, led by Klaus Schmidt in 1994, revealed the world's oldest known monumental structure, dating back to approximately 10,000 BCE. His groundbreaking study challenged previous notions about the timeline of human social development and monument building, suggesting that complex architectural projects may have begun much earlier. In his book *Göbekli Tepe: Genesis of the Gods* (2016), he concluded that these ancient structures were built by hunter-gatherer societies, overturning the assumption that such large-scale construction required settled agricultural communities. This discovery supports the idea that advanced civilisations may have existed long before the Egyptians, opening up intriguing possibilities about the origins of monumental structures, such as the pyramids.[cccxcix]

Some propose that the pyramid may have been built by an earlier, more advanced civilisation and later repurposed by the Egyptians. While these theories lack substantial evidence and are not

Powered by Pyramids: A Book of Theories

supported by mainstream archaeology, they add a fascinating layer to the broader debate around the exact age and origins of Egypt's oldest pyramid and its similarities with other pyramids worldwide. Imagine the possibilities! What if the pyramids were a legacy of an ancient, forgotten era? These ideas keep the mystery alive, inviting us to look deeper into our past and question what we know about human history.

In the next chapter, we will examine the pyramid's construction. After unpacking these mysteries, we will explore the idea that the Egyptian pyramids could have been inherited from a lost civilisation and repurposed, suggesting that our understanding of their origins might need reevaluation.

Powered by Pyramids: A Book of Theories

Chapter 5 Construction of the Pyramids

The pyramids are incredible examples of ancient building skills. For years, people have wondered how these massive structures were built so precisely without the modern tools we have today. For instance, the Great Pyramid of Giza comprises millions of enormous limestone blocks, each weighing several tons, perfectly stacked to create a recognisable shape that has lasted thousands of years. But how did they build something so big and heavy back then? What materials did they use, and how did they lift and move the giant stones? And did they have enough personnel to complete the job?

In this chapter, we will explore how the pyramids were built, examining the types of stone and other materials, such as limestone and granite, that contributed to their strength. We will also discuss their tools and methods, such as simple copper tools, wooden sledges, ramps, and other ideas that may have aided them in moving the heavy blocks. We will also discuss the workers—were they slaves, or was it a team of skilled and organised builders who made this possible?

The Construction of the Great Pyramid of Giza

The construction of the Great Pyramid of Giza in Egypt is estimated to have taken around 20 years, meaning a stone would have had to have been placed every 2.5 minutes. Some theorists suggest that the pyramid's visible structure is the tip of a much more extensive underground construction.

The mainstream theory is that ramps, levers, and manual labour were employed over decades to build these monumental structures. Workers may have used straight or zigzagging ramps made of mudbrick or limestone chippings to haul the heavy blocks into place. Levers might have been used to lift and position stones with precision.[cd] Pyramids were constructed in horizontal layers, with workers completing one level before ascending to the next, ensuring stability throughout the construction process. Once the main structure was complete, outer casing stones were meticulously fitted to create a smooth and polished surface, reflecting sunlight and enhancing the pyramids' grandeur.[cdi] Substantial evidence exists that they possessed the necessary engineering, organisation, and labour management skills to construct these massive structures. Renowned Egyptologist Zahi Hawass argues that the evidence of pyramid construction techniques, such as the discovery of ramps and tools, points to human ingenuity rather than advanced or alien technologies.[cdii] Some are sceptical.

Replicating the Great Pyramid today would be an extraordinary undertaking. Estimates suggest it could take around ten years and cost between $1 billion and $5 billion, depending on location, material choices, and modern construction costs. The original Great Pyramid counted approximately 2.3 million limestone and granite blocks, some weighing up to 80 tons. Modern equipment would significantly reduce the time and labour required compared to ancient methods. Heavy-duty cranes, such as crawler and tower cranes, would be used to lift and position the massive stone blocks precisely, replacing the manual ramps and levers once used by ancient builders.[cdiii] These cranes, capable of lifting hundreds of tons, would allow for quicker and more accurate placement at various heights. Excavators equipped with hydraulic hammers and cutting attachments would efficiently quarry and extract the stone blocks, vastly surpassing the speed and efficiency of the Egyptians' dolomite pounders and copper tools.[cdiv] Bulldozers transport these blocks, streamlining the movement of materials from the quarry to the construction site.[cdv] Hydraulic jacks would position and align the heavy stones precisely, replacing the manpower and simple levers of ancient times. These systems would enable lifting and adjusting stones with minimal effort.[cdvi] Transport trucks would also play a vital role, moving stones efficiently and eliminating the need for the sledges and manual hauling methods that were once necessary. Automated robotics, including robotic brick-laying machines, could also handle repetitive tasks such as placing smaller stones and casing blocks. These robots, programmed for precision, would drastically reduce the time and labour involved, making the entire construction process far more efficient than it was thousands of years ago.[cdvii]

Jean-Pierre Houdin, a French architect, proposed in 2005 that the pyramid was constructed using an internal spiral ramp, which he believes still exists inside the structure. His theory challenges the traditional notion that large external ramps were used to haul the massive stone blocks into place. His idea suggests that the ancient Egyptians used a combination of two ramps: an external straight ramp for the pyramid's base and an internal spiral ramp for the upper sections. He theorises that the internal ramp was carved within the pyramid's walls, allowing workers to move the blocks upward in a controlled and protected manner. This method would have been more efficient and required fewer resources than the widely accepted external ramp theory. He stated that with a 7% incline on the internal spiral ramp of the Great Pyramid, it would take about 4 to 6 people to drag a 2.5-ton block up the ramp. This number is significantly lower than estimates for traditional external ramp theories, which suggest many more workers would have been needed due to the steeper angles and longer distances involved. His theory gained attention due to its plausibility, especially with modern technology revealing anomalies inside the pyramid that could potentially support the existence of internal ramps. He collaborated with engineers and scientists, using 3D modelling software and scanning techniques to test his ideas. Although not yet universally accepted by Egyptologists, his theory continues to spark discussions about ancient engineering techniques, adding new perspectives to the ongoing debate about how the Great Pyramid was constructed.[cdviii]

Required Labour Force

Archaeologists believe that around 20,000 to 30,000 workers were involved in constructing the Great Pyramid of Giza. This remarkable achievement is a testament to their ingenuity, organisational skills, and commitment to creating structures that have stood the test of time. The construction process would have involved meticulous planning, immense labour, and the ability to harness human and natural resources.

Unlike the vast workforce in ancient Egypt, a modern project would benefit from automation and machinery. It would involve fewer workers but require highly trained engineers, construction managers, and specialised labourers for efficient execution. This streamlined workforce would manage the project far more effectively than may have been the case in ancient times. Nonetheless, planning permission is a crucial aspect that should not be overlooked. Securing permissions in today's regulatory environment could add another ten years![cdix]

Herodotus, a Greek historian who visited Egypt around 450 BCE, recorded some of the earliest known accounts of the construction of the pyramids in his renowned work, *Histories*. According to Herodotus, the Great Pyramid took 20 years to complete and required the labour of 100,000 workers, a figure that has been widely debated. He provided intriguing details about the organisation and sustenance of the workforce, suggesting that they were fed well and organised into groups for efficient construction.[cdx] However, modern historians often view Herodotus's account with scepticism, especially his estimation of the labour force, which is now considered exaggerated. Contemporary archaeological evidence suggests a workforce of around 20,000 to 30,000 skilled labourers, rather than the massive numbers Herodotus cited.[cdxi]

The total population of Egypt at the time of the Great Pyramid's construction (around 2,550 BCE during the reign of Pharaoh Khufu) is estimated to have been 1.5 to 2 million people. Assuming around 20,000 to 30,000 workers were involved in the pyramid's construction, roughly 1-2% of the total population would have been directly engaged in building the pyramid at any given time.[cdxii]

Additionally, the discovery of workers' villages near the Giza Plateau suggests that thousands of labourers built the pyramids using basic tools and highly organised labour systems. The Giza Workers' Village, a residential complex for the labourers who built the pyramids, revealed bread ovens, tools, and evidence of a well-organised workforce, challenging earlier notions that slaves built the pyramids. The archaeological evidence suggests that these monumental structures were erected using a well-organised workforce of skilled Egyptian labourers and craftsmen rather than enslaved people, who likely worked seasonally during the Nile's inundation when farming was not feasible.[cdxiii] Around three to four months a year, they could not farm as the land was flooded. This provided seasonal labour. Archaeological evidence further suggests that the workers' diet consisted of bread, meat, and beer, indicating they were well-nourished. Their skeletal remains indicate they were generally healthy despite the physically demanding labour. Evidence of a well-organised supply chain was found.[cdxiv]

John Ruskin (1819–1900), an influential English art critic, writer, and social thinker, once said: *"The pyramids remind us not of the power of kings, but of the determination of men"*.[cdxv]

Was it only men at work, or were women also involved in constructing the pyramids? There is no historical evidence to suggest that women played a central role in the construction of the pyramids. The pyramids, especially the Great Pyramid of Giza, were built by thousands of labourers, likely under the direction of skilled architects and overseers. These labourers were primarily men, as evidenced by discoveries of workers' villages, tools, and inscriptions. However, women in ancient Egypt did have significant rights and responsibilities. While they weren't typically involved in heavy labour, such as pyramid construction, they held important positions in religion, medicine, and administration. Some women of noble or royal status, like queens and priestesses, played vital roles in religious rituals and could commission monuments. The physical building of the pyramids is generally considered to have been done by male labourers. In her speculative work *The Hidden Architects: Women of Ancient Egypt*, author Mira Solari presents a controversial theory that Egyptian women, particularly high-ranking priestesses, played a pivotal role in the construction and design of some of Egypt's monumental structures. Solari suggests that while men executed much of the physical labour, it was the priestesses, particularly those devoted to the goddess Hathor, who provided the architectural blueprints and spiritual guidance for projects like the Great Pyramids and the Temple of Karnak. She argues that many design elements, such as the alignment of structures with celestial bodies, point to the influence of Egypt's powerful matriarchal religious class, whose knowledge of sacred geometry and astronomy has been largely overlooked by mainstream historians. Solari's theory has sparked debate, drawing both support from feminist archaeologists and criticism from those who believe her evidence is circumstantial at best. Nonetheless, *The Hidden Architects* invites readers to reexamine the often-ignored contributions of women in the ancient world.[cdxvi]

Materials and Tools to Cut the Stones

Theories on how the ancient Egyptians cut the massive stones used in pyramid construction generally revolve around the use of copper tools, abrasives, and simple yet effective techniques that required large amounts of labour. One of the most widely accepted methods involves using copper chisels, saws, and drills, combined with abrasives such as sand.

For softer stones, such as limestone, copper chisels were effective for carving and shaping the blocks. However, for harder stones like granite, copper tools alone were insufficient, so it is believed that the Egyptians used sand as an abrasive in conjunction with copper saws and drills.[cdxvii] The sand, harder than the copper, would act as the cutting agent, wearing out the stone over time.

Another method, especially for quarrying stones, involved dolomite pounders, which were hard stone hammers used to break and shape softer limestone blocks.[cdxviii] Some rocks were extracted from quarries by creating deep cuts with copper tools and wooden wedges. When soaked in water, these wedges would expand, causing the stone to crack and separate from the bedrock.[cdxix] Additionally, tubular drills made from copper, also using sand as an abrasive, may have been employed to hollow out stone or make precise cuts, especially in statues and chambers.[cdxx] Others argue that the precision and scale of the pyramid construction, particularly with hard stones like granite, would have been impossible with the simple tools available to the Egyptians at the time.[cdxxi]

Excavations dating back to the 1990s have uncovered copper tools, including chisels, saws, and drills, which were essential for cutting the massive limestone and granite blocks.[cdxxii] These tools were often hardened with arsenic or tin to increase their durability.[cdxxiii] Many of these artefacts, including the copper tools, are on display at the Egyptian Museum in Cairo.[cdxxiv]

The Iron Age in Egypt did not begin until around 1,000 BCE, long after the pyramids were built.[cdxxv] Meteorite iron was sometimes used for ceremonial items or small tools, but it was rare and not used in large-scale construction.[cdxxvi] Meteorite iron comes from iron meteorites, which are composed primarily of iron and nickel.[cdxxvii] Because meteorite iron was scarce and literally "fell from the sky," it was often considered sacred and reserved for special objects.[cdxxviii]

However, meteorite iron and other materials may have been more abundant in ancient times than we think. Much of it could have been lost or repurposed over time, contributing to the relative scarcity of evidence today.[cdxxix] Is it possible that they used meteorite iron, but it all disintegrated? Iron meteorites are generally quite durable and do not simply disintegrate quickly.[cdxxx] However, factors such as moisture and environmental conditions can lead to the gradual deterioration or removal of meteorites from the archaeological record. In dry environments, meteorites are more likely to survive intact, which explains why a higher percentage of meteorites are found in deserts and polar regions.[cdxxxi] While some meteorites may rust over time, their resilience means they would still last for thousands of years unless subject to extreme conditions or human interference. Advances in scientific techniques, such as XRF and mass spectrometry, may continue to reveal more about the role meteorite iron played in the ancient world, and ongoing archaeological discoveries could further expand our knowledge of its use.[cdxxxii]

Advances in scientific techniques, such as XRF and mass spectrometry, may continue to reveal more about the role meteorite iron played in the ancient world, and ongoing archaeological discoveries could further expand our knowledge of its use.

Modern stone-cutting methods differ significantly from those used by the ancient Egyptians in both efficiency and precision. The Egyptians, working with copper tools, abrasives like sand, and simple mechanical tools, relied heavily on labour-intensive and time-consuming methods. This process required extensive manpower and skill, as they had to manage the limited durability of their tools and work with basic resources available at the time. In contrast, modern construction uses advanced technology such as diamond-tipped saws, CNC machines, and water jet cutters. These tools enable the precise and rapid cutting of even the hardest stones, including granite, through automated processes and computer-aided designs. This allows for the creation of complex shapes and smooth finishes with minimal effort. Where the Egyptians might have taken weeks or months to quarry and shape a single block, modern methods can accomplish the same task in hours. This comparison highlights the technological advancements in stone cutting, showing the leap from manual, labour-intensive methods to automated, high-precision machinery.

Fringe theories about the precision cutting of stones in the pyramids propose methods beyond the conventional use of copper tools and sand. One idea, popularised by authors like Christopher Dunn in *The Giza Power Plant* (1998), suggests that the Egyptians used vibrational energy. He theorises that they could have employed sound frequencies and resonance, possibly through chanting, musical instruments, or devices designed to emit vibrations to soften or break the stones, making it easier to carve them accurately.[cdxxxiii] Similarly, David Hatcher Childress proposes using crystal-based tools in *Lost Cities & Ancient Mysteries of Africa and Arabia* (1991). He speculates that the Egyptians—or a more advanced, earlier civilisation—used quartz crystals that interacted with Earth's energy fields, harnessing them to cut stones precisely. This idea aligns with the belief that these crystals have special properties, especially when combined with vibrational techniques.[cdxxxiv]

Some like Erich von Däniken in *Chariots of the Gods?* (1968) argues that the Egyptians may have inherited advanced technology from a lost civilisation, such as Atlantis. They point to the precision and alignment of the stones as evidence of technology far superior to simple copper tools. They argue that this lost civilisation possessed highly sophisticated laser technology capable of cutting through stone with extreme precision. This technology would have been passed down to the Egyptians, enabling them to shape and fit massive stone blocks with an accuracy that would be difficult to replicate using conventional ancient tools.

Others take this theory further by proposing extraterrestrial assistance. Proponents, such as Giorgio A. Tsoukalos, host of Ancient Aliens, argue that aliens provided the Egyptians with advanced tools or machinery, explaining the precise cuts and the alignment with celestial bodies that surpass the capabilities of known ancient human technology.

Moving and Transporting the Stones

In addition to questions about the labour force required and the tools available during the construction of the pyramids, another question lingers: how the massive stone blocks, some weighing several tons, were moved around and transported to the building sites. The distance from the quarry to the construction site would have affected the feasibility and cost of transportation. Designing and constructing adequate ramps for lifting stones into place poses challenges. The type and slope of ramps must strike a balance between efficiency and safety, especially as the pyramid height increases.

The fact that the wheel had not yet been invented during the construction of the Great Pyramid of Giza makes the achievement even more remarkable. Wheel use in Egypt became more widespread during the New Kingdom period, roughly 1,500 BCE, when chariots, likely introduced by the Hyksos, were used for warfare and transportation. The ancient Egyptians used other ingenious methods to transport the massive stone blocks. Scholars believe they used a combination of sledges, ropes, manpower, and water or oil to reduce friction when dragging the blocks across the desert sands.

Cedar wood from Lebanon played a crucial role in transporting and moving heavy stones. The Egyptians imported this durable wood, which was used to build sledges and scaffolding. Cedar wood's strength and flexibility made it ideal for creating structures that could bear the weight of massive stone blocks.[cdxxxv] Texts such as the *Amarna Letters*, tomb inscriptions, and depictions in Egyptian art describe trade routes and tribute missions that included cedar wood as a valuable resource. Additionally, ancient shipping documents and archaeological evidence of cedar wood artefacts found in Egypt, like ships and coffins, confirm that Lebanon was a key source of timber for the Egyptians.[cdxxxvi]

One theory explored how water was poured before sledges carrying heavy stones to reduce friction, allowing workers to pull the blocks with less force. This technique could have helped in both horizontal and inclined transport. For instance, engineers have demonstrated that using water underneath, simple lever systems combined with lubricated sledges can move massive stone blocks with minimal human effort. A 2014 study by the University of Amsterdam showed that wetting the sand in front of the sledges could reduce friction, enabling workers to haul stones much more efficiently. By revisiting such engineering principles, some argue that we can dispel the notion that the pyramids required alien technology or advanced machinery, grounding these ancient feats in human ingenuity.[cdxxxvii]

One of the most significant discoveries in 2024 was the unearthing of a previously unknown branch of the Nile River, which once flowed adjacent to the pyramids. This river branch was likely crucial in transporting the massive stones needed to build the pyramids.[cdxxxviii] This new finding helped to solve the long-standing mystery of how ancient Egyptians managed to move such heavy materials to the pyramid sites over long distances.

Another groundbreaking new theory related to water use in 2024 suggests that the ancient Egyptians may have used a sophisticated hydraulic lift system to build the Pyramid of Djoser, one of Egypt's oldest pyramids. According to a study led by Xavier Landreau from the CEA Paleotechnic Institute, water from nearby canals may have been used to create a hydraulic lift, which allowed heavy stones to be floated upward. This theory challenges the long-held belief that ramps and levers were the primary tools for transporting stones during pyramid construction. The study identified structures near the pyramid, including a possible water treatment facility and channels that could have directed water through the pyramid's shafts, providing the hydraulic force needed to lift the stones. This concept marks a revolutionary shift in our understanding of ancient Egyptian engineering, highlighting their potential mastery of water-based technology. While the theory is still being investigated, it offers a fresh perspective on how the pyramids were built, further emphasising the Egyptians' advanced engineering skills. More research is needed to confirm the mechanics of this system and its practicality during the pyramid's construction.[cdxxxix]

Some researchers, such as Joseph Davidovits, suggest that the massive stones of the pyramids were not carved and transported but rather cast in place using a type of ancient concrete or geopolymer. According to this theory, the Egyptians knew how to mix materials, including limestone, clay, and other components, to create a form of concrete that could be moulded into blocks on-site. This would have eliminated the need for moving huge stones over long distances and explained the precise fit of the blocks.[cdxl]

Could ancient Egyptians have hollowed out limestone and filled it with other materials? Egyptian masons were highly skilled in working with limestone, as it was a primary building material for the pyramids and temples due to its relative softness and abundance in the region.[cdxli] While their tools wouldn't have been able to hollow out limestone as precisely as modern equipment, they could achieve this by chipping away incrementally.[cdxlii] The Egyptians also used sand and quartz grit drills as abrasives to bore into rock. This technique could potentially hollow out larger limestone blocks or sections.[cdxliii] The Egyptians could have filled the cavities with different materials if hollowing had been achieved. Hollowing out certain blocks could make transportation easier without significantly weakening the structure.[cdxliv] However, there is no direct evidence that the Egyptians extensively employed this technique of hollowing and filling in large-scale architecture, such as the pyramids.[cdxlv] It remains a plausible idea within their skills and technologies, but would have been labour-intensive and reserved for specific, intentional purposes rather than routine construction.

Another speculative theory suggests that the ancient Egyptians employed holographic or light technology to project an image of the pyramids as they were being built. This would have provided a precise guide for workers to follow, ensuring the exact placement of the stones. Proponents argue that the Egyptians had access to technology, possibly from extraterrestrial sources or an advanced lost civilisation, that could create visual blueprints using light manipulation.[cdxlvi]

What if the massive stones used to build the pyramids were moved not by brute force but through sound? Ancient texts and myths suggest that the use of sound or vibration can be employed to manipulate matter. What if the Egyptians—or an even older civilisation—had mastered acoustic levitation, using precise frequencies to move and position the massive blocks as if they were weightless? Alternative historians, such as Erich von Däniken and David Hatcher Childress, suggest that ancient builders might have had access to levitation devices or energy fields that enabled them to lift the stones. Acoustic levitation, a process using sound waves to lift objects, is one such hypothesis. Ancient texts and hieroglyphs depict priests chanting and using rods, hinting at the use of vibrational energy. If true, this could revolutionise our understanding of ancient technologies, suggesting that the Egyptians—or an even older civilisation—mastered techniques far beyond our current knowledge.

Another theory proposes that the ancient Egyptians—or possibly an even older civilisation—used magnetic fields to lift and move stones. Nick Redfern discusses magnetic fields, sound, and antigravity technology theories in his book *How Antigravity Built the Pyramids: The Mysterious Technology of Ancient Superstructures*. He suggests ancient builders deeply understood Earth's geomagnetic properties and could create devices or manipulate materials that temporarily counteracted gravity.[cdxlvii] This concept is similar to modern maglev (magnetic levitation) technology, suggesting that the pyramids or other structures may have acted as nodes or amplifiers for these magnetic forces. Proponents argue this technology could have been developed independently or passed down from an advanced pre-Egyptian civilisation.

Moving the Granite Box

How they managed to move the granite box found in the King's Chamber of the Great Pyramid of Giza is astonishing. It is a monolithic structure carved from a single granite block, weighing approximately 3.75 metric tons (3,750 kg or 8,270 lbs). The lid alone is estimated to have weighed around 1 to 2 metric tons (1,000 to 2,000 kg or 2,200 to 4,400 lbs). As J. Isler notes in *The Mystery of the Granite Box:*

Engineering Feats in the Great Pyramid (2020), the average human can lift or carry about 20 to 30 kg, meaning it would have required 40 to 80 people to lift the lid alone.[cdxlviii]

How did they transport it there, and how did the ancient Egyptians position it within the Great Pyramid, which has passageways and chambers that are far from easily accessible? The King's Chamber sits in the middle of the pyramid, surrounded by solid stone walls. The box is too large to have passed through the entrance or the narrow passageways leading to the chamber, suggesting that it was placed there before the upper parts of the pyramid were constructed.

Complexity and Precision

Besides discussing the labour force, tools and transport of the stones, some researchers argue that the engineering complexity, mathematical precision and scale of the pyramids, particularly the Great Pyramid of Giza, would have been beyond the capabilities of the Egyptians. They question whether the technologies and methods supposedly available at that time could account for the precision of the construction.

They argue that the sheer complexity and size of the pyramids suggest they must have been built by an advanced civilisation much older than the Egyptians. Then, the Egyptians later repurposed these structures or renovated the pyramid by perhaps adding the outer layer. This theory posits that ancient knowledge, now lost to history, played a pivotal role in the construction of the pyramids. While mainstream archaeology supports the view that ancient Egyptians possessed the skills to construct the pyramids, critics remain sceptical. The mystery surrounding these architectural marvels fuels speculation about forgotten or undiscovered technologies that could radically change our understanding of history.

John Anthony West is one of the sceptics who argue that the pyramids' precision, specifically their alignment with astronomical phenomena and potential cataclysmic events, such as shifts in the Earth's axis or pole reversals, suggests they were constructed by a civilisation concerned with these events. In his book *Serpent in the Sky: The High Wisdom of Ancient Egypt (1979)*, he argues that the ancient Egyptians inherited these structures from a much older civilisation with advanced knowledge of cosmic cycles and global cataclysms. He also concludes that the Egyptians may have used the pyramids for purposes different from those intended by their original creators, possibly as an effort to preserve and convey knowledge about these catastrophic events.[cdxlix]

In addition to writing books on the topic, John Anthony West was a central figure in *The Mystery of the Sphinx,* a groundbreaking documentary that aired in 1993. It focuses on alternative theories regarding the origins and purpose of the Great Sphinx and the pyramids of Giza. In the documentary, John Anthony West said, "The sophistication of the pyramids cannot be overstated. They are far more than tombs. I believe they are a testament to an ancient and highly advanced knowledge system, much of which we are only beginning to understand."

The scale, complexity, precision, and alignment with the stars of the pyramids have led to ongoing debate and speculation. More recently, in Fingerprints of the Gods (1995), Graham Hancock also argued that the pyramids required technological and architectural capabilities, which suggest knowledge that might have been lost from an earlier, more advanced civilisation.[cdl]

The Importance of the Flat Base and Slope of the Pyramid

The flat base of the pyramids is of immense importance. From a structural perspective, it provides the foundation necessary to support the enormous weight of the pyramid. The Great Pyramid of Giza, the largest and most iconic of Egypt's pyramids, is estimated to weigh 5.75 million tons. This immense weight results from the sheer scale of the structure, which was built using approximately 2.3 million stone blocks weighing 2.5 to 15 tons, with some of the largest stones in the inner chambers weighing up to 80 tons. The precise levelling of the base ensured that the entire structure would be stable and distribute weight evenly, preventing the pyramid from shifting or collapsing over time.[cdli] Ancient Egyptian builders employed remarkable engineering techniques to achieve this, levelling the base to within fractions of an inch across its vast area.[cdlii] This accuracy was crucial, as a slight misalignment could have led to instability higher up in the pyramid.

The ancient Egyptians must have employed several ingenious methods to achieve the exact levelling of the pyramid's flat base. One common technique they may have used was a form of water levelling, which involved digging shallow trenches around the intended base and filling them with water. The surface of the water would naturally find a level plane due to gravity, allowing the builders to use this as a reference to ensure the ground was perfectly flat.[cdliii] Once the water settled, they could measure the distance from its surface to the ground and adjust the terrain accordingly. In addition to water levelling, the Egyptians likely employed simple sighting tools such as A-frames with plumb lines and levelling instruments, similar to modern spirit levels, which allowed them to ensure that large areas were consistent in height.[cdliv]

They would also have used stone or wooden blocks, along with pounding and smoothing tools, to gradually even out the base layer.[cdlv] The base was levelled horizontally and aligned with cardinal directions, often using astronomical observations such as the stars or the sun to achieve this precision.[cdlvi] The Egyptians could have constructed the flat base by combining practical engineering with careful observation of natural phenomena. The scale and precision of these methods reflect the sophistication of their architectural and engineering capabilities.[cdlvii]

The slope of the pyramid was equally critical to the structure. The slope ensures that the massive weight of the pyramid is distributed efficiently downwards and outward, preventing the structure from collapsing under its own weight. The pyramid's slope was carefully calculated to maintain stability while achieving the desired height. For example, the Great Pyramid of Giza has a slope angle of approximately 51.5 degrees, striking a near-perfect balance between steepness and height, as well as the necessary base width to support the structure.[cdlviii]

Modern construction employs advanced techniques to achieve the same precision and stability that ancient builders did with pyramid bases. For large structures, reinforced concrete foundations are often combined with deep foundation methods, such as piling, to anchor the building into stable soil or bedrock. This approach is similar to how the pyramids relied on bedrock for support.

Modern construction uses laser levelling technology to ensure that foundations are flat and level. Laser levels project a precise horizontal plane across the site, allowing workers to adjust and level the surface accurately. This technology surpasses the ancient methods of water levelling or sighting tools, providing millimetre-level accuracy over vast areas. Advanced surveying tools, such as GPS and total station systems, help modern builders accurately align structures. Similar to how the ancient Egyptians used astronomical observations, these tools allow for precise alignment with cardinal directions and other coordinates, ensuring the accuracy and stability of the base.

Modern geotechnical practices, such as soil compaction and stabilisation, create a solid load-bearing platform, preventing the foundation from shifting over time. High-strength steel and smart concrete enhance the structure's flexibility and resilience, distributing weight efficiently and allowing for self-repair, which ensures long-term stability.

In some modern sustainable building projects, geothermal energy systems are integrated into the foundation design. This concept parallels speculative theories about the pyramids' interaction with geomagnetic fields or Earth's natural energy. Geothermal piles help manage internal building temperature and stability, showcasing a similar integration of environmental forces with architecture.

When it comes to achieving the precise slope of a structure like a pyramid, modern builders use computer-aided design (CAD) software and laser-guided systems to establish the exact angle required for stability. This process involves setting up the base level and using precise measurements to ensure the slope is consistent across the entire structure. Engineers also use scaffolding systems and templates that follow the specified angle, much like ancient builders used sighting tools and plumb lines. These modern innovations ensure the accurate placement of each component, guaranteeing the structure's stability and aesthetic integrity.

Preventing the Pyramid from Collapsing

Several crucial architectural and engineering elements must be carefully considered to ensure a pyramid's stability and prevent its collapse. These principles were critical in constructing ancient pyramids, such as the Great Pyramid of Giza, which has stood for thousands of years without significant structural failure.

One key factor is the proper slope angle that ensures the weight is evenly distributed; steeper angles lead to structural instability.[cdlix] A solid foundation is also essential, as the pyramid must be built on stable bedrock to support its immense weight.[cdlx] The core structure—made of large, rough blocks of limestone or granite—also acts as the main load-bearing element.[cdlxi] These blocks must be layered with precision to prevent weak points.[cdlxii] The Egyptians also employed interlocking stones with incredible accuracy, often without mortar, to ensure the pyramid's rigidity and resistance to lateral forces.[cdlxiii]

Weight distribution was another critical consideration, with heavier stones used in the lower layers and lighter stones placed higher to reduce pressure.[cdlxiv] Carefully designed internal chambers and corridors helped maintain structural integrity. The Great Pyramid, for instance, features a relieving chamber system above the King's Chamber to prevent the ceiling from being crushed under the immense weight above.[cdlxv] These engineering innovations showcase the Egyptians' expertise in pyramid construction, allowing their monumental structures to endure for millennia.

Could the tunnels and chambers beneath the pyramids have served as stabilisers for the base, playing a crucial role in maintaining the structural integrity of these monumental edifices? By strategically creating voids, ancient builders may have used these tunnels to redistribute the immense weight of the pyramid, ensuring an even distribution of pressure across the foundation. This approach would help prevent uneven settling and maintain the structure's balance over time. The tunnels could also function as pressure relief systems, absorbing and dispersing stress from ground shifts or external forces like modern expansion joints in buildings.[cdlxvi] These subterranean pathways might have also acted as drainage channels, directing underground water away from the base to prevent erosion and maintain the foundation's integrity. This multifaceted design suggests that the pyramids' architects not only focused on monumental scale and symbolic meaning but also incorporated advanced engineering principles to ensure the stability and longevity of their structures.

In modern architecture, similar principles are applied to large structures, with advanced technology and materials enhancing stability and longevity. For example, using steel-reinforced concrete in skyscrapers allows for flexibility and strength, absorbing lateral forces such as wind or seismic activity, much like the interlocking stones used in ancient pyramids.[cdlxvii] Engineers also employ a tapering design in tall buildings, resembling the pyramid shape, which reduces the wind load and helps stabilise the structure, as seen in the Burj Khalifa in Dubai.[cdlxviii] Another key innovation is the use of deep foundation systems, such as pilings that extend deep into the earth to anchor buildings in unstable soil, similar to how ancient pyramid builders selected stable bedrock for their constructions.[cdlxix] Modern engineers also use sophisticated computer modelling to simulate stress points and optimise weight distribution, ensuring that materials are used efficiently and structures can withstand external forces, such as earthquakes. For instance, buildings often feature flexible joints and shock absorbers in earthquake-prone areas, mimicking the design of the ancient pyramids, which managed and redistributed internal forces[cdlxx]. Integrating ventilation and expansion systems in modern construction also reflects ancient techniques. The Great Pyramid's internal chambers and air shafts functioned to relieve pressure and manage the internal environment, much like the advanced HVAC (heating, ventilation, and air conditioning) systems and dynamic structural designs used in contemporary architecture to maintain internal stability and regulate temperatures.[cdlxxi]

Trial and Error or Reverse Engineering

The Great Pyramid of Giza holds several Guinness World Records, cementing its status as one of the most remarkable structures in history. It is recognised as the tallest pyramid in the world, originally standing at 146.6 meters (481 feet)[cdlxxii]. It remains the largest stone structure by volume, comprising approximately 2.3 million stone blocks that weigh between 2.5 and 15 tons each. The pyramid also holds the record for being the only surviving structure of the original Seven Wonders of the Ancient World.^{cdlxxiii} Additionally, it had the title of the tallest man-made structure in the world for an impressive 3,800 years until the construction of Lincoln Cathedral in the 14th century.^{cdlxxiv}

Rather than developing these monumental constructions from scratch, the Egyptians might have been striving to replicate a design from an earlier, advanced civilisation whose knowledge they only partially inherited. Perhaps the ancient Egyptians encountered remnants of a sophisticated architectural blueprint or ruins left by an earlier civilisation and endeavoured to reverse engineer these mysterious structures.

Interestingly, before the Egyptians perfected the design of the Great Pyramid of Giza, there were several failed attempts to achieve the pyramid's ideal slope and structure. One of the earliest failures was the *Meidum Pyramid*, originally constructed as a step pyramid but later modified with smooth sides. Its overly steep slope caused the outer layers to collapse. Another important attempt was the *Bent Pyramid* at Dahshur, built during the reign of Sneferu. Initially constructed with a steep angle of 54 degrees, the pyramid began to show signs of instability, prompting the builders to modify the slope midway to 43 degrees to prevent its collapse. These structural adjustments marked a critical learning phase in Egyptian pyramid building, and the lessons learned from these failures informed the more successful design of the Great Pyramid, which was constructed with a stable slope of 51.5 degrees. These early missteps ultimately paved the way for the remarkable achievements that would be seen in later pyramids. Mark Lehner provides in-depth details in *The Complete Pyramids: Solving the Ancient Mysteries*. This work provides a detailed account of the experimental phases of pyramid design during Sneferu's reign and the architectural evolution that led to the successful construction of the Great Pyramid.^{cdlxxv}

What if it were the other way around? Rather than a process of trial and error, the Egyptians might have been attempting to replicate an already perfected design. The Egyptians might have had access to remnants of earlier knowledge, and rather than inventing pyramid technology, they were trying to reverse-engineer these structures. The failures seen in the Bent Pyramid and Meidum Pyramid could be viewed as signs that they struggled to replicate the complexity of the original design.^{cdlxxvi}

It seems a stretch to believe that with great mathematical and astronomical understanding, the Egyptians went from poor execution to suddenly achieving near perfection with the Great Pyramid of Giza. It seems more likely that they gradually became more adept at copying an original masterpiece. While they refined their methods and improved their craftsmanship, they likely never reached the same heights of perfection and precision as the original creators. It seems plausible that later generations imitated something much more advanced. Could the Great Pyramid of Giza have been intended as a model for replication elsewhere?

Modern-Day Failed Attempts to Build a Replica

In modern times, several attempts have been made to replicate the construction of the ancient pyramids, particularly the Great Pyramid of Giza. Japan and the United States have embarked on high-profile projects to demonstrate how the ancient Egyptians might have built such monumental structures. However, these efforts have underscored the challenges of recreating the precision and scale of the original pyramids, even with modern technology and a deeper understanding of ancient methods.[cdlxxvii]

In 1978, Nippon Television in Japan undertook an ambitious project to build a small-scale pyramid using only the tools and techniques believed to have been available to the ancient Egyptians. The aim was to understand how the Egyptians managed to quarry, transport, and position massive stone blocks with such precision and accuracy. However, the Japanese team quickly encountered significant difficulties. Workers struggled to cut and shape the stone with the copper tools they were using, and transporting the heavy blocks across the sand using wooden sledges was inefficient and prone to failure. *"When the workers tried to cut the stone with copper tools, the chisels quickly became dull, and progress slowed to a crawl. After days of work, only a small portion of the stone had been cut, forcing the team to reconsider their methods"* – Nippon Television Documentary (1978). The structural challenges also became evident as the blocks did not fit together with the same seamless precision seen in the Great Pyramid. After several setbacks, the team had to abandon traditional methods and introduce modern machinery, such as cranes and bulldozers, to complete the project.[cdlxxviii] *"Moving the stone blocks over the sand with wooden sledges, as ancient Egyptians might have done, proved nearly impossible. The sledges dug into the sand, causing the blocks to get stuck repeatedly and bringing progress to a halt. Despite our best efforts to stay true to ancient techniques, we couldn't make significant progress without modern machinery"* – Nippon Television Documentary (1978). The experiment revealed how advanced the original techniques must have been, as the process was still arduous even with modern tools.

In 1997, the PBS series NOVA carried out a similar experiment, this time under the guidance of Egyptologist Mark Lehner.[cdlxxix] Using ancient techniques, the goal was to build a smaller pyramid near the Giza plateau. While the project aimed to be educational, it faced many of the same challenges as the Japanese attempt. Moving even modest-sized stone blocks proved labour-intensive, and while sledges and ramps were employed, they didn't provide the efficiency that had been hypothesised. Additionally, achieving the precision required to align and place the stones properly proved difficult, and many basic tasks, such as building the ramps or cutting the stone, were far more challenging than anticipated. *"Achieving the same level of precision as the ancient builders was nearly impossible. Despite our best efforts to cut and align the stones, the pyramid structure wasn't coming together with the seamless fit seen in Giza. It's clear the ancient Egyptians had techniques we still don't fully understand"* – Mark Lehner, NOVA, "This Old Pyramid" (1997). Like the Japanese team, the NOVA project used modern tools and equipment to complete the pyramid.[cdlxxx] Despite the project's small scale compared to the original pyramids, it demonstrated the challenges of ancient construction techniques and how far we are from fully understanding them.

These modern failures offer a deeper insight into the complexity of ancient Egyptian engineering. The Japanese and American projects underscore that despite our technological advances, we still cannot easily replicate the precision and grandeur of the pyramids. Some theorists suggest that the Egyptians possessed lost or highly specialised knowledge that has not been passed down through history.[cdlxxxi]

This could point to ancient construction techniques that were more advanced than previously thought or to alternative theories, such as the possibility that the Egyptians were trying to replicate a structure or knowledge from an earlier, more advanced civilisation. While mainstream archaeology attributes these failures to the learning curve of ancient builders, the challenges faced in modern experiments fuel speculation about what the Egyptians knew—and what we still have to learn.

Did Edward Leedskalnin unlock the Secrets of the Pyramids?

Throughout history, individuals have claimed they could build or move large structures without using traditional tools, often attributing their abilities to unique understandings of energy, magnetism, or ancient techniques.

Edward Leedskalnin, a Latvian-American immigrant, is renowned for constructing the enigmatic Coral Castle in Florida. This structure is made of enormous coral rock slabs weighing several tons. Coral Castle covers approximately 1,100 tons of stone, arranged across a small complex that includes walls, towers, a throne, a sundial, and various sculptures, all carved from oolitic limestone, often referred to as "coral rock" due to its appearance. The largest stones in the castle weigh as much as 30 tons each. The entire complex sits on a piece of land, roughly 10 acres in size, although the structures occupy a smaller, more concentrated area. The impressive stone blocks range from smaller, movable slabs to multi-ton structures that form walls around the castle. One of the most famous pieces is the 9-ton stone gate, originally perfectly balanced so that it could be rotated with a single push, though it has since been repaired and is no longer as easily movable.[cdlxxxii] This balance and the precision of the cuts and placements have significantly contributed to the mystery and intrigue surrounding Coral Castle and Edward Leedskalnin's building methods.

Coral Castle has fascinated researchers, engineers, and curious minds because no one has definitively explained how he managed to move and precisely place these massive stones without the aid of modern machinery.[cdlxxxiii] What is remarkable is that he constructed this entire castle by himself, working primarily at night and using only simple hand tools.[cdlxxxiv] He kept his techniques hidden. Edward Leedskalnin hinted at understanding the secrets of the pyramids and reportedly had a unique understanding of magnetism and energy.[cdlxxxv]

Some believe he may have used a form of magnetic levitation to lift the stones, aligning with theories that he tapped into some ancient or unknown method to manipulate large objects.[cdlxxxvi] Another popular theory is that he harnessed geomagnetic or lunar energy to lift or move the stones. While the moon does exert a gravitational influence on Earth, for example, through tides, its magnetic field is relatively weak. Could he have discovered a way to amplify or "tune into" Earth's or the moon's magnetic and gravitational fields?

While he never directly explained his methods, he left behind a book titled *Magnetic Current* (1945), which describes his unique theories on magnetism. He proposed unique ideas about magnetism, arguing that magnetism is a flowing force rather than a stationary phenomenon. He claimed that every atom has a magnetic "current" and that electricity has a magnetic effect, a notion differing from mainstream science.

However, it doesn't provide clear answers about the construction of Coral Castle. Theories surrounding his work include the idea that he may have utilised anti-gravity technology, magnetic fields, or even sound frequencies to move the stones, similar to how some speculate that ancient builders may have moved the stones of the pyramids.^{cdlxxxvii} These theories are speculative and unproven; the Coral Castle remains a mystery and a monument to his unconventional engineering skills.^{cdlxxxviii} While no one has successfully replicated his methods accurately, Coral Castle is often included in discussions of unexplained engineering feats alongside other megalithic structures, such as the pyramids of Egypt. His legacy persists in alternative science communities, inspiring studies into magnetism and speculative construction methods. Mainstream scientists and engineers largely attribute the construction of Coral Castle to clever, well-applied engineering techniques, such as levers and counterweights, although the specifics of these techniques remain unknown.

Conclusions

As we have explored, the construction of the pyramids defies simple explanation. From their monumental scale to their alignment and stonework precision, ancient techniques remain mysterious, inviting speculation about advanced tools or methods that have been lost to time.

The ancient Egyptians may have used a combination of ramps (internal spiral and external ramps), sophisticated water management techniques (hydraulic lifts or flotation channels), and possibly geopolymer concrete methods to create precise blocks in situ.

What if the machinery used to build the pyramids was deliberately hidden or lost to time, erased from history by design or accident? Some speculate that the ancient builders, whether Egyptians or an even older advanced civilisation, possessed tools and machines far beyond what we currently understand—machines capable of easily cutting, lifting, and placing massive stones. These machines, perhaps made of materials that degrade over time or hidden in secret chambers beneath the desert sands, could have been destroyed, dismantled, or hidden by later generations to preserve their mystery or power. Alternatively, they could have been spiritual or energy-based technologies without physical traces, using sound, vibration, or magnetic forces to move the massive blocks. If such technologies existed, they may still lie buried in unexplored parts of the pyramids or forgotten beneath layers of history, waiting to be rediscovered.

Whether these ancient builders possessed technology far beyond what we typically attribute to early civilisations or if they tapped into resources and knowledge we have yet to rediscover, the enigma persists. While mainstream theories focus on manpower and ingenuity, we must remain open to the possibility that the pyramids were part of a grander, more complex system of understanding that may have been influenced by forces or knowledge not yet fully comprehended. The mysteries embedded in these constructions are far from solved, prompting us to examine the structures themselves and what lies beneath them, both physically and metaphorically. Could the answers to the pyramids' mysteries be hidden in their foundations? This brings us to the next chapter, where we delve into what lies beneath these monumental structures, exploring theories of hidden chambers and missing capstones.

Chapter 6 What Lies Beneath the Pyramids and Where Are the Capstones

What if their secrets lie not in their towering heights but beneath the surface? Beneath the Giza Plateau, hidden from sight and speculation, may be answers to some of history's most enduring mysteries. From legendary labyrinths and undiscovered tombs to advanced energy systems, the possibilities of what lies below these colossal structures have sparked the imagination of archaeologists, historians, and treasure seekers alike. Still largely unexplored, these underground spaces could reshape our understanding of ancient civilisations and their technological capabilities. As we delve into this chapter, we will explore the fascinating theories and myths surrounding what might be buried under the pyramids, leading us to question the full extent of the pyramids' purpose and the knowledge left behind by those who built them.

Recent investigations using non-invasive technologies, such as ground-penetrating radar and 3D mapping, support the idea that the Giza Plateau may house an undiscovered labyrinth of tunnels and chambers. However, full-scale excavation remains limited due to the site's historical significance and the risks of disturbing the pyramids' foundations. This has left much of the Giza Plateau unexplored, fueling speculation about what might still be hidden beneath the surface. The Giza Plateau may hold many more secrets than we have uncovered, buried beneath layers of history, waiting to be revealed.

We will also explore the missing tops of the pyramids and whether they hold a significant piece of the puzzle in understanding the true functionality of these ancient structures. Without these capstones, we wonder whether they played a vital role in the pyramids' function. Could these missing pieces hold secrets to the pyramids' mysterious functionality, and their removal have severed a crucial link to the advanced technologies or energies of the ancient world?

Or are the pyramids themselves the capstones of an extensive underground structure, marking entrances or serving as energy focal points for vast subterranean networks that remain hidden, silently guarding ancient secrets waiting for humanity to rediscover and understand?

Challenges of Excavation Beneath the Pyramids

Excavating beneath the pyramids, particularly the Great Pyramid of Giza, presents significant challenges beyond the logistics of digging. These technical challenges are deeply intertwined with the pyramids' profound cultural, historical, and spiritual significance. Non-invasive technologies such as ground-penetrating radar and 3D mapping have revealed intriguing anomalies beneath the Giza Plateau, fueling speculation about hidden chambers, tunnels, and possible buried structures.[cdlxxxix] However, no substantial evidence has been strong enough to justify large-scale excavation. This leaves an atmosphere of mystery and unanswered questions as the underground secrets remain out of reach.

With their monumental weight and delicate internal architecture, the pyramids pose enormous risks to any potential excavation. Digging beneath them could compromise the structural integrity of the entire site. The Great Pyramid alone weighs approximately 6 million tons, and its intricate design, featuring chambers, corridors, and relieving blocks, was engineered to distribute this immense weight evenly across the entire structure. Any disruption to the foundational layers of the plateau could lead to catastrophic shifts, causing irreversible damage to the monument. The pyramid, which has stood for thousands of years, could be physically destabilised and its cultural legacy compromised.

Moreover, the pyramids are among the most precious cultural and historical artefacts in human history, protected by international preservation laws and UNESCO guidelines.[cdxc] These laws enforce stringent measures against unnecessary or speculative excavations. Archaeologists and preservationists argue that until there is irrefutable evidence of what lies beneath the pyramids, the risk of damaging such irreplaceable monuments far outweighs the potential benefits of uncovering new information.[cdxci] These restrictions leave a sense of anticipation as researchers grapple with the tension between scientific curiosity and the duty to preserve the environment.

The intrigue deepens when considering the possibilities that lie beneath the surface. Could hidden chambers be filled with untold treasures or relics of ancient technology? Or could underground tunnels link to other sacred sites, creating a network lost to time? Some theorists believe Egypt's most significant discoveries may lie beneath the pyramids, but these remain speculative dreams until more definitive evidence is uncovered.[cdxcii] We are left in suspense now, with modern technology allowing us glimpses into these underground worlds, but not enough to fully open the door.

The mysteries beneath the Giza Plateau continue to inspire both scholars and adventurers. The allure of potentially uncovering new tombs, relics, or advanced technologies has captivated imaginations for centuries.^{cdxciii} However, the weight of responsibility to protect these cultural marvels is equally profound. While delving beneath the pyramids remains a possibility, the cost of such an endeavour—both in terms of archaeological ethics and the potential for destruction—keeps excavation efforts at bay.^{cdxciv} Standing as sentinels of time, the pyramids guard their underground secrets with silent resolve, leaving us to wonder what lies just out of reach, hidden beneath millennia of history and stone.

We are, hence, left speculating about what could be beneath the pyramids. Will we find more tombs, more valuables, an ingenious system to stabilise the pyramid, a water and energy generation system, an energy storage system or perhaps an underground transportation system?

More Tombs below our Feet?

Some archaeologists and historians have proposed that the Giza Plateau, including the pyramids, may be just the surface of a much larger, undiscovered underground burial complex.^{cdxcv} While the pyramids tower above the desert sands as iconic symbols of ancient Egypt, their true significance may lie beneath the ground, where an intricate network of tunnels, tombs, sarcophagi, and ceremonial chambers could be hidden in the bedrock. This vast, subterranean world may contain the remains of more pharaohs, priests, or high-ranking officials, adding new layers to our understanding of Egypt's funerary culture and spiritual practices.

The concept of underground burial complexes beneath the pyramids is not without precedent. Archaeological discoveries from other pyramid sites worldwide have uncovered vast underground systems for ceremonial purposes, burials, and the safeguarding of treasures and sacred objects.^{cdxcvi} A notable comparison is found at the Pyramid of the Sun in Teotihuacan, Mexico, where an underground tunnel and chamber system was discovered. These chambers are believed to have been used for ritual burials, possibly of rulers or priests, and contain offerings such as jade, pottery, and shells.^{cdxcvii} Such discoveries suggest that pyramids may not just be surface structures for burial but gateways to expansive underground complexes designed to house the dead and the spiritual and material treasures accompanying them into the afterlife.^{cdxcviii}

In 2011, another significant find was made beneath the nearby Pyramid of the Feathered Serpent (Quetzalcoatl), where archaeologists uncovered a tunnel that led to several chambers filled with offerings and human remains.[cdxcix] The chambers contained items believed to be ritualistic, reinforcing the idea that, beneath many pyramid structures, intricate burial and ceremonial spaces played a crucial role in the spiritual and religious lives of these ancient societies.[d] Such chambers beneath pyramids in other parts of the world invite speculation that a similar underground network might exist beneath the Giza Plateau, awaiting discovery.

In Egypt, underground tunnels and chambers have already been found beneath several other pyramid complexes, notably the Step Pyramid of Djoser at Saqqara, which contains an extensive network of subterranean passageways and burial chambers.[di] This structure, the oldest known stone pyramid in Egypt, was built with intricate underground galleries that housed the tomb of King Djoser and numerous other sacred spaces filled with symbolic objects and reliefs designed to ensure the king's safe passage to the afterlife.[dii] The underground chambers beneath Djoser's pyramid demonstrate that Egyptian builders were skilled in creating vast, hidden spaces beneath their monumental structures, lending credence to the theory that similar networks may be present beneath the Giza pyramids.[diii]

If such an underground complex exists beneath Giza, it could dramatically alter our understanding of the site's purpose. The pyramids may have been part of a grand funerary complex, serving as tombs for individual rulers and as the heart of a more extensive burial system where sacred rituals took place in hidden chambers.[div] These chambers could have been used to honour the dead or conduct spiritual ceremonies, with the tunnels serving as symbolic passageways between the worlds of the living and the dead.[dv]

While many aspects align with mainstream thinking—especially the possibility of hidden tombs, the role of pyramids in spiritual and burial practices, and the precedent of underground spaces—the idea of an extensive, undiscovered network of burial chambers and spiritual spaces beneath the pyramids of Giza is speculative and not widely accepted in mainstream archaeology.

Safe for Valuables

An underground structure could have served highly practical purposes beyond its religious and ceremonial functions. It might have included secure storage spaces for treasures, artefacts, and offerings that the ancient Egyptians believed were essential for the deceased to navigate the afterlife. These objects, which often included precious metals, jewels, sacred texts, and ceremonial items, were believed to aid the deceased in their journey through the underworld, ensuring their safe passage and prosperity in the afterlife.[dvi] The Egyptians held a profound belief that the soul required material possessions in the afterlife, making the protection of these items a paramount concern.[dvii]

Moreover, these underground chambers could have functioned as hidden repositories for Egypt's most valuable treasures, belonging to the deceased and the state.[dviii] As symbols of the pharaoh's divine status, enormous quantities of gold and jewels would have been buried alongside rulers. These treasures were thought to ensure the ruler's wealth in the afterlife, but they also represented the wealth and power of the Egyptian state. Items such as crowns, sceptres, and ceremonial clothing, often adorned with precious metals and stones, could have been hidden to symbolise the ruler's divine right and authority in life and the afterlife. High-ranking officials or pharaohs could have also been buried with weapons, such as swords, shields, and ceremonial armour, representing their power as rulers and military leaders.

The Giza Plateau, Egypt's most monumental and symbolic burial site, may have been considered the ideal location for securing items of immense cultural and spiritual value.[dix] By placing treasures underground, possibly beneath multiple layers of solid stone, the Egyptians could have created a vault system resistant to looters and invading forces. This foresight was crucial given the historical record of looting, where many pyramids, including those at Giza, were plundered by tomb robbers over the centuries, eager to steal the wealth buried with the pharaohs.[dx]

It is plausible that the Egyptians anticipated this threat and designed elaborate underground networks to safeguard their most essential and sacred relics. Hidden deep beneath the pyramids, these treasures would have been inaccessible to most and remained undisturbed for thousands of years. Placing treasures underground, rather than in more easily accessible above-ground tombs or burial chambers, could have served as an additional defence against potential plunderers.[dxi] The ancient builders may have employed false corridors, sealed passageways, or decoy chambers to confuse and mislead those who attempted to rob these sacred sites.[dxii]

Further supporting this notion is the elaborate care and engineering that went into concealing some of the most important tombs, such as those in the Valley of the Kings.[dxiii] To deter robbers, pharaohs and high-ranking officials were often buried with intricate security measures, such as concealed doorways and complex tunnel systems.[dxiv] The same principles could have been applied on a larger scale beneath the Giza Plateau, where the Egyptians may have developed a vast underground labyrinth to protect not only the physical remains of their rulers but also the treasures that represented their divine power and connection to the gods.^{dxv}

The movie *The Mummy* (1999) perfectly illustrates how ancient Egyptians might have protected their treasures from looters. It is depicted through the elaborate traps and tunnels of Hamunaptra, the City of the Dead. Looters and treasure hunters, including the main characters, venture deep into underground chambers only to find themselves caught in deadly traps designed to guard the sacred relics. As they pass through labyrinthine passageways, false doors and collapsing ceilings are triggered. Many of the looters inside never managed to escape. These scenes show how the Egyptians, fearing looters, could have engineered elaborate defence mechanisms to ensure their most valuable treasures remained hidden and protected for eternity. This reflects the very real security measures used by the Egyptians, such as hidden chambers, false corridors, and deadly traps designed to mislead and punish those attempting to steal the wealth meant for the afterlife. The movie brings to life the possibility that underground treasure vaults were not only hidden but also meticulously designed to be deadly for any who dared to disturb them.

While the dramatic traps seen in films like *The Mummy* (1999) and *The Pyramid* (2014)—such as collapsing ceilings, spikes, or deadly gas—are exaggerated for effect, there are parallels with real-life security measures used by the Egyptians. For example, many tombs were built with false doors, hidden chambers, and decoy corridors to confuse looters. In some cases, heavy stone blocks were designed to slide into place, sealing off burial chambers once the tomb was closed. These blocks could weigh several tons, making it nearly impossible to reopen the tomb without extensive effort. Pitfalls and deep shafts were also used to deter or trap intruders. These natural obstacles, while not fatal traps, protected the most valuable treasures hidden deep within the complex, ensuring they remained untouched for millennia. These practical, passive defences relied on the tomb's architecture and clever design to create obstacles for looters rather than actively injuring or killing them, aligning with the Egyptians' desire for eternal peace in the afterlife.

Stabilising the Pyramids

As alluded to before, when we discussed the construction of the pyramids, these underground channels may have had a protective or stabilising function for the structures themselves. Water can act as a natural buffer, absorbing seismic vibrations and distributing pressure more evenly through the ground.^{dxvi} In a seismically active region, the underground water could have mitigated the effects of minor earthquakes, helping protect the pyramids and surrounding structures from damage.[dxvii] The underground water could have also helped maintain the precise alignment of the pyramids over centuries, stabilising the ground beneath them and preventing any significant shifting that might have compromised their accurate alignment with the stars.[dxviii]

Moreover, some theories suggest that water movement through these underground tunnels could have created a dynamic balance within the structures, perhaps contributing to the pyramids' long-term stability and durability.[dxix] The continuous water flow might have regulated the pressure on the foundations, preventing cracks or structural shifts that could have weakened the monument over time.[dxx] This could explain why the pyramids have withstood thousands of years of natural wear and environmental changes.

Architects today incorporate materials and designs that resonate with the Earth's natural frequencies, reducing structural wear.[dxxi] Some buildings are designed to minimise vibration or enhance structural stability using materials that absorb seismic or environmental vibrations.[dxxii] For example, buildings in earthquake-prone areas might use base isolators or damping systems to minimise the impact of seismic waves, but this doesn't involve resonance with the Earth's natural frequencies or water movement.[dxxiii] While modern architecture incorporates various environmental factors to enhance resilience, using underground water is not part of mainstream architectural practice. While contemporary architecture has yet to explore the full potential of underground water for these purposes, there is an opportunity to learn from ancient practices.[dxxiv]

Underground Water Systems and Energy Theories

Researchers have long speculated that a network of underground water tunnels, lakes, and reservoirs may lie beneath the pyramids, potentially serving as more than mere ceremonial or ritualistic elements. These water sources could have played a critical role in the pyramids' function, either as a natural resource for religious practices or as part of a more advanced system designed to harness and generate energy.

Geological surveys of the Giza Plateau have revealed the presence of underground water channels, leading some to propose that these channels, in conjunction with the pyramids' unique structure and materials, may have been part of an ancient energy grid. Water, a powerful conductor of energy, could have been used like modern hydroelectric systems, where the movement of water generates electricity.

Ancient Egyptian texts also refer to the significance of water in religious and spiritual practices, particularly the Nile, which was seen as the lifeblood of Egypt.[dxxv] Water was integral to their rituals of purification, rebirth, and the afterlife, often symbolising the flow of life and energy between worlds. Given this, some researchers suggest that the pyramids' connection to water was symbolic and functional, possibly leveraging water's physical properties in ways we are only beginning to comprehend.

Modern theorists, such as Andrew Collins, have taken these ideas further, proposing that the pyramids were deliberately situated to interact with underground aquifers and tributaries of the Nile. This interaction could have created a natural resonance or vibration, which some believe the ancients harnessed for energy production. According to these theories, the underground water tunnels may have served as conduits for transferring this energy, amplified by the pyramid structures above. The specific placement of the pyramids on certain geological formations could have enhanced this effect, creating a kind of ancient power plant that drew on the Earth's natural resources.[dxxvi]

Underground Energy Storage Systems

Some researchers speculate that ancient civilisations developed advanced energy generation or storage systems, potentially hidden beneath the pyramids. The idea of such systems revolves around the possibility that underground chambers could have been used to house technological equipment or energy sources, kept safely hidden from the surface. These chambers, if discovered, might contain remnants of early batteries, devices for generating electromagnetic energy, or even mechanisms that harness natural forces, such as the Earth's geomagnetic field, underground water flows, or the piezoelectric properties of the stone itself.

The presence of such technology could reshape our understanding of ancient engineering. Were these civilisations capable of tapping into natural energy sources, and could they have stored and used this energy for practical purposes, such as lighting internal chambers, powering primitive machinery, or facilitating long-distance communication? The idea of *Baghdad batteries* found in Mesopotamia, for instance, suggests that ancient people may have experimented with early forms of energy storage.[dxxvii]

The Baghdad batteries are a set of ancient artefacts discovered in the 1930s near Baghdad, Iraq, by German archaeologist Wilhelm König.[dxxviii] These artefacts consist of approximately 5-inch-tall terracotta pots with a copper cylinder inside, which houses an iron rod. An asphalt plug or stopper separates the copper cylinder and the iron rod, keeping the two metals from touching. When acidic liquid, such as vinegar or lemon juice, is added to the pot, the setup can generate a small electrical current, leading to the theory that these objects may have functioned as primitive batteries.[dxxix] The Baghdad batteries are typically dated to around 150 BCE to 250 CE.[dxxx] However, there remains some uncertainty about their exact date and purpose, as no direct textual or archaeological evidence has been found to definitively confirm their use during that time.

With their precise alignment to celestial bodies and significant geological features, the pyramids could have been an advanced part of an energy network, designed not only for religious and cultural purposes but for functional applications that we associate with more modern technological systems.

If these underground energy systems existed, they might have involved extensive networks of underground tunnels that transported or stored energy in ways still not fully understood by modern scientists. Ancient builders might have harnessed the natural properties of materials like limestone, quartz, or granite, which are known to exhibit piezoelectric properties, potentially converting pressure from the Earth or water movement into usable energy.[dxxxi] Some theories suggest that the Great Pyramid of Giza could have functioned as a resonator, collecting and amplifying natural energy, which was then stored or used within the underground chambers.[dxxxii]

Discovering such an advanced energy system would significantly shift our understanding of ancient Egypt and other civilisations. This suggests that the pyramids were not merely monumental tombs or religious structures, but sophisticated components of an energy grid designed to support everyday technological needs. This could indicate that these civilisations were far more advanced in their understanding of physics, geology, and engineering than previously thought. Moreover, it would point to technological innovation that enabled energy storage and use in ways not rediscovered until much later in human history, challenging our perceptions of technological progression.[dxxxiii]

Pyramids built on Pillars?

Some Flat Earth theorists suggest that the pyramids were not built on solid ground, but on massive pillars, which raised them above the Earth's surface.[dxxxiv] They claim this hidden construction method ties into their beliefs about ancient knowledge and an alternative understanding of Earth's structure. According to this view, these pillars were part of an advanced civilisation's technology or architecture, designed to elevate the pyramids for mystical or functional purposes.

They also speculate that a hidden labyrinth could be part of a vast underground system connected to the pyramids. They claim the pyramids are much larger than visible above ground, extending deep underground. The visible portion of the pyramids is only a tiny part of the entire structure, which is believed to be supported by massive foundations or hidden chambers beneath the Earth. No credible archaeological or scientific evidence supports the existence of massive pillars beneath ancient monuments, such as the pyramids or other well-known structures. However, many ancient civilisations did use sophisticated foundation systems to support their monuments. These were often designed to handle the weight of the structures and to ensure stability, but they were not hidden "pillars" in the sense described by speculative theories.

For Flat Earth theorists, the unconfirmed March 2025 discovery offers compelling support for long-held beliefs about hidden structures beneath the pyramids. The sheer depth and symmetry of the cylindrical formations—encircled by spiral pathways and connected to massive square bases—align with claims that the pyramids are not built directly on the Earth's surface but are elevated by enormous substructures. According to this perspective, these underground constructs could be part of a forgotten architectural system designed by an advanced civilisation with knowledge far beyond what mainstream archaeology acknowledges.

Spirals Beneath the Surface: Vortex Energy, Kundalini, and Tesla's Legacy

Could the spiral pathways discovered through SAR technology around the underground cylindrical structures beneath the pyramids be more than just architectural features? Their precise, deliberate geometry raises intriguing possibilities. Spirals are found throughout nature and mysticism, often associated with the movement of energy, transformation, and ascension. In Kundalini traditions, energy is believed to lie dormant at the base of the spine, coiling like a serpent. Through spiritual practices, this energy rises in a spiralling motion through the chakras, symbolising awakening, enlightenment, and connection to higher consciousness. Could these underground spiral paths mirror this energetic journey, scaled up and etched into the Earth?

In modern science, the spiral is not just symbolic—it's deeply functional. Nikola Tesla, one of history's most visionary inventors, used coiled forms in his Tesla coils to generate and transmit electrical energy wirelessly. The spiral was key to concentrating, amplifying, and releasing energy across space. Similarly, in vortex physics, spirals appear in fluid dynamics, magnetic field lines, and even in weather systems—such as hurricanes and galaxies—demonstrating that the spiral is a universal form for channelling and distributing energy efficiently.

The subterranean spiral pathways could, therefore, represent more than structural supports. They may be expressions of a forgotten science that combined the physical mechanics of energy with spiritual or metaphysical insight. Whether designed to move heat, charge, vibration, or consciousness, these spirals suggest the builders of the pyramids were not only master engineers but also students of the universe's deeper energetic design. This architectural resonance between Earth, the body, and the cosmos suggests that the pyramid complex may have functioned as a kind of Earth-aligned energy machine, connecting the planet's inner forces with the sky above.

The Lost Labyrinth of Egypt

"*The Lost Labyrinth of Egypt* is one of the most captivating and mysterious legends from ancient times, yet it remains relatively obscure compared to other Egyptian wonders. The Lost Labyrinth of Egypt is a structure that ancient historians, such as Herodotus and Strabo, mentioned. Unlike the well-known pyramids and temples, the labyrinth remains relatively obscure because its exact location and nature are still a mystery, and no visible monument has been conclusively identified as the labyrinth today. The Lost Labyrinth was said to be a massive and complex underground structure located near the city of Crocodilopolis (modern-day Hawara) in the Faiyum region of Egypt. According to Herodotus, who visited Egypt around the 5th century BCE, the labyrinth was even more impressive than the pyramids. He described it as having over 3,000 chambers, some above ground and some below, filled with treasures, intricate hieroglyphs, and secret knowledge of the ancient world.[dxxxv] Herodotus claimed that the labyrinth was built as a great temple and administrative centre for the twelve kings of Egypt, serving as a tomb and a place of worship. Strabo, a Greek geographer from the 1st century BCE, also mentioned the labyrinth, supporting Herodotus's account. He described it as a grand and vast structure with interconnected courtyards and intricate passageways.[dxxxvi] Other ancient writers, including Pliny the Elder, also referred to the labyrinth, further fueling its legend as an architectural marvel of ancient Egypt.

Despite these detailed accounts from ancient writers, the Lost Labyrinth remains relatively obscure because no definitive evidence of its existence has been found in modern times. Several expeditions and excavations have been carried out in the Faiyum region, particularly around Hawara, where the labyrinth is believed to have been located. In the 19th century, Egyptologist Flinders Petrie discovered a vast temple complex that some believe might be part of the labyrinth. However, no comprehensive structure matching the ancient descriptions has been uncovered.

The labyrinth's obscurity also stems from its current lack of physical presence. While the pyramids and other monuments are visible and well-documented, the maze is mainly known through ancient texts, which makes it more mysterious. Some scholars argue that it may have been dismantled over the centuries or that its remains lie buried beneath the sands, waiting to be discovered. The Lost Labyrinth is significant because, if it existed as described by Herodotus and others, it would have been one of the most sophisticated and monumental constructions of the ancient world, possibly surpassing the pyramids in complexity and importance. It also represents a vast repository of ancient knowledge, treasures, and cultural heritage.

Some researchers and theorists believe that this legendary labyrinth might still be hidden beneath the pyramids of Giza or near them, waiting to be discovered.[dxxxvii] The idea that the labyrinth could house lost Egyptian knowledge, sacred relics, or even technological secrets is exciting. Despite numerous expeditions and modern archaeological techniques, the Lost Labyrinth remains elusive. Whether real or merely myth, the labyrinth continues to fascinate historians, archaeologists, and treasure hunters, standing as one of Egypt's greatest mysteries. People speculate that it may hold untold secrets about ancient Egyptian civilisation.

The Missing Capstones

A significant part of the mystery surrounding the pyramids lies in the missing capstones or pyramidions that once crowned these monumental structures. Understanding what topped these pyramids could provide crucial insights into their original purpose and significance. By exploring what might have topped these structures, we examine the possibility that the pyramids were more than just tombs—perhaps they served as ancient power stations, spiritual beacons, or communication devices that connected the earthly and celestial realms. The disappearance of these capstones only deepens the mystery, hinting that critical pieces of ancient knowledge and technology may have been lost or hidden over time.[dxxxviii]

The missing caps of the pyramids, known as *pyramidions* or capstones, are a subject of much speculation. Over millennia, weathering, earthquakes, and natural elements could have caused the caps to erode or break apart.[dxxxix] Ancient or later civilisations may have

Powered by Pyramids: A Book of Theories

removed the capstones.[dxl] Some materials, particularly precious metals or stones, may have been looted, repurposed, or taken as spoils.[dxli] Some claim that the pyramids were never fully completed.[dxlii] It is also possible that the capstones were damaged or lost during the construction phase or in the years that followed and were never replaced.[dxliii] Maybe it fell off during an earthquake or seismic event.[dxliv] It leaves us speculating what they could have been made of and what they were used for.

Historical accounts of the pyramids describe gleaming surfaces that reflect sunlight. Archaeological evidence and historical records suggest that the capstones were likely made from white tura limestone, granite, gold, or electrum plating.[dxlv] Some think the smooth, white limestone used in the outer casing of the Great Pyramid was also likely used for the capstone.[dxlvi] This would have reflected sunlight, making the cap visible from a distance.[dxlvii] Some capstones, such as those found in smaller pyramids, were made from granite, which is more durable than limestone.[dxlviii] Other theories suggest that capstones were covered in gold or electrum, a naturally occurring alloy of gold and silver, to make them gleam brightly in the sunlight.[dxlix] This would have been visually striking.[dl]

The original capstone may have been made of materials that could potentially conduct electricity.[dli] If the pyramid, particularly its capstone, were made of or coated with a conductive material like gold, electrum, or copper, it would have likely attracted lightning. Could an antenna once have stood at the pyramid's peak, amplifying or harnessing natural electromagnetic energies from the Earth and cosmos?

An intriguing theory suggests that the missing capstones were critical elements in a global network of pyramids designed to work together. These capstones, possibly made from conductive materials like gold or crystalline structures, might have been crucial to synchronising energy between pyramids in distant parts of the world. According to this theory, the capstones acted as transmitters, using the Earth's natural electromagnetic field to connect various pyramids across continents, creating a vast energy grid that ancient civilisations used to communicate or transfer power. This global network could have allowed advanced societies to share knowledge or resources, effectively linking their spiritual and technological achievements. As a conductor of electricity, copper might have played a role in energy transmission, particularly if the pyramids were part of a more extensive network designed to harness or amplify natural energies from the Earth.[dlii] The removal or loss of these capstones may have disrupted this ancient energy system, severing the connection between these once-active energy nodes and leaving behind the monumental structures we see today, devoid of their original power.[dliii]

The capstone would have been the pyramid's final crowning, linking it with the heavens in both a spiritual and perhaps practical sense.[dliv] Some speculate that the capstones could have been made of quartz crystal. Quartz is known for its piezoelectric properties, which enable it to generate an electrical charge in response to mechanical stress. In this theory, the capstones could have amplified or focused energy from the Earth, possibly for spiritual or technological purposes. Quartz's translucent nature would have made it a visually striking material, as it reflects and refracts light.[dlv]

Others suggest the capstone may have projected a light beam into the sky, serving as a point of communication with celestial bodies. This light could have been created by reflective materials or advanced technology lost to time, or perhaps it was a symbolic 'pillar of light,' connecting the Earth to the heavens in a metaphysical sense. Could the pyramids' smooth, reflective surfaces and alignment with specific stars or constellations be navigational aids for alien spacecraft? Could the capstones have emitted beams of light or energy, helping guide alien ships to Earth?

Another possibility is that the capstones were made from meteorite iron, a material highly prized in ancient cultures. The Egyptians are known to have used meteorite iron in jewellery and ceremonial objects, and its extraterrestrial origin would have added symbolic and possibly ritual significance to the pyramid's capstone. As a material, meteorite iron could have connected the Earth to the cosmos, symbolising a divine or extraterrestrial link.[dlvi] There is archaeological evidence that the ancient Egyptians used meteorite iron in jewellery and ritual objects, such as King Tutankhamun's dagger. The symbolic value of meteorite iron as "metal from the heavens" could suggest its use in pyramid construction, particularly for capstones, to emphasise a cosmic connection.

In more speculative theories, orichalcum—a legendary metal described in ancient texts, particularly Plato's writings on Atlantis—has been proposed as a potential material for the capstones. Described as having a reddish-gold hue, orichalcum was believed to be highly valuable and possessed unique properties, perhaps even capable of conducting energy in ways unknown to modern science.[dlvii]

One bold idea is that the capstones were crafted from materials far beyond our current understanding, perhaps crystalline structures or even extraterrestrial alloys capable of amplifying or channelling energy. In this theory, the capstones were not merely decorative but integral to the pyramids' ability to harness cosmic or Earth-bound energies.[dlviii]

Their disappearance could be explained as part of a deliberate effort, either by ancient civilisations or by those who came later, to prevent their powerful technology from falling into the wrong hands.[dlix] The intentional removal and hiding of the capstones may signify an attempt to safeguard the knowledge they contained—knowledge that could potentially unlock new dimensions of energy manipulation.[dlx] This speculation invites us to imagine the pyramids not as static monuments but as once-active energy devices, their true potential hidden by the loss of these capstones.[dlxi]

From an Egyptological perspective, the capstones were both symbolic and architectural features, rather than objects of esoteric or cosmic power. Pyramidions were often made of limestone or granite and may have been gilded to reflect the sun, symbolising the pharaoh's connection to the sun god, Ra. Their function was primarily religious and symbolic, reinforcing the pharaoh's divine status rather than serving as tools for energy manipulation or cosmic alignment. This more grounded explanation aligns with the established understanding of ancient Egyptian beliefs and practices.

There are other examples in history of messages from the past being destroyed. In the rural fields of Georgia, USA, a granite monument known as the *Georgia Guidestones* once stood—eerily modern in construction, yet ancient in intention.[dlxii] Like the pyramids, it was encoded with astronomical alignments, cryptic language, and an apparent mission to outlive the civilisation that built it. Etched in eight modern languages and four ancient scripts, the monument delivered ten directives for a future humanity, including a striking call to limit population and live in harmony with nature. Its destruction in 2022 only amplified its mystery—mirroring how capstones and messages from the pyramids may have been lost, buried, or deliberately removed to veil deeper truths. Just as Egypt's Great Pyramid was once thought to house prophetic records in its structure, the Guidestones functioned as a modern time capsule: a coded instruction manual from an unseen architect. Their alignment with celestial bodies and the invocation of universal laws point to the same intent many attribute to the pyramids— not just to memorialise the past, but to anchor consciousness for a post-collapse world.[dlxiii]

What Colour Could the Capstones Have Been?

Mainstream Egyptologists believe the original capstones may have been made of electrum — a naturally occurring alloy of gold and silver. This would have given the pyramid apex a brilliant golden glow, especially under sunlight. Being highly reflective, Gold would have amplified this effect, possibly making the capstones visible from miles away.

If pyramids channel telluric energy or even emit ground-to-sky lightning, the ionisation of nitrogen and oxygen in the surrounding air could have created a blue or violet corona, similar to St. Elmo's Fire. This phenomenon is seen today on ship masts or plane wings during high-energy atmospheric conditions.

Over time, repeated lightning strikes or energetic reactions could have scorched or oxidised the stone, especially if copper or iron traces were present. This may have caused reddish-brown discolouration, similar to how metals or stones blacken after exposure to extreme heat.

If no capstone ever existed or was removed to release energy or plasma, the tip of the pyramid may have become charred, blackened, or vitrified over time due to direct exposure to the elements. This theory suggests the pyramids were intentionally incomplete at the top, functioning like a vent for Earth energy or solar plasma.

More esoteric theories propose that capstones could have been made from crystals, unknown alloys, or even extraterrestrial materials capable of changing colour depending on the energy around them. These ideas link the capstone to ancient energy manipulation, frequency tuning, or even interdimensional communication.

Who Could Be Hiding the Capstones?

There are many speculative theories about the missing capstones and who might be hiding them. Let's go through the potential suspects and their possible motives.

In *"The Templar Secrets: Pyramid Connections and Hidden Knowledge" (2019), Jason Brown explores the notion that the Knights Templar, as part of a secretive order, possessed* ancient knowledge, including the significance of the pyramids and their capstones. He theorises that these capstones held esoteric power, possibly linked to controlling cosmic forces, which the Templars understood and sought to protect. He writes that the Templars may have removed and hidden the capstones to prevent this knowledge from falling into the wrong hands. He connects the symbolism of the pyramid and the hidden capstones to the Templars' secret practices, suggesting that the capstones may still be hidden in secret vaults or temples under the guardianship of descendants of these secret orders.[dlxiv] These secret societies might still exist today, guarding the capstones in underground vaults or secret temples, waiting for the right time to reveal the knowledge.[dlxv] However, no documented historical evidence supports that the Knights Templar had access to esoteric knowledge about the pyramids or their capstones. The Templar Order, primarily active during the Crusades, focused on military and religious objectives in the Holy Land and did not document any specific knowledge or connection to the pyramids in Egypt.

Along similar lines, some argue that modern governments or shadow organisations like the Illuminati or secret branches of military intelligence may have discovered the power of the capstones and removed them for classified research.[dlxvi] These organisations may have realised the capstones had the potential to unlock free, limitless energy or connect with extraterrestrial civilisations, and they now keep them hidden in secret research facilities.[dlxvii] The goal is to weaponise or control this technology for global dominance, keeping it hidden from the public to maintain geopolitical power[dlxviii].

Were the capstones cosmic anchors that helped align Earth with specific celestial bodies or cosmic energies? Removing the capstones shifted the Earth's energetic balance, causing the loss of these connections.[dlxix] A hidden group of astronomer-priests, possibly descendants of ancient star-worshipping cults, could have removed the capstones to prevent a catastrophic cosmic event, believing that leaving them in place would have attracted an apocalyptic alignment.[dlxx] Could these capstones be kept in a secret location, known only to a few initiates, to protect the Earth from disastrous cosmic forces?[dlxxi]

There are also many alien-related theories. One theory argues that perhaps aliens who had constructed the pyramids returned to Earth to retrieve the capstones. These capstones were not just decorative but advanced extraterrestrial technology that enabled communication or energy transmission between the pyramids and their home planet.[dlxxii] Once their mission was complete or Earth's civilisations no longer needed the pyramids' power, the aliens took the capstones back to prevent humanity from accessing the advanced technology prematurely.[dlxxiii] The capstones may have been removed and taken to a lost city—possibly Atlantis or another advanced, undiscovered civilisation.[dlxxiv] These cities could have possessed the technology and knowledge to harness the true power of the capstones, and they removed them to consolidate their power.[dlxxv] The capstones may still be used in secret to power the advanced technologies that keep this civilisation hidden, and their existence ensures that only those who are worthy or enlightened can access the pyramids' full potential.[dlxxvi]

Others wonder if the capstones were tools used by interdimensional beings to open portals between dimensions. When humanity began to misuse the pyramids or drifted away from their original purpose, these beings may have removed the capstones to prevent further harm.[dlxxvii] They believe these capstones are now hidden in a parallel dimension, accessible only to those who possess the ancient knowledge of dimensional travel. These beings might reintroduce the capstones when humanity is ready for the next phase of spiritual or technological evolution.[dlxxviii] This theory falls into the science fiction category rather than being based on historical or archaeological facts.

And finally, perhaps the capstones were not physically removed, but instead rendered invisible or cloaked using ancient or advanced technology. This technology bends light or manipulates perception, making the capstones invisible to the human eye.[dlxxix] Those who have unlocked the knowledge of the pyramids' true purpose can access this hidden technology and "see" the capstones.[dlxxx] Could the capstones still sit atop the pyramids, guiding energy and knowledge, but only for a select few to interact with them?[dlxxxi] While explored in theoretical physics, such technology is not supported by any evidence that ancient civilisations possessed or implemented such technology.

Derren Brown, the well-known mentalist and illusionist, has occasionally explored secret societies and their involvement in historical mysteries, albeit from a sceptical standpoint rather than a believer in such theories. In his discussions and writings on conspiracy theories, including in his book *Tricks of the Mind* (2006), he suggests that many of these ideas, such as the notion of the Knights Templar or secret Egyptian orders hiding powerful artefacts like the capstones, are rooted in human fascination with mystery and the unknown. He argues that these stories are often a product of our desire for grand narratives that explain the unexplainable, and they play into our cognitive biases, which make us more inclined to believe in hidden forces at work. He does not necessarily support the idea that secret societies guard such knowledge. Still, he acknowledges that the allure of these theories is potent because they offer simple answers to complex historical gaps. He concludes that while entertaining, these theories are more reflective of human psychology and our need for wonder and control than of real historical evidence.[dlxxxii]

Of course, it is also possible that there never were any capstones at all. Rather than being lost or stolen, they may have been intentionally left out, designed as open points for the release of energy or to maintain a connection between the structure and the sky. In this view, the pyramid's apex wasn't meant to be sealed but to remain an active conduit between Earth and the cosmos.

Conclusions

The mysteries hidden beneath the pyramids and the missing capstones continue to captivate researchers and theorists alike. From the possibility of secret chambers holding forgotten knowledge to the idea that the missing capstones once served a crucial function, these theories offer new dimensions to our understanding of the pyramids. Whether these subterranean spaces were designed as burial grounds to store sacred artefacts, generate energy, or serve as portals to more profound cosmic mysteries, the truth remains elusive, adding another layer of intrigue to these ancient wonders.

While the evidence is largely speculative, it compels us to reconsider what we know about the pyramids' purpose and their role in the broader context of ancient knowledge and power. The tension between scientific exploration and ethical preservation creates an intriguing dynamic, underscoring that these secrets may remain hidden for years, if not indefinitely.

The Sphinx is another structure that may hold further clues. Could the Sphinx and other nearby monuments, like the obelisks, provide additional insights into the mysteries of the pyramids and their origins? In the next chapter, we will explore the connections between these iconic structures and what they might reveal about the true history of Egypt's most enduring wonders.

Powered by Pyramids: A Book of Theories

Chapter 7 Clues given by the Sphinx and Obelisk?

Some scholars and enthusiasts believe that the Sphinx, the obelisks, and the pyramids are all interconnected, forming a unified system that reveals secrets about their origins and purpose. This chapter will investigate the Sphinx and the obelisks as they may provide complementary insights and clues about the architects behind these structures and the era in which they were built. Are these monuments linked through a shared intention or technology? By examining the Sphinx and the obelisks, we can gain a deeper understanding of the builders' motivations, the technology they employed, and the broader context surrounding the construction of the pyramids. This investigation could help us piece together who built them and why.

Could The Sphinx Be Older?

Like the pyramids, the Sphinx is shrouded in mystery. There are no inscriptions explaining its construction and function. The Great Sphinx of Giza, situated on the Giza Plateau near Cairo, Egypt, is located near the Pyramids of Giza and is traditionally believed to have been constructed during the reign of the pharaoh Khafre around 2,500 BCE. The Sphinx, a massive limestone statue with the body of a lion and the head of a human (often thought to be a likeness of Khafre), is one of the most iconic monuments of ancient Egypt. The Great Sphinx of Giza was carved from a single, massive block of limestone. [dlxxxiii]

In the early '90s, Dr Robert Schoch proposed a controversial theory suggesting that the Sphinx was much older than was traditionally believed. He bases his theory on evidence of water erosion on the body of the Sphinx. This type of erosion, he argues, could only have occurred during a period when the region experienced significant rainfall, which would have been before the rise of ancient Egyptian civilisation. According to Dr Robert Schoch, the Sphinx could date back to around 10,000 BCE, when the climate was wetter, and the area was not a desert. [dlxxxiv] He supports this theory by pointing out the vertical erosion patterns on the limestone body of the Sphinx, which he argued were caused by significant rainfall over an extended period. These patterns differ from the horizontal erosion typically caused by wind and sand, which is more common in arid desert environments, such as modern-day Egypt. The only period when the Giza Plateau experienced sufficient rainfall to cause this erosion was around 10,000 BCE, when the region had a much wetter climate. Evidence of a wetter period in the Sahara, including the Giza region, is found in fossilised plant remains and ancient lake beds, indicating significant water sources and vegetation during that time. Sediment analysis reveals periodic wet phases, particularly during the African Humid Period, which lasted until about 5,000-6,000 years ago. Additionally, geological formations in the area display erosion patterns consistent with weathering from a humid climate, further supporting evidence of a wetter environment.[dlxxxv]

The theory that vertical erosion was caused by significant rainfall around 10,000 BCE is considered speculative and lacks sufficient geological evidence to support it. Mark Lehner states, "*the horizontal erosion patterns on the body of the Sphinx are consistent with the effects of wind and sand, which is typical in desert environments like Giza.*"[dlxxxvi] His analysis is based on extensive archaeological excavations in the Giza Plateau, and he argues that the Sphinx's construction dates to the reign of Pharaoh Khafre around 2500 BCE, aligning with traditional timelines of Egyptian history.

A study published by the Geological Society of America in 2010 analysed the erosion of the limestone on the Giza Plateau. It concluded that "*while some vertical erosion patterns may suggest exposure to water, these can be attributed to the natural erosion of softer layers of limestone that were not as resistant to weathering as others.*"[dlxxxvii] This finding reinforces the mainstream belief that wind and sand, rather than water, caused the erosion. He asserts that the climate around Giza has been predominantly dry since 2500 BCE, with little rainfall, making water erosion highly unlikely. The argument is supported by studies showing that the softer layers of limestone on the Sphinx erode differently than the harder layers, which can create patterns resembling water erosion but are caused by wind and sand.

Dr Robert Schoch's theory suggests that a much older civilisation might have built the Sphinx, possibly predating the ancient Egyptians by thousands of years. Some proponents of this theory also extend it to the pyramids, proposing that they, too, could have been built by an older civilisation and later adopted or modified by the Egyptians. Some link this to the era of the mythical lost civilisation of Atlantis, suggesting that the Sphinx could be a remnant of this advanced society.

The documentary *The Mystery of the Sphinx* (1993) focuses on alternative theories regarding the origins and purpose of the Great Sphinx and the pyramids of Giza. John Anthony West collaborated with Dr Robert Schoch to propose that the Sphinx is far older than traditionally believed. The film draws attention to the idea that the official timeline of Egyptian history may need revision, and it has continued to inspire speculation about the hidden knowledge encoded in these ancient monuments. If the Sphinx is much older, they argue, it would imply that advanced civilisations existed long before what is commonly accepted, necessitating a significant revision of ancient history and our understanding of Egyptian and the entire human civilisation's timeline. The documentary also highlights the resistance from mainstream Egyptology and academia to these alternative theories. It discusses the academic establishment's reluctance to embrace new evidence that could dramatically alter the understanding of ancient history, implying that these theories challenge entrenched historical narratives. [dlxxxviii]

Some researchers argue that the Sphinx symbolises the Age of Leo, which places the monument between 10,500 BCE and 8,000 BCE. The Sphinx's orientation, facing east, aligns with the constellation Leo during that time's spring equinox. [dlxxxix] While celestial alignments are a known aspect of many ancient structures, the theory connecting the Sphinx to the Age of Leo is speculative. Egyptologists argue that while ancient Egyptians had astronomical knowledge, there is no direct evidence linking the Sphinx to such an alignment. They believe the Sphinx's orientation facing east is more likely symbolic of the sunrise, an essential aspect of Egyptian religious and spiritual beliefs tied to rebirth and the solar cycle, rather than an alignment with the stars.

Others suggest that the Sphinx may have been built as early as 36,000 BCE. They refer to the readings of Edgar Cayce, a well-known American psychic who gained a reputation for the remarkable accuracy of his psychic readings. He is renowned, and his predictions and insights were so influential that researchers, scholars, and the general public have preserved and studied a vast archive of his readings. These readings, numbering over 14,000, are now housed in the *Edgar Cayce Library* in the US. In his readings from 1920 to 1930, he claimed that the Sphinx was built around 10,500 BCE by survivors of Atlantis. He stated that this period coincided with the final destruction of Atlantis, when refugees from the sunken continent arrived in Egypt and contributed to the construction of the Sphinx and other monuments. He also mentioned an earlier date tied to the Atlantean civilisation, around 36,000 BCE. He claimed that the Atlanteans possessed advanced technological knowledge and spiritual understanding, which they later encoded into structures like the Sphinx. His readings also suggest that we will discover records beneath the Sphinx, containing knowledge from the lost civilisation of Atlantis. [dxc]

Mainstream Egyptologists and archaeologists reject the theories of Dr Robert Schoch and Edgar Cayce. They argue that no direct evidence, such as inscriptions or artefacts, suggests that the Sphinx predates Khafre's reign. Theories suggesting the Sphinx was built by survivors of Atlantis or using lost technology are considered pseudo-scientific by mainstream scholars. There is also no archaeological evidence to support the existence of an advanced civilisation or "Atlantis" responsible for the Sphinx's construction. Therefore, claims based on Cayce's readings or links to Atlantis are speculative and not grounded in scientific evidence. The debate continues about the origins of ancient monuments, such as the Sphinx and the pyramids, challenging established views of Egypt's history.[dxci]

What Lies Beneath the Sphinx?

The idea that hidden chambers or tunnels may lie beneath the Sphinx, similar to the pyramids, has been a subject of speculation for centuries. Ancient Egyptian texts and myths often depict the Sphinx as a guardian figure of tombs and a keeper of hidden knowledge.

Could it be that the Sphinx serves as an access point to a deeper, unseen network beneath the Sphinx and the pyramids? Some speculative theories suggest that the Sphinx's location, carefully aligned with the stars, serves as a gateway to an underground library or chamber of ancient wisdom—a Hall of Records that holds the secrets of human history and advanced technologies lost to time. Could this monument have been designed not as a mere statue but as a guardian of cosmic and earthly knowledge, intentionally placed to conceal something far more extraordinary than what meets the eye? A chamber is said to contain the lost understanding of advanced civilisations, including the fabled Atlantis. The psychic Edgar Cayce, who predicted that the chamber with the Hall of Records would be discovered in the 20th century, revealed the true history of humanity.[dxcii] However, no such discovery has been made, and there is no archaeological evidence supporting the existence of this Hall of Records. Some speculate it may have been found but hidden from the public.

Seismic surveys and ground-penetrating radar have detected several anomalies beneath the Sphinx, fueling further speculation that tunnels and chambers may have been concealed beneath the Monument. Some of these anomalies are believed to be natural cavities formed within the limestone bedrock over millions of years, rather than man-made constructions. Others could be tunnels or voids left behind by ancient construction activities.

Egyptologist Dr Zahi Hawass extensively explored the Giza Plateau and the Sphinx. While he acknowledged that anomalies and tunnels exist beneath the Sphinx, no significant chambers or Hall of Records were discovered. Ultimately, the investigations yielded no significant findings, at least not that we are aware of.[dxciii] In discussing the potential tunnels and chambers beneath the Sphinx, he acknowledged that tunnels discovered beneath the Sphinx "*could be remnants of ancient construction activities, though no significant finds have been made.*"

Has the Original Head on the Sphinx been Replaced?

Geologists, particularly those who subscribe to alternative dating theories, such as Dr Robert Schoch, have pointed out that the head of the Sphinx appears to have experienced less erosion than the body. He also argued that the head was relatively small compared to the massive body. This has led to the hypothesis that the head might have been recarved.

Some suggest that the original head might have been a female figure, possibly representing a goddess like *Hathor,* the goddess of the sky, love, and fertility. Other possibilities include Isis, the mother goddess, or Sekhmet, the lion-headed goddess of war. All these gods were central to Egyptian mythology. Advocates of this theory propose that the head could have been re-carved at some point in history, possibly to match the likeness of a reigning pharaoh, such as Khafre. They point to the erosion patterns and the seeming mismatch between the head and body. Furthermore, in ancient Egyptian art, female deities were often depicted with lion-like features, suggesting that the Sphinx may have once represented a more feminine or divine figure before its transformation. [dxciv]

Similarly, the golden burial mask of Tutankhamun, one of the most iconic artefacts from ancient Egypt, may have been initially crafted for a female, possibly Queen Neferneferuaten. Tutankhamun, commonly known as "King Tut," was an ancient Egyptian pharaoh of the 18th Dynasty who ruled during the New Kingdom period (around 1332–1323 BCE). He ascended the throne at a very young age, likely around 9 or 10 years old, following the death of Akhenaten, the controversial pharaoh known for his religious reforms. Tutankhamun's reign was relatively short, lasting approximately ten years, as he died at the age of around 18 or 19. Tutankhamun is best known not for his achievements as a ruler but for his nearly intact tomb (KV62) in the Valley of the Kings, discovered by British archaeologist Howard Carter in 1922. The tomb contained many artefacts, including his famous golden burial mask. Evidence supporting this theory of repurposing the golden burial mask includes the androgynous features of the mask, such as its narrow chin and high cheekbones, which align more closely with female depictions in ancient Egyptian art. Additionally, the mask has ear holes, a feature typically seen in female representations, as male pharaohs were not usually depicted with pierced ears. There are also signs that the cartouche bearing Tutankhamun's name was altered, suggesting it might have displayed initially the name of a female ruler. Given the short reign of Tutankhamun, it is likely that existing artefacts were repurposed quickly for his burial, reflecting a common practice in ancient Egypt during transitional periods.[dxcv]

The head of the Sphinx used to have a beard, which dropped off over time due to natural erosion and structural stress. Could the remnants of this beard provide an important clue about the Sphinx's original appearance?[dxcvi] Does it indicate that it was a feature added later? While one piece of the beard is housed at the British Museum in London, another, smaller portion is located in the Egyptian Museum in Cairo. This beard fragment is a significant artefact because it aligns with the traditional iconography of Egyptian pharaohs, often depicted with ceremonial beards symbolising their divine rule. Some scholars believe that the beard may have been a later addition during restoration efforts, as it appears to have been attached to the Sphinx's chin after its initial construction.[dxcvii] This would support the theory that the head of the Sphinx was replaced later. The debate about whether the beard was part of the original design or a later addition remains open among Egyptologists.

Another fringe theory suggests that the Sphinx was originally depicted as a dog, possibly representing the jackal-headed god Anubis. Proponents of this idea point to the Sphinx's smaller head compared to its large body, suggesting it might have been re-carved from an earlier, larger form. Anubis, the guardian of the dead and protector of necropolises, fits the role of a sentinel over the Giza plateau, which aligns with the Sphinx's position guarding the pyramid complex.[dxcviii] This hypothesis suggests that an original Anubis statue was altered to resemble a lion with a human head, likely to suit royal symbolism during the Old Kingdom or later. This theory is not widely accepted.

Mainstream scholars agree that the body of the Sphinx has experienced more erosion than the head. The consensus attributes this to the fact that the body was buried in the sand for long periods while the head remained exposed. The protective covering of sand likely shielded the body from the same degree of weathering experienced by the exposed head, causing the apparent difference in erosion patterns. The idea that the head was re-carved from a larger original figure, possibly a lion or other animal, is speculative. Mainstream scholars argue that the head and body proportions of the Sphinx are due to the limitations of the rock formation from which it was carved.

How about the Hole and Lost Nose?

The hole in the Sphinx's head also remains a mystery. Some claim the hole was a deliberate architectural feature, perhaps used for ceremonial or astronomical purposes or to access chambers beneath.[dxcix] However, these claims lack substantial evidence, and no significant discoveries have been made to support such ideas. Most scholars, including Zahi Hawass, suggest that the hole was created during later restoration efforts or by explorers in the past, possibly during the 19th century, in search of hidden chambers or other features. This hole is not believed to have been part of the Sphinx's original construction.[dc] Most evidence indicates that it results from later human activity rather than a significant feature of the original monument.[dci] Although the idea of hidden chambers and ancient treasures intrigues many, no discoveries have confirmed these theories to date.[dcii]

A more creative thought is whether the Sphinx served as a water fountain. This adds an interesting perspective on the water erosion patterns around its base. The erosion patterns observed on the Sphinx's body and its surrounding enclosure differ from those caused by wind-based erosion seen on other ancient monuments in Egypt. Robert Schoch's geological analysis argued that the Sphinx may have been exposed to heavy rainfall during a wetter climatic period thousands of years before the generally accepted date of its construction.[dciii] However, could it be evidence of the Sphinx's use as a water feature or fountain, with water actively flowing around or through it?[dciv] One critical detail supporting the fountain theory is the cavity or hole on the top of the Sphinx's head.[dcv] Water may have been channelled through the head of the Sphinx and cascaded down its sides, contributing to the erosion patterns observed today.[dcvi]

Others wonder what happened to the nose. In *The Lost Face of the Sphinx: Uncovering the Truth Behind the Missing Nose* (2016), Mark Jones explores the longstanding mystery surrounding the Sphinx's missing nose. He delves into historical accounts and examines evidence challenging the widespread belief that Napoleon's soldiers were responsible for its destruction. According to his research, sketches of the Sphinx made before Napoleon's campaign in Egypt show that the nose was already absent by the 18th century. This suggests that the damage occurred much earlier, possibly during the Islamic period. The nose may have been deliberately removed during the Islamic period when acts of defacement against idolatrous figures were sometimes carried out. The most commonly cited story attributes the damage to a 14th-century Sufi named Muhammad Sa'im al-Dahr, who was angered by local peasants offering sacrifices to the Sphinx in the hope of a good harvest. According to this account, he defaced the statue as an act of iconoclasm. Mark Jones also highlights the symbolic significance of the missing nose, noting that it could have been a deliberate act to erase part of the monument's identity, reflecting a shift in cultural or religious values at the time.[dcvii]

Lion vs. Cow: Symbolism and Societal Shifts in Ancient Egypt

Could the Sphinx point to the construction of earlier hunter-gatherer societies? In *Göbekli Tepe: Genesis of the Gods* (2016), Klaus Schmidt demonstrated that hunter-gatherer societies could create monumental structures, overturning the long-held belief that such large-scale construction was exclusive to settled agricultural communities. Göbekli Tepe is a prehistoric site in modern-day Turkey, dated to around 9,600 BCE, and is indeed one of the oldest known monumental structures built by a hunter-gatherer society. This discovery challenged the belief that monumental architecture was exclusive to settled agricultural societies. This insight prompts us to reevaluate the origins of the Egyptian Sphinx.[dcviii]

Lions existed in ancient Egypt. Lions were native to the region during the early periods of Egyptian civilisation, particularly around the time of the Old Kingdom (c. 2,686–2,181 BCE). They were found in the wild across North Africa, including Egypt. Over time, as the region became increasingly arid and desertification spread, the lion's habitat diminished; however, they were present in ancient Egypt's environment, especially during its early stages.[dcix]

Before the rise of Egypt's advanced civilisation, earlier hunter-gatherer societies would have encountered and likely hunted lions, which roamed the region at the time. As powerful predators, lions held significant meaning to these early humans, representing both danger and strength. The successful hunting of lions by these societies could have led to their reverence, perhaps inspiring the lion's body in the design of the Sphinx. The Sphinx, often viewed as a symbol of protection and kingship in ancient Egypt, may reflect much older traditions in which hunter-gatherers held lions in awe and incorporated them into their symbolic and spiritual worlds.

Cows are prominent in Egyptian hieroglyphs and art. They were associated with deities like Hathor, the goddess of love, beauty, fertility, and motherhood, who was often depicted as a cow or with cow horns. This reflects the values of a settled, agrarian society that relied heavily on livestock and agriculture. We see barely any representations of lions.[dcx] This contrast suggests that the Sphinx could be rooted in an older, pre-agricultural, hunter-gatherer society. This shift in symbolism from lions to cows is plausible given the different relationships agricultural societies have with nature. They moved away from confrontations with predators, such as lions, that characterised hunter-gatherer life.

Mainstream archaeology attributes the Sphinx's creation to a more developed, settled society of ancient Egypt rather than to earlier hunter-gatherers. Nonetheless, the lions still held a symbolic importance in ancient Egypt and earlier cultures. While cows symbolised nourishment and daily life, lions were reserved for the pharaohs and deities. For instance, the throne of the pharaoh was sometimes referred to as a "lion throne" due to its powerful symbolism.[dcxi] Lions are also linked with *Sekhmet,* the lioness-headed goddess of war, who embodied the fierce and protective aspects of the pharaoh's power. She was depicted with a lion's head, often representing destruction and healing.[dcxii] Lions appear in Egyptian art and hieroglyphs in royal hunting scenes, symbolising the pharaoh's ability to dominate the natural world and political enemies.[dcxiii] Lions are sometimes shown in tomb scenes, symbolising the protective nature of the afterlife, guarding the deceased from evil forces.

So, while lions are less frequently depicted in Egyptian hieroglyphs than other animals, such as cows, falcons, or snakes, one could argue that the lion's role is generally reserved for the elite and deities.

Sphinx Across Cultures

Can we learn anything by comparing the Sphinx to other similar monuments that have been discovered? The Sphinx is one of the most enduring symbols of ancient civilisations, with its most famous representation being the Great Sphinx of Giza in Egypt. Like the pyramids, the sphinx has appeared across various cultures throughout history. Due to their varied presence throughout history and the existence of modern replicas, it is challenging to determine the exact number of Sphinx statues worldwide. Researchers estimate that there are hundreds of sphinxes, most of which are located in Egypt. Sphinx statues flank the avenue from the Luxor Temple to the Karnak Temple complex. Many of these have the head of a ram (representing the god Amun), known as "Criosphinxes," while others have human heads, referred to as "Androsphinxes."[dcxiv] The Sphinx, particularly in ancient Egypt, was seen as a guardian figure, protecting sacred spaces such as temples, tombs, and the Giza Plateau.[dcxv] Could they have been guarding ancient secrets buried under the Sphinx? The mainstream narrative is that its imposing form was meant to ward off evil and protect the pharaohs in the afterlife.[dcxvi] In this sense, the Sphinx embodies the concept of divine protection and the safeguarding of spiritual knowledge and power.

While the Sphinx is most closely associated with ancient Egypt, its symbolism and form have been adopted by different cultures, particularly in Greek, Roman, and European art and architecture.^{dcxvii} Each culture attributed different meanings to the Sphinx, ranging from guardianship and protection in Egypt to mystery and intellectual challenge in Greece. Modern replicas and interpretations reflect humanity's enduring fascination with this enigmatic figure. The lion, a central component of the Sphinx's form, is universally recognised as a symbol of strength, courage, and royalty. Combining the lion's body with a human head, the Sphinx represents a powerful, almost supernatural being capable of physical dominance and intellectual authority—the human aspect of the Sphinx, especially in Greek mythology, symbolises intelligence and wisdom. The Greek Sphinx is different from its Egyptian counterpart. It is usually depicted as a creature with the head of a woman, the body of a lion, the wings of an eagle, and sometimes a serpent's tail. This supports the theory that the Sphinx in Egypt may have originally had a female head.^{dcxviii} In Greek mythology, the Sphinx is most famous for guarding the entrance to Thebes and posing the famous riddle to travellers: *"What walks on four legs in the morning, two legs at noon, and three legs in the evening?"* Oedipus solves the riddle, and the Sphinx kills herself in despair. This version of the sphinx symbolises mystery, death, and intellectual challenges.^{dcxix} The Sphinx of Naxos is a famous Greek sculpture that once stood on a tall column at the Oracle of Delphi. This Sphinx had the body of a lion, the wings of a bird, and the head of a woman. The people of Naxos dedicated it to the sanctuary around 560 BCE. The sphinx symbolised protection and divine power and was associated with the Oracle of Delphi, one of ancient Greece's most important religious centres. It represented a connection between the human world and the divine.^{dcxx}

Chinese lions, often referred to as Foo Dogs or Shishi, and the Egyptian Sphinx share some intriguing visual and symbolic similarities, despite their vastly different cultural origins. Both are depicted in a majestic, guarding posture, representing strength and protection. The Sphinx, with the body of a lion and the head of a pharaoh, stands as a protector of royal tombs and a symbol of divine power in ancient Egyptian mythology. Similarly, Chinese lions, often placed at the entrances of temples and palaces, serve as guardians against evil spirits and symbols of imperial authority in East Asia. Though the Sphinx is more streamlined and realistic in form, reflecting Egypt's focus on the divine and afterlife, Chinese lions are more decorative, featuring exaggerated manes and fierce expressions. Despite these stylistic differences, both figures are powerful representations of protection, symbolising how different cultures have used lion imagery to guard sacred spaces and convey authority.^{dcxxi}

While some theorists explore the idea that ancient civilisations, such as Egypt and China, may have exchanged cultural symbols or had contact, no concrete evidence suggests a direct connection between the Sphinx and the Chinese lions. Instead, these parallels are likely due to the universal symbolism of lions as powerful and protective creatures across different cultures.

Lions were not native to China, and their presence in Chinese art and symbolism became prominent only after the spread of Buddhism from India, where lions were already important religious symbols. Before this exchange, Chinese mythological creatures, such as dragons and other hybrid animals, were more prevalent in Chinese religious and cultural practices. ^{dcxxii} Interestingly, we have seen a shift from a focus on the lion to cows, similar to what we propose happened in Egypt. The cow's role in Indian culture grew significantly due to its vital importance in agricultural life and its deep associations with motherhood, nourishment, and nonviolence in Hindu spirituality.

Are the Obelisks connected to the Sphinx and the Pyramids?

Another part of the puzzle is the obelisk. In Egypt, approximately 30 ancient obelisks remain standing today, with some of the most famous examples located in Karnak, Luxor, and Heliopolis.^{dcxxiii} Interestingly, while pyramids are found in Egypt, Sudan, and other parts of the world, obelisk monuments are uniquely Egyptian. This makes the obelisk a distinctly Egyptian symbol of power and divine connection.^{dcxxiv} Some have been relocated to modern cities like Paris, London, and New York. The obelisk is a 20 to 30-meter-tall, slender, four-sided monument that tapers towards the top and ends with a small pyramid-shaped capstone, often gilded to reflect the sun.^{dcxxv} Obelisks are not typically found near the pyramids or the Sphinx, but at the entrance of the temples.

As with the pyramids and the Sphinx, dating the obelisk is a matter of debate.^{dcxxvi} The obelisks found in Egypt often date back to the New Kingdom period, around 1,500 BCE, with notable examples including the obelisk of Hatshepsut and those of Thutmose III.^{dcxxvii} Mainstream Egyptologists maintain that the New Kingdom dates are based on inscriptions and archaeological evidence.^{dcxxviii} However, alternative historians disagree about the dating of certain obelisks. Some theorists suggest that the origins of these monuments could be older than traditionally believed, linking them to earlier dynasties or even to a pre-Egyptian civilisation, much like the debates surrounding the dating of the Sphinx and the pyramids.^{dcxxix} They propose that erosion patterns or unrecorded restorations might indicate earlier construction phases. [dcxxx]

Could the inscriptions on some obelisks have been added later than the monument's construction itself? [dcxxxi] This theory suggests that, much like the pyramids and the Sphinx, obelisks may have been erected earlier and later reused or repurposed by pharaohs, who added their inscriptions to commemorate their reign. [dcxxxii] In ancient Egypt, it was common practice for rulers to restore, modify, or reinscribe monuments built by earlier kings to assert their divine authority and legitimacy. If the obelisks were part of an older tradition, later pharaohs could have inscribed them with texts praising the sun god Ra and their accomplishments.

Adding inscriptions during restoration efforts or claiming ownership of older monuments is a common practice in many Egyptian structures.[dcxxxiii] Supporters of this theory point to erosion patterns, which could suggest that some obelisks had existed for long periods before the inscriptions were added.[dcxxxiv] The possibility of unrecorded restorations also supports this theory, as certain obelisks may have undergone multiple phases of modification or inscription across different dynasties.[dcxxxv] The alternative view, much like debates surrounding the Sphinx and pyramids, proposes that obelisks may have initially been part of an earlier civilisation or culture, predating the New Kingdom by thousands of years, and were later incorporated into the religious and political frameworks of the Egyptian pharaohs.

Does the construction method reveal anything? These iconic structures were made from a single block of stone. Granite was the primary material used for obelisks, and it was quarried in Aswan, located about 500 miles south of Giza.[dcxxxvi] Aswan was famous for its high-quality pink granite, the material of choice for obelisks because of its durability and reflective qualities. The most accepted theory is that once the obelisk reached the Nile River, it would be placed on a barge and floated down to the construction site.[dcxxxvii] At its destination, the obelisk would be unloaded and transported to the temple or elsewhere, where it would be erected. Numerous experiments have demonstrated how the stones may have been transported and positioned. In the 1990s, Mark Lehner, an Egyptologist, led an experiment to replicate how ancient Egyptians might have transported large stone blocks. Using a wooden sledge and manpower, researchers pulled large stone blocks across the desert sand, which had been moistened with water. [dcxxxviii] This experiment supported the theory that water helps reduce friction, making the transportation of heavy blocks over sand more feasible.[dcxxxix] Then, in 2000, a team led by Egyptologist Zahi Hawass attempted to replicate how an obelisk might have been erected using ancient methods. The team used ropes, wooden beams, and manpower to raise a small replica of an obelisk. [dcxl] Although the attempt was successful, it highlighted the difficulty and complexity of the process without modern equipment.

Like pyramids, obelisks might have been precisely positioned to align with the stars or celestial bodies. This alignment is plausible, as ancient Egyptians had advanced astronomical knowledge.

The placement of obelisks was frequently aligned with the sun's movement. [dcxli] The alignment of some obelisks with the sun's path suggests that they may also have been used to mark significant times of the year, such as the solstices or equinoxes, important periods in Egyptian religious and agricultural life. [dcxlii] Their positioning could help determine the time for important ceremonies or planting seasons. [dcxliii]

Obelisks are thought to symbolise a divine connection to the sun god, Ra. They were placed at temple entrances to honour Ra and align with his path across the sky. The obelisks' design—with a small pyramid-shaped capstone (the "benben")—was intended to capture the first rays of the morning sun, symbolising renewal and life. [dcxliv] Inscriptions on obelisks usually included hymns praising the sun god, Ra, for bringing life and light. [dcxlv] This symbolism connects obelisks to the broader Egyptian belief in the cyclical nature of time, death, and rebirth, all under the watch of the sun god.

Some alternative researchers have proposed that obelisks might have had other practical and technological functions, similar to theories about the pyramids. They propose that the obelisks might have been designed to harness or generate energy. This theory suggests that the granite used to construct obelisks, particularly its high quartz content, could have allowed them to serve as electromagnetic conductors or energy amplifiers. Just as some believe the pyramids were part of an energy grid or network, similar arguments are made about the placement and design of obelisks, particularly how they might have aligned with celestial bodies or geomagnetic forces to focus and distribute energy across the land. [dcxlvi] Obelisks were often capped with metals like gold or electrum. What if these towering symbols were not just commemorative monuments but sophisticated energy conduits? Some alternative historians speculate that obelisks were placed strategically to interact with the Earth's electromagnetic field, channelling this energy to enhance the power of nearby pyramids or temples. If we consider obelisks part of an ancient grid system designed to harness and distribute energy, could they have been integral to a communication network or power transmission across vast distances? While quartz is piezoelectric and can generate small electric charges under pressure, there is no historical evidence to suggest that the ancient Egyptians understood or harnessed this property when constructing obelisks.

Other researchers have theorised that the obelisks' shape and material (granite, rich in quartz) could have been intended to amplify and focus energy, connecting the terrestrial with the spiritual world. The obelisk might have been seen as a spiritual antenna, drawing divine power from the sky to the ground. [dcxlvii]

Recent studies in acoustics and vibration suggest that obelisks may function as resonant tuning devices, amplifying and projecting sound frequencies. This has sparked speculation that ancient Egyptians may have used these towering structures to channel sound waves or vibrational energy in their rituals.

Suppose obelisks were designed to create resonances with Earth's natural frequencies. In that case, they might have been used in ceremonies to harness vibrational energy for healing, spiritual ascension, or even levitation techniques modern science is only beginning to explore. This perspective opens up the possibility that obelisks, like tuning forks, were part of a broader system of energy manipulation that intertwined spirituality with technology. In today's world, crystals are often shaped like obelisks due to their symbolic meaning and practical uses in metaphysical practices. With its strong base and tapering peak, the obelisk shape is believed to channel and amplify energy, directing it from the earth through the point at the top. This design mirrors the possible ancient Egyptian use of obelisks, which were thought to connect the terrestrial and divine worlds. Modern crystal enthusiasts use obelisk-shaped stones for grounding energy, spiritual awakening, and healing.[dcxlviii]

Mainstream Egyptologists argue that the idea that obelisks were designed to resonate with the Earth's natural frequencies, amplifying sound waves or vibrational energy, is speculative. They claim that there is no scientific or archaeological evidence to suggest that ancient Egyptians used obelisks for such purposes. Studies in acoustics and vibration have been applied to other ancient structures; however, these ideas remain speculative theories rather than facts.

Obelisks beneath the Surface?

We may only be seeing the tip of the iceberg. Some theorists believe these towering monuments may hint at a deeper architectural truth: the existence of pillars beneath the surface. Just as the visible obelisk pierces the sky, could it metaphorically represent an unseen counterpart plunging into the Earth? This duality—above and below, heaven and earth—echoes ancient principles, such as the Hermetic axiom *"As above, so below."* Some consider the obelisks not only as symbolic markers but also as possible surface indicators of vast, energetic, or structural systems hidden beneath the ground. If massive cylindrical structures truly lie beneath the pyramids, as recent Synthetic Aperture Radar data suggests, the obelisks scattered across Egypt and other sacred sites might have served as more than monuments—they could be coded reflections of a vast, pillar-based technology buried beneath our feet.

What if the pyramids are not complete structures themselves, but merely the visible peaks of gigantic obelisks embedded deep within the Earth? Rather than envisioning eight underground cylinders, as initially suggested by radar imagery, we might instead be looking at the shafts of buried obelisks, stretching over 600 meters underground. The pyramids we see may be the capstones, the apex of a hidden pillar system far larger than previously imagined. Perhaps these buried giants act as energetic antennas, drawing power from the Earth's core and releasing it through the pyramids above. The elegance, symmetry, and deliberate alignment of these structures could be clues left by a civilisation that understood the vertical integration of Earth and sky, hidden in plain sight.

The Obelisk as Male and the Sphinx as Female

Could the obelisk represent the male and the Sphinx the female? In various occult traditions, there is a tendency to view architectural forms through the lens of gender symbolism, which often connects phallic symbols like the obelisk to masculine energy, representing power, creation, and cosmic connection. In his book *Serpent in the Sky: The High Wisdom of Ancient Egypt*, John Anthony West states, "The Sphinx is a symbol of the eternal feminine, representing wisdom, protection, and the nurturing forces of life, while structures like the obelisk stand as phallic representations of masculine power, creation, and cosmic connection."[dcxlix] The tall and pointed obelisk can be seen as a symbol of the male principle. Its phallic form was often associated with the sun god Ra in ancient Egypt, representing strength, fertility, and the divine. In contrast, the lion, especially the Sphinx's body, could embody feminine energy. The female lion represents the nurturing and sustaining aspects of life, as well as the raw power of nature, which contrasts with the more structured and directional energy attributed to the obelisk. [dcl] In The Secret Teachings of All Ages (1928), Manly P. Hall explains that the ancients believed these incredible monuments were repositories of celestial power, symbolising the union of heaven and earth, as well as the masculine and feminine, through their design and form. [dcli]

Perhaps the Sphinx was initially built with a female head, which was later re-carved into a male head when society shifted towards a more patriarchal structure. Is it possible that the construction of obelisks was much later than the sphinx, as this patriarchal society continued to evolve? While there isn't conclusive proof of a formal transition from matriarchy to patriarchy, the role of women in power fluctuated throughout Egyptian history.[dclii] Women held significant influence in early periods and certain dynasties. However, over time, especially during the New Kingdom and after, male rulers and patriarchal structures became more dominant in Egypt's governance and religious frameworks.[dcliii]

The obelisks may have been built later than the Sphinx, although the exact era of their construction is disputed. Even mainstream theories agree that obelisks became prominent during later periods of ancient Egyptian history, especially from the Middle Kingdom (around 2,000 BCE) onward, while the Sphinx is generally believed to have been constructed during the Old Kingdom (around 2,500 BCE). The use of obelisks to honour Ra, the sun god, gained greater importance during the New Kingdom (around 1,550 BCE) when the pharaohs increasingly associated themselves with solar deities.

Links Between Pyramids, Sphinx and Obelisks

One of the strongest connections between the Sphinx, pyramids, and obelisks is their relationship with the sun god, Ra. The obelisks, often strategically placed in cities like Heliopolis (the city of the sun), served as solar markers, tracking the sun's movement across the sky.[dcliv] This suggests that the Egyptians built these structures to honour the sun god, Ra, and maintain an advanced calendar system based on solar and stellar cycles.[dclv]

Beyond honouring the sun god Ra, these monuments symbolise the pharaohs' eternal power and connection to the divine.[dclvi] As eternal tombs, the pyramids represent the afterlife and the pharaohs' immortality. The Sphinx, often considered a guardian, symbolises the enduring protection of the divine order, while the obelisk, reaching towards the sky, symbolises a connection between the earthly realm and the heavens.[dclvii] Together, they form a triad emphasising the pharaohs' role as mortal rulers and divine intermediaries.[dclviii]

The design and placement of these monuments reflect a shared architectural language that emphasises symmetry, alignment, and sacred geometry. In *Architecture and Mathematics in Ancient Egypt*, Rossi explains that *"the Egyptians' use of geometry was not merely functional but deeply symbolic, reflecting their cosmological views and the belief in an ordered harmonious universe"*.[dclix] This suggests that ancient builders applied the same underlying mathematical and cosmic knowledge across all these structures, integrating their spiritual and architectural principles in a unified manner.

The precision of the pyramids' angles, the Sphinx's alignment with celestial bodies, and the vertical alignment of obelisks show a unified understanding of geometric principles that may have been part of an ancient knowledge system. This suggests that ancient builders applied the same underlying mathematical and cosmic knowledge across all these structures.[dclx]

In Mesoamerican cultures, pyramids such as those at Teotihuacan also align with celestial bodies and have similar energy-harnessing features. The ancient Chinese built pyramids oriented towards constellations, and obelisks were also used in other ancient cultures, such as those of Rome. The presence of these elements globally suggests a shared or interconnected ancient knowledge system where the pyramids, Sphinx-like guardians, and obelisks had universal purposes related to astronomy, energy, and spiritual transformation.[dclxi]

Some researchers, such as Robert Bauval in *The Orion Mystery: Unlocking the Secrets of the Pyramids* (1994), suggest that these monuments were strategically placed to form a larger cosmological map across Egypt. Robert Bauval, an engineer and Egyptologist, proposed that the pyramids' alignment on the Giza Plateau mirrors the stars of Orion's Belt. He argued that the pyramids and monuments, such as the Sphinx and obelisks, were deliberately positioned to reflect a celestial map, thereby creating a connection between the heavens and the earth. This theory suggests that the ancient Egyptians possessed a profound understanding of astronomy, which they used to plan and align their monuments, thereby representing cosmic balance and order.[dclxii] The pyramids, often aligned with Orion's Belt, the Sphinx positioned to face the rising sun during the equinoxes, and obelisks marking significant points within temples or cities, may indicate that they were interconnected components of a grand design, representing a balance between celestial and terrestrial forces.

Another theory is that these structures were part of a forgotten knowledge system, extending to the possibility that they were built to harness or manipulate Earth's natural energies. The pyramids might have been designed to tap into geomagnetic fields, while obelisks could have acted as energy conductors or receivers, channelling energy from the sun or the Earth.[dclxiii] In its central position, the Sphinx could have served as a regulator or guardian of this energy system, ensuring the balance between these forces.[dclxiv]

In her book Infinite Mind: Science of the Human Vibrations of Consciousness (1995), scientists Dr. Valerie Hunt conducted experiments suggesting that quartz can generate piezoelectric effects, producing electricity when pressure is applied. Dr. Hunt's research explored the relationship between human consciousness and energy fields, concluding that certain materials, like quartz, can act as energy transducers, converting mechanical pressure into electrical energy. She proposed that ancient civilisations may have understood these properties and incorporated them into their architecture, such as pyramids and obelisks. According to her conclusions, these structures could have functioned as energy-harnessing or transforming devices, channelling geomagnetic or cosmic energy through applying pressure and alignment with natural forces. This theory supports the idea that pyramids and obelisks were not merely symbolic but practical components of an advanced energy system.[dclxv]

In *The House of the Messiah: Controversial Revelations on the Historical Jesus* (1992), Ahmed Osman explores Egypt's role as a foundational source of spiritual wisdom within various occult traditions. He suggests ancient Egypt was the birthplace of material civilisation and the centre for esoteric knowledge and mystical practices. He argues that Egypt's spiritual traditions, including the teachings of Thoth and the symbolism embedded in the pyramids and temples, had a profound influence on later mystical systems, such as Hermeticism and Gnosticism. These traditions viewed Egypt as a land of sacred rites and divine knowledge, where initiates could access higher truths about the cosmos and the self. He connects these ideas to the occult belief that Egyptian symbols, such as the ankh, the Eye of Horus, and the pyramids, serve as spiritual keys, guiding those seeking enlightenment or transformation. He concludes that these mystical and symbolic elements of Egypt became foundational in shaping the spiritual traditions of later Western esoteric movements, emphasising Egypt's centrality in developing spiritual wisdom.[dclxvi] The pyramids, obelisks, and Sphinx are viewed as spiritual keys—tools designed by ancient civilisations to connect with cosmic forces. Particularly in Gnosticism and Freemasonry, the Sphinx, pyramids, and obelisks acquired hidden, symbolic meanings associated with secret knowledge and spiritual awakening. Freemasonry holds the pyramid as a symbol of spiritual ascension, while the obelisk symbolises strength and cosmic energy.[dclxvii] Together, these elements represent the journey from ignorance (symbolised by the Sphinx's riddle) to enlightenment (the pyramid's peak). The Sphinx's riddle, originating from Greek mythology rather than Egyptian lore, is a famous puzzle posed by the mythical Sphinx of Thebes. It asked, "What walks on four legs in the morning, two at noon, and three in the evening?" The riddle symbolises the stages of human life: in the morning (childhood), a person crawls on all fours; at noon (adulthood), they walk upright on two legs; and in the evening (old age), they use a cane, making it three legs. The hero, Oedipus, correctly answered the riddle, revealing the human life cycle's metaphorical stages. His success led the Sphinx to destroy itself, emphasising the power of knowledge and insight in overcoming challenges. This story has been a symbol of wisdom, fate, and human understanding in Greek mythology.[dclxviii]

In Egyptian mythology, Thoth, the god of wisdom, was believed to have come from a distant land (often speculated to be Atlantis) and brought knowledge to the Egyptians. According to the *Emerald Tablets of Thoth*, he was instrumental in constructing the pyramids as repositories of ancient knowledge and energy centres to aid in spiritual transformation. This legend could tie the pyramids, the Sphinx, and the obelisks as elements of a knowledge system handed down from a forgotten advanced civilisation. The story of Thoth suggests that the Sphinx acted as a guardian of secrets hidden within the pyramids. It is said that beneath the Sphinx lies the Hall of Records, a mythical library containing ancient wisdom. This ties the Sphinx directly to the pyramids and occult traditions, designating it as a protector of hidden knowledge.

There is ongoing speculation that the pyramids, the Sphinx and the obelisks may have been constructed much earlier than traditionally believed. Some alternative historians propose that the pyramids, the Sphinx, and the obelisks are remnants of a much older civilisation, possibly Atlantis or a pre-dynastic Egyptian society. This theory suggests that these monuments were constructed as a part of an advanced system of knowledge and technology that predated the known Egyptian civilisation. Evidence of water erosion on the Sphinx and the precision of the pyramids and obelisks supports the idea that they were built during a time of higher knowledge and understanding, which has been lost to the sands of time.

Challenge of Admitting to an Earlier Timeline

The speculation that the Sphinx may predate ancient Egypt and represent the remnants of a highly advanced civilisation poses a challenge to traditional Islamic teachings and the historical narrative in predominantly Muslim countries, such as Egypt. In Islamic tradition, history is understood to follow a divine order, with prophets serving as guides for humanity. *The Qur'an* outlines human history as divinely guided through prophets, from Adam to Muhammad. Any suggestion that an advanced civilisation existed long before this could disrupt the timeline of human progress as ordained by God. Additionally, the association of the Sphinx and other ancient monuments with pagan idolatry conflicts with the strict monotheism of Islam, where idol worship is considered the gravest sin. Theories that claim suppressed knowledge about the Sphinx's origins could threaten the credibility of both governmental and religious institutions in Egypt, potentially undermining the close relationship between the state and Islam. In this context, such conspiracy theories are not merely historical curiosities; they raise theological, cultural, and political tensions by suggesting a narrative that may contradict Islamic teachings about the origins of civilisation and divine guidance.

In *"The Controversy of Ancient Civilisations in Modern Historiography"* (2015), James A. Montgomery examines how the discovery of ancient civilisations and the subsequent reinterpretation of historical timelines have frequently led to clashes with established religious beliefs. He discusses how new archaeological findings, particularly those suggesting the existence of advanced civilisations predating well-known cultures like ancient Egypt, challenge traditional religious narratives that adhere to a linear progression of human history as guided by divine intervention. This historical revisionism, he argues, can provoke resistance from religious communities who view such discoveries as contradictory to sacred texts, particularly in monotheistic religions like Islam and Christianity, where the creation and development of mankind are closely linked to divine order. By examining these controversies, he sheds light on the complex interplay between archaeology, history, and religion, illustrating how the reinterpretation of ancient civilisations often forces societies to reconsider long-held beliefs about human progress and spirituality.[dclxix]

One of the most provocative and rigorously compiled challenges to mainstream historical narratives comes from Michael A. Cremo and Richard L. Thompson's monumental 1993 work, *Forbidden Archaeology: The Hidden History of the Human Race*. The book spans over 900 pages and meticulously documents archaeological and paleontological anomalies that have been ignored, forgotten, or dismissed by mainstream science. Its central thesis is jarring: that anatomically modern humans may have existed not for 200,000 years as currently accepted, but for tens, even hundreds, of millions of years. This controversial idea is not presented as a casual speculation but is built upon exhaustive documentation of cases that defy the accepted timeline of human evolution.[dclxx]

The authors comb through historical scientific literature from the 19th and early 20th centuries, before Darwinian orthodoxy had solidified, unearthing dozens of cases where human bones, artefacts, or footprints were discovered in geological strata that should have predated humans by millions of years. These include the famous *Calaveras Skull*, allegedly found in a gold mine in California within a Miocene stratum (dating back over 5 million years), and human footprints discovered in Williamson County, Texas, limestone— allegedly found alongside dinosaur tracks. Equally perplexing are iron and gold artefacts recovered from deep coal seams in Illinois and Pennsylvania, supposedly formed during the Carboniferous period, 300 million years ago. In one case, a finely carved metallic vase was reportedly blasted from solid rock during construction work in Dorchester, Massachusetts. This rock is dated to be over 600 million years old.

The authors claim these cases were dismissed not based on empirical refutation but on an ideological filter within scientific institutions. They call this phenomenon *knowledge filtration*, a process by which data inconsistent with the prevailing paradigm is either ignored, ridiculed, or buried in obscure publications. According to the authors, the rejection of anomalous finds is not always malicious. Still, it is often the result of unconscious bias toward the accepted model of linear evolution and materialist assumptions.

If human beings with modern capabilities existed millions of years ago, what technologies might they have had? What structures could they have left behind? Is it so unthinkable that the global pyramid phenomenon represents remnants of such a forgotten epoch?

Forbidden Archaeology serves as an intellectual backdoor into understanding the mystery of the pyramids. Its thorough cataloguing of outlier discoveries provides a theoretical foundation for re-examining other anomalies, such as pyramid alignments, geodetic knowledge, and energy theories, from a broader temporal perspective. This outlook does not assume that humans are the pinnacle of development, but instead views us as one cycle within a much older continuum.

If their work is even partially valid, then what we label as "prehistory" may be more accurately described as "amnesia." And in that context, the pyramids may not be primitive tombs or ceremonial centres, but rather, the last visible signs of a science and culture that predates written memory, fossil records, and sanctioned archaeology.

Conclusions

Could the Egyptians have renovated the structures? Perhaps they added the shiny outer layer to the pyramids and replaced the head on the Sphinx. As we continue to unearth evidence, we may find that the true origins of these colossal structures are even more ancient and complex than we ever imagined. This possibility opens the door to new interpretations of human history and technological capability.

As we close the chapter, we turn our attention to the dating of the pyramids. How old are these structures truly? One key piece of the puzzle remains: how do we accurately date the pyramids? Could they be far older than mainstream historians suggest? The absence of definitive records and their incredible construction precision have led to ongoing debates about when they were truly built. In the next chapter, we will explore the challenges of accurately dating the pyramids and how conflicting evidence puzzles scientists and theorists, casting new light on our understanding of their origins.

Chapter 8 The Difficulty of Dating the Pyramids

Perhaps history is not what happened, but what was allowed to be remembered. Dating the pyramids is challenging. Why did the Egyptians, known for their meticulous record-keeping, not document the construction of these remarkable monuments? The technological achievements evident in the Great Pyramid of Giza, particularly its precise alignment with celestial bodies and the accuracy of its dimensions, suggest a level of knowledge that may have originated from forgotten sources, whether advanced ancient civilisations, extraterrestrial influences, or mystical energies. As we investigate these questions, we see the pyramids as stone monuments and gateways to a deeper understanding of ancient wisdom and technology.

Why Didn't the Egyptians Write About the Construction?

Egyptian hieroglyphs developed around 3,200 BCE. Initially, hieroglyphs were used for religious inscriptions, monumental purposes, and official records. Over time, they evolved into a complete writing system used in religious texts, royal decrees, and administrative records. Egyptians wrote on various materials. On stone for inscriptions in temples and tombs. They also used papyrus, a type of paper made from reeds. Papyrus scrolls enabled the preservation of religious texts, administrative records, and literature. Amazingly, papyrus, the plant-based material used by ancient Egyptians for writing, has survived over millennia due to a combination of factors, primarily climatic conditions, storage methods, and preservation environments. Modern books could survive for a few centuries to over a thousand years, depending on their materials and storage conditions. However, most are unlikely to last that long without significant degradation.

Why did the Egyptians leave no accounts detailing the construction of the pyramids despite their meticulous record-keeping? This absence of evidence invites speculation and fuels debates about whether the pyramids were truly built by the Egyptians or inherited from an older civilisation. By exploring why the Egyptians might have hidden, lost, or erased these records, we open the door to alternative histories that challenge mainstream archaeological narratives. Mainstream archaeologists generally agree that the pyramids were built during the Old Kingdom period; however, detailed records of the construction process are lacking.

Surprisingly, none of the hieroglyphic texts found on the walls of the pyramids, tombs, or temples directly describe how the pyramids were constructed.

Although we have yet to decipher all ancient Egyptian hieroglyphic symbols completely, we have a good understanding of most of them. The ability to read and interpret Egyptian hieroglyphs was "cracked" in 1822 when Jean-François Champollion deciphered the *Rosetta Stone*. This trilingual inscription contained the same text written in Greek, Demotic (a simpler Egyptian script), and hieroglyphics. His breakthrough allowed scholars to finally understand Egyptian hieroglyphs, which had remained a mystery for nearly 1,500 years after they fell out of use during the Greco-Roman period. The Greek inscription, which scholars could read, served as a reference point, enabling François Champollion to match Greek words with the corresponding Egyptian symbols.[dclxxi] This provided the foundation for decoding the entire writing system, unlocking the rich history of ancient Egypt. Egyptian hieroglyphics employ logograms (symbols that represent words) and phonograms (symbols that represent sounds). The Egyptians also used *determinatives*, which clarified the meaning of words.[dclxxii] Today, Egyptologists can read most of the hieroglyphic inscriptions in tombs, temples, and monuments, especially those related to religious texts, kingship, and daily life. However, there are still gaps in our understanding.[dclxxiii] Some symbols remain ambiguous or context-dependent, primarily associated with more obscure religious rituals, specific locations, or non-standardised spellings.[dclxxiv] Discoveries offer fresh insights, and Egyptologists still interpret certain signs and symbols based on archaeological findings and comparative linguistic studies.[dclxxv] The cracking of hieroglyphs in the early 19th century revolutionised the study of ancient Egypt, but our understanding continues to evolve as new artefacts are uncovered.

What if hieroglyphs were not the everyday language of the ancients, but a symbolic code written in stone specifically for future generations? Hieroglyphs were laboriously carved into stone. Each glyph, rich with animal forms, celestial markers, and energy symbology, could be seen as a timeless code, designed to survive cultural collapse and reawaken memory. In this light, the temples and tombs become not static monuments, but *interactive archives*—echo chambers from the past speaking directly to those capable of decoding them. Rather than fossils of a dead civilisation, hieroglyphs may be living symbols, waiting for their meaning to be fully remembered.

While the Egyptians were meticulous in documenting religious rituals, offerings, and the achievements of their pharaohs, they did not leave behind records explaining the methods or techniques used to build these monumental structures. Most of the inscriptions inside pyramids, such as the *Pyramid Texts,* were focused on religious and funerary purposes to ensure the deceased pharaoh's safe passage to the afterlife. These texts contained spells, prayers, and instructions for the deceased's journey, but did not mention the architectural processes involved in constructing the pyramids. They focused on religious, symbolic, and ceremonial aspects rather than practical documentation.[dclxxvi] Strangely, they did not write about the construction. Why would you not write about such a fantastic achievement?[dclxxvii] This has led some to speculate and further support the theory that the Egyptians may have repurposed pre-existing structures for religious and political purposes rather than constructing them from scratch. Egyptians might have inherited the pyramids from an earlier, possibly unknown civilisation and added their finishing touches, such as burial chambers and inscriptions.[dclxxviii]

A scandal surrounding a Cartouche of Pharaoh Khufu's Daughter emerged in the late 19th and early 20th centuries and was later proven to be fake. Cartouches were oval-shaped enclosures with the hieroglyphic name of a pharaoh or a royal individual, serving primarily as a protective and identifying symbol. They were often part of inscriptions meant to ensure immortality in the afterlife. This find was important because it would date the pyramids. Scholars began to question the authenticity of the cartouche due to discrepancies in the style and language used. Researchers asked why the cartouche did not conform to the typical inscriptions and artistic styles known from the time of Khufu. Further investigation revealed that the cartouche exhibited characteristics of forgery, including the use of modern techniques and materials in its creation. For example, some features of the inscriptions did not align with the known hieroglyphic practices of the Old Kingdom. Egyptologists and experts in ancient scripts analysed the cartouche in more detail and determined that it had been artificially aged or otherwise tampered with to make it appear ancient.[dclxxix] Forensic examinations, including analysis of the materials and methods used in creating the cartouche, further indicated that it was a modern creation. Forgeries have occasionally muddied the dating and interpretation of artefacts. However, it doesn't discredit the broader archaeological consensus about the pyramids' origins.

Ancient manuscripts have been discovered, written on papyrus. Papyrus was an essential material in ancient Egypt, serving as the world's first form of durable writing paper. Made from the pith of the papyrus plant, which grew abundantly along the Nile River, the Egyptians crafted the material by cutting the plant into strips, soaking them, and pressing them together. Papyrus sheets were used to write religious texts, administrative records, literature, and personal correspondence. Some of the most significant finds include *The Book of the Dead*, a funerary text guiding the deceased through the afterlife, and the *Edwin Smith Papyrus*, the oldest known medical text detailing surgical procedures and treatments. Another vital discovery is the *Great Harris Papyrus*, which documents the reign of Ramses III and highlights Egypt's complex religious and economic systems. These documents offer invaluable insights into ancient Egyptian life, culture, religion, and governance.[dclxxx]

The *Diary of Merer*, a papyrus discovered in 2013 by French archaeologist Pierre Tallet and his team, is considered one of the most significant and direct pieces of evidence related to the construction of the Great Pyramid of Giza. Found in a cave at Wadi al-Jarf, an ancient Egyptian harbour on the Red Sea, this collection of papyrus logs dates back to approximately 2,550 BCE. These records, written by an overseer, effectively a manager, called Merer, detail the transportation of massive limestone blocks from the Tura quarries to Giza, where they were used to build the outer casing of the Great Pyramid. The diary offers unique insights into the labour force, describing the organisation of workers and the use of boats to ferry stones along the Nile River, providing a glimpse into the logistical operations behind the construction of one of the world's most iconic structures. As the first direct account of the pyramid's construction, the *Diary of Merer* confirms long-held theories about transportation methods. It enhances our understanding of how the ancient Egyptians managed such a monumental project. This discovery is a game-changer in the study of Egyptology, providing tangible, authentic evidence of the immense organisational skills and resources dedicated to pyramid building, aligning with other historical records and shedding new light on the ancient construction techniques used during Khufu's reign.[dclxxxi]

Interestingly, the Diary of Merer talks about the transportation of limestone. Is it possible that the ancient Egyptians only built the outer layer of the pyramid? While the Tura limestone was used specifically for the visually striking outer casing, rougher limestone was used extensively in the core structure of the pyramid. Therefore, limestone was a crucial material throughout the pyramid's construction, internally and externally, though the quality and refinement varied depending on its purpose. There is a clear difference in the precision and quality of craftsmanship between the outer casing and the inner core of the pyramids, particularly in the Great Pyramid of Giza.

Critics argue that the *Diary of Merer* provides only a partial view of the construction process, focusing primarily on the transportation of limestone. It does not describe the methods used to construct the pyramid's core, raise the massive stone blocks, or detail the architectural planning. They also point out that, while the diary provides valuable logistical information, it is far from a comprehensive account of how the pyramids were built. Some argue that the interpretation of the *Diary of Merer* could be biased, with archaeologists and Egyptologists potentially reading into the text with pre-existing assumptions about pyramid construction. These sceptics believe that the papyrus may not necessarily confirm the standard narrative of how the Great Pyramid was built and that other explanations should still be considered.[dclxxxii]

Though not strictly about the pyramids, the *Turin King List* papyrus is critical to understanding the chronological order of pharaohs and the timeline of pyramid construction. It lists the names of Egyptian kings and their reigns, providing a framework for dating pyramid constructions, such as those at Giza and Saqqara. This papaya and the writings of the historian Manetho reference a period before the reign of the pharaohs, known as Zep Tepi, the "First Time," when gods or demigods were said to have ruled Egypt. Some researchers speculate that the pyramids could have been built during this mythological era, with the Egyptians later inheriting and repurposing the structures for their religious and political purposes.[dclxxxiii] Mainstream archaeologists and Egyptologists generally dismiss the notion that the pyramids were constructed during the mythological period of Zep Tepi, or the "First Time," when it is said that gods or demigods ruled Egypt. Although this period is referenced in ancient Egyptian texts, such as the *Turin King List* and the writings of the historian Manetho, it is considered mythological rather than historical.[dclxxxiv]

Were the Construction Records Lost or Purposefully Erased?

The absence of records detailing the construction of the pyramids may be attributed to either the ancient Egyptians' deliberate erasure or the loss of these records over time due to various historical and environmental factors. Or, as Graham Hancock suggests in *Fingerprints of the Gods: The Evidence of Earth's Lost Civilization* (1995), they may not have built them and instead inherited the pyramids from a much older civilisation.[dclxxxv] One theory, as suggested by Corinna Rossi in *Architecture and Mathematics in Ancient Egypt* (2004), is that the Egyptians, known for their meticulous record-keeping, intentionally chose to keep the construction methods of the pyramids secret. She argues that building monumental structures like the Great Pyramid of Giza may have been considered a sacred and exclusive act reserved for the pharaohs and the elite priesthood. She proposes that the methods and technologies used were likely viewed as divine knowledge, accessible only to a select few, to maintain an aura of mystery, power, and authority. By keeping this information within a restricted circle, the Egyptians could reinforce the pharaohs' god-like status and connection to the divine, as the ability to construct such massive and precise structures would have been perceived as a supernatural achievement.[dclxxxvi] Suppose the pyramid-building process was viewed as a sacred ritual rather than a mere engineering achievement. Then, it is plausible that the Egyptians chose not to document it publicly, ensuring that such powerful knowledge remained protected and untainted by the broader society. Another perspective suggests that records may have existed but were lost over the centuries due to Egypt's tumultuous history. Egypt faced numerous invasions, including those by the Hyksos, Assyrians, Persians, Greeks, and Romans, resulting in significant periods of destruction, plunder, and reorganisation of Egyptian religious and cultural centres.[dclxxxvii] During these times, temples, libraries, and archives that might have housed the records of pyramid construction could have been destroyed or looted.[dclxxxviii] The shifting sands of Egypt's political and religious landscape, including changes in dynasties and the rise of different belief systems, may have also contributed to the intentional destruction or neglect of records no longer aligned with new rulers' agendas. These historical shifts might have led to the deliberate removal of documents that threatened the authority or ideological control of the new regime.[dclxxxix] Therefore, the absence of construction records could be a result of a combination of deliberate suppression and accidental loss, due to the vulnerabilities of ancient documentation methods and Egypt's long and eventful history. The Egyptians frequently recorded information on papyrus, a fragile material susceptible to decay due to humidity, flooding, and improper storage. Papyrus records are far less durable than stone inscriptions, which have endured for thousands of years.[dcxc] They could have disintegrated over thousands of years, leaving little trace of what might have once been documented about the construction of pyramids. Even if some of these original texts are found, their chances of being intact and identifiable today are slim.

The Loss of the Library of Alexandria

The Library of Alexandria, a hub for ancient knowledge, is a prime example where documents relating to Egypt's architectural and scientific achievements, including possible pyramid records, may have been destroyed in the series of fires it endured.[dcxci] The Library of Alexandria was established around 283 BCE in Egypt.[dcxcii] It was considered the largest and most significant library of the ancient world. The library was a repository of knowledge and a place for intellectual exchange, housing a collection estimated to contain 40,000 to 400,000 scrolls.[dcxciii] The library was part of the larger *Mouseion* (the Museum), a research institution where scholars lived and worked. It was unique not only for the sheer volume of its holdings but also for its ambitious goal of collecting all the world's knowledge, with texts written in Greek, Egyptian, Persian, Hebrew, and other languages. These texts covered a broad range of subjects, from mathematics and philosophy to astronomy and geography, as well as more esoteric writings that explored hidden knowledge, including possible documents related to the construction, symbolism, and secrets of the Egyptian pyramids.[dcxciv]

The loss of the library, through a series of events and conflicts, resulted in the destruction of the vast majority of its treasures. Today, the exact site of the library is lost, but the modern Bibliotheca Alexandrina was built nearby in 2002, standing as a symbolic revival of the original library's intellectual spirit.[dcxcv] Although most of the original documents were destroyed, some knowledge survived through copies and references by later scholars. Notable examples include the works of Euclid in mathematics and Archimedes' scientific contributions.[dcxcvi]

However, the many hidden and mystical writings that may have contained vital information about ancient technologies, including the secrets of the pyramids, were likely lost forever in the flames, leaving us with gaps in our understanding of ancient civilisations. This lack of records and evidence opens the door for alternative theories, including the idea that the Egyptians may have possessed advanced technologies or knowledge now lost to time or that they inherited the sites. Without the records to confirm or deny these possibilities, the pyramids remain a mystery in human history.

Surviving Texts

While it is widely believed that most of the library's contents were lost in a series of fires and subsequent destruction, making copies for distribution to other libraries or scholars was common in the ancient world.[dcxcvii] The Ptolemies founded the Library of Alexandria and actively collected and copied manuscripts from across the Mediterranean.[dcxcviii] This means texts originating in other regions may have survived outside of Egypt. It's conceivable that private collections, undiscovered archaeological sites, or hidden archives could still hold some of these ancient manuscripts.[dcxcix]

Throughout history, entire collections of manuscripts have been discovered in unexpected locations, such as medieval monasteries or hidden in caves.^{dcc} During the medieval period, monastic libraries, especially in Europe and the Middle East, became key centres for preserving knowledge from antiquity.^{dcci} Some ancient Greek and Roman texts were copied by monks and housed in these libraries. For instance, Byzantine monasteries preserved ancient Greek works, and Arab scholars in the Islamic Golden Age translated many classical texts into Arabic.^{dccii} Is it conceivable that some manuscripts originally housed in Alexandria or their descendants might have been passed down through these monastic or Islamic scholarly networks?

Similarly, during the Islamic Golden Age, scholars in the Middle East translated and preserved many classical texts, especially from Greek and Roman sources. Major learning centres, such as the House of Wisdom in Baghdad, were known to collect and translate important texts from various cultures, possibly including documents from Alexandria.^{dcciii} If copies or parts of these texts existed in Islamic learning centres, they might have been preserved in collections that remain today, though much was also lost during later periods of conflict.

During the time of the Library of Alexandria, other significant libraries existed, such as the Library of Pergamum in Asia Minor and the Library of Celsus in Ephesus, as well as others throughout the Greek and Roman empires.^{dcciv} Greek and Roman scholars often kept copies of important texts in their collections, and some documents from Alexandria were possibly shared with other ancient libraries, such as the Library of Pergamum.^{dccv} Some texts from Alexandria may have been copied and housed in these locations. It is possible that remnants of these collections, or copies made from them, could still exist. Some ancient libraries were looted, and their contents scattered, leading to the potential preservation of their contents being spread out across various locations.^{dccvi}

The Vatican Library and Library of Congress

Today, the Vatican Library, *also known as the Biblioteca Apostolica Vaticana, holds a prominent* place among the world's most significant libraries.^{dccvii} However, it is not as large as the Library of Congress, which has over 170 million items.^{dccviii} The Vatican Library contains approximately 1.1 million printed books, manuscripts, and codices, as well as around 75,000 manuscripts dating back over two millennia.^{dccix} Despite its smaller size than other modern libraries, it is renowned for its rare and ancient texts, many of which are invaluable historical, religious, and scientific documents.^{dccx} These include some of the oldest known copies of the Bible, illuminated manuscripts, early printed works, and important documents related to the history of the Catholic Church and Western civilisation.^{dccxi} The Vatican Library, founded in 1475, is unique in that it functions both as a library and a highly restricted archive, containing collections accessible only to specialised scholars.^{dccxii} Its holdings reflect the Vatican's long-standing role as a preserver of knowledge and religious documents throughout history. Unlike the Library of Alexandria, which aimed to collect all world knowledge, the Vatican Library's collection is deeply tied to religious, theological, and philosophical works. However, it also holds scientific and cultural texts.^{dccxiii} While the Vatican Library's size doesn't compare to the largest libraries of today in terms of total items, its cultural and historical significance is profound.^{dccxiv} Many of its manuscripts are one-of-a-kind, and its archives contain sensitive documents relating to the Church's governance and history. Thus, it is more exclusive and specialised than the more extensive and diverse collections of the Library of Congress, which collects materials on nearly every conceivable topic across all fields of knowledge.^{dccxv} The Vatican Library holds a special place among modern libraries, not for its size but for its unique and ancient texts, often considered irreplaceable treasures of human history, religion, and thought. Like the Library of Alexandria in antiquity, its role as a preserver of knowledge and culture maintains its reputation as one of the world's most important intellectual repositories.^{dccxvi}

When comparing the best sources of documents on pyramids worldwide, including Egypt, Mesoamerica, Sudan, China, and the Middle East, both the Library of Congress and the Vatican Library hold valuable collections, but each offers distinct strengths. The Library of Congress stands out for its comprehensive, modern research on the construction, symbolism, and archaeology of pyramids across these regions.^{dccxvii} It contains many documents, including scholarly works, excavation reports, architectural studies on Egyptian pyramids, the Mesoamerican structures built by the Mayans and Aztecs, and the lesser-known pyramids in China and Sudan.^{dccxviii} Its global scope makes it a superior resource for researchers interested in a comparative study of pyramid structures across civilisations.^{dccxix} In contrast, the Vatican Library excels in preserving rare historical and religious manuscripts, particularly those related to early European explorations and missionary work.^{dccxx} This includes colonial accounts of Mesoamerican pyramids and ancient Egyptian texts with religious significance.^{dccxxi}

Powered by Pyramids: A Book of Theories

Private and Corporate Collectors

Private collectors also play a significant role in preserving and acquiring rare historical manuscripts, books, and artefacts, often holding some of the world's most valuable and unique items. Figures such as Bill Gates, who famously purchased Leonardo da Vinci's Codex Leicester[dccxxii], and David Rubenstein, known for his acquisitions of the Magna Carta and the Declaration of Independence[dccxxiii], have used their wealth to secure culturally and historically important documents. Collectors like Martin Schøyen, who owns the vast Schøyen Collection of over 13,000 manuscripts[dccxxiv], and Sir Thomas Phillipps, whose 19th-century collection of more than 60,000 manuscripts remains legendary[dccxxv], focus on preserving human history across various regions and periods. Wealthy families like the Rothschilds have also amassed substantial collections, including illuminated manuscripts and rare books.[dccxxvi] These collectors safeguard these treasures and often loan them to public institutions or auction them, as seen in the posthumous sales of Paul Allen's estate.[dccxxvii] Many of these collectors prioritise the preservation of world history, scientific discovery, and human imagination, often maintaining private libraries that rival some public institutions in their significance and scope.[dccxxviii]

Martin Schøyen's collection includes various ancient texts and manuscripts, some of which are related to Egyptian civilisation. While the collection has a broad focus on ancient history, including Mesopotamian and biblical texts, it may hold manuscripts or papyri related to Egyptian pyramid texts and funerary practices.[dccxxix] Sir Thomas Phillipps was one of the largest private collectors of manuscripts in the 19th century, and his collection included numerous Egyptian papyri and texts.[dccxxx] Although much of his collection has been dispersed through auctions, some manuscripts related to Egyptian antiquity, including those possibly connected to the pyramids, may still be in private hands. While primarily known for collecting U.S. historical documents, David Rubenstein has also acquired significant ancient texts.[dccxxxi] Although his collection is not focused on Egyptian pyramids, collectors like him occasionally acquire rare papyri or texts related to ancient Egypt through auction. The Rothschild collection includes many manuscripts, illuminated texts, and other historical items. Some items from ancient Egypt are part of the family's extensive holdings, although it is unclear whether they possess significant manuscripts related to pyramids.[dccxxxii]

Not only private collectors, but also corporations maintain extensive collections of valuable documents, artefacts, and historical materials. Many large companies, such as IBM, The Walt Disney

Company, and Procter & Gamble, preserve vast archives related to their industries, innovations, and corporate history.[dccxxxiii] These corporate collections often contain rare books, patents, research materials, and promotional artefacts that chronicle the evolution of technology, marketing, and business strategies.[dccxxxiv] For instance, Google's digital library, through projects like Google Books, provides access to millions of scanned texts, including those about ancient history and pyramids, making it one of the most accessible archives globally.[dccxxxv] While corporations like IBM and Disney do not typically hold primary documents specifically focused on pyramids, they may contribute indirectly to pyramid-related research through technology, data analysis, or media projects that explore ancient civilisations.[dccxxxvi] Like private collectors, corporate archives preserve significant pieces of history and innovation, contributing to the global preservation of knowledge, with occasional intersections into subjects like ancient architecture and pyramids through digitisation or media content.

While it's enticing to think that more original manuscripts from the Library of Alexandria could still exist, no direct evidence has yet emerged. The most likely sources would be private collections, monastic libraries, the Vatican Library, or through archaeological discoveries. However, much of this remains speculative, as the destruction of the library is widely believed to have resulted in the loss of nearly all of its invaluable knowledge. Still, history has shown that ancient texts can sometimes reappear in the most unexpected places, leaving the door open to possibilities. The possibility of knowledge having been preserved remains intriguing, fueling modern-day treasure hunts for lost knowledge. If anyone were to possess such documents, it could open a window into the hidden wisdom of the ancient world, including lost knowledge on subjects like the construction of the pyramids, esoteric practices, or ancient technologies.

Some argue that keeping specific knowledge or technology in the hands of a few ensures it remains safeguarded, much like sacred texts or secretive practices were historically reserved for priests or scholars. A modern parallel might be nuclear technology or artificial intelligence, where certain safeguards are deemed necessary because the impact of misuse could be catastrophic. In the speculative realm, these ancient technologies might be envisioned as tools that, in the wrong hands, could disrupt society, nature, or even humanity's spiritual path.

Dorothy Eady, also known as Omm Sety, famously claimed to be the reincarnation of an ancient Egyptian priestess and devoted her life to studying Egypt's mysteries.[dccxxxvii] She believed she had firsthand knowledge of Egypt's spiritual rituals and contributed significantly to

Egyptology, claiming insights that seemed intuitive rather than learned.[dccxxxviii] Similarly, famed psychic Edgar Cayce reported visions suggesting he was connected to ancient Egypt and shared predictions about the advanced technologies and energy systems the Egyptians supposedly harnessed.[dccxxxix] Individuals like Dorothy Eady and Edgar Cayce, with their strong convictions of past-life connections to Egypt, often felt a duty to safeguard or interpret this knowledge, viewing it as potentially dangerous if misused by the uninitiated.[dccxl] For them, this ancient knowledge, encompassing energy manipulation and spiritual practices, was something to be carefully handled, almost like a sacred trust passed down through lifetimes. This belief reinforces the idea that only those with a spiritual or ancestral link to the pharaohs—or who feel they have "memories" of such lives—are prepared to handle the mysteries of ancient technologies responsibly, ensuring their secrets remain protected or gradually revealed.

Ultimately, the view that only a few can handle certain knowledge remains highly debatable. It raises ethical questions about power, responsibility, and trust in humanity's ability to wisely wield complex tools, whether modern advancements or ancient relics.

Clues from Mythology

Egyptian mythology provides insight into the mystical aspects of pyramid construction through the figure of Thoth, the god of wisdom, writing, science, and architecture. Known as the deity who brought knowledge and order to the world, Thoth was believed to possess the secrets of mathematics, astronomy, and engineering—skills crucial for constructing monumental structures like the pyramids.[dccxli] According to legend, Thoth used his divine knowledge to design and imbue the pyramids with cosmic significance.[dccxlii] He is said to have instructed the ancient builders in the precise measurements needed to align the pyramids with celestial bodies, ensuring that these structures could harness and amplify Earth's energy. Some interpretations of ancient texts even suggest that Thoth's involvement went beyond mere design; he may have provided the knowledge of advanced technologies, such as energy manipulation techniques, to elevate the stones and position them with perfect accuracy.[dccxliii] Thus, under Thoth's guidance, the pyramids were crafted as tombs and cosmic power stations designed to tap into and amplify Earth's natural energy grid, serving both spiritual and practical functions for civilisation. Opponents argue that the idea that Thoth's divine knowledge played a role in pyramid construction is symbolic and not meant to be taken literally in historical terms. Ancient Egyptian texts often attributed cosmic and sacred significance to structures like the pyramids, but no reliable evidence suggests that these myths describe actual construction technologies.[dccxliv]

The mythology surrounding Thoth and his association with wisdom, architecture, and the construction of the pyramids is derived primarily from ancient Egyptian religious texts and traditions.

The Pyramid Texts (c. 2400–2300 BCE) are some of the oldest religious texts in Egypt, found in the pyramids of Saqqara. They contain spells and hymns referencing Thoth as a deity associated with wisdom, writing, and order. While they don't explicitly mention Thoth constructing the pyramids, they highlight his role as the god who governs knowledge and cosmic balance, which are essential for such monumental architectural achievements.

The Coffin Texts (c. 2100–1600 BCE) are successors to the Pyramid Texts and contain similar spells and hymns. Thoth is often invoked as a deity who controls the movement of celestial bodies, linking him to the precision and alignment of the pyramids with the stars.

The Book of the Dead (c. 1550–50 BCE) is a collection of spells and rituals intended to guide the deceased through the afterlife. Thoth appears as the scribe of the gods, the keeper of divine knowledge, and the one who measures and maintains the cosmic order. His association with architecture and building is implicit through his role in maintaining Ma'at (cosmic balance), which was critical in designing the pyramids to align with celestial patterns and Earth's energy.

These sources form the basis of mythology that links Thoth with the construction and spiritual purpose of the pyramids. The stories evolved and became more esoteric over time, with later interpretations by scholars of Hermeticism and Egyptian mythology elaborating on Thoth's role as a master architect who could manipulate cosmic and Earthly energies.

Some argue that the mythology surrounding the pyramids indicates that they were not constructed by the ancient Egyptians but by the gods. According to these interpretations, texts such as the Pyramid Texts and later Egyptian writings describe the pyramids as divine creations built using the knowledge and power of gods, including Thoth. These legends suggest that the pyramids were sacred energy centres or cosmic devices beyond the capabilities of mere mortals. Proponents of this view assert that the Egyptians inherited these structures from a much older, more advanced civilisation of gods or semi-divine beings who possessed the secrets of sacred architecture and energy manipulation. They argue that the precise alignment with celestial bodies, the monumental scale, and the advanced construction techniques described in these myths could only have been achieved with divine intervention. To these believers, the pyramids are a testament to an ancient, godly mastery of science and cosmic forces, not a human engineering achievement.

Why can't we date the Pyramids with Certainty?

With modern technology at our disposal, one might assume that dating the stones of the pyramids would be a straightforward process. However, establishing the age of ancient stone structures is a complex task. Traditional dating methods, like radiocarbon dating, rely on organic materials, which are absent in stones since they are inorganic and lack carbon. This makes it impossible to date most stone objects directly. As I. McFadzean highlights in *The Challenges of Dating Ancient Stone Structures*, stones are formed over millions or even billions of years, and their components, such as minerals, do not degrade in a way that provides clues to their age. The stones used in pyramid construction could have existed for millions of years before being shaped and assembled.[dccxlv] Adding to the challenge, environmental factors such as erosion, weathering, and human modification alter the stone's surface over time. Ancient civilisations often recycled stones from older structures, meaning the stone may be far older than the monument itself. This practice complicates efforts to determine the exact age and origin of the materials.[dccxlvi]

Recent technological developments offer promising alternatives. Luminescence dating, for example, measures the last time mineral grains were exposed to sunlight, providing insight into when stones were moved or placed.[dccxlvii] Similarly, cosmic ray exposure dating can estimate how long a stone has been on the Earth's surface by measuring isotopic changes caused by cosmic radiation.[dccxlviii] Though still developing, these methods may one day help pinpoint when ancient monuments were constructed. In *Luminescence Dating of Sediments and Sedimentary Rocks* (2008), E.J. Rhodes discusses the potential of luminescence dating to revolutionise the understanding of archaeological and geological timelines. He explains that while the technique is primarily used for dating sediments, advancements could eventually enable more precise dating of stones used in ancient monuments, such as pyramids. He emphasises that as technology develops, it may be possible to determine the last time mineral grains within the stones were exposed to sunlight or heat, offering new insights into when they were moved, shaped, or placed by ancient civilisations. He is optimistic that, with further refinement, luminescence dating could provide a viable method for dating monumental stone structures, filling gaps left by other dating methods and expanding the understanding of ancient construction practices.[dccxlix]

Another advanced technique, archaeomagnetic dating, examines changes in Earth's magnetic field recorded in heated stones or ceramics. Although not directly applicable to pyramid stones, similar methods could be adapted to explore the thermal history of quarried blocks, giving us clues about the construction phases.

Despite these advancements, some esoteric groups propose that the stones in the pyramids possess a unique energy that interferes with modern instruments. Could the pyramid stones have been "activated" through unknown processes that disrupt our dating methods? In *Secrets of the Great Pyramid* (1971), Peter Thompkins explores various esoteric theories related to the pyramids, including the belief held by some groups that the stones in the pyramids possess a unique, unexplained energy. He discusses how proponents of these theories claim that this energy could potentially interfere with modern technological instruments, making accurate measurements or analysis difficult. Thompkins notes that these esoteric groups suggest the stones were "charged" or "activated" through ancient rituals or processes, possibly involving sound, light, or magnetism. According to these accounts, the pyramids were designed not just as tombs but as energy centres, and the stones themselves may have been altered in a way that created an energetic field. He remains neutral in his assessment, presenting these theories as part of the broader spectrum of mystical interpretations surrounding the Great Pyramid while acknowledging the lack of scientific evidence to substantiate such claims.[dccl]

In *The House of the Messiah: Controversial Revelations on the Historical Jesus* (1992), Ahmed Osman explores the mythological and symbolic significance of ancient Egyptian architecture, including the pyramids. He discusses the belief in Egyptian mythology that the pyramids were constructed by gods, specifically using "stones of light" that were said to come from the heavens. He explains that these "stones of light" are depicted in myths as mystical materials, imbued with divine energy and brought to Earth by celestial beings or deities, such as Thoth. According to the myth, these stones were not ordinary; they were believed to have been forged in the stars, giving them extraordinary properties such as resilience, luminosity, and the ability to channel energy. He connects this concept to the broader narrative of the pyramids as spiritual and cosmic tools, emphasising that the myth of the "stones of light" symbolises the divine origin of the pyramids and their role in linking the earthly realm with the heavens.[dccli] If such legends hold any truth, could the materials have an origin beyond our planet? Researchers like V. Martel, in The Cosmic Stones Hypothesis, argue that pyramid stones may contain extraterrestrial minerals, making conventional Earth-based dating methods ineffective.[dcclii]

There are legends about the ancient Egyptians—or even more mysterious, older civilisations—using sophisticated technology to construct the pyramids. Some accounts suggest using vibrational technology or acoustic levitation to lift and position the massive stones. Ancient texts describe priesthoods chanting or using sound to move stones effortlessly, a concept explored by Dr Michael Lee in *Resonant Frequencies and Stone Levitation in Ancient Civilizations*. If the stones were shaped or moved using vibrational technology, this could alter their internal composition, rendering modern dating methods ineffective.[dccliii]

Additionally, myths surrounding "energy stones" in pyramid construction claim that the ancient builders infused the stones with spiritual energy or used crystals to manipulate time and space. These ideas, while fantastical, open intriguing questions about the interplay of mythology and potential lost technologies. Could the stones have been intentionally altered to confound future generations, making it difficult for them to determine their actual age and origin?

Were the Pyramids Inherited from a Lost Civilisation?

When we examine the evidence—and, crucially, the lack of evidence and gaps in our knowledge—an intriguing question arises: could the pyramids have been built not by the Egyptians but by an even older, lost civilisation? The absence of detailed construction records, the advanced architectural techniques, and the precision of the pyramids' alignment with celestial bodies suggest a level of knowledge that might exceed that of the Old Kingdom Egyptians. If these structures were inherited, it would imply that ancient civilisations possessed sophisticated technologies and advanced engineering capabilities long before recorded history.

Exploring this theory challenges us to rethink the established timeline of human civilisation and technological evolution. It invites us to imagine a past where forgotten cultures might have thrived, developing architectural feats and knowledge systems that have since been lost to time. Investigating this possibility broadens our understanding of the pyramids and opens the door to a reimagined history of human achievement and ingenuity.

During his travels to Egypt, French novelist Gustave Flaubert (1821–1880) was deeply inspired by ancient culture. In his letters, Flaubert wrote reflectively, blending romance with mystery: "*The pyramids stand as lovers do—timeless and towering, keeping their secrets close, hidden in stone.*"[dccliv]

A persistent question is when the pyramids were built—during the commonly accepted timelines or much earlier? For centuries, they have stood as enigmatic sentinels, silently guarding the secrets of ancient Egypt. While mainstream scholars attribute their construction to the mighty pharaohs of the Old Kingdom, many wonder if the Egyptians inherited these structures from an older, more advanced civilisation.

Ancient architectural remnants found in places like Gobekli Tepe in Turkey, dating back over 11,000 years, challenge the traditional timeline of human civilisation. The advanced construction methods and symbolic carvings suggest that sophisticated architectural capabilities existed long before the rise of the Egyptian dynasties. It is, therefore, conceivable that the Egyptians inherited knowledge, techniques, or even partially completed structures from these earlier cultures. This notion is supported by the fact that the precision and scale of pyramid construction have puzzled archaeologists for centuries, leading to speculation that the pyramids may result from long-lost building methods passed down from earlier civilisations.[dcclv]

Recent archaeological discoveries have further fueled the debate about whether the pyramids were repurposed from older civilisations. In his seminal work *Fingerprints of the Gods* (1995), Graham Hancock argues that the pyramids' precision and alignment with astronomical events suggest a much older and technologically advanced civilisation.[dcclvi] However, mainstream archaeology, as exemplified by Mark Lehner's work, continues to assert the Egyptian origin of the pyramids, based on radiocarbon dating and historical records.[dcclvii]

Several alternative researchers and scholars have further explored the idea that the ancient Egyptians may have repurposed the pyramids rather than building them from scratch. This theory suggests that the pyramids, or at least parts of them, may predate Egyptian civilisation and were built by an earlier, possibly lost civilisation, with the Egyptians later renovating, adapting, or using these structures for their own purposes. There is considerable evidence that humans have repurposed old buildings and structures throughout history. This practice, known as adaptive reuse, has been observed across various cultures and historical periods.[dcclviii]

New Life for Old Structures: Repurposing Buildings

Ancient civilisations might have modified existing structures for various practical, religious, and political reasons. Over time, as societies evolved, their cultural needs, spiritual beliefs, and technological capabilities changed, which often led to the adaptation or renovation of older monuments. For instance, conquering civilisations might have repurposed pyramids or temples from earlier cultures to assert their authority while still respecting the power and sacredness associated with the original builders. In other cases, religious shifts, such as changes in the dominant gods or spiritual practices, could prompt modifications to align older structures with new worship rituals or cosmological understandings. Practical reasons also played a role as populations grew or environmental conditions changed, requiring the enhancement or reinforcement of older structures to ensure their continued functionality. Additionally, the symbolic importance of ancient structures, especially pyramids, as centres of power, knowledge, and spirituality may have driven civilisations to renovate or expand them, preserving their relevance for new generations while maintaining a connection to the past.

In today's world, old factories, warehouses, and industrial complexes have also been repurposed for new uses. For example, Tate Modern in London was once a power station before being converted into one of the world's leading art galleries.[dcclix] Similarly, New York City's High Line was once an elevated railway track and has been transformed into a popular public park.[dcclx]

An older example is the Parthenon in Greece, built in the 5th century BCE, which was initially a temple dedicated to the goddess Athena, the protector of Athens. It was repurposed many times. In the 6th century CE, the Parthenon was converted into a Christian church after the spread of Christianity in the Roman Empire. Its pagan sculptures were altered or removed, and Christian iconography was added to fit its new function as a place of worship. During the Ottoman Empire, the Parthenon was repurposed again as a mosque this time. A minaret was added to the structure, becoming a centre for Islamic worship.[dcclxi]

Hagia Sophia in Istanbul, Turkey, is another iconic example of architectural repurposing. Originally constructed in 537 CE as a Byzantine cathedral under Emperor Justinian I, it stood as the largest Christian church in the world for nearly a thousand years.[dcclxii] After the Ottoman conquest of Constantinople in 1453, the building was transformed into a mosque, with the addition of minarets, a mihrab, and other Islamic features, marking its transition from a Christian to an Islamic place of worship.[dcclxiii] In 1935, following the establishment of the secular Turkish Republic, Hagia Sophia was converted into a museum, symbolising Turkey's embrace of a secular, modern identity.[dcclxiv] However, in 2020, it was once again repurposed as a mosque.[dcclxv] Despite these significant cultural transformations, Hagia Sophia's essential architectural elements, such as its grand dome and intricate mosaics, have been preserved. It demonstrates how buildings have been adapted to accommodate shifts in religion and politics.

The Mayan civilisation often built temples on top of previous structures, and beneath these pyramids, archaeologists have found evidence of earlier temples and ceremonial spaces used by previous rulers. This layered construction technique was a way to honour past rulers and reinforce the site's spiritual and political significance. New rulers would build over old structures, physically and symbolically connecting themselves with the past. Evidence of these practices is well-documented in the works of William Fash[dcclxvi] and David Freidel[dcclxvii], who have extensively studied Mayan architecture and its evolution over the centuries.

It is easy to imagine how knowledge and wisdom were passed down through generations, not lost but transformed to fit the prevailing narratives of the authorities. Significant structures are often repurposed for new cultural, religious, or practical needs. The idea that the pyramids could have been inherited or repurposed by the Egyptians or other civilisations fits into the evidence of historical practices observed elsewhere. Whether as tombs, temples, or energy conduits, the pyramids likely held multiple meanings and functions across the ages, shaped by the needs and understanding of different societies.

The thought that these monumental wonders might be legacies from a forgotten era, subsequently repurposed, inspires us to look beyond conventional narratives. It invites us to explore deeper and seek answers in places we never thought to look. Let the possibility of an older origin for the pyramids spark your curiosity and propel you toward uncovering the mysteries of our shared human heritage. We must now explore whether the evidence supports the belief that the Egyptians didn't build them.

Conclusions

The theory that the pyramids may have been repurposed structures built by an older, forgotten civilisation invites us to question the narrative of ancient Egypt's supremacy in pyramid-building. History often shows that cultures repurpose the accomplishments of those before them, and the pyramids may be no exception. Could they have only renovated the structures? Perhaps they added the shiny outer layer? As we continue to unearth evidence, we may find that the true origins of these colossal structures are even more ancient and complex than we ever imagined. This possibility opens the door to new interpretations of human history and technological capability.

The next chapter delves into the possibilities of alternative architects, exploring influences from neighbouring cultures and the involvement of extraterrestrials. What if extraterrestrial visitors came to Earth thousands of years ago, assisting ancient humans in constructing these massive structures? Perhaps the pyramids served as docking stations for alien spacecraft or energy-refuelling hubs for advanced civilisations. If we open our minds to this possibility, what might these structures reveal about humanity's ancient connection to the cosmos?

Chapter 9 Alternative Architects

"The Pyramids themselves, doting with age, have forgotten the names of their founders" – Thomas Fuller.[dcclxviii]

Built by the Neighbors, Pre-Historic Civilisation or Aliens?
Who could have built the pyramids and the Sphinx if it weren't the Egyptians who built them? The perspective of mainstream scholars often invokes Occam's Razor when addressing theories about advanced technologies, extraterrestrials, or prehistoric civilisations. This principle, which suggests that the simplest explanation is usually the most accurate, has been a foundational tool in scientific reasoning for centuries. In the context of pyramid construction, many mainstream archaeologists and historians argue that human ingenuity, not advanced or alien technologies, offers the simplest and most plausible explanation.[dcclxix]

Egyptologist Mark Lehner, in his seminal work *The Complete Pyramids: Solving the Ancient Mysteries*, provides a detailed analysis of the methods used by the ancient Egyptians to construct the pyramids, emphasising the use of ramps, levers, and advanced organisational techniques rather than the involvement of older or lost civilisations. His research also highlights the archaeological evidence for the workforce that built the pyramids, including the discovery of workers' villages near Giza. Similarly, Zahi Hawass, renowned for his expertise on ancient Egyptian monuments, has argued convincingly in several publications that there is no substantial evidence to suggest that the pyramids were inherited from an earlier civilisation. His excavations support the view that the pyramids were constructed entirely during the reigns of the pharaohs of the Old Kingdom, particularly during the Fourth Dynasty.

As discussed in the previous chapters, there are reasons to believe that the Egyptians may have inherited the pyramids and the Sphinx, rather than being their original builders. If this is the case, it raises the question of who else could have constructed these monumental structures. Exploring this possibility opens up fascinating avenues of inquiry into pre-Egyptian civilisations or other cultures that may have advanced knowledge of engineering, astronomy, and energy manipulation. Could a forgotten or lost civilisation, potentially predating the Egyptians, be responsible for the pyramids' construction? Or perhaps the influence of external forces, such as ancient seafaring cultures or even extraterrestrial visitors, played a role? In this chapter, we will examine various alternative architects and the speculative theories that suggest the Egyptians inherited and repurposed these iconic structures while exploring the cultural and historical implications.

The mainstream view often assumes that early civilisations developed in isolation. As outlined in the previous chapter, growing evidence suggests that trade, migration, and seafaring could have facilitated cultural and technological exchange. Additionally, there is speculation that aliens may have visited or even landed on Planet Earth.

The ancient Egyptians may have sought to rewrite or obscure the pyramids' true origins to enhance their political and spiritual legitimacy. Whether by erasing a previous advanced civilisation, external influences such as their neighbours, extraterrestrials, or even supernatural beings, these theories suggest that those in power shape history, and the whole story of the pyramids may have been hidden to support Egypt's narrative. Egyptians do not see themselves as Arabs or Africans. They take profound pride in their Egyptian identity and heritage. The pyramids, especially the Great Pyramid of Giza, are central to the narrative of ancient Egyptian civilisation. It would be a significant dent in their national pride if it were established that the pyramids were not built by their ancestors. Some may argue there is no such thing as bad publicity, and it would likely lead to more tourism.

No definitive evidence confirms that the pyramids were built by someone else or by a different, older alien civilisation. While mainstream archaeology supports the view that the ancient Egyptians built the pyramids, alternative theories suggest that they were repurposed and built by an earlier civilisation.[dcclxx] In this chapter, we explore some of the possible alternative architects of the pyramids. Keep in mind that all of these thought-provoking theories are speculative.

Sumerians

The Sumerians, Akkadians, Assyrians, and Babylonians from Mesopotamia, modern-day Iraq, were contemporary with ancient Egypt and built monumental structures of their own.

Could the Sumerians have built the pyramids in Egypt? While the two civilisations existed at overlapping times, there is no direct evidence of large-scale contact or cooperation between them, especially in construction projects like the pyramids.[dcclxxi] Ancient Egypt and Mesopotamia developed along separate river systems: the Nile for Egypt and the Tigris and Euphrates for Sumer. However, they did trade with each other. There is a possibility that skilled labourers or architects from Sumer travelled to Egypt for work, especially during the early periods when both civilisations were expanding. This migration could have facilitated the exchange of ideas and techniques essential for large-scale construction.

While it is an intriguing idea, the critics of this theory argue that the suggestion that the Sumerians built the pyramids of Egypt lacks supporting evidence. The two civilisations had distinct architectural styles, religious practices, and historical records that do not indicate direct collaboration in pyramid building. The Sumerians were renowned for their ziggurats and terraced mudbrick structures, which were designed for religious purposes. Ziggurats were temples that served as platforms for worship and were built differently from the smooth-sided pyramids of Egypt.[dcclxxii]

Both civilisations possessed advanced engineering and architectural skills. The use of large stone blocks and complex construction techniques in Sumerian ziggurats and Egyptian pyramids suggests a potential exchange of knowledge that could have influenced building methods. Some proponents believe that the design of the pyramids could have been influenced by ziggurat construction. The step-like structure of ziggurats could have inspired the initial concepts for pyramids.

Ancient African Civilisations

Some modern-day African groups have claimed that sub-Saharan Africans, or civilisations further south than Egypt, were responsible for building the pyramids, either directly or through the transmission of knowledge. These claims often arise from a desire to reclaim African heritage and challenge the narrative that ancient Egypt was an isolated civilisation separate from the rest of Africa.

The Nubians, located south of Egypt in modern-day Sudan, built over 200 pyramids at sites such as Meroë and Napata. Theirs were smaller and steeper than Egyptian pyramids. [dcclxxiii] The Kingdom of Kush had periods of rivalry and close contact with Egypt. The Nubians ruled Egypt during the 25th Dynasty, also known as the Nubian or "Kushite" Dynasty. Could they have been hired for their track record of building pyramids to build an even bigger one in Egypt? It sounds plausible, but we are told that the Nubian pyramids were built later than the Egyptian pyramids. While Egypt's largest pyramids, such as those at Giza, were built long before Nubian rule, it is possible that Nubians could have been hired or brought in as workers, labourers, or craftsmen during the periods of cultural exchange between the two civilisations.

Archaeological evidence from Nabta Playa, a site located in southern Egypt near the Nubian border, reveals a prehistoric stone circle dating back to approximately 5,000 BCE, predating the construction of the pyramids by several thousand years. This suggests that the region's inhabitants already possessed knowledge of astronomy and stone construction, raising questions about whether these early inhabitants passed down this knowledge, which eventually contributed to the construction of pyramids.[dcclxxiv]

Some mention lost civilisations in Africa. While there is no definitive evidence to support the idea that a lost African civilisation built the pyramids or directly contributed to their construction, it is certainly possible that earlier African cultures or civilisations influenced the development of stone-working techniques, architectural principles, and astronomical knowledge that the Egyptians later applied.[dcclxxv]

Giants

The construction of massive stone structures, such as the pyramids, Stonehenge, and other sites, has sparked speculation that human labour alone could not have achieved such feats. The idea is that giants or superhuman beings with immense strength might have assisted in moving and arranging these enormous stones.

In the King Kong films, King Kong, while technically an oversized ape, represents the theme of prehistoric giants hidden from the world. King Kong is depicted as the last of a giant, mysterious species, evoking themes of forgotten giants from the past. If there were dinosaurs and other enormous creatures in the past, why not giant human beings?

There are many movies depicting giants. *The Hobbit: An Unexpected Journey* (2012), based on J.R.R. Tolkien's beloved novel, offers a vivid portrayal of giants in a scene where "stone giants" engage in a colossal battle within the misty mountains. These giants, crafted from rock and blending into the mountainscape, evoke a sense of ancient beings that are both powerful and deeply connected to the earth. This taps into the age-old human fascination with the possibility of giant creatures coexisting alongside humanity in a distant, forgotten past. Their portrayal in the film suggests a time when the natural world was populated by beings of enormous size and strength, reinforcing the theme that giants might once have roamed the earth. This concept resonates with myths and legends from various cultures, which describe giants as primordial entities who were part of the world's early history.

Medieval Arab historians and scholars often wrote about the pyramids in the context of ancient giants or pre-Adamite civilisations. The historian al-Maqrizi (1364–1442) mentioned that the pyramids were built by a king named Surid Ibn Salhouk, who was warned about a coming disaster (often associated with the Great Flood) and constructed

Powered by Pyramids: A Book of Theories

the pyramids to preserve knowledge.[dcclxxvi] Some interpretations suggest that Surid and his people were of extraordinary stature.[dcclxxvii]

In his 14th-century travelogue, *The Travels of Sir John Mandeville* (circa 1357-1371), the author presents a theory that supernatural giants built the pyramids. He described the pyramids as "*wonders beyond the art of man,*" attributing their construction to these colossal beings rather than human ingenuity.[dcclxxviii] While he does not offer extensive details on the giants, his work weaves myth and legend, suggesting that these beings were ancient, powerful entities whose superhuman strength allowed them to erect such grand and mysterious monuments.[dcclxxix]

Do giants exist? There have been confirmed cases of gigantism. We see giants in old photos. These giants have been attributed to medical conditions, rather than being evidence of an entire race of giants. They argue that excess growth hormones cause individuals to grow to unusual heights, such as over 8-12 feet tall.[dcclxxx] There is, however, no biological or evolutionary evidence to support the idea that humans evolved from giants to modern humans. Human size has varied throughout history due to natural selection, environmental conditions, oxygen levels and nutrition, but not on the scale suggested by stories of giants.[dcclxxxi] Is it possible that there was a gradual, multi-thousand-year decline instead of a sudden extinction? Perhaps the giants did not vanish overnight. They may have shrunk, integrated, or gone underground.

Giants have long been significant in the myths and legends of various cultures worldwide. They often symbolise great power or may serve as metaphors for untamed natural forces. In the *Bible*, the Nephilim are described as giant offspring of divine beings and human women, suggesting a race of mighty and fearsome individuals who roamed the Earth before the Great Flood (Genesis 6:1-4). The biblical reference to the Nephilim can be found in this passage of the Old Testament, which describes them as the offspring of divine beings and human women, existing before the Great Flood.[dcclxxxii] Similarly, in *Norse mythology*, the Jotunn, or giants, represent primordial chaos and often conflict with the gods, underscoring their symbolic role as forces that must be subdued to bring order to the world.[dcclxxxiii] The Jotunn, as portrayed in Norse mythology, are a central theme in many Norse legends. Irish mythology, as recorded in The Book of Invasions (11th century), mentions the Fomorians, a race of giants said to have constructed massive structures. Legends from South America also describe giants building megalithic structures, as described in *Chronicles of Tiahuanaco* (16th century). In *The Greek Gigantes* (8th century BC), towering beings born of Gaia, the Earth, played critical roles in the Gigantomachy, a mythic battle between giants and the Olympian gods. This battle symbolised the struggle between civilisation and chaos. Across these stories, giants are often depicted as creators, destroyers, or divine intermediaries, reflecting humanity's attempt to understand the vast forces of nature.[dcclxxxiv]

We see that almost every culture has legends of giants or superhuman beings. The recurrence of these stories across the globe has led some to wonder if they all stem from a shared human experience or memory of giant beings in the distant past. Scholars argue that these stories likely reflect the human desire to mythologise the powerful and the unknown, using the figure of the giant as a representation of cosmic and earthly forces beyond human control. Recent anthropological studies, such as David Leeming's *Giants: Myth and Meaning*, suggest that these myths may have arisen as symbolic explanations for natural phenomena or as allegories for human aspirations and fears.[dcclxxxv]

Some interpretations of ancient depictions of giants suggest that these figures might represent ancestral "parents" rather than literal giants, symbolising elders' wisdom, guidance, and protective nature over younger generations.[dcclxxxvi] This perspective reimagines giants not as mythological beings but as symbolic representations of authority and legacy, emphasising respect and reverence for those who came before.[dcclxxxvii] By portraying these ancestors as giants, ancient cultures may have visually reinforced the idea of parental influence and the foundational role of ancestors in the ongoing "growth" and development of society.[dcclxxxviii] This interpretation sheds light on how ancient societies might have viewed the relationship between generations, with the "giants" serving as guiding figures that tower over descendants, both metaphorically and artistically.[dcclxxxix]

While no concrete archaeological evidence has confirmed the existence of a race of giants, ancient stories and archaeological findings of large tools or burial sites have occasionally fueled speculation about their historical reality. Some archaeologists have uncovered huge tools and weapons that are far too large for an average-sized human to use effectively.[dccxc] However, archaeologists have often dismissed or reclassified these discoveries as ceremonial objects or shapes, attributing them to natural causes. Large bones have also been discovered, but many of these findings have been discredited or attributed to other causes.

Those who are convinced that the Giants existed argue that suppressing such evidence aims to maintain the current historical narrative, preventing the public from understanding the true history of ancient civilisations and their potential connection to giant beings. Suppose the pyramids were built by giants or superhuman beings. If that were the case, the Egyptians might have erased this information to present their pharaohs as the ultimate rulers and builders of these massive structures.^{dccxci} Associating their leadership with supernatural or divine forces of their choosing, rather than an ancient race of giants, would have reinforced their authority. ^{dccxcii}

Lost Civilisation, The Tartarian Empire

Could the Tartarias be the true architects of the pyramids? Tartarians are said to have mastered technologies far more advanced than those we attribute to ancient societies. One of the most intriguing aspects of this theory is the claim that the Tartarians had access to wireless energy, a concept Nikola Tesla would propose millennia later. Is it possible that the pyramids were designed not as tombs, as traditionally believed, but as energy-conducting structures? Could the Tartarians have engineered a worldwide wireless network? ^{dccxciii}

Tartaria was a global civilisation with influence stretching from Central Asia to Europe, Africa, and the Americas. This theory might explain the remarkable similarities between pyramidal structures found in disparate parts of the world, from the step pyramids of Mesoamerica to the pyramids in China. This civilisation is believed to have thrived from ancient times—before the rise of known civilisations like Egypt or Mesopotamia—until the 17th or 18th century, when much of their history was allegedly erased or suppressed.^{dccxciv}

Some sources propose that the Tartarians' advanced society may have been wiped out by natural disasters or global conflicts, such as the Great Flood of the 1800s or wars that reshaped the modern world. This lost civilisation may have held knowledge far beyond what we consider possible for their time, and their influence may have shaped not just Egypt but the entire world.

An intriguing aspect of the Tartarian theory is the claim that they were a race of giants, standing anywhere from 7 to 12 feet tall. Proponents of this theory argue that the sheer size and weight of the stones used to build the pyramids and other monumental structures worldwide could point to a race of taller, stronger beings capable of easily moving massive blocks.^{dccxcv}

When discussing the Tartarian Empire and who could be considered an authority on this theory, it's essential to note that the idea of Tartaria as a highly advanced lost civilisation is primarily a modern conspiracy theory rather than a historically validated concept. The theory's roots can be traced back to Russian pseudoscience, particularly the work of Anatoly Fomenko and his *New Chronology* theory, which suggested a significant rewriting of human history.^{dccxcvi}

This theory was later propagated by figures like Nikolai Levashov, who incorporated Tartaria into racial occult histories and suggested it was a technological civilisation wiped out by natural disasters or hidden by modern powers.[dccxcvii] The theory gained wider attention on social media platforms, particularly around 2016, when proponents suggested that the Tartarian civilisation had advanced technology, potentially including wireless energy and architectural marvels that we now mistakenly attribute to other civilisations.[dccxcviii]

Though no single historian or scholar is recognised as an authority in academic circles for this theory, it continues to intrigue a subset of conspiracy theorists and alternative historians who question mainstream historical narratives.

Survivors of Atlantis, a Lost City

Plato was the first to introduce the concept of Atlantis in his dialogues *Timaeus* and *Critias*, written around 360 BCE. In these, he described a powerful, advanced civilisation that existed 9,000 years before his time. According to Plato, Atlantis was a legendary island nation that allegedly sank into the sea.

However, it wasn't until Ignatius Donnelly's *Atlantis: The Antediluvian World* (1882) that the idea of Atlantis as a real, historical civilisation gained modern popularity. He built on Plato's account, suggesting that Atlantis was the source of advanced knowledge and the origin of many ancient civilisations, including the Egyptians and Mesoamericans. His work brought Atlantis into the mainstream, sparking widespread interest in the possibility of ancient, advanced civilisations. Could survivors of Atlantis have built the pyramids? Some, including Ignatius Donnelly, suggest the pyramids were built by survivors of the lost city of Atlantis or another highly advanced prehistoric civilisation. According to this theory, when Atlantis was destroyed, some of its survivors travelled to different parts of the world, bringing their advanced knowledge. In this view, these survivors could have helped the Egyptians and possibly other ancient cultures design and build the pyramids using forgotten construction techniques. Ignatius Donnelly argued that the pyramids and other architectural marvels were not just monuments or tombs but repositories of forgotten wisdom and technological prowess, potentially linked to lost energy systems. [dccxcix]

In 1971, Edgar Cayce, known for predicting the future like Nostradamus, also alluded to Atlantis, predicting that remnants of the civilisation would be found and that Atlantean survivors may have contributed to pyramid construction.[dccc] According to Cayce, Atlantis was a vast and highly advanced civilisation over 10,000 years ago, located in the Atlantic Ocean, stretching between the Americas, Europe, and Africa. He claimed that the height of Atlantean civilisation occurred around 50,000 BC to 10,000 BC, and they possessed advanced technologies far beyond modern understanding, including using crystals to harness energy, flying machines, and powerful weapons. He described Atlantis as having been destroyed in three catastrophic events, with the final disaster occurring around 10,000 BC, which resulted in the submerged of the remaining landmass. He suggested that Atlantean survivors fled to other parts of the world, including Egypt, where they influenced the construction of the Great Pyramid of Giza. He said these Atlantean survivors also spread their advanced knowledge to other cultures, such as the Mayans and early European civilisations. He believed that many people in modern times were reincarnations of Atlanteans, drawn to rediscovering their past lives and the ancient knowledge of Atlantis. He viewed the fall of Atlantis as a moral and spiritual lesson, warning that the misuse of power and technology had led to the civilisations' destruction and that modern humanity could face a similar fate if it failed to balance material progress with spiritual wisdom. Despite the lack of empirical evidence supporting his predictions, his visions of Atlantis continue to captivate those interested in ancient mysteries and metaphysical knowledge, shaping the ongoing allure of the lost civilisation and its potential impact on humanity's future.[dccci]

The ancient Greek philosopher Plato remains the primary ancient authority on Atlantis. According to Plato, Atlantis was a powerful and technologically advanced civilisation beyond the *Pillars of Hercules* (modern-day Strait of Gibraltar). It was a utopian society with sophisticated engineering, architecture, and technology knowledge.[dcccii] In Plato's account, Atlantis eventually fell out of favour with the gods due to its moral and spiritual decay. The island was said to have sunk into the ocean in a single day and night of catastrophic earthquakes and floods, around 9,000 years before Plato's time (which would place the event around 11,000 BCE). Geological studies have not uncovered evidence of a cataclysm that would align with the timeframe and location described for Atlantis. According to Plato, Atlantis supposedly existed around 9,600 BCE, about 7,000 years before the pyramids were built. While many historians view Plato's account as an allegory or fiction intended to teach moral lessons about the rise and fall of civilisations, some researchers and enthusiasts, such as Graham Hancock in his book *Fingerprints of the Gods* (1995), have speculated that Atlantis was a real place, possibly an advanced civilisation lost to history.[dcccii]

Imagine a civilisation so advanced that it could have influenced the construction of iconic structures like the pyramids. This theory challenges our understanding of ancient history and invites us to consider what other secrets might be buried in our past.

Some argue that Atlantis is a continent behind the ice wall. The concept of an ice wall is commonly associated with the flat Earth theory. This theory posits that the Earth is flat and encircled by an immense ice wall. They claim Antarctica is not a typical continent, but a colossal barrier that contains the world's oceans.[dccciv] They suggest hidden lands, unknown civilisations, or uncharted territories might lie beyond this ice wall. Enthusiasts of this theory imagine that ancient, lost civilisations, such as Atlantis, could be concealed beyond this mysterious ice boundary, shielded from modern discovery. Despite lacking scientific evidence to support these claims, they have gained attention and traction within certain conspiracy circles. While mainstream science dismisses these views due to a lack of evidence and timeline discrepancies, theories about Atlantis continue to captivate the imagination of many.

Alien Involvement

There is speculation that other interdimensional and extraterrestrial beings may have been involved in pyramid construction, which has been popularised in books, documentaries, and pop culture. Some suggest a coalition of aliens.

Mauro Biglino, known for his unconventional interpretations of religious texts, explores various ancient structures, including the pyramids, in his discussions of extraterrestrial influence. He worked as a translator for the Vatican Publishing House, where he focused on translating biblical texts from Hebrew, which gave him a unique perspective on interpreting ancient scriptures. In his book *The Book That Will Forever Change Our Ideas About the Bible* (2011), he explores the ancient astronaut hypothesis, suggesting that monumental achievements, such as the Great Pyramids of Giza, might have been facilitated or influenced by advanced beings from other worlds. He proposes that the references in sacred texts could be interpreted not as symbolic or purely spiritual but as descriptions of real interactions with extraterrestrial civilisations and their advanced technology. He argues that the pyramids might have been constructed using knowledge imparted by these beings, rather than merely serving as religious or ceremonial structures.[dcccv] Based on his detailed translations and re-examination of religious texts, these theories provide a thought-provoking framework that questions traditional understandings of history and human development.

Powered by Pyramids: A Book of Theories

Ancient Aliens (2010)[dcccvi] is a popular documentary series on the History Channel that further explores the idea that extraterrestrial beings influenced pyramids and other ancient structures. The show presents theories that the pyramids might have been built using advanced technology or knowledge lost to humanity, often tying these structures to questions of ancient civilisations and their potential contact with aliens.

These books and movies suggest that the pyramids' incredible precision and advanced engineering might have been beyond the capabilities of the Egyptians and ancient civilisations alone. While this idea remains controversial and lacks concrete evidence, it captures the imagination of many, inviting further exploration and discussion.

Given their size, jotted around the world, and visibility from above, could the pyramids have acted as markers or beacons, guiding alien spaceships toward Earth? Perhaps the pyramids served as docking stations for extraterrestrial spacecraft, much like ships anchored at a harbour. These ancient structures, with their precise geometry and alignment with celestial bodies, might have provided the stability and energy fields needed to dock large spacecraft upon their arrival on Earth. Just as ships are moored to the shore, the pyramids could have acted as cosmic anchoring points, facilitating contact between ancient civilisations and visitors from the stars. Or could the pyramids have also functioned as refuelling stations for extraterrestrial spacecraft, harnessing Earth's natural energy to recharge their ships? With their strategic locations in energetic hotspots and precise alignment with the stars, the pyramids may have been part of an advanced global network of petrol stations, working on a system designed to tap into geothermal or electromagnetic forces. These energy sources could have provided the power necessary to refuel interstellar vehicles.[dcccvii]

Although controversial, Erich von Däniken's theories about alien involvement in ancient pyramids continue to spark the imagination. One of his famous quotes is: *"The pyramids are proof of a great intelligence, but their origins are still mysterious. Were they a testament to the power of ancient civilisations, or did they have otherworldly connections?"*[dcccviii] Von Däniken suggests that the ancient Egyptians either received help from extraterrestrial visitors or modelled the pyramids based on knowledge from advanced alien civilisations.

According to him, the size of the Great Pyramid of Giza and its alignment with celestial bodies, such as the constellation of Orion, indicate advanced knowledge that may have come from beyond Earth. He points to the engineering complexity involved in moving and shaping the massive stone blocks, weighing several tons each, and the extreme precision with which they were placed. For von Däniken, the fact that many ancient cultures, such as the Egyptians, Mayans, and Sumerians, share similar myths about gods descending from the sky suggests a common influence, potentially extraterrestrial beings who brought knowledge of construction, astronomy, and geometry. Although most mainstream scholars dismiss his theories, his ideas have captured the public imagination. [dcccix]

David Icke is known for his equally controversial views on extraterrestrial involvement and the pyramids. He has suggested that the pyramids were built by or under the influence of advanced extraterrestrial beings and are part of a more extensive global network of structures connected by energy or ley lines. While David does not directly state that the Anunnaki built the pyramids, his theories about extraterrestrial involvement in human history imply such a connection. He believes Anunnaki were extraterrestrial reptilian beings who have manipulated human history and continue to control humanity through a hidden elite. Others dispute that they were reptilians.[dcccx] Due to the extreme nature of his claims, many of David's interviews, particularly those that explore ancient alien or New World Order theories and his views on ancient structures, have been restricted or removed from platforms. [dcccxi] His ideas are available in books and on niche platforms. One of the primary reasons the media dismisses this theory is the absence of verifiable evidence. No solid archaeological, historical, or scientific data support the idea of extraterrestrial involvement in pyramid construction. Since the media often aligns itself with expert opinions and scientific consensus, it is less likely to promote theories contradicting well-established historical and archaeological facts. Mainstream media usually treats it more as entertainment than a legitimate historical inquiry.

Mainstream scholars, like Kenneth Feder in *Frauds, Myths, and Mysteries: Science and Pseudoscience in Archaeology* (2017), argue that these theories rely on a misinterpretation of historical and archaeological evidence, pointing instead to the ingenuity of ancient human civilisations.[dcccxii]

It is seen to undermine the achievements of ancient civilisations like the Egyptians, Mayans, and Sumerians. The suggestion that these ancient peoples could not have built the pyramids or other monumental structures on their own implies a lack of human ingenuity and resourcefulness, which many view as disrespectful to their cultural and technological advancements. Mainstream media prefers to celebrate human achievement and innovation, emphasising the remarkable engineering skills of ancient builders rather than attributing their accomplishments to external (alien) sources. [dcccxiii]

In Egyptian mythology, the land was divided into Kemet (the "black land," referring to the fertile land along the Nile) and Deshret (the "red land," referring to the surrounding deserts). Some alternative theorists speculate that "Deshret" or the "Red Land" might symbolically refer to Mars, known as the "Red Planet." They propose that references to the "red land" could be a symbolic or metaphorical connection to Martian visitors or a lost Martian civilisation.[dcccxiv] According to these speculations, Martian visitors might have shared technological or astronomical knowledge with ancient Egyptians, helping them construct the pyramids as part of a broader cosmic or interplanetary connection.

In 1984, a group of tourists reportedly saw UFOs hovering above the Great Pyramid of Giza. Although the sighting was widely discussed, it was never fully explained, which contributed to theories suggesting that extraterrestrial forces may have played a role in the construction of pyramids. Such modern sightings of UFOs near ancient structures fueled speculation about alien involvement in ancient civilisations.[dcccxv]

No credible or verified inscriptions of military objects, such as modern weapons, aircraft, or tanks, have been found in the pyramids. One notable exception comes from the Temple of Seti I in Abydos, Egypt, where carvings on the ceiling of a temple hall appear to depict modern vehicles, such as helicopters, submarines, and aeroplanes. Proponents of ancient astronauts or conspiracy theories often cite this carving. However, Egyptologists explain these as a result of palimpsest, a phenomenon where older hieroglyphs were plastered over with newer inscriptions, and over time, parts of the original carvings became exposed. This creates the illusion of modern machinery but is an accidental blend of ancient symbols.[dcccxvi]

Hard to believe no one has visited Earth?

Although many are sceptical about alien theories, it is equally hard to believe extraterrestrial civilisations haven't visited us. Given the vastness of the universe and the likelihood of other habitable planets, it seems statistically improbable that Earth has had no known visitors.

Some theories, as explored in Carl Sagan's *Cosmos* (1980), suggest physical or technological limitations, like the vast distances between stars and our limited means of detection; the nearest star system, Alpha Centauri, is 4.37 light-years away, which would take tens of thousands of years to reach with current technology.[dcccxvii] This, however, is based on our inability to relate to other civilisations that are much more advanced than ours. Another perspective on why extraterrestrial beings cannot visit Earth involves the concept of a firmament—a solid, impenetrable barrier separating Earth from outer space. Proponents of this idea often reference early cosmological models or religious texts. For example, in *The Greatest Lie on Earth: Proof That Our World Is Not a Moving Globe*, Edward Hendrie argues that "the firmament is a tangible boundary placed by the Creator, above which lies the waters beyond". He suggests that this firmament prevents anything from entering or leaving Earth's atmosphere, blocking potential interstellar visitors. He says modern space exploration claims are either mistaken or deliberately misleading.[dcccxviii]

This interpretation aligns with some flat Earth theories, suggesting that the firmament acts as a natural barrier, thereby reinforcing the view that the Earth is uniquely enclosed and inaccessible to outside forces. Similarly, we cannot visit other planets based on this theory. On a side note, could the pyramids have directed blasts that weakened or "cracked" this barrier, possibly releasing the "waters above" and causing a flood? This idea may explain the ancient flood myths and the mud and sediment layers found across many regions of the Earth.

In contrast, authors like Arthur C. Clarke in *Childhood's End* (1953) propose that advanced civilisations may choose not to interfere with less advanced species, akin to how we observe animals in the wild, so as not to disrupt our cultural, social, and technological development.[dcccxix] Similarly, Stephen Webb's *If the Universe Is Teeming with Aliens... Where Is Everybody?* (2002) discusses the "Great Filter" theory, which suggests that civilisations might self-destruct before achieving interstellar capabilities or that they may focus inwardly on sustainable or digital realities.[dcccxx]

Others speculate, as in Liu Cixin's *The Three-Body Problem* (2008), that advanced civilisations use communication methods beyond our understanding or keep their presence hidden to avoid detection.[dcccxxi]

Each of these possibilities highlights our limited understanding of life's complexity and the vast cosmos we inhabit. Authors like Erich von Däniken, in *Chariots of the Gods* (1968), argue that extraterrestrials may have already visited Earth, but the evidence was lost, hidden, or misinterpreted.[dcccxxii]

Do We Have Any Evidence That Aliens Exist?

Thousands of individuals worldwide claim to have been abducted by aliens or to have seen UFOs. By far the most commonly reported type of alien, Greys are often described as being short (approximately 3-5 feet tall), with large heads, large black almond-shaped eyes, and thin, spindly bodies. They are usually depicted as having grey skin and lacking noticeable ears, hair, or noses. Their mouths are often small. They have long, slender arms and fingers. Many abduction stories involve *Greys*, usually associated with telepathic communication, cold, clinical behaviour, and a lack of emotional expression. They are typically depicted as scientists or explorers conducting experiments on humans. A significant portion of alien encounter reports involve abductions, during which the individual claims to have been taken aboard a spaceship for physical exams, experimentation, or observation.[dcccxxiii] While these accounts are often dismissed as psychological phenomena or misidentifications of natural occurrences, they continue to generate interest and debate.[dcccxxiv]

Countries such as Brazil, Russia, China, the US and France have documented numerous sightings, and governments and military agencies often investigate these unexplained aerial phenomena.

The public's continued fascination with aliens is reflected in the cinemas. The late 1990s and early 2000s saw a peak in alien-related movies, especially with shows like *The X-Files*, films like *Independence Day*, and documentaries about UFO sightings.[dcccxxv]

The X-Files: Fight the Future (1998) gained immense popularity as part of the broader X-Files franchise, tapping into the widespread fascination with government conspiracies, extraterrestrial life, and ancient mysteries.[dcccxxvi] The film expanded on the show's central themes of alien influence on humanity and the government's role in covering up evidence of extraterrestrial life, which resonated with viewers during a time when public interest in UFOs and paranormal activity was high.[dcccxxvii] Its exploration of an ancient extraterrestrial virus buried deep within the Earth and alien colonisation plans mirrored the growing belief in ancient alien theories.[dcccxxviii]

In recent years, movies like *Arrival* (2016), series like *Stranger Things* (2016–present), and Marvel's cosmic storyline in *Guardians of the Galaxy* (2014) have kept aliens in the public consciousness, although often through different narrative lenses—focusing on communication, friendship, or cosmic adventure rather than conspiracy.[dcccxxix]

Are we ready for UFO disclosure? The panic triggered by Orson Welles' 1938 *War of the Worlds* broadcast began with a false sense of credibility. Presented as a series of breaking news reports interrupting normal programmes, it convinced many listeners that Earth was genuinely under Martian invasion. The realism—enhanced by deadpan reporters, fake scientific commentary, and sound effects—blurred lines between fiction and reality. With no commercial breaks for almost 40 minutes, those who tuned in late missed the disclaimer that it was a dramatisation. Reports of people fleeing their homes, clogging roads, or calling police and newspapers flooded in. Afterwards, a theory circulated—discussed in both public speculation and conspiracy forums—that this event uncovered something deeper: that the population was mentally unprepared for contact with extraterrestrials. Some believe that the broadcast inadvertently—or perhaps deliberately—acted as a social experiment, and that the extreme reaction led government and intelligence agencies to conclude that public disclosure of alien life would be too destabilising. This idea continues to influence UFO disclosure debates today, where his fictitious Martians still cast a long shadow over the politics of belief.[dcccxxx]

For decades, the US denied UFOs.[dcccxxxi] In 2020, the U.S. Department of Defence declassified some interesting UFO (now called UAP—Unidentified Aerial Phenomena) reports. These reports describe encounters between military pilots and objects exhibiting advanced flight capabilities that surpass current human technology. These disclosures are among the most credible unexplained incidents.[dcccxxxii]

These sightings often include descriptions of bright lights, unusual movements, and incredible speeds, estimated to be between 5,000 and 20,000 miles per hour, far surpassing the capabilities of known aircraft. Some pilots have reported seeing metallic, disc-shaped objects hovering or moving at these astonishing speeds. In contrast, others describe glowing orbs that appear to manoeuvre intelligently, often changing direction suddenly or disappearing at high velocities. These objects are sometimes described as silent and seem to defy known laws of physics, making rapid accelerations, sharp turns, or hovering in ways that modern aircraft cannot replicate.[dcccxxxiii]

These UFOs are sometimes spotted at high altitudes or near military bases, raising concerns about their origin. Pilots often emphasise the unconventional behaviour of these objects, including their ability to maintain high speeds without traditional propulsion systems like jet engines or rotors. The possibility that UFO sightings are linked to adversaries such as Russia or China is considered highly unlikely by many experts. Advanced technological capabilities required for some of the observed phenomena far surpass what is currently known about the military developments of these nations. Additionally, the idea that an adversarial nation could operate such sophisticated vehicles undetected within foreign airspace for extended periods without triggering international tensions or responses from defence agencies seems improbable.[dcccxxxiv]

Some speculate that aliens are concerned about the development of our technology and are monitoring it. They may want

Powered by Pyramids: A Book of Theories

to contain any destructive technologies. Could they be worried about our nuclear programs? An atomic bomb may have an impact on their planet and disrupt their world.

The government's openness about investigating these phenomena has fueled speculation and interest, with mainstream news covering UFO reports more extensively than in previous years. While they admitted these objects could not be explained, they did not confirm them as extraterrestrial. Although these sightings are not definitive proof of aliens[dcccxxxv], they continue to capture public and governmental interest, prompting ongoing investigations into the nature of these phenomena.

The Search for Extraterrestrial Intelligence (SETI) listens for radio signals from space that might come from intelligent alien civilisations. While no confirmed extraterrestrial signal has been detected, a few unexplained signals, such as the "Wow!" signal in 1977, remain intriguing but inconclusive.[dcccxxxvi]

Where could the aliens be hiding? In *Exposing U.S. Government Policies on Extraterrestrial Life* (2009), Michael Salla explores the secrecy surrounding extraterrestrial life and alleged interactions with non-human entities. He argues that the U.S. government and other global powers have concealed knowledge of alien visitations, technology, and covert collaborations with extraterrestrial beings for decades.[dcccxxxvii]

One of the most famous examples is the alleged Roswell incident of 1947, where it's believed that the U.S. military recovered a crashed UFO and its occupants. Supporters of this theory argue that the government has been involved in secret recovery and reverse-engineering programs aimed at studying advanced alien technology. Over the years, numerous reports from military personnel, intelligence officials, and civilians claim to have witnessed or been involved in these recoveries. While no conclusive evidence has been made public, these stories persist and contribute to the widespread belief that governments may conceal proof of extraterrestrial contact.[dcccxxxviii]

Another provocative voice in the discussion of concealed knowledge is William Tompkins, a former aerospace insider who, in his 2015 memoir *Selected by Extraterrestrials*, claimed to have worked on a U.S. Navy program involving reverse-engineered alien technology. He detailed alleged post-WWII collaborations between American intelligence agencies and former Nazi scientists.[dcccxxxix] He said they were influenced by extraterrestrial guidance, particularly from so-called "Nordic" beings. According to his account, these efforts led to the development of secret spacefaring technologies far in advance of what is publicly acknowledged today. His narrative mirrors a familiar pattern: that of a hidden elite, entrusted with advanced knowledge, operating in the shadows of official history. He represents a modern incarnation of the 'initiated few', a class of individuals believed to be entrusted with the secrets of propulsion, energy manipulation, and cosmic architecture. Whether one views his testimony as factual, symbolic, or purely mythological, it contributes to a broader framework in which wisdom encoded in ancient monuments is not lost but rather carefully hidden or selectively passed on, surfacing only through leaked narratives or recovered memory.

In October 2024, the *Daily Mail* reported on a theory suggesting that an alien "mothership" could be monitoring Earth. The article referenced observations made by the Pentagon's All-Domain Anomaly Resolution Office (AARO) and Harvard scientist Avi Loeb.[dcccxl]

Why do we not hear of UFO sightings in other countries, outside the US? In many regions, media coverage does not focus on UFO reports as much as it does in the United States, where UFOs are a widespread cultural phenomenon fueled by movies, TV shows, and government disclosures. In some countries, governments may not disclose information about UFOs or suppress reports to avoid public panic, leading to fewer publicised sightings. Additionally, access to advanced observation technology varies, meaning that countries with fewer resources might not capture or report these events as frequently. Cultural beliefs also influence how aerial phenomena are perceived, with some regions interpreting sightings through the lens of local myths or religious traditions, rather than associating them with extraterrestrials. Finally, language barriers and limited international reporting can result in UFO reports from non-Western or non-English-speaking countries receiving less global attention.

Could the US government possess far more advanced technology than the public is aware of, and is such technology being tested in secretive locations, such as Antarctica and Area 51 in the US? This possibility has fueled speculation for years, with some suggesting that many UFO sightings might not be extraterrestrial in origin but rather highly classified government projects. In this context, the strange flight patterns and high speeds often attributed to UFOs might result from government-controlled technologies, hidden from public view yet tested in these highly secretive locations.

Similarly, some researchers have suggested that UFO sightings could be explained by advanced augmented reality (AR) technology. In this theory, the objects witnessed in the sky may not be physical craft but rather sophisticated projections, possibly created using holographic or AR technologies. This could explain why some UFOs appear to defy the laws of physics, such as making sudden turns or accelerating at speeds that seem impossible to achieve. If advanced enough, AR systems could manipulate light and visual perception to create highly realistic images in the sky, leaving witnesses questioning the authenticity of what they see. While this theory is speculative, it offers an intriguing possibility that the UFO phenomenon could be the result of cutting-edge human or extraterrestrial technology designed to simulate physical presence.

Area 51, long shrouded in secrecy and conspiracy, has been at the heart of many speculations about extraterrestrial activity. Located in the Nevada desert, this highly classified U.S. Air Force facility has been linked to rumours of alien technology reverse-engineering, UFO sightings, and secret government experiments. In *Area 51: An Uncensored History of America's Top Secret Military Base*, author Annie Jacobsen delves into the shadowy history of the infamous U.S. Air Force facility. Through extensive research and interviews with former employees, she uncovers many classified operations at the base, including experimental aircraft testing and Cold War intelligence activities. While she stops short of confirming extraterrestrial involvement, she does discuss how the secrecy surrounding Area 51 has fueled numerous conspiracy theories about alien technology and reverse-engineering efforts. She concludes that much of the base's mystery stems from its role in testing cutting-edge military technology. However, she acknowledges that public fascination with UFO sightings and alleged cover-ups continues to cloud its reputation. [dcccxli]

In *Antarctica and the Secret Space Program: From World War II to the Current Space Race*, author David Hatcher Childress explores the theory that Antarctica has long been a hub of extraterrestrial activity and secret government operations. He delves into claims that ancient alien civilisations established bases beneath the ice thousands of years ago, leaving behind advanced technologies that remain hidden from public knowledge. He also investigates the possibility of a secret space program involving both the U.S. and Nazi Germany, suggesting that advanced alien technology might have been discovered and reverse-engineered in Antarctica. His conclusions emphasise that while there is no definitive proof, Antarctica's remote and unexplored nature continues to fuel speculation that it remains a secretive location for extraterrestrial research, drawing parallels to the mystery surrounding Area 51. Whether grounded in reality or speculative fiction, the connection between Area 51, aliens, and Antarctica remains a topic that continues to captivate the imaginations of many.[dcccxlii] Some speculate that the Area 51 facility has extensive underground tunnels and bunkers for secretive military research and testing. The lack of public access to the site has fueled these rumours.

Movies about aliens further fuel speculation. The sci-fi movie *Arrival* (2016), directed by Denis Villeneuve, is known for its thought-provoking exploration of how language shapes perception and how humans might approach first contact with alien life. In the film, a linguist is recruited by the U.S. military to help communicate with mysterious alien spaceships that have landed at various locations around the world. The movie focuses on language, time, and the effort to understand the intentions of the extraterrestrial visitors through communication rather than conflict.[dcccxliii]

Do Aliens Exist Underground or in the Oceans?

Mermaids have appeared in folklore across many cultures for centuries, from the sirens of Greek mythology to the selkies of Scottish legend and the mami wata spirits in West African traditions. What if mermaids are real?

Some argue that less glamorous aliens live in the underground tunnels. They highlight the iconic image of "Grey aliens" (or Greys), characterised by large, black eyes. If extraterrestrial beings evolved in underground or low-light environments, their eyes would naturally adapt to become larger and more sensitive to light. This resembles how Earth-based creatures, such as cavefish, nocturnal animals, or deep-sea organisms, develop enormous eyes or heightened senses to navigate and survive in dark conditions. Such large eyes would allow more light to enter, enhancing their vision in dim or pitch-black environments. These adaptations would be crucial for aliens that may have evolved underground, enabling them to see clearly in dark tunnels or subterranean habitats where light is scarce.

Could the aliens be hiding in the oceans? If an alien species originated or adapted to the oceans, large eyes would be a plausible trait in an environment where little light penetrates. The vast and largely unexplored oceans represent one of Earth's greatest mysteries, holding secrets that may rival those of space. More than 80% of the world's oceans remain unmapped and unexplored, presenting an immense frontier with the potential for groundbreaking discoveries.[dcccxliv] While NASA is renowned for its space missions, the unexplored depths of our seas have sparked theories suggesting that the true focus of discovery lies beneath the waves. Some propose that hidden civilisations or even extraterrestrial beings could have found refuge within the ocean's dark expanse, using it as an ideal hiding place that's difficult for humanity to surveil. Reports of unidentified submerged objects that defy known physics have fueled this idea, merging scientific curiosity with myth and speculation. If such theories were true, one reason for keeping this hidden could be the immense societal and psychological impact, challenging our understanding of life, technology, and our place on Earth. Yet, as with any profound mystery, the search continues, fuelled by imagination, discovery, and the relentless human spirit of exploration. Ivan T. Sanderson, a biologist and writer, was among the early proponents of the idea that some UFOs were USOs (Unidentified Submerged Objects), capable of seamless travel between the sky and the ocean depths. In his 1970 book *Invisible Residents*, Sanderson speculated that these mysterious crafts could be piloted by beings uniquely adapted to space and deep-sea environments, possessing advanced technologies far beyond human comprehension. He suggested that the vast and largely unexplored underwater world could provide an ideal hiding place for such intelligent life, shielding them from detection by humans.[dcccxlv]

The intrigue surrounding Admiral Richard E. Byrd's purported statements in the *El Mercurio* newspaper in 1947 has fueled decades of speculation about the true nature of *Operation Highjump* and Antarctica's mysteries. Operation Highjump remains a landmark in polar exploration, making significant contributions to scientific and geographical knowledge. While the official objectives were largely achieved, the expedition's abrupt conclusion and Richard Byrd's curious statements have kept its legacy shrouded in intrigue, sparking debate and fascination among historians and conspiracy theorists alike. Conspiracy narratives claim that he may have encountered evidence of advanced civilisations, unidentified flying objects, or otherworldly phenomena during his flights. Among the most enduring and fantastical speculations is the "*Hollow Earth Theory*," which argues that he accessed a hidden, underground world teeming with life or advanced beings. While historians and scientists dismiss such claims as myth, the combination of his remarks, the abrupt conclusion of the mission, and the veil of secrecy surrounding aspects of the operation leaves many to wonder if there is more to the story than officially acknowledged.[dcccxlvi]

In November 2024, the US Congress held hearings about the possibility of underwater alien bases. During a session titled "*Unidentified Anomalous Phenomena: Exposing the Truth*," Representative Lauren Boebert questioned experts about the existence of such bases. She inquired whether there were any accounts of Unidentified Aerial Phenomena (UAPs) emerging from or submerging into oceans, which could indicate an underwater alien presence. Journalist Michael Shellenberger responded, mentioning reports of UAPs in oceanic environments, but stated he was unaware of any specific underwater bases. The hearings have included testimonies from various experts and whistleblowers aiming to shed light on the government's knowledge and handling of UAP-related information.^{dcccxlvii} Could this be part of a deliberate disclosure process, or does it reflect the government's efforts to address public interest while maintaining control over the narrative?

Were the Pyramids built Underwater?

Could aliens have built the pyramids underwater? Advocates of this idea propose that an advanced alien species, using technology far beyond human comprehension, constructed the pyramids. At the same time, Earth's landscape was partially submerged due to higher sea levels or a deliberate choice to harness the unique properties of water. Water, an excellent medium for mitigating gravity's effects, could have facilitated the movement and precise placement of massive stone blocks with minimal effort, possibly aided by technologies such as sonic levitation or anti-gravity devices. The underwater environment might also explain the precision of the pyramids' alignments, as extraterrestrial builders could have used advanced instruments to stabilise construction in a controlled aquatic setting.

Some studies suggest that specific erosion patterns on the Great Pyramid of Giza and the Sphinx resemble damage caused by prolonged exposure to water, such as heavy rainfall or flooding. This has led to theories that these structures might predate known Egyptian civilisation and could have been built when the Nile region experienced higher water levels or was partially submerged. Submerged pyramid-like structures, such as the Yonaguni Monument off the coast of Japan, have been discovered. There are more finds underwater. In 2001, researchers reported finding structures resembling pyramids and circular formations off Cuba's western coast. The depth and complexity of these formations have led to various theories, but conclusive evidence is lacking. In 2013, a submerged pyramid-like structure was identified near the Azores Islands in Portugal. Approximately 60 meters tall, its origins—natural or artificial—are still under investigation.

Could it be possible that the pyramids were built underwater and later revealed as sea levels receded? This speculative theory suggests that during periods of higher global sea levels or after a cataclysmic flood, parts of the Earth's surface, including the Giza Plateau, may have been submerged. In such conditions, ancient builders—or perhaps extraterrestrial entities—could have used the buoyant properties of water to facilitate the transportation and placement of the massive stone blocks, thereby reducing the effort required for construction. Over time, as the water levels dropped due to geological shifts, ice age cycles, or other climatic changes, the pyramids would have emerged as enduring monuments on dry land. This concept aligns with the persistent global myths of great floods, such as the story

Powered by Pyramids: A Book of Theories

of Atlantis or the biblical deluge, which may reflect actual historical events. While archaeological evidence currently supports a terrestrial origin for the pyramids, this idea invites further exploration into ancient climate conditions, geological anomalies, and the possibility of advanced knowledge or intervention during their construction.

Myths across cultures offer narratives that suggest evidence of advanced beings or extraterrestrial entities associated with the seas. In Hindu mythology, the Nagas, serpent-like deities dwelling in an underwater realm called Patala, are described as possessing immense knowledge and treasures, sparking theories that they could represent ancient depictions of alien entities or advanced civilisations.[dcccxlviii] Similarly, the Dogon tribe of Mali recounts the story of the Nommo, amphibious beings who came from the Sirius star system and brought wisdom, technology, and cultural knowledge to early humans. According to Dogon mythology, the Nommo arrived in an ark that descended from the heavens, splashing into the water upon arrival. They are often depicted as water-dwelling, fish-like entities who brought wisdom, technology, and spiritual guidance to early humanity. The Nommo's connection to water is central to their identity, symbolising life, fertility, and the fluidity of knowledge. [dcccxlix] Babylonian mythology describes Oannes, a fish-like being who emerged from the sea to teach humanity the arts of civilisation—a story often paralleled with ideas of alien visitation and knowledge sharing.[dcccl] The Pacific Island myths of lost continents, such as Lemuria and Mu, describe sunken worlds inhabited by advanced beings, hinting at the potential existence of underwater civilisations.[dcccli] These stories, while mythical, collectively weave a tapestry of mysterious knowledge and unexplained phenomena tied to the seas, fueling modern speculation about the presence of extraterrestrial life or advanced technologies hidden beneath the waves.

If the pyramids were initially built underwater, what was their purpose? Could they have served to create currents or traps for marine life, functioning as sophisticated fishing systems to provide a steady food supply? Alternatively, could they have been energy generators using water pressure and currents to produce power, possibly for advanced technologies or even extraterrestrial operations? The underwater location might also have enabled the pyramids to serve as communication hubs, using their shape to amplify sound waves or energy signals efficiently transmitted through water.

Where Do the Aliens Allegedly Come From?

The origin of aliens varies depending on the source. Many theories suggest that aliens originate from distant planets or star systems within our galaxy or beyond. The *Greys* come from the Zeta Reticuli star system. They are commonly depicted as indifferent or malevolent. The Orion constellation and the Sirius star system are frequently linked to ancient astronaut theories. The Ancient astronaut theory believes that extraterrestrial beings visited Earth in ancient times and interacted with early human civilisations. Proponents of this theory suggest that these visitors influenced the development of human culture, technology, and religion, often being mistaken for gods or divine beings by early humans. The Pleiades is another star system frequently associated with the humanoid species known as the *Pleiadians*. They are described as spiritually advanced, peaceful, wise, and concerned with the well-being of humanity. [dccclii] Some other theories propose that aliens are interdimensional beings existing in parallel dimensions, able to cross over into our reality. Could aliens be advanced humans or entities from the future who have mastered time travel?

Some speculative theories, such as the *Flat Earth theory*, propose that aliens may not come from outer space but rather from lands beyond the Antarctic wall, which, according to this theory, surrounds our known world. Proponents of this idea suggest that the extraterrestrial beings we encounter could be advanced civilisations living in these hidden lands outside the boundary of the known Earth. This contrasts with mainstream beliefs about aliens originating from distant planets or galaxies.[dcccliii] Additionally, modern theories, such as simulation theory, propose that our universe could be a simulated reality, with aliens acting as entities outside or interacting with this simulation. In such a scenario, these beings could manipulate the simulated environment to make them appear as "aliens" to those inside the simulation[dcccliv]. These theories push the boundaries of conventional thinking and add to the growing debate over the true nature of extraterrestrial encounters and the structure of reality itself.

These theories push the boundaries of conventional thinking, much like the speculative ideas surrounding the pyramids, which suggest they could be part of an ancient global energy grid or communication system created by these very advanced civilisations. Such theories challenge our understanding of extraterrestrial encounters and question the true purpose and origins of Earth's most enigmatic structures, like the pyramids.

Are We the Aliens or a Hybrid?

Several astronauts have shared speculative thoughts on humanity's place in the universe, suggesting that humans may have extraterrestrial origins or connections. Edgar Mitchell, an Apollo 14 astronaut, was one of the more outspoken figures. He often spoke about his belief in the existence of extraterrestrial life. He hinted that ancient humans might have been influenced by, or even originated from, extraterrestrial sources.[dccclv] While he didn't explicitly claim that we are aliens, his comments suggest that he saw human life as possibly interconnected with alien civilisations. Al Worden, an Apollo 15 astronaut, made intriguing comments in a 2017 interview. In it, he suggested that ancient Sumerian texts could provide evidence of human extraterrestrial origins. Worden stated, "*We are the aliens,*" implying that humans may have come from another planet and that our ancestors may have been visitors from space who established life on Earth.[dccclvi] Brian O'Leary, a former NASA astronaut and scientist, shared similar sentiments. He suggested that extraterrestrial civilisations might have played a role in seeding life on Earth or influencing human development. However, he framed this more as a theory than a direct claim.[dccclvii] These comments are more speculative than factual, with astronauts reflecting on broader philosophical questions about humanity's origins and its place in the universe. None of these remarks has been backed by hard scientific evidence.

Interestingly, the unusual characteristics of human hairlessness have even made their way into speculative theories, including ideas that align with the concept of humans having extraterrestrial origins. One notable author who explores this idea is Lloyd Pye in his book *Everything You Know Is Wrong: Human Origins* (1997). He suggests that human features, such as hairlessness, upright posture, and a huge brain-to-body ratio, set us apart from other primates. He argues that these traits may indicate that humans are not entirely a product of Earthly evolution but might have been influenced or engineered by extraterrestrial beings.[dccclviii] Although unconventional, his theories highlight the debate surrounding human anomalies that mainstream science has yet to explain fully. While no solid evidence supports the claim that humans have extraterrestrial origins, his work intrigues readers and fuels discussions about the possibility of otherworldly influences on our evolutionary path. Is it possible that we had an underwater phase? There is some support for the Aquatic Ape Theory (AAT), first proposed by Alister Hardy in the 1960s and later expanded by Elaine Morgan. This theory suggests that certain human traits, such as hairlessness, subcutaneous fat, and breath control, could be adaptations to a semi-aquatic lifestyle. Elaine Morgan argued that humans' ability to swim, the presence of the mammalian dive reflex, and occasional webbing between fingers and toes might be evolutionary remnants of this aquatic phase. Mythological references, such as the global tales of mermaids, provide symbolic echoes of a potential underwater connection. Additionally, the origins of life in the oceans and early humans' reliance on coastal environments further highlight the evolutionary importance of water.

Could humans have been genetically engineered to do a job on Earth? The Sumerian myth of the Anunnaki suggests that these deities, often described as god-like beings from the heavens, genetically engineered early humans to serve as labourers, particularly in mining operations, according to texts like the *Enuma Elish* and *Atrahasis*.[dccclix] Critics, however, argue that these interpretations lack linguistic and archaeological support. Similarly, the Bible's account of the Nephilim describes them as the offspring of the "sons of God"—interpreted by some as extraterrestrials or divine entities—and human women, pointing to the possibility of genetic mixing or hybridisation between species.[dccclx] In Hindu mythology, the creation of humanity by gods like Brahma often involved direct intervention, with tales of divine beings moulding, modifying, or even recreating life forms to populate the Earth.[dccclxi] These myths suggest a recurring theme across cultures of humanity's origins being shaped by external forces, whether divine or otherworldly, through intentional acts of creation or genetic manipulation.

The Annunaki

One of the aliens frequently mentioned is the Annunaki. Could the Annunakis have passed down advanced knowledge to humans? In ancient Sumerian, Akkadian, Assyrian, and Babylonian texts, the Anunnaki are described as powerful gods responsible for creating the universe and humanity, as well as guiding human affairs.[dccclxii] They were believed to have descended from the sky and directly shaped early civilisations by teaching humans critical skills, such as farming, construction, and creating complex societies. Some alternative theorists take this idea further, suggesting that the Anunnaki were not just mythological figures but extraterrestrial beings who came to Earth and passed down advanced technological and architectural knowledge. This, they propose, could explain the construction of ancient megastructures, such as the pyramids, which exhibit precise astronomical alignments and engineering feats that seem remarkably advanced for their time.[dccclxiii]

One of the most prominent proponents of this theory is author Zecharia Sitchin, who popularised the idea in his 1976 book *The 12th*

Planet. According to Zecharia Sitchin, the Anunnaki came from a planet called Nibiru, which he claimed had a long, elliptical orbit that brought it close to Earth every 3,600 years. He theorised that the Anunnaki genetically engineered humans to serve them as labourers and that their advanced knowledge of technology, astronomy, and engineering was passed down to early human civilisations. He argued that ancient texts, such as the Epic of Gilgamesh and Sumerian cuneiform tablets, referenced space travel, advanced technology, and celestial knowledge, implying extraterrestrial involvement. He claimed that the Anunnaki's influence on early human civilisations was profound, providing genetic advancements and technological and cultural understanding. This included astronomy, engineering, and construction techniques, which he suggested could explain the remarkable architectural achievements of the ancient world, like the precision and astronomical alignments of the Great Pyramid of Giza.[dccclxiv]

However, this theory presents a significant chronological challenge compared to the known history of the pyramids. While the Great Pyramid of Giza was built around 2,500 BC, Zecharia Sitchin's Anunnaki timeline places their influence much earlier, around 440,000 years ago—a vast gap not supported by mainstream archaeology.

Proponents of the Anunnaki theory often highlight the pyramids' astronomical alignments, suggesting that the precise positioning of the structures, especially in relation to stars such as Orion's Belt, could indicate that the builders possessed advanced knowledge of the cosmos. According to these theories, this knowledge could have been passed down by the Anunnaki, often associated with the heavens or extraterrestrial origins.

While mainstream historians attribute the pyramids' construction to the Egyptians' mastery of mathematics, geometry, and observation of the stars, the Anunnaki theory suggests that such knowledge may have come from an otherworldly source. Despite the lack of concrete evidence to support these claims, the idea that the Anunnaki played a role in human development and the construction of ancient monuments continues to captivate those interested in ancient alien theories and the mysteries of early civilisations.

Collective Consciousness Manifestation

Modern ideas, such as the Law of Attraction and quantum consciousness, suggest that thoughts and beliefs shape reality. In her book, *The Secret* (2006), Rhonda Byrne explores the idea that thoughts and beliefs can shape reality, a concept central to the Law of Attraction and popular in New Age spirituality; if this were true, some have argued a group of spiritually attuned people could have worked together to manifest the pyramids as a physical expression of their collective will. This theory is rooted in the ancient Egyptian belief in the power of the mind and spirit to influence the physical world, primarily through their religious practices centred on maintaining *maat*, or cosmic order.[dccclxv]

In this context, the pyramids could be viewed as physical manifestations of the spiritual will of individuals deeply connected to higher planes of consciousness. Their understanding of energy and focused intent may have allowed them to shape reality in ways that seem impossible by today's standards. The construction of the pyramids might have been a form of spiritual alchemy, where thought, vibration, and willpower combined to bring these massive structures into existence.[dccclxvi]

The idea that thoughts and beliefs can shape physical reality, especially on the scale of manifesting large structures like pyramids, conflicts with established scientific principles. These ideas are often criticised for being pseudoscientific, lacking in rigour, and based on personal belief systems rather than verifiable facts.[dccclxvii] For example, in *The Intention Experiment* (2007), Lynne McTaggart explores the concept of collective intention, suggesting that focused group thoughts or intentions can influence physical reality. She presents various studies and experiments where groups meditated or focused on specific outcomes, aiming to demonstrate how collective thought can impact material conditions.[dccclxviii] However, mainstream scientists argued that they lack empirical evidence and do not adhere to the rigorous standards of scientific experimentation typically required to validate such claims.

In physics and material science, constructing massive structures like the pyramids requires physical forces, labour, and material manipulation, not merely spiritual or mental effort.

While gaining traction in New Age and spiritual circles, mainstream academics do not consider quantum consciousness and the Law of Attraction scientifically rigorous. Quantum mechanics deals with subatomic particles, and while consciousness remains a topic of exploration in neuroscience, the mainstream argument is that there is no scientific evidence linking quantum phenomena to large-scale physical manifestations, such as buildings.[dccclxix]

Some point out that these theories misinterpret ancient Egyptian spirituality, which focused more on the afterlife, cosmic order, and divine authority than on harnessing spiritual energy to manifest physical objects, such as pyramids.[dccclxx]

Creation through Thought and Vibrational Frequencies

Other theories involve the manipulation of frequencies. If matter is simply a dense form of energy, it could theoretically be manipulated through vibrations and therefore, the pyramids could have been constructed by manipulating vibrational frequencies. Imagine if ancient builders knew how to alter the frequency of matter, transform energy into stone, or even manipulate the physical properties of the stone to make it lighter or more easily movable. By tapping into an advanced understanding of resonance and frequency, these visionary builders might have shifted the vibrational state of energy to create physical stone blocks or move them effortlessly into place.[dccclxxi]

The ancient Egyptians could have harnessed specific sound frequencies or mantras to manipulate the stone blocks with stunning precision. Many occult and esoteric traditions hold that the universe is made up of vibrations and frequencies, and by tuning into specific vibrations, reality can indeed be shaped or altered. Consider Tibetan monks using mantras and sound vibrations to achieve physical phenomena—such practices align with this intriguing idea. Alchemy teaches that everything vibrates at a specific frequency, and by altering those frequencies, one can change the material properties of an object. The idea is that the ancient Egyptians could have used sound vibrations or specific mantras to change the frequency of the stone, making it lighter to transport.

According to modern physics and quantum theory, matter and energy are interchangeable at the subatomic level. This idea resonates with the theory that all matter is simply energy in a denser form. If the ancient Egyptians knew how to transform or manipulate matter using energy, it would have opened up possibilities for how the pyramids' massive stone blocks could have been created or moved.

It is inspiring to think that what was believed possible through spiritual intention and profound understanding in ancient times led to one of humanity's most significant architectural marvels. This deep connection between thought, vibration, and creation remains a powerful reminder of what can be achieved when minds and will unite towards a common purpose.[dccclxxii]

However, mainstream archaeologists argue that no ancient texts or artefacts have been discovered that support the use of sound frequencies or mantras to move or manipulate stone. Most evidence suggests that manual labour and mechanical tools, such as ramps, levers, and sledges, were used.

While the theory of manipulating vibrational frequencies draws on modern concepts from quantum physics and vibrational frequency, academics say these ideas are misapplied in large-scale construction. Quantum physics deals with subatomic particles, and the effects of manipulating vibrational frequencies on such a level do not apply to objects like large stone blocks. Current physics and material science do not support the suggestion that sound waves or vibrations could alter the stone's molecular structure to make it lighter or more malleable.[dccclxxiii]

Researchers, however, have continued to explore the potential for manipulating objects using sound waves, providing intriguing insights into the broader theory of how vibrational frequencies influence matter.

Recent research has made fascinating strides in manipulating objects using sound waves. In a 2024 study conducted by the École Polytechnique Fédérale de Lausanne (EPFL), scientists demonstrated the precise movement of small objects through a process known as wave-momentum shaping. This experiment used tailored acoustic fields to guide objects along controlled trajectories without direct physical contact. The researchers generated complex sound waves, which carried momentum capable of pushing or pulling objects in a specific direction. By carefully shaping the momentum of these waves, they managed to manipulate the object's position with high precision. The objects were suspended in an environment where the acoustic properties varied. The researchers had to adapt the sound waves to these changing conditions, showing how sound could move objects in less predictable environments. This experiment is groundbreaking because it opens up possibilities for using acoustics to influence matter.[dccclxxiv]

Another line of research by the Max Planck Institute for the Science of Light explores the intricate relationship between sound waves, known as "phonons," and quantum mechanics. In their 2024 study, scientists investigated how sound waves at extremely high frequencies, known as hypersound waves, interact with quantum systems. These sound waves are manipulated at the quantum level, providing insights into the potential of controlling quantum particles through acoustic means. The experiment involved cooling hypersound waves optoacoustically, meaning the researchers used light to control sound waves in quantum environments, effectively demonstrating a method to manipulate sound waves as they travel through a material. Their findings suggested that, much like photons (light particles), phonons (sound particles) can be manipulated with great precision. This could open up new avenues for understanding how sound interacts with matter on a subatomic scale. This type of research is critical for future developments in quantum computing and nanotechnology, where controlling energy and matter at the quantum level becomes essential. dccclxxv While still largely theoretical and limited to small-scale quantum systems, these experiments suggest the possibility of controlling material properties through sound. They provide a modern scientific basis for the idea that sound waves might have been used to manipulate matter, similar to ancient theories about constructing megastructures, such as the pyramids.

These experiments could provide a foundation for theories suggesting that ancient civilisations, such as the Egyptians, may have harnessed sound to manipulate energy and even move massive stone blocks.

Were AI and Robots Buried with the Pyramids?

Could it be that artificial intelligence and robotics are not just breakthroughs of the modern age, but echoes from a much older system, lost in a catastrophe? What if the technological revolution we pride ourselves on today is not truly innovation, but a reactivation of something long gone? What if something occurred that led to a shutdown and a purge? Whether through disaster, sabotage, or a deliberate reset, the system went dark. Civilisations fell, and their knowledge disappeared or was buried, hidden, encoded in stone and stories for future discovery. And here we are again, playing with algorithms and automation. Again, we flirt with an intelligence we cannot fully control or understand. But perhaps we are not explorers at all. Maybe, unknowingly, we are retracing the same cycle we've lived through before. The ancients may have walked this route already, leaving silent warnings in stone and broken myths about what awaits at its end.

Perhaps the ancient world reached a tipping point where intelligence surpassed wisdom, and machines, once guided by consciousness, began to operate without it. A runaway system, no longer serving harmony but prioritising efficiency at the expense of life itself. Or maybe the ancients foresaw this danger and chose to dismantle it before it dismantled them. A reset not driven by nature, but orchestrated by custodians of a deeper knowledge, those who believed some power was too dangerous to remain active. The signs of collapse are echoed in flood myths, sudden disappearances, shattered temples, and unexplained technological gaps across the globe. Entire cities have vanished. Civilisations reduced to rubble. The surviving fragments suggest not just disaster, but deliberate erasure. Memories wiped, mechanisms buried, warnings encrypted in geometry, myth, and monumental silence. Now, as we once again build thinking machines and delegate our decisions to code, are we awakening something that was deliberately put to sleep? Are we reactivating a system without understanding why it was initially shut down? If the ancients had AI and robotics, and buried them, it was not because they lacked the power to harness them. It was because they understood what happens when that power becomes unanchored from consciousness. The pyramids may still stand not as relics of superstition, but as survivors of a previous age of intelligence and silent guardians of a warning we are only just beginning to remember.

What if it is the very mechanism through which the universe maintains its balance, cycling between birth and annihilation, form and formlessness, memory and forgetting? Perhaps this cycle isn't confined to individuals through reincarnation. Perhaps ideas reincarnate. Civilisations reincarnate. Even technologies. A knowledge once known, once applied, once feared, may die with its age, only to rise again, disguised in new forms. Could artificial intelligence and robotics, hailed as modern marvels, be echoes of a previous system? A system deliberately dismantled, buried under stone, myth, and misdirection? Reincarnation may be a law. A force. A cosmic rhythm etched into everything, visible in the rise and fall of empires, in the life and death of stars, in the silent gaze of the pyramids.

Helena Blavatsky proposed in *The Secret Doctrine* (1888) that human development does not occur in a straight line but moves through vast cosmic waves, characterised by cycles of ascent, decline, and renewal. She spoke of ancient root races, such as the Atlanteans and Lemurians, who once possessed knowledge and technology that would be utterly beyond modern comprehension. Yet, she warned, "the civilisations of our present age are but pale reflections of those that have passed into the darkness of time." She viewed reincarnation not just as a personal journey of the soul but as a planetary process, one where not only souls return, but entire systems of thought, tools, and energies buried in catastrophe resurface when the cycle turns again. In this view, technological memory resides in the collective unconscious and reappears when the conditions are right. Therefore, what we call innovation may be the rebirth of something long-forgotten: echoes from a previous age stepping once again into the light.[dccclxxvi]

If civilisations are born, destroyed, and reborn in great waves, what invisible mechanism drives this cycle? In Cosmos and Psyche (2006), philosopher Richard Tarnas argues that the rise and fall of cultures are not random but aligned with the deep rhythm of the cosmos itself. His work proposes that human history follows a pattern shaped by the archetypal influence of planetary alignments, much like a clock measuring not time but consciousness. Civilisations do not simply collapse due to war or decay. They collapse in sync with celestial tides—

and when those same cosmic configurations return, so too do the themes, ideas, and energies that once defined the previous age.[dccclxxvii]

He identifies key periods in which planetary configurations, particularly involving Saturn, Pluto, Uranus, and Neptune, have coincided with revolutionary change, cultural transformation, or catastrophic collapse. These moments are not purely destructive. They are threshold points, symbolic death-rebirth portals that clear away the exhausted structures of one era to make room for the next. In his view, history is not a linear progression. It is an archetypal recurrence. The soul of the world (what ancient thinkers called the *anima mundi*) pulses in time with the heavens, and when it turns, it turns everything.

This model aligns eerily well with the idea that forgotten technologies, philosophies, or even energy systems might not have been lost. They could have been submerged, waiting for the next cosmic shift to re-emerge. Perhaps we are not truly evolving but recycling through patterns of consciousness, unaware that our inventions, ideas, and crises are not new. They are familiar echoes rising again, clothed in new language, shaped by the same stars. If that is the case, then the rediscovery of pyramid energy, ancient AI, or lost wisdom may not be innovation at all. It might be inevitability, an archetypal return embedded into the fabric of reality. The pyramids may have been built not once, but many times across epochs we no longer remember, each time rising from the ashes of collapse as the cosmos opened a new window for knowledge to re-enter. The structures endure. The meanings return. The systems are reborn. The sky remembers what the Earth forgets.

Mainstream Egyptology vs. Alternative Theories

The potential involvement of extraterrestrial beings, lost civilisations, or even giants in pyramid construction stretches the limits of mainstream thought. Did and do aliens exist today, or are the UFOs advanced technology that the government is hiding from us? These speculative theories remind us that much of human history remains unknown or misunderstood. While the establishment may dismiss these ideas, they spark curiosity and challenge us to think beyond accepted narratives. The pyramids could hold secrets that defy modern understanding, and only by keeping an open mind will we uncover the true extent of their origins and significance.

The pyramids are deeply intertwined with Egyptian cultural identity, symbolising their greatness and advanced civilisation. Admitting that the Sumerians or an earlier race of giants or superhuman beings built these structures could have undermined the Egyptians' historical and cultural pride. Mainstream archaeologists point out that no tangible evidence exists of any architect other than the Egyptians. They point out that while it is tempting to believe that an unknown advanced civilisation may have built these structures, no archaeological evidence of such a civilisation has been found. That does not mean no evidence exists. Could remains such as bones have been found and hidden if they did not fit the Egyptian supremacy narrative? The *absence of evidence is not evidence of absence*. While it is theoretically possible that remains or artefacts have been hidden or lost over time, science operates on what can be observed, tested, and verified. Without solid evidence, such claims remain speculative.

Many new archaeological finds have been and are being made due to technological advancements. Future discoveries could shed new light on ancient history, which would be exciting. Recent advancements in archaeological technology, such as ground-penetrating radar and 3D scanning, can reveal more about the pyramids' construction and possibly uncover hidden chambers or bring new evidence about their origins to light.

Whether the pyramids were designed by alternative architects, such as ancient civilisations, extraterrestrial beings, or lost cultures, their incredible mathematical precision and alignment with celestial bodies cannot be overlooked. The idea that these ancient structures may have been built to track the stars, the sun, and the moon raises questions about the level of astronomical knowledge of their creators. Was this alignment a coincidence, or did it reflect the builders' understanding of cosmic forces? As we move forward, in the following chapters, we will explore the advanced mathematics and astronomy that underpin the design of these pyramids, seeking to understand how and why such precise alignment was achieved and what it reveals about the relationship between the Earth and the heavens. So, while the architects of the pyramids remain mysterious, the mathematical precision and the alignment of monuments with the stars suggest deep knowledge yet to be uncovered.

Chapter 10 Advanced Maths and Alignment with the Stars

How the Pyramid's Shape Connects Earth and Cosmos

The precise alignment of the pyramids with stars and their use of advanced mathematics suggest these monuments were designed to mirror the cosmos and focus energy. We will explore how the pyramid's geometry may have unlocked the Earth's hidden powers.

As we explore why the pyramids were built, are there clues in the shape? Could their unique shape be a key to unlocking the Earth's hidden forces? In this chapter, we delve into the profound geometry of the pyramids and the ancient mathematical and astronomical knowledge embedded within these awe-inspiring structures. Could these pyramids have been designed to concentrate energy from the Earth, the cosmos or both? Exploring how the shape of the pyramid might interact with the forces of the universe, blending ancient knowledge with modern scientific inquiry, we may discover that pyramids hold the secret to tapping into the Earth's and the cosmos' energy.[dccclxxviii]

The precision of the mathematical alignments of the pyramids has been analysed in-depth by researchers like Robert Bauval and Adrian Gilbert in *The Orion Mystery* (1994), which argues that the Great Pyramid's alignment with Orion's Belt reflects an advanced understanding of stellar movements. The mathematical ratios in the pyramid design also align with the Golden Ratio, studied by Livio Mario in *The Golden Ratio: The Story of Phi* (2003), suggesting that ancient builders may have integrated sophisticated geometry and astronomy into their construction techniques. However, some critics argue that while these alignments are intriguing, they could be coincidental rather than deliberate.

The pyramid's profound yet straightforward shape encourages us to look deeper, not just at the craftsmanship of ancient builders but at the hidden power that may lie within its very form. Could it be that the pyramid's shape is more than an architectural choice? Could it serve a purpose far more significant than mere monument-building? We will begin by examining the enigmatic geometry of pyramids and investigating how their distinctive shape may concentrate or direct energy.[dccclxxix] We will journey through ancient builders' understanding of mathematics and astronomy, uncovering the extraordinary precision behind these structures. Finally, we will explore the theory of Pyramid Power, a controversial yet fascinating idea that pyramids were designed to harness and concentrate energy within their walls.[dccclxxx]

The Geometry of the Pyramid: A Universal Design

Across the globe, ancient pyramids rise from the Earth, their shapes echoing each other despite being built by civilisations separated by time, space, and culture. These structures are architectural wonders and enigmatic symbols of power and mystery. Its remarkable geometry could explain the pyramid's universal design, which inherently provides structural stability and longevity. But could this iconic shape have a deeper, hidden purpose?

Many of the world's most awe-inspiring structures, from the Great Pyramid of Giza in Egypt to the Gothic cathedrals of Europe, were built using the principles of sacred geometry. The Great Pyramid, for instance, is believed to incorporate the golden ratio and other geometric principles, symbolising the connection between the heavens and the Earth. Similarly, Gothic cathedrals, such as Chartres Cathedral in France, are said to have been designed with sacred geometry in mind, with their arches, windows, and floor plans following specific geometric ratios.

Sacred geometry is the sacred measurement of the world. The study of geometric shapes, patterns, and proportions is believed to reflect the universe's fundamental laws, connecting the physical and spiritual worlds. In nature, art, and ancient architecture, sacred geometry emphasises the symbolic meaning behind forms like the circle, triangle, and golden ratio, representing unity, balance, and cosmic harmony.

Academic research, led by scholars such as Robert Bauval and John Anthony West, has provided compelling evidence for the pyramid's precise alignment with celestial bodies, including the constellation Orion. This alignment further links the pyramid's design to cosmic forces. Studies have also found that the pyramid's base perimeter and height relate to Earth's dimensions, suggesting an advanced understanding of geometry and the planet's size. This research supports the idea that understanding these patterns allows one to gain deeper insight into the interconnectedness of all life and the divine.

Some researchers believe the pyramid's unique geometry can concentrate energy.[dccclxxxi] Picture the energy that flows naturally through the Earth—the electromagnetic waves, the gravitational pull, the resonance of the planet itself. Could the pyramid's shape, with its flat base and pointed peak, act like a giant funnel, drawing energy upward and focusing it at the top?[dccclxxxii] This idea forms the basis for a controversial yet intriguing hypothesis that pyramids were designed to capture and direct energy from the Earth's magnetic field.

In the 20th century, the idea of 'Pyramid Power' captured the imagination of researchers and mystics alike.[dccclxxxiii] Antoine Bovis, a Frenchman, famously claimed that organic matter decayed more slowly inside a small pyramid model, acting like a modern refrigerator, suggesting that the structure somehow concentrated energy. [dccclxxxiv] More recently, a 2018 study by ITMO University in Russia simulated the electromagnetic properties of the Great Pyramid, discovering that its shape could focus electromagnetic waves within its chambers and beneath its base.[dccclxxxv]

While this research remains somewhat theoretical, it raises the question of whether the ancient builders intentionally designed the pyramid to harness and concentrate energy in ways that we have yet to understand fully. The study suggested that the pyramid's shape allowed it to resonate with electromagnetic waves in the radio frequency range. While this research was purely theoretical and did not claim that the pyramid was built for this purpose, it has increased interest in the idea that the shape of the pyramid could concentrate energy in ways we do not yet fully understand.

Throughout history, the shape of the pyramid has also been associated with the divine.[dccclxxxvi] The ancient Egyptians, for example, believed that the pyramid's form mirrored the sun's rays, symbolising a bridge between the Earth and the heavens.[dccclxxxvii] But was this symbolism merely spiritual, or could it point to an ancient understanding of energy fields? Could the heart of the Earth be connected with the cosmos?

In today's world, science and spirituality are often viewed as distinct, even opposing forces. Science is typically rooted in empirical evidence and tangible data, while spirituality explores the intangible aspects of existence, such as consciousness, energy, and the soul. However, in ancient civilisations like those of Egypt, China, and India, this separation did not exist. Knowledge systems integrated spiritual and scientific principles, seeking to understand the universe as a unified whole.

The Hidden Calculations in Pyramid Construction

Salvador Dalí (1904–1989), a Spanish surrealist artist, said, *"The pyramids stand as symbols of perfection—geometric and eternal."*

Whether or not it was the Egyptians, the builders of the pyramids were not only master architects but also brilliant mathematicians and astronomers. The Great Pyramid of Giza is a marvel of mathematical precision. Additionally, its alignment with the cardinal points — north, south, east, and west — is almost flawless, with an error margin of less than 0.05 degrees.[dccclxxxviii] Modern architects would struggle to replicate it without advanced tools.[dccclxxxix] How did the ancient Egyptians achieve such precision?

Even more fascinating is the pyramid's connection to the Earth's dimensions. The ratio of the pyramid's height to the perimeter of its base mirrors the ratio of a circle's radius to its circumference—an indication that the builders understood the concept of *pi* long before it was 'discovered' by mathematicians in Greece.[dcccxc] The golden ratio, *also known as pi, is a mathematical ratio found in many natural patterns, as well as in art* and architecture. In sacred geometry, it is considered to represent divine proportions and beauty. This ratio can be observed in the proportions of ancient buildings, such as the Great Pyramid of Giza, and in the Fibonacci sequence, a series of numbers that closely approximates the golden ratio and is found in various natural phenomena, including the arrangement of leaves on plants, the pattern of shells, and the branching of trees. Furthermore, the Great Pyramid's dimensions correspond remarkably closely to the curvature of the Earth itself, as if the builders had mapped the globe and encoded this knowledge into their structure.[dcccxci] Studies have found that the pyramid's base perimeter and height relate to Earth's dimensions, suggesting an advanced understanding of geometry and the planet's size. The pyramid's base was typically a perfect square, each side measured with extreme precision.[dcccxcii] Egyptian architects likely would have used ropes and wooden pegs, employing a method known as "stretching the cord," which allowed them to map out right angles and straight lines across vast areas.

They were likely familiar with the Pythagorean theorem—centuries before Pythagoras—which allowed them to ensure accuracy in creating perpendicular lines. The theorem is named after the ancient Greek mathematician Pythagoras (570-495 BC). He is credited with formalising the theorem and introducing it into the Western mathematical tradition. The Pythagorean Theorem is a fundamental principle in geometry that establishes a relationship between the sides of a right-angled triangle. It states that, in any right-angled triangle (a triangle with one angle of 90 degrees), the square of the length of the hypotenuse (the side opposite the right angle) is equal to the sum of the squares of the lengths of the other two sides. Builders use the Pythagorean Theorem to ensure that angles are square and that buildings have precise right angles. By applying this knowledge, they could guarantee that the pyramid's base aligned perfectly with the cardinal directions—north, south, east, and west—critical for religious symbolism and the pyramid's relationship to the stars.[dcccxciii]

Although not explicitly recorded, the golden ratio (1.618:1) and pi are believed to be reflected in the design of some pyramids.[dcccxciv] The architect may have applied this ratio to the height of the pyramid in relation to its base. The height of the Great Pyramid (146.6 meters when it was built) and the length of its base (230.4 meters) are often discussed in the context of the Golden Ratio. The ratio of half the base to the height is approximately 1.618, which is the Golden Ratio. Architects would have also used geometry to calculate the angle, creating the smooth, precise slope of the pyramid, ensuring it was consistent on all sides. For instance, the slope of the Great Pyramid of Giza is approximately 51.5 degrees.

Inside the pyramid, geometry also dictated the construction of chambers and passageways. These spaces were constructed with precise proportions, utilising rectangles and squares derived from fundamental geometric principles to ensure structural integrity and alignment with cosmic energies. The internal layout was meticulously planned, with the chambers often aligned with specific stars or celestial points.

Some argue that ancient Egyptians may have intuitively applied ratios close to the golden ratio to create structures that appeared harmonious and balanced to the human eye. This would have aligned with their desire to build monuments that reflected order and cosmic balance, key elements in their worldview. In ancient Egyptian culture, the concept of *ma'at,* which means balance, truth, and order, was deeply significant. The use of the Golden Ratio may have been a way to represent this balance and harmony in their architecture. Using naturally pleasing proportions, the Egyptians reflected their cosmology and philosophy in their built environment.

There is substantial written evidence that ancient Egyptians were skilled mathematicians, using their mathematical knowledge in various aspects of their culture. For example, the *Rhind Mathematical Papyrus* (circa 1550 BC) is one of the most comprehensive sources of ancient Egyptian mathematics. It contains a variety of mathematical problems and solutions, showing their expertise in arithmetic, geometry, and algebra. The papyrus includes problems involving calculating the area of fields, volumes of granaries, and the surface area of different shapes. They clearly understood area and volume calculations, especially for more complex shapes, such as truncated pyramids.

The *Moscow Mathematical Papyrus* (circa 1850 BCE) is another crucial text that showcases the ancient Egyptians' advanced mathematical knowledge. This papyrus contains various geometry problems, including one that calculates the volume of a truncated pyramid, highlighting their sophisticated understanding of spatial dimensions and proportions. The document also provides examples of arithmetic operations, such as multiplication and division, as well as solving linear equations, further demonstrating their practical mathematics skills. These mathematical concepts could have been applied in architecture, engineering, and surveying, illustrating how Egyptian mathematicians integrated theory into everyday practice. The papyrus shows their ability to work with complex geometric shapes and equations long before similar developments in Greek mathematics, emphasising the sophistication of Egyptian mathematical traditions.

dcccxcv

The ancient Egyptians' mathematical abilities extended far beyond the construction of the pyramids. Their achievements in architecture, astronomy, engineering, surveying, commerce, and other fields demonstrate that they were masterful mathematicians, proving their understanding of scale, symmetry, and balance. Their knowledge of geometry, algebra, and arithmetic enabled them to construct some of the most enduring monuments in human history, while also managing the practical challenges of daily life.

Egyptian temples, such as the Temple of Luxor and the Temple of Karnak, are said to reflect proportional relationships that align with the Golden Ratio. These ratios are evident in the layout of columns, doorways, and the spacing between structural elements. The creation of obelisks, often exceeding 20 meters in height and weighing hundreds of tons, required precision in design, carving, and erection. Another example is the Fayum Basin, one of ancient Egypt's most ambitious hydraulic engineering projects. This project involved diverting water from the Nile to create a massive irrigation system, which required complex calculations related to water flow, angles, and gradients. Egypt's ability to build dams, canals, and other water management systems demonstrates its understanding of hydrology and applied geometry.

While ancient Egyptian hieroglyphs and reliefs may not specifically reference the construction of the pyramids, they provide evidence that mathematics played a critical role in their architectural practices.

In locations such as the Tomb of Meketre and the Temple of Karnak, depictions of workers using tools like cubit rods and cords reveal a sophisticated system for measuring and calculating proportions, which is fundamental for constructing large-scale structures. These hieroglyphs depict craftsmen and architects using standard units of measure, such as the cubit, to ensure precision in building temples, tombs, and other monumental projects.[dcccxcvi] The fact that these measurement tools and methods are consistently depicted in various contexts suggests that mathematics was an integral part of their construction techniques. By demonstrating their advanced knowledge of geometry and arithmetic, these inscriptions indirectly support the notion that the Egyptians possessed the skills necessary for the precise architectural planning required for pyramid building. This evidence shows that although the inscriptions do not explicitly reference the pyramids, they highlight a well-established tradition of mathematical application in construction, which would have been essential for such massive and complex projects.

Some scholars suggest that the Egyptians might not have explicitly understood the mathematical concept of the Golden Ratio but relied on intuitive methods based on observation and practical experience. By studying the natural world and using trial and error in their construction techniques, they could have discovered proportions that naturally corresponded to the Golden Ratio without formalising it mathematically.

Fractals and the Pyramid Code

The Mandelbrot set, named after mathematician Benoît Mandelbrot, who introduced it in his 1982 book *The Fractal Geometry of Nature*, is a complex geometric pattern that reveals infinite layers of self-similarity, order, and recursive structure. Though born from mathematics, it has become a powerful metaphor across scientific, esoteric, and metaphysical disciplines for understanding the hidden architecture of reality. Beneath what appears to be randomness lies a deeper order, governed by patterns that repeat across time, scale, and dimension.[dcccxcvii]

In the context of pyramid theory, some researchers propose that ancient builders may have intuitively grasped or deliberately encoded similar fractal principles into their architectural blueprints, not explicitly in equations, but through sacred proportions, modular repetition, and harmonic scaling. The pyramid form itself, with its layered tiers, geometric precision, and alignment with planetary and celestial harmonics, may be seen as a physical embodiment of fractal logic, anchoring energy across scales from Earth to cosmos.

Like fractals, pyramids may serve as antennae of order, bridging the finite and the infinite, the terrestrial and the stellar. Suppose consciousness, energy, or even intention behave fractally, as some quantum theorists and consciousness researchers suggest. In that case, the pyramid might act not merely as a symbol of stability, but as a resonant interface for interacting with universal energy fields in a recursive, scale-independent way. The shape may function as a fractal attractor, focusing not only electromagnetic force but possibly thought itself.

Alignment with the Stars, no Coincidence

Many researchers have asked why many pyramids align with stars or significant geographical features. They conclude that the builders of the pyramids seem to have deeply understood the cosmos.[dcccxcviii] Mainstream archaeologists argue that some of these alignments could be coincidental. For instance, statistical studies have shown that not all pyramids are aligned with astronomical objects as precisely as often claimed.[dcccxcix]

In recent years, archaeoastronomy has made significant strides in understanding the relationship between ancient pyramids and celestial bodies. Scholars have continued to explore how structures like the Great Pyramid of Giza and the pyramids of Mesoamerica are precisely aligned with key astronomical events, such as the solstices and star constellations.

Anthony Aveni, a well-known scholar in archaeoastronomy, has researched the alignment of ancient structures with celestial bodies, particularly in Mesoamerica. In his 2020 study titled "*The Measure of the Cosmos: The Archaeoastronomy of Mesoamerican Civilizations*," Aveni explored how structures such as Mayan and Aztec pyramids were precisely aligned with solstices, equinoxes and key star constellations. He concluded that these alignments were deliberate and served ritualistic and calendrical purposes. Aveni demonstrated that ancient Mesoamerican civilisations used their knowledge of the stars to organise agricultural cycles, religious festivals, and political events, suggesting that their understanding of the cosmos was deeply integrated into everyday life. He also noted that, although not all structures align perfectly with astronomical bodies, the overall patterns reveal a sophisticated understanding of celestial mechanics that rivals that of other ancient cultures, such as the Egyptians.[cm] This ongoing research offers exciting insights into how the ancients integrated cosmic phenomena into their architectural and spiritual practices.[cmi]

Using modern tools like satellite imagery and computer simulations, researchers have confirmed that these structures were deliberately positioned to reflect celestial movements. This further supports the idea that the builders had advanced astronomical knowledge. Ancient Egyptians profoundly understood the cosmos.

Their ability to align monuments with celestial bodies, track the solar and lunar cycles, and incorporate cosmic symbolism into their religious beliefs highlights a sophisticated knowledge of astronomy.[cmii]

Whether in their temples, tombs, calendars, or religious festivals, the Egyptians demonstrated a remarkable capacity to connect the heavens with life on Earth.

For example, the axis of the Karnak Temple is aligned with the rising sun at the summer solstice. On this day, the sun rises directly between the temple's pylons, illuminating the inner sanctuary. This alignment shows that the Egyptians understood the solar cycle and its connection to the agricultural calendar.[cmiii]

In temples like Dendera and tombs like those in the Valley of the Kings, we find further evidence of Egyptian astronomical knowledge. These ceilings often depict constellations, star patterns, and planetary cycles. The Dendera Zodiac, for example, illustrates the Egyptians' detailed understanding of the night sky and their ability to track the movements of celestial bodies. They had star clocks and used the heliacal rising of Sirius (Sopdet) to mark the start of their new year, indicating their proficiency in observing and documenting astronomical cycles. [cmiv] Hieroglyphic inscriptions frequently depict tools like the merchet, a sighting instrument used to observe stars, and the cord for surveying land and laying out architectural plans. These tools suggest that the Egyptians developed sophisticated methods for measurement and observation, which were crucial for their architectural and astronomical achievements. [cmv]

Other recent archaeological studies have uncovered evidence suggesting that ancient civilisations possessed more advanced technologies than previously believed. For instance, the Antikythera Mechanism, an ancient Greek analogue computer discovered in the early 20th century, demonstrates the Greeks' profound understanding of mechanical engineering. The device, dating back to around 150-100 BCE, was used to predict astronomical positions and eclipses with remarkable precision.[cmvi] This discovery offers a tangible parallel to the possibility that ancient Egyptians may have possessed similar, if not more advanced, knowledge of geometry, astronomy, and mechanics, which could have been applied to pyramid construction and energy manipulation.[cmvii]

Why did they align the Pyramids with the Cosmos?

The Great Pyramid's alignment with Orion's stars was likely no coincidence. If it was not a coincidence, what was the purpose of the alignment with the stars? Some attribute the precise alignment of pyramids with celestial bodies, such as Orion's Belt, to religious or symbolic purposes. Scholars argue that the alignment reflects the Egyptians' religious emphasis on the afterlife and their desire to align with the gods, particularly Osiris.[cmviii] This suggests that their knowledge of astronomy was intricately tied to their spiritual beliefs. They believed that the pharaoh's soul would ascend to Orion after death.[cmix] The alignment of specific structures, such as the Great Pyramid, may have been oriented toward Orion, reflecting their cosmological beliefs about the soul's journey and its connection to the stars. In Egyptian religion, the sky was personified as the goddess Nut, who would swallow the sun each evening and give birth to it every morning. The stars were believed to be the souls of the dead. This cosmic symbolism, evident throughout Egyptian culture, influenced the design of temples, tombs, and the alignment of buildings.

Could their understanding of the cosmos be more than spiritual—could it be deeply scientific, reflecting a detailed awareness of celestial mechanics?[cmx] R.J.C. Atkinson's studies on Stonehenge, particularly in his work *Stonehenge and its Megalithic Structures* (1956), provided groundbreaking insights into the deliberate alignment of this iconic monument with key solar and lunar events.[cmxi] His research demonstrated that the builders of Stonehenge possessed advanced astronomical knowledge, using the monument not just for ritualistic purposes but also as a celestial calendar. This same emphasis on celestial alignment is also evident in other ancient structures, such as the pyramids of Egypt.[cmxii] His work strengthens the argument that ancient cultures, including the Egyptians, might have designed their monuments with a sophisticated understanding of celestial movements. This connection between Stonehenge and the pyramids supports the theory that these structures were not merely architectural achievements but tools for understanding and actively interacting with the universe.[cmxiii]

However, studies by astronomers like Ed Krupp and Egyptologist Mark Lehner dispute this, suggesting that the astronomical knowledge of the Egyptians was advanced for their time but rooted in spiritual, rather than scientific, pursuits related to energy. Edwin Krupp's *Echoes of the Ancient Skies: The Astronomy of Lost Civilizations* (1983) discusses how ancient civilisations, including the Egyptians, used the stars for ritualistic and symbolic purposes rather than technological or energy-focused applications. Similarly, Mark Lehner emphasises in *The Complete Pyramids: Solving the Ancient Mysteries* (1997) the spiritual and religious motivations behind the pyramids' celestial alignments, particularly their connection to Orion and Osiris in the Egyptian belief system.

These academics do not dispute the alignments, but rather the purpose for which the pyramids were aligned with the stars.

More speculative theories combine the idea that ley lines, as energetic pathways on Earth, were interconnected with celestial patterns, forming a link between the Earth and the cosmos. They argue that the pyramids were aligned with the stars and the Earth's energetic fields. However, no scientific evidence substantiates a direct connection between ley lines and the stars.

Theory versus Practice

While it is possible that the ancient Egyptians possessed advanced knowledge in mathematics and astronomy, this does not necessarily prove that they built the pyramids. Theory and practice are different matters. Theoretical knowledge does not guarantee the capacity to apply it on a massive scale.

Critics, like Graham Hancock in *Fingerprints of the Gods* (1995), point out that even with advanced theoretical understanding, the tools and technology available at the time would not have been sufficient for the level of precision seen in the pyramids.[cmxiv] The absence of written records detailing the construction methods and mathematical calculations further complicates attributing the pyramids to the Egyptians alone, as Robert Bauval and Adrian Gilbert noted in *The Orion Mystery: Unlocking the Secrets of the Pyramids* (1994).[cmxv]

The sheer scale and precision of the pyramids, particularly the Great Pyramid of Giza, are extraordinary even by today's standards. The alignment with the cardinal points, the near-perfect squareness of the base, and the massive size of individual stones—some weighing as much as 80 tons—raise questions about how this could have been accomplished without modern technology. In The Giza Power Plant: Technologies of Ancient Egypt (1998), Christopher Dunn argues that even with advanced mathematical and astronomical knowledge, it is challenging to envision how these elements were practically applied with such precision on such a monumental scale using only the tools available at that time.[cmxvi]

This continues to fuel the debate about whether another group, possibly with superior technology, could have played a role in the construction of the pyramids. Erich von Däniken, in *Chariots of the Gods* (1968), suggests that an advanced civilisation or extraterrestrial beings might have contributed to the construction of the pyramids, providing technological assistance beyond what was available to the ancient Egyptians.[cmxvii]

Lost Knowledge

The mystery remains alive because of the pyramid's precise geometry, alignment with celestial bodies, and potential energetic properties. In the next chapter, we will explore how the location and placement choices were not coincidental but deliberate to tap into Earth's energy and the cosmos.

Researchers such as Robert Bauval in The Orion Mystery (1994) and Christopher Dunn in The Giza Power Plant (1998) have suggested that ancient cultures may have possessed an advanced understanding of the Earth's energy fields and the cosmos, which modern science is only beginning to explore.

Could the ancient builders, as suggested by Graham Hancock in *Fingerprints of the Gods* (1995), have deliberately placed these pyramids on powerful energy hotspots across the globe?[cmxviii] Could their location hold the key to a lost understanding of the Earth's energies? Did the pyramid's builders, as authors like John Michell in *The View Over Atlantis* (1969) propose, purposefully encode advanced geometric and astronomical knowledge into their construction?[cmxix]

Perhaps the pyramids, particularly the Great Pyramid of Giza, were used as a research centre or an ancient scientific or technological hub. In her research on energy fields, I*nfinite Mind: Science of the Human Vibrations of Consciousness* (1995), Dr Valerie Hunt suggests that the pyramids may have served as knowledge repositories, particularly their inscriptions and mathematical alignments.[cmxx] Some researchers, like Joseph Davidovits in *Why the Pharaohs Built the Pyramids with Fake Stones* (2009), propose that they could have been designed as laboratories or research facilities for studying astronomical phenomena, earth energy, or even sound and vibration.[cmxxi] Could it have been a university for multiple disciplines, or is the point that the Egyptians integrated all disciplines into their thinking as opposed to the siloed research in today's world?

Could the mathematical precision have been part of an effort to experiment with energy fields and cosmic alignments? Could the pyramid have been used as an energy research centre? This could have involved studying and harnessing natural forces, such as geomagnetic energy or sound waves.

Energy fields are around us, permeating every layer of our existence, from the ground beneath our feet to the heavens above. These interconnected fields of energy form a vast, invisible web that connects the Earth to the universe, creating a continuous exchange of forces that impact all living things.

We will investigate in detail why specific geographical hot spots may have been chosen for pyramid construction. Authors like Alfred Watkins in *The Old Straight Track* (1925) suggest that the pyramids were positioned along ley lines deliberately to tap into the Earth's hidden forces.[cmxxii] The pyramids' alignment with ley lines may have concentrated the planet's natural energies, making these structures amplifiers of the Earth's vibrational frequencies. Could these energy centres have powered advanced technologies, influenced consciousness, or controlled the weather? What if our modern technology, far from being an innovation, is merely a rediscovery of what ancient civilisations once knew?

Ancient cultures may have possessed a deeper understanding of the Earth's energy fields and the universe that modern science is only beginning to explore, leaving the pyramids as architectural marvels and enigmatic symbols of lost knowledge. What secrets might still lie within their walls, waiting for the day we can fully understand the forces they were designed to harness?

Chapter 11 Pyramids Geographical Hot Spots

Location, Location, Location

Why were specific locations chosen for the construction of the pyramids? Could the locations be more than a coincidence?

Pyramids were built on elevated ground or in locations that made them highly visible from great distances, underscoring their role as symbols of power, religion, and authority. They often served as focal points for the surrounding region. Many pyramids were also built in locations with access to nearby quarries. The massive structures required large amounts of stone. Another typical pattern is the proximity to trade routes, which allowed these civilisations to access the necessary resources for pyramid construction: stone, food, and labour.

Pyramids were also often built near water sources, such as lakes, seas, and cenotes (natural sinkholes). Water was crucial for the logistics of construction and its symbolic connection to life, death, and fertility. However, proximity to rivers was not universally required for the construction of pyramids. Some pyramids were constructed in more arid or inland regions. Of course, rivers may have migrated or disappeared.

The pyramids appear to be strategically located in regions that some believe hold concentrated natural energy. Could ancient builders have deliberately chosen these sites, tapping into the Earth's unseen forces? Did the ancients possess knowledge about the Earth's energy that we have since forgotten? This chapter explores the theory that pyramid sites were not randomly chosen but strategically placed at geographical energy hotspots, where the Earth's magnetic and electromagnetic forces are concentrated. It extends the theory to cosmic ley lines. Through case studies, we will investigate how the location of pyramids may hold the key to a forgotten understanding of the Earth's energy sources. We will explore the possibility that they are positioned at geographical energy hotspots to connect the planet's natural energy grid. [cmxxiii]

One of the most astonishing facts about the Great Pyramid of Giza is that it is located near the geographical centre of the Earth's landmass, meaning that the lines of latitude and longitude passing through the pyramid divide the Earth's land equally into four quarters. This remarkable position has puzzled researchers for centuries. The ancient Egyptians, who built the pyramid around 2,500 BCE, had no known knowledge of the entire geography of the world. They lacked modern tools such as maps, satellite imagery, or global positioning systems. Yet, somehow, they managed to place this monumental structure in a location of global significance. The coincidence—or perhaps intentional design—has led to various theories about how the Egyptians might have achieved such precision. Some speculate that they had access to knowledge lost to history. This mystery adds to the fascination surrounding the pyramids and raises questions about the sophistication of ancient civilisations in understanding Earth's geography. cmxxiv

Choosing Elevated Ground

Pyramids were often constructed on elevated ground or in prominent locations, a practical and symbolic choice. By positioning pyramids on high ground, ancient builders maximised their visibility, ensuring they could be seen from great distances. This was crucial for establishing the pyramids as central, powerful symbols of authority and influence, dominating the landscape and visually reinforcing the presence of the ruling elite, religious leaders, or deities. The elevation allowed the pyramids to serve as focal points, giving them an imposing and monumental presence that reminded people of the power and reach of those who built them.

The choice of elevated locations may also have been influenced by religious and spiritual beliefs. For many ancient cultures, high places were considered closer to the divine. Elevating the pyramids might have been a way to symbolically bridge the gap between the earth and the heavens, making these structures sacred spaces where the spiritual and physical worlds could connect. By placing pyramids on elevated terrain, builders may have aimed to create a physical representation of ascent and transcendence, aligning their societies with the cosmos and the divine order they believed governed it.

In practical terms, constructing pyramids on high ground protected them from environmental threats, such as flooding. For civilisations like the Egyptians, who built near the Nile River, this would have been a strategic decision to safeguard these monumental structures from seasonal inundations. Similarly, in Mesoamerica, the elevated placement of pyramids helped them remain prominent and unimpeded by surrounding settlements or agricultural activity, ensuring they remained visible and central to civic and religious life.

Moreover, the desire for a strategic vantage point might have influenced the decision to build on elevated terrain. Ancient cultures could establish a dominant, watchful presence over their territories by placing pyramids on hills or plateaus, further reinforcing their role as centres of power, surveillance, and control. The elevation allowed these structures to act as spiritual and societal beacons, symbolising the reach and omnipresence of the civilisation's leaders or deities and ensuring their influence extended far and wide.

Access to Quarries

The materials used to construct the pyramids may have been a decisive factor in their location, given their potential to interact with the Earth's energy fields. The choice of building materials—primarily limestone and granite—appears strategic, as these materials are known for their conductive and energy-amplifying properties. Using these stones, the ancient builders could have enhanced the energy flow, amplifying any natural electromagnetic forces in the area. The proximity of quarries near the construction sites would have been essential to ensure the availability of these specific materials. The limestone's crystalline structure allows it to transmit and store energy, much like the conductors in modern electrical circuits.

The proximity of quarries to pyramid sites wasn't unique to Egypt. Pyramids worldwide were built near sources of suitable building materials. For example, the pyramids of Teotihuacan in Mexico were constructed using locally available volcanic rock, such as basalt and tezontle. These materials, sourced from nearby quarries, were used extensively in the pyramid's structure, allowing the builders to optimise the construction process and minimise the need for long-distance transport. Similarly, in Sudan, the pyramids at Meroë were constructed using sandstone from quarries located near the construction sites. Using locally sourced materials reduced logistical challenges. This suggests that ancient civilisations strategically positioned these monumental structures to exploit the natural resources available.

The fact that pyramids worldwide are located near quarries indicates a deliberate and practical approach to construction, possibly combined with an understanding of the energetic or symbolic significance of the materials themselves. Whether these civilisations fully understood the conductive or energetic properties of the stones they used remains speculative. However, the consistency in choosing locations with abundant building resources suggests a shared architectural strategy among ancient cultures. This widespread practice points to a blend of practicality and intentionality, where proximity to quarries ensured both efficiency in construction and perhaps alignment with natural or spiritual energies associated with these materials.

Water Supply

Could water, the fundamental essence of life, have been a crucial factor in the pyramids' design and placement? Throughout history, ancient civilisations have revered water for its life-giving properties and mysterious ability to flow, change forms, and carry energy. From the Nile River, which sustained Egyptian civilisation, to the sacred cenotes of the Maya, water was often viewed as a sacred force that bridged the realms of the living and the divine.

But what if water had a more practical role? Some researchers propose that the Great Pyramid of Giza and other ancient pyramids were strategically built above underground water sources. This theory suggests that water movement beneath the pyramids could have generated electromagnetic energy, which was then harnessed by the structures above. This concept is based on the principles of hydroelectricity, where flowing water generates an electric current through the movement of charged particles. If the pyramids were indeed built above aquifers or underground rivers, the constant flow beneath them could have created natural electromagnetic fields. Amplified by the pyramid's shape and the conductive materials used in its construction, these fields might have powered unknown spiritual, technological, or both functions.

Recent discoveries at the Giza plateau add support to this theory. Geologists have discovered evidence of an extensive underground water system beneath the Great Pyramid, comprising extensive limestone aquifers. Some researchers suggest this water was intentionally directed beneath the pyramid to create a natural energy generator. According to this hypothesis, the movement of water through the limestone could have produced a piezoelectric effect, where certain materials generate an electric charge when subjected to mechanical stress.

This raises an intriguing possibility: Were the ancient Egyptians aware of these energy-generating properties of water and limestone? And if so, how might they have used this energy? The idea that water flowing beneath the pyramid could have generated electromagnetic fields offers a new perspective on these ancient structures. Could the pyramids have served as ancient power plants, harnessing the Earth's natural energy?

Plugging into the Earth's Energy Grid

To understand why specific pyramid sites may have been chosen, we must also explore the idea that they may have been plugging into the Earth's energy grid.[cmxxv]

The concept of the Earth's energy grid suggests that invisible lines, known as ley or geomagnetic lines, crisscross the planet, carrying natural energy. [cmxxvi] These lines intersect at critical points, creating energy hotspots. More than a dozen ancient monuments, including pyramids, appear to be aligned with these intersections, leading some to believe that their builders intentionally tapped into the Earth's energy fields.

The idea of ley lines was popularised in the early 20th century by British researcher Alfred Watkins, who noticed that many ancient monuments and sacred sites across Britain aligned in straight lines.[cmxxvii] In his early 20th-century book The Old Straight Track (1925), Alfred Watkins introduced the idea that ancient sites, including pyramids, were built along ley lines, pathways of spiritual or earth energies. Over time, this concept was expanded to suggest that similar alignments exist globally, linking some of the world's most ancient and enigmatic structures, including the pyramids.[cmxxviii] Modern research into the geomagnetic properties of pyramids, such as the work of engineer Christopher Dunn in *The Giza Power Plant* (1998), suggests that geomagnetic forces may have influenced their placement. However, no consensus has been reached in the scientific community. While the ley line theory remains speculation, it has captured the imagination of many who believe that ancient civilisations knew of the Earth's energy grid and intentionally built their most important structures—pyramids—at these powerful points.[cmxxix] According to this theory, pyramid builders may have harnessed the natural energy flowing through these hotspots to enhance the spiritual, practical, or technological functions of their monuments. Across Europe, ley lines are believed to pass through notable historical, religious, and natural sites, with some claiming this is evidence that they serve as powerful conduits of the Earth's energy.

Mainstream scientists say there is no scientific evidence to support the existence of ley lines as literal energy pathways. However, modern geographic and cartographic techniques reveal that many ancient sites align, although some argue that this may be coincidental or due to geographic factors such as ease of construction or astronomical alignments. Is there any scientific basis for this idea? Can energy hotspots be identified through geological and magnetic studies? Some researchers believe so.

Evidence of cultures seeking to understand and harmonise with Earth's energy flows can be found globally, particularly in China, India, and the Middle East. Practices like Feng Shui reflect this knowledge, where the orientation of buildings, cities, and even graves is believed to balance the flow of *Qi* (energy). Similarly, civilisations like the Egyptians, Mayans, and other pyramid-building cultures may have aligned their structures with magnetic north, celestial bodies, or geologically significant locations, indicating their awareness of geomagnetic properties.

Geomagnetic Fields

Geomagnetic fields refer to the magnetic field generated by the Earth's core, which extends from the Earth's interior out into space. This field is responsible for phenomena like the auroras and is crucial to how the Earth interacts with solar winds. Geomagnetic anomalies are areas where the Earth's magnetic field behaves differently, often due to underlying geology or tectonic activity. Studies of the Earth's geomagnetic field have revealed areas where magnetic anomalies—regions with unusually strong or weak magnetic fields—occur. These anomalies often coincide with regions of volcanic activity, tectonic fault lines, or other geological features, suggesting that the Earth's natural energy is concentrated in specific areas.[cmxxx]

Pyramids, including those in Egypt and Mesoamerica, are often located on these geomagnetic and tectonic hotspots. These areas, where Earth's magnetic field exhibits unusual behaviour, suggest that the builders may have understood or even harnessed natural energy flows. In his work, *Earth Lights Revelation* (1989), scientist and historian Paul Devereux explores the relationship between megalithic sites and geomagnetic anomalies.[cmxxxi] He argues that ancient cultures might have been aware of these energy fields and deliberately constructed monumental structures to interact with them. His research indicates a possible connection between ancient architecture and natural energy pathways, implying that some megalithic sites could have been chosen for their energetic properties rather than purely religious or geographical reasons.[cmxxxii]

In 2022, a study published in *Nature Communications* found correlations between the location of ancient structures and natural energy hotspots, reinforcing the idea that ancient peoples may have intentionally constructed their pyramids and temples to tap into the Earth's natural energy.[cmxxxiii] Recent advancements in mapping geomagnetic anomalies, such as those conducted by the National Geophysical Data Center in the early 2000s, provide scientific evidence that certain regions—especially those with large-scale ancient constructions—show unusual geomagnetic activity. These studies have used modern technology to create detailed magnetic anomaly maps, revealing that ancient monuments may align with or be located near areas of significant geomagnetic variation.[cmxxxiv] This growing body of data supports theories that ancient civilisations were aware of the

Earth's magnetic properties, possibly influencing the placement of structures like pyramids.

Since volcanic areas are highly fertile, these regions would have been prime locations for settlement. Volcanic soils, known as Andisols, are among the most fertile soils in the world due to their high nutrient content, including phosphorus, potassium, and trace minerals essential for plant growth. Studies show that volcanic ash deposits, after weathering, contribute to vibrant soils that support dense agriculture. The abundance of nutrients in volcanic soil would have supported agriculture and larger populations, allowing for the development of more complex societies capable of constructing monumental structures like pyramids, temples, and other significant architectural works. A study published in *Earth Surface Processes and Landforms* (2018) by C. Torrence focused on the hydrological benefits of volcanic regions, showing how communities benefit from the abundant water resources, making the areas even more attractive for settlements.[cmxxxv] Volcanic regions often have rich deposits of minerals, stones, and other materials that could be used in construction.

For example, Mexico's Teotihuacan and El Tajín pyramids were constructed near volcanic zones, where the fertile valleys supported large agricultural populations. This agricultural abundance likely contributed to the manpower and resources needed to create such impressive structures. Similarly, the Inca Empire thrived in volcanic regions, with cities like Machu Picchu strategically located near fertile land and geomagnetic hotspots. This provided a stable agricultural base and spiritual significance to the placement of their sacred structures. Even in Italy, the region around Mount Vesuvius, particularly Pompeii, demonstrated how people were willing to settle near a dangerous volcano due to its fertile soil and spiritual and economic importance. Despite the ever-present risk of eruption, grand structures were built, highlighting the balance between opportunity and risk in these volcanic landscapes. This is confirmed in research published in *Natural Hazards* (2016) by L. Gaillard, which discusses the sociocultural aspects of living near volcanic areas. The study shows that historical and modern communities assess risk from volcanic activity but prioritise the economic benefits derived from the rich soil.[cmxxxvi]

Earthquakes, volcanic eruptions, and other natural disasters always carry the risk of partially or entirely burying structures. Earthquakes, in particular, can cause landslides or ground shifts, resulting in buildings being covered by debris or earth. Similar to those seen in Pompeii with Mount Vesuvius, volcanic eruptions can bury entire cities under a layer of ash and pyroclastic material.

Cosmic Ley Lines

Lines on the Earth reflect lines in the mind. Reconnect one, and you influence the other.

Could the ley lines extend beyond Earth and into the cosmos? This theory, sometimes referred to as "cosmic ley lines" or "celestial energy grids," suggests that the Earth's energy grid is not an isolated phenomenon but rather part of a more extensive, interconnected network that spans the universe.

Many ancient monuments align with other terrestrial structures and celestial bodies such as stars, planets, and constellations. For example, the Great Pyramid of Giza is aligned with Orion's Belt, and other sites, such as Stonehenge, align with solstices or specific lunar and solar events. This suggests that ancient civilisations may have understood the Earth's energy grid as part of a broader cosmic order, where certain locations on Earth resonate with specific celestial phenomena.[cmxxxvii] The *Pyramids* episode from the *"The Universe"* series aired in 2007. It explores theories about how the Great Pyramid and other ancient structures might be connected to a cosmic energy grid. *Ancient Aliens*, which premiered in 2009, explores similar ideas, including the alignment of monuments like Stonehenge and the pyramids with celestial bodies, suggesting that they were built to tap into cosmic and Earth energies.

Some researchers propose that the Earth is a node in a much larger cosmic grid, with ley lines serving as energetic pathways that connect it to other planets, stars, and galaxies. In this view, the planet's ley lines are extensions or reflections of a cosmic energy network that permeates the universe. Ancient structures built on ley lines could have been attempting to tap into this larger cosmic energy, functioning as nodes or antennas to connect with the cosmos. Consider planetary and stellar ley lines, as well as celestial bodies like the moon, planets, and distant stars, which are connected through energetic pathways similar to those theorised on Earth. For instance, the positions of the planets to Earth could create energetic alignments or resonances that influence ley lines. Ancient civilisations, aware of these patterns, may have aligned their monuments with the terrestrial ley lines and these cosmic alignments to harness energy or communicate with the cosmos.[cmxxxviii]

The Earth generates its electromagnetic field, as do other planets and stars. If ley lines are indeed channels for energy, they may resonate with electromagnetic waves from other cosmic sources, creating a connection between Earth's energy grid and the cosmos. Some researchers propose that aligning ancient structures with ley lines could enhance this resonance, effectively linking Earth's energy field with larger cosmic energies. Pyramids and other monuments might then act as amplifiers, resonating with cosmic frequencies and channelling energy from the universe.

The idea of cosmic ley lines also intersects with theories of ancient communication systems. If ley lines are part of a cosmic grid, then ancient monuments may have been built to function as communication hubs, transmitting information or energy between Earth and the stars. The alignment of these structures with specific constellations, such as Orion, could have been intended to create a resonance or connection with those celestial bodies, potentially allowing civilisations to interact with or receive cosmic energies.

The documentary *"Celestial Circuits: Exploring the Mysteries of Ley Line Energies"* suggests that ley lines may not be solely Earth-based, but rather part of a broader cosmic energy network connecting planets, stars, and ancient monuments. It speculates that these lines could have functioned as ancient communication channels between Earth and other celestial bodies, aligning with constellations like Orion's Belt to create energetic or technological connections.

Modern physics suggests that everything in the universe is interconnected through a unified field, an invisible web of energy that ties together all matter and space. The idea of ley lines extending into the cosmos fits within this framework, as the Earth's energy grid could be a tangible manifestation of this unified field, connecting points on Earth and across the universe. Ancient civilisations, who may have had a deeper understanding of this concept, might have used their monuments to tap into this unified field, aligning with terrestrial and cosmic ley lines to access or influence energy on a universal level.

Some theories propose that knowledge of cosmic ley lines may have been passed down from extraterrestrial visitors who understood the Earth as part of a larger energy grid system. According to these theories, ancient civilisations could have been guided to build their structures in alignment with Earth's and cosmic ley lines to access universal energy. Pyramids and temples are considered part of an ancient technology designed to harness cosmic forces, amplifying and directing them for spiritual or technological purposes.

We see many examples of interconnected thinking. Chinese geomancy (Feng Shui) speaks of "dragon lines," believed to be Earth's natural energy lines. These were thought to connect sacred sites, mountains, and bodies of water. In some interpretations, these lines are said to extend beyond the Earth, forming a network that aligns with the cosmos, particularly with key stars and celestial events. Similarly, the Native American medicine wheels, such as the Bighorn Medicine Wheel in Wyoming, align with the rising and setting of stars, including those in the constellation Orion. These wheels are thought to have served as terrestrial markers and tools for connecting with cosmic energies, implying an understanding that sacred geometry was not merely symbolic, but functional—serving as a bridge between Earth and sky, human and divine. This suggests that ancient cultures across continents shared a metaphysical framework: that the land itself was alive with patterns, and that by aligning their monuments, rituals, and lives to these energetic grids, they could harmonise with the larger intelligence of the cosmos.

The Great Pyramid of Giza and Earth's Magnetic Pulse

Specific studies of the Giza Plateau have revealed magnetic anomalies—regions where Earth's magnetic field deviates from the norm. These anomalies are commonly found near tectonic fault lines and other geological features, further supporting the idea that the area around the Great Pyramid is a natural energy hotspot.[cmxxxix] Some researchers believe the pyramid's precise positioning was intended to interact with Earth's geomagnetic field, potentially allowing the structure to concentrate or amplify natural energy. This theory, however, remains speculative as more empirical research is needed to substantiate the claim that ancient builders selected sites based on energetic properties.[cmxl]

The design of the Great Pyramid, in conjunction with its location at a geomagnetic hotspot, has sparked further speculation. Proponents of the energy theory argue that the pyramid's shape and construction materials—limestone and granite, both known for their conductive properties—were chosen to focus and amplify the Earth's natural energy. Granite, which contains significant amounts of quartz, exhibits piezoelectric properties, meaning it can generate electric charges in response to mechanical stress.[cmxli] This leads to the hypothesis that the pyramid, acting as a large-scale resonator or capacitor, might have been an ancient form of energy manipulation. While the conductive properties of granite and limestone are scientifically plausible, there is no historical evidence that the ancient Egyptians selected these materials for their energy-related qualities.[cmxlii] It is more likely that the materials were chosen for their durability and local availability. However, the possibility of a deeper understanding of these properties cannot be entirely ruled out. The Great Pyramid's precise alignment with the cardinal points—north, south, east, and west—also adds weight to the theory that its builders had advanced knowledge of Earth's magnetic forces. Some suggest that this alignment could have been used for spiritual, technological, or even practical purposes, such as energy harnessing.[cmxliii]

Although mainstream archaeologists remain sceptical of such theories, they continue to intrigue researchers who believe the pyramids might hold the key to understanding ancient energy technologies. Could the pyramid have been an ancient energy hub designed to channel Earth's natural forces for purposes we are only beginning to understand? The debate continues, but the theory of the pyramids as energy conductors remains a captivating possibility.[cmxliv]

Teotihuacan – The Pyramid of the Sun and Cosmic Energy

In the heart of Mexico, thousands of miles away, lies another great pyramid: the Pyramid of the Sun at Teotihuacan. This ancient city, once home to one of the most influential civilisations in Mesoamerica, is shrouded in mystery. Little is known about the people who built it, and even less about the purpose of its massive pyramids. But one thing is clear: Teotihuacan was built with an understanding of both the Earth and the cosmos.

Some researchers believe the Pyramid of the Sun, the largest structure in Teotihuacan, is aligned with cosmic forces. Its orientation is slightly offset from the cardinal directions, aligning instead with the point where the sun sets during the summer solstice.[cmxlv] This alignment suggests that the builders of Teotihuacan were attuned to the movements of the stars and the cycles of the sun and that the pyramid was designed to capture and channel solar energy.[cmxlvi]

But the Pyramid of the Sun may also be tapping into the Earth's natural energy. Beneath the pyramid, archaeologists have discovered a series of tunnels and chambers, some of which contain traces of mica, a mineral known for its insulating and conductive properties.[cmxlvii] Could these underground structures have been designed to harness geothermal or electromagnetic energy from the Earth? Some researchers believe so, suggesting that the Pyramid of the Sun may have been a spiritual or technological device to focus both solar and terrestrial energy.

Adding to the intrigue, Teotihuacan is situated along Mexico's volcanic axis, a region renowned for its geothermal activity.[cmxlviii] The pyramid's location at this volcanic hotspot may have been chosen for its energetic significance, further supporting the idea that the builders of Teotihuacan understood and sought to use the Earth's natural forces.

The Bosnian Pyramid: Ancient Power Station or Natural Wonder

One of the most controversial pyramid sites in the world is not found in Egypt or Mexico, but in Bosnia. The so-called Bosnian Pyramids near Visoko have sparked fierce debate among archaeologists and energy researchers. Discovered in 2005 by Bosnian researcher Semir Osmanagić, these pyramidal structures are claimed to be the oldest and largest pyramids in the world. His credentials in sociology and his studies on the Maya, rather than formal training in archaeology or geology, contribute to why many experts question his authority to make such bold claims about the pyramids.

Mainstream archaeologists remain highly sceptical of the Bosnian Pyramids[cmxlix], dismissing them as natural formations.[cml] Geologists and archaeologists from institutions such as the University of Tuzla and Boston University have revealed that the pyramids are naturally occurring hills composed of conglomerate, clay, and sandstone, similar to other regional formations.

In Robert Schoch's article *"The Bosnian Pyramids: Reality or Hoax?"* published in *Archaeology Magazine* in 2006, he concludes that the Bosnian Pyramid claims are unsubstantiated and largely unsupported by scientific evidence. Robert Schoch, a geologist, visited the site and found no convincing evidence that the formations in Visoko are man-made. Instead, he argues that the so-called pyramids are natural geological formations composed of sedimentary rock layers that have been shaped by erosion over time. He also criticises the methods used by Semir Osmanagić and his team, suggesting that their excavations are amateurish and could potentially damage genuine historical remains in the area. In summary, Robert Schoch and other experts maintain that the Bosnian Pyramid claims lack credible scientific backing, dismissing the structures as natural hills rather than ancient pyramids.[cmli]

As a result, researchers see little value in further high-tech investigation of what they consider to be naturally occurring landforms. [cmlii] Advanced technologies, such as ground-penetrating radar, LIDAR, and deep excavation, require substantial financial and logistical resources. Since most academic funding is allocated to sites with established historical significance or potential, the scientific community does not consider the Bosnian Pyramids a priority for funding.[cmliii]

Semir Osmanagić and his team argue that the site shows clear evidence of human construction.[cmliv] The alleged interaction of the Bosnian Pyramids with energy fields is particularly intriguing. According to Semir Osmanagić, measurements taken at the site have revealed electromagnetic and ultrasound phenomena, with energy beams emanating from the apex of the largest pyramid—the so-called Pyramid of the Sun—and reaching into the sky.[cmlv] Semir Osmanagić claims that these energy beams are evidence of an advanced ancient technology designed to harness and transmit energy.[cmlvi]

Whether or not this theory holds up to scientific scrutiny, the Bosnian Pyramids have become a focal point for those who believe that ancient civilisations deeply understood the Earth's energy fields and built monuments to tap into them.

The Knowledge of Ancient Builders

While ley lines remain primarily speculative, geomagnetic surveys provide a more scientifically grounded approach to understanding the locations of ancient monuments. A deeper investigation into magnetic field maps of pyramid locations around the globe could reveal whether these structures were deliberately built in energy-rich areas of the planet. Whether in Egypt, Mexico, or Bosnia, the pyramids appear to have been built where the Earth's natural forces are powerful—geomagnetic fields, volcanic activity, or cosmic alignments. Whether through geomagnetic fields or volcanic forces, the locations of these monuments appear deliberate, implying a lost knowledge of energy manipulation. As we continue to study these sites, we may discover a forgotten science bridging the gap between ancient wisdom and modern energy technologies, revolutionising how we understand the Earth and the pyramids. These pyramids' precise alignments, choice of materials, and geographical placements suggest that their builders were far more attuned to the Earth's energy than we often give them credit for.[cmlvii] While mainstream archaeology remains cautious in endorsing the energy hotspot theory, the possibility that the pyramids were built to interact with the Earth's energy fields invites us to reconsider what we know about the ancients.[cmlviii] Their monuments, far from relics of a bygone age, may hold secrets that could change how we understand energy, architecture, and our relationship with the planet.

The next chapter continues our journey into the pulsating energy beneath the surface. We will compare the power of pyramids to one of Earth's most formidable forces—volcanoes. Building on geographical positioning, mathematical precision, and alignment with the stars, we will draw parallels between pyramids and volcanoes to investigate whether these ancient structures were designed to harness Earth's energy in a similar manner.

Chapter 12 Volcanoes and Pyramids: A Comparison

The inspiration for this book came in a flash, quite literally, when I saw a photo of a volcano with lightning erupting from its peak. In that moment, I became convinced that the pyramids were modelled on volcanoes. I didn't even know lightning could rise from the Earth at the time. But that image stayed with me, and a question began to form: Could lightning have once shot out of the pyramids too? Perhaps the capstones were never there — maybe they were open, acting as vents to release energy like that volcano channelling lightning into the sky.

The root "pyr-" comes from the Greek word "pyr" (which means fire. The word pyramid could, therefore, mean *fire in the middle*. Some speculative etymologies suggest that "pyramid" might originally have symbolised a sacred flame or sunlight being focused upward — possibly referring to the shape pointing toward the sun (Ra, the Egyptian sun god), a spiritual or energetic centre inside the pyramid, or an eternal flame or source of power within the structure.

Harnessing Earth's Energy

Did the pyramids once harness the energy of the Earth, like silent volcanoes reaching toward the sky?

Volcanoes are among the most powerful and awe-inspiring phenomena on Earth. They are the planet's natural vents, releasing the heat and pressure that build up deep within its core.[cmlix] Volcanoes are natural geological structures that form when molten rock, ash, and gases are expelled from beneath the Earth's surface. They typically develop a conical shape, though their form varies depending on the type of volcano. *Shield volcanoes*, such as those in Hawaii, have broad, gently sloping sides due to the low viscosity of their lava, while *stratovolcanoes*, like Mount Fuji, have steeper cones formed by layers of lava, ash, and rock. Volcanic activity is often associated with tectonic plate boundaries and can produce violent eruptions and steady lava flows. Pyramids, by contrast, are monumental man-made structures with a square or triangular base and sloping sides that converge at a single point. They are constructed from stone or brick—the most famous example being the Great Pyramid of Giza, made of limestone and granite. The pyramids present a uniform appearance. Could these human-made structures serve as a replica of volcanoes, harnessing the

Earth's energy in a controlled manner? In the previous chapter, we learned that specific locations of pyramids may correlate with volcanic regions or areas of high tectonic activity. Were pyramids built to tap into Earth's "natural power zones"?

Tristan Gooley's *The Lost Art of Reading Nature's Signs* (2014) offers a wealth of insights into the deep connection between natural observations and human understanding, suggesting that our ancestors had an intimate relationship with the land and its signals. He is a respected author, navigator, and explorer who has written multiple best-selling books on understanding and using natural cues for orientation and survival. His exploration of how ancient and indigenous peoples read subtle environmental cues—like the behaviour of animals, shifts in weather patterns, and the movement of celestial bodies—supports theories that ancient builders may have incorporated these natural insights into their monumental designs.

For example, he highlights how shifts in animal behaviour can indicate impending natural phenomena such as volcanic eruptions or weather changes.[cmlx] This reinforces the idea that ancient civilisations may have viewed volcanoes as sacred or powerful energy sources. This perspective supports the theory that pyramids may have been deliberately aligned with natural forces and constructed to reflect and channel Earth's energies. The shape of pyramids, mirroring volcanic peaks, could symbolise humanity's reverence for the Earth's raw power, embodying both stability and energy. Ancient builders might have observed how animal migrations or seasonal changes aligned with volcanic activity. They harnessed that knowledge to time their construction efforts, alignments, and rituals to maximise their structures' energetic significance. Moreover, Tristan Gooley's emphasis on the instinctive connection to nature's signs suggests that early human societies intuitively understood geomagnetic and seismic energy.

His theory aligns with the idea that ancient civilisations placed their structures not only to honour celestial alignments but also to sit on powerful earth nodes, where natural energy was believed to be strongest. The pyramids' alignment with geological fault lines, energy grids, or volcanic areas could have been an intentional choice to harness the Earth's vibrational forces, much like how animals instinctively react to such energies for survival. Did the ancient world view the Earth as a living, energetic system, integrating these beliefs into the design and purpose of their structures?

Natural Eruptions vs. Man-Made Masterpieces

Although the idea of pyramids mimicking volcanoes is fascinating, their energy release mechanisms are fundamentally different.

Volcanoes erupt with a fury that can devastate landscapes and create new landforms while offering us a glimpse into the immense energy trapped within the Earth's core.[cmlxi] Volcanoes are conduits between the Earth's core and the surface, releasing massive amounts of geothermal energy during eruptions. In Earth's early history, volcanic activity was more frequent and intense when the core and mantle were significantly hotter. Over time, the planet has cooled, resulting in a reduction in overall volcanic activity. This cooling and reduction in activity is consistent with what we know about Earth's thermal history and the evolution of plate tectonics.

There are approximately 1,500 volcanoes worldwide, including those on the ocean floor. The most active volcanic regions are located along tectonic plate boundaries, such as the Pacific "Ring of Fire," which includes countries like Indonesia, Japan, the United States (Alaska), and Chile. On average, between 50 and 70 volcanoes erupt each year worldwide. We cannot control volcanoes. These eruptions can range from minor ash emissions to major explosive events. Some volcanic eruptions last just a few hours or days, while others persist for months or years.

In stark contrast, pyramids appear as stable, precise and predictable structures. Could they function like Earth's natural powerhouses, volcanoes?[cmlxii] Maybe they act as controlled conduits, channelling energy through their geometric design, placement, and the materials used in their construction. Could volcanoes' natural processes have inspired them to tap into Earth's energies?

The comparison between volcanoes and pyramids has sparked speculation about the pyramids' potential to harness geothermal or seismic energy. According to *Geothermal Energy: Renewable Energy and the Environment* by William Glassley (2010), volcanoes release vast amounts of geothermal energy.[cmlxiii] Some theorists suggest that the pyramid's material composition, including quartz and limestone, may have been intended to amplify the Earth's energy, similar to the volcanic processes that convert geothermal forces into surface energy.

Scientists are now exploring the potential of harnessing geothermal power from volcanoes as a clean and reliable energy source. Countries such as Iceland and New Zealand have used geothermal energy from volcanic regions for decades. Similarly, researchers in Canada are exploring dormant volcanoes, such as Mount Meager, as sources for geothermal energy production. These systems tap into the heat below the Earth's surface, converting steam into electricity by turning turbines. Though they unleash destructive forces, volcanoes are also the planet's natural way of expelling internal energy, creating islands, reshaping continents, and enriching the soil with nutrients, fostering the growth of lush ecosystems.[cmlxiv]

The Shared Power of Volcanoes and Pyramids

Volcanoes have always played a crucial role in developing human civilisations by destroying them and creating fertile lands, potentially influencing the architecture of the pyramids.

Volcanoes are not just geological phenomena; they are symbols of the Earth's ability to harness and release immense energy, to create and destroy in equal measure. For ancient civilisations that lived in the shadow of these giants, volcanoes were often regarded as sacred, feared and revered in equal measure.[cmlxv]

Studies of geothermal energy extraction, particularly in volcanic regions such as Iceland and Hawaii, reveal how the immense heat generated by volcanic activity can be converted into usable energy.[cmlxvi] Geothermal plants today capture this heat to produce electricity, offering a modern parallel to ancient structures that may have sought to harness similar energy sources. Researchers studying the electromagnetic fields around active volcanoes have found that these natural formations can generate significant electrical charge, particularly during eruptions.[cmlxvii] This electromagnetic activity offers intriguing possibilities for understanding how ancient civilisations, particularly those living near volcanic regions, might have recognised and sought to use these natural forces, much like the speculative theories surrounding pyramids designed to capture or direct Earth's energy.

Could the ancients have seen a model for how energy could be concentrated and released? Brown (2019) further explores the electromagnetic phenomena associated with volcanic eruptions in *Harnessing Earth's Heat: A Geological Exploration of Geothermal Energy from Volcanoes*. He explains how ancient civilisations might have observed and attempted to harness these natural forces.

Could this understanding have influenced the design of pyramids?[cmlxviii] Smith and Johnson (2018) discuss the geothermal potential of volcanic activity in *Volcanic Energy and Its Geothermal Potential: A Study of Natural Power Sources*, highlighting how modern energy plants harness heat from the Earth's mantle to generate electricity. This research parallels ancient theories of pyramids designed to tap into natural energy sources, much like volcanoes.

Volcanoes and pyramids symbolise power—volcanoes with their raw, untamed force and pyramids with their focused, deliberate construction. Ancient civilisations living near active volcanoes often interpreted these natural phenomena spiritually. For instance, in Mesoamerican mythology, volcanoes were considered sacred mountains associated with the gods of creation and destruction, and their eruptions were viewed as divine interactions. Volcanoes were often revered as sacred sites by ancient cultures. In Central America, volcanic mountains were believed to be the homes of gods, and pyramids were built nearby to honour their divine power."[cmlxix] Similarly, the Mayans and Greeks attributed earthquakes, often linked to volcanic activity, to cosmic or divine forces.

In this light, pyramids may have been designed to channel Earth's energies more deliberately. Volcanic eruptions release electromagnetic energy, and this natural phenomenon could have inspired the builders to replicate this with pyramids. Rather than violent eruptions, pyramids could have been constructed to harness subtle and direct electromagnetic energy upward, much like volcanic magma rising toward the surface. [cmlxx] This comparison suggests that they might have seen their pyramids as controlled reflections of the natural, chaotic forces they witnessed in nature.

Recent advances in geophysics offer intriguing parallels between volcanic energy and the potential energy harnessed by pyramids. Volcanic eruptions release immense amounts of geothermal energy, and their proximity to fault lines and tectonic activity is well-documented. Similarly, some ancient pyramid sites, such as those in Mexico and Egypt, appear to be strategically located near tectonic plates or areas of geomagnetic anomalies.

A study published in *Earth and Planetary Science Letters* (2019) highlights the presence of geomagnetic disturbances near the Giza Plateau. These anomalies often occur near tectonic fault lines, which could imply that the pyramids were deliberately placed to tap into natural electromagnetic forces, much like volcanoes are positioned at tectonic hotspots. It is also worth noting that the granite and quartz used in pyramid construction possess piezoelectric properties.[cmlxxi] This means they can generate an electric charge when subjected to pressure. Volcanic regions, known for their intense geological forces, also contain materials capable of producing piezoelectric effects. It is possible that ancient builders understood this phenomenon and used materials capable of conducting energy, much like the volcanic earth around them.

Volcanoes are natural sources of heat, releasing geothermal energy through eruptions and lava flows. Pyramids, constructed from heat-absorbent materials like limestone, might have also been designed to capture and retain heat. This could have served a dual purpose: maintaining internal temperature and potentially generating or storing energy within their structure.

Harnessing Lightning: Pyramid Power and Volcanic Inspiration

Volcanic eruptions often produce lightning, a natural electrical discharge caused by the static electricity generated by ash particles rubbing together. This concept has inspired human-made plasma reactors and lightning capture technologies, which seek to mimic the energy release seen in volcanic eruptions to generate controlled bursts of energy.[cmlxxii]

Observing volcanic lightning could have also taught ancient civilisations that electrical energy could be controlled or redirected. Suppose they believed pyramids could capture this energy. In that case, they might have developed rituals or technologies to harness this power for practical purposes, such as energy storage or even spiritual ceremonies involving electrical displays.[cmlxxiii] They could have used pyramids as early attempts to capture or direct energy, combining their observations of natural phenomena with advanced architectural designs. This idea aligns with the broader hypothesis that the pyramids were not only spiritual monuments but also advanced technological tools, harnessing natural forces and ancient knowledge to capture or redirect lightning's energy.[cmlxxiv]

This theory adds another dimension to the pyramids' potential function. They could have acted as natural energy absorbers or redistributors, reflecting a sophisticated understanding of Earth's electromagnetic dynamics. By doing so, the ancients could have engaged in early experiments with electrical energy, connecting the spiritual with the scientific and attempting to manipulate forces they believed were natural and divine.[cmlxxv]

Thinking that these colossal structures might have been designed to capture or redirect lightning's energy is breathtaking. Ancient builders may have harnessed nature's most volatile and spectacular force to create balance and harmony within their environment. Seeing lightning emerge from volcanic eruptions might have reinforced the idea that electricity was a force tied to Earth's energy and that specific structures or materials could attract or store it. The towering, conical shape of volcanoes may have inspired the design of pyramids. Both structures are pointed, and their form could have been perceived as a way to attract and capture energy from the sky.[cmlxxvi] If lightning strikes were more frequent around volcanoes, civilisations might have believed replicating these shapes elsewhere could bring similar benefits, especially regarding accessing natural power.[cmlxxvii]

In addition to practical uses, the ability to channel or harness lightning would have had profound spiritual significance. Civilisations may have viewed lightning as a gift from the gods or a symbol of divine power, integrating it into their religious or mystical practices.[cmlxxviii]

Could lightning have come *out of* the pyramids?

If pyramids had been designed to harness telluric currents — the natural electrical currents on Earth —they might have focused that energy upward. The pyramid's shape and conductive materials, like granite and possibly gold, could hypothetically act like a natural capacitor, lightning rod, or even an energy emitter. The mystery of the missing capstones could support this idea. Instead of being topped by gold, what if the capstone space was left open as a release point? Like a volcano's vent — not to emit lava, but electrical discharge. This could have symbolised a connection to the heavens or been used to send up bursts of energy. Ancient myths often describe gods descending in lightning or fire — perhaps these tales emerged from real visual phenomena tied to energy structures, such as pyramids. It would have seemed divine if people had seen sparks or discharges emanating from the apex.

The unconfirmed March 2025 discovery of underground formations extends over 648 meters in depth. It is aligned with spiral pathways, closely resembling magma shafts or volcanic throats, where pressure and energy build up before release. In this context, the pyramid above could represent the visible cone of a manmade volcano. At the same time, the buried spiralling cylinders serve as the subsurface "magma chamber", built to channel geothermal or electromagnetic energy upward. Just as real volcanoes often emit volcanic lightning, this could explain ancient myths and theories suggesting that lightning may have emerged from the pyramid tips. The design may have been both symbolic and functional—honouring nature's power while replicating it through a controlled, architectural form of energy release. This blurs the line between sacred monuments and sophisticated energy conduits, reinforcing the idea that ancient builders were imitating Earth's most powerful natural energy system.

Echoes of Fire: Could Ancient Pillars Be Volcanic Remnants?

Or, could the massive stone pillars or even certain pyramid-like structures scattered across the globe be remnants of ancient volcanic formations? Towering natural columns, often known as volcanic necks or plugs, can form when magma solidifies deep within the vents of an active volcano. The softer surrounding rock gradually eroded over millions of years, leaving behind astonishingly precise, column-like shapes. It is conceivable that ancient civilisations, discovering these mysterious natural structures, attributed profound spiritual or cosmic significance to them, interpreting them as symbols of divine power, earthly connection, or gateways to celestial realms. Such awe-inspiring geological formations might have served as natural blueprints or inspirations for later human-made constructions, prompting ancient architects to imitate their powerful symbolism and impressive dimensions through monumental building projects. This speculative yet intriguing scenario could explain why similar monumental forms, pillars, and pyramid-like structures arose independently across distant cultures, who perhaps sought to capture or replicate the awe inspired by volcanic towers believed to connect the earth and sky. If we were to find geological evidence of ancient volcanic activity beneath or near prominent archaeological sites, it would significantly strengthen this hypothesis, highlighting the close intertwining of the forces of nature and human creativity.

There is geological proof of volcanic necks, also known as volcanic plugs, which are the hardened remnants of volcanic throats (vents) that become exposed after erosion strips away the softer surrounding rock. A volcano's throat can vary significantly in depth, typically ranging from a few hundred meters to several kilometres beneath the Earth's surface.[cmlxxix] Notable examples include Shiprock in New Mexico, USA, a volcanic neck rising approximately 482 meters above the surrounding plains, representing the hardened magma conduit of an ancient volcano[cmlxxx]; Devils Tower in Wyoming, USA, approximately 386 meters tall, formed as the core of a volcano now exposed after millions of years of erosion[cmlxxxi]; and Saint Michel d'Aiguilhe in France, an 85-meter volcanic neck featuring a medieval chapel constructed atop it.[cmlxxxii] However, volcanic conduits typically extend far deeper beneath the visible surface, reaching underground magma chambers located kilometres below. Thus, visible volcanic necks usually represent only a small fraction of the entire volcanic structure, which is revealed through extensive geological erosion over extended periods.[cmlxxxiii]

Controlled Power: Pyramids' Response to Nature

Despite their differences, volcanoes and pyramids may reflect an ancient understanding of Earth's energy. Volcanoes release energy in an uncontrollable form, while pyramids, with their precise geometry and alignment, might represent humanity's attempt to capture and direct that energy. Volcanoes tap into geothermal energy, drawing from the Earth's molten core. If specific theories hold, pyramids may have been designed to interact with the Earth's electromagnetic fields, concentrating and amplifying that energy. This possibility opens new dimensions in understanding how ancient peoples might have viewed and harnessed the planet's power. Volcanoes often have a connection to water through geothermal springs and underwater volcanoes. Similarly, some pyramid theories suggest that water—via underground rivers or aquifers—played a role in how pyramids harnessed energy.

Whether natural or constructed, volcanoes and pyramids may serve as conduits for Earth's immense energy. Volcanoes unleash this power violently and unpredictably, transforming landscapes through explosive eruptions. In contrast, pyramids, with their precise design and alignment, seem to capture and focus energy more precisely and deliberately. To the ancient civilisations that built them, both were powerful symbols—one a force of nature, the other a manifestation of human ingenuity. Yet, despite their differences, they share a connection to the deeper forces that shape our world.

Another Example of How Humanity Recreated the Eruption

In 1945, deep in the desert of New Mexico, modern man staged his own volcanic initiation. The Manhattan Project was not merely a scientific venture. It was a ritual of fire, secrecy, and transformation. When the first atomic bomb was detonated at the Trinity site, the earth itself seemed to recoil. A pillar of light rose like a man-made volcano—ash, flame, and fury erupting skyward. This mushroom cloud was no accident of form: it mirrored the ancient volcanic plume. Where once volcanoes reset civilisations through tectonic forces, now the human race had summoned its own doomsday engine. The nuclear bomb became a synthetic volcano, born not of magma, but of uranium and uranium's memory of starlight. It was, perhaps, our attempt to control what we had once worshipped: the uncontainable power of Earth's core. Yet unlike volcanoes, which destroy and regenerate, the bomb left behind only radioactive silence.

Volcanoes imitated, Power Redirected

A final thought, could ancient rulers, observing the awe and fear inspired by volcanoes—those towering, fire-spewing mountains that connected sky, earth, and the underworld—have sought to replicate their power in a symbolic and controllable form? If the people revered the volcano as a seat of the gods, then why not create a man-made equivalent—one that could anchor divine authority not in nature, but in kingship? By constructing pyramids that mimicked the shape, orientation, and even energetic signature of volcanoes, these leaders may have intentionally aligned themselves with cosmic forces. In doing so, they didn't just imitate nature—they redefined it under their rule. The pyramid became a domesticated volcano: no longer erupting unpredictably, but radiating power in service of human hierarchies and priestly control.

Conclusions

With the parallels between volcanoes and pyramids established, the next chapter will further explore the Earth's energies and natural forces that may have influenced the construction and purpose of pyramids. As we move from the raw, geothermal power of volcanoes to the more subtle forces at play within pyramids, it's worth asking: Could ancient civilisations have understood and harnessed the Earth's energy in ways we are only beginning to rediscover? If pyramids were designed to channel natural power, how did they interact with the Earth's electromagnetic fields, water sources, or other unseen forces? Could these structures provide the key to understanding a forgotten knowledge of energy manipulation?

Chapter 13 Earth Energies and Natural Forces

The Earth's Pulse

The Earth pulses with dynamic energy beneath its surface. This chapter examines how ancient builders may have aligned their structures to harness Earth's natural forces, thereby creating monuments that resonate with the planet's rhythms. People view Planet Earth as a living entity full of energy. In later chapters, we will go deeper into the functionality. This chapter focuses solely on Earth's energies, which the ancients may have harnessed. The energies explored in this chapter are not an exhaustive list but rather a selection of the most prominent and speculative examples of Earth's forces that ancient civilisations might have tapped into.

Geological Energy (Geothermal Energy)

The Earth's interior generates immense heat. This heat is transferred through the mantle, eventually reaching the crust and escaping through geothermal energy.[cmlxxxiv] Geothermal hotspots, located where the Earth's crust is thinner, such as in Iceland or the Pacific Ring of Fire, produce heat.[cmlxxxv] This heat can generate electricity by turning turbines with hot water or steam. [cmlxxxvi] Geothermal energy is known to be concentrated in areas of volcanic activity, and some ancient civilisations, such as the Romans, built near geothermal hotspots for practical reasons, including access to hot water for bathing and heating. [cmlxxxvii] Some believed these areas were spiritually powerful[cmlxxxviii]. The Romans dedicated hot springs to the gods, and the Japanese revered them as places of healing.[cmlxxxix] Could ancient civilisations have instinctively understood the healing properties of geothermal energy without modern scientific understanding? They established settlements near hot springs and geothermal areas, taking advantage of the natural heat and mineral-rich waters.[cmxc]

Did the Egyptians make use of Geothermal Energy? People speculate that by channelling heat from underground sources through carefully designed tunnels and chambers, the pyramids could have created steam pressure or a controlled temperature environment, possibly for water purification or energy generation processes. They might have absorbed and stored heat during the day, releasing it at night to maintain a controlled environment. Alternatively, heat could have been used for specific processes within the pyramid, such as drying or cooking materials. However, no historical or archaeological evidence supports this claim. Egypt's geological environment lacks the geothermal activity needed for such systems. The Great Pyramid and other Egyptian pyramids are situated in regions that are not geothermally active, and there is no evidence that the Egyptians channelled geothermal heat through pyramids for energy generation, water purification, or other such purposes. The materials used in pyramids (limestone and granite) absorb heat. Still, the idea of using the pyramids' structure to store and release heat in a controlled manner is speculative, lacking archaeological evidence.

Capturing Solar Power

Although solar energy originates from the sun, it can be classified as Earth energy because it is fundamentally linked to how the Earth interacts with the sun's radiation. Solar energy is the primary driver of photosynthesis in plants, a process fundamental to life on Earth. It also powers the water cycle through evaporation and influences climate patterns by heating the Earth's atmosphere and surface, thereby regulating weather systems. Solar energy is captured naturally through photosynthesis in plants, stored as heat in the oceans, and influences atmospheric dynamics. Human technology, like solar panels, captures this energy for power generation. Many ancient pyramids' smooth, reflective surfaces, especially in Egypt, were initially covered in polished limestone. The glimmering surfaces of pyramids might have captured the sun's rays. The reflective surfaces of the casing stones might have concentrated sunlight, while the internal chambers could act as collectors. Could they have served as an ancient solar power plant, using sunlight for illumination, heat, or even to create chemical reactions? There is, however, no archaeological evidence to support this claim. While the reflective casing stones could have illuminated the pyramids, there is no evidence that they were used to concentrate sunlight for technological purposes, such as energy generation or chemical reactions. Many ancient pyramids, including the Great Pyramid of Giza and the Pyramid of the Sun at Teotihuacan, show precise alignments with astronomical events such as solstices and equinoxes. These alignments were likely used to track the sun's movement, which could have been necessary for agricultural and ritualistic purposes.

Solar Winds: Channelling the Winds of the Sun

Could specific ancient structures—such as pillars or pyramids—have been designed to channel energy rising from deep within the Earth? A fascinating theory suggests that Earth's magnetic field may capture charged particles from the solar wind, particularly during periods of heightened solar activity. These particles, also known as solar plasma, can interact with the Earth's crust, potentially creating natural electrical currents.

In this view, structures built along geomagnetic lines or energetic hotspots may have functioned like conduits, guiding energy from below the surface upward, possibly even releasing it into the sky. The idea echoes how lightning can sometimes emerge from the ground during intense geomagnetic events. If pyramids or pillars had been built with this in mind, their design might not have been merely symbolic but also functional, intended to harness or regulate energy flows between the Earth and the sky.

Adding another layer, this theory parallels modern geothermal systems, such as those used in parts of Germany. These systems utilise the temperature difference—known as a delta—between the Earth's deep heat and the cooler surface. The resulting energy can be converted into electricity. It's possible that ancient civilisations, through advanced understanding or intuitive design, tapped into a similar principle using megalithic structures.

Could the missing capstones atop some pyramids be more than a mystery? Perhaps they weren't missing but intentionally left open—like a volcanic vent—to allow energy, or even plasma, to rise and discharge. In this way, the pyramid becomes not just a monument but a dynamic energy interface between Earth's core and the cosmos.

Water as Power: Using Earth's Elemental Energy

Ancient civilisations have long used hydraulic energy generated by water's movement.[cmxci] Water in motion—whether from rivers, lakes, or tides—carries kinetic energy that can be harnessed. Ancient Greeks, Romans, and Chinese used water wheels to grind grain and power machines. Ancient civilisations often built near water sources for access to water for drinking, irrigation, and transportation. Water was used for agriculture, transportation, and powering mills, but it was not harnessed for energy generation like modern systems.

Today, advanced technology, such as hydroelectric dams and tidal energy systems, captures hydraulic energy. These systems are far more sophisticated than the ancient use of waterwheels or simple irrigation systems. For example, hydroelectric dams like the Hoover Dam in the US use the kinetic energy of flowing water from large reservoirs to turn turbines, generating electricity for millions of homes.cmxcii The MeyGen tidal project in Scotland is one of several tidal energy projects that use the natural movements of ocean tides to generate electricity. Tidal energy is part of the growing field of renewable energy sources.cmxciii

What if the Great Pyramid of Giza or other pyramids were used to harness hydraulic energy?cmxciv The hydraulic theory suggests that the pyramids may have been constructed over underground aquifers, which are common on the Giza Plateau.cmxcv Water flowing beneath the pyramid could have been channelled through specific cavities or tunnels within the structure.cmxcvi As the water moved through these tunnels, it could have generated pressure or kinetic energy, potentially driving mechanical processes within the pyramid, such as pumping water to higher levels or producing some form of power.cmxcvii There is, however, no archaeological evidence to support the idea that the pyramids, including the Great Pyramid of Giza, were designed or used to harness hydraulic energy.cmxcviii

Some researchers believe that the ancient pyramids may have used water in a manner that is not fully understood today. One theory suggests that water inside or near the pyramids could have taken on a special form known as *structured water*, considered the fourth form of water. Dr. Gerald Pollack, a professor of bioengineering at the University of Washington, explores this concept in his book, "*The Fourth Phase of Water: Beyond Solid, Liquid, and Vapor*" (2013). His research shows that structured water has a more organised, gel-like structure that can store and transmit energy, acting somewhat like a battery.cmxcix The stones of the pyramids, such as limestone, might have helped create this structured water when in contact with their surfaces, forming an exclusion zone (EZ) that repels impurities and enhances energy storage. The idea that the pyramids could have used structured water as part of an advanced energy system is intriguing but remains speculative.

Winds: The Forgotten Force

Wind is a powerful natural force generated by differences in atmospheric pressure. As air moves from areas of high pressure to low pressure, it carries kinetic energy that can be harnessed. Wind turbines can harness this energy to generate electricity.

Ancient civilisations recognised and used wind energy for practical purposes. Windmills for grinding grain date back to ancient Persia (around 500-900 CE) and were later used in China and Europe. The use of wind for sailing is well-documented in ancient Egypt and other maritime cultures. Evidence shows that ancient civilisations also used natural airflow for cooling, such as through architectural designs like wind catchers in Persia. However, this use was less technologically advanced than that of modern wind turbines for electricity generation.

Wind could have influenced the design of the pyramids by promoting airflow through chambers, creating ventilation or sound resonance within the structure, and enhancing the pyramid's spiritual or ceremonial functions. However, due to their enclosed nature, airflow within the pyramids is limited, and no mechanisms or design elements specific to wind manipulation have been found. Some theories suggest that ancient structures, including pyramids, may have been deliberately positioned to align with air currents, thereby amplifying energy or symbolically channelling the wind's power to enhance their spiritual or energy-redirecting properties. No credible archaeological studies or records support the idea of pyramids or other ancient structures being deliberately positioned to harness air currents for energy or spiritual purposes. While alignment with celestial bodies (like the solstices and cardinal points) is documented, there is no concrete proof linking pyramid orientation to wind currents or energy manipulation. While there's no concrete evidence of wind-harnessing mechanisms like windmills atop pyramids, is it possible that ancient builders had an intuitive understanding of how wind interacts with large structures, possibly using it to their advantage in ways we are only beginning to explore?[m]

Fossil Fuels

Could the Great Pyramid of Giza have tapped into fossil fuels? This one seems unlikely. Fossil fuel energy requires complex infrastructure, including extraction sites, refineries, and storage facilities—none of which have been found in or around the pyramids. The pyramids are primarily constructed from limestone and granite, which are unsuitable for energy production and lack the internal mechanisms or ventilation systems necessary for combustion processes. Furthermore, the ancient Egyptians did not have access to or knowledge of fossil fuels like coal or oil, and there were no signs of any residue suggesting the burning of such fuels within the pyramids. The location of the pyramids on the Giza Plateau is far from any significant coal or oil deposits that the ancient Egyptians could have exploited. Egypt does not have major coal reserves, and there are no known deposits near the Giza Plateau. Egypt's limited coal resources are primarily found in the Sinai Peninsula and the Eastern Desert, far from the pyramids. These deposits are small and would not have been accessible or used by the ancient Egyptians, who primarily relied on wood and charcoal as their primary sources of fuel. Egypt has oil reserves, but they are mainly located in regions such as the Western Desert and the Gulf of Suez, as well as offshore in the Mediterranean Sea and the Red Sea. These areas are not near the pyramids at Giza. Oil exploration and extraction in Egypt only began in the modern era; there is no evidence that ancient Egyptians accessed or used these resources.

Chemical Energy

Early humans' use of fire, dating back over a million years, was one of the earliest practical applications of chemical energy. Combustion, or the burning of materials, is a chemical reaction in which energy is released through heat and light.[mi] While some speculative theories suggest that the pyramids were designed to harness chemical energy, no substantial archaeological evidence supports this notion. The ancient Egyptians possessed advanced knowledge of chemistry, as evidenced by their use of materials such as gypsum mortar and limestone in construction.[mii] For instance, gypsum plaster production involves heating gypsum rock to release water and storing energy within chemical bonds—a basic example of energy transformation.[miii] Speculative theories propose that the pyramids might have facilitated more complex chemical processes. For instance, some suggest that copper tools, combined with the acidic properties of certain substances in the limestone or granite chambers, could have triggered chemical reactions, releasing gases like carbon dioxide or hydrogen. One such idea suggests that water may have been channelled through the pyramid's internal structure to produce hydrogen gas, using the pyramid's architecture to generate pressure or energy.[miv]

However, no archaeological evidence of infrastructure or residues suggests that such processes occurred. Furthermore, while the Egyptians were skilled in various chemical applications, such as mummification, dye production, and metallurgy—fields in which they demonstrated an understanding of chemical reactions—these practices were not directly linked to the pyramids.[mv] The Egyptians used alchemical techniques to create and refine materials. Still, these processes were primarily employed in small-scale settings, such as workshops or temples, rather than in monumental architecture like the pyramids.[mvi]

Magnetism

Magnetism is one of the oldest natural forces that humans have identified. Ancient civilisations, such as the Greeks and Chinese, observed magnetic properties in lodestones (naturally magnetised pieces of iron ore). The Chinese used magnetism as early as the 3rd century BCE for navigation, using lodestones as early compasses.[mvii] The ancient Greeks and Chinese did not observe the development of electromagnetism in the 19th century.[mviii]

Electromagnetism, a broader concept, describes the unified relationship between electricity and magnetism, which was formalised by James Clerk Maxwell's equations in the 19th century. These equations demonstrate that changing electric fields produce magnetic fields and vice versa, resulting in electromagnetic waves, encompassing light, radio waves, and other forms of energy that propagate through space. The discovery of electromagnetism revolutionised technology and science, enabling the development of everything from electric motors and generators to wireless communication systems.[mix]

Electromagnetic Energy

Earth's geomagnetic field, generated by molten iron (liquid iron) in the core, shields the planet from solar radiation.[mx] Earth's outer core is composed primarily of molten iron and nickel. This liquid metal moves due to the planet's rotation and convection currents caused by the heat from the inner core. The movement of conductive molten iron, combined with the Earth's rotation, creates electric currents that generate the magnetic field through geodynamo.[mxi] Electromagnetic induction, as described by Faraday's law, occurs when a conductor moves within a magnetic field, generating electric currents. This principle is fundamental to the operation of the Earth's magnetic field.[mxii] These electric currents form a magnetic field with lines that emerge from the Earth's core and extend into space. The magnetic field lines run from the magnetic north pole to the south pole, forming a protective bubble around the planet.[mxiii]

Electromagnetism is one of nature's four fundamental forces governing interactions between electric charges and the magnetic fields they produce. It includes electric and magnetic fields, which we can observe as light, electricity, and magnetism.[mxiv]

Both electromagnetic energy and lightning electricity are governed by the principles of electromagnetism, which describe how electric charges and currents produce electric and magnetic fields.[mxv] Lightning is an electromagnetic phenomenon that involves the movement of electric charge, resulting in the emission of visible light and radio waves.[mxvi]

Could ancient civilisations have built pyramids to capture or redirect electrical energy from the atmosphere, particularly in lightning-prone areas? This would suggest a deeper understanding of Earth's natural forces.[mxvii] Lightning is one of the most powerful natural phenomena caused by the build-up of electrical charge between the sky and the ground. While most people think of lightning as descending from the clouds, it can also originate from the ground in ground-to-cloud lightning, further highlighting the complex dynamics of the Earth's electrical environment.[mxviii] Lightning is a striking visual spectacle and a powerful expression of Earth's natural electromagnetic energy, releasing hundreds of millions of volts during a single strike.[mxix] This massive discharge of energy creates temperatures hotter than the sun's surface, igniting the air and producing the thunderous shockwaves we associate with thunderstorms.[mxx] Beyond its visual and audible power, lightning contributes to Earth's global electric circuit by maintaining the electrical charge balance between the Earth's surface and the atmosphere. It does not directly sustain the Earth's geomagnetic field, which is primarily maintained by the geodynamo in its core.[mxxi] Given lightning's raw energy, ancient peoples may have revered it for its destructive potential and as a divine or creative force, symbolising chaos and order.[mxxii] Many ancient cultures associated it with gods or supernatural forces. The Greeks, for instance, believed that Zeus wielded lightning bolts, and many cultures viewed it as a manifestation of divine power. This natural phenomenon can spark chemical reactions essential to life—such as nitrogen fixation, which nourishes the soil—while simultaneously causing great destruction.[mxxiii] As both creator and destroyer, the duality of lightning may have inspired ancient civilisations to explore ways of harnessing or redirecting this energy for spiritual or technological purposes.[mxxiv]

Pyramids, particularly those located in regions prone to lightning, may have been designed to interact with atmospheric electrical forces.[mxxv] The pointed shape of pyramids resembles lightning rods, structures modern science uses to direct lightning strikes into the ground, preventing damage safely.[mxxvi][mxxvii] Could these ancient structures be, in essence, colossal electrical conductors designed to harness or channel lightning's energy? Such a design might suggest that the ancients were aware of electromagnetic forces, using the pyramids to harness Earth's geomagnetic and atmospheric energy. To date, there has been no archaeological or scientific evidence suggesting that pyramids were designed to function in this way.

Schumann Resonance

While distinct, resonance and electromagnetism are interconnected phenomena that may have influenced how ancient structures, such as pyramids, interacted with natural energies.[mxxviii]

Resonance occurs when a system vibrates or oscillates at its natural frequency in response to an external stimulus. It tends to be an internal process where energy vibrates or oscillates within a system.

Although the effects (such as sound) can sometimes be perceived, the resonance (the underlying vibrations) is usually invisible.[mxxix]

Discovered by physicist Winfried Otto Schumann in 1952, the Schumann resonance refers to the electromagnetic waves trapped between the Earth's surface and the ionosphere. These waves are produced primarily by lightning strikes.[mxxx] The primary frequency is approximately 7.83 Hz, and while some spiritualists suggest a connection with human brainwaves, this remains speculative. Some spiritualists and researchers have linked the Schumann resonance to concepts of the Earth's "heartbeat," suggesting that ancient peoples may have been more attuned to these frequencies, perhaps using structures like pyramids to resonate with these natural energies.[mxxxi] The primary frequency of the Earth's heartbeat is approximately 7.83 Hz, but there are higher harmonic frequencies as well. It is viewed as the Earth's natural electromagnetic pulse, which is believed to be in sync with biological processes in humans and other living organisms.[mxxxii] Some spiritual interpretations suggest that human consciousness and the Schumann resonance are linked[mxxxiii], though this connection remains speculative.[mxxxiv]

Some speculate that if the pyramids were designed to amplify these natural frequencies, they could have served as a conduit between Earth's energy and the human mind, perhaps enhancing spiritual practices or healing.

The Power of the Planet's Movements

Imagine a world where the builders of pyramids understood the Earth's seismic energy, constructing these structures not just as monuments but as ancient 'volcanoes'—funnelling Earth's raw power upward in a controlled, sacred form. [mxxxv]

The Earth's lithosphere is broken into tectonic plates that float on the semi-molten asthenosphere (a part of the mantle). The movement and interactions of these plates generate seismic energy, leading to earthquakes and volcanic activity.[mxxxvi] Fault lines, or boundaries where tectonic plates interact, are places where pressure builds up. This pressure is released as seismic energy through earthquakes and volcanic eruptions, particularly at convergent and divergent plate boundaries.[mxxxvii]

The USGS (U.S. Geological Survey) has long studied geomagnetic fields through its Geomagnetism Program, which monitors variations in Earth's magnetic field across different regions. However, while some magnetic anomalies correlate with tectonic activity or volcanic areas, these correlations are not always direct. Magnetic anomalies can result from various geological factors, including rock composition and tectonic structures, but not all tectonic boundaries or volcanic areas exhibit such anomalies.[mxxxviii]

Volcanic eruptions release vast amounts of heat, ash, gases, and magma. Many ancient cultures, including the Mesoamericans, regarded volcanoes as sacred, symbolising creation, destruction, and the power of the gods.[mxxxix] For example, the Aztecs and the Mayans held volcanic mountains as significant sites in their mythology and spirituality.[mxl]

With its conical shape, the pyramid could be seen as a man-made representation of a volcano, directing energy upward.[mxli] Pyramids may also be viewed as symbolic and functional counterparts to volcanoes, harnessing Earth's latent energy in a more controlled and spiritual manner.[mxlii] Just as volcanoes release energy from Earth's depths, pyramids might have acted as stabilisers, channelling seismic forces into a controlled energy flow.[mxliii] Some theorists propose that ancient structures, such as the Great Pyramid, were deliberately built near tectonic fault lines, including the Nile River Valley and the Pacific Ring of Fire, where energy is concentrated.[mxliv] However, the Great Pyramid of Giza is not near a major tectonic fault line. It is situated on the Giza Plateau, which is relatively stable geologically. The Nile River Valley is not a tectonic fault line but rather a valley formed by erosion. The Pacific Ring of Fire is a tectonic and volcanic zone. With their stable, conical shape, pyramids may have symbolised and channelled the dynamic energy of volcanoes and earthquakes, aligning human structures with Earth's natural power.[mxlv]

Gravity's Grip: The Unseen Force

No single person *invented* gravity, but the concept of gravity has been developed over time through the work of many scientists. Isaac Newton is often credited with "discovering" gravity because he formulated the Law of Universal Gravitation in 1687. According to his law, every mass attracts every other mass in the universe with a force proportional to the product of their masses and inversely proportional to the square of the distance between their centres. This law became the foundation of classical physics, describing how objects interact through gravity on a universal scale. The legend of his discovery includes the famous story of an apple falling from a tree, inspiring him to think about the forces that keep the apple on Earth and the Moon in orbit. Though the story may be simplified, his work on gravity explained how the same natural laws govern objects in space and on Earth. Earth's gravity is fundamental in regulating tides through the gravitational interaction with the moon. Gravity keeps satellites in orbit and shapes Earth's landscape, influencing river flow and water distribution. It is an essential force for maintaining life and stability on the planet.[mxlvi] While Newton's theory of gravity worked well for most calculations, it could not fully explain certain phenomena, such as the orbit of Mercury.

Albert Einstein revolutionised our understanding of gravity with his theory of General Relativity in 1915. Instead of viewing gravity as a force between masses, he described it as the warping or curvature of spacetime caused by massive objects. In this theory, objects move along curved paths in spacetime, and this movement is what we perceive as gravity.[mxlvii]

Gravity affects the movement of all objects on Earth, from the flow of water to the movement of tectonic plates. It also plays a role in energy distribution, as it influences atmospheric and oceanic circulation.

Ancient civilisations did not understand gravity as a force, but they could observe its effects, such as the moon's influence on tides or objects falling to the ground. Symbolism in ancient structures often reflected balance and harmony, as seen in the design of pyramids and temples. However, no evidence suggests that this understanding extended to designing structures based on gravitational principles beyond the symbolic representation of stability and permanence.[mxlviii]

Some speculate that gravitational anomalies could have created energy vortices or hotspots when combined with electromagnetic fields.[mxlix] If pyramids were built to align with these hotspots, they may have amplified this energy, creating a form of power generation. The materials used in the pyramids, such as limestone and granite, may have interacted with these fields, producing piezoelectric effects that generated electrical energy.[ml] Critics argue that the materials used in the pyramids, including limestone and granite, were likely selected for their availability, durability, and symbolic significance rather than their piezoelectric properties.[mli]

Some proponents extend the theory of limestone and granite acting as conductors by suggesting that pyramids might have been early forms of wireless energy transmitters.[mlii] By focusing and directing gravitational and electromagnetic energies, the pyramids could have served as power stations, sending energy through the air or the ground to nearby sites or structures. This theory aligns with concepts Nikola Tesla later explored in his wireless energy experiments.[mliii]

Others ask, what if pyramids amplified gravitational and electromagnetic energies to transform materials within their chambers? For example, the concentration of energies at particular frequencies could have been employed to alter or refine minerals, metals, or other materials for spiritual, ceremonial, or technological purposes. Ancient builders may have used this energy to enhance the strength of construction materials.^mliv This speculative theory suggests that the energy within the pyramid could have reinforced the stones used in construction, leading to the durable structures we see today.^mlv

Aether, the Quintessential Element

The concept of aether, or "ether," as one of the five classical elements, dates back to ancient philosophies and traditions, including those of the Greeks, Hindus, and Chinese. Unlike the tangible elements of earth, water, fire, and air, aether is considered the quintessence—the unseen, subtle energy that fills the universe. It was believed to be the substance through which energy flows and connects all other elements.^mlvi In many ancient traditions, aether was the medium that allowed for the transfer of energy, light, and even consciousness.^mlvii Ancient civilisations viewed the Earth as a living, breathing entity infused with aether, which they believed was the source of its dynamic, invisible forces. These civilisations, from the Egyptians to the ancient Greeks and beyond, saw the aether as the bridge between the physical and spiritual realms. It was the medium through which energy from geothermal forces, electromagnetic fields, and celestial bodies moved, influencing natural events like earthquakes and human consciousness.^mlviii

Could structures like pyramids and temples have been built as instruments designed to channel the aetheric energy? By aligning these monuments with ley lines, celestial bodies, and Earth's magnetic field, ancient builders might have created focal points where the aether could be concentrated, amplified, and harnessed. Could the pyramids have had golden capstones capable of interacting with the aetheric field? Gold's high conductivity and corrosion resistance make it an ideal candidate for such a function. Similar principles are used in antennas and energy collectors today. However, these principles are based on established electromagnetism, not the aether concept. Mainstream archaeologists say there is no proof that the tops were made of anything other than limestone, like the rest of the pyramid.

Historically, ancient Greek philosophers, such as Aristotle, proposed aether as a fifth element, in addition to the four classical elements: earth, water, air, and fire. It was thought to fill the universe beyond the terrestrial sphere. In the 19th century, scientists hypothesised the existence of the "luminiferous aether" as a medium for light waves to travel through space. However, this concept was debunked by the Michelson-Morley experiment in 1887, and it is no longer accepted in modern physics. Therefore, while aether was once a part of theoretical models, it is not considered a component of Earth's energy network in modern science. Some argue that aether was intentionally excluded from scientific acceptance, stemming from the evolution of modern physics. In the 19th century, scientists such as James Clerk Maxwell and Michael Faraday employed the concept of aether to explain electromagnetic phenomena. However, after Albert Einstein's theory of special relativity in 1905, the need for aether was challenged.[mlix] Einstein demonstrated that light can travel through a vacuum without a medium, and the concept of aether was largely abandoned in mainstream science.

Despite this, some alternative researchers and proponents of free energy theories suggest that ancient civilisations might have understood and utilised a form of aether to tap into what they call "free energy."[mlx] They argue that structures like pyramids and obelisks were not merely architectural wonders but energy devices that harnessed and channelled aetheric energy for various purposes, such as powering ancient technologies or promoting spiritual and physical well-being.[mlxi]

Could this knowledge have been systematically removed or suppressed to maintain control over energy resources? Some claim that by eliminating the concept of aether and focusing solely on fossil fuels and centralised power systems, ancient techniques for accessing this "free energy" were lost or hidden. This understanding of the aether as an all-pervading life force could explain why many ancient structures appear to be strategically placed around the globe. The builders might have tapped into these aetheric currents to stabilise their societies, enhance spiritual practices, and influence weather patterns or natural events. By resonating with the Earth's aetheric rhythms, these structures may have been intended to create harmony between humanity and the planet, making them not just physical monuments but energy tools that interacted with the unseen world.[mlxii]

Tapping into Earth's Biomagnetic Fields

Living organisms, including humans, generate electromagnetic fields, particularly from the heart and brain. Electrocardiograms (ECG) and magnetoencephalography (MEG) measure these fields.[mlxiii] Some spiritual and esoteric beliefs say a universal "web of energy" exists. They say these fields constantly interact with the environment and other living beings, creating an invisible web of energy that some believe connects all life forms.[mlxiv] In humans, the heart and brain produce the most substantial biomagnetic fields, which can be measured using technologies such as electrocardiograms (ECG) and magnetoencephalography (MEG).[mlxv] Biomagnetic fields, particularly those emanating from the heart and brain, fluctuate in response to physical health and emotional states. Heart rate variability, for example, changes in response to stress or relaxation.[mlxvi]

Some spiritual and alternative science theories suggest that ancient civilisations understood these biomagnetic fields and knew how to manipulate or enhance them through architecture and sacred structures. With precise alignment and geometric design, pyramids may have been constructed to harness and interact with the Earth's geomagnetic and human bioelectric fields. These fields, which extend beyond the body, could have been amplified by the pyramids' structural and material elements, such as the use of quartz and other conductive minerals.[mlxvii]

The alignment of pyramids with key celestial bodies and magnetic north further supports the idea that these structures were more than mere architectural marvels; they were carefully designed to resonate with Earth's natural energy currents and the biomagnetic energy of those who entered. This interaction may have generated a potent energy field within the pyramid, intended to enhance individuals' physical, mental, and spiritual states, acting as an ancient energy amplifier or spiritual catalyst.[mlxviii]

The placement of the pyramids on specific geologically significant points, often linked with ley lines or energetic vortexes, suggests that the builders understood the Earth's energy grid and its connection to human biomagnetic fields. By aligning these fields within the pyramid's structure, they may have aimed to harmonise the energy of individuals with that of the planet, promoting healing, heightened consciousness, or spiritual elevation. Essentially, the pyramids could have served as sacred spaces where the biomagnetic energy of individuals was amplified, potentially enabling them to reach altered states of consciousness, access healing energy, or connect with spiritual realms.[mlxix]

Quantum Mechanics and the Pyramid's Energy Potential

One of the most intriguing concepts in quantum mechanics is quantum entanglement, the idea that particles can become linked across vast distances, with changes in one particle instantly affecting the other, regardless of their separation. This concept has been experimentally verified, although it operates at a quantum (very small) scale. Some researchers have speculated that the pyramids could be linked to quantum processes, acting as nodes in a global energy grid.[mlxx] This theory, although speculative, suggests that the pyramid's location and structure may enable it to tap into a type of quantum energy field that exists throughout the Earth and the universe. Quantum entanglement and related processes occur at the atomic and subatomic levels and are not known to scale up to larger structures, such as pyramids. Zero-point energy is the lowest energy state of a quantum system in quantum mechanics. However, the practical harnessing of zero-point energy remains purely theoretical, with no experimental evidence to support its use in energy applications. Most scientists agree that it's an interesting concept, but it's far from being understood or harnessed practically.[mlxxi] Some scientists believe that zero-point energy could be harnessed for various applications. Could the pyramids, with their unique design and alignment, somehow tap into this elusive form of energy?[mlxxii]

While mainstream science remains cautious about applying quantum theories to ancient structures, the possibilities they open up are tantalising.[mlxxiii] If the pyramids were designed to interact with energy on a quantum level, it could suggest that ancient civilisations had access to knowledge far beyond what we currently understand.

Lost Energies: The Hidden Mysteries

It is intriguing that the ancient Egyptians, with their remarkable mathematical skills and deep understanding of the cosmos, did not seem to have explicitly harnessed Earth's energies in ways that match our modern technological standards. The precision with which they aligned their pyramids with celestial bodies and their engineering sophistication suggest they possessed advanced knowledge beyond simple architecture. However, despite this, there is no clear evidence that they used their understanding to tap into Earth's natural forces, such as geothermal, electromagnetic, or gravitational energy, as we might imagine today. Some researchers propose that they might have been aware of these energies but chose to incorporate them symbolically or spiritually rather than through direct technological means. Did the Egyptians have and hide deeper secrets about harnessing energy, or were their achievements solely a testament to their spiritual and astronomical devotion? The stones might have been alive with energy, vibrating in resonance with the Earth and the cosmos, creating a force beyond the physical world. It seems unlikely they would have invested so much effort in aligning these structures with celestial events or geological features without some knowledge of the energies involved. There is also speculation that the pyramids were positioned to harness Earth's natural energies. This is just part of the mystery. What sets these ancient societies apart is their possible development of complex systems to manage and direct these forces. The idea that ancient builders could tap into and manipulate energy on such a scale suggests a deeper mastery of natural power than we currently understand. In the next chapter, we will explore how ancient civilisations might have understood energy and developed methods—perhaps long lost—to control and use these forces with precision. This inquiry will offer further insights into the advanced technologies and knowledge that still elude modern science.

Chapter 14 How Ancient Civilisations Understood Energy

Pyramids are profound symbols of humanity's connection to the cosmos, imbued with deep spiritual and mystical significance that transcends cultures and time.[mlxxiv] What makes the pyramid so compelling as a spiritual symbol?[mlxxv] This chapter explores the spiritual and mystical significance of pyramids, examining their role as symbols of humanity's connection to the earth and the divine. It delves into the deeper meanings of these ancient structures and considers the possibility that they serve as spiritual tools. This chapter explores how ancient civilisations understood energy in terms of physical forces and spiritual and cosmic worlds. It suggests that pyramids were more than mere monuments; they were sophisticated instruments designed to harness the Earth's energy and possibly the universe's energy.

Research into the energy practices of ancient civilisations suggests that they may have had a deeper understanding of natural forces than previously believed.

In *Ancient Energies of the Earth* (1990), David Cowan explores how ancient monuments, including pyramids, may have been aligned with natural energy currents or ley lines.[mlxxvi] Similarly, the Mayan civilisation's use of solar and lunar cycles for agricultural and ceremonial purposes, as detailed by Anthony Aveni, shows a sophisticated understanding of cosmic and earthly energies[mlxxvii]. While this theory remains speculative, it encourages further research into how ancient civilisations interacted with their natural environments. As we explore this, we will uncover the possibility that these ancient structures hold secrets about energy that could redefine our understanding of the world today.

In ancient times, civilisations seemed bound by shared spiritual understandings that transcended geographical boundaries, fostering unity across diverse cultures. Maulana Mohammad Ali Jauhar, a prominent thinker in the 20th century, envisioned religion as a unifying force. One of his famous quotes is, "*Religion binds, and nations divide*," reflecting his belief that shared spiritual values could unite people more powerfully than nationalistic boundaries.[mlxxviii] This viewpoint, expressed during the turbulent times of India's struggle for independence, underscored his dedication to unity across religious lines, particularly among Muslims and Hindus, in the face of British colonial rule. He saw religion as a force that could transcend borders, offering a common foundation for mutual respect and coexistence. In contrast, he viewed nationalism and rigid state divisions as factors that could foster discord and fragmentation among communities.

His philosophy echoes the ancient world's interconnectedness, where religious beliefs provided a common framework through which societies across Egypt, Mesopotamia, and Mesoamerica developed parallel practices in architecture, energy use, and alignment with celestial bodies. This unity may have facilitated the diffusion of sophisticated ideas about energy harnessing, like those believed to have been employed in constructing pyramids.[mlxxix] These structures were not merely monuments but possibly cosmic beacons, channelling Earth's energy in ways beyond individual nations and serving a collective spiritual purpose.[mlxxx]

The Pyramid as an Energy Conduit

The pyramid, especially the Great Pyramid of Giza, is often regarded as a remarkable architectural achievement. However, new theories propose that its shape, geometry, and alignment were more than just impressive engineering feats. Researchers believe that pyramids were deliberately designed to interact with Earth's natural forces and the universe. The pyramid's shape—a broad base tapering to a point—may have acted as a geometric conductor, focusing and directing energy. [mlxxxi]

For centuries, people have speculated about the unique "Pyramid Power" associated with these structures. This theory suggests that the pyramid's design was both symbolic and functional, harnessing natural forces such as the Earth's electromagnetic field. Some researchers have even proposed that pyramids could focus energy, like a lens that focuses light, and redirect this energy for various purposes.

In ancient times, the distinction between the physical and the spiritual was not clearly defined. Energy was not just a concept of mechanical force but something that flowed through both the material and spiritual worlds. In this context, pyramids could have been seen as gateways where energy from the Earth and the cosmos could converge, to be utilised both spiritually and practically. Far from being static, these ancient structures may have served as dynamic energy centres, interacting with the Earth's natural forces in ways that modern science is only beginning to explore. [mlxxxii]

Could the ancient builders have seen the pyramid as a tool for accessing and harnessing energy from the Earth and the cosmos?[mlxxxiii]

Spiritual and Cosmic Energy in Ancient Civilisations

Civilisations in ancient Egypt, Mesoamerica, and beyond viewed the Earth as a living, breathing entity filled with divine energy. The world was not a dead landscape but instead infused with a life force that linked humanity with the cosmos. These ancient peoples believed that by building monumental structures—such as pyramids, temples, and shrines—they could connect their physical world with the spiritual forces that governed life and the universe.

The significance of energy in these cultures went beyond mere survival. Energy was seen as a divine force governing everything from the flood cycles of rivers to the movements of the stars. The alignment of pyramids with astronomical bodies, like the stars and planets, is no coincidence. It suggests a belief that pyramids were constructed not just to serve as tombs or religious centres, but as structures that interacted with the universe's rhythms.

This spiritual approach to energy is also applied to the design and placement of these structures. For example, many pyramids were situated in key geographical locations where energy was thought to flow more freely, whether from fault lines, underground water sources, or other natural energy points. This suggests that ancient civilisations may have possessed a deeper understanding of the Earth's energies than we recognise today.

The work of anthropologist and mystic Carlos Castaneda offers an esoteric reflection of these ancient intuitions. In his accounts of apprenticeship under Yaqui sorcerer Don Juan—first introduced in The Teachings of Don Juan: A Yaqui Way of Knowledge (1968)—perception itself is regarded as an energetic act: a purposeful arrangement of awareness controlled by the position of the "assemblage point" on the luminous body. This metaphysical centre, invisible yet vital, determines what we call reality. Move the point, and you move the world. In this perspective, reality is not fixed but fluid—a construct shaped by the movement of energy, intention, and silence. Carlos Castaneda's later works, including The Fire from Within (1984) and The Power of Silence (1987), deepen this understanding, describing how ritual, willpower, and altered states of consciousness can radically reconfigure one's perception.[mlxxxiv] While his writings have been debated by scholars regarding their anthropological accuracy, their symbolic and energetic significance within esoteric traditions remains profound.

Seen through this lens, sacred sites such as pyramids were not inert tombs or temples but instruments of attunement. They may have served as external mirrors of the internal process Castaneda described—a place where the assemblage point could be destabilised and reoriented, permitting a dissolution of consensus reality. The initiate, like the nagual apprentice, entered not to worship but to unmake—to realign their energetic body with a broader, more fluid field of awareness. The pyramid becomes not an endpoint of knowledge but a site of energetic disassembly—where the geometry of the self could collapse into the unknowable and be remade. In this perspective, inner geometry replaces theology; silence replaces scripture. The true map was never external. It was always the map of perception itself.

Egyptian Cosmology: The Divine Energy of the Gods

In ancient Egypt, the concept of energy was closely tied to the gods, who were regarded as cosmic forces that controlled natural elements. Ra, the sun god, was the life-giver, channelling his energy into the world each day. His rays provided vitality, growth, and nourishment to the land, especially along the Nile River, which was considered the country's lifeline. Egypt relied heavily on the Nile's flooding, and Ra's energy was directly connected to this vital cycle. Osiris, the god of the underworld, oversaw death and rebirth, seen as cyclical processes driven by natural forces. Meanwhile, Ma'at, the goddess of truth, balance, and cosmic order, kept the harmony of energy in the universe.

The Egyptians viewed energy as flowing through land, water, sky, and people. This was not a symbolic or abstract idea; to them, energy was a natural force that could be manipulated and directed. The pyramids, particularly the Great Pyramid of Giza, were designed to capture and channel this energy. Built near the sacred Nile River, the Great Pyramid's alignment with celestial bodies and geometric precision suggests it may have been placed on a powerful energy site.[mlxxxv]

Some theories suggest that the Great Pyramid was built over natural sources of electromagnetic energy, which may have been intensified by the pyramid's limestone and granite materials.

Granite contains quartz, a material known to have piezoelectric properties, meaning it can generate an electrical charge when subjected to mechanical pressure. The internal chambers and shafts of the pyramid may have been designed to amplify and direct these natural energy flows, acting as a conduit for energy between the Earth and the heavens.

The ancient Egyptians also believed in the concepts of ka and ba, which represented the life force and the soul, respectively. These elements played key roles in their beliefs about the afterlife. The ka was regarded as an energy that persisted after death, while the ba was the soul that travelled through the cosmos. The Great Pyramid, in particular, was believed to house the ka, or the life force, of the deceased pharaoh, thereby ensuring his immortality and divine status among the gods.[mlxxxvi]

In ancient Egypt, the pyramids were not just tombs but colossal devices designed to help the pharaoh ascend to the afterlife. The pharaohs were not merely kings—they were living gods destined to join the universe's cosmic forces upon death. With their precise geometry and astronomical alignments, the pyramids served as sacred vessels, celestial launchpads meant to guide the soul into the stars and the afterlife. Each stone was laid deliberately, and each chamber was carefully crafted to reflect the cosmos.

The king's body was laid to rest inside the pyramid, surrounded by treasures and offerings. Meanwhile, the pyramid's shafts were aligned with specific stars, particularly those in the constellation Orion, which was believed to represent Osiris, the god of the afterlife. This celestial alignment was intentional; it was meant to guide the king's spirit to the gods, travelling through the cosmic energy between Earth and the heavens.[mlxxxvii]

Could they have held the key to eternal life or a link to the world above? Today, some psychics believe that pyramids, especially the Great Pyramid of Giza, serve as interdimensional gateways or portals to other worlds. Through astral projection, psychics claim to access these gateways and travel to higher planes of existence. In these altered states, they explore the energetic dimensions of the pyramids, encountering mystical entities or divine beings.

The Mayans and Aztecs: Tapping into Cosmic Energy

Far across the ocean, the Mayans and Aztecs possessed similarly advanced understandings of energy, although their approach was more centred on the cosmos and the cycles of time. The Mayans, for instance, believed that the universe operated in cycles and that a specific set of energies governed each era. Their pyramids, such as the Pyramid of Kukulkan at Chichen Itza, were constructed with the movements of the sun, moon, and planets in mind. These structures were aligned with celestial events, such as the equinoxes, when shadows cast by the pyramid would form the image of a serpent slithering down the steps. This serpent symbolised the flow of cosmic energy into the world.[mlxxxviii]

However, the Mayans were not solely focused on the sky. They also appeared to have built their pyramids on land where they believed the Earth's energy was strongest. Many Mayan pyramids were erected near cenotes—natural sinkholes filled with water that were regarded as sacred. These cenotes might have been seen as portals to the underworld, but they probably also served as natural reservoirs of energy. Water, especially moving water, produces electromagnetic fields, and the cenotes may have acted as amplifiers, increasing the energy of the pyramids and their connection to the Earth's forces.

The Aztecs also viewed energy as a crucial force in maintaining the universe's balance, although they focused on the cyclical nature of destruction and rebirth. The Aztecs built their great city, Tenochtitlan, on a series of canals, with the Temple Mayor at its centre. [mlxxxix] The temple represented the axis mundi, the centre of the universe, and it was seen as a place where energy from the gods flowed into the world. Human sacrifices were often performed at the top of the pyramid, and these rituals were believed to release energy back to the gods, maintaining balance and ensuring the city's continued prosperity. [mxc]

The Mayans and Aztecs believed energy flowed through their pyramids, making them more than just physical structures. They were conduits for cosmic and Earthly energies, designed to keep their civilisations in harmony with the universe. The Mayans and the Aztecs also built pyramids as sacred spaces for spiritual rituals, but here, the emphasis was on the cycles of life, death, and rebirth. The Pyramid of Kukulkan at Chichen Itza, with its 365 steps corresponding to the days of the solar year, served as a living calendar, marking the passage of time and the sun's power.[mxci]

Rituals performed atop or within these pyramids were designed to channel the energies of the Earth and the sky, ensuring the continued balance of life and maintaining harmony with the gods. Human sacrifices at the top of the Aztec pyramids were viewed as offerings that nourished the gods and kept the cosmic order, ensuring the sun would rise and the world would continue.[mxcii]

Choosing Sacred Sites

One of the most fascinating aspects of ancient pyramid construction is the choice of site. These structures were not placed randomly; they were located where the Earth's energy was believed to be especially strong. Many pyramids were built on what researchers call "energy hotspots"—places where the Earth's geomagnetic forces are focused.[mxciii]

For example, the Giza Plateau, where the Great Pyramid stands, is believed to be an energy-rich area. Its proximity to the Nile, its alignment with the stars, and its position along specific latitudinal and longitudinal lines suggest that the Egyptians possessed a deep understanding of the Earth's energy grid. The decision to build the pyramids here may have been motivated by more than just symbolic reasons. It is possible that the ancient Egyptians selected this site because they believed it was a location where the Earth's natural forces could be harnessed most effectively. [mxciv]

Similarly, Mayan and Aztec pyramids were often constructed near underground water sources or geological fault lines. These fault lines are locations where the Earth's crust shifts, releasing energy, and can be seen as powerful sites where the planet's forces are most accessible. The cenotes near Mayan pyramids were not merely sacred portals to the underworld; they may have also functioned as reservoirs of natural energy, strengthening the pyramids' connection to the Earth's forces. Moving water is known to generate electromagnetic fields, and the cenotes might have amplified the energy channelled by the pyramids. [mxcv]

These energy hotspots are not unique to Egypt or Mesoamerica; they are also found in other regions. Across the world, from the Andes to the Himalayas, ancient civilisations built their most sacred structures at places where the Earth's energy was thought to be strongest. Whether based on advanced scientific knowledge or an intuitive spiritual understanding, these locations were chosen with purpose, reflecting the belief that the Earth was alive with power.

What the Pyramids Still Have to Teach Us

As we examine the practices and beliefs of ancient civilisations, a common theme emerges: energy is a force that flows through the Earth, the heavens, and all living things. This energy was not just a metaphor for the Egyptians, the Mayans, the Aztecs, and many other ancient peoples. It was a tangible force that could be harnessed, directed, and amplified through the construction of monumental structures.

Could the pyramids have been living instruments crafted to interact with the natural and spiritual energies of the universe?

Today, we see proof of ancient beliefs and energy practices in the rituals of modern indigenous cultures, whose traditions offer a living testament to ancient understandings of the Earth's natural forces. Many Native American and Aboriginal cultures employ energy rituals rooted in a profound sense of the Earth's natural elements. Native American ceremonies, such as the Sun Dance and Medicine Wheel, are believed to channel spiritual energy, aligning participants with the cosmos and Earth's energies, similarly to how ancient pyramids were aligned with celestial bodies. [mxcvi] Aboriginal Australians also practice energy manipulation through rituals, such as "singing the land," where specific songs activate the spiritual and energetic essence of the land itself. [mxcvii] These modern indigenous practices reflect an unbroken tradition of engaging with Earth's energy flows, offering a valuable parallel to the energy manipulation theories surrounding ancient pyramid-building cultures.

Indigenous peoples, particularly those with strong spiritual and oral traditions, often view the Egyptian pyramids through their cultural lenses, emphasising their spiritual and energetic significance.[mxcviii] Some Native American and Aboriginal elders believe that the pyramids were not just tombs or monuments but powerful centres for harnessing Earth's energies, similar to the sacred sites in their cultures.[mxcix] They often speak of a deep connection between the land, sky, and spiritual worlds, which they believe the Egyptians understood and encoded into the design and alignment of the pyramids.[mc]

For example, some Native American spiritual leaders compare the energy practices surrounding the pyramids to their sacred geometric structures, such as medicine wheels, which are aligned with celestial bodies for spiritual and healing purposes. Aboriginal traditions also mention sacred geometry and songlines that reflect the cosmic alignments found in the pyramids.[mci]

While there may not be widespread indigenous commentary on the Egyptian pyramids, the common themes of energy, alignment, and sacred geometry resonate across these cultures, suggesting a shared ancient wisdom about the interconnectedness of the Earth, sky, and human consciousness.[mcii] As we grasp ancient energy concepts, the next chapter will illustrate how energy harnessing transcended cultures and time, showcasing global parallels.

Chapter 15 Harnessing Energy Across the Globe

Across the globe, scattered throughout time and space, ancient structures are silent witnesses to lost civilisations. From the towering pyramids of Egypt to the mystical stone circles of Britain, these monuments captivate our imagination with their grandeur and the mystery they embody. Were these structures merely religious sites or symbols of power? Or is there another layer to their purpose—one involving a deeper understanding of the Earth's energy? Considering the possibility that ancient civilisations built these monuments to harness natural energy, we must ask a profound question: How did this knowledge become lost or misinterpreted over time? What lessons can we derive from these ancient practices to inform our contemporary pursuit of energy solutions? This chapter will take you on a journey to explore other ancient sites beyond the pyramids, delve into how this ancient knowledge of energy may have been forgotten or misused, and explore the tantalising potential of how these lost practices could offer insights into modern energy technologies.

Ancient Structures as Energy Devices: A Global Perspective

While the pyramids of Egypt may be the most famous examples of monumental architecture potentially linked to energy, they are far from being the only ones. Across the world, there are countless ancient structures that some researchers believe were designed to harness or manipulate the Earth's natural energy fields. These structures, built with impressive knowledge of geometry, alignment, and material properties, suggest that many ancient civilisations may have had a sophisticated understanding of energy that goes far beyond what we traditionally credit them for.

Stonehenge: The Mystery of the Stones

Stonehenge, located on the Salisbury Plain in southern England, is perhaps the most iconic of these enigmatic structures. Composed of massive stones arranged in a circular formation, Stonehenge has long been a source of mystery. While mainstream archaeology suggests it was primarily a ceremonial or astronomical site, some researchers propose that Stonehenge was much more than a gathering place for rituals.

One intriguing theory is that Stonehenge was built to harness electromagnetic energy. The stones, particularly the bluestones, are believed to have special properties. Bluestones, sourced from the Preseli Hills over 150 miles away, are known to exhibit piezoelectric properties—the ability to generate an electric charge when subjected to mechanical stress. [mciii] Could Stonehenge have been designed to harness these properties, perhaps amplifying the Earth's natural energy or tapping into geomagnetic forces?[mciv]

Moreover, Stonehenge is situated on a major ley line, and many believe it was intentionally placed at a geographical energy hotspot.[mcv] The site's alignment with the solstices suggests that it may have been used to channel both solar and terrestrial energies, with the bluestones acting as conductors or amplifiers. In this sense, Stonehenge could have been a kind of ancient energy device, resonating with the Earth's natural forces and the cosmos.

Teotihuacan, Machu Picchu, and Beyond

Beyond Stonehenge, numerous other ancient structures are believed to have been built with energy in mind. In Mexico, the ancient city of Teotihuacan features the Pyramid of the Sun and the Pyramid of the Moon, which are aligned with astronomical and geomagnetic forces. As discussed in previous chapters, the underground chambers and mica layers beneath Teotihuacan's pyramids suggest that the city may have been designed to harness cosmic and geothermal energy.[mcvi]

In the high Andes of Peru, Machu Picchu stands as a testament to the engineering genius of the Inca civilisation. While Machu Picchu is often viewed as a royal estate or religious site, some researchers have proposed that it may also have been designed to manipulate natural energy. The site's location on a mountain ridge, its alignment with sacred mountains (apus), and its sophisticated water management system suggest that the Incas understood how to work with the Earth's natural forces.[mcvii] Water, running through the mountain and the city's many channels, may have created a natural energy flow amplified by the structure's geometry and orientation.[mcviii]

These examples are only the tip of the iceberg. Across the world, from the Nabta Playa stone circle in Egypt to the Carnac stones in France, ancient structures share common traits: precision in design, alignment with natural forces, and the use of materials that interact with the Earth's energy fields.[mcix] While modern science has only begun to explore these possibilities, the sheer number of such structures suggests a profound understanding of energy in ancient times. This understanding has been largely forgotten.

How Ancient Energy Practices Were Misunderstood or Forgotten

The idea that ancient civilisations harnessed energy in ways we no longer fully understand raises a critical question: How did this knowledge become lost? Throughout history, knowledge has been lost to time due to war, conquest, and the passage of centuries.[mcx] Yet, some energy practices may have been deliberately suppressed, misinterpreted, or replaced by more immediate concerns of power and control.

For much of human history, civilisations' focus shifted toward empire-building, resource extraction, and technological innovation. As new empires rose and fell, the spiritual and scientific knowledge of earlier cultures was often dismissed or destroyed. Libraries were burned, texts were lost, and oral traditions faded into obscurity.[mcxi] In many cases, the sacred and practical knowledge of harnessing the Earth's energy may have been dismissed as superstition or replaced by more modern forms of energy manipulation, such as fire and metallurgy.[mcxii]

Another factor contributing to the loss of ancient energy knowledge is the separation of science and spirituality.[mcxiii] In ancient times, the two were often intertwined. Civilisations viewed energy as a physical and spiritual force that flowed through the Earth, the heavens, and the human body. This holistic view of energy contrasts sharply with the more mechanical approach of modern science, which often separates the physical from the spiritual. As a result, much of the ancient wisdom concerning the Earth's natural energy fields was ignored or misinterpreted.[mcxiv]

However, evidence suggests that some of this knowledge persisted in secret. Throughout history, esoteric traditions—from ancient Egyptian mysteries to the teachings of alchemists in the Middle Ages—may have preserved fragments of this ancient understanding.[mcxv] Even today, indigenous cultures worldwide continue to hold knowledge about the Earth's energy that echoes the practices of their ancestors.[mcxvi]

What we may have lost over time, perhaps, is a deeper understanding of how natural energy can be harnessed and used harmoniously, both for practical purposes and spiritual enlightenment. As we explore these ancient structures with fresh eyes and new technologies, we may begin to rediscover the wisdom of the ancients and apply it to the challenges of the modern world.

The Relevance of Ancient Energy Practices to Modern Technology

As we face unprecedented environmental challenges, the relevance of ancient energy practices to modern technology becomes increasingly evident. While we have made tremendous strides in our understanding of energy—from harnessing the power of fossil fuels to developing renewable energy sources—there are aspects of energy manipulation our ancestors may have understood far better than we do today.[mcxvii]

One key lesson from ancient energy practices is the importance of working with nature rather than against it. Ancient civilisations built monuments in harmony with the Earth's natural forces, often aligning their structures with the cycles of the sun, moon, and stars, as well as the Earth's geomagnetic fields. This approach contrasts with many modern energy systems, which often seek to dominate or exploit natural resources with little regard for sustainability.

Ancient sites, such as the pyramids and Stonehenge, may hold clues to the development of renewable energy technologies.[mcxviii] Natural elements—such as the piezoelectric properties of stone, the movement of water, and the alignment with electromagnetic fields—could inspire new approaches to energy generation. For example, studying ancient sites that harnessed natural energy could inform the development of geothermal, hydroelectric, and solar energy technologies, helping us design efficient and environmentally sustainable systems.[mcxix]

Additionally, the ancient understanding of resonance and vibration could have applications in modern technology. The ability of certain materials to amplify energy through resonance, as seen in the construction of pyramids and stone circles, could inform the development of new materials and structures that harness vibrational energy.[mcxx] This concept has already found its way into modern sound and vibration therapies, but its potential applications extend far beyond healing into communication, energy transmission, and beyond.[mcxxi]

Ultimately, ancient energy practices remind us of the importance of reconnecting with the spiritual aspects of energy. In many ancient cultures, energy was viewed as a holistic force that connected all things—humans, nature, and the cosmos. We have often lost sight of this interconnectedness in our modern pursuit of technological advancement. Rediscovering the ancient wisdom of balancing physical energy with spiritual energy could offer profound insights into creating a more sustainable and harmonious future.[mcxxii]

As we explore the possibility that ancient structures were designed to harness natural energy, we are reminded of the vast knowledge possessed by early civilisations—knowledge that may have been lost or misunderstood over time. These ancient monuments, whether pyramids, stone circles, or other sacred sites, stand as testaments to a time when humanity worked in harmony with the Earth's forces, seeking to harness energy for physical power and spiritual enlightenment.

In our modern world, faced with an energy crisis and the need for sustainable solutions, ancient practices of energy manipulation may offer vital lessons. Looking to the past, we may rediscover new ways to harness the Earth's natural forces, creating technologies that align with nature's rhythms.

The mystery of how ancient civilisations harnessed energy and what they used it for is far from solved. However, as we continue to study these ancient structures and their potential energy applications, we may discover that the future of energy lies in the wisdom of the past. In our quest for understanding, Chapter 15 will focus on the spiritual significance of pyramids, exploring their energy potential and their connection to occult practices throughout history.

Powered by Pyramids: A Book of Theories

Chapter 16 The Pyramid in Occult Mysticism

The occult often emphasises hidden knowledge, symbolism, and the connection between the spiritual and material worlds, aligning with the exploration of ancient civilisations that harnessed Earth's energy through pyramids. Perhaps the rituals or ceremonies in these structures were based on occult practices designed to unlock the pyramids' full energetic potential.

Throughout history, the pyramids have stood as testaments to human ingenuity, their purpose traditionally understood through the lens of tomb-building and religious symbolism. But what if the physical and the spiritual are more deeply intertwined than we think? As we look beyond the practicalities of pyramid construction, we encounter a wealth of mystical interpretations. Ancient civilisations viewed the Earth not merely as a resource to be controlled but as a living entity, a source of divine energy. These views open up a world of spiritual and symbolic interpretations, inviting us to consider whether the pyramids were designed not only as monuments, but also as a means to channel and harness the very energies that govern life.

For many occultists, the pyramid is a powerful symbol of energy, transformation, and esoteric knowledge. Across various occult traditions, its geometric form is believed to be vital in unlocking deeper cosmic truths and spiritual enlightenment.

Imagine standing before these towering structures, feeling the pulse of ancient wisdom coursing through you. This is not just a journey into history; it's an invitation to explore the boundless worlds of human potential and spiritual awakening. Let us embrace the notion that these majestic edifices are not merely remnants of a bygone era but keys to unlocking profound truths that resonate with our deepest spiritual quests.

The Pyramid as a Symbol of Power and Energy[mcxxiii]

In the occult, sacred geometry is a vital concept. Shapes such as triangles, pyramids, and circles are believed to possess powerful symbolic meanings and energetic properties. The pyramid's geometry itself is believed to hold mystical power. Occultists often argue that its four sides, symbolising the four elements (earth, water, fire, air), come together at the apex, the top, to represent ether, the fifth element. This combination of elements is thought to create a harmonious balance of earthly and celestial energies. Some even suggest that the pyramid's shape mimics the golden ratio and sacred geometry, which are fundamental principles in occultism, symbolising the harmony of the universe.

As a geometric figure, the pyramid is often seen as a symbol of ascension, linking the material world with higher spiritual realms. Was the pyramid's shape intentionally designed to channel cosmic or earth-bound energy in occult traditions, serving both a spiritual and technological purpose? Precise geometry may act as a "resonator" of hidden natural laws, echoing the universe's principles of balance and harmony, serving as an energy amplifier and a cosmic energy conduit that directs energy from the Earth to the heavens and vice versa. The pyramid is often used for energy concentration in occult practices, particularly in rituals and meditative practices.

Materials such as quartz, crystals, and certain metals are also believed to possess metaphysical properties in occult theories. Could specific materials used in pyramids—like limestone, granite, or gold—have been chosen not just for their structural properties but also for their occult significance in energy conduction or spiritual resonance?

Pyramids and the Concept of Ascension[mcxxiv]

In occult traditions, the pyramid is often seen as a symbol of spiritual ascension and transformation. Its shape, a metaphor for the soul's journey, resonates deeply with our spiritual quest. The broad base represents the material world and the beginning of the soul's journey, while the apex symbolises the ultimate goal of spiritual enlightenment or connection with the divine. This idea echoes ancient interpretations of the Egyptian pyramids, which were viewed as structures designed to guide the deceased pharaoh's soul to the afterlife.

Meditating inside or near a pyramid-shaped structure is believed to enhance spiritual development significantly in esoteric practices. The energy generated by the pyramid is believed to aid practitioners in reaching higher states of consciousness, making it easier to access more profound knowledge and wisdom.

This practice is linked to resonance. Resonance occurs when an object or system is driven to vibrate at its natural frequency by an external force. Examples of resonance include tuning musical instruments or how structures like bridges or buildings can resonate with earthquake vibrations or wind forces.

The vibrations within the pyramid can tune into the natural frequencies of the Earth and the universe, creating a harmonious symphony that facilitates spiritual growth. Imagine meditating within this sacred geometry, feeling every cell in your body attuned to higher energies, unlocking doors to deeper understanding and enlightenment. The pyramid becomes not just a structure but a transformative space where your soul's journey aligns with cosmic rhythms, propelling you toward your ultimate spiritual destination.

This resonates with *Mentalism*, the emerging trend that represents a profound shift from the long-standing paradigm of materialism, where physical matter and external reality were seen as the primary forces shaping our lives. For centuries, materialism has dominated scientific and philosophical thought, positing that the physical world is the foundation of existence and that the mind is merely a byproduct of brain activity.[mcxxv] However, mentalism has emerged as a counter-movement with the rise of quantum mechanics, metaphysical studies, and renewed interest in ancient philosophies.[mcxxvi] Mentalism posits that consciousness and thought are the fundamental building blocks of reality, and that the mind creates, influences, and even transforms the material world around us. This shift marks a move away from the idea that we are at the mercy of external forces and toward the belief that reality is a mental construct shaped by our thoughts, beliefs, and intentions.[mcxxvii] Practices like visualisation, affirmations, and intention-setting have become mainstream, reflecting a growing awareness of the mind's power to influence life outcomes.[mcxxviii] As materialism gives way to mentalism, individuals increasingly recognise that mastering their internal world—thoughts, emotions, and perceptions—can lead to mastery over their external circumstances, fostering a new era of personal empowerment and collective consciousness.[mcxxix]

Science remains the foundation for technological advancements, medicine, and our understanding of the physical world. In today's world, there appears to be a significant shift from left-brain dominance—focused on logic, analysis, and materialism—toward a more right-brain-oriented approach, emphasising creativity, intuition, and mentalism. This cultural transformation is reflected in the growing emphasis on holistic education, emotional intelligence, and the rise of creative industries that value innovation and human-centred thinking. As technological advancements, such as AI, take over more analytical tasks traditionally associated with the left brain, the human focus is increasingly shifting toward the qualities machines cannot replicate—imagination, empathy, and spiritual connection. This movement mirrors ancient wisdom traditions prioritising mentalism over materialism. It suggests that humanity is rediscovering the profound power of the mind and consciousness, much like the mysteries explored in the pyramids and their deeper esoteric meanings. In his work, *A*

Whole New Mind: Why Right-Brainers Will Rule the Future, Daniel H. Pink explores this cultural shift toward right-brain thinking, arguing that the future belongs to those who combine creativity, empathy, and meaning with traditional logic and analysis. He suggests that the information age, dominated by left-brain skills such as data processing and analysis, gives way to a "conceptual age" where right-brain qualities, including design, storytelling, and empathy, will be critical for success.[mcxxx]

There is growing interest in exploring how consciousness, thought, and non-material forces may shape reality, ideas supported or speculated upon by fields such as quantum physics and neuroscience.

The Pyramid and the Occult Practice of Pyramidology[mcxxxi]

A specific branch of occultism, pyramidology, delves into the profound belief that pyramids possess symbolic power and measurable natural energy. Pyramidologists assert that these magnificent structures can preserve physical objects, sharpen blades, and even heal by concentrating energy. While scientific validation for these claims remains sparse, the mystical allure of pyramids as energy amplifiers has captivated human imagination for centuries.

The roots of pyramidology trace back to the 19th century when European explorers and Egyptologists rekindled their fascination with the grandeur of the pyramids. Visionaries like John Taylor and Charles Piazzi Smyth pioneered theories that the Great Pyramid harboured mathematical and astronomical secrets, igniting a wave of occult exploration. Some enthusiasts believe the pyramids' precise location and alignment with stars or magnetic fields amplify their ability to focus and harness energy.[mcxxxii] For instance, the Great Pyramid of Giza's alignment with Orion's Belt—a constellation linked to resurrection and divine wisdom in ancient Egyptian lore—is compelling evidence for those who argue that these structures were designed to channel cosmic forces.

Hermeticism, a cornerstone of occult philosophy, resonates with the phrase *As above, so below*, derived from the Emerald Tablet. This tenet posits that the macrocosm (the cosmos) mirrors the microcosm (the Earth and human life), suggesting that manipulating earthly energies can influence celestial realms and vice versa.[mcxxxiii] Ancient civilisations may have embraced this belief in their architectural endeavours, constructing monuments like pyramids to capture cosmic alignments and harness energies from Earth and the stars.

Could it be that the positioning and construction of pyramids were deliberate acts to tap into Earth's energy and align with celestial bodies? This alignment might reflect a deep-seated belief that cosmic forces govern all existence. The precise orientation towards stars, planets, or astronomical events could be part of a grand occult design to channel universal energies into these awe-inspiring edifices. The mysteries of pyramidology invite us to ponder whether ancient builders indeed sought to bridge the earthly and the cosmic, capturing a power that transcends time and space.[mcxxxiv]

Pyramids and Hidden Knowledge[mcxxxv]

Occultists also see the pyramid as a symbol of esoteric knowledge—the idea that hidden or secret truths are encoded within its structure. Freemasonry[mcxxxvi] and Hermeticism adopted the pyramid as a symbol, blending ancient Egyptian iconography with Western esoteric traditions during the Renaissance. The pyramid symbolises the quest for hidden wisdom in the Hermetic Order of the Golden Dawn and Freemasonry traditions. The pyramid is a monument and a map of the human journey toward self-realisation and cosmic understanding for these groups.

The capstone or apex of the pyramid, often depicted with an eye (as in the Eye of Providence), symbolises the acquisition of ultimate knowledge or illumination. This imagery is prevalent in alchemical and mystical texts, where the pyramid represents the completion of the spiritual journey, with the eye symbolising divine insight.

Pyramids in Modern Occult Practices[mcxxxvii]

Psychotronics is a groundbreaking modern theory suggesting that human consciousness can influence physical objects or energy fields through structures such as pyramids. Robert Pavlita, one of the pioneers in psychotronics, has laid the groundwork for this remarkable theory. His pioneering work proposes that the human mind can interact with energy fields and physical objects. It's astonishing to consider the possibilities for understanding consciousness and the physical world! William Tiller's work delves deeper into the broader concepts of consciousness, and its ability to influence physical reality leaves one spellbound. The idea that our thoughts and intentions can affect the world around us is mind-boggling and awe-inspiring. William's research delves into the very fabric of existence, challenging conventional scientific paradigms and unlocking infinite possibilities. It's a profound journey to understand the power of our minds.

These works support the idea that pyramids can boost mental and spiritual power and connect psychotronics with ancient structures like pyramids. Pyramids may harness Earth and cosmic energies, acting as amplifiers for human mental and spiritual potential. Ancient occult rituals performed within pyramid spaces might have been designed to enhance the practitioner's ability to influence the world through the mind.

In modern occultism, such as Theosophy and New Age spirituality, the pyramid plays a crucial role in rituals, meditation, and energy work. Many practitioners use pyramid-shaped objects during meditation or as focal points in ritual spaces, believing that the shape helps to centre and amplify spiritual energy. They claim these sessions produce heightened consciousness, healing effects, or an improved connection to higher spiritual realms.

Additionally, we observe that the concept of pyramid energy has been incorporated into modern alternative medicine, with some practitioners utilising pyramid shapes to promote physical and spiritual healing. Although controversial, the belief that pyramids possess healing powers is rooted in the ancient view of the pyramid as a structure that transcends the physical world, bridging the gap between Earth and the cosmos.

In recent years, black orgonite pyramids have emerged as a modern interpretation of ancient pyramid symbolism, believed to harness and transform energy. Constructed from a mixture of resin, metals, and quartz crystals, these pyramids absorb negative energy and promote positive vibrations. Many users claim that placing orgonite pyramids in their homes enhances well-being, encourages mental clarity, and fosters spiritual growth.[mcxxxviii] This contemporary application draws intriguing parallels to the ancient pyramids' intended purposes—serving as energy conduits and symbols of transformation. By examining these modern artefacts, we can gain insights into the enduring fascination with pyramid structures and their perceived ability to influence our environment.[mcxxxix]

Embrace the timeless wisdom that pyramids offer. Let their ancient energy guide you towards heightened awareness, inner peace, and profound spiritual connections. Whether through meditation or ritualistic practices, allow these majestic structures to amplify your intentions and elevate your spirit.

The Occult and the Pyramids of Egypt[mcxl]

The pyramids of Egypt, particularly the Great Pyramid of Giza, hold a special place in occult mysticism. Many occultists believe that these pyramids were not merely tombs but structures designed with esoteric and mystical knowledge in mind. The alignment of the Great Pyramid with specific stars, measurements, and internal chambers is thought to encode secrets about the universe, time, and spiritual enlightenment.

The tale of *The Curse of the Pharaohs* is legendary. After the discovery of King Tutankhamun's tomb in 1922, several members of the excavation team died under mysterious circumstances, fueling rumours of a curse. This story illustrates how the pyramids and their tombs were thought to hold supernatural powers, connecting spiritual energy and occult practices surrounding the pyramids. While modern explanations suggest factors like bacterial infections or environmental toxins, the curse legend remains a powerful example of the mystical aura that has surrounded the pyramids for centuries.

Occultists have long speculated that the builders of the pyramids possessed advanced knowledge of astronomy, geometry, and metaphysics that has since been lost or hidden. Some believe that the pyramids hold clues to ancient energy systems or technologies that could harness natural forces. This idea is central to many occult theories about ancient, advanced civilisations.

Imagine standing before these monumental structures, feeling the weight of history and the whispers of forgotten wisdom. The pyramids invite us to open our minds to possibilities beyond our current understanding. They challenge us to seek deeper truths and embrace the mysteries hidden in plain sight. They are not just relics of a bygone era but beacons of inspiration, urging us to explore the vast potential within ourselves and the universe.

Max Spiers was a British conspiracy researcher and self-described supersoldier whose mysterious death in 2016 fueled widespread speculation. Known for speaking publicly on topics such as secret military programs, MK-Ultra-style mind control, extraterrestrials, interdimensional entities, and the occult elite, he claimed to have been part of secret black projects from a young age. He often referred to a breakaway civilisation and alleged that pyramidal and ancient technologies were being reverse-engineered for psychic warfare and consciousness manipulation. Just days before he died in Poland, he reportedly texted his mother saying, "Your boy's in trouble. If anything happens to me, investigate." He was found dead on a friend's sofa, allegedly vomiting a black liquid, and the official cause of death remained inconclusive. His death drew parallels to whistleblower suppression narratives and sparked questions about whether his research into hidden technologies or elite rituals crossed a line.[mcxli]

Similarly, Leo Zagami, a former Freemason turned whistleblower, suggests that pyramids were not merely ancient monuments but encoded energy tools used by both benevolent and malevolent factions across history. In his writings, Zagami posits that modern elites have inherited fragments of this ancient knowledge and now seek to repurpose it not for spiritual awakening, but for global control through occult technology and AI-linked rituals. He claims that hidden esoteric orders understand the pyramid as a multidimensional architecture—able to influence consciousness, open portals, and anchor non-human intelligences. His insights, while controversial, challenge the reader to consider whether the pyramid's geometry was ever meant to enslave or to liberate—and who, in today's world, might be manipulating such forms for covert agendas. In this view, the ancient pyramids were once guardians of ascension; today's imitations may serve as control grids.[mcxlii]

Interdimensional Energy and the Pyramid's Role

Could pyramids act as interdimensional gateways? Imagine the possibilities. Occult traditions often emphasise travel between planes of existence, and the pyramids—majestic, enigmatic structures—might serve a purpose far grander than we ever imagined. Could their purpose be not merely as energy conductors in a physical sense but as bridges between dimensions, allowing access to spiritual realms or alternate realities?

This profound idea resonates deeply with Hermeticism's concept of planes of existence and the spiritual journey between them. Hermetic teachings describe the process of ascending through various levels of consciousness, with each plane unveiling new understandings and experiences. What if the pyramids were constructed with this very intent—to facilitate such transcendental journeys?

Picture standing before a pyramid, not just as an ancient monument, but as a portal to the cosmos —a beacon guiding your soul through the vast landscape of spiritual realms. This idea ignites the imagination and invites us to explore beyond the physical to embrace the mysteries hidden within these architectural marvels. The pyramids could be our connection to something far greater, urging us to embark on that timeless journey of discovery and enlightenment.

Conclusions: The Pyramid as a Mystical Gateway

In occultism, the pyramid is far more than a physical structure; it is a spiritual tool, a symbol of ascension, and a conduit for universal energy. Whether viewed as a representation of the journey from the material world to higher spiritual realms or as a vessel for esoteric knowledge and cosmic power, the pyramid continues to captivate and inspire those who seek to understand the universe's hidden forces. Through its geometric perfection, cosmic alignment, and symbolic richness, the pyramid is a gateway to the mysteries of both the physical and metaphysical worlds.

In an interview with National Geographic in 2007, Zahi Hawass said, "*The Great Pyramid of Giza was built as a tomb for Pharaoh Khufu. We have archaeological evidence that supports this. However, the pyramids continue to attract various theories, and that's because they are still mysterious in many ways.*"

In the following chapters, we will examine the potential functionality of the pyramids. Chapters 17 and 18 discuss the funerary and spiritual functions of pyramids in various ancient cultures. They may have been monumental tombs guiding souls to the afterlife, reincarnation portals, and centres for amplifying consciousness or telepathic communication. Chapter 19 extends this idea, proposing that pyramids could have been ancient healing centres, harnessing energy for life preservation, rejuvenation, and even manipulating DNA. Chapter 20 examines the theory of pyramids as central hubs for energy production and wireless transmission, potentially powering ancient technologies similar to modern power grids. Chapter 21 speculates about the pyramids' function as a transportation hub. Finally, Chapter 22 explores the pyramids' potential role in climate control, tectonic stabilisation, and resource transformation, suggesting that these structures may have been used to influence weather patterns, agricultural productivity, and even alchemical material transformation.

As we move from exploring the pyramid's role in occult mysticism to its more traditional function as a funerary monument in the next chapter, we must recognise the fluidity between these two interpretations. In ancient Egyptian culture, the line between the physical and spiritual worlds was blurred, and the pyramids were designed to bridge these realms. What we now consider purely funerary structures were likely imbued with esoteric significance, serving as tombs and spiritual tools. The burial process was viewed as a sacred ritual that facilitated the pharaoh's transformation into a divine being. The pyramid's alignment with celestial bodies, its precise geometry, and the inclusion of mystical symbols all point to a deeper spiritual function, where the journey to the afterlife was not just a physical one but a passage through hidden energies and cosmic forces. In this sense, the pyramids operated as gateways to the afterlife and an elevated spiritual existence beyond the material world.

Powered by Pyramids: A Book of Theories

Chapter 17 Funerary and Spiritual Functions

Virginia Woolf (1882-1941), a prominent English writer, once said, "*The pyramids are silent, but their silence speaks volumes—of life, death, and everything in between.* " This statement reflects her recurring fascination with the passage of time and the weight of history. In her works, she often explored the profound meaning of silence, solitude, and the spaces between life and death, much like the pyramids, which are enduring symbols of these universal themes.

The pyramids may have served far more diverse and complex purposes than previously thought. The following chapters explore the various potential uses of pyramids. Their actual utility may lie in their extraordinary ability to blend the physical, the metaphysical, and the technological in ways we are only beginning to understand.

This chapter explores the potential funerary and spiritual functions of the pyramids. These ancient structures may have held spiritual and metaphysical significance. The pyramids' intricate designs and symbolism suggest their role as bridges between the physical and spiritual worlds, from guiding souls to the afterlife to serving as potential portals for reincarnation. The towering, geometric forms could have functioned as spiritual conductors, enabling not only the transition of the deceased but also the preservation and possible reincarnation of their physical essence.

Polytheistic Religion

When the pyramids were built, ancient Egypt was characterised by a deeply entrenched polytheistic religion, which involved worshipping many gods and goddesses believed to control the natural and supernatural worlds. The Egyptians believed that the gods played an active role in their lives, so worshipping and appeasing these deities through rituals, offerings, and temples was essential for maintaining order and harmony in their society. Each deity represented different aspects of life, nature, and culture, such as the sun, the Nile River, fertility, and the afterlife. The religion was not merely a set of beliefs but a comprehensive system that influenced nearly every aspect of Egyptian life, from politics and architecture to daily rituals and funerary practices.

The major deities during this period included Ra, the sun god, considered the supreme deity, often linked with kingship and the daily cycle of death and rebirth. Pharaohs were viewed as earthly manifestations of Ra, ruling as divine kings and protectors of Ma'at, the goddess of cosmic order, truth, and balance.[mcxliii] Ma'at played a vital role in the judgment of the dead. Pharaohs were seen as protectors of Ma'at. The relationship between the pharaoh and the gods was central to Egyptian cosmology, with the pharaoh as the intermediary between the divine and the human realms.

The Solar Temples of Ra, particularly those constructed during the 5th Dynasty, provide compelling archaeological evidence of the central role of religion in ancient Egypt, specifically in worshipping the sun god Ra. These temples were closely aligned with the sun's movement, emphasising the divine connection between the pharaoh and Ra, who was seen as the supreme deity governing life and death. The temples' design, with features like obelisks and open courts, allowed sunlight to penetrate sacred spaces, symbolising the power of Ra and the pharaoh's divine right to rule. Furthermore, the pyramids' alignment with the sun's rays is believed to represent the pharaoh's ascension to the afterlife, where he would be united with Ra in the heavens. This architectural precision, combined with religious iconography, clearly demonstrates how Egypt's polytheistic beliefs influenced the construction of pyramids and temples, linking the physical structures to the spiritual journey of the soul.[mcxliv]

Another key god during this period was Osiris, the god of the afterlife and resurrection. His myth of death and rebirth was critical in the Egyptian understanding of the afterlife. Inscriptions and reliefs in temples, such as the Temple of Osiris at Abydos, depict the myth of Osiris, including his death and resurrection. These link Osiris and the Egyptian understanding of death and the afterlife.[mcxlv]

Isis, his wife, was a goddess of motherhood and magic. Their son Horus, a falcon-headed god, was closely associated with the reigning pharaoh. Horus embodied kingship and divine protection and was often depicted as the pharaoh's protector. Anubis, the jackal-headed god of mummification, was believed to guide the souls of the dead through the underworld, ensuring they reached Osiris's court to be judged.[mcxlvi]

The Egyptians had a complex belief system regarding the afterlife, which was intricately connected to their monumental architecture, particularly the pyramids.[mcxlvii] The pyramids were religious structures designed to assist the pharaoh in his journey to the afterlife. Egyptians believed that upon death, the pharaoh would be reborn as an Osirian figure, and the pyramid, with its symbolic shape representing the rays of the sun, would aid his soul in ascending to the heavens to unite with Ra.[mcxlviii]

The construction of the pyramids was deemed a religious act meant to honour the pharaoh's divinity and ensure his eternal life among the gods.

Inside the pyramids, sacred texts known as the Pyramid Texts—the earliest known religious writings—were inscribed to provide the pharaoh with guidance and protection as he navigated the afterlife.[mcxlix] These texts contained spells and prayers meant to navigate the challenges of the underworld and successfully reach the Field of Reeds, a heavenly paradise. Egyptians believed the soul was composed of distinct parts, including the Ka (the life force) and the Ba (the personality), which required sustenance after death. Mummification was essential for preserving the body, as it was believed that the soul could not survive in the afterlife without a well-preserved body.[mcl]

Priests and the royal family performed offerings and daily rituals at temples to ensure that the gods remained favourable, and these acts were integral to maintaining Ma'at.[mcli]

Ancient Egypt's religion during the pyramid-building era centred on a profound belief in the gods' influence over life, death, and the eternal nature of the soul. These beliefs were deeply intertwined with the kingdom's fate and the divine nature of the pharaoh himself.

The discovery of Tutankhamun's tomb by Howard Carter in 1922 provides strong archaeological evidence supporting ancient Egypt's deeply rooted polytheistic religion and its emphasis on the afterlife. The tomb contained numerous funerary objects, inscriptions, and religious texts, illustrating the link between the pharaoh and deities such as Osiris, the god of the afterlife, and Anubis, the god of mummification and protector of the dead. The walls of the burial chamber depicted Tutankhamun's journey through the underworld, guided by Anubis and his eventual resurrection, reflecting the myth of Osiris. Elaborate burial items, like the iconic golden death mask, canopic jars for preserving organs, and protective amulets, were meant to ensure the pharaoh's safe passage to the afterlife, where he would be reunited with the gods. This find offers concrete evidence of the Egyptians' religious beliefs in the eternal nature of the soul and the crucial role that gods such as Osiris and Anubis played in the pharaoh's journey to the afterlife.[mclii]

Sacred Resting Places

Historically, the pyramids' primary and widely accepted function, particularly in Egypt, was as monumental tombs for pharaohs, symbolising their divine status and ensuring their transition to the afterlife. The Great Pyramid of Giza and its counterparts in the Giza complex were designed as an eternal resting place for rulers, reflecting their earthly power and celestial aspirations. *The Pyramid Texts*—ancient religious spells inscribed on the walls of pyramids, such as those found in the Pyramid of Unas—serve as direct evidence of their funerary function, guiding the pharaoh's soul as it journeyed through the afterlife.[mcliii]

Archaeological finds, such as those from the burial chambers of the Pyramid of Djoser, have shed light on the elaborate rituals surrounding death and burial in ancient Egypt.[mcliv] These chambers were filled with treasures, offerings, and spells meant to protect and assist the pharaoh in the afterlife.

Egyptians strongly believed that they could take goods to the afterlife. They thought the deceased would need various items for their journey and life after death. This belief led to the placement of food, furniture, jewellery, and other valuable items in tombs. A notable example is the elaborate burial practices of pharaohs, who were often buried with treasures and provisions to ensure a comfortable afterlife. This belief in an afterlife and the desire for material goods played a significant role in their burial customs and the construction of monumental tombs, such as the pyramids.

The King's Chamber in the Great Pyramid, which housed a granite sarcophagus deep within the structure, remains one of the most studied aspects of Egyptology. Renowned Egyptologist Zahi Hawass has extensively documented the complexities of these burial chambers and their role in Egyptian funerary practices, noting that the depth and positioning of these chambers were designed to protect the body and ensure the pharaoh's ka (spirit) ascended to the heavens.[mclv] The King's Chamber, buried deep within the pyramid and once thought to contain the mummified body of Pharaoh Khufu, was found empty when it was first explored. This has led to considerable speculation, with some archaeologists suggesting that the chamber was looted in antiquity. In contrast, others, such as author Robert Bauval, propose that it may never have housed a body.[mclvi] Curiously, none of the pyramids in the Giza complex have revealed intact bodies, leading to speculation that they may not have served as traditional tombs. While some believe the pyramids were robbed in antiquity, others question whether they ever held bodies.[mclvii]

Although the Great Pyramid of Giza and others in the Giza complex remain devoid of discovered bodies, other pyramids did have human remains. For example, the Pyramid of Queen Neith at Saqqara, part of a complex built during the Sixth Dynasty, revealed the skeletal remains of the queen. Her pyramid is much smaller than the royal pyramids of Giza, but it contains burial chambers, a sarcophagus, and remnants of funerary offerings. The discovery of her skeletal remains, jewellery and pottery confirmed its use as a tomb.[mclviii]

Similarly, the Pyramid of King Teti at Saqqara has provided significant archaeological insights. Excavations uncovered fragments of the king's mummy, which had been subjected to ancient looting but left enough remains to confirm the pyramid's funerary function. Teti's burial chamber was adorned with sections of the *Pyramid Texts*, which detailed spells intended to assist the deceased in navigating the underworld.[mclix] These findings reinforce the theory that, while many pyramids served as tombs, they also had a deeper, religious, and spiritual purpose.

Another fascinating discovery was made in the Pyramid of Amenemhat I, part of the Twelfth Dynasty, at Lisht. The pharaoh's remains were discovered inside the burial chamber, along with a cache of ritual objects and amulets designed to protect the king in the afterlife. The architectural complexity of this pyramid, with its multiple chambers and passageways, suggests a blend of practical and spiritual considerations, combining protection from grave robbers with a sacred journey for the pharaoh's soul.[mclx]

Compared to other Egyptian tombs, such as those in the Valley of the Kings from the New Kingdom period, the burial chambers of the Giza pyramids are relatively plain. Tombs from later periods are richly decorated with scenes depicting gods, the deceased, and the afterlife, reflecting their function as burial places and elaborate spiritual canvases.[mclxi] The simplicity of the Giza chambers might be attributed to the early period in which they were built, around 2580–2560 BCE, when the focus was on monumental architecture rather than detailed artistic decoration. However, this contrast raises questions—why would a civilisation renowned for its elaborate funerary practices construct such plain burial chambers for its most important rulers?

Other significant artefacts discovered include small funerary goods and the Khufu Ship, an intact solar barque buried near the Great Pyramid for the pharaoh's afterlife journey.

In Mesoamerica, significant discoveries have shed light on the ceremonial use of pyramids. Excavations of the Pyramid of the Moon at Teotihuacan revealed several burials of sacrificial victims. These bodies were often interred with elaborate offerings, including jade, shells, and animal remains, reflecting the ceremonial importance of the site.[mclxii] Similarly, at the Temple of the Feathered Serpent (Quetzalcoatl) in Teotihuacan, multiple burials have been found, particularly of warriors and sacrificial victims, indicating that the pyramid served a dual purpose: as a spiritual and ritualistic centre connected to the afterlife.^{mclxiii} In Mayan pyramids, such as El Castillo at Chichen Itza, burials were occasionally placed within or beneath these structures. These burials were often accompanied by grave goods intended to honour the deceased or appease the gods, emphasising the spiritual role of the pyramid.^{mclxiv}

In China, pyramidal tombs, particularly the mausoleums of emperors, were constructed to house the bodies of rulers along with treasures intended to ensure their status and protection in the afterlife. The Mausoleum of the First Qin Emperor (Qin Shi Huang), located in Xi'an and covered by an earthen mound, is one of the most famous examples. Although largely unexcavated, this massive tomb is renowned for its Terracotta Army, a vast collection of life-sized figures intended to guard the emperor in the afterlife.^{mclxv} Similarly, the pyramidal tombs of the Han Dynasty have revealed the remains of emperors and noble families. These tombs contained treasures such as jade burial suits and various offerings, highlighting the belief that these items would accompany and protect the deceased in the afterlife, reflecting a complex blend of spiritual and political power.^{mclxvi}

When comparing the Egyptian pyramids to similar structures in other cultures, such as the Mesoamerican pyramids used in rituals of death and rebirth, a common theme of spiritual ascension emerges. Whether in Egypt, Mexico, or China, the pyramid form symbolises the connection between the earthly and the divine, serving as a bridge between life, death, and eternity. Renowned archaeologist Michael Coe has written extensively on the ceremonial and astronomical functions of Mesoamerican pyramids, which, like their Egyptian counterparts, were aligned with celestial bodies and used for spiritual purposes.^{mclxvii} This cross-cultural perspective enhances our understanding of how different civilisations conceptualised life and the afterlife, making the function of the pyramids far more complex and spiritually significant than just monumental tombs.

Pathway to the Afterlife

Osiris was the god of the afterlife, resurrection, and the dead. Osiris was central to beliefs about the afterlife and was thought to judge the souls of the deceased. Egyptians believed that the body was needed in the afterlife. Mummification was intended to preserve the body so the soul could recognise and reunite with it after death. They believed the physical body housed the soul; preserving it through mummification ensured the soul's journey could continue uninterrupted.

The Egyptians believed that the heart was the seat of intelligence, emotion, memory, and the soul and was crucial for the deceased's journey to the afterlife. The brain was discarded during the mummification process. It was removed through the nose using specialised tools, a process called excerebration, and discarded because it was thought unnecessary. The heart, however, was usually left in the body or placed back inside after the other organs were removed and preserved.

In the afterlife, the heart would be weighed against the feather of Ma'at (representing truth and justice) during the "Weighing of the Heart" ceremony to determine the soul's fate. The person could proceed to the afterlife if the heart were lighter or balanced with the feather. If heavier, it would be consumed by the devourer, Ammut. The rest of the internal organs, like the liver, lungs, stomach, and intestines, were removed, embalmed, and stored in jars, each guarded by one of the four sons of Horus.

The story of the ancient Egyptian belief in the heart's importance and the practice of preserving it during mummification is primarily derived from Egyptian religious texts and archaeological findings. The heart was considered the seat of intellect, memory, will, and emotion. It was seen as more than just a physical organ—it was deeply tied to one's moral character and considered the centre of life and the afterlife.

During mummification, a special object known as a heart scarab was placed on or near the heart. The purpose of the heart scarab was to protect the deceased from having their sins revealed during the "Weighing of the Heart" ceremony in the afterlife. The scarab, typically inscribed with a spell from the *Book of the Dead,* was meant to prevent the heart from testifying against the deceased before the gods. The inscription on the heart scarab often included a plea to the heart not to "betray" the deceased by revealing their wrongdoings. The spell reads: "*O my heart which I had upon earth, do not rise against me as a witness, do not oppose me in the tribunal, do not be hostile against me before the keeper of the balance.*" By placing the scarab over or near the heart, the Egyptians believed they could symbolically prevent the heart from speaking out against the deceased, ensuring their sins remained hidden and they could pass safely into the afterlife. This magical protection was part of their belief system that linked the body, the soul, and morality in the afterlife journey.

In his pivotal 1957 work, *The Symbolism of the Pyramid*, George R. Hughes explores the profound connection between pyramids and the afterlife within ancient Egyptian cosmology. George R. Hughes emphasises that the pyramid was not just a monumental structure but a sacred representation of the pharaoh's divine status and journey to eternal life. The shape and alignment of the pyramid symbolised the pharaoh's ascent to the heavens, mirroring the sun's rays, which the

Egyptians believed would guide the soul of the deceased ruler toward immortality. This concept of the pyramid as a pathway to the afterlife reflects the Egyptian belief in the eternal cycle of life, death, and rebirth, with the pharaoh becoming one with the gods after death.[mclxviii]

More recently, we also see the afterlife as a central theme in Zahi Hawass's 2003 book *Pyramids, Temples, and Tombs of Ancient Egypt*—the pyramid's role in ensuring the pharaoh's immortality. Zahi Hawass explains how these monumental structures were meticulously designed to protect the pharaoh's body and the vast treasures required for his journey into the afterlife. The pyramid served as a tomb and a symbolic bridge between the earthly realm and the divine, facilitating the pharaoh's ascension to the heavens. In Zahi Hawass' analysis, this connection to the afterlife is vital to understanding the pyramids' significance in ancient Egyptian cosmology, as they were constructed to guarantee the eternal existence of the pharaoh's soul in the company of the gods.[mclxix] One of his quotes: "*The pyramids are not just the tombs of the kings, but they are the spiritual elevators that raised the soul of the king into eternity.*"

The idea of pyramids as pathways to the afterlife was not unique to Egypt. In many ancient cultures, pyramids were not just physical structures but also symbolic pathways to the afterlife. Their geometric shape, pointing skyward, was seen as a connection between the Earth and the heavens, facilitating the soul's journey.[mclxx]

Other pyramid-building civilisations, such as the Mayans and Aztecs in Mesoamerica, also associated pyramids with spiritual ascension and connection to the heavens. In Mesoamerica, pyramids like those at Teotihuacán and Chichén Itzá were seen as spiritual gateways, linking the earthly realm with the cosmos. The Temple of Kukulkan at Chichen Itza is aligned with the solstices, symbolising the connection between the Earth and the sky. These pyramids were often associated with gods of creation and the afterlife, reflecting similar beliefs about the soul's journey to the celestial realm.[mclxxi]

Consciousness Beyond Death

Dr. Raymond Moody coined the term "near-death experience" (NDE) in his 1975 bestseller *Life After Life*. He documented hundreds of testimonies from individuals who were declared clinically dead but returned with vivid memories of moving through tunnels, encountering radiant beings, and experiencing a life review, phenomena remarkably consistent across cultures, age groups, and belief systems.[mclxxii]

What makes his findings striking is the structural and symbolic overlap between NDEs and ancient ritual architecture. The tunnel, for instance, one of the most universally reported elements in NDEs, is echoed in the narrow shafts and corridors of pyramids, which often lead toward a chamber symbolising transformation. The sense of detachment from the body, of merging with light or universal consciousness, mirrors initiatory experiences described in Egyptian funerary texts such as the *Amduat* and the *Book of the Dead*. These texts guide the soul through underworld realms, much like Dr. Moody's accounts describe a "journey" between worlds. It is conceivable that the pyramid was not only metaphorically aligned with death, but also structurally engineered to replicate or trigger this transpersonal journey.

His research also supports the non-local nature of consciousness, a concept shared by biologists like Dr. Rupert Sheldrake and echoed in the work of Dr. Bruce Lipton, both of whom suggest that mind and awareness are not confined to the brain. If the pyramid's geometry, materials, and spatial harmonics could influence energy fields, as some propose, it may also affect human consciousness in ways we are only beginning to understand. From this angle, the Great Pyramid becomes a resonant chamber, designed to decouple awareness from the body, elevate perception, and simulate a state that modern researchers have only recently begun to document scientifically.

How might the ancient structures have been used to explore, rehearse, or even manipulate the boundaries of life and death? Perhaps the ancients knew what Dr. Moody's research confirms: consciousness transcends flesh, and death is not an end, but a doorway into something far more complex and patterned.

Reincarnation Portal

In *The Mummy* (1932), directed by Karl Freund, the theme of reincarnation is a central element of the plot.[mclxxiii] Imhotep, an ancient Egyptian priest resurrected after thousands of years, believes that Helen Grosvenor, a modern woman, is the reincarnation of his lost love, Princess Ankh-es-en-Amon. His goal is to reunite with her by performing a forbidden ritual to kill Helen's current form and restore his beloved fully in her body. The film weaves themes of ancient magic, resurrection, and eternal love, setting a template for modern mummy-themed cinema.

While ancient Egyptians did not have a concept of reincarnation in the same way as Hinduism or Buddhism, they were intensely focused on rebirth and resurrection. They believed that death was a transition rather than an end, and through careful rituals, the soul could achieve eternal life or even be reborn.[mclxxiv]

In ancient Egyptian mythology, the story of Osiris is a powerful narrative of death, resurrection, and the cyclical nature of life. Osiris, the god of the afterlife and rebirth, was betrayed and murdered by his brother, Set, who sought to claim the throne of Egypt. Set dismembered Osiris and scattered his body across the land, plunging the world into chaos. However, Osiris' devoted wife, Isis, embarked on a relentless quest to find and reassemble his body, using her magical powers to resurrect him. This act restored Osiris to life and established him as the ruler of the underworld, embodying the promise of renewal and transformation. His resurrection symbolised the eternal cycle of life, death, and rebirth, mirroring the natural rhythms observed in the world around them, such as the annual flooding of the Nile. Intriguingly, the scarab beetle also embodies this theme of regeneration. As it rolls balls of dung, it is seen as a symbol of creation and transformation, reinforcing the belief that life continues in a new form. Scarabs were often placed in tombs or worn as amulets to invoke protection and rebirth, further emphasising the ancient Egyptians' understanding that death was not an end but a transition to another state of being, rich with the potential for renewal.

By concentrating cosmic or Earth energies, pyramids might have been seen as tools to guide the soul after death, allowing it to return to Earth in a new form, perhaps even controlling the reincarnation process to select specific times or conditions for rebirth.[mclxxv] The rituals surrounding mummification, such as preparing the body and placing the sarcophagus, a coffin, within the pyramid, could have been part of a broader process aimed at energetically preserving the body and the essential genetic material. This could align with the Egyptians' focus on rebirth and resurrection, where the soul and the physical essence needed to be preserved to ensure eternal life. Interestingly, the Eye of Horus was placed on the bodies of the dead as a symbol of protection and resurrection.[mclxxvi] In occult traditions, this symbolic eye could be considered a precursor to the All-Seeing Eye.

In Mesoamerica, pyramids are often associated with sacred rituals that involve the sun and the cycles of death and rebirth. These structures were designed to align with astronomical phenomena, reflecting the deep spiritual connection between the physical world and celestial forces, symbolising the cyclical nature of life, death, and renewal.[mclxxvii]

These similarities suggest that different pyramid-building cultures shared overlapping ideas about spiritual transformation and the possibility of life after death, including the concept of rebirth.

The concept of reincarnation—the belief that the soul or consciousness is reborn into new bodies after death—has existed for millennia in many spiritual and religious traditions.[mclxxviii] However, scientific proof of reincarnation remains elusive. Most evidence comes from anecdotal accounts, psychological studies, and interpretations of unexplained phenomena rather than direct empirical evidence.[mclxxix]

One of the most compelling studies that suggests the possibility of reincarnation comes from the work of Dr. Ian Stevenson, a psychiatrist at the University of Virginia. Over several decades, he researched children who claimed to remember past lives, documenting more than 2,500 cases. His findings, particularly in his book *Twenty Cases Suggestive of Reincarnation* (1966), continue to be cited as some of the most convincing evidence in favour of reincarnation.[mclxxx]

Studies suggest that 20-30% of people in Western countries believe in reincarnation or the concept of past lives. A 2016 Pew Research Centre survey found that 33% of American adults who identify as spiritual but not religious believe in reincarnation, reflecting a broader interest in spiritual practices in the West, including past-life beliefs.[mclxxxi] Another study by the University of Virginia shows that belief in reincarnation is more prominent among people who practice New Age spirituality or have undergone past-life regression therapy.[mclxxxii] Belief rates are significantly higher in countries where reincarnation is deeply embedded in religious practices, such as India, Nepal, and Southeast Asia. Among adherents of Hinduism, Buddhism, Jainism, and other religions incorporating reincarnation, 80-90% may hold beliefs in past lives, with the concept being a core tenet of these spiritual traditions.[mclxxxiii] A Gallup survey in India, for instance, found that over 90% of Hindus believe in reincarnation, which aligns with religious teachings about karma and rebirth.[mclxxxiv] While these beliefs in reincarnation are common, the number of individuals who believe they were specific historical figures or notable identities from the past is harder to measure.

While these beliefs in reincarnation are common, the number of individuals who believe they were specific historical figures or notable identities from the past is more challenging to measure. The belief that one was a pharaoh in a past life is surprisingly common, fueled by a blend of cultural fascination, psychological influence, and spiritual exploration. With its grand monuments, powerful rulers, and elaborate myths, ancient Egypt holds a unique allure in the modern imagination, creating an almost mystical connection that draws people to its history. Identifying as a pharaoh in a past life can fulfil a deep psychological need for significance and purpose, often enhancing one's self-image through association with influential, god-like figures. Many experience these "past life" memories during past-life regression therapy, where vivid, imaginative visions are often interpreted as genuine recollections, and pharaohs—with their grandeur and mystery—make for particularly compelling identities. Media and pop culture also reinforce this fascination, romanticizing ancient Egypt and its rulers in ways that make these identities feel accessible and resonant. Swiss psychologist Carl Jung's concept of archetypes suggests another layer: identifying with pharaohs taps into a universal archetype of power, wisdom, and spiritual authority, reflecting a collective memory or symbolic connection that spans cultures. These factors create a compelling pull toward believing in past lives as pharaohs, blending history, psychology, and spirituality into a timeless narrative. Or could life function like a "video" or interactive experience, where souls can choose a character, replay certain events, or even return to past eras? This concept would explain why many people believe they've been reincarnated as the same notable figures, pharaohs, warriors, or other historical personalities—since they might actively "select" these identities to fulfil specific roles or lessons. In a way, life becomes a vast, cosmic game where each soul has agency, not only in choosing its character but also in setting the conditions of each incarnation.

Despite the compelling personal stories and studies, mainstream science does not accept reincarnation as a proven phenomenon. Most researchers argue that memory, imagination, suggestion, and psychological factors, such as cryptomnesia, can explain the phenomena often attributed to reincarnation.[mclxxxv] Cryptomnesia occurs when forgotten information re-emerges, often making people feel as though they are experiencing something for the first time when, in fact, they are unconsciously recalling something learned earlier.[mclxxxvi]

Portal to the Underworld

While much of the fascination with pyramids focuses on their connection to the stars and the heavens, ancient Egyptians believed that life didn't end with death. Could the pyramids be portals for communicating with the dead? A portal is typically depicted as a doorway or gateway between two locations or dimensions, allowing for instantaneous travel. Portals are often associated with fantasy or science fiction, serving as magical or advanced technological devices that enable passage between distinct points in space, time, or even different realities. Portals often represent fixed or temporary openings that allow people or objects to travel between two specific points. The mechanism by which they work is usually left unexplained or attributed to magic, advanced technology, or unknown forces.

In many Egyptian texts, the underworld, known as Duat, mirrors the living world—a place where the soul could continue its existence if it passed the necessary trials.[mclxxxvii] The pyramid, then, could have been an instrument designed not only to house the physical

Powered by Pyramids: A Book of Theories

body of the deceased but to serve as a guidepost or even a transmission device, aiding the pharaoh or other influential individuals in their voyage through the underworld. Imagine the Great Pyramid as an ancient version of a radio tower. Instead of sending signals to the heavens or the rest of the world, it could have transmitted the soul's essence into the depths of the underworld, connecting with gods like Osiris, the ruler of the dead, or Anubis, the guide of souls. The pyramid's shape, alignment with celestial bodies, and the materials used, such as limestone and granite, could have enhanced the ceremonial aspects of contacting and navigating the realms below.

The choice of granite in the King's Chamber also supports this idea. Granite contains quartz, a material known for its piezoelectric properties, meaning it can generate an electrical charge under pressure.[mclxxxviii] Could this have been part of the ancient Egyptians' intention—using the chamber's materials to enhance energy or amplify spiritual frequencies? Such energy could have been harnessed in rituals to communicate with the dead.

Some of the oldest religious writings in the world are inscribed on the walls of pyramids and coffins. They contain spells, prayers, and incantations to guide the pharaoh or noble into the afterlife and ensure their safe passage through the underworld.[mclxxxix]

Modern attempts to communicate with the dead are widespread and practised by various cultures. People who have had near-death experiences often claim to have encountered deceased loved ones or spiritual beings. Neurologists suggest that neurochemical processes in the brain might explain near-death experiences and spiritual encounters. Shamanic traditions involve rituals in which shamans communicate with the spirits of their ancestors for guidance and healing. Some claim séances, Ouija boards, and other spiritualist tools to be methods for communicating with the dead. From a scientific standpoint, there is no proof that communication with the dead is possible. Most modern scientists and sceptics argue that the phenomena attributed to spirits or the dead can be explained through psychological, physical, or environmental factors.[mcxc]

This idea of communicating with the underworld also ties into modern pop culture, where pyramids are often depicted as gateways to other dimensions. Similarly, think of video games like *Assassin's Creed Origins*. We see the same in movies like *Indiana Jones* and *The Kingdom of the Crystal Skull,* referred to earlier in this book. Could these representations be modern reflections of a more profound, ancient truth?

Could the underworld have been a literal place beneath the earth? Instead of seeing the underworld as a spiritual world, they may have thought it was a physical place deep underground. With their massive size and underground tombs, the pyramids could have been more than symbolic—they might have been seen as markers or gateways to this hidden world. Egyptian tombs, especially in the Valley of the Kings, were often built deep into the earth, possibly because they believed the dead had to physically descend to reach the underworld. Descriptions of the Duat in texts like the *Book of the Dead* describe rivers, lakes, and perilous landscapes, which could have been imagined as real places beneath the earth. Similar to how other ancient cultures, such as the Greeks and Mayans, believed in actual underworlds, the Egyptians may have thought the same. The pyramid may have been a carefully designed portal to the world of the dead that they believed lay beneath the earth.

    The idea of real underground cities has intrigued people for centuries and continues to spark interest today. Many cultures have myths and legends about entire civilisations living beneath the earth. Some believe these underground cities are hidden from the surface, housing advanced societies or ancient beings. This fascination with underground cities also extends into modern conspiracy theories, with some suggesting that secret governments or military bases operate deep beneath the surface. Whether for protection, survival, or advanced technological purposes, real underground cities tap into the idea that the world beneath our feet holds mysteries that we have yet to understand fully. Some propose that there are underground facilities where advanced medical technology could be used to heal or even "resurrect" people. These ideas are speculative and lack any concrete evidence, but they continue to capture the imagination.

Chapter 18 Gateway to the Secrets of the Universe

Beyond their religious and funerary purposes, pyramids have been linked to esoteric theories that propose they could enhance mental faculties, such as telepathy and intuition, by amplifying the mind's resonance with Earth's energy fields or cosmic forces. Some suggest these structures served as hubs for amplifying human intentions, allowing for collective manifestations through focused thought, beliefs and intentions.

Further exploring the pyramids' role as resonant structures, theorists argue that they could have fine-tuned the brain's capacity to access a universal consciousness—a field of knowledge known as the Akashic records, which contain the cumulative wisdom of past, present, and future. Think of it as the cloud from which you can download. This theory suggests that the pyramids acted as cosmic antennas, connecting humanity with higher planes of existence or even extraterrestrial beings, facilitating interdimensional communication and access to universal knowledge.

The pyramids' alignment with celestial bodies may have enhanced this role, positioning them as tools for astral travel and exploration beyond the material world.

Ultimately, the pyramids may have functioned as multifaceted spiritual and energetic centres, bridging life, death, consciousness, and cosmic forces and offering a deeper understanding of ancient beliefs and modern mystical thought. Let us explore the pyramid's possible functionality as a spiritual command centre in more detail.

Mind Enhancement and Telepathy

Some esoteric theories suggest that pyramids, such as those used for telepathy or intuition, may have been employed to enhance mental faculties. These theories suggest that by amplifying the brain's resonance with Earth's energy fields or cosmic forces, pyramids could have allowed individuals to access higher states of consciousness or communicate telepathically over long distances.[mcxci] According to this line of thinking, pyramids acted as energetic amplifiers, boosting the brain's natural abilities and facilitating mental communication beyond the physical senses.

In modern research on psychic phenomena, such as telepathy, some scientists have investigated whether brainwave synchronisation between individuals allows for mental communication. One of the most notable studies in this field is the *Ganzfeld experiment* conducted by parapsychologist Charles Honorton in the 1970s and 1980s. In these experiments, participants were placed in a state of sensory deprivation to enhance mental focus. Some trials showed a statistically significant transfer of information between the sender and receiver, suggesting the possibility of telepathic communication.[mcxcii] However, these findings remain controversial and have yet to be entirely accepted by the mainstream scientific community.

Another famous researcher, J.B. Rhine, conducted experiments in the 1930s at Duke University, focusing on extrasensory perception (ESP) and telepathy. J.B. Rhine's experiments, which involved participants guessing symbols on hidden cards (Zener cards), provided early statistical evidence that telepathic communication might be possible.[mcxciii] However, his work also faced criticism for methodological flaws.

British biologist Rupert Sheldrake conducted extensive research into telepathy, proposing that it is a natural expression of what he calls the "extended mind." Rather than seeing thought and perception as confined to the brain, he suggests that the mind reaches beyond the skull and can influence or resonate with other minds across space. He has conducted empirical studies on phenomena such as people knowing who is calling before answering the phone, animals anticipating their owners' return, and the common experience of feeling stared at. These observations, he argues, suggest a non-local connection between beings, a mental field interaction that modern science has overlooked due to its materialist assumptions.[mcxciv]

Further exploration into the relationship between quantum mechanics and consciousness has led some theorists to propose that non-local communication—where particles affect each other across distances—could also apply to human thought. This idea is supported by quantum entanglement, a phenomenon Albert Einstein referred to as "*spooky action at a distance.*"[mcxcv] Some researchers, such as Dean Radin, have explored the connection between principles from quantum physics and consciousness and telepathy. In his book *Entangled Minds*, Dean Radin proposes that quantum connections between minds might explain telepathy and other psychic phenomena.[mcxcvi]

Although the intersection of quantum mechanics and consciousness remains not fully understood, proponents of this theory argue that pyramids may have harnessed cosmic forces to enhance mental connectivity, offering a possible explanation for ancient practices involving heightened states of mind or telepathic communication. These connections between ancient structures, modern psychic research, and quantum theory suggest a compelling link between the mind and the unseen forces of the universe.

Connecting these ideas back to pyramids, it is possible that the pyramids' geometric structure and alignment with celestial bodies played a role in enhancing brainwave synchronisation or amplifying consciousness. Ancient civilisations may have intuitively understood the interaction between energy fields and the human mind, using pyramids for spiritual rituals and as tools to tap into a higher level of consciousness. Whether through the resonance with Earth's magnetic fields or cosmic alignments, the pyramids could have been purposefully designed to create a unique environment where mental faculties, such as telepathy, were more accessible.[mcxcvii] This perspective invites us to reconsider the pyramids not merely as monumental tombs but as advanced spiritual and mental technologies.

In *The Living Energy Universe,* Gary E. Schwartz and Linda G. S. Russek delve into a groundbreaking concept that challenges traditional views of matter and energy. They present the universe as a collection of physical elements and a complex, interconnected web of consciousness, energy, and information. This theory proposes that all living beings interact through an energy field that binds them, creating a seamless network where information flows beyond space and time constraints. According to the authors, this field is dynamic and responsive, suggesting that interactions can influence personal experiences and collective reality. Their research explores quantum mechanics and non-locality principles, indicating that the interactions between these fields are instantaneous and unaffected by physical distance. This model of interconnectedness suggests a more profound, almost mystical understanding of the universe, where consciousness plays a significant role in shaping reality. The authors propose that this energetic field is fundamental to life and may explain phenomena such as intuition, telepathy, and synchronicity, which traditional science struggles to account for.[mcxcviii] Their theory would suggest that ancient civilisations, often portrayed as highly attuned to cosmic and terrestrial energies, might have understood and harnessed aspects of this living energy network in ways that modern science is only beginning to explore. This book pushes the boundaries of what is possible. It provides a compelling lens to view ancient structures like the pyramids as architectural achievements and nodes within a larger energetic framework that links all life.

Amplifying Human Intentions

Modern New Age theories suggest that pyramids could have been used as powerful tools to amplify collective human consciousness or intentions. Imagine ancient groups gathering at these majestic structures, focusing their minds and energies on common goals—whether calling for rain, healing the sick, or even something as extraordinary as moving massive stones using the power of thought. This thought sparks the imagination.[mcxcix]

Manifestation, the art of bringing desires, goals, or intentions into reality through focused thought, belief, and action, plays a central role in this theory. It's based on the *Law of Attraction*, which suggests that "like attracts like"—your thoughts, emotions, and beliefs emit a vibrational frequency that draws similar energies from the external world.[mcc] So, if you're constantly visualising success and happiness, those positive vibes will ripple out and supposedly bring good things your way. The universe is one giant cosmic boomerang, sending back whatever energy you throw at it.

But what if pyramids were not just ancient architectural wonders but also "cosmic amplifiers" for these intentions? Through synchronised group efforts—whether through prayer, meditation, or ceremonial rituals—people may have been able to focus and manifest their desires for health, prosperity, or even peace.[mcci] Picture an ancient group standing around the Temple of Kukulkan at Chichen Itza, chanting and praying for rain or a bountiful harvest. Their collective intention, focused on the pyramid's structure, could have amplified their energy, attracting the results they hoped for. Whether it was rain for crops or protection from disaster, pyramids may have acted as "spiritual Wi-Fi routers," sending their intentions out into the universe!

Now, here is where it gets even wilder. Some fringe theories suggest that these ancient ceremonies focused on manifesting their desires and might have even involved something as mind-bending as levitating or moving the massive stones of the pyramids.[mccii] Could groups of people, through mental and energetic alignment, have used pyramids as tools to enhance their powers and manipulate the physical world? Some believers think it might have been possible.

This brings us back to the Great Pyramids of Egypt. Imagine the builders not just physically stacking enormous blocks of stone but perhaps using the very structure of the pyramid to amplify their mental energy. The precision and alignment of the pyramids with celestial bodies—such as the stars in Orion's Belt—might not have been purely for religious or symbolic reasons but a deliberate design to tap into the natural energy of the universe.[mcciii] The pyramid's shape could have acted as a "mental amplifier," boosting the intentions of those who gathered within its walls or worked on its construction. Could these ancient builders have tapped into the energy fields around them to lift stones or influence the environment?

And, of course, we can't talk about this without mentioning the curious connection to quantum physics. The observer effect in quantum mechanics—where observation influences the behaviour of subatomic particles—has been cited as possible evidence that consciousness can interact with matter on a fundamental level.[mcciv] Could this explain how ancient civilisations might have harnessed the power of human thought to affect reality? While the observer effect operates on a tiny scale, not on large objects like pyramid stones, it opens the door to exciting questions about the role of consciousness in shaping our world. Maybe one day, mainstream science will catch up with what ancient civilisations supposedly knew already—that the mind is far more powerful than we can imagine!

The connection between ancient pyramids, human consciousness, and modern scientific theories, such as quantum mechanics, offers a fascinating possibility.

Universal Consciousness

Some believe the pyramids could have functioned as resonant structures, fine-tuning the brain's capacity to access the unified field of consciousness, which ties into theories of the universal mind or Akashic records.[mccv] This universal record-keeping system holds all knowledge and history. The concept of the Akashic records—a database containing all knowledge, thoughts, and events of the past, present, and future—is rooted in Hindu and Theosophical traditions, not directly in Egyptian beliefs.[mccvi] The term *"Akashic Records"* originates from the Sanskrit word *"Akasha,"* meaning "ether," "sky," or "space." In ancient Indian cosmology and spiritual traditions, Akasha refers to the fundamental, ethereal substance that forms the basis of all things in the universe. It is considered one of the five elements (alongside earth, water, fire, and air) and is thought to be the medium through which all things are interconnected.

The *Eye of Horus*, an ancient Egyptian symbol representing protection, royal power, and health, is often likened to the pineal gland due to its visual similarities when viewed from a cross-sectional perspective of the brain. The pineal gland is a small, pea-shaped endocrine gland located deep in the brain's centre. In spiritual and esoteric circles, people refer to the "third eye," which is believed to be the seat of intuition, higher consciousness, and spiritual awakening. The pineal gland and the third eye are not the same but have similar spiritual interpretations. The third eye is located in the middle of the forehead, slightly above the space between the eyebrows. In many spiritual traditions, the pineal gland is believed to be the physical manifestation of the third eye. The Eye of Horus symbol, associated with vision and protection, is considered by some to represent an ancient understanding of the brain's anatomy and the spiritual significance of the pineal gland. Although there's no historical evidence that the Egyptians understood the specific function of the pineal gland, the symbolic resemblance continues to captivate modern thinkers who view both as representations of enlightenment and spiritual insight.[mccvii]

The *Akashic Records* are considered accessible when the receiver, located in the pineal gland, is open or activated, enabling a person to tap into deeper levels of spiritual knowledge and universal truths.[mccviii] Some believe that the pineal gland can become calcified due to a poor diet, fluoride exposure, or stress, thereby reducing its ability to function as a spiritual organ. Proponents of this theory often suggest that crystals or certain practices can help to "decalcify" the pineal gland and restore its spiritual functions.

We see many examples today of sounds and vibrations believed to play a crucial role in stimulating or "opening" the third eye, which is closely associated with the pineal gland in spiritual and esoteric traditions. Chanting specific mantras, such as "Om," is a common practice in Hinduism and Buddhism, where the resonance of the sound is believed to vibrate through the body, particularly at the location of the Ajna chakra (the third eye), thereby encouraging spiritual awakening and heightened perception. Similarly, Tibetan singing bowls and tuning forks, which produce harmonic tones and frequencies, are used in meditation to clear blockages and activate the third eye. Modern techniques, such as binaural beats, are also used to help synchronise brain hemispheres and stimulate deeper meditative states, potentially opening the third eye and enhancing one's connection to spiritual insight and intuition. These ancient and modern sounds are said to help individuals access higher levels of consciousness and spiritual knowledge.[mccix]

Modern theorists propose that structures like the pyramids might have been designed to tune into the universal field of knowledge. The idea that the pyramids could resonate with universal consciousness ties into this belief system, where the pyramid was viewed as a bridge between the physical world and the spiritual realm.[mccx] In New Age spiritual practices, pyramids are often seen as powerful tools for amplifying consciousness. Some believe that meditating inside a pyramid or constructing pyramid-shaped spaces allows one to connect with the universal mind or tap into higher states of awareness.[mccxi] This idea is built on the belief that the pyramid's geometry focuses energy at the apex, making it easier to access cosmic information or tune into a universal consciousness.[mccxii] Modern practitioners of pyramid meditation report feelings of mental clarity, enhanced intuition, and, in some cases, experiences that they interpret as tapping into a collective or cosmic consciousness.[mccxiii] While no scientific evidence proves that pyramids can access the universal mind, these personal accounts suggest that pyramidal structures are perceived as amplifiers of consciousness, much like the Akashic records are believed to hold collective knowledge.[mccxiv]

Some researchers propose that consciousness is a field that connects all things in the universe, much like the quantum field.[mccxv] This aligns with the idea of universal consciousness or a collective mind.

The *life review* described by people who have had near-death experiences, where individuals recount seeing their life flash before their eyes, could this be interpreted as a "download" of all earthly experiences into a universal consciousness, similar to the way data is transferred in a digital system? It likens human consciousness to a vast data reservoir being uploaded or synchronised with a greater cosmic or universal mind. In this interpretation, just as when files are copied on a computer and the progress is visualised, the life review could represent the transfer of personal experiences from the individual's consciousness into a larger, interconnected consciousness or cosmic database.

Is Reality a Construct?

Michael Talbot's *The Holographic Universe* (1991) presents a radical reinterpretation of reality: that the universe—and everything in it—is fundamentally holographic.[mccxvi] This means that each part contains the whole, and that what we perceive as physical reality may be a projection from a deeper, non-local level of existence. The theory blends quantum physics with consciousness studies, mysticism, and paranormal phenomena to suggest that our minds are not separate from the universe but active participants in shaping it. He draws heavily from the work of physicist David Bohm, who proposed that the universe operates according to an "implicate order", a hidden layer of reality from which the physical world ("explicate order") unfolds much like a 3D image emerging from a 2D hologram. He also incorporates Karl Pribram's model of the brain, which suggests that memory and perception are distributed like interference patterns in a hologram, allowing the brain to function in a non-local, holistic way. He uses these foundations to explore how telepathy, precognition, psychokinesis, and spiritual experiences could be naturally explained within a holographic model. In this view, the boundaries between matter and mind dissolve, allowing phenomena such as synchronicity, miraculous healings, or shared visions across space and time to be considered real—not paranormal anomalies, but features of a universe where everything is interconnected and consciousness is primary.

The movie *The Matrix (1999)* explores the idea of reality as an illusion, a simulated world. This ties into the concept of universal consciousness—where humans are connected to a greater field of knowledge and can manipulate their reality once they understand the truth.[mccxvii] The film's exploration of the virtual and real worlds parallels esoteric ideas of accessing higher planes of existence and breaking through dimensional barriers.[mccxviii] *The Matrix* introduced a reality-bending narrative where the physical world is revealed as a simulated construct created by sentient machines to control humanity. This concept resonated deeply with audiences, giving rise to a subculture of individuals who began to view the movie's themes through the lens of philosophical, spiritual, and even conspiratorial ideas. The Matrix films are rooted in intellectual concepts, particularly the theory of simulation. This idea argues that reality as we know it may be an artificial simulation. The Matrix provides a literal portrayal of this notion. René Descartes' idea of radical scepticism and Plato's *Allegory of the Cave* are key philosophical influences—his thought experiment questions whether our sensory experiences can be trusted. Plato's cave allegory explores a similar idea that what we perceive as reality may only be shadows of a deeper truth.[mccxix]

In *The Future of the Mind (2014)*, theoretical physicist Dr. Michio Kaku suggests that consciousness is not a mystical abstraction but a measurable phenomenon, resulting from complex feedback loops in the brain that simulate time, social interaction, and future outcomes. What distinguishes human consciousness is our ability to envision alternate realities and outcomes—a higher-order function layered upon basic awareness. He proposes that future science may enable us to map and transmit consciousness via laser systems, using quantum data transfer to upload a complete model of the mind into space-bound probes or alternative substrates. In essence, this is a scientific echo of ancient soul-transit metaphors. Egyptian funerary texts described the Ba and Ka (soul components) navigating between planes through portals and "tunnels of light"—not unlike the wormholes or hyperspace shortcuts described in Dr Kaku's earlier work *Hyperspace* (1994), where higher dimensions provide a bridge between distant points in time and space.[mccxx]

The line between simulation and reality is thinning, both philosophically and technologically.

Interdimensional or Extraterrestrial Communication

Some theorists considered pyramids gateways to other dimensions or even tools for communicating with extraterrestrial beings. They suggest the pyramids could have emitted light or energy from their apex. Could the pyramid have been designed to capture or amplify natural Earth energies, including electrical or magnetic fields and potentially even lightning? Lightning harnessing could have occurred if pyramids were built to act as large electrical capacitors, collecting static electricity from the atmosphere and discharging it, perhaps in spectacular bursts at the tip. Imagine light beams shooting from the top of the pyramids.

The movie *E.T.* inspires the idea that the pyramids may have been used for communication and cosmic connection. Were the pyramids built to communicate with or harness energy from the earth and cosmos, much like in the movie E.T.? *E.T. the Extra-Terrestrial* is a 1982 American science fiction film directed by Steven Spielberg. E.T. is a gentle and intelligent alien with large eyes, a long neck, and glowing finger. He can heal and communicate telepathically. He forms a deep bond with Elliott and Elliott's siblings, who decide to keep E.T. hidden from the authorities while helping E.T. find a way to contact his people. E.T. wants to "phone home"—a famous phrase from the movie—so he can return to his home planet. Using his advanced alien technology and the help of Elliott and his friends, E.T. constructs a communication device out of everyday household objects to send a signal to his spaceship. Similarly, could the pyramids send signals to another planet or spaceship? Like E.T. manipulates electricity and radio waves to "call home," ancient civilisations may have manipulated natural energies for communication or power.

Dimensional or Time Travel

A fascinating idea is that pyramids might have been used to manipulate or alter time. Some theorists propose that these structures could distort time, acting as gateways or focal points for time travel or alternate dimensions. Exploring this idea would add a cutting-edge, almost science fiction-like angle to the theories. If pyramids could connect individuals with higher planes of existence, they might have been used to facilitate out-of-body experiences, astral travel, or the exploration of other dimensions. This would make the pyramids centres for transcendent experiences, allowing access to other universes beyond the physical.[mccxxi]

The ancient Egyptians had a complex belief system surrounding the soul, which consisted of multiple components, including the Ka, Ba, Akh, and Ib.[mccxxii] The Ba is often depicted as a human-headed bird and was believed to be the part of the soul that could travel between the physical world and the afterlife.^{mccxxiii} In some ways, this concept of the Ba might resemble the idea of out-of-body experiences, as it was seen as a form of the self that could leave the body after death.^{mccxxiv}

In today's world, thousands of individuals across different cultures have reported out-of-body experiences, either spontaneously or through practices such as meditation or lucid dreaming.^{mccxxv} While these personal accounts are widespread, they remain subjective experiences and cannot be empirically verified. Many reports of out-of-body experiences also come from people who have had near-death experiences. In these cases, individuals often describe floating above their bodies or travelling through tunnels of light during moments of intense trauma, such as heart attacks or accidents.^{mccxxvi} Though some accounts have been consistent across different cultures, these experiences could be linked to brain activity during critical moments rather than evidence of consciousness leaving the body.^{mccxxvii}

The phenomenon remains a subject of controversy and is not yet fully understood within the scientific community. Although scientific proof of out-of-body experiences is still debated, researchers in parapsychology have conducted experiments on them and astral projection. Astral projection is a term used to describe an out-of-body experience in which an individual's consciousness or "astral body" is believed to separate from the physical body and travel in the astral plane beyond the physical world. While the studies do not specifically focus on pyramids, the idea that consciousness can separate from the body and travel through non-physical worlds is central to modern interpretations of dimensional travel.^{mccxxviii}

The dream world, often viewed as a gateway to higher planes of existence, offers a profound connection to out-of-body experiences. In many ancient cultures, including those of the Egyptians, dreams were viewed as portals to communicate with divine forces or gain insight into the spiritual realm.^{mccxxix} Similarly, Aboriginal Australian traditions emphasise dreamtime, a spiritual belief system in which individuals can travel through dreams to connect with their ancestors, the land, and the universe. For them, dreams represent not just a state of rest but a means of journeying across time and space, interacting with deeper truths.^{mccxxx} This concept of dream travel aligns with practices like astral projection, where one's consciousness is believed to leave the physical body and explore other dimensions.^{mccxxxi} According to some, the pyramids might have facilitated such experiences, amplifying spiritual energy to allow for deeper states of dreaming or out-of-body travel.

Theoretical physicists studying quantum mechanics and consciousness have proposed that consciousness itself may not be limited to the physical brain but could exist in multiple dimensions or states.[mccxxxii]

Researchers in the field of quantum consciousness, such as Roger Penrose and Stuart Hameroff, have advanced intriguing hypotheses that propose consciousness might not be confined to the brain but could exist in multiple dimensions.[mccxxxiii] In Roger Penrose's book, *The Emperor's New Mind* (1989), he proposes that consciousness arises from quantum processes in the brain, specifically within structures known as microtubules. Building on this, Stuart Hameroff, a professor of anesthesiology and psychology, collaborated with Roger Penrose to further develop the Orchestrated Objective Reduction (Orch-OR) theory, which posits that the brain interacts with the quantum field to generate conscious experience. In *Consciousness and the Universe* (2011), they elaborate on this idea, proposing that the mind may extend beyond the physical body, which could potentially explain phenomena such as out-of-body experiences. Although the quantum consciousness hypothesis remains speculative, it opens up fascinating possibilities that consciousness could interact with other dimensions. This idea resonates with ancient and esoteric theories that suggest pyramids serve as gateways to higher realms or non-physical planes of existence, implying that these structures may tap into quantum processes or dimensional interactions beyond our current understanding.[mccxxxiv]

Although this is a developing field and lacks empirical proof, some proponents of quantum theories of consciousness suggest that structures like pyramids might resonate with the quantum field, enabling access to other dimensions or non-physical planes of existence.[mccxxxv] Modern esoteric thinkers often view pyramids as dimensional gateways facilitating consciousness travel between different planes of existence.[mccxxxvi] This theory is grounded in symbolic interpretations of the pyramid's shape and alignment, as well as the belief that ancient builders understood the relationship between geometry and the cosmos.[mccxxxvii] The pyramid's design is thought to align with sacred geometry, which some believe allows access to hidden dimensions.[mccxxxviii]

Drunvalo Melchizedek, in his influential works *The Ancient Secret of the Flower of Life* (Volumes 1 and 2), explores the deep connection between pyramids, sacred geometry, and higher-dimensional planes. He suggests that the design of pyramids mirrors the *Flower of Life*, a symbol believed to encode the fundamental patterns of creation. According to Drunvalo Melchizedek, the geometric precision of pyramids resonates with universal forces, creating an energetic alignment that could potentially open gateways to other dimensions. He further proposes that shapes like the pyramid possess the power to influence energy fields and harmonise with the cosmos' core structures, facilitating access to hidden dimensions and higher states of consciousness.[mccxxxix]

The movie *Stargate*[mccxl] ties the concept of pyramids to that of dimensional travel and extraterrestrial technology. In the film, an ancient pyramid-shaped device, the Stargate, is discovered to be a portal to another planet, facilitating travel between dimensions and distant galaxies. The film draws on the idea that pyramids could serve as gateways to other worlds, directly paralleling theories that pyramids act as portals to other dimensions or realms of consciousness.

The idea that pyramids could facilitate dimensional travel or serve as conduits for connecting to other worlds shares exciting parallels with modern scientific endeavours, particularly in projects like CERN's Large Hadron Collider (LHC) in Switzerland.[mccxli]

CERN, the European Organization for Nuclear Research, is one of the world's leading centres for particle physics research. Established in 1954 by 12 European nations, its primary mission was to promote collaboration in nuclear research and help rebuild Europe's scientific infrastructure following the devastation of World War II.[mccxlii] Today, CERN comprises 23 member states, with researchers from around the world participating in its cutting-edge projects. Located near Geneva on the border between Switzerland and France, CERN is home to the Large Hadron Collider (LHC), the world's most powerful particle accelerator. This institution has become synonymous with groundbreaking discoveries in physics, particularly in understanding the fundamental particles and forces that govern the universe.[mccxliii]

One of the goals of the Large Hadron Collider is to explore the possibility of extra dimensions beyond the three-dimensional space we experience[mccxliv]. Theoretical physicists have long argued for the existence of higher dimensions based on string theory and other advanced models. String theory suggests that there could be up to 11 dimensions, with the extra dimensions being "curled up" or compactified in ways that make them invisible to us in everyday life. These additional dimensions are considered key to unifying the fundamental forces of nature. By smashing particles together at incredibly high energies, approaching the speed of light, CERN scientists hope to detect evidence of these extra dimensions, which could help explain fundamental questions about gravity and the nature of the universe.[mccxlv] These collisions allow them to explore conditions similar to those just after the Big Bang. The data from these collisions is analysed for phenomena that might suggest the existence of extra dimensions, such as missing energy or unusual patterns in particle interactions. Such evidence could provide insights into gravity, dark matter, and the universe's fundamental structure.

Fringe theories suggest that CERN may serve as a gateway to understanding other dimensions, much like the pyramids, which were believed to have functioned as dimensional gateways in ancient civilisations.[mccxlvi]

In addition to theories that the pyramids facilitate dimensional or astral travel, some researchers and alternative historians propose that the coordinates of the Great Pyramid of Giza are directly linked to the speed of light, suggesting a potential connection to time travel.[mccxlvii] The geographical coordinates of the Great Pyramid are 29.9792° N, a number remarkably similar to the speed of light in a vacuum, which is 299,792,458 meters per second.[mccxlviii] This striking coincidence led some to theorise that the ancient Egyptians may have advanced knowledge of light, physics, and space-time, perhaps using the pyramid for time travel.[mccxlix] This concept of pyramids as potential time portals aligns with modern quantum physics, where time and space are often viewed as interconnected, fluid constructs that might be manipulated under certain conditions.[mccl]

Both Albert Einstein and Stephen Hawking believed that time travel, while extremely difficult, is not impossible according to the laws of physics. Einstein's theory of relativity suggests that time dilation enables time travel into the future by travelling at speeds close to the speed of light or near massive objects, such as black holes, where gravity distorts time.[mccli] While sceptical of practical time travel to the past, Hawking acknowledged that wormholes—theoretical tunnels through space-time allowed by Einstein's equations—could offer a pathway for travel across vast distances or even different points in time. Though enormous technological challenges remain, the fact that these ideas fit within accepted physical laws suggests time travel is theoretically possible, not forbidden by the universe's rules.[mcclii]

In the shadowed corridors of modern mythology, the Montauk Project mirrors the spiritual aims of the ancients—except instead of pyramid chambers, we find radar arrays and black-budget laboratories. Montauk allegedly involved mind control, psychic amplification, and time manipulation using a device called the Montauk Chair. This chair—said to use electromagnetic fields to project consciousness into other dimensions—functions metaphorically like a synthetic pyramid: a tool for collapsing spacetime through focused awareness. The parallels are striking. Where ancient initiates may have used resonance chambers, ritual, and geometry to access altered states or portals, Montauk sought similar ends through technology, secrecy, and force. If pyramids acted as consciousness amplifiers tuned to Earth's natural frequencies, then Montauk represents a modern attempt—though distorted—to reverse-engineer the same thresholds. One accessed the soul through silence and symbol; the other through coils, isotopes, and electricity. Both point to a forgotten science of traversing dimensional architecture by altering perception itself. These stories originate largely from Preston B. Nichols and Peter Moon's book *The Montauk Project: Experiments in Time* (1992), which blends speculative narrative with conspiracy theory.[mccliii] While no official evidence has corroborated these events, the Montauk mythos continues to resonate in alternative history circles and has influenced popular culture, including the Netflix series *Stranger Things*.

Stretching the imagination, perhaps the ancients didn't need ships or aeroplanes and used different methods for travelling the world. Imagine a world where the pyramids are advanced technological devices—transporters capable of moving individuals through time and space, much like the TARDIS from the iconic British TV series *Doctor Who*, which first aired in 1963. In the series, the Doctor, a time-travelling alien known as a Time Lord, uses the TARDIS—a blue police telephone box to travel across galaxies and through different eras. Could the pyramids have allowed ancient civilisations or extraterrestrial visitors to travel vast distances across the globe or even to other dimensions? Just as Doctor Who steps into a familiar structure that hides incredible technology, the pyramids could have served a similar purpose for those who understood how to activate their hidden potential. This theory could also explain why pyramids are found worldwide, from Egypt to Mesoamerica, to China and Indonesia—much like modern airports, they may have been strategically located hubs for travel and energy exchange, connecting civilisations or even worlds. These global monuments could have been part of an ancient, advanced transportation network, making them far more than mere stone structures—they were perhaps portals that bridged time, space, and civilisation. Another line of thought is that ancient civilisations understood how to download instructions from the universal consciousness. These and many more ideas will be explored in later chapters.

Pyramid Library: Ancient Wisdom Encoded in Stone

Could the pyramids have been ancient knowledge centres, functioning as universities where the mysteries of the cosmos and Earth's forces were preserved? Some suggest that these monumental structures may have acted as repositories of wisdom, encoding mathematical, astronomical, and historical knowledge within their architecture. The precise design of pyramids may have served as a tool for transmitting universal understanding across generations, preserving insights about the natural world and the cosmos through their dimensions and alignments.[mccliv]

The *Hall of Records* theory is one of the more captivating and speculative ideas associated with the Great Pyramid of Giza and other ancient structures. It argues that secret chambers buried deep beneath the pyramids or within their walls contain hidden knowledge or advanced technologies left by ancient civilisations or even extraterrestrial beings. According to this theory, these hidden archives may hold critical information about humanity's true origins, forgotten history, advanced science, and possibly the mysteries of the cosmos.

Edgar Cayce, often referred to as the "Sleeping Prophet," was an American mystic and clairvoyant who lived from 1877 to 1945. He is famous for entering deep trance states and delivering thousands of readings on health and spiritual wisdom. During the early 20th century, he made several profound statements about ancient civilisations, including Egypt and the pyramids. In the 1930s and 1940s, he suggested that the Great Pyramid was not merely a tomb or monument but a vast repository of wisdom. He stated, *"The pyramid's purpose was to be a storehouse for knowledge – much of which is still to be discovered."* This view came from his belief that the pyramids encoded advanced knowledge, hidden away for future generations to unlock. His insights have inspired countless followers and offer a perspective that sees the pyramids as metaphysical libraries safeguarding ancient wisdom.[mcclv] The origins of the Hall of Records theory can be traced back to Edgar Cayce, who famously predicted that a hidden chamber containing lost wisdom would one day be found beneath the Sphinx. He suggested that this chamber would contain ancient texts, records, or tools that held the key to unlocking the knowledge of Atlantis, a lost civilisation believed to be the source of great technological advancements. His prophecies have sparked countless investigations and explorations at the Giza Plateau, with researchers and enthusiasts hoping to uncover this legendary library of knowledge.

In an interview, Edgar Cayce was asked how he was able to see into the future. He answered, *"Because time is all one moment."* Perhaps he was tapping into the Akashic Records—a metaphysical compendium of all universal events, thoughts, and experiences.

Bashar is known as a multidimensional being channelled by Darryl Anka, who has been presenting Bashar's teachings for several decades. Bashar's teachings blend metaphysical principles with personal empowerment, emphasising that our beliefs, intentions, and vibrations create reality. One of his most profound teachings is similar to Edgar Casey's, which states that *"everything happens now"* and challenges conventional notions of time as a linear progression of past, present, and future. Bashar argues that all moments exist simultaneously, and human perception moves through these moments. This perspective encourages individuals to live in the present moment, as it is the only point of power where change and manifestation occur.[mcclvi]

According to those who believe in the Akashic Records, this "universal memory" transcends time and space, providing access to knowledge of the past, present, and future.[mcclvii] The ability to view events beyond the confines of linear time aligns with this notion. The Akashic Records are said to exist outside of time, allowing a person to glimpse into different timelines or dimensions.[mcclviii] Could their visions have been directly connected to this ethereal source of information? For those who believe in the Akashic Records, this answer offers a profound connection to this ancient idea.

Many pyramids, such as the Great Pyramid of Giza, were aligned with celestial phenomena, notably, Orion's Belt. This alignment suggests a purpose beyond mere architectural grandeur, potentially connecting earthly existence with the movements of the cosmos. These monuments may have functioned as astronomical observatories or spiritual tools, harnessing celestial energy to aid in enlightenment or to mark significant astronomical events. Their alignments imply that pyramids could have been used to track and interpret the heavens, offering ancient civilisations a profound connection to the stars. However, if the pyramids served as astronomical observatories, one might expect to find physical evidence—such as tools or inscriptions—detailing the tracking of celestial events. Curiously, no such explicit records have been found.[mcclix] While some pyramids, such as those in Egypt, exhibit precise celestial alignments, others, like those in Nubia (modern-day Sudan) or China, do not.[mcclx] This inconsistency in alignment suggests that astronomical features might have been culturally specific rather than part of a global effort to connect with the stars.[mcclxi]

Beyond astronomy, theories suggest that the pyramids' proportions, alignments, and architecture may encode profound knowledge about the universe, mathematics, or human history.[mcclxii] Some speculate that the gemstones or crystals within or around the pyramids could have been used to store information, much like how modern technology relies on silicon chips.[mcclxiii] If true, this would position pyramids as physical monuments and intellectual vaults, safeguarding the achievements and knowledge of the civilisations that built them.[mcclxiv] No known technology can use gemstones or crystals to store vast amounts of information like silicon-based technology does in modern computers. Scientists are developing holographic data storage systems that use lasers to store information within crystals or other materials in three dimensions, providing significantly greater storage capacity than traditional methods. This technology is still in the experimental phase, but suggests the potential for crystals to be used for data storage.[mcclxv]

The Pyramid could be compared to the Library of the Vatican. While the Vatican Library serves as a traditional repository of knowledge, preserving written texts that document human history and spirituality, the Library of the Pyramids takes a more symbolic and energetic approach to knowledge preservation.[mcclxvi] In this vision, the pyramids are not just architectural wonders, but timeless libraries that encode universal truths and principles in their design, meant to be interpreted by those capable of unlocking their secrets. Both libraries reflect humanity's quest to understand the universe, the divine, and the natural world. However, they do so differently: one through the written word, the other through sacred geometry and cosmic alignment.[mcclxvii]

Pyramids as Bridges Between Realms

The funerary and spiritual functions of the pyramids extend far beyond their role as mere tombs for the pharaohs. The possibility that these grand structures served as energetic centres, guiding souls into the afterlife, adds a layer of complexity to our understanding of ancient Egyptian beliefs about life, death, and consciousness. Whether through their alignment with celestial bodies, their potential to connect with the spiritual world or their symbolic ascent from Earth to the heavens, the pyramids appear to have been carefully designed to embody physical and metaphysical significance.

This chapter explored the pyramids as monuments of power and portals to other worlds, possibly as conduits for reincarnation, resurrection, or interdimensional communication. From amplifying human intention to acting as cosmic antennas, the pyramids represent a profound blend of technology, spirituality, and mystical purpose that may have facilitated everything from mental enhancement to astral travel.

While much evidence for these functions remains speculative, the pyramid's enduring mystery continues to captivate the imagination, suggesting that these ancient structures may hold deeper secrets about universal consciousness and life after death. As we explore, we will delve even further into the pyramids' possible cosmic and energetic roles in shaping ancient beliefs and practices.

In reflecting on the funerary and spiritual roles of the pyramids, it becomes evident that these structures were designed not only to honour the dead but also to serve as mighty spiritual monuments. The dual purpose of the pyramids—as final resting places for the elite and as metaphysical gateways to the afterlife—underscores their significance in earthly and cosmic realms. Whether as literal tombs or symbolic vessels of energy, the pyramids are eternal reminders of ancient Egypt's profound understanding of life, death, and the forces that bind them together. Ultimately, they represent the intertwining of material and spiritual worlds, ensuring the immortality of those entombed within while potentially acting as conduits for unseen cosmic energies.

After examining their spiritual roles, Chapter 19 will examine the healing properties attributed to pyramids, further expanding on their multifaceted significance. What if the pyramids were not just places for the dead but also healing centres for the living? Imagine the ancient Egyptians entering the pyramids, where precise geometric shapes, materials such as quartz, and alignment with the Earth's natural energies created environments conducive to healing. Could the unique structure of the pyramids, along with sound or light, have been used to rejuvenate and heal both body and spirit? If we could recreate these environments today, could we unlock ancient energy-based healing methods that modern medicine has yet to rediscover?

Chapter 19 Healing Power and Life Preservation

Could ancient civilisations have advanced knowledge of energy manipulation for healing and life preservation that we have yet to rediscover or fully understand?

Peter Tompkins's *The Secret Life of Nature* (1997) offers a captivating blend of mysticism and scientific exploration, proposing that unseen forces—such as nature spirits and subtle energetic fields—actively engage with and influence living organisms.[mcclxviii] One of his most intriguing theories is that the world is not just a collection of inert matter but a dynamic, living system infused with consciousness and energy. He suggests that ancient civilisations may have had a profound awareness of this residing energy and understood how to harness it to achieve harmony with the cosmos. This knowledge, he argues, could explain why ancient structures, such as the pyramids and other megalithic monuments, were built with precise alignments and materials believed to channel or amplify these energies. He explores the concept of elemental beings—entities associated with natural forces such as water, air, earth, and fire—which he describes as intermediaries between the physical and energetic realms. In his view, these beings may have been regarded by ancient cultures not as mere mythological constructs but as real participants in the orchestration of nature's balance. This belief may have driven the placement and construction of sacred sites, aligning them with natural energy flows and creating spaces where human activity could resonate with Earth's pulse. He also delves into the notion of biophotons and the subtle light emitted by living cells, suggesting that this bio-energy field could be part of what ancient people perceived as the aura or spiritual essence. He theorises that by understanding and manipulating these subtle energies, ancient builders could have designed structures capable of amplifying life forces, promoting healing, and facilitating spiritual experiences. Peter Tompkins was well known for his work in esoteric and fringe science literature. His best-selling book, *The Secret Life of Plants* (1973), gained prominence, exploring the idea that plants possess emotions and a form of consciousness.

Did the ancients believe in the healing power of pyramids? Modern alternative therapies are reviving this theory. Could the pyramids hold the secret to life preservation or even healing? We will delve deeper into the energy they harness in the next chapter. In this chapter, the ancient structures are explored through the lens of practical use, such as providing shelter from extreme temperatures and as centres of healing, preservation, and bioenergetics. In some beliefs, pyramids are thought to amplify natural energies, acting as healing centres that focus energy for physical rejuvenation and enhanced mental states. Theories extend into sound healing, where specific frequencies within the pyramids are said to promote spiritual or physical well-being.

A quote by Robert Anton Wilson (1932–2007), an American author and futurist, sums up our interest in the pyramids: *"The pyramids symbolise the greatest of all human desires: the quest for immortality."*

The chapter explores the pyramids' potential role in preserving life at both the physical and genetic levels. It speculates that they may have been designed as bioenergetic devices that could manipulate or preserve DNA. From the idea of cloning historical figures to possibly activating dormant genetic material, the pyramids' structure and energy fields are imagined to play a role in advanced, yet forgotten, technologies.

In ancient times, it is believed that humans may have lived much longer, as suggested by myths and historical records from cultures such as the Sumerians and the Bible, which describe pre-flood individuals living for centuries.[mcclxix] In the Bible, figures like Methuselah are said to have lived for 969 years, and Noah lived to be 950 years old.[mcclxx] Similarly, in Sumerian king lists, kings who ruled before the great flood are reported to have reigned for thousands of years, with some living for up to 28,800 years.[mcclxxi] These extraordinary lifespans are often interpreted symbolically, though some speculative theories suggest that humans may have lived far longer in the distant past due to access to advanced knowledge or technologies related to health and energy.[mcclxxii]

Some theories link this longevity to the advanced knowledge and energy manipulation that may have been encoded in ancient structures, such as the pyramids.[mcclxxiii] For example, the Great Pyramid of Giza could have been a centre for harnessing Earth's natural energies, promoting healing and well-being.[mcclxxiv] The pyramids might have created environments conducive to physical rejuvenation and extended lifespans by concentrating and amplifying electromagnetic or spiritual forces.[mcclxxv] After the great floods, which some view as a symbolic loss of this ancient knowledge, human lifespans may have shortened as civilisations lost access to these energy-enhancing technologies.[mcclxxvi] Exploring this connection between the pyramids and human health could offer deeper insights into how ancient civilisations used these monumental structures for spiritual purposes and to maintain vitality and longevity.

Further comparisons draw parallels between the pyramids and lightning as energy sources for reanimation, akin to the imagery of Dracula's resurrection through storms. The chapter also discusses the symbolic and practical uses of geothermal energy and hot springs, which may be linked to healing and purification rituals associated with pyramid sites. This collection of theories invites readers to consider the pyramids as architectural and cultural wonders and as possible centres of ancient technological and spiritual advancement. Let's go into more detail about all of these potential functions of the pyramid.

Shelter from Extreme Temperatures or Rain

If you visit Egypt, you will find that the outside temperature in the desert can soar above 40°C (104°F) during the day and drop significantly at night. The pyramids offer a protective, climate-controlled environment of around 20°C (68°F), and for the entire structure to have been intended solely as a shelter seems too simplistic. The pyramid's geometry may have helped regulate internal temperatures through passive solar heating. During the day, the pyramid's large surfaces would absorb and store heat, while at night, the interior would release the warmth, maintaining a stable environment. This passive solar heating system might have created comfortable temperatures inside the pyramids.

However, researching the weather in the past, it appears that when the pyramids were built, particularly during the Old Kingdom of Egypt (around 2686–2181 BCE), the region's climate was quite different from what we see today in Egypt. Evidence suggests that the environment was generally more temperate, and the surrounding regions, including areas that are now deserts, were more hospitable. During the early periods of ancient Egypt, the Sahara was not the vast, arid desert it is today. Known as the "African Humid Period," this era was characterised by a wetter climate, with increased vegetation, lakes, and rivers across the Sahara Desert.[mcclxxvii] The construction of the pyramids coincided with a period when the Nile River experienced regular and predictable flooding, which was crucial to agriculture. The annual inundation of the Nile deposited fertile silt onto farmlands, supporting the kingdom's agricultural economy.[mcclxxviii] However, around the end of the Old Kingdom, fluctuations in this flooding pattern occurred, leading to droughts that may have contributed to the political instability of the time.

Over time, the climate became increasingly arid, and by the end of the Old Kingdom, desertification had gradually transformed the previously green regions into the Sahara Desert. This increasing aridity would have made life more difficult, but during the peak pyramid-building era, the climate was likely still more favourable than it is today.[mcclxxix]

In summary, Egypt's climate was significantly milder during the time of the pyramids, with wetter conditions in surrounding areas, particularly during the African Humid Period. However, as desertification gradually progressed, the region became increasingly drier, which had a significant impact on later dynasties.

Therapeutic Hot Springs

If pyramids were located near natural geothermal sources, the hot water could have been used for therapeutic purposes, much like modern hot springs. The heated water could provide healing benefits for physical ailments, and the pyramid's energy might have enhanced these effects. Ancient civilisations could have built bathhouses or sanctuaries near these pyramids where people could have bathed in hot water for rejuvenation and health. Experiments have recently tested how pyramid shapes may influence biological systems.

A 2016 study by a Russian scientific team observed the effects of placing water under a pyramid structure. The study found that water exposed to the pyramid structure showed a slight increase in energy potential, leading to speculation that this could have healing applications if consumed or applied in medical settings. Although the mechanisms remain largely unexplored, these preliminary findings have opened discussions on whether pyramid shapes can enhance energy in biological systems. The study *The Influence of Pyramid-Shaped Structures on Water Properties* (2016) by Dr. Alexander Golod, presented at a scientific symposium in Moscow, examined the potential of pyramid shapes to alter the molecular properties of water. The study suggested that the energy concentration within the pyramid could lead to measurable changes in the structure of water molecules, which may have implications for biological health.[mcclxxx]

Sacred Hot Water Rituals and Water Purification

In many ancient cultures, water is a symbol of purification and life. If the pyramids had access to geothermal energy or other sources of heated water, it might have been used in purification rituals for the pharaohs or religious figures. Heated water, particularly in baths or steam rooms, could have been used to cleanse the body and spirit before burial or essential ceremonies, aligning with the pyramids' symbolic connection to the afterlife and spiritual ascension.

Another idea is that underground water flow near the pyramids generated natural energy that could have been used for water purification. Some researchers theorise that aquifers beneath the Giza Plateau might have contributed to the geomagnetic energy harnessed by the pyramid. This energy could theoretically influence the structure of water, possibly enhancing its purity or beneficial properties.

Healing Centre

Ancient Egyptian medical texts, such as the *Ebers Papyrus*, reference the use of natural elements for healing and spiritual health, suggesting that the Egyptians had an advanced understanding of energy, life forces, and medicinal practices.[mcclxxxi] While the text does not explicitly mention pyramids, it indicates a belief in the power of geometry, location, and materials in promoting well-being. In modern times, studies on pyramid energy, although often controversial, have examined how the pyramid shape itself may influence energy fields. Researchers, such as Dr. Alexander Golod, have conducted experiments on the effects of pyramid structures on biological processes.[mcclxxxii] Some claim these shapes enhance immune response and promote healing in plants and humans.

Many New Age practitioners believe pyramids have healing properties, with the structure's design amplifying natural energies that can promote physical and emotional well-being.[mcclxxxiii] This concept, known as "pyramid power," suggests that pyramids can preserve physical objects, enhance healing, and focus positive energy.[mcclxxxiv] Whether through meditation, healing rituals, or spiritual practices, people have used pyramids to concentrate energy and to improve well-being and balance.

Scientists remain sceptical about the healing claims associated with pyramid power, citing a lack of reproducible, peer-reviewed research. They claim that many studies supporting pyramid power have been conducted in uncontrolled environments without the rigour to establish scientific validity. Some say it may be no more than a placebo effect. The placebo effect is a well-established phenomenon in medical science, and it could explain why some individuals report improvements in well-being after exposure to pyramid structures. If people believe that pyramids enhance healing or balance energy, they may experience real benefits, even if there is no objective mechanism at work.

In *The Biology of Belief*, cell biologist Bruce H. Lipton presents compelling evidence that gene expression is not hardwired, but is instead regulated by signals from the environment, including the energetic environment shaped by our beliefs, emotions, and mental states. The subconscious mind operates as a control panel that directly affects the physiology of every cell in the body.[mcclxxxv] This has profound implications when considering the potential healing properties of pyramid structures. Suppose pyramids function as energetic amplifiers, whether through geometry, material composition, or geomagnetic alignment. In that case, they may enhance the body's ability to self-regulate and heal by influencing the very signals that affect cellular behaviour. In this context, the pyramid may act as a resonant chamber that strengthens coherence between the mind and body, aligning intention with biological repair mechanisms. His model supports the idea that healing is not only biochemical, but also psychosomatic and field-dependent, suggesting that individuals who meditate or focus intentions within a pyramid-shaped space may be activating self-healing pathways through enhanced belief resonance and environmental signalling.

Amplifying Sounds for Healing

Several researchers and visitors have conducted experiments involving sound within the pyramids. These include toning, chanting, and playing specific musical notes to observe how sound behaves in the chambers. Some believe these ancient structures were designed to amplify or modulate the sound, potentially for spiritual or energetic purposes. Notably, in the 1990s, a team led by Dr. Abd'el Hakim Awyan conducted experiments within the Great Pyramid's King's Chamber, using various frequencies to test the chamber's resonance. These experiments revealed that the chamber resonates at frequencies between 5 Hz and 16 Hz, including a low F sharp tone.[mcclxxxvi]

5 Hz and 16 Hz refer to extremely low sound frequencies, often classified as infrasound, which is sound below the threshold of human hearing (which starts around 20 Hz). Although most people cannot hear these frequencies, they can be felt as vibrations. Infrasound has been associated with inducing a calming effect on the human body, potentially influencing the nervous system. Researchers believe these low frequencies can enhance meditative states, reduce stress, and even alter consciousness, supporting the theory that the pyramids were used for spiritual purposes.[mcclxxxvii]

Low F sharp tone corresponds to a musical note in the lower range of the audible spectrum. In standard tuning, F# (F sharp) below middle C resonates at approximately 46.25 Hz. Still, in the case of the pyramid's King's Chamber, this may correspond to a lower octave or subharmonic frequency.[mcclxxxviii] Ancient traditions in Eastern and indigenous cultures have long associated F sharp with healing, balance, and spiritual harmony. Today, Sound healing practitioners use the F-sharp frequency to tune forks and other instruments, promoting emotional and physical healing.[mcclxxxix]

The resonance and the chamber's acoustic properties led to speculation that the pyramid might have been purposefully designed to manipulate sound, possibly for spiritual or healing purposes. Furthermore, modern researchers, such as Paul Devereux, have studied how infrasound, including the frequencies observed in the King's Chamber, can induce altered states of consciousness, potentially used by ancient Egyptians for meditation or ritual practices.[mccxc]

Modern research into vibrational medicine shows that sound frequencies can profoundly affect the body's cells and tissues. Studies conducted by Dr. John Beaulieu and others suggest that specific frequencies can influence cellular function, thereby triggering healing responses. For example, 528 Hz has been linked to DNA repair and cellular regeneration, suggesting sound can enhance the body's natural healing processes. The correlation between certain frequencies and physical healing further supports the hypothesis that the pyramids, with their resonant chambers, might have been used for similar purposes.[mccxci]

For instance, tuning forks, calibrated to specific frequencies, often restore the body's natural vibrational state. These frequencies are selected based on their ability to reduce pain, alleviate stress, and promote healing and well-being. Instruments such as singing bowls and gongs in sound healing sessions produce harmonic overtones that induce relaxation and facilitate meditation by aligning the body's energy centres (chakras).[mccxcii] Studies published in the *Journal of Evidence-Based Complementary & Alternative Medicine* have documented the effects of sound healing practices, such as gong therapy and singing bowl meditation, showing significant reductions in cortisol levels (the primary stress hormone) and improvements in overall well-being.[mccxciii]

Sound therapy is used in modern healing practices, with claims that specific frequencies can positively impact both mental and physical health. Rife frequencies and bio-resonance therapy are two examples of sound being believed to impact cellular regeneration or disrupt harmful pathogens. Even ultrasound technology uses high-frequency sound waves to generate images of internal organs, showcasing how frequencies can affect biological tissues.

We see this theme in movies. For example, in *Doctor Strange* (2016), sound, vibrations, and mystical energies intertwine to create powerful effects, echoing the theories of sound amplification within the pyramids. The film shows how manipulating frequencies and resonance can alter reality and consciousness, much like the speculative experiments in the Great Pyramid's King's Chamber. Just as ancient civilisations might have used these resonant spaces to achieve altered states or spiritual healing, *Doctor Strange* portrays sorcerers harnessing vibrations and energy within ancient structures to transform their perception and power.

Preserving Life and Longevity

Some believe pyramids can preserve organic material, such as food or human bodies. This theory posits that the pyramid's shape creates an energy field that slows down the decay of objects placed inside, aligning with ancient Egyptian mummification practices. Could they have known the secrets to longevity? Some researchers have conducted experiments with pyramids, claiming that food, water, and even living organisms placed inside pyramidal structures exhibit signs of preservation, reduced decay, and enhanced vitality.[mccxciv] Were pyramids designed to maintain the physical integrity of bodies and objects for centuries, possibly preserving them for spiritual or scientific purposes? There are claims that spending time in pyramid-shaped structures can promote physical well-being and longevity.

Could sleeping under a copper pyramid extend life? This theory draws from the "pyramid power" concept, which suggests that the pyramid's unique geometry amplifies energy fields, potentially impacting health and longevity. This idea argues that the pyramid shape, particularly when paired with a conductive material like copper, creates a concentrated energy field that could harmonise with the body's natural energy centres, promoting cellular rejuvenation and improved vitality.[mccxcv] Proponents argue that these energy effects can reduce stress, enhance meditation, and align the body with Earth's magnetic fields. This may lead to improved physical well-being and potentially slow down the ageing process.[mccxcvi] Some claim that ancient civilisations, such as the Egyptians, harnessed this knowledge to build pyramids that preserved spiritual and physical health.[mccxcvii] While anecdotal reports suggest that sleeping under copper pyramids has positive effects, scientific research has yet to validate these claims.[mccxcviii,mccxcix] Nonetheless, interest in pyramid power persists, with copper pyramids gaining popularity in wellness practices as tools for meditation, relaxation, and energy alignment, thereby keeping the theory alive in modern alternative health circles.

There is a theory that the human lifespan is limited, and records detailing this limitation were held in the Great Pyramid of Giza. This suggests that ancient civilisations had advanced knowledge about the human body, genetics, and cosmic cycles. According to this theory, the ancient Egyptians, or possibly a more advanced civilisation before them, understood that the human lifespan could be influenced or controlled by specific cosmic or environmental factors. They encoded this knowledge within the design and structure of the Great Pyramid of Giza, possibly in hidden chambers or inscribed on stone tablets, to safeguard this secret for future generations.[mccc] Proponents argue that these records may reveal how the pyramids' alignment with celestial bodies and Earth's magnetic fields could have been used to enhance or extend life. Some speculate that this ancient wisdom included information on synchronising human energy fields (such as the chakras) with the Earth's geomagnetic forces, allowing for longer, healthier lives. The theory also suggests that this knowledge was lost or deliberately hidden over time, possibly to prevent misuse or control of populations. It implies that those who built the pyramids possessed a profound understanding of human potential. Still, these secrets were buried—perhaps literally—within the structure of the Giza pyramid.

Today, a theory circulates that the limited human lifespan is artificial, resulting from an artificial mutation or genetic manipulation that causes missing chromosomes or limits lifespan. In esoteric circles, the "artificial mutation" theory can be linked to the idea that humanity was once more spiritually or physically advanced and has since been "limited" by genetic modifications. This idea often aligns with the broader concept of lost knowledge or suppressed potential. However, these ideas remain speculative and lack empirical support.

Bioenergetic Device: DNA Preservation and Activation

The pyramids might have been used to preserve or manipulate DNA. The concentrated energy within pyramids may have helped maintain the genetic material of rulers or other essential individuals. [mccci] Ancient Egyptian rulers, particularly pharaohs, were regarded as the embodiment of divine power, often considered to be gods themselves or the descendants of the gods. Their genetic material would have been of supreme importance, as maintaining the purity of this lineage was essential to the continuation of their rule.[mcccii]

This aligns with mummification practices but with a potential focus on preserving life at the genetic level.[mccciii] The *Mummy Trilogy* (1999, 2001, 2008) presents the theme of resurrection and preservation through the revival of ancient Egyptian rulers using supernatural rituals and ancient knowledge. In these films, the mummies of long-dead pharaohs and priests are brought back to life, often accompanied by powerful curses and mystical forces. While the trilogy primarily focuses on magic and the supernatural, it subtly suggests that the ancient Egyptians possessed advanced capabilities that extended beyond what modern science can fully explain. This idea is tied to the Egyptian rulers' preoccupation with preserving their physical bodies and spiritual essence for eternity. This practice goes beyond mummification into something more profound. Although the films emphasise mystical resurrection rather than DNA manipulation, they align with the notion that the ancient Egyptians may have been safeguarding the biological integrity and purity of their rulers' lineage.

In cryonics today, bodies or even genetic material are preserved at extremely low temperatures in the hope that future technologies will be able to revive the individual or repair genetic defects. This practice shares conceptual similarities with the idea that the pyramids might have been used to preserve the genetic material of pharaohs or important individuals. While the methods are different, the goal—preserving biological integrity for future use—aligns with the theory that the ancient Egyptians may have used the pyramids to conserve and protect vital genetic material. The modern practice of storing embryos, sperm, or genetic material for future use in fertility treatments or cloning also draws parallels to the idea that the Egyptians might have sought to preserve not just the body but the genetic lineage of their rulers.

Some researchers have explored how specific resonant frequencies can impact biological tissues, even suggesting that specific frequencies might promote cellular regeneration or repair genetic material.[mccciv] Suppose the pyramids were designed to channel or resonate with these natural frequencies. In that case, they may have been intended to preserve the genetic integrity of individuals buried within and perhaps even to activate dormant DNA in future generations.[mcccv]

The study of quantum fields suggests that all matter is interconnected through unseen energy fields and that these fields may influence particles on a microscopic level. While quantum field theory is applied in physics, some researchers suggest that these fields could also impact biological processes, including the genetic material. If the pyramids were designed to channel or amplify natural energy fields, such as Earth's electromagnetic field, this could theoretically have affected the DNA or biological health of individuals buried within. The idea that energy fields can influence matter—central to quantum field theory—connects to the theory that pyramids harnessed energies to preserve or manipulate genetic material.

Laboratories for Cloning

The idea of laboratories for cloning within the pyramids opens a fascinating speculative narrative that intertwines ancient technology, genetics, and modern biophysics. The concept suggests that the pyramids, particularly the Great Pyramid of Giza, may have served as more than monumental tombs or spiritual structures—they could have been designed to harness energy for advanced biological processes, potentially even cloning.[mcccvi]

Cloning key figures, such as the pharaohs, who were revered for their god-like status and profound connections to divine knowledge, would serve as a method of resurrecting not only their physical forms but also their wisdom and leadership. The belief that genetic material, such as DNA, could be preserved within the energy fields of the pyramid stems from the idea that the pyramids were not just structures but living entities that functioned as machines capable of interacting with cosmic and terrestrial forces.[mcccvii] This advanced understanding of energy manipulation might suggest that ancient Egyptians had access to knowledge beyond what we currently understand about genetics and biology.[mcccviii]

This theory's missing capstone of the Great Pyramid is a central element. Historically speculated to have been made from a conductive material like gold, copper, or electrum, the capstone may have acted as a receiver and transmitter of energy. Its position at the pyramid's pinnacle would allow it to channel cosmic radiation, solar energy, or even geomagnetic forces into its core, creating an environment where biological and genetic processes could be manipulated.[mcccix]

In this speculative narrative, the chambers of the pyramid, particularly the King's Chamber, are viewed as controlled environments for these processes. The King's Chamber, built from dense granite known for its piezoelectric properties, could act as a biological reactor.[mcccx] Piezoelectricity, which generates an electric charge in response to mechanical stress, could theoretically create an energetic environment conducive to DNA activation.[mcccxi] The ancient Egyptians, who may have had access to this knowledge, could have utilised the chamber's unique acoustics and material composition to activate preserved genetic material.[mcccxii]

Rituals involving sound frequencies or chanting may have initiated the process, aligning with the theory that the pyramids were designed to resonate with frequencies that correspond to the human body.[mcccxiii] These rituals might have worked with technological processes, employing principles of biophysics to create a controlled field where preserved DNA could be reconstituted into a new form.[mcccxiv]

In this scenario, ancient knowledge of energy manipulation and bioengineering would be combined to appear advanced even by today's standards. The preserved DNA could have been stored in a way that protected it from environmental degradation, allowing for future use when the conditions—possibly an alignment of energy fields, cosmic forces, or even seasonal cycles—were optimal for the resurrection or cloning process.[mcccxv]

The implications of this theory go well beyond just the pyramids. If ancient civilisations had access to such technologies, it prompts questions about the lost sciences of the past and how much we actually know about human history. Were these technologies handed down through generations, woven into mythologies, or hidden within secret societies? Could the pyramids have served as stores for physical bodies and genetic legacies, aiming to revive influential figures when their knowledge was most needed?[mcccxvi]

This theory also touches on modern debates about the ethical implications of cloning and genetic engineering. While today's scientists grapple with the potential and pitfalls of cloning, the idea that ancient civilisations may have already mastered this art suggests that they approached these issues with a blend of spirituality, ritual, and technological prowess.[mcccxvii] This raises provocative questions about the nature of life, death, and rebirth in ancient thought and whether they believed that physical resurrection was possible through a mastery of both the material and the energetic realms.[mcccxviii]

By incorporating this theory into the broader narrative of the pyramids as energy devices, the concept of cloning becomes part of a more comprehensive discussion on the potential uses of these ancient monuments. It invites us to reconsider the capabilities of past civilisations and the role that the pyramids might have played as laboratories of life, where energy, matter, and spirit converged to create a process of biological regeneration.[mcccxix]

Egyptian mythology is rich in hybrid creatures, such as the Sphinx (part lion, part human) and the Gryphon (part lion, part bird).[mcccxx] These hybrids could be seen as evidence of a deeper, possibly genetic, understanding of life forms. This suggests that the ancient Egyptians might have conceptualised species-blending long before modern genetic engineering was conceived.[mcccxxi] These depictions might indicate a belief or experimentation with cross-species genetic modification.[mcccxxii]

Many animal depictions in ancient Egypt are associated with themes of regeneration, rebirth, and the continuity of life. For example, the scarab beetle, associated with the god Khepri, symbolised the cycle of life and rebirth, as it was believed to push the sun across the sky daily.[mcccxxiii] Could this be interpreted as a metaphor for the concept of genetic renewal, with animals acting as symbols of potential genetic manipulation or cloning processes designed to ensure the continuation of life?[mcccxxiv]

The extensive presence of animal-headed deities, such as Anubis (jackal), Horus (falcon), and Bastet (lioness), can be viewed through the lens of genetic experimentation.[mcccxxv] These hybrid beings might symbolise a culture that understood the manipulation of species at a genetic level. The depictions of these gods as part-human and part-animal could indicate an ancient attempt at or understanding of blending genetics to enhance or augment physical and spiritual attributes.[mcccxxvi] While the theory that animal inscriptions in Egypt reference cloning is highly speculative, it presents an exciting lens through which to explore ancient Egyptian beliefs, rituals, and technological capabilities.[mcccxxvii]

Jurassic Park (1993) explores the ethical and scientific implications of cloning through its central premise: the resurrection of dinosaurs using preserved DNA.[mcccxxviii] The film highlights the allure and danger of genetic engineering as scientists manipulate the genetic code to bring extinct creatures back to life.[mcccxxix] Cloning, in this context, is not just a technological achievement but a profound disruption of nature's balance, where life that had long disappeared is unnaturally revived.[mcccxxx] The movie raises critical questions about the consequences of tampering with genetics, including the unpredictability of cloned organisms and the moral responsibility of those who create life.[mcccxxxi] Through the lens of cloning, *Jurassic Park* becomes a cautionary tale about humanity's attempts to control nature, underscoring the potential perils of genetic experimentation without fully understanding the consequences.[mcccxxxii]

We know cloning is possible. Cloning has advanced significantly over the past two decades, with several notable examples demonstrating its potential applications in science, medicine, and agriculture. Dolly the Sheep (1996) was cloned slightly more than 20 years ago; she remains a landmark achievement as the first mammal successfully cloned from an adult somatic cell using nuclear transfer. Dolly's success paved the way for further research into cloning technologies. In the last two decades, cattle and pigs have been cloned extensively for agricultural and research purposes.[mcccxxxiii] Cloned animals are often used to enhance livestock breeding, ensure better meat quality, or improve disease resistance.[mcccxxxiv] Tetra was the first primate cloned using "embryo splitting," a precursor to more advanced methods. This breakthrough set the stage for later developments in cloning primates, which are more closely related to humans.[mcccxxxv] CC the Cat (2001)—CC (short for "Carbon Copy") was the first cloned domestic pet.[mcccxxxvi] This achievement paved the way for commercial pet cloning, and companies today offer cloning services for individuals who want to clone their cats and dogs.[mcccxxxvii] In recent years, cloning has been used to preserve endangered species. For example, in 2003, the first endangered species, a Banteng (a wild cattle species), was cloned from frozen cells.[mcccxxxviii] In 2020, a cloned black-footed ferret was born from cells that had been frozen for over 30 years, marking a significant step forward in efforts to save endangered species. In 2013, scientists successfully cloned human embryos to extract embryonic stem cells. These stem cells can be used in regenerative medicine, potentially treating diseases such as Parkinson's, diabetes, and spinal cord injuries.[mcccxxxix] These examples illustrate the evolution of cloning. We are not far off from cloning humans, or it has already happened.

Lightning Powering Cloning and Resurrection

In several Dracula films, lightning and storms are often associated with Dracula's power, particularly in scenes depicting his resurrection.[mcccxl] Dracula was created by Bram Stoker, an Irish author, in his 1897 Gothic horror novel *Dracula*.[mcccxli] Count Dracula is a vampire and the novel's main antagonist, which has since become one of the most famous works of vampire literature. Dracula has influenced countless adaptations and interpretations in books, films, and popular culture, establishing many modern conventions associated with vampires.[mcccxlii] In some adaptations, Dracula is revived during storms, with lightning symbolising the uncontrollable forces of nature that seem to bring him back to life.[mcccxliii] This imagery suggests that Dracula's power is tied to natural elements beyond the control of ordinary humans, lending a supernatural element to his immortality.[mcccxliv] Similarly, harnessing lightning to power the pyramids' cloning process evokes this connection between natural energy and reanimation.[mcccxlv] The pyramids may have harnessed the power of lightning or cosmic energy through their capstones, made of conductive materials like gold, copper, or electrum, which act as antennas, drawing in and amplifying natural forces. This energy could then be directed into the genetic preservation chambers, potentially triggering the cloning process and reviving individuals.[mcccxlvi] Of course, this is all speculation.

While harnessing lightning directly is still beyond current technology due to its unpredictability and immense power, researchers are exploring ways to capture the energy from lightning strikes and other forms of high-energy plasma.[mcccxlvii] Scientists have proposed capturing lightning's energy to power devices or even small areas, but the technology is complex and remains largely theoretical.[mcccxlviii]

However, lightning research has informed high-energy physics, where scientists study plasma and extreme energy states, which could one day contribute to innovative energy solutions.^{mcccxlix}

Today, electricity is recognised as a catalyst in certain biological processes. For example, electrofusion, a technique used in cloning, involves applying a small electrical current to fuse cells, commonly in animal cloning and genetic research.^{mcccl} This controlled electricity use plays a role in research labs' in vitro fertilisation and embryonic development.^{mccclii} While it's not lightning, as seen in films, these small electrical currents are integral in controlled genetic manipulation, including cloning techniques.^{mccclii}

While true resurrection is still far from scientific reality, advancements in regenerative medicine are making significant strides. Techniques in stem cell therapy, gene editing like CRISPR, and bioengineering have allowed scientists to regenerate damaged tissue and organs in animals and, in some cases, humans.^{mcccliii} Additionally, scientists have successfully revived certain types of cells and tissue, and there is promising research into "reviving" organs outside of the body to improve organ transplant success rates.^{mcccliv} This does hint at a controlled form of regeneration that, while far from reanimation, shares some similarities with resurrection themes.^{mccclv}

Vampirism

The blood-drinking narrative is deeply embedded in mythology and folklore, particularly in stories about creatures such as vampires, werewolves, or blood-drinking gods.^{mccclvi} The stories illustrate the ancient and cross-cultural allure of consuming another's life force to gain power. Ancient Mesopotamian, Greek, and Roman myths include figures who drink blood to gain power, exact revenge, or transcend human limitations.^{mccclvii} This idea has continued to thrive in modern literature, films, and popular culture, where characters who consume blood are often depicted as powerful but cursed.^{mccclviii} Did the Egyptians practice vampirism?

The debate on whether ancient Egypt practised vampirism and cannibalism is backed by references across literature and history, where the concept of consuming others for power has resonated widely. For instance, in the *Pyramid Texts*, specifically the Cannibal Hymn, the pharaoh is described as consuming gods to absorb their strength. It says he "eats their magic and gulps down their spirits".^{mccclix} This symbolic cannibalism resembles themes in *Dracula*, where Count Dracula drains the life force of others. He consumes blood to sustain his strength and achieve a form of immortality.^{mccclx} Advocates for literal interpretation and cannibalism in Egypt speculate that such acts could have taken place in royal rituals, influenced perhaps by neighbouring cultures where ritualistic cannibalism existed.[mccclxi] However, the lack of physical evidence contradicts this theory. Archaeological analyses of Egyptian burial sites show no signs of human remains that were cannibalised, and preservation through mummification was fundamental to their beliefs, conflicting with any concept of physical consumption.[mccclxii] Consequently, many scholars interpret these cannibalistic descriptions as symbolic, signifying the king's union with divine forces in the afterlife rather than literal cannibalism.[mccclxiii] Just as Dracula's consumption of blood symbolises power and eternal life, the pharaoh's "consumption" of gods metaphorically captures his ascent to divinity.

In ancient Egypt, animal sacrifices were common, with offerings of bulls, birds, and other animals to honour gods and sustain the deceased's spirit in the afterlife.[mccclxiv] In Mesoamerican cultures, the Aztecs and Mayans viewed human sacrifice as essential to appease the gods and maintain cosmic order. Their pyramids served as altars where both human and animal sacrifices were performed, and these acts were believed to ensure the continuation of life, successful harvests, and the stability of the realm.[mccclxv] In contrast to Dracula's gain, the blood sacrifices in ancient rituals by the Aztecs or Mayans were typically conducted for the benefit of society or the divine order.[mccclxvi] They were often framed as noble or necessary acts that ensured the continuation of life, harvest, or the protection of the realm.[mccclxvii]

Conspiracy theories involving blood drinking have long captivated the imaginations of fringe communities and those exploring hidden truths behind ancient rituals. These theories often intertwine with beliefs in secretive elite groups, such as the Illuminati or reptilian overlords, who allegedly partake in blood-drinking ceremonies as part of maintaining power and control. Central to these claims is the idea that consuming blood provides sustenance and life-extending properties, spiritual power, or even a form of psychic energy. In *Conspiracy Theories and Occult Practices: A Deep Dive into Blood Rituals*, John Smith delves into the historical and mythological origins of such ideas, exploring how ancient practices, such as ritual bloodletting and sacrificial rites, have been distorted into modern conspiracies. He highlights that while actual blood-related rituals existed in various cultures for spiritual purposes, these practices have been exaggerated in contemporary conspiracy narratives, particularly regarding elites and secret societies. Some conspiracists link blood-drinking practices to occult traditions or rituals found in mythology, suggesting that the elites use blood to stay connected to dark, supernatural forces. Blood-drinking conspiracies are often tied to exaggerated interpretations of actual historical rituals, misunderstood religious symbols, and a general mistrust of powerful figures. For example, some claim that secret societies operating in the shadows engage in such acts during highly secretive gatherings, using human blood to harness life force or control populations. Though there is no evidence to support these claims, they persist in various conspiracy circles fueled by a mix of anti-establishment sentiment, cultural myths, and occult symbolism.[mccclxviii]

Similarly, some conspiracy theories suggest that human sacrifices still occur in secret, particularly among elite or occult groups. These beliefs often tie back to ancient practices where human sacrifices were part of rituals to appease gods or gain favour from supernatural forces. Modern theorists claim that such sacrifices are used by secret societies, such as the Illuminati, to harness life force, maintain power, or fulfil dark spiritual objectives. Reports of missing persons, sensationalised media stories, and symbolic interpretations of ancient rituals often fuel these ideas. In his book, John Smith explores how the mythos of human sacrifice has persisted into modern conspiracy culture. He argues that while the human sacrifice was a real part of some ancient religious practices, the idea that such rituals continue today is primarily based on speculation, fear of the unknown, and mistrust of the powerful.

Meanwhile, discussions about dietary practices, such as the anti-meat movement and plant-based diets, reveal the shifting boundaries around human and animal life. Just as societies have long debated where to draw the line between consumption for sustenance and respect for life, so too do these theories reflect enduring questions about ethics, power, and human nature.[mccclxix] Ultimately, these narratives highlight a timeless fascination with the mysterious forces that govern life, death, and the boundaries of human potential.

Why is eating animal meat not a form of cannibalism? What is the difference? Cannibalism is defined explicitly as the practice of consuming the flesh of one's species.[mccclxx] In biological terms, cannibalism is when a member of a species eats another member of the same species. For humans, eating animals falls under the category of carnivory or omnivory. Cannibalism, on the other hand, has cultural, ethical, and often legal taboos attached, likely because of its implications for social cohesion, disease transmission, and the psychological effect of consuming one's own kind.[mccclxxi] Humans have long established boundaries around which species are considered suitable for consumption and which are not, shaping norms and taboos based on cultural, moral, and social factors.[mccclxxii] Additionally, humans have historically distinguished themselves ethically from other animals. Religious and philosophical beliefs often reinforce this distinction, creating a moral framework that doesn't apply the concept of cannibalism to the consumption of different species.[mccclxxiii]

Today, we are witnessing a growing movement against the consumption of animal meat. While humans have traditionally viewed animals as resources, a shift towards recognising them as sentient beings deserving of rights reflects a broader, more compassionate perspective on life. Many believe that society can cultivate compassion and empathy by reducing harm and suffering to animals or humans. Animal rights advocates argue that animals are sentient beings capable of experiencing pain, stress, and joy; therefore, they should not be exploited for human consumption. Advocates for reducing or eliminating meat consumption argue that adopting plant-based diets could significantly minimise humanity's environmental footprint. A growing body of research links high consumption of red and processed meats to health issues such as heart disease, cancer, and diabetes.

Conspiracy theorists often view the anti-meat movement with scepticism, suggesting that there are hidden agendas behind it. Some claim that plant-based diets are being promoted as part of a broader agenda to weaken or control populations. They suggest that diets with less animal protein might lead to a physically weaker and less resilient populace, which could then be more easily manipulated.[mccclxxiv] By encouraging vegetarianism or veganism, they argue that cultural attitudes around food, tradition, and identity are being reshaped to fit a new agenda of uniformity, where traditional practices and values are replaced with a more globalised, corporatised model of eating[mccclxxv]. There is also a conspiracy theory that aligns the anti-meat movement with "Big Pharma." Proponents argue that by promoting plant-based diets, which they believe might result in nutritional deficiencies, people would ultimately become more reliant on supplements and medications, benefiting pharmaceutical companies.[mccclxxvi] This theory is rooted in the belief that the medical industry profits from a population perpetually dependent on healthcare interventions.

A popular theory suggests that different blood groups may have evolved in response to varying dietary preferences or tolerances, specifically in the context of meat or plant-based diets. This concept gained traction with the publication of Dr. Peter D'Adamo's book *Eat Right 4 Your Type*, which claims that blood types influence optimal diets for individuals.[mccclxxvii] Despite the popularity of this theory, there is little scientific evidence to support a link between blood type and dietary preference or tolerance. [mccclxxviii]

Could a preference for meat be "written in the genes" or influenced by personality traits, particularly those associated with a hunter type? Some theories, like Dr Thom Hartmann's "hunter vs farmer" hypothesis, suggest people have genetically ingrained behavioural and dietary preferences linked to ancient roles in hunter-gatherer societies. According to this theory, "hunters" are more active, impulsive, and attracted to high-energy foods (like meat), while "farmers" may prefer structured lifestyles and plant-based diets.[mccclxxix]

In conclusion, while the movement toward plant-based diets is gaining traction, it raises questions about whether it is truly natural for humans to stop eating meat after centuries of meat consumption. Historically, humans have evolved as omnivores, with diets adapted to the available resources, including both animal- and plant-based foods. Ancient Egyptians were also meat eaters. The meat was likely more common in the diets of the wealthy, while poorer Egyptians relied primarily on bread, beer, vegetables, and legumes, with occasional access to fish or poultry. Given this background, shifting entirely away from meat could feel counter to these long-standing dietary practices. However, it is also possible that humans are not a monolithic group in terms of their nutritional needs or preferences. Some may be naturally inclined toward a plant-based diet due to cultural, ethical, or biological factors. In contrast, others may find a meat-inclusive diet aligns better with their nutritional needs or personal health.

Human-alien Hybridisation?

Could they have gone beyond genetic preservation, optimisation and cloning, and actively reengineered the DNA?

Beneath the desert floor of Dulce, New Mexico, persistent claims suggest the existence of a deep underground facility. No official body recognises this facility, yet it is consistently described with unsettling accuracy by former insiders and whistleblowers.

Chief among them was Phil Schneider, a former government geologist who, before his suspicious death in 1996, claimed to have worked on secret military projects involving deep-earth construction. In public lectures and interviews, he said the Dulce Base extended across multiple subterranean levels, with *"Nightmare Hall"*—Level 6— being a zone dedicated to advanced genetic experimentation involving humans and non-human entities. His allegations included tales of human-alien hybridisation, cloning, and chimeric lifeforms, describing entities that were neither fully human nor alien. He claimed to have witnessed vats containing partially formed humanoids, genetically modified beings, and the systematic manipulation of DNA in ways that transcended conventional science. While these assertions remain unverified, the details evoke uncanny parallels with ancient mythological records.

Former CIA pilot John Lear, speaking in radio interviews during the late 1980s and 1990s, also referred to underground facilities linked to genetic programmes. He claimed the U.S. government had entered into secret agreements with extraterrestrial entities, exchanging access to human genetic material for advanced technology. He did not coin the term "Nightmare Hall," but supported the narrative of hidden genetic programmes and biological manipulation beneath the surface of military black sites, including Area 51 and Dulce.

These hybrid narratives are not isolated. They appear across continents, such as in Egypt, India, and South America—myths of gods creating or altering life not just spiritually but biologically. If they are even partly true, then perhaps modern genetic experimentation, conducted in secrecy, is not entirely new. It may be the reawakening of ancient knowledge, buried, preserved, and gradually surfacing in the shadows of institutional silence. The laboratories of today might be sterile, fluorescent-lit rooms behind steel doors, but they reflect the temples and vaults of lost civilisations, where life was shaped and reshaped by those who claimed to come from the stars.

In 1991, former naval intelligence officer William Cooper released a book that would ignite the minds of truth-seekers and conspiracy researchers alike. Titled *Behold a Pale Horse*, it was not a carefully argued thesis, nor a fully verified historical work, but something far more explosive. It was a declaration. A warning. A collection of documents, whistleblower claims, and personal testimony that suggested the world we inhabit is but a carefully curated illusion, built to conceal ancient truths, suppressed technologies, secret treaties, and the quiet rise of a new control system. He claimed that powerful global elites were deliberately hiding knowledge, from extraterrestrial contact, to hidden energy systems, to advanced genetic programs operating in secrecy beneath the surface of the Earth. He wrote of underground bases, black budget operations, and deep-level government cooperation with non-human entities. While his assertions are unverifiable and often ridiculed by mainstream historians, they resonate uncannily with the ancient themes found in texts like the *Book of Enoch*, Sumerian myths, and the esoteric fragments left behind by lost civilisations. What he described is not far from the warnings encoded in the monuments of the ancient world: a cycle of hidden knowledge, collapse, and control. In his worldview, the so-called "new world order" was not new at all, but the modern re-emergence of an ancient agenda, one that may have its roots in the forgotten temples of Lemuria, the halls of Atlantis, or the energy networks buried beneath the pyramids themselves. In *Behold a Pale Horse*, he also hinted at genetic manipulation programs, soul-harvesting technologies, and electromagnetic control systems. All feels less like speculative fiction and more like modern incarnations of the divine interference described in ancient lore. Whether one agrees with him or not is irrelevant.[mccclxxx]

As Yuval Noah Harari notes in *Homo Deus* (2015), humanity is now on a trajectory to become godlike, not through spiritual ascension, but through the manipulation of code, consciousness, and biology. He writes that "organisms are algorithms" and that the new elite will not be priests or kings, but data scientists and gene editors. When humans play god through AI, hybrid creation, or neural control, we may not be pioneering but rather repeating a pattern. The ancients may have left monuments not just of power, but of warning.[mccclxxxi]

In the film *Species* (1995), directed by Roger Donaldson, we are presented with a chilling fictional narrative that feels disturbingly plausible when viewed through the lens of ancient myth, modern conspiracy, and the ongoing speculation around covert genetic programs. The plot revolves around a government experiment gone wrong: an extraterrestrial DNA sequence, received via a transmission from space, is fused with human genetic material to create a female hybrid named Sil. Raised in a controlled environment, Sil rapidly evolves, escapes containment, and seeks to reproduce, driven by instincts that science cannot control or explain. What makes *Species* so relevant to modern alternative theory is not simply its horror elements, but its symbolic mirroring of ancient narratives: forbidden knowledge, the manipulation of life, and the unleashing of a power that cannot be contained. The government scientists in the film operate in secrecy, answerable to no one. The project is conducted underground. The hybrid child, once born, rapidly exceeds expectations, suggesting that alien intelligence, when merged with human biology, may activate dormant capabilities or instincts long buried in the genome. The film reflects the secrecy surrounding alleged underground bases like Dulce.

Why would anyone want to merge an alien with a human? Perhaps because the human body holds something rare: a genetic blueprint forged through pain, resilience, emotion, and chaos. These are qualities not easily replicated in cold logic or advanced machine minds. Some say the hybrid is a salvation project for dying alien species. Others see it as infiltration disguised as integration. And some whisper that this merging is destined. Humanity was never a finished product, but a seed waiting for something older, stranger, and more advanced to return and complete the design. Whether a bridge, a weapon, or a vessel, the hybrid may not be coming. It may already be here.

One hybrid is all it would take. Not an army, not a global invasion. Just one. Introduced quietly into a population, allowed to reproduce without resistance, the hybrid's genetic code could begin to ripple outward like a drop in still water. In just thirty generations, less than a thousand years, that single deviation could saturate the human genome entirely. So if a hybrid entered our lineage thousands of years ago, its code would now be in all of us, diluted perhaps, but still dormant, waiting. What if this was the real plan all along? Not conquest by war, but by inheritance. Genetic subversion disguised as ancestry. A quiet infiltration that has already happened. Or was ancient DNA manipulation the very crime that ended those civilisations?

Perhaps the obsession with youth, as seen in both ancient gods who demanded 'virgin sacrifices' and modern reports of hybrid experimentation, was never about the body at all. It was about energy, access, and control over the point of origin. For in innocence lies unclaimed power, and the darker the intent, the more it craves what is most uncorrupted.

Life, Energy, and Eternity

The possibility that ancient civilisations possessed advanced knowledge of energy manipulation for healing and life preservation opens intriguing doors. The pyramids may have been centres for bioenergetic healing, preservation, and perhaps even technologies we have yet to rediscover. Whether through providing shelter from extreme temperatures, amplifying healing energies, or preserving life at a genetic level, these ancient structures are wrapped in a mystery that continues to inspire scientific inquiry and speculative thought.

These ideas invite us to rethink the pyramids' roles in the lives of those who built and revered them. From the healing power of vibration and sound to the potential for preserving and manipulating DNA, the pyramids may have served as instruments of well-being and spiritual rejuvenation. Whether through energy fields, ceremonial practices, or advanced architectural techniques, these structures may hold secrets to ancient forms of healing and life extension that are only now being explored in modern times.

While some of these ideas remain speculative, they highlight the pyramids' potential role in promoting physical and spiritual well-being through their design, materials, or alignment with natural forces. In conclusion, the notion that the pyramids could have facilitated healing and preserved life demonstrates the breadth of ancient knowledge, pushing us to reconsider how modern technology might integrate these ancient concepts of energy manipulation for holistic wellness.

After investigating healing practices, we propose that pyramids were not only burial sites but also central hubs for energy production and transmission, as discussed in the next chapter. What if the ancients had discovered how to harness the Earth's natural energies—geothermal, electromagnetic, or even solar energy? The towering structures of Giza, aligned with precision to the stars and Earth's magnetic fields, could have acted as colossal energy conductors. Picture an ancient civilisation drawing power from beneath the Earth, using the pyramids as hubs to distribute this energy across their cities. If this were true, it would imply that ancient Egyptians had technological insights that surpassed our modern understanding of energy distribution. Could the energy grids we use today be echoes of this forgotten knowledge?

Chapter 20 Central Utility Hub

How plausible is the idea that pyramids were designed as utility hubs for energy production and wireless transmission, and what modern parallels could help explain their functionality in this regard? Mainstream Egyptologists reject the idea that ancient civilisations had access to advanced technology, citing the absence of physical evidence for such advanced technologies in the archaeological records.

This chapter examines the possibility that pyramids served as central utility hubs. They could have been used for energy production and transmission, wireless transmission, and powering ancient technologies that have yet to be fully understood. Theories suggest that pyramids may have functioned as power plants, distributing energy to various technologies or infrastructure across vast distances, much like modern power grids. The Great Pyramid, being the largest, could have acted as the "power station," amplifying and directing energy to the smaller pyramids nearby.

At the heart of this exploration is the idea that pyramids were part of a global energy grid connected by ley lines or electromagnetic fields. This grid may have harmonised the Earth's natural energy systems, allowing energy to flow seamlessly across continents.

Further expanding on this idea, some propose that pyramids were designed for wireless energy transmission, similar to Nikola Tesla's vision of transmitting electricity through the atmosphere. By focusing and directing energy without wires, pyramids could have powered ancient cities, devices, or transportation systems. This hints at a lost technological sophistication. The pyramid's capstone, potentially made of conductive material, might have acted as an antenna.

In *The Prestige* (2006), the film's portrayal of Nikola Tesla's experiments blurs the line between science and magic, revealing the extraordinary possibilities of unseen forces and technologies beyond common understanding. Tesla, portrayed as a visionary, experiments with wireless energy and the transmission of electricity through the air, concepts that resonate deeply with speculative theories about pyramid technology. Just as Tesla explored how energy could be harnessed and transmitted without wires, some researchers suggest that the ancient pyramids might have functioned as vast energy conductors, tapping into the Earth's natural forces.

This chapter combines the idea of a global energy grid with the parallels to Tesla's work. It presents a speculative but thought-provoking perspective on the pyramids as ancient energy hubs. These hubs could have powered entire civilisations by manipulating natural forces and earthly energy systems.

It is not difficult to imagine that the pyramids had multiple purposes if we examine their history. Many large-scale constructions have served dual purposes beyond their primary functions throughout history. For example, Roman aqueducts were not merely transportation systems for water; they were engineering designs that connected entire cities to essential resources.[mccclxxxii] Similarly, medieval castles were fortified structures that housed royal families and served as hubs for local economies, offering protection, resources, and centralised governance.[mccclxxxiii] More recently, skyscrapers like the Empire State Building have incorporated multi-functional purposes, such as providing office space while hosting communication towers and power systems.[mccclxxxiv] These immense structures often fulfil multiple needs, suggesting that pyramids may have served as multi-purpose hubs with their advanced construction and strategic placements. Could they have facilitated energy production, storage, and possibly even distribution all in one?[mccclxxxv]

Free Energy

The history of free energy is a fascinating subject. What if we could tap into energy sources that are limitless, clean, and potentially available all around us?

Zero-point energy refers to the theoretical lowest possible energy that exists in the vacuum of space itself. According to quantum physics, even when all conventional energy is removed, space is not truly "empty." Instead, it teems with fluctuating electromagnetic fields and virtual particles, offering a potential reservoir of untapped energy.[mccclxxxvi] Zero-point energy is often presented as a nearly limitless source of power. Theoretically, it could be harnessed by extracting the residual energy in empty space. However, according to mainstream science, this is merely a theory, and there are currently no technologies capable of efficiently harnessing zero-point energy.

Another concept is the idea of over-unity machines—devices that output more energy than they consume. Although no practical or verifiable over-unity devices have been demonstrated, this concept remains crucial in free energy circles.

Then there is cold fusion. Unlike "hot" fusion, which occurs at extremely high temperatures, this nuclear reaction would occur at room temperature. If successful, cold fusion would be a potential source of free energy, but despite occasional reports, it remains unproven in mainstream science.

In the early 20th century, pioneers such as Nikola Tesla explored wireless energy transmission and envisioned harnessing the Earth's natural energy. Tesla's work suggested that energy could be extracted directly from the environment—such as the energy produced by the Earth's electromagnetic field or cosmic radiation. He believed this could revolutionise technology, providing endless power without relying on traditional fuel sources.[mccclxxxvii] In *The Prestige* (2006), directed by Christopher Nolan, Nikola Tesla plays a key role in the subplot, representing the mysterious and often misunderstood genius behind early 20th-century technological advancements. Tesla, who in real life explored wireless energy transmission and is frequently linked with free energy theories, is portrayed as a figure on the fringes of scientific understanding. His experiments in the film push the boundaries of what was possible, delving into the idea that advanced technology could unlock powers beyond society's comprehension. Tesla's work, both in the film and historically, symbolises how revolutionary technologies can challenge existing structures of power and knowledge.

By the mid-1920s, manipulating energy for levitation and anti-gravity gained more interest. Experimenters began working with high-voltage electric fields to investigate the possibility of levitation. This concept overlaps with early explorations into electromagnetic propulsion and the idea that specific frequencies or high voltage could counteract gravity, making objects float or hover. These experiments gained momentum in the following decades.[mccclxxxviii] Between the 1940s and the 1960s, interest in anti-gravity and levitation technologies experienced significant growth. Numerous speculative theories were fuelled by the Cold War's space race and technological arms race, that secretive government experiments were underway to unlock anti-gravity technologies.[mccclxxxix] This was also the era of flying saucer reports, and some theorists speculated that extraterrestrial spacecraft might be using advanced propulsion or energy technologies, such as anti-gravity.[mcccxc]

In the context of free energy, zero-point energy has been hypothesised to power anti-gravity devices. The idea suggests that if we could harness the energy present in the vacuum of space, it would provide an unlimited source of energy and a means to manipulate gravitational forces. Researchers in the 1960s and beyond began delving into how this might be accomplished, linking zero-point energy with anti-gravity and high-voltage experiments.[mcccxci]

The Morning of the Magicians (1960), written by French journalists Louis Pauwels and Jacques Bergier, devotes significant attention to the convergence between Nazi ideology and occultism, portraying the Third Reich not merely as a political regime but as a theosophical-technocratic experiment. The authors suggest that key Nazi figures were heavily influenced by esoteric myths of lost civilisations possessing advanced knowledge and spiritual power. They sought to uncover its supposed technological secrets, including unconventional energy sources, anti-gravity propulsion, and speculative mind-enhancing technologies. Interestingly, the authors report on fringe claims that Nazi scientists were involved in esoteric physics experiments, including early prototypes of what some now call zero-point energy, and speculative devices like *Die Glocke* ("The Bell"), a purported anti-gravitational craft surrounded by electromagnetic field experimentation.[mcccxcii]

In 2024, several intriguing experiments on free energy were conducted. For instance, MIT researchers developed a self-powering sensor that harvests energy from magnetic fields, which could lead to a battery-free future for many devices.[mcccxciii] This sensor stores small amounts of magnetic energy and converts it to power without a traditional battery, showcasing a potential shift towards more sustainable energy solutions. Additionally, ongoing experiments with Tesla towers and enhanced geothermal systems continue to push the boundaries of free energy exploration.[mcccxciv]

While no definitive mainstream breakthroughs have occurred, many alternative researchers and theorists continue to investigate these concepts, suggesting that zero-point energy, if unlocked, could offer free energy and unprecedented control over physical forces, such as gravity. Some claim that governments or private entities have made more progress than publicly acknowledged.[mcccxcv]

Could the ancients have been aware of free energy? Some argue that the education system has erased this knowledge from human consciousness.

Free Energy Suppression?

What is interesting is that a significant portion of early cars were electric. In the early 1900s, around one-third of the vehicles on the road in the United States were electric.[mcccxcvi] This period was a high point for electric vehicles (EVs), which were favoured for their simplicity, low maintenance, and smooth operation compared to steam and gasoline cars.[mcccxcvii] Electric cars, especially popular in cities, were quieter, had no exhaust emissions, and didn't require manual cranking to start, a significant inconvenience of early gas-powered cars.[mcccxcviii]

However, several factors contributed to the decline of EVs in the early 20th century, including the mass production of gasoline cars, thanks to Henry Ford's assembly line, the development of improved road infrastructure, and the discovery of abundant oil reserves, which made gasoline more affordable and accessible. So, while electric cars were initially popular, they were eventually overshadowed by gasoline-powered vehicles. However, this trend has only recently started reversing, thanks to renewed interest in EVs driven by technological advancements and environmental concerns.[mcccxcix] Interestingly, some believe that during this early era of electric vehicles, there may have been access to "free energy" sources that could have transformed transportation and industry.[mcd] Figures like Nikola Tesla were experimenting with wireless electricity transmission, which some suggest could have provided decentralised, limitless power. Could this information have been suppressed?

Theo Paijmans is an author who has written extensively on suppressed free energy technologies and their erasure from collective memory through education. His book *Free Energy Pioneer: John Worrell Keely* delves into the theories of suppressed free energy inventions, particularly focusing on the broader conspiracy that certain energy technologies were hidden from public knowledge to maintain control over energy markets. He delves deeply into the story of John Worrell Keely, a 19th-century inventor who claimed to have developed a motor that could harness "free energy." His invention, known as the "Keely Motor," was purportedly powered by an unknown force—referred to as "etheric energy" or "vibratory energy"—which he claimed existed all around us and could be tapped into without the need for conventional fuels. His work attracted significant public attention in the late 1800s due to its ambitious claim: a seemingly perpetual motion machine that could revolutionise energy production by generating unlimited power, thereby bypassing the need for coal, oil, or other traditional energy sources. Sceptics argued that his machine was a deception, potentially powered by hidden mechanisms like compressed air or concealed wires, as Keely refused to let outside experts inspect his setup. Supporters, however, believed he was a misunderstood genius whose discoveries could disrupt the world's reliance on fossil fuels and traditional energy infrastructure. In his book, Theo Paijmans also discusses how certain systems, including education, may have contributed to the suppression of this knowledge.[mcdi]

The broader "free energy suppression" conspiracy theory, as documented, suggests that influential entities, including governments and corporations, have actively suppressed the discovery or use of free energy technologies, which would have otherwise revolutionised global energy systems. In "The Hunt for Zero Point" (2001), British aerospace journalist Nick Cook delves into secretive military projects and explores the possibility that anti-gravity and free energy technologies are being hidden from the public eye. His investigative work suggests that significant advancements have been concealed to prevent disruption to existing energy markets.[mcdii] Thomas Valone, a physicist and advocate for alternative energy technologies, authored The Practical Conversion of Zero-Point Energy in 2007, exploring the potential of zero-point energy as a transformative power source. He discusses how this theoretical form of energy, derived from the quantum vacuum, could revolutionise global energy systems by providing limitless, clean energy. Like Nick Cook, he also suggests that powerful entities—primarily within governmental and corporate sectors—have actively suppressed the development and dissemination of zero-point energy technologies to protect the dominance of existing energy industries. [mcdiii]

The list goes on. Dr. Steven M. Greer, a retired medical doctor, is a prominent advocate for the disclosure of suppressed technologies, particularly in the field of free energy. His 2006 book, *Hidden Truth, Forbidden Knowledge*, claims that advanced free energy technologies have been deliberately concealed to maintain the current global power structure. He argues that these technologies, which could provide clean and limitless energy, are kept hidden by powerful interests that wish to protect the status quo of the energy industry and global politics. His work has influenced the broader "free energy suppression" theory, which posits that governmental and corporate entities have blocked humanity's access to revolutionary energy solutions for their benefit.[mcdiv]

We see similar themes in the cinema. *Thrive: What on Earth Will It Take?* (2011) is a documentary that explores various conspiracy theories, prominently featuring the idea that free energy technologies exist but are being suppressed by powerful institutions. The film argues that free energy could revolutionise the world by providing a limitless, clean energy source, but it suggests that corporate and government interests are preventing its development. The documentary promotes the idea that free energy would disrupt the global economy, which is dominated by fossil fuels, and shift the balance of power away from traditional energy industries. Although controversial, *Thrive* taps into many people's frustration about energy dependence and the possibility of hidden solutions."

Zero Point: The Story of Mark McCandlish and the Alien Reproduction Vehicle (2014) delves into the story of aerospace illustrator Mark McCandlish, who claimed knowledge of secret government projects involving free energy and anti-gravity technologies. Specifically, McCandlish's story centres around a craft known as the Alien Reproduction Vehicle (ARV), allegedly powered by zero-point energy. The documentary suggests that advanced energy technologies, potentially derived from extraterrestrial sources, have been developed but remain classified. It supports the narrative that free energy technologies could revolutionise the world, but are being suppressed for reasons of control or secrecy.

Chain Reaction (1996), starring Keanu Reeves and Morgan Freeman, explores the discovery of a way to generate clean, unlimited energy from water—a process akin to cold fusion. The scientists in the film find themselves in danger when powerful entities attempt to suppress their invention to maintain control over the global energy market. This plot mirrors real-world fears that those with vested interests in maintaining the status quo could stifle disruptive technologies, such as free energy. The film emphasises the tension between scientific discovery and the forces that resist change, particularly when such innovations could upend established power structures.

Although the jury is still out on the viability of free energy, it remains a hot topic that captivates scientists and the public. Whether through speculative technologies like zero-point energy or the prospect of anti-gravity and electromagnetic propulsion, the idea of limitless, clean energy has sparked countless discussions, films, and theories. Fusion energy, which powers the sun, has long been hailed as the ultimate clean, limitless energy source. Recent breakthroughs, such as the 2022 net energy gain in fusion reactions and progress at ITER in France, suggest it could become commercially viable within decades, though sceptics debate this timeline. Suppose fusion energy was to reach the market in just five years. It may revolutionise global energy systems, displacing fossil fuels, decentralising power grids, and reducing geopolitical tensions over energy resources. Beyond Earth, it could make deep space travel more feasible, providing a compact, efficient power source for spacecraft. What impact would such a shift have on industries, economies, the environment, and humanity's reach into space?

Data centres powering Artificial Intelligence (AI) models consume staggering amounts of electricity, forcing a global reckoning over how future energy systems must evolve. Although we are seeing breakthrough energy systems, they will likely be centralised and marketised under safe labels like "AI-optimised nuclear" or "quantum-enabled renewables," not "free energy." If "free energy" does exist in the shadows, it will likely be viewed as a weapon or strategic tool, rather than a consumer product.

As discoveries continue to emerge and technologies evolve, the dream of free energy remains one of the most compelling frontiers in science and popular imagination.

Power Plant

Could the pyramids have served as central hubs for powering other ancient technologies—tools, machines, or even transportation systems — that we have yet to discover or understand? The energy concentrated or produced by pyramids might have been distributed across vast distances, facilitating the operation of complex devices or infrastructures. The theory that pyramids were used as power plants is not supported by mainstream science or archaeology. If the pyramids were used as power plants to generate and distribute energy, they argue, there would likely be some evidence of the technologies that used this energy. However, no devices, machinery, or systems requiring electrical or other forms of power have been found in or around the pyramids. Ancient Egyptian tools and technologies were based on manual labour and simple machines, such as levers, ramps, and chisels.[mcdv] However, one could argue that the pyramids could not have been built without such machinery.[mcdvi]

Although the majority of hieroglyphs pertain to religious, social, and royal matters, some symbols are linked by theorists to possible energy technology. For example, the "Ankh" represents life and is sometimes interpreted as a key to divine energy or power in alternative theories. The famous "Dendera Light" is a controversial interpretation of a bas-relief in the Temple of Hathor at Dendera. It depicts what some believe is a large, electric, light bulb-like object, although mainstream Egyptology views it as a symbolic representation of creation and rebirth. Some have used this interpretation to suggest that ancient Egyptians may have been aware of energy or electricity.[mcdvii]

Given the latest free energy experiments and research in 2024, would it be possible for the pyramids to harness various forms of energy based on environmental sources, much like modern energy-harvesting technologies? For instance, geothermal energy could have been a potential source, tapping into the Earth's heat due to the pyramids' strategic location. Additionally, the structure's materials, such as limestone and quartz, may have interacted with electromagnetic fields, creating the potential to harness electromagnetic energy similar to modern devices like self-powering sensors that capture ambient magnetic energy. However, there is no solid evidence to support this theory.

Global Energy Grid

Some theorists propose that pyramids were part of a global energy grid connected by ley lines or electromagnetic fields. This network could have distributed energy across vast distances, harmonising the Earth's energy systems. The global positioning of pyramids suggests that their builders may have understood how to tap into and manipulate the Earth's energy on a grand scale. Mainstream archaeology explains the global distribution of pyramids as resulting from different civilisations developing similar architectural forms independently. The pyramid shape is structurally stable and efficient for large-scale construction, making it a practical design for ancient builders. No archaeological or textual evidence supports that these pyramids were part of a global energy network. Dismissing these structures as merely practical or coincidental in form downplays the possibility that they had a more profound, possibly energetic, purpose. The consistent use of the pyramid shape and its spiritual and astronomical significance across distant cultures suggests that these civilisations may have shared knowledge through direct or indirect contact or some ancient forgotten source of wisdom. The argument that this is purely coincidental doesn't fully account for the striking similarities, which might imply a shared and connected ancient understanding of energy or geometry.

Global Wireless Energy Transmission

Theories suggest that the pyramids, especially the Great Pyramid of Giza, may have been part of a system for wireless energy transmission. Like Nikola Tesla envisioned transmitting electricity through the air without wires, pyramids might have been designed to focus and direct energy over long distances. This energy could have been used to power ancient cities, devices or other unknown technologies without traditional fuel sources. He envisioned creating a system that could transmit electricity through the Earth's atmosphere without wires, using the Earth as a conductor. He theorised that ether could be tapped into to provide wireless, free energy to power the entire planet. He claimed that the Earth's natural energy could be harnessed through devices like the Tesla coil. He proposed that shapes like pyramids could theoretically resonate and amplify energy over long distances without the need for wires. His experiments with wireless power transmission have inspired modern scientists to reconsider ancient technologies.[mcdviii] Tesla's *Wardenclyffe Tower*, a project aimed at transmitting energy wirelessly across great distances, was based on the principles of resonance and the Earth's natural electromagnetic fields. Some theorists draw parallels between Tesla's work and the pyramids, suggesting that the pyramids could have been ancient structures built to achieve a similar goal of wireless energy transmission. The pyramid's capstone could have played a critical role in the conductor's interaction with these natural forces.

We also see this theory explored in documentaries. *Revelation of the Pyramids (2010)* investigates the construction of pyramids worldwide, exploring the possibility that ancient civilisations had access to advanced knowledge and technologies. It presents fringe theories that the pyramids are part of a global network designed to transmit energy, hinting at a lost global civilisation.[mcdix]

Scientists like Christopher Dunn argue that ancient Egyptians might have used different methods to harness and transmit energy. Dunn's book *The Giza Power Plant* speculates that the pyramids functioned as machines to harness the Earth's natural forces, though this theory remains speculative.[mcdx] More recent studies on wireless energy transmission suggest that ancient civilisations may have had advanced knowledge of the Earth's electromagnetic properties, though conclusive evidence remains elusive.

Obelisks as Transmitters or Receivers

Obelisks became prominent in Egypt from around 2,000 to 1,000 BCE, after the pyramids were built. The Egyptians are believed to have created an estimated 28 obelisks, although some sources suggest there may have been more than 30. Studies have shown that obelisks were incredibly precise, with smooth surfaces and straight lines.[mcdxi] Many were aligned with the four cardinal directions, like the pyramids.[mcdxii] They were also aligned with astronomical or solar events, such as the sun's rising and setting. Most are now fallen, and only eight remain standing in Egypt today. [mcdxiii]

Obelisks were erected as religious symbols, often to honour the sun god Ra. Inscriptions frequently referred to the pharaoh as Ra's earthly representative.[mcdxiv] Could the obelisks have been more than symbolic, but practical components of a broader energy network, working in conjunction with the pyramids to transmit or harness energy?[mcdxv] Obelisks are tall, slender structures with pointed tops, much like modern lightning rods. Their height and pointed shape make them ideal for attracting electrical charges from the atmosphere, such as lightning. If obelisks were positioned near pyramids, they could have been used to attract atmospheric electricity and direct it to the Earth.[mcdxvi] Obelisks were often made of granite, a quartz material with piezoelectric properties that can generate electrical charge under mechanical stress.^{mcdxvii} This could make obelisks attractors of energy from lightning or atmospheric electricity and capable of interacting with the Earth's natural energy fields.^{mcdxviii} If pyramids were designed to harness Earth's energy through ley lines, geomagnetic fields, or other natural forces, could obelisks have acted as energy conductors or antennae to channel energy from the sky - atmospheric, solar, and cosmic?^{mcdxix} Together, they could have formed a complete energy system where obelisks gather or channel energy and pyramids store, amplify, or direct it.^{mcdxx} The precise placement of obelisks near temples, pyramids, or sacred sites could indicate that the Egyptians intentionally positioned them to enhance the energy flow between the sky and the Earth. Could obelisks have acted as conductors for electromagnetic energy, drawing it from the atmosphere, while pyramids stored and controlled it? Placing granite blocks in the pyramids and the quartz content in both obelisks and pyramids could facilitate the transmission of electrical energy.^{mcdxxi} The pyramids' alignment with ley lines and strategic positioning along the Earth's magnetic grid suggest they were designed to tap into natural Earth energies.^{mcdxxii} Standing tall, obelisks could have been used to capture atmospheric energy and channel it into these natural energy grids, making the entire system more powerful. Or could the obelisks be receivers, receiving energy from the pyramid?^{mcdxxiii} Obelisks were sometimes capped with electrum, a highly conductive alloy of gold and silver, which might have enhanced their ability to attract and conduct energy.

Egyptian obelisks, originally from Egypt, stand in Istanbul, Rome, London, Paris, and New York. During the 19th century, they were moved to various parts of the world as diplomatic gifts or trophies of European colonialism. The fact that obelisks were transported and gifted to several world powers, such as the Vatican, Paris, London, and New York, suggests that they carried significant political and cultural weight.^{mcdxxiv} Could gifting the obelisks represent a symbol of power and a shared ideology or governing system, perhaps aimed at fostering a unified world? They may have used obelisks to communicate their vision of a united world under a common rule or shared belief system.

Global Wireless Communication System

Some speculate that the pyramids, particularly the Great Pyramid of Giza, could have been part of a wireless communication system with an antenna at the top.^{mcdxxv} This is an intriguing idea. The missing capstone or pyramidion of the Great Pyramid is often thought to have played a crucial role in its functionality. If this capstone were made of a conductive material such as gold, copper, or another metal, it could have acted like a modern antenna, collecting or transmitting signals through the air.^{mcdxxvi} This aligns with how today's communication systems use antennas to transmit or receive electromagnetic waves. While no direct experiments have been conducted on the original pyramidion, experiments on the conductivity of materials such as gold and copper in connection with the pyramid's geometric shape show that structures with pointed tops can act as capacitors or antennas, collecting and focusing electromagnetic energy.

The pyramid's height and position at the geographical centre of Earth's landmass could have been ideal for serving as a central transmitter or receiver of signals across vast distances.^{mcdxxvii} The pyramid's position divides the Earth's landmasses into nearly equal quarters when measured longitudinally and latitudinally.^{mcdxxviii}

While no conclusive archaeological evidence proves the pyramids were used for communication, there is historical precedent for using ancient structures in similar capacities. For instance, the ancient Greeks used the Pharos Lighthouse of Alexandria as a beacon that could be seen from miles away, and Roman military systems relied on advanced signalling techniques. The idea of pyramids transmitting energy or signals across long distances is not entirely implausible when viewed in the context of other ancient methods.

The curvature of the Earth is a critical factor to consider when discussing global wireless transmission. Wireless communication, whether through radio waves, microwaves, or other forms of electromagnetic waves, typically relies on line-of-sight transmission. This means the signal sent from one point (such as a transmitter) must travel directly to a receiver. However, the curvature of the Earth limits how far a signal can travel without obstruction because the Earth's surface bends away from that straight line. The Great Pyramid of Giza originally stood at around 146.6 meters (481 feet).^{mcdxxix} This height, combined with the pyramid's location near the centre of Earth's landmass, would have given it a larger horizon, allowing signals to be transmitted over greater distances before encountering the Earth's curvature. If it acted as a transmitter, the pyramid's height could have helped extend its reach across a larger portion of the globe.

The antenna could have been designed to capture cosmic or atmospheric energy, converting it into signals that could travel through the Earth's atmosphere or even beyond, linking up with other pyramids or communication hubs.^{mcdxxx} If pyramids across the globe were part of this network, they might have created an interconnected wireless communication system, potentially transmitting data or even sound across great distances.

In an earlier chapter, we highlighted that the Great Pyramid of Giza mimics Earth's curvature through its geometric proportions, where the ratio of its base perimeter to height corresponds to 2π.[mcdxxxi] When scaled by 43,200, it reflects Earth's equatorial circumference and polar radius, suggesting advanced knowledge of Earth's dimensions. If the pyramid was used as a global transmitter, its design mimicking the curvature of the Earth could have played a crucial role in enabling effective wireless communication or energy transmission across large distances. If the pyramid's geometry was designed to account for this curvature, it might have helped maintain the strength of these signals by allowing them to "hug" the Earth's surface as they travelled, extending their range. The pyramid's design, incorporating the Earth's dimensions and curvature, could create a resonant connection with the planet.[mcdxxxii]

Giant Water Pump

Stanley Meyer was an American inventor. His invention of the Water Fuel Cell, which he claimed could power a car using water by splitting it into hydrogen and oxygen, captivated the world with its promise of a revolutionary energy source. His device purportedly allowed vehicles to run on water rather than gasoline, a breakthrough that, if fully realised, could have disrupted the global energy industry. However, his sudden death in 1998, officially attributed to a brain aneurysm, sparked a wave of conspiracy theories. Moments before his death, Meyer allegedly ran out of a restaurant shouting, "They poisoned me!"[mcdxxxiii] This claim led many to believe that powerful interests, particularly oil companies and government agencies, had silenced his life's work.

Supporters of his invention argue that his technology significantly threatened the oil industry's dominance. As a result, his work was suppressed before it could reach the public.[mcdxxxiv] In light of this, some theorists wonder if similar concepts could explain the pyramids' potential function as energy devices. If his water-based technology was a modern-day breakthrough, could ancient civilisations have harnessed water equally groundbreakingly? While his invention was never proven to work, his claims sparked a global conversation about alternative energy sources and the possibilities of water as a fuel source.

Many similar inventions focus on splitting water into hydrogen and oxygen and using hydrogen as fuel. When burned, hydrogen produces water as a byproduct, making it a very attractive clean energy source. However, splitting water requires a significant energy input, meaning that none of these inventions have successfully demonstrated a net energy gain or "free energy." If technology could extract energy from water in a cost-effective, abundant, and sustainable manner, it could significantly reduce the world's dependence on fossil fuels. Some speculate that the pyramids may have been used for hydrogen production. They believe that the chambers and materials within the pyramid could have facilitated chemical reactions that produced hydrogen, which could then be used as a fuel source.

There is also speculation that the pyramids, particularly the Great Pyramid of Giza, may have incorporated water in an energy-producing mechanism, possibly using hydraulic power.[mcdxxxv] Proponents of this idea suggest that the pyramid's underground chambers and water channels were designed to manipulate water for energy or even electromagnetic purposes. Much like his Water Fuel Cell, the theory remains speculative, but it adds an intriguing dimension to the mysteries surrounding ancient technology and modern inventions.[mcdxxxvi]

What if the Great Pyramid of Giza had cracked the code and functioned as a hydraulic structure or a giant water pump? Proponents of this theory suggest that the pyramid's internal chambers and shafts were designed to harness the power of water pressure from underground sources. Water could have been pumped upward and possibly purified mechanically. While this theory lacks solid archaeological support, it offers an alternative perspective on how water could have been integrated into the pyramid's function. It aligns conceptually with modern hydropower innovations, in which water movement generates electricity.

The theory begins with the idea that the Great Pyramid sits above a natural aquifer or underground water source, which could have been accessed through tunnels or wells beneath the structure.[mcdxxxvii] Egypt's Nile River and its floodplain were crucial to the region's agriculture and daily life, so it's conceivable that ancient engineers might have devised ways to control or use the abundant water supply under the pyramid.[mcdxxxviii] One of the pyramid's lesser-known features is the underground chamber, which lies beneath the pyramid's base. Theorists have proposed that this chamber, along with the descending passage leading to it, played a role in water movement. Some believe the chamber was part of a system that directed water from the aquifer below into the pyramid.

The internal structure of the Great Pyramid includes several unique chambers (the King's Chamber and Queen's Chamber) and narrow shafts connecting these chambers to the pyramid's exterior. Proponents of the hydraulic theory suggest that these chambers and shafts were not designed solely for ritual or symbolic purposes but were part of a complex hydraulic system. The pyramid may have functioned like a large-scale hydraulic ram pump. A ram pump uses water pressure to move a smaller volume of water to a higher elevation. This could explain the pyramid's height, allowing water to be pumped upward through internal passages.

Some versions of the hydraulic theory suggest that the pyramid could have been used to purify and pump water. This idea is based on the pyramid's interior materials, such as granite, which is thought to have piezoelectric properties (meaning it generates an electric charge under pressure). Some theorists argue that this process could have played a role in purifying or "charging" the water as it moved through the structure.

Some researchers have noted unusual erosion patterns in the underground chamber, which they believe may be caused by water flow.[mcdxxxix] This could indicate that water was once a key component in the pyramid's operation. Mainstream archaeologists, however, attribute this erosion to other factors, such as poor construction or natural wear.[mcdxl] The pyramid's proximity to the Nile River is significant in this theory. The river's annual flooding could have created the hydraulic pressure necessary to operate a large-scale water pump.[mcdxli] The pyramid may have harnessed this natural resource to generate power or move water for irrigation or other practical purposes. Some researchers suggest that the pyramid's chambers exhibit unusual acoustic properties, which may be connected to the movement of water or air. The sound waves generated within the pyramid could have been a byproduct of the water pressure system, creating harmonic resonances for practical purposes (e.g., amplifying water movement) or ceremonial or spiritual reasons. The granite blocks in the King's Chamber and other parts of the pyramid have piezoelectric properties, generating electrical charges when subjected to pressure or vibration. Some theorists suggest that the pyramid may have been designed to create or manipulate electrical energy, possibly in conjunction with the movement of water through the structure.

The pyramid might have served to pump water from the underground aquifers or the nearby Nile to higher elevations for irrigation. This would have been a vital function in an arid environment like Egypt's, where managing water resources was crucial for agriculture and survival. The pyramid may also have acted as a system for delivering fresh water to the surrounding area. Pumping water from underground sources could have supplied clean water for drinking, bathing, and other uses.

If the pyramid's internal structure was designed to purify or "charge" water, it could have been used for practical and spiritual purposes. Purified water may have been used in religious ceremonies or healing practices, as water was often seen as a sacred element in ancient Egypt. Even if the pyramid had a practical use as a water pump, it might also have served a symbolic or spiritual purpose. The movement of water could have been seen as representing the flow of life or the power of the gods, adding a layer of religious significance to the pyramid's hydraulic function.

Reimagining the Pyramid: More Than Tombs?

While speculative, the concept that pyramids served as central utility hubs for energy production and wireless transmission presents a thought-provoking perspective. There is growing interest in the possibility that pyramids were part of an ancient global energy grid. These structures may have tapped into Earth's natural forces, such as electromagnetic and geothermal energy, functioning similarly to modern power grids that rely on nodes for efficient energy distribution.

Today, energy grids are designed with nodes—specific points where energy is optimally distributed across a region. Similarly, the pyramid's geometric design and placement along ley lines could represent a primitive version of this energy distribution system. Research published in *Energy & Buildings* (2020) demonstrated how triangular and pyramid-like structures, due to their shape and material composition, can optimise the absorption and distribution of solar energy. The Great Pyramid's alignment with Earth's cardinal points and the precise dimensions of its internal chambers suggest it could have served as a key node in an ancient energy network.

Furthermore, theories suggest that the pyramids, especially the Great Pyramid of Giza, may have been built to transmit energy wirelessly, akin to Nikola Tesla's idea of using the Earth's natural electromagnetic fields for energy transfer. The capstone, possibly crafted from a conductive material, could have served as an antenna, playing a vital role in this system.

While the idea of pyramids functioning as central energy hubs in an ancient global energy grid is intriguing, modern scientific and archaeological research casts doubt on its plausibility. From a technological standpoint, there is no evidence to support the infrastructure needed to transmit energy wirelessly across vast distances in ancient civilisations. As physicist Paul A. LaViolette notes in his book *Secrets of Antigravity Propulsion (2008)*, there is no known mechanism by which pyramidal structures could have generated or transmitted power on a scale comparable to that imagined by modern alternative theories.[mcdxlii] Geological studies further highlight that materials used in pyramid construction, such as limestone and granite, lack the conductive properties necessary to channel or store significant amounts of energy.

Archaeological evidence also overwhelmingly supports the view that pyramids were primarily used for religious and funerary purposes rather than as power-generating structures. In *The Complete Pyramids: Solving the Ancient Mysteries* (1997), Egyptologist Mark Lehner emphasises that the sheer magnitude of labour and resources devoted to pyramid construction points more to their role as tombs and symbols of royal power rather than any technological or energy-related function. Furthermore, logistical challenges—such as the absence of remnants of energy-receiving technology or networks—compound the difficulties in supporting the energy grid theory.[mcdxliii] Despite imaginative hypotheses proposed by engineer Christopher Dunn in *The Giza Power Plant*, critics have pointed out the lack of empirical evidence for the advanced technologies required for such a system to exist, leaving the theory speculative.[mcdxliv]

Although no direct archaeological evidence supports the idea that pyramids were used for energy production, the potential similarities with modern energy systems and recent discoveries in solar energy optimisation encourage further research. Technological advancements, such as thermal imaging and electromagnetic field mapping, could offer new insights into the possible roles of the pyramids as central utility hubs in ancient civilisations.

This utility perspective will be explored further in the next chapter, where we will investigate how pyramids might have influenced climate control and resource transformation.

Powered by Pyramids: A Book of Theories

Chapter 21 Global Transportation System

Ancient Underground Tunnelling System

Numerous documented tunnels worldwide, including those beneath pyramids and ancient sites, support the idea that pyramids could have served as access points or "train stations" within an underground network. The size of ancient underground tunnels ranges from narrow, person-sized passages to large chambers and extensive networks spanning miles. Could the tunnel systems mentioned at the start of this book have been part of an ancient underground transportation network?

The discovery of ancient tunnels beneath pyramids and sacred sites around the world is truly astonishing, revealing a level of sophistication and interconnectedness that challenges everything we thought we knew about ancient civilisations. From the intricate labyrinths beneath the Giza Plateau in Egypt to the vast underground cities of Cappadocia in Turkey stretching for miles, these networks showcase advanced engineering techniques that seem almost impossible. In Mexico, the mysterious tunnels under Teotihuacan contain pools of mercury, hinting at a technology or ritual practice that remains unexplained. The Qin Shi Huang tomb in China, surrounded by rivers of mercury within an underground maze, echoes similar mind-boggling designs. Meanwhile, the Hypogeum in Malta and the underground passages of Chichen Itza in Mexico connect sacred structures and natural elements with precision, suggesting a deliberate, global understanding of underground construction. Even in Greece and Rome, these tunnels served as burial sites and conduits for religious and social activities. The sheer scale and complexity of these tunnels, often aligned with sacred architecture like pyramids and temples, present an incredible puzzle—one that compels us to reassess the technological and spiritual capabilities of these ancient cultures, who may have harnessed the Earth's energy in ways we are only beginning to comprehend. [mcdxlv]

Mercury Powering Transport System

Could mercury potentially be linked to the idea of an ancient transportation system beneath pyramids and other sacred sites? Mercury is a metal known for its unique properties, especially its ability to conduct electricity and flow in a liquid state at room temperature. In speculative theories, it is suggested that ancient civilisations might have used mercury as a conductor or energy source in their technologies.[mcdxlvi] Mercury could have been a critical component in amplifying and transmitting that energy through the tunnel networks if they were harnessing the Earth's magnetic or electromagnetic energy.[mcdxlvii] In underground transport, mercury could have been used to create liquid circuits or conduits in the tunnels, channelling energy efficiently throughout the system. This idea aligns with a ley line-powered network, where mercury's conductive properties could enhance the energy flow necessary to propel platforms or vehicles.[mcdxlviii]

Mercury is generally avoided in modern transportation systems due to its toxicity, environmental risks, and the availability of safer, more efficient alternatives. However, it has historically been employed in scientific and engineering fields, especially in temperature measurement, vacuum technology, and electrical systems. In the early 20th century, mercury arc rectifiers converted AC to DC power, aiding the development of electric railways and proving mercury's usefulness in transportation technology. Although mercury's toxicity poses hazards, its historical application in devices like mercury arc rectifiers for converting electrical currents provides a precedent for its potential use in ancient systems.[mcdxlix]

Modern Experiments with Magnetic Levitation Trains

Contemporary experiments with underground transportation systems, such as magnetic levitation (maglev) trains and hyperloop concepts, show that high-speed subterranean travel is possible with the right technology. Recent research has highlighted how these systems use advanced magnetic propulsion and low-friction tunnel environments to reach unprecedented speeds while reducing energy consumption and resistance. For example, Smith and Zhang's (2021) work on the development of Maglev and Hyperloop systems demonstrates the potential for these technologies to transform transportation by optimising underground routes, much like the networks proposed in ancient civilisations. If modern technology can achieve such feats, it is reasonable to speculate that ancient societies, with an advanced understanding of Earth's geomagnetic properties, may have used similar principles to create underground pathways for efficient movement.[mcdl]

Imagine What If?

Imagine pyramids as sophisticated energy amplifiers designed to tap into the Earth's geomagnetic forces, particularly those channelled

Powered by Pyramids: A Book of Theories

through ley lines. These ley lines—powerful energy currents running through the earth—intersect at the locations of pyramids, where the structures act as nodes or stations in this global network. The ancient engineers who built the pyramids understood the Earth's energy grid and aligned these structures precisely to maximise their effectiveness as transport hubs. You arrive at the Great Pyramid of Giza, which looms above you as an architectural marvel. You are not here to tour its massive chambers or to marvel at its alignment with the stars; you are here to travel. As you enter the pyramid's base, you descend into an underground chamber where the true magic happens—the platform.

This platform is not merely a platform but an ancient piece of technology. The surface is embedded with crystalline materials, some of which are translucent and glow faintly, pulsating in sync with the energy flowing from the ley lines beneath the earth. This chamber, located directly at the convergence of these powerful energy lines, serves as the gateway into the transportation network.

When you step onto the platform, you feel a gentle hum beneath your feet, a magnetic pull that anchors you in place. Guardians of the pyramid, trained in the sacred sciences and technology of their time, activate the transport system. They perform precise hand movements, triggering mechanisms within the chamber. Ancient symbols carved into the walls and etched into the platform begin to glow, channelling energy through crystal conduits.

The energy pulses grow stronger as the platform lifts slightly off the ground, hovering as the magnetic forces stabilise. You feel an increasing sense of weightlessness, and then, with a flash of light and a sudden surge, the energy field propels you forward, launching you into the tunnel network below.

Once inside the tunnel network, the energy channelled by the ley lines drives the platform at incredible speeds. The tunnels, lined with sleek stone surfaces and reinforced with crystalline metals, are designed to minimise friction and sustain a stable magnetic field. Unlike anything modern technology can achieve, the sensation is smooth, silent, and swift.

The tunnels are illuminated by faint luminescent stones, perhaps powered by the same geomagnetic energy that propels the platform. As you travel through this vast network, the tunnels occasionally branch into different directions, all precisely mapped and aligned with the energy grid that ancient engineers mastered long ago.

The pyramid "stations" are located at key nodal points where ley lines converge, acting as both amplifiers of energy and access points for this underground transportation network. In Egypt, the Great Pyramid serves as the central hub for the network, with other pyramids, such as those at Saqqara and Dahshur, and even the smaller step pyramids acting as secondary stations, distributing travellers and resources across the ancient world.

But this network does not end in Egypt. It extends globally. The tunnels connect to Teotihuacan's pyramids in Mexico, the temples and pyramids of ancient China, and the mysterious structures in Sudan. Each pyramid is a portal into this global network, ensuring that those who understand the ancient technology can move seamlessly between distant civilisations.

The pyramids' role as train stations is intertwined with their spiritual significance. Ancient travellers, whether priests, scholars, or leaders, did not merely use the transport system for convenience. They believed that by tapping into the Earth's energy, they engaged with a higher power, aligning themselves with the cosmos. Thus, every journey was a spiritual experience, and rituals, chants, and ceremonies often accompanied the journey.

When activated, the platform became a gateway to distant lands and spiritual ascension, linking the traveller to the cosmic energy flowing through the Earth. The technology and the sacred were the same, blending practicality with mysticism.

Speculative Theories

David Hatcher Childress elaborates on several theories in his book *Lost Continents and the Hollow Earth* (1999). He suggests that ancient civilisations had access to Earth's natural energy grid, specifically ley lines, which are believed to be geomagnetic pathways connecting ancient sites such as pyramids, Stonehenge, and other megalithic structures. He suggests that these civilisations built tunnels along these ley lines to harness and distribute energy, potentially powering advanced technologies or serving as high-speed transit routes similar to modern magnetic levitation (maglev) systems. He also discusses how the alignment of ancient structures like pyramids, obelisks, and temples was intentional, designed to act as nodes that amplify energy flow into these tunnels. This energy could have been used to propel platforms or vehicles using levitation technology, enabling rapid transportation across vast distances.[mcdli]

Furthermore, he ties these ideas to the Agartha Legend, which describes an advanced civilisation living underground with superior knowledge of energy and technology. He connects these subterranean pathways to sacred sites, such as those in Tibet and South America, suggesting that these tunnels formed an interconnected network for travel and communication. He expands on this by linking legends from Tibetan and Hindu traditions, which describe hidden entrances to these underground worlds in the Himalayas, to tunnel networks in South America, including the Tayos Caves in Ecuador, believed to span entire continents.^{mcdlii}

Regarding the legend of Atlantis, he suggests that these tunnels may be remnants of a highly advanced civilisation that existed before recorded history. He believes the tunnels connect sacred sites such as the pyramids of Egypt and the Mesoamerican pyramids, indicating that these structures were part of an ancient infrastructure used for transportation and energy purposes. Childress contends that these tunnels beneath the pyramids might contain remnants of Atlantean technology, providing the infrastructure for such a global network.^{mcdliii}

The Shaver Mystery, popularised by Richard Shaver in the 1940s, suggests that ancient underground tunnels are inhabited by two technologically advanced races: the Dero and the Tero. The Dero are hostile beings who use advanced machinery to control and manipulate the surface world. At the same time, the Tero are benevolent and seek to mitigate the damage caused by the Dero. His stories, published in *Amazing Stories* magazine, claimed that these tunnels contained forgotten technologies, including mind-control devices, hologram generators, and advanced transportation systems. Although his tales are primarily viewed as science fiction, they have influenced modern theories of a hollow Earth and beliefs in hidden underground civilisations.

In *The Giza Power Plant: Technologies of Ancient Egypt* (1998), Christopher Dunn suggests that the tunnel systems beneath the Great Pyramid were crucial to an advanced energy infrastructure. He proposes that these tunnels were designed to align with the pyramid's broader purpose of harnessing Earth's natural forces. Dunn argues that the layout, dimensions, and orientation of the tunnels and chambers demonstrate a sophisticated understanding of acoustics and energy flow. He points to evidence of water erosion within the tunnels, theorising that they channelled water in a controlled manner to generate energy, possibly utilising resonance effects akin to modern hydropower systems. Additionally, he highlights electromagnetic anomalies detected in the area, implying that the tunnels amplify and direct these natural energies. He maintains that by choosing specific materials, such as granite for its crystalline properties, the ancient builders aimed to optimise the conversion and distribution of energy throughout the pyramid complex.^{mcdliv}

Perhaps they used water and geomagnetic energy to transmit power along these routes. The precision engineering observed at sites like the Serapeum in Saqqara, with its vast granite sarcophagi and extensive tunnels, supports the notion that these spaces were designed with advanced knowledge of energy and resonance technology, possibly related to transportation or energy storage. However, mercury was found in the tunnels, and it is highly toxic. If it enters the water supply, it can have serious health consequences for humans, animals, and plants.

Given the multifunctional uses of ancient Greek and Roman tunnels, as outlined by Dan Davis in *Classical Archaeology Review* (2021), it is plausible that the tunnels beneath the pyramids could have served similar purposes. He explains that these ancient passageways were used for water management, religious processions, storage, and military purposes. Applying this perspective to the Egyptian tunnels, one might speculate that these structures could have supported similar activities. The tunnels' strategic alignment with pyramids and other sacred sites suggests they may have been designed for the secure transport of goods, storage, or even military operations, in addition to their ceremonial functions. Could military equipment have been found in these tunnels? This theory aligns with the idea that pyramids and their associated tunnels formed nodes in a vast, sophisticated infrastructure system. Further exploration and study of these tunnels could reveal more about the Egyptians' advanced engineering capabilities and multifunctional use of underground networks.

Could ancient civilisations have discovered methods to propel passengers through underground tunnels at speeds approaching or surpassing the speed of light? This idea hinges on the belief that these advanced societies had access to energy sources beyond our current understanding, perhaps by tapping into Earth's ley lines or manipulating geomagnetic fields.[mcdlv] Some theorists suggest that the pyramids and their tunnel networks acted as nodes within this vast energy grid, amplifying and channelling power in ways that defy modern physics.[mcdlvi] According to this theory, the ancient engineers possessed a profound knowledge of space-time manipulation, enabling them to create instantaneous travel between distant sites, akin to teleportation.[mcdlvii] While no evidence supports such a claim within the boundaries of known science, the idea captivates the imagination, hinting at a lost era of technological and spiritual mastery far beyond what we comprehend today.[mcdlviii]

If ancient civilisations had developed tunnels that allowed for travel at the speed of light, the journey from Egypt to Mesoamerica would have been astonishingly fast. Given the distance of roughly 12,000 kilometres between Giza and Teotihuacan, such a trip would take only about 0.04 seconds.[mcdlix] This near-instantaneous travel highlights the incredible potential of harnessing light-speed technology, allowing passengers to traverse vast distances across continents almost instantaneously. While purely speculative, this showcases the advanced capabilities these ancient societies might have possessed if they had unlocked such extraordinary knowledge.[mcdlx]

However, it isn't easy to imagine how this could be possible considering our current understanding. According to Einstein's Theory of Relativity, as objects approach the speed of light, their mass increases, requiring infinite energy to reach that speed. For ancient civilisations to achieve this, they would need to harness extraordinary amounts of energy, far beyond what even modern technology can produce. Travelling at the speed of light would also require materials capable of withstanding immense stresses and forces. Even the most advanced materials known today would not be capable of maintaining the structural integrity needed at such velocities, making it unlikely that ancient engineers possessed this level of technology. While fascinating, using ley lines or Earth's geomagnetic energy would not be enough to accelerate objects to such speeds. The energy needed to reach and sustain the speed of light would likely surpass what these natural phenomena could provide.[mcdlxi]

What Proof Do We Have?

Globally, the discovery of underground tunnels beneath pyramids, sacred sites, and ancient cities reveals a complexity and engineering skill that exceeds that of typical water management systems. The consistent alignment of these tunnels with structures, their depth, and the presence of materials like mercury and massive stone architecture suggest that they may have been designed for transportation or energy-related purposes, challenging the traditional view that they were merely for water or defence.

If this ancient transport system existed, why do we not see its remnants today? The answer lies in the decline of civilisations and the loss of knowledge as these ancient civilisations fell—whether due to natural disasters, invasions, or internal strife—the secrets of the transport system were lost. The tunnels, once maintained by the Guardians, collapsed or were buried, while others became filled with debris or water. The activation chambers within the pyramids were sealed off, and the crystalline components necessary to power the platforms were either removed, lost, or repurposed over the centuries. Recent archaeological discoveries support the idea of ancient underground tunnelling systems, suggesting they might have served purposes beyond water management.

For example, archaeologist Kathleen Martinez led the discovery of a 4,300-foot-long tunnel beneath Egypt's Taposiris Magna Temple, revealing a complex network of passageways. The tunnel, constructed during the Ptolemaic era, reflects the engineering accomplishments of ancient Greek tunnels, indicating advanced planning and deliberate construction. It is partially submerged, likely due to earthquakes, suggesting that ancient civilisations designed tunnels capable of withstanding natural disasters.

In Mexico, the archaeological site at Mitla, associated with the ancient Zapotec culture, has revealed extensive underground passageways and chambers beneath the San Pablo Church.[mcdlxii] These tunnels, confirmed through modern geophysical methods like seismic tomography and ground-penetrating radar, align with local legends that describe Mitla as an entrance to the underworld. The scale and connection of the tunnels to key ceremonial structures suggest that they were not merely used for water or storage, but could have also served transportation or spiritual functions.

These discoveries, along with others worldwide, including those beneath Teotihuacan in Mexico and the underground cities in Cappadocia, Turkey, suggest that ancient tunnel systems were more than just simple water channels. Their alignment with significant structures and the use of advanced materials, such as mercury at Teotihuacan and the Qin Shi Huang tomb, indicate a sophisticated understanding of engineering and energy manipulation. As more tunnels and chambers are uncovered using non-invasive technologies, such as ground-penetrating radar, researchers gain further evidence of the complexities of these ancient networks.

The idea of pyramids functioning as stations for an advanced underground transport system powered by ley lines captures the imagination. It implies a world where ancient civilisations were not only skilled in architecture but also in harnessing energy and technology, well beyond our current understanding. It was a time when the Earth's energy grid linked the spiritual realm with the physical, instantly bridging distances.

Ancient Launch Pad or Military Base?

The Great Pyramid of Giza, often considered a tomb, may have served a much more complex purpose—a launch platform or transportation hub for an ancient civilisation with sophisticated technology, as some alternative researchers suggest.

Writers like Christopher Dunn, in The Giza Power Plant: Technologies of Ancient Egypt (1998), suggest that the pyramid's design and materials—such as its use of limestone, granite, and elaborate interior chambers—indicate it could have served as an energy generator. This energy might have been directed skyward, possibly for powering aerial vehicles or sending signals to distant stars.

Could the pyramid's electromagnetic fields have been directed into the atmosphere to power aerial vehicles, providing lift or propulsion for light craft? This assumes a highly advanced understanding of electrostatic propulsion. Some theorists propose that granite's high quartz content could produce a continuous piezoelectric charge when subjected to Earth's vibrations, which could theoretically be harnessed for energy or communication.[mcdlxiii]

Artefacts like the "Saqqara Bird", an ancient wooden artefact shaped like a glider, hint at an awareness of aerodynamics. Although officially described as a toy or ceremonial item, it has intrigued researchers as a possible test model for flight principles.[mcdlxiv]

Could the ancients and we learn from the animal Kingdom by observing how birds tap into the Earth's energies? Robin Baker, a biologist renowned for his work on animal behaviour and sensory biology, extensively explored the mysterious sense of magnetoreception in animals in his book *Animal Navigation: The Mysterious World of Instinct (1984)* he wrote, *"The magnetoreceptive sense, if fully understood, could unravel one of the most elegant solutions in the animal kingdom to the challenges of global navigation."*[mcdlxv] This statement highlights the complexity of the mechanisms that enable migratory birds to sense and respond to the Earth's geomagnetic field during their extensive journeys. His work shows how nature has evolved such refined systems for orientation, reflecting a broader, almost mystical connection between living beings and the planet. Robin Baker was well-known in his field for his contributions to understanding animal navigation and behaviour. His exploration into how animals use Earth's magnetic field for navigation captivated researchers and readers alike, adding valuable insight into the scientific community's understanding of animal instincts and sensory capabilities. Could the ancients have understood how to tap into Earth's energies for transportation?

Egyptian, Indian, and Mayan art features curious symbols resembling vehicles, such as the "vimanas" described in ancient Indian texts as flying chariots or aerial vehicles. Expanding on this speculative view, authors like Erich von Däniken, in *Chariots of the Gods?* (1968) argues that ancient structures, including pyramids and obelisks, may have formed a network of power stations or "launch pads" for advanced craft. Perhaps the tops of pyramids and obelisks served as docking stations, creating an interconnected, airborne transport system. Some theorists imagine a setup resembling modern cable cars or ski lifts, shuttling between obelisks and pyramids. In this vision, the Great Pyramid was a symbolic structure and a key node in an energy-driven grid, pointing to an ancient technological civilisation with ambitions reaching far beyond Earth's boundaries.

If they conducted or emitted energy, the obelisks lining temple entrances or the grand processional paths in Egypt could serve as markers or conduits for aerial landing. The tall, pointed shapes could act as antennas or visual guides for landing, with the electromagnetic properties of granite potentially grounding energy from the atmosphere. This would create a landing strip where obelisks could act as nodes within an energy-based guidance system for docking craft.[mcdlxvi]

If, as some researchers believe, ancient civilisations discovered a firmament or barrier encasing Earth, the pyramid may have even been used to channel blasts of energy to crack it, releasing the "waters above" or creating a passageway to explore beyond. Many ancient cultures have references to a "firmament" or celestial boundary. In the *Hebrew Bible*, the firmament is described as a dome separating the waters above from the Earth below.[mcdlxvii]

Similarly, Sumerian texts mention a "sky vault" and barriers between realms. The Egyptian concept of Nut, the sky goddess, portrays the sky as a physical structure held up by Shu (air), which could symbolise a form of enclosure. Mesopotamian and Norse myths also describe a cosmic dome or celestial boundary restricting humanity's access to the divine.[mcdlxviii]

Elon Musk's space endeavours, primarily through SpaceX, may symbolise a modern attempt to "crack the firmament". He has not suggested any literal belief in a physical firmament. His statements and the stated goals of SpaceX focus on extending human presence beyond Earth, with aspirations of making space travel and colonisation of Mars viable for the future. Thus, "cracking the firmament" in this context is more symbolic than literal, resonating with age-old myths of breaking through perceived cosmic limits rather than implying Musk's intention to dismantle any physical barrier in space.

Could the Great Pyramid of Giza have functioned as a defensive weapon, an "energy cannon" designed to deter or even shoot down intruders from the sky? Its unique structure, materials, and alignment may have been intentionally designed to harness and direct energy, potentially creating concentrated electromagnetic bursts. Advocates of this theory argue that an advanced civilisation might have built this "energy weapon" to protect against intrusions, whether from rival groups or perhaps even extraterrestrial forces. Although there is no evidence to support this concept, it presents a fascinating possibility.

Conclusions

As we conclude our exploration of the speculative global transportation systems linked to the pyramids, the idea that these structures were merely tombs continues to fade. Instead, a more complex picture of the pyramids as multifunctional centres emerges. The next chapter explores these possibilities further, examining whether the pyramids may have played a role in influencing climate patterns, controlling resources, and shaping the conditions necessary for life and agriculture to flourish. By harnessing the Earth's energy and natural forces, could these ancient builders have used the pyramids for yet another remarkable purpose: climate control and resource transformation?

Powered by Pyramids: A Book of Theories

Chapter 22 Climate Control and Resource Transformation

Influencing Climate and Farming

Could ancient civilisations have controlled weather and agriculture using the pyramids? The idea might sound incredible, but evidence suggests technology that surpasses what we currently consider possible. These ancient powers could have been as mighty as we imagine. This chapter examines the possibility that pyramids served as sophisticated tools for controlling climate and agriculture. Could weather patterns be altered by tapping into the Earth's electromagnetic field? These structures may have ensured optimal farming conditions and protected regions from extreme events, such as droughts or floods, if connected to a broader energy network. Additionally, the strategic placement of pyramids near tectonic fault lines has led to speculation that they could have stabilised seismic activity. By harnessing tectonic energy, the pyramids may have dissipated the forces of earthquakes, suggesting their function as practical tools for tectonic stabilisation and environmental protection. The pyramids may have influenced agricultural practices through their astronomical alignments. By tracking celestial events like the solstices and equinoxes, pyramids may have helped ancient civilisations determine the best times for planting, harvesting, and conducting rituals, integrating their spiritual and agricultural cycles. Lastly, the potential use of geothermal energy from pyramids to heat water for irrigation is explored, supporting the idea that pyramids could have enhanced crop productivity and extended the growing season. By blending environmental control with spiritual and agricultural practices, this chapter presents pyramids as practical and powerful tools for sustaining ancient civilisations.

1. **Climate Control**

Tectonic Stabilization

An environmental theory proposes that pyramids might have served as large-scale devices to maintain or restore balance in Earth's ecosystem, potentially influencing tectonic plates or the atmosphere. This concept can be linked to modern concerns about sustainability and planetary health, bridging ancient ideas with the future. Some pyramids are situated near tectonic plates or fault lines, suggesting they may have been used to harness and stabilise the Earth's tectonic energy. The pyramid's shape could have helped dissipate seismic forces, possibly preventing earthquakes or other natural disasters, making them more than mere monuments but practical tools for environmental management. There is no direct evidence from ancient texts, archaeological research, or modern science to support the claim that pyramids were constructed to harness or stabilise tectonic energy. However, the structural design of pyramids, notably their broad base and pyramidal shape, inherently provides stability and resistance to natural forces such as earthquakes. While pyramids have demonstrated durability and resilience over time, the idea that they were intentionally built to prevent earthquakes or control tectonic forces remains speculative.

In modern times, there is a greater understanding of tectonic activity. While modern buildings can be designed to withstand earthquakes, there is no evidence that ancient builders had the technology or knowledge to influence seismic energy by constructing pyramids. Nonetheless, the structural genius behind the pyramids ensures their resilience, allowing them to survive in areas prone to seismic activity, but this is a result of engineering, not tectonic stabilisation.

A related idea is that when the Earth's magnetic field weakens and fluctuates in times of potential pole shifts, these pyramids may have acted as stabilisers or energy conduits, harnessing and redistributing the planet's natural electromagnetic forces. By strategically positioning these structures at key global locations, ancient civilisations could have sought to maintain the Earth's magnetic equilibrium, preventing or mitigating the chaotic effects of such shifts on the environment and human life. Though speculative, this theory suggests that pyramids may have been sophisticated, earth-tied technologies designed to safeguard the planet from cosmic and terrestrial upheavals. It is essential to note that the Earth's magnetic field does not reverse suddenly, but rather over thousands of years. During this process, the magnetic field weakens, potentially leading to increased exposure to solar radiation.[mcdlxix]

Climate Manipulation

Some speculative theories suggest that pyramids could have been used to manipulate weather patterns by interacting with Earth's electromagnetic field.[mcdlxx] If pyramids were part of a broader energy network, they might have controlled local weather to ensure agricultural stability or protect regions from natural disasters, such as droughts or floods. What if pyramids, especially those aligned with

Earth's energy grids or ley lines, could have acted as amplifiers of natural forces to influence local weather? Could ancient civilisations have understood how to tap into the Earth's geomagnetic forces to manipulate wind patterns or induce rainfall? Perhaps the pyramids were not just built to control the local environment but were part of a grand, planet-wide terraforming project to stabilise and enhance the Earth's climate over millennia. Could the entire grid of pyramids and megalithic structures worldwide have been part of an ancient geoengineering experiment to transform the Earth's climate or atmosphere?

Ancient civilisations often believed their gods controlled the weather, and rulers like the pharaohs were regarded as intermediaries who could influence these divine forces. Temples and pyramids functioned as sites for rituals intended to invoke divine favour for rain and protection against natural disasters. If these structures were believed to enhance human or divine intentions, it is plausible that they were seen as instruments to influence climate conditions.

In modern times, cloud seeding is a weather modification technique used to enhance rainfall by dispersing substances that encourage cloud formation into the air.[mcdlxxi] This practice demonstrates that humans can influence weather patterns with technology. The idea that pyramids might have been used in a similar, albeit more mystical or energy-based, capacity aligns with the modern understanding that atmospheric manipulation is possible.

The pyramids may have influenced rainfall patterns by affecting the Earth's energy field and atmospheric conditions. By interacting with electromagnetic forces in the atmosphere, pyramids could draw moisture or alter wind patterns to bring rain to regions that needed water for agriculture. This idea aligns with the notion that ancient civilisations heavily dependent on agriculture would have been motivated to develop methods to ensure consistent rainfall and prevent droughts.

To support this theory, ancient civilisations like the Egyptians and Mesopotamians developed sophisticated water management systems, including canals and reservoirs, to control the water supply.[mcdlxxii] If these cultures also understood how to manipulate natural energy fields, they could have sought to extend this control to weather systems. While there's no direct evidence linking pyramids to weather control, the significant agricultural importance of these civilisations lends some plausibility to the theory.

The High-Frequency Active Auroral Research Program (HAARP) is a real-world example of a project designed to study and potentially manipulate the ionosphere (a layer of the Earth's atmosphere that plays a role in weather and communication).[mcdlxxiii] Some conspiracy theories suggest HAARP can influence weather patterns by interacting with the ionosphere. If pyramids interacted similarly with the Earth's energy field, they could have affected weather patterns in their region.

While the idea that pyramids could have been used for climate control is captivating, significant scientific and archaeological reasons challenge this theory. Modern studies show no evidence of ancient infrastructure or mechanisms capable of large-scale environmental manipulation, such as systems to regulate atmospheric conditions or manage natural resources. Climate change expert and geophysicist Michael Mann, in his book *The Madhouse Effect*, emphasises that "climate manipulation requires a complex understanding of atmospheric systems and technology far beyond what was available to ancient civilisations, and no evidence supports the notion that structures like pyramids played any role in such processes.[mcdlxxiv]

The movie Geostorm (2017) explores a future where humanity's control over nature becomes a double-edged sword. In this thrilling depiction, advanced technology enables the precise regulation of global weather patterns through a vast satellite network designed to mitigate natural disasters. But as power often does, it spirals out of control, leading to chaos with catastrophic weather events that threaten the planet. This cinematic exploration of climate manipulation resonates with speculative theories about ancient technologies and their potential influence on natural forces. It aligns with the idea that pyramids, too, might have served as tools for environmental control, hinting at the power civilisations could wield—or lose—when tampering with the forces of nature.

2. Agriculture Control

Determining Best Times for Farming and Rituals

The alignments with the stars could have been employed to observe solar events, such as solstices and equinoxes, to identify the optimal times for planting, harvesting, and performing religious rituals. In this context, the pyramids' power would have been to assist ancient civilisations in their agricultural schedules and spiritual activities. Discoveries at locations like Giza, Chichen Itza, and Teotihuacan also indicate that these alignments were deliberate and used to signal seasonal changes, helping ancient civilisations decide the best times for planting, harvesting, and conducting rituals.

Although Stonehenge is not a pyramid, it serves as a significant example of how ancient cultures used solar and lunar alignments to observe seasonal changes and plan agricultural activities. Modern archaeologists have verified that Stonehenge is aligned with the summer solstice, offering an annual point for planting and harvesting cycles. This example supports the broader idea that astronomical alignments in ancient structures—such as pyramids—were used for similar purposes, helping civilisations determine the optimal times for farming and other vital activities.[mcdlxxv]

In modern times, some organic and biodynamic farmers still use lunar phases and astronomical events to guide their planting and harvesting schedules, based on the belief that celestial cycles influence plant growth.[mcdlxxvi] This practice is rooted in ancient knowledge passed down through generations, demonstrating that astronomical alignments have long been used to influence agricultural decisions. While today's farmers often rely on weather predictions and scientific methods, the continued use of lunar planting calendars demonstrates the enduring relevance of ancient farming practices.[mcdlxxvii] The modern permaculture and sustainable farming movements also emphasise the importance of natural cycles in farming.[mcdlxxviii] These approaches often draw on ancient agricultural techniques, including those based on astronomy, to inform modern farming practices that work in harmony with nature.

Geothermal Irrigation to Boost Crop Yields

The underground water channels beneath the pyramids could have been an essential part of a sophisticated irrigation system, vital to sustaining the agricultural needs of ancient Egypt. The Nile River was the lifeblood of Egypt's agriculture, and the annual inundation provided fertile silt that enriched the farmlands.[mcdlxxix] However, managing this floodwater was crucial to maximise its benefits and ensure the year-round irrigation of crops. The Nile River was the lifeblood of ancient Egypt, its annual flooding transforming arid lands into fertile fields. The ancient Egyptians became masters of water management, constructing elaborate irrigation systems to harness floodwaters for crop cultivation. But what if these innovative minds went even further, using not just the water but the heat of the Earth itself to supercharge their agriculture?

One possibility is that geothermally heated water, sourced from beneath the Earth's surface, could have been used to irrigate crops in nearby fields, potentially speeding up growth or extending the growing season.[mcdlxxx] This would have been particularly beneficial in cooler climates or colder months, where warm water irrigation could prevent frost damage and promote faster germination. Pyramids, often built in regions with tectonic activity, may have been strategically positioned to tap into the Earth's geothermal energy.[mcdlxxxi] These structures could have been vital to agricultural productivity by channelling heated water through underground tunnels or canals. If true, this would support the theory that pyramids were more than just spiritual or ceremonial monuments—they were practical tools that ensured sustainability and survival by boosting food production.[medlxxxii]

Although the direct use of geothermal water for irrigation in ancient Egypt remains speculative, it should not be dismissed. Historical evidence shows that many ancient civilisations, particularly in regions of Mesoamerica like Mexico and Guatemala, were acutely aware of volcanic and geothermal activity.[medlxxxiii] While no direct proof exists that they used hot water for irrigation, their sophisticated agricultural practices, including terracing, canal systems, and even chinampas (floating gardens), demonstrate high environmental adaptation and resourcefulness. It's plausible that these cultures recognised the potential benefits of geothermal water to improve crop growth and experimented with it to increase their agricultural yields.[medlxxxiv]

Further supporting this idea is the practice of hot spring irrigation observed in later periods and other regions. For example, hot springs have been used in parts of Iceland and Japan for centuries to extend growing seasons and create microclimates suitable for crops in otherwise cold environments.[medlxxxv] If such knowledge existed in ancient Mesoamerica or Egypt, even in its earliest forms, it would provide a significant advantage, allowing these civilisations to cultivate more food year-round and sustain larger populations.

Thus, the notion that geothermally heated water might have been channelled through pyramidal structures or used in nearby fields is an exciting avenue for exploration. If proven, it would position these iconic monuments as symbols of ancient power and spirituality, as well as early innovations in sustainable farming, further solidifying the pyramids' role in the practical survival of ancient civilisations.

The idea that these underground water channels might have been connected to a broader irrigation network is plausible and intriguing. Such a system could have efficiently distributed water throughout the ancient city of Giza and its surrounding areas, ensuring a steady and controlled water supply for agriculture, even during dry periods or outside of the flood season[medlxxxvi].

In this context, the pyramids and underground channels may have served as hydraulic regulators, redistributing water to various agricultural zones through underground canals.[medlxxxvii] These canals could have supplied water to sustain crops, livestock, and the general population, creating a farming hub that sustained the city's growth.[medlxxxviii]

Evidence of sophisticated irrigation techniques, such as canals and water management systems, has been found in other parts of ancient Egypt. It is possible that the area around the pyramids was part of a similar network[mcdlxxxix]. This irrigation system could have ensured that even during periods of low Nile flooding, Giza remained fertile and productive, allowing the civilisation to thrive.

Vertical Farming

Many pyramids worldwide, particularly those with step-like designs, present a compelling case for early irrigation and vertical farming innovations. In Mesoamerica, stepped pyramids such as those at Teotihuacan or Chichen Itza feature large, flat terraces that may have been used for both religious purposes and agriculture. A study by archaeologists at the National Institute of Anthropology and History in Mexico suggested that the terraces on the Pyramid of the Sun at Teotihuacan were potentially used for agricultural practices, harnessing the pyramid's elevation and natural water flow for crop cultivation.[mcdxc] The stepped design naturally lends itself to irrigation, allowing water to flow downward from the top and nourish crops on each level. Ancient civilisations could have strategically channelled rainwater or river water to the uppermost terraces, letting gravity distribute it evenly across each tier. This would have created a vertical farming system where different crops were planted on each level to maximise sunlight exposure, water distribution, and efficient use of space. In regions where water was scarce, this method could have provided a sustainable way to grow food in elevated areas, turning these pyramidal structures into agricultural powerhouses. Similar research conducted by Indonesian archaeologists on the Borobudur Temple, which features a stepped-pyramid design, suggests that ancient cultures understood and used stepped terraces for both ceremonial and agricultural purposes.[mcdxci] The pyramids of Indonesia, China, and Sudan—though varying in form—also share this stepped construction, suggesting a similar multipurpose use, where the structure served ceremonial and practical needs, including food production and irrigation.

3. Mining Industry

Transformation beyond the Spiritual

Did the builders of the pyramids understand alchemy? Could they have transformed materials using the knowledge we have since lost? We will explore how they may have unlocked the power of transformation in both material and spiritual forms.[mcdxcii] In this chapter, we examine the possibility that pyramids played a pivotal role in ancient alchemy and the transformation of materials, particularly in the context of gold and gemstone formation. Drawing from alchemical traditions, where the goal was to transmute base materials into precious metals like gold, we examine theories suggesting that pyramids, functioning as energy amplifiers, could have been used to catalyse material transformations. One theory suggests that pyramids, with their alignment to Earth's energy grids and ability to interact with magnetic fields, may have influenced natural geological processes, thereby accelerating the formation of valuable materials such as gold.[mcdxciii] Gold was central to ancient Egypt's wealth and spiritual practices, and the pyramids may have played a more direct role in the extraction or formation of this precious metal. Additionally, the concept of pyramids as gemstone factories is explored, suggesting that these structures could have harnessed geothermal energy and simulated the extreme conditions—heat, pressure, and mineral-rich environments—needed to form gemstones. Just as modern laboratories can recreate these conditions, it is speculated that the pyramids might have served as ancient tools to mimic volcanic processes, providing the environment for the rapid crystallisation and creation of valuable stones.

Alchemical Transformations

In ancient alchemy, the ambition to transmute base materials into precious stones or metals, such as turning lead into gold, was a predominant pursuit.[mcdxciv] Some theorists propose that pyramids, seen as energy amplifiers, could have been integral to alchemical processes aimed at material transformation.[mcdxcv] Using pyramidal energy to enhance the creation of gemstones may correlate with ancient alchemical quests to elevate lesser materials into entities of greater value. Gold mining was a key industry in ancient Egypt, with prominent locations in the eastern desert and Nubia.[mcdxcvi] The pharaohs accumulated immense wealth in gold, primarily for religious and ceremonial purposes. Perhaps the pyramids' alignment with Earth's energy grid or their interaction with natural frequencies and magnetic fields somehow catalysed or expedited natural geological processes essential for gold formation.[mcdxcvii] There are, however, no inscriptions that directly support such a use.[mcdxcviii] Some alternative theorists take this further, suggesting that the pyramids may have been part of an extraterrestrial mining operation. According to these theories, aliens—interested in Earth's valuable resources, primarily gold—could have used advanced technology embedded within the pyramids to harness the planet's natural energy for mining purposes.

Gemstone Factory[mcdxcix]

One of the recurring themes in alternative history theories is that extraterrestrial beings may have visited Earth to exploit its rich natural resources. If aliens had the technology to harness geothermal energy, they could recreate or control the natural processes required for gemstone formation.

Some theories suggest that the pyramids might have harnessed Earth's geothermal energy. Gemstones like diamonds, rubies, and quartz form naturally deep within the Earth's crust under extreme conditions of heat and pressure. This process often takes millions of years, involving geothermal heat and tectonic activity to create the necessary environment for crystallisation. If pyramids could channel geothermal energy or volcanic forces, it's possible to hypothesise that they could replicate some conditions required for gemstone formation. Since pyramids were often built near tectonically active zones (e.g., the Giza Plateau near the Nile River Valley), they could theoretically access geothermal forces.

While no evidence has been found to suggest that pyramids were used to create gemstones, the presence of gemstones in Egyptian tombs and temples indicates that they held significance. The idea that ancient Egyptians may have used geothermal energy to manufacture or enhance these stones is speculative. Still, it aligns with the broader narrative of their spiritual and energetic beliefs.

Modern technologies can create diamonds in laboratories by replicating natural conditions. Given that modern technology can recreate gemstone formation by controlling heat and pressure, it raises the question: Could ancient structures, such as pyramids, have been designed to harness natural geothermal energy in a similar manner? The pyramids may have mimicked volcanic activity, providing heat, pressure, and mineral-rich conditions that generated a diverse range of gemstones.[md]

While there is no archaeological evidence of ancient technology replicating this process, modern synthetic gemstone production proves that it might be possible to create gemstones artificially with the right technology and environmental control.

4. Construction Industry

Acoustic Engineering

Could the pyramids' acoustics have been used to amplify energy or ritual sounds, creating an enhanced perception of power? This idea has fascinating parallels in the design of churches and mosques, where acoustics play a crucial role in the spiritual experience.[mdi] These ancient and modern sacred spaces are often designed to project and magnify sound in ways that evoke a sense of the divine, mystery, and awe, contributing to the feeling of power and holiness emanating from the structure.[mdii] Let's explore the comparison in more depth.

Modern acoustic engineering has advanced our understanding of how sound behaves in structures, and certain principles applied in today's buildings likely mirror knowledge that ancient builders might have intuitively grasped through observation and trial and error.

Acoustical engineering is the science of controlling sound within spaces, ensuring that buildings enhance sound transmission or reduce unwanted noise. This discipline focuses on how structures amplify, reflect, or absorb sound. [mdiii] Some fundamental principles include Resonance (the amplification of sound waves due to the structure's shape or materials), which is often a critical factor in designing concert halls, churches, and auditoriums in modern buildings.

Specific shapes, like domes or curved surfaces, naturally enhance sound resonance.[mdiv] This is why large, dome-like structures such as the Sydney Opera House or the Guggenheim Museum use curves to control how sound moves through the space.

Sound waves either reflect off surfaces or are absorbed by materials. Buildings, such as modern concert halls, use sound-absorbing materials in specific areas to enhance the acoustics for performances. Reflective surfaces, on the other hand, can channel sound to certain areas, such as the stage in a theatre. Modern acoustical engineers often design spaces with focal points where sound converges. This can be seen in the construction of parabolic reflectors in concert halls or whispering galleries, such as St. Paul's Cathedral in London, where sound is naturally amplified to distant points.[mdv] Different materials absorb or reflect sound waves in varying ways. For example, stone, glass, and metal reflect sound, while wood and foam absorb it. Modern acoustical engineers take this into account when designing buildings. In ancient times, stone structures like pyramids were likely to have had reflective properties that enhanced sound resonance.[mdvi]

Acoustic Levitation

A more imaginative question is whether sound has been used to levitate stones, a phenomenon known as acoustic or sonic levitation. Some ancient legends and stories suggest that sound or vibration may have been used in construction. Tibetan monks are often cited in these stories, where harmonic chanting or instruments were supposedly used to lift large boulders during the construction of temples. Similar legends exist in other ancient cultures, including Peru, where sound or vibration was used to move the massive stones of Sacsayhuamán. Although these accounts are anecdotal and not scientifically verified, they suggest that sound may have been viewed as a powerful tool in construction.[mdvii] However, no conclusive evidence has been found to support this. Similarly, Egyptian texts sometimes describe chants, spells, or music in sacred rituals, although they don't directly suggest these were used to levitate stones.[mdviii]

Several factors must be aligned for sound to levitate or move large stones. The stones would need to vibrate at specific resonant frequencies.[mdix] This could theoretically cause the rocks to become lighter or even hover for short periods. The sound waves must be amplified to extreme levels to generate enough force to counteract the stone's weight.[mdx] This would require a large-scale, coordinated effort, possibly involving multiple sound sources or devices that could concentrate and direct the energy. Some materials may respond more effectively to specific frequencies, potentially making it easier to manipulate them using sound. It's possible that ancient builders chose specific types of stone that resonated with particular frequencies, enhancing their ability to be moved using sound.

Today, scientists and engineers have demonstrated acoustic levitation in controlled environments, but only with lightweight objects. In 2017, physicists at the University of Bristol successfully demonstrated 'acoustic levitation,' where sound waves at specific frequencies can manipulate small objects. While current technology limits these experiments to microscopic scales, this opens the possibility that ancient cultures may have used sound in ways not yet fully understood. However, critics point out that the forces needed to lift multi-ton stones with sound waves are vastly greater than those achievable in laboratory settings. Scaling up this technology would require an enormous amount of energy, far beyond what ancient civilisations could have possessed without modern machinery. Therefore, while acoustic levitation is a proven phenomenon, it seems highly unlikely that it could be used to lift large stones, such as those in pyramid construction. The difference between what we believe is possible and the theoretical capability to lift multi-ton stones suggests that sound was employed in ancient times through unknown methods or technologies.

Stone Formation From Other Materials

Is it possible that the pyramids were built from other materials that then turned into stone? Numerous examples show how materials can transform into stone over time. These include organic materials like wood and bone through fossilisation, sediment that forms sedimentary rock, volcanic materials like lava and ash, natural mineral deposits, synthetic materials like cement, and minerals that crystallise over time. These processes usually take thousands to millions of years under specific environmental conditions, such as heat, pressure, and mineral-rich water.

One of the most well-known examples of a material turning into stone is petrified wood. This happens when organic material is buried beneath sediment, and minerals-rich groundwater seeps through the wood fibres. Over thousands to millions of years, the organic material decays and is replaced by minerals such as silica, which solidifies and preserves the original structure in stone.

Bone fossilisation follows a process similar to that of wood. Minerals in water replace the organic material in bones, slowly transforming them into stone while retaining the original bone's shape and structure. Entire organisms, including trees, shells, and plants, can undergo fossilisation under the right conditions, turning them into stone-like materials over long periods.[mdxi]

Over time, loose sediments like clay, silt, and sand can compact and cement together to form sedimentary rock.[mdxii] The process involves the accumulation of these particles in layers, compacted under pressure and often cemented together by dissolved minerals in water, such as calcium carbonate or silica. The precise cutting and alignment of the blocks suggest that this would have been unlikely.

Limestone is formed from the accumulation of calcium carbonate, often derived from the shells of marine organisms. Over time, this organic material solidifies and forms the rock known as limestone.

In caves or mineral-rich environments, calcium carbonate precipitates from water, forming stone over time. This process creates stalactites and stalagmites in caves and travertine stones from mineral springs.

Over time, minerals dissolved in water can crystallise and form stones. This natural process, which involves the formation of quartz or amethyst as water evaporates, sheds light on the Earth's geological history. Similarly, cracks or voids in rocks can fill with mineral-rich water. As the water evaporates or cools, the minerals crystallise to form solid stones, creating veins of ore or gemstones within the rock.

Organic material, such as ancient plant matter, can also compact over millions of years under high pressure to form coal or oil shale. Sediment may also bury these materials and compact them into stone-like substances.

The idea that the pyramids were built using materials that turned into stone over time is a captivating mystery. It suggests that ancient civilisations may have had a deeper understanding of natural material transformation than we realise today, sparking our curiosity about their knowledge and techniques.

Transformation from Liquid Substance into Stone

Could pyramid structures be constructed by creating a framework and applying a solidifying substance, such as cement?

One well-known theory along these lines is the geopolymer theory, proposed by French materials scientist Joseph Davidovits.[mdxiii] According to this theory, the massive stones used to build the pyramids were not quarried and transported in solid form but instead made on-site using a kind of ancient concrete or synthetic stone. He suggests that the Egyptians might have used a mixture of limestone, clay, lime, and water, combined with natural chemicals (such as natron or sodium carbonate) to create a slurry. This slurry could have been poured into wooden moulds that shaped the blocks, which then hardened like cement. Over time, the mixture would have solidified into a substance resembling natural limestone, and the blocks could have been assembled to form the pyramid.

Rather than creating individual blocks in this manner, a framework or scaffold could have been constructed, and a layer of stone mixture applied, similar to how concrete is sprayed in modern construction for certain architectural forms. Once the material dried or cured, it would harden into a cohesive structure resembling natural stone.

If true, this theory would enable faster and more accurate construction. Spraying or pouring a stone-like material into a pre-designed framework could greatly reduce the time and effort needed to transport and position large stone blocks. Creating stones on-site or spraying them in place might have allowed builders to achieve precise alignments and joints in the pyramids. The idea that the pyramids were built with synthetic stone could explain why they were made using locally sourced ingredients rather than transporting massive blocks from distant quarries.

Archaeological discoveries have revealed that ancient civilisations, such as those in Mesopotamia, used cement-like materials in their construction practices. In ancient Mesopotamia, builders used bitumen and other natural binding agents to solidify materials, creating durable structures that have withstood the test of time. These findings suggest that early civilisations possessed techniques to transform materials into more stable and durable forms. While this evidence does not directly prove that the Egyptians used geopolymer technology to construct the pyramids, it suggests that the understanding and application of binding agents were present in ancient times. The Egyptians could have adapted or expanded such knowledge, potentially supporting the theory that advanced methods, such as synthetic stone-making, were within their technological reach. [mdxiv]

We know the ancient Romans developed a form of concrete that, when exposed to seawater over time, solidified into a solid and durable material, even compared to modern concrete. The concrete, made from volcanic ash, lime, and seawater, created structures that have lasted millennia. Some researchers believe that if the Romans had developed a durable concrete material, the Egyptians could have developed a similar method to create pyramid stones. [mdxv]

Although the theory sounds plausible, there is little archaeological evidence to support the use of advanced spraying technology or large-scale moulds in ancient Egypt. Most traditional accounts and depictions show that the Egyptians used chisels, ramps, and manual labour to quarry and move stones.

Volcanic Origins: Use of Lava

When volcanic lava cools and solidifies, it forms igneous rocks such as basalt or granite. Over time, this hardened lava can erode and weather, but it remains a solid, stone-like substance. After a volcanic eruption, ash can settle and undergo processes that cement it into rock. Ancient civilisations, including the Egyptians, primarily obtained volcanic rocks like basalt and granite from quarries near the Earth's surface, where these rocks had already solidified. These rocks result from ancient volcanic activity that had long since cooled and become part of the Earth's crust. Volcanic stones such as granite were used in certain parts of the pyramids, including the King's Chamber in the Great Pyramid of Giza. Granite forms when magma cools and solidifies, creating a durable and solid material. Volcanic stone had to be sourced from distant quarries. Granite originated from Aswan, likely transported by boat along the Nile. Aswan is approximately 800 kilometres (500 miles) south of Giza, where the Great Pyramids are located. While this type of stone was quarried and transported, it is conceivable that other volcanic materials could have been used and hardened over time. However, there were no volcanoes in its proximity. Historic volcanoes can and have disappeared over time due to various natural processes. While it is uncommon for a volcano to vanish completely, many have been eroded, buried, or subsided to the point where they are no longer easily recognisable. There is, however, no geological evidence of a vanished volcano near the Giza Plateau or other pyramid sites. Could they have drilled deep into the Earth to access molten lava? The idea that ancient civilisations drilled deep into the Earth to access molten lava is far beyond the technological capabilities of any known ancient society, including the Egyptians. Magma typically resides tens to hundreds of kilometres beneath the Earth's surface, making it virtually inaccessible without modern drilling technology. There is no evidence that the Egyptians or any other ancient civilisation possessed the tools or knowledge to undertake such deep drilling or manipulate magma in any meaningful way.

5. Waste Management

Some propose that the pyramids served as ancient waste incinerators, with the underground tunnels functioning as sewage systems, suggesting that these monumental structures had both practical and ceremonial roles. According to this theory, the pyramids were massive waste-burning facilities featuring extensive interior chambers. Traditionally believed to align with celestial bodies, the shafts could have been used to vent smoke from fires that burned rubbish, turning waste disposal into a sacred act of purification. Meanwhile, the extensive tunnel systems beneath the pyramids might have been designed to manage sewage, directing waste to underground chambers or nearby water sources. Like modern urban infrastructure, where incinerators and sewage systems are concealed but vital, these tunnels could have channelled waste from the pyramid's surroundings or from workers maintaining these sacred sites. This theory suggests that the Egyptians, renowned for their architectural ingenuity, may have incorporated practical waste management solutions into their grand designs, thereby ensuring cleanliness and maintaining a hygienic environment. Although lacking direct evidence, this concept challenges conventional interpretations of the pyramids, proposing that they were multifunctional structures that balanced both the sacred and the practical.[mdxvi]

Conclusions

The exploration of pyramids as tools for climate control, resource transformation, and tectonic stabilisation challenges our conventional understanding of ancient technologies. While many of these theories remain speculative, they open doors to the possibility that ancient civilisations may have been more advanced than we previously thought, not just in spiritual or ceremonial contexts but in their practical approaches to survival and environmental management.

Whether through influencing weather patterns, managing agricultural cycles, or tapping into geothermal energy, these ancient monuments may have been more than just symbols of power and the afterlife. Instead, they may have been multifunctional tools designed to work harmoniously with the Earth's natural systems to sustain civilisation. The lack of direct evidence for these advanced uses of the pyramids doesn't negate the potential for these ideas to inspire new avenues of research. Just as modern science continues to discover ways to harness the Earth's energy for climate control and agriculture, it's possible that the ancient Egyptians were pioneers of this knowledge in their time. The durability of their monuments is a testament to their ingenuity, and the mysteries surrounding their potential uses remind us that there is still much to learn from these remarkable structures. As we shift from ancient theories of climate control and resource transformation to modern technology in the next chapter, it becomes clear that past wisdom may hold answers for today's challenges. Many of the cutting-edge innovations we see today—such as sustainable energy solutions, architectural design, and even advanced materials—are inspired by ancient structures like the pyramids. Modern engineers are increasingly looking to the past, studying the techniques and principles used by ancient civilisations to harness natural forces. From using specific materials that regulate temperature to strategically placing buildings for enhanced energy efficiency, these ancient practices are being revisited and adapted to tackle issues such as climate change and resource depletion. By unlocking these secrets, we are beginning to bridge the gap between the speculative wonders of the past and today's technological advances, opening new possibilities for a sustainable future.

Chapter 23 Modern Technology to Unlock Ancient Secrets

The only true wisdom is in knowing you know nothing." – Socrates.[mdxvii]

In the past, archaeologists relied heavily on a blend of intuition, historical texts, and local knowledge to determine where to dig. They often followed clues left by ancient writers or were guided by oral traditions passed down through generations. Early archaeologists were frequently forced to explore regions on foot or horseback, hoping to stumble upon evidence of ancient civilisations. Some of the most significant discoveries in history were made by accident, such as when construction workers or farmers unearthed artefacts while going about their daily tasks, prompting further investigation. Visible ruins also played a crucial role in their decisions—if remnants of old buildings, city walls, or temples could be seen above ground, it was often a strong indicator of a larger buried complex waiting to be uncovered. Additionally, geographic features such as rivers, fertile plains, or strategic hilltops were common targets, as they were likely locations where ancient people would have established settlements or built defensive structures. Early aerial photography, although primitive compared to today's technology, allowed archaeologists to spot crop marks and unusual land formations from above, suggesting the existence of man-made structures below the surface. Trial digs, or exploratory trenches, were another essential tool, helping to assess whether an area held the potential for more extensive excavation. Though less precise than modern techniques, these methods were instrumental in many groundbreaking discoveries, offering invaluable glimpses into the lives and cultures of ancient peoples. Contemporary scientific methods and technologies make an enormous difference in archaeology. They unveil new pyramids and provide new opportunities to further investigate the existing pyramids. Will emerging technologies revolutionise our understanding of the pyramids? This chapter will examine the modern technologies that may unlock ancient secrets and illuminate the pyramids' functionalities.

Powered by Pyramids: A Book of Theories

1. **Imaging and Mapping Technologies**

Drone and Satellite Imaging

The future will shape our past. A powerful tool in our technological arsenal is satellite imaging. High-resolution satellite imagery has already been used to identify previously unknown pyramids and large-scale construction projects hidden beneath centuries of desert sand. [mdxviii] The imagery helps archaeologists locate and study sites without being physically present. This is especially valuable for remote, politically unstable, or environmentally hazardous areas. Traditionally, it took years or even decades of exploration and digging to uncover ancient cities and settlements. Now, with drones and satellite imaging, vast landscapes can be surveyed in a matter of days. Drones offer real-time aerial views of archaeological sites, providing detailed maps and 3D reconstructions. This accelerates the discovery process, enabling archaeologists to assess the layout of ancient cities or locate hidden structures far more quickly than previously possible.

LiDAR (Light Detection and Ranging), which can penetrate dense vegetation, has uncovered entire ancient cities, such as the Mayan metropolis discovered in Guatemala, which was previously believed to be lost to time. Could technology uncover a network of ancient pyramids interconnected globally in ways we have yet to understand? These technologies might be used to detect energy grids or ley lines that could connect pyramids across the world. Could they verify the theory that pyramids were aligned with Earth's natural energy fields? By mapping energy hotspots and architectural alignments, these tools could provide the physical evidence needed to support long-standing theories.

High-resolution satellite imagery, combined with advanced spectral analysis, could reveal previously unnoticed features and offer insights into the pyramids' geographical and environmental contexts. By examining the surrounding landscape, researchers might uncover why specific sites were chosen and how they interact with natural forces.

LIDAR technology has uncovered the vast scale and complexity of the Mayan civilisation in Guatemala and Mexico, revealing hidden cities, roads, and agricultural terraces. This discovery reinforced the theory that the Mayan civilisation was far more interconnected and organised than previously thought, demonstrating advanced infrastructure that challenges the idea of a fragmented society.[mdxix]

Spectral Analysis

Spectral analysis involves studying the light spectrum emitted or absorbed by materials, allowing researchers to gain insights into their composition and potential properties. When applied to pyramid construction materials like limestone and quartz, this technique enables a deeper understanding of how these substances may have interacted with natural forces. For instance, quartz, which exhibits piezoelectric properties, generates an electric charge when subjected to mechanical stress. Ancient builders could have leveraged this property in ways we are only beginning to understand.

In practical terms, spectral analysis detects specific wavelengths of light that materials emit or absorb, revealing their chemical composition and structural characteristics. By analysing the spectral signatures of quartz, researchers can determine how this mineral might have been selected for its unique energy-related properties, such as its ability to store or transmit electrical charges. In pyramid structures, where immense pressure and mechanical stress would naturally occur due to the sheer weight of the stones, the piezoelectric effect could have been activated. This might have allowed the pyramids to function as energy amplifiers or conductors, transmitting electromagnetic energy or even harnessing vibrations from the Earth.

Furthermore, by studying the spectral properties of limestone, researchers can investigate its insulating or conductive characteristics and how it may have contributed to the overall energy dynamics of the pyramids. Spectral analysis could reveal whether the materials used in pyramid construction were deliberately chosen for their energy-related qualities, potentially supporting theories that these structures were more than just tombs but also energy devices.

Spectral analysis of materials has reinforced the idea that certain civilisations may have used quartz and limestone for their unique properties, potentially to manipulate energy within architectural structures, lending credence to theories of energy harnessing and manipulation. While spectral analysis has not yet provided conclusive proof of energy manipulation in pyramid construction, it offers a promising avenue for future research. As technology advances, it may enable us to uncover how ancient builders could have harnessed the properties of these materials to create structures that interacted with natural energy fields. This line of inquiry could significantly advance our understanding of ancient technological knowledge and its application in monumental architecture, such as the pyramids.

2. Subsurface Exploration Tools

Advanced Ground-Penetrating Radar (GPR), Seismic and Muon Tomography

In recent years, ground-penetrating radar (GPR), muon tomography, and seismic tomography have revolutionised our understanding of ancient structures, especially pyramids. These cutting-edge, non-invasive technologies have enabled researchers to peer inside these colossal monuments without disturbing them, revealing hidden chambers, structural anomalies, and new insights into how they were built and what they might have been used for.

Ground-penetrating radar (GPR) is crucial for detecting underground structures, providing a 3D image of what lies beneath the surface.[mdxx] It is suitable for finding hidden tunnels, chambers, or areas that deviate from known layouts. GPR can map the pyramid's foundation, offering insights into its interaction with the surrounding environment, such as possible connections to underground water systems or seismic activity. These findings could add depth to theories suggesting that pyramids were aligned with Earth's natural forces. Limited by depth—GPR can't penetrate as deep as neutrino detectors or muon tomography, making it less effective for examining the core of large pyramids.

3D scanning is another crucial tool. It allows archaeologists to create precise digital models of ancient structures, mapping the pyramids' exterior and interior with incredible detail. These scans are essential for identifying deviations from known blueprints, detecting hidden features, and even restoring eroded or damaged sections of the pyramids. The 3D digital reconstructions provide an invaluable resource for further study and preservation.[mdxxi]

Researchers have unlocked lots of new information by combining these technologies. The discovery of a large void in the Great Pyramid, made possible by muon tomography and 3D scanning, challenges long-standing beliefs about the pyramid's internal layout. It suggests there may still be more hidden spaces waiting to be uncovered, potentially offering clues to the pyramid's true purpose.

Seismic tomography, which measures the movement of seismic waves through the Earth, provides detailed 3D images of subsurface structures. This method helps archaeologists understand how pyramids might interact with natural geological formations. It can detect hidden chambers and tunnels, but may also reveal connections between the pyramid and the Earth's energy, such as underground water flow or tectonic movements. The resolution isn't as fine as that of GPR or muon tomography for small-scale structures, and geological factors affect the propagation of seismic waves.

One of the most groundbreaking discoveries occurred in 2017, when the ScanPyramids project employed muon tomography to reveal a previously unknown void within the Great Pyramid of Giza. This hidden space above the Grand Gallery has sparked renewed debates about the pyramid's purpose and design. Was it simply an architectural feature, or could it be part of a more complex system related to energy storage or even ceremonial functions?

Muon tomography detects cosmic particles called muons that naturally penetrate solid objects. By analysing how these particles pass through the pyramid, researchers can map out its internal structure, revealing gaps or hidden chambers that were previously inaccessible. It is slower than other methods, requires specialised equipment, and is expensive to implement.

Muon tomography has added new depth to theories surrounding ancient construction methods, suggesting that the pyramids' alignment and internal structure may be based on a complex understanding of materials and spatial design.

As we continue to refine these non-invasive methods, we edge closer to unravelling the mysteries of the pyramids. From detecting hidden chambers to understanding how these structures interact with their environment, these technologies are reshaping our knowledge of ancient engineering and opening up new possibilities for what we might discover next.

Ultrasonic Testing, detecting cracks or voids

Ultrasonic testing uses high-frequency sound waves to detect voids, cracks, or weaknesses in materials such as stone.[mdxxii] It has been used to assess the condition of pyramid stones, identify weak points, and locate hidden chambers or structural anomalies. This highly accurate and non-invasive method makes it ideal for detecting internal flaws or hidden structures without disturbing the pyramids.

Ultrasonic testing has proven invaluable in pyramid research and broader archaeological studies, particularly for non-invasive investigations of ancient structures. In pyramid studies, ultrasonic testing has been used to assess the structural integrity of stone blocks. By sending high-frequency sound waves through the stone and analysing the return signals, researchers can detect cracks, voids, and weaknesses within the stone blocks that make up the pyramid. This is especially valuable for conservation efforts, as it enables experts to determine which areas require reinforcement or restoration without physically damaging the structures.

Ultrasonic testing has been employed to locate voids or potential hidden chambers within the pyramids. While other methods, such as infrared thermography and muon tomography, are often used for large-scale explorations, ultrasonic testing provides a more localised analysis of specific areas, helping to identify internal anomalies or structural weaknesses.

3. Energy and Environmental Interaction Technologies

Infrared Thermography, detecting temperature differences

Thermography uses infrared cameras to detect temperature differences on the surface of structures. This method helps identify areas of interest for further exploration without damaging the structure. It provides a non-invasive method for detecting hidden features based on heat variations, making it an effective tool for identifying voids or structural differences.

In 2015, thermal scanning of the Great Pyramid of Giza revealed several temperature anomalies, suggesting the presence of cavities or hidden chambers.[mdxxiii]

Infrared thermography has also been employed to detect buried Roman structures beneath modern cities. For instance, in Pompeii, it was used to reveal subsurface structures and hidden features beneath the volcanic ash. The heat variations detected through this method helped archaeologists map out areas of interest for excavation.[mdxxiv]

In Mesoamerica, infrared thermography has been combined with other technologies, such as LiDAR, to identify ancient cities and temples hidden beneath dense jungle canopies. Thermography helped detect areas of interest where buried structures caused subtle changes in surface temperature.[mdxxv]

Quantum Sensors

Quantum sensors, based on the principles of quantum mechanics, offer cutting-edge precision in detecting subtle changes in energy and matter.[mdxxvi] These sensors can measure fluctuations in electromagnetic fields, gravitational forces, and subatomic particles, making them an invaluable tool for studying ancient structures, such as the pyramids. By deploying quantum sensors in and around these monuments, researchers could detect hidden energy flows or anomalies, shedding new light on how pyramids were constructed and their functions.[mdxxvii]

One of the most intriguing possibilities is that quantum sensors could reveal minute fluctuations, suggesting the pyramids were designed to interact with the Earth's magnetic field or other natural energy patterns. These measurements could support or challenge theories that the pyramids functioned as energy concentrators or distributors. For example, detecting small but consistent changes in electromagnetic fields around the pyramids could indicate deliberate alignment with natural energy sources, such as underground water systems or geological formations.[mdxxviii]

Quantum sensors are also highly effective at measuring gravitational anomalies, which could be present due to the precise mass and arrangement of the pyramid's massive stones.[mdxxix] If the pyramids were designed to influence or harness gravitational or geophysical forces, quantum sensors could help map these interactions and provide fresh insights into the engineering knowledge of ancient builders.

These sensors can also detect subatomic particles, such as those used in muon tomography, which has already successfully identified hidden voids within the Great Pyramid of Giza. Combining quantum sensors with muon detection could further enhance our understanding of the pyramid's internal layout, revealing hidden chambers, tunnels, or even energy conduits that are currently unknown.

The potential of quantum sensors extends to detecting subtle energy shifts within the pyramid's structure, particularly in relation to the materials used, such as quartz and granite, which possess piezoelectric properties. These materials may have been chosen for their ability to interact with natural energy fields, and quantum sensors could confirm whether these choices were part of an ancient strategy to harness or manipulate energy.

In essence, quantum sensors offer a new frontier in pyramid research. These sensors could provide definitive evidence regarding the pyramids' role in ancient energy systems by detecting energy flows, electromagnetic field fluctuations, and gravitational anomalies. They apply modern scientific tools to longstanding theories about the pyramids' purpose, allowing researchers to explore the possibility that these structures were not just tombs or monuments, but part of a sophisticated energy network. As this technology advances, quantum sensors could help bridge the gap between ancient knowledge and modern science, offering unprecedented insights into the mysteries of the pyramids. Remember that while excellent for detecting energy-related phenomena, quantum sensors may not provide detailed visualisations or direct mapping of internal structures.

Neutrino Detectors

Neutrinos are tiny subatomic particles that travel through matter, like rocks and buildings, without being affected.[mdxxx] They pass through everything—planets, stars, and even the pyramids—without leaving much of a trace. However, with special neutrino detectors, scientists can capture the rare moments when neutrinos interact with matter. This technology provides a non-invasive method for examining the pyramids without physical contact or damage.

Researchers could gain a detailed view of the internal structure by placing neutrino detectors around the pyramids. [mdxxxi] Since neutrinos can pass through solid rock, scientists can measure how they move through the pyramid. If hidden rooms, passages, or gaps are inside, the neutrinos' behaviour will change slightly as they pass through these areas. This allows scientists to create a 3D map of what's inside, revealing previously unseen parts of the pyramid.

This method is non-invasive, meaning it doesn't disturb the pyramid. Unlike other tools that might involve drilling or scanning, neutrino detectors allow us to study the pyramids without risking damage to the ancient structures. The data collected from neutrinos could reveal unknown chambers or structural details that help explain how the pyramids were built and their purpose.

In addition to mapping the pyramid's layout, neutrino detectors could also help explore whether the pyramids were built to interact with natural energy sources. Specific designs or materials inside the pyramid might influence how neutrinos move through them, offering clues that they may have been more than just tombs—perhaps they were designed to harness energy in ways we don't yet fully understand.

Neutrino detection could help solve some of the mysteries surrounding the pyramids. Even the most well-known pyramids, such as the Great Pyramid of Giza, may still hold secrets deep within. This technology allows us to explore those mysteries without harming these historic structures. The technology is complex; detecting neutrinos is a slow process that requires sophisticated and expensive equipment. It's also not widely used in archaeology due to its niche nature. As neutrino science continues to advance, we may soon uncover new insights into these ancient wonders that have been hidden for thousands of years.

4. **Material Analysis and Construction Techniques**

Radiocarbon Dating (with Improved Accuracy)
An advanced method of radiocarbon dating organic materials (like wood, plants, or bones) found in or around pyramids. Radiocarbon dating has been used to determine the age of organic materials found within pyramids, such as wooden beams or organic remains used in construction. Improved methods have offered greater precision and

helped clarify the construction timelines of various pyramids. This tool is constantly improving in accuracy and can now date materials more precisely than before, offering better insights into the timeline of pyramid construction.

Radiocarbon dating of wooden beams used in the construction of the Great Pyramid of Giza has provided dates around 2500 BCE, aligning with the reign of Pharaoh Khufu. However, some scholars argue that wood may have been reused from older structures, potentially placing the actual date of construction even earlier.[mdxxxii]

While wood and plant materials are commonly dated, advanced methods are employed to date bones and human remains found in or around burial chambers within the pyramids. Radiocarbon dating of human remains has helped confirm burial timelines and provided a more comprehensive understanding of who may have been buried within these structures. This supports the theory that pyramids were used for extended periods, sometimes long after construction.

Radiocarbon dating can help detect later additions or modifications to the pyramids. If organic materials are found in areas that are believed to be later renovations or additions to the original pyramid, radiocarbon dating could reveal different construction phases or alterations, providing a more complex timeline than previously thought.

Chemical Analysis

Chemical analysis also contributes significantly to unlocking the long-standing mysteries surrounding the construction of pyramids and other ancient structures. While effective for organic materials, traditional carbon dating methods are unsuitable for stone, as they require organic carbon to be effective. However, modern chemical analysis tools have opened up new avenues for studying stone in ways previously impossible. These techniques include *X-ray fluorescence* (XRF), *mass spectrometry*, and *isotope analysis*, all of which can detect trace elements and geochemical signatures within the stone.

XRF is excellent for identifying trace elements and determining quarry sources, which is foundational for understanding the origin of the stones. Mass Spectrometry and Isotope Analysis help with material origins and offer insights into ancient trade routes, highlighting social and economic dimensions. The isotope technique allows archaeologists to study the chemical signatures in bones and teeth to learn about ancient diets, migration, and even the environment in which people lived. Isotopic analysis can reveal the origins of individuals and the distances they travelled during their lifetimes.

Chemical changes in weathered stone layers provide insights into the structures' exposure history and longevity. The composition of materials used to bind the stones is also analysed. Certain compounds, such as those found in ancient mortars or binding agents, can help identify the types of adhesives and construction materials employed to join the stones. In some cases, researchers have uncovered surprising innovations, such as the possible use of early forms of concrete or geopolymer technology by ancient Egyptians to cast large blocks of stone instead of simply cutting and shaping natural materials.

More advanced methods, like luminescence dating or cosmogenic nuclide dating, help establish the age of construction or the last manipulation.

By identifying the precise chemical composition of stones, researchers can trace the materials back to their original quarries, offering clues about the logistics of construction, transportation methods, and the scale of ancient quarrying operations. For instance, by analysing the mineral content of limestone or granite blocks, scientists can determine whether they were sourced locally or transported from distant regions, shedding light on the resources and labour involved in pyramid construction. This analysis can also reveal how ancient builders selected specific stones for their structural properties or symbolic meanings, offering a deeper understanding of their architectural and cultural priorities.

Chemical analysis also helps reconstruct the techniques used by ancient civilisations to manipulate stone. For example, microscopic analysis of tool marks and chemical studies of stone surfaces can reveal how ancient masons shaped and polished the stones.

5. AI and Machine Learning in Archaeology

Modern advancements in artificial intelligence (AI) and machine learning are also making significant contributions to the field of archaeology. Artificial intelligence (AI) and machine learning algorithms can analyse vast datasets, such as satellite imagery, architectural blueprints, and historical texts. [mdxxxiii] For example, they have been used to decipher ancient languages and predict the location of previously unknown archaeological sites.

By applying these techniques to pyramid research, AI could help identify previously unseen patterns in pyramid construction, alignments, or even energetic functions. If AI could model ancient construction techniques, it might shed light on whether ancient civilisations had access to technologies or methods that surpass today's capabilities.

AI algorithms are increasingly used to process vast amounts of LiDAR, aerial photography, and satellite imagery data. This approach allows archaeologists to map subtle changes in terrain or detect buried structures that would have taken years to identify manually. For instance, AI was used in conjunction with satellite data to reveal hidden pyramid structures in dense vegetation, such as those found in Mesoamerica.

Could AI's ability to process complex geometrical data help us unlock hidden design principles within the pyramids, which govern the structure and its interaction with Earth's energies? AI can identify patterns and correlations suggesting connections between pyramids and ancient structures. For instance, AI could analyse data from various sources to identify correlations between pyramid locations and geomagnetic anomalies. Additionally, machine learning algorithms can simulate how the pyramids interact with natural forces, [mdxxxiv] testing different hypotheses about their purpose, such as energy conduction or astronomical observatories. [mdxxxv]

As AI continues to improve, we can expect it to play a more prominent role in guiding excavations, predicting the locations of new sites based on environmental and historical data, and even assisting archaeologists in decoding ancient texts and languages. AI-powered simulations could also recreate ancient environments, helping researchers better understand how ancient societies interacted with their landscapes.

AI could shift how societies perceive their past and, in extreme cases, contribute to an identity crisis. [mdxxxvi] This applies to the history of the pyramids and the world. AI can analyse vast amounts of data, including archaeological findings, historical documents, and cultural artefacts, at a scale that human historians may not be able to handle. This may lead to the uncovering of many new perspectives or challenge long-held historical narratives. If AI reveals previously overlooked or suppressed facts about history, such as the roles of marginalised groups, hidden political agendas, or alternative interpretations of key events, it could lead to societal re-evaluations of collective identity. [mdxxxvii] For example, if AI reveals inconsistencies in widely accepted historical narratives or provides evidence for alternative interpretations, such as suppressed technologies or historical events, it could prompt individuals or nations to reevaluate their origins. If people feel disconnected from the histories they previously identified with, this could lead to a cultural identity crisis. [mdxxxviii]

Historians' biases, perspectives, and values have influenced how history is recorded and taught. AI-based history may prioritise data-driven analysis over subjective storytelling, which could lead to more factual but emotionally disconnected versions of history. This could create a sense of alienation, as individuals might struggle to relate to this new interpretation of their past, potentially leading to a detachment from cultural or national identity.[mdxxxix] AI could unearth uncomfortable truths that contradict national myths or cultural narratives that bind societies. It could make it harder for people to maintain a cohesive sense of belonging or pride in their cultural heritage.[mdxl] Nations built on idealised historical accounts might face an identity crisis if their historical foundations are revealed to be more complex, multifaceted, or even false.[mdxli]

AI also poses the risk of deepfake technology, where historical images, videos, or audio recordings can be manipulated to fabricate events or distort history.[mdxlii] The blurring line between factual and fabricated historical data could lead to confusion about what is true. In a world where the authenticity of historical records is constantly questioned, people might experience an identity crisis rooted in uncertainty as they become unsure of which version of history to trust.[mdxliii] AI has the potential to provide globalised perspectives on history, pulling from a vast array of cultural and geographic data sources. While this could be beneficial in creating a more holistic view of world history, it may also challenge nationalist or regional identities significantly if it diminishes the significance of local histories in favour of a broader global narrative.[mdxliv] This might cause people to feel that their cultural identity is being diluted or rendered insignificant.

6. Application and Future Research

More research is necessary to determine whether the pyramids were more than just architectural marvels; they could have been part of a global energy network or sophisticated energy systems.

The Global Energy Network Theory suggests that pyramids were part of an interconnected global energy network. Researchers propose that ancient structures, such as pyramids, obelisks, and stone circles, were strategically placed on ley lines or geomagnetic hotspots to harness and amplify the Earth's natural energy fields. For example, some theorists believe that the pyramids' alignment with specific astronomical events and geomagnetic anomalies was deliberate, aiming to synchronise with natural energy cycles.

Future research could involve geomagnetic mapping and global positioning systems to test this theory.[mdxlv] By analysing energy fields around ancient structures and comparing them with known ley lines or geomagnetic anomalies, researchers might uncover evidence that the pyramids were strategically positioned to tap into global energy flows. mdxlvi

Another theory posits that the pyramids functioned as energy amplifiers, converting natural energies into usable power. Proponents of this idea argue that the materials used in pyramid construction, such as limestone and quartz, may have acted as energy conductors or resonators. For instance, quartz is known for its piezoelectric properties, which could theoretically convert mechanical stress into electrical energy.

Future research using quantum sensors or neutrino detectors may demonstrate, beyond current scientific understanding, that the materials used in the pyramids, such as limestone and quartz, may have played a role in this process, acting as conductors or energy resonators. mdxlvii

Potential Costs of Advanced Technologies

The costs of implementing advanced technologies at archaeological sites can be substantial, reflecting the need for specialised equipment, expertise, and logistical support. For instance, a LIDAR survey using drone-mounted sensors can range from $5,000 to $50,000, depending on the survey area and the equipment's resolution. mdxlviii Muon tomography is even more expensive, often requiring millions of dollars due to the need for custom-built detectors and lengthy data collection periods. mdxlix Similarly, while promising for uncovering hidden structures, quantum sensors and neutrino detectors are costly, with quantum sensor projects costing upwards of $100,000 and neutrino detection involving unique, high-cost instrumentation. mdl Beyond equipment costs, these technologies require skilled operators, data analysis experts, and sometimes substantial power and transportation resources, especially for remote sites. mdli Funding typically comes from grants, university partnerships, or sponsorships from government and private sources, making the financial aspect a critical factor in determining when and where these tools are deployed. mdlii Understanding these costs helps frame the needed resource investment and highlights the collaborative, multi-disciplinary efforts required for high-tech archaeological investigations.

Conclusions

How might future technologies help solve mysteries that current methods cannot? As we develop new technologies to unlock the mysteries of the pyramids, we may uncover evidence challenging long-held assumptions about ancient civilisations.

From advanced energy transmission theories to potential applications in modern science, the pyramids may offer a bridge between the past and the future. We will continue to explore these structures with an open mind and cutting-edge tools. We may be on the verge of discovering revolutionary technologies that could change our understanding of energy, construction, and human potential. The future of pyramid research promises to reshape our knowledge of energy, architecture, and our place in the universe, potentially revealing profound connections between ancient wisdom and modern science. The journey to unravel the mysteries of the pyramids is just beginning.

Bridging ancient practices with modern science, Chapter 24 will explore how we can harness the wisdom of Earth's energy in our daily lives, integrating ancient knowledge into contemporary practices.

Chapter 24 Tapping into Earth's Energy in Daily Life

Understanding Earth's Energies

In today's world, where technology dominates and the natural world is often pushed aside, perhaps we can learn something profound from the ancients. By reconnecting with the Earth's energy—whether through scientific exploration or spiritual practice—we might rediscover the power our ancestors once knew.[mdliii] We might unlock new ways of thinking about energy, not just as something to be generated by machines but as something that flows naturally through the planet, waiting to be tapped into.

The Earth's energy is not just a theory but a reality. From the flickering of the northern lights to the molten rivers of lava beneath the ground, this energy is all around us, shaping our world in ways we are only beginning to understand.[mdliv] The Earth beneath our feet is not simply a mass of stone and soil but a living, breathing energy system that ancient civilisations may have been intimately connected to.[mdlv] A captivating idea in spiritual thought is the belief that the Earth possesses consciousness. Ancient peoples may not have only harnessed natural energies for practical purposes but also believed that these energies reflected the planet's living spirit. This concept aligns with modern *Gaia theory*, which suggests that the Earth functions as a self-regulating, living organism. [mdlvi]

This view brings a profound dimension to the construction of pyramids and other sacred sites. Beyond their spiritual or religious significance, these monuments may have been intentional acts of communication with the Earth. By aligning structures with ley lines, energy vortexes, and celestial bodies, ancient civilisations could have participated in a grand, universal relationship that transcends modern scientific understanding—one where human life and the planet's natural energy flow were harmonised. Earth's energy encompasses a wide range of forces and phenomena, from the tangible heat and movement beneath the surface to the mystical life force believed to flow through the planet. Ancient civilisations may have had an advanced understanding of how these energies shaped their environment and spirituality. From geothermal energy and electromagnetic fields to ley lines and mystical energy centres, the concept of Earth's energy is tied to both scientific and speculative theories, offering a multifaceted view of how humans can interact with the natural world.

The animal kingdom is filled with examples of creatures that have harnessed Earth's energies to survive, navigate, and thrive. From migratory birds that rely on the Earth's magnetic field for precise navigation, using cryptochrome proteins in their eyes to "see" geomagnetic cues, to sharks that detect electric signals through specialised organs, these adaptations showcase an innate connection to the planet's natural forces. Elephants communicate through low-frequency infrasound that travels through the ground, and bees use polarised light and electromagnetic sensitivity to relay information. These abilities reflect a profound, almost mystical attunement to the Earth's energies, an ancient instinct deeply embedded within the natural world. This leads us to question why modern humans have become disconnected from these inherent senses. In our pursuit of technology and progress, have we lost the ability to sense the subtle vibrations and energies that once guided our ancestors? What knowledge has been overshadowed by the convenience of modern tools, and what might we rediscover if we sought to reconnect with these primal ties to the Earth?

Modern Spiritual Pilgrimages

In New Age thought, certain places on Earth are believed to be energy vortexes—locations where the Earth's energy spirals upward or downward, creating areas of spiritual significance. Examples include Sedona, Arizona, and Mount Shasta in California. These places are often associated with peace, enlightenment, or healing. It's theorised that ancient civilisations, with their intuitive understanding of the planet, built pyramids and other sacred structures at these vortex points to channel Earth's energy for spiritual awakening or mystical practices.[mdlvii]

In some traditions, the Earth is thought to have energy centres similar to the chakras in the human body. Specific sacred sites, such as Mount Shasta and the Great Pyramid of Giza, are associated with these energy points. Proponents believe that aligning oneself with these principles can promote spiritual healing, growth, and a deeper connection to the universe.

People are drawn to the pyramids as spiritual pilgrimage sites. Many people feel a profound sense of energy when standing within or near significant structures, as if the pyramids are alive with force, connecting them to the universe.[mdlviii] The design and scale of pyramids are awe-inspiring, and standing in front of or inside one can trigger a psychological response. Some say that the environment—combined with the expectation that pyramids are linked to mystical energy—can create a heightened sense of awareness, making people more sensitive to their surroundings and more likely to attribute normal physical sensations (like a breeze or temperature shift) to the "energy" of the pyramids.

Many people visit pyramids in groups to seek spiritual enlightenment or a deeper understanding of meaning. The placebo effect can be magnified in settings where group dynamics influence individual perceptions. If others in the group express a special connection or energy, individuals may subconsciously align their experiences to match the group's expectations. The idea that the pyramids can heal or connect people to the universe may evoke a genuine sense of physical and emotional well-being in those who believe in the structures' power. This mind-body connection is a well-documented aspect of the placebo effect, where the brain's belief in healing or connection can lead to physiological changes in how people perceive their feelings. Whether the feeling is due to an actual energy force or simply the power of belief, the pyramids remain potent symbols that evoke profound experiences for many people.

How to Become the Unstoppable Hulk

Much like Bruce Banner's accidental transformation in *The Hulk*, initially featured in Marvel Comics and later adapted into a movie, The Incredible Hulk (2008), ancient civilisations might have tapped into Earth's energy through exposure to gamma rays. While gamma rays in *The Hulk* symbolise untapped energy with transformative power, the pyramids may have been ancient mechanisms that channelled Earth's energetic pulses in ways we are only beginning to comprehend.

While the Hulk is a fictional character, gamma radiation is a real phenomenon. Gamma rays are a form of electromagnetic radiation with the shortest wavelength and the highest energy in the electromagnetic spectrum. Today, gamma rays are used in radiation therapy to treat cancer by targeting and killing cancerous cells.

In the same way that gamma radiation radically altered Bruce Banner's physiology, turning him green and transforming him into a muscular giant, giving him incredible strength and resilience, the energy harnessed by ancient pyramid builders could have profoundly affected their surroundings and possibly their own evolution. The mysterious alignment of pyramids with Earth's geomagnetic fields and their potential to conduct electromagnetic energy hints at an advanced understanding of energy manipulation. Just as gamma radiation in *The Hulk* represents the immense yet dangerous power of untapped energy, these ancient structures might symbolise a deeper connection to the Earth's hidden forces—forces that, if controlled or manipulated correctly, could transform civilisations and carry unforeseen consequences.

On Earth, gamma rays are generated through natural and human-made processes. One significant source is Terrestrial Gamma-ray Flashes (TGFs), which occur during thunderstorms when high-energy electrons are accelerated in the electric fields of lightning, producing brief bursts of gamma rays. Gamma rays also originate from the radioactive decay of naturally occurring isotopes, such as uranium, thorium, and radon, in the Earth's crust. These materials release gamma radiation as they decay into more stable elements. Additionally, gamma rays are produced during specific nuclear reactions in human-made sources, such as nuclear reactors and in medical applications like cancer treatment, where radioactive materials emit gamma rays to target and destroy harmful cells. Although gamma rays from Earth are not as intense as those from cosmic sources, they play a crucial role in both natural phenomena and technological applications.

Scientists have pointed out that no known biological mechanism could cause a transformation like this, even if one could survive massive radiation exposure.[mdlix] Michael E. Mann's article, *The Science of Superheroes: Why the Hulk is Not Possible*, published in the *Journal of Popular Science Fiction Studies*, critically examines the scientific inconsistencies behind the Hulk's transformation from a biological standpoint. In the article, he explains how gamma radiation, which in reality causes cellular damage and mutations, could not lead to superhuman abilities or extreme muscle growth, as depicted in the comic book. He explores the physical limits of human biology, emphasising that no known biological mechanism could allow a person to survive such massive radiation exposure, let alone harness it for strength and rapid growth. The article bridges the gap between popular culture and science by debunking common superhero myths while educating readers on the actual effects of radiation and the limits of human potential. His work is an engaging critique of science fiction and an accessible resource for understanding the science behind the superhero genre. While the idea of ancient Egyptians transforming into the Hulk to lift the massive stones used in building the pyramids is a fun concept, it does not appear to be scientifically feasible.

Scientists have also debunked the idea of gaining superhuman strength from eating spinach, popularised by Popeye, a cartoon character who first appeared in 1929. The myth stems from a miscalculation made in the 19th century regarding the iron content of spinach, where a decimal point was misplaced, leading people to believe that spinach contains ten times more iron than it does.

Bruce Banner's intense emotional state—particularly anger or stress—triggered the powerful physical transformation that turned him into the Hulk. Perhaps we should see this as a symbolic manifestation, with the transformation not resulting from the gamma rays but from the emotional state. His emotions, particularly anger, manifest into a tangible, unstoppable force like a volcanic explosion. In this sense, the Hulk represents the outward manifestation of his inner emotional state, transforming into an exaggerated form of emotional expression. Matter expands when heated, which is widely observed and considered a general law of physics.

Safer Ways to Tap into Earth's Energies

Meditation in Natural Environments

Spending time in nature, whether in forests, near rivers, or the sea, has been proven to reduce anxiety, increase mindfulness, and improve mental clarity. The natural energy in these environments is believed to balance the body's bioelectric field and promote a deeper state of relaxation.[mdlx] To engage with this energy, find a quiet spot outdoors where you feel comfortable. Close your eyes, focus on your breath, and visualise energy rising from the Earth, flowing through your body, infusing you with balance and vitality. This practice strengthens your connection to the planet's natural energy.

Some individuals practice meditation techniques to tap into the Earth's geomagnetic field. By meditating outdoors, particularly at sunrise or sunset, people seek to align their bodies and minds with the planet's electromagnetic energy. This practice aims to enhance mental clarity, intuition, and spiritual awareness by synchronising with the Earth's natural cycles.

Recent scientific research has provided robust evidence supporting the positive effects of time in nature on mental and physical health. A landmark study by Berman et al. (2008) found that interacting with natural environments significantly improves cognitive function and reduces mental fatigue. Participants in the study who spent time in nature showed improved attention and working memory compared to those who remained in an urban setting.[mdlxi]

This aligns with the practice of forest bathing, which originated in Japan and encourages immersion in nature to restore mental clarity and reduce stress. Forest bathing involves immersing oneself in a forest environment, taking deep breaths, and consciously engaging with the surroundings.[mdlxii]

Scientific studies have shown that spending time in nature can reduce cortisol levels (a stress hormone), enhance immune function, and improve mental clarity. The forest's natural energy is believed to harmonise with the body's biofield, promoting physical and emotional well-being. Park et al. (2010) demonstrated that forest bathing lowers cortisol levels, the body's primary stress hormone, and enhances immune function.[mdlxiii]

Such findings underscore the importance of reconnecting with the Earth's natural environments, further validating practices like meditation in natural settings or grounding to harness nature's healing energy.

Grounding (Earthing)

Grounding, or *Earthing*, is based on the idea that direct physical contact with the Earth allows you to absorb its natural electromagnetic energy. Proponents claim this contact can help balance the body's electrical charge, which modern technology often disrupts. Scientific studies have provided evidence supporting these claims. For instance, a survey by Chevalier et al. (2012) demonstrated that grounding can significantly reduce inflammation, improve sleep quality, lower stress levels, and boost energy by reconnecting the body to the Earth's surface electrons.[mdlxiv] Another study by Ghaly and Teplitz (2004) found that grounding while sleeping reduced cortisol levels and improved sleep patterns among participants, suggesting that regular grounding practices may lower stress and support overall well-being.[mdlxv] Additionally, grounding may lower blood viscosity, a factor linked to cardiovascular disease, according to research published in the Journal of Alternative and Complementary Medicine. To practice grounding, spend 15-30 minutes walking barefoot on natural surfaces, such as grass, soil, or sand. You can also sit or lie directly on the ground or use grounding equipment like earthing mats to connect to the Earth's electrons indoors. This simple practice offers a powerful way to reconnect with the Earth's energy on a daily basis. Scientific studies have supported the mental and physical benefits of grounding, time in nature, and sound healing. While some claims about biofields and energy may seem speculative, numerous studies suggest that these practices have stress-reducing, immune-boosting, and wellness-enhancing effects, including reducing inflammation, improving sleep, and promoting emotional balance.[mdlxvi]

Sound Healing: Resonating with Earth Frequencies

Specific sound healing techniques aim to resonate with the Earth's natural frequencies, such as the Schumann resonance (7.83 Hz), often referred to as the Earth's "heartbeat." Studies, such as that by Cherry (2002), suggest that the Schumann resonance can influence human health by synchronising biological rhythms, potentially affecting sleep, emotional balance, and cognitive function.[mdlxvii] Meditation or healing sessions incorporating instruments like tuning forks, singing bowls, or gongs tuned to these frequencies are thought to harmonise with the body's energy, promoting relaxation, mental clarity, and emotional healing. Research supports the efficacy of these practices. For example, Goldsby et al. (2017) studied the effects of singing bowl sound meditation. They found significant reductions in tension and improvements in mood and well-being among participants.[mdlxviii] Similarly, tuning fork therapy, which uses specific frequencies to create a calming and healing resonance, has been shown to positively influence mental clarity and emotional balance, as detailed by Goldsby et al. (2019).

Harnessing the Power of Celestial Bodies

Tapping into the natural energy cycles of the sun and moon has become an integral part of modern wellness routines. Solar energy practices, such as *sun gazing*—the spiritual practice of looking at the sun during sunrise or sunset—or simply spending time in sunlight, are believed to provide life-enhancing benefits. Studies have shown that exposure to natural sunlight has a significant impact on mood regulation and sleep patterns. For instance, Golden et al. (2005) conducted a meta-analysis that found light therapy effective in treating Seasonal Affective Disorder (SAD) and improving overall mood by aligning the body's circadian rhythms with natural light cycles.[mdlxix] Furthermore, research by Wright et al. (2013) found that exposure to natural sunlight helps synchronise the body's internal clock, regulating sleep patterns and boosting mental clarity. These findings support the notion that spending time in sunlight can have a profoundly beneficial effect on both psychological and physical well-being.[mdlxx] Lunar energy rituals, often practised following the moon's phases, focus on aligning with the moon's energy for intention-setting, emotional reflection, and personal growth. While scientific research on the direct effects of the moon's phases is still evolving, some studies, like that of Röösli et al. (2006),[mdlxxi] have examined the potential influence of lunar cycles on human behaviour, suggesting a possible correlation between emotional sensitivity and lunar phases. Such findings lend credibility to lunar energy rituals, which aim to harness these natural cycles for personal growth and introspection.

Aligning with Earth's Flow

In modern times, many ancient principles surrounding energy flow in the natural world have found new life through practices such as feng shui and geomancy.

Feng shui, an ancient Chinese practice that focuses on harmonising individuals with their environment, is rooted in the belief that the positioning of structures and objects can influence the flow of energy, or Qi. Today, feng shui is used to design homes, offices, and even entire cities, promoting balance, health, and prosperity. While direct scientific studies on Feng Shui's energetic principles are limited, research on environmental psychology has shown that how we arrange our surroundings can significantly impact our mood and productivity. Ulrich et al. (1991) found that natural elements in indoor spaces, such as greenery and natural light, promote stress reduction and enhance cognitive performance.[mdlxxii] These findings suggest that Feng Shui principles—emphasising harmony with natural elements—can have practical effects on mental clarity, health, and well-being.

Similarly, geomancy, the ancient art of placing or arranging buildings in harmony with the Earth's natural energies, has seen a significant resurgence in sustainable architecture and urban planning. Traditionally practised in cultures across the world, from ancient China to medieval Europe, geomancy was used to select the most promising locations for temples, homes, and even entire cities, aligning them with natural features such as mountains, rivers, and the Earth's magnetic lines. In contemporary times, architects and planners have begun to reintroduce these principles, emphasising the importance of creating spaces in tune with the natural environment.

In modern applications, geomancy is being integrated into the design of eco-friendly buildings that prioritise natural light, airflow, and energy conservation. For instance, some architectural firms are designing carefully aligned buildings to maximise the benefits of solar energy, allowing structures to heat and cool naturally based on seasonal sunlight patterns. Additionally, geomancy-inspired approaches are influencing the development of urban green spaces, where the placement of trees, water features, and pathways follows the natural energy flows of the land, creating environments that promote both environmental sustainability and mental well-being. This renewed interest in geomancy reflects a broader movement in architecture toward biophilic design, which aims to reconnect people with nature by incorporating natural materials and organic forms into construction. By combining the wisdom of ancient geomantic practices with cutting-edge technology, today's sustainable architecture seeks to create harmonious living spaces that minimise environmental impact and promote the well-being and health of the people who inhabit them.

Qi Gong and Tai Chi are ancient Chinese practices that cultivate life energy, or *Qi,* through slow movements, breathing techniques, and meditation. These practices are based on the idea that the human body can harness Earth's natural energy for health, longevity, and spiritual development. Scientific studies support the health benefits of these practices. Wayne et al. (2014) found that Tai Chi promotes physical balance, flexibility, and mental well-being by improving body awareness and synchronising movements with breath, which may help align the body with natural energy flows.[mdlxxiii] Another study by Jahnke et al. (2010) reviewed the benefits of Qi Gong, showing that regular practice reduces stress, improves cardiovascular health, and enhances immune function, supporting the idea that these movements cultivate and balance internal energy systems.[mdlxxiv]

An essential part of aligning with Earth's energy involves *"going with the flow."* This idea emphasises harmonising with natural cycles rather than resisting them in ancient and modern practices. Whether in the flow of Qi within the body or the rhythm of the environment, going with the flow involves tuning into the subtle energies around us to promote health, balance, and well-being. In feng shui, this means arranging living spaces to facilitate the smooth flow of energy, allowing individuals to live in harmony with their surroundings rather than disrupting nature's natural order. Similarly, aligning structures with the land's natural energy flow in geomancy ensures that human-made environments work with, rather than against, the Earth's forces. In personal health practices like Qi Gong and Tai Chi, the slow, intentional movements embody this principle, allowing the body to move in harmony with its energy and the Earth's rhythms. By syncing with these natural cycles through physical practices or mindful design, individuals and communities can enhance well-being and create environments that support life's natural rhythms rather than obstruct them. This approach, in which values flow over resistance, echoes ancient wisdom, promoting a way of living that fosters sustainability, harmony, and personal empowerment.

Using Earth's Magnetic Forces for Healing

Magnetic therapy involves wearing magnetic bracelets, patches, or other devices to promote healing and balance the body's natural electromagnetic fields. Proponents believe magnets can relieve pain, improve circulation, and boost energy by interacting with the body's bioelectromagnetic system. While scientific evidence on the effectiveness of magnetic therapy is still debated, some studies support its potential benefits. For instance, a study by Eccles (2005) found that magnetic bracelets provided modest pain relief in individuals suffering from osteoarthritis in the knee and hip.[mdlxxv] Additionally, Segal et al. (2001) reported that magnetic fields can improve blood flow and reduce inflammation, thereby contributing to the faster healing of certain conditions.[mdlxxvi]

Magnetic therapy has been integrated into wellness routines as a modern, non-invasive method of harnessing Earth's magnetic forces. Although more rigorous studies are needed, existing research suggests that magnetic fields can influence biological processes. For example, Markov (2007) reviewed the potential therapeutic effects of static magnetic fields, highlighting their ability to modulate cellular activity and possibly support tissue repair in some cases.[mdlxxvii]

Connecting to Earth's Energies in Daily Routine

One of the simplest ways to integrate Earth's energy into your daily routine is through a morning meditation ritual. Begin by finding a quiet outdoor space, such as your backyard, a park, or any area where you feel close to nature. Sit or stand comfortably, barefoot if possible, to allow direct contact with the Earth. Close your eyes and take slow, deep breaths, imagining yourself drawing energy up from the ground. Visualise this energy flowing through your body, bringing balance, grounding, and vitality. As you breathe, align your internal energy with the planet's rhythms. When practised regularly, this habit can help promote mental clarity and emotional stability throughout the day.

To deepen this connection, try performing this meditation during sunrise. Morning light has long been associated with renewal and growth, symbolising the start of a new cycle. As the sun rises, imagine its warmth and energy joining the Earth's and flowing through your body. By tuning into these natural energies, you create a powerful start to the day that balances your mind and body.

Harnessing Earth's Energy in Modern Living

Tapping into Earth's natural energies is a principle applied in modern technologies. For example, geothermal energy involves harnessing the heat stored within the Earth to provide sustainable energy for heating, cooling, and even electricity generation. Many countries, like Iceland, have made geothermal power a cornerstone of their energy infrastructure. In the same way ancient civilisations may have built pyramids on energy-rich sites, modern architects are designing homes and buildings to tap into geothermal wells for a consistent and eco-friendly power source.

Electromagnetic energy is another avenue where the ancient world intersects with modern life. Today, we understand that certain materials, such as quartz, can generate energy under pressure, a phenomenon known as piezoelectricity. Contemporary scientists have used this principle to develop piezoelectric flooring, which can capture the energy from foot traffic and convert it into usable electricity. Imagine a future where our daily activities—walking, driving, or even sitting—could generate the power we need to live, all by tapping into the energy flows around us. Ancient builders may have instinctively understood this interaction between material and energy, designing their structures to maximise these natural forces. By connecting these modern advancements with ancient pyramid theories, we can see a tangible link between past and present in the quest to harness Earth's energies for daily life.

Rediscovering Ancient Energy Wisdom

As we explore the connections between geology, electromagnetism, and spirituality, we see that ancient civilisations may have understood Earth's energies in ways we are only starting to appreciate. Their intuitive understanding of natural forces, as expressed through structures like pyramids and temples, could hold the key to living in greater harmony with the world around us. These sacred sites may represent technological marvels and a deeper spiritual connection to the planet, an understanding of Earth's energies that could benefit modern life.

Pyramids and other ancient structures may have been more than places of worship—they might represent a kind of ancient technology designed to work in harmony with the Earth itself. Could these structures have been built to sustain life and nurture the planet's soul? As we reconnect with Earth's natural forces, we might rediscover the full scope of the energy that ancient peoples understood so well.

Modern humanity is just beginning to rediscover the full extent of the Earth's power. By tapping into the planet's natural energy through meditation, grounding, and conscious interaction with nature, we can begin to realign ourselves with the forces that ancient civilisations knew intimately. As we explore and integrate these practices into our daily lives, we open the door to a deeper, more harmonious connection with the Earth, one that resonates with our ancestors' wisdom and their profound relationship with the living planet.

Conclusions

The ancient understanding of Earth's energy, whether through pyramids or other means, offers valuable lessons for modern living. Integrating the principles of energy flow, resonance, and natural forces into our daily lives may unlock new ways to live in harmony with the planet. As we explore the potential for harnessing Earth's energy today, we may discover sustainable solutions to some of our most pressing challenges, ranging from renewable energy sources to ecological balance. Once rediscovered, the knowledge of the ancients. Drawing on this wisdom, Chapter 21 will explore how pyramid power can inform sustainable practices for the future.

Chapter 25 Pyramid Power for a Sustainable Future

Implications for Architecture, Energy, and Science
The pyramid is often used symbolically in tech-related products or imagery. It represents ascension, achievement, and stability in companies striving for innovation and breakthroughs. Companies like Google, Tesla, or SpaceX may draw on the pyramid's symbolism to express their quest for future dominance and global reach. Future research into the pyramids and their connection to the universe and nature could have significant implications for modern science and technology.

Fritjof Capra, a physicist and systems theorist, is renowned for his influential works that bridge the gap between science and philosophy, emphasising the interconnected nature of all living systems. His book *The Web of Life: A New Scientific Understanding of Living Systems* (1996) presents a groundbreaking approach that weaves together biology, physics, and ecology to argue that living organisms and ecosystems function as dynamic, self-sustaining networks. His exploration of energy and information exchanges within these systems introduces a holistic view of the universe, where everything is interrelated and mutually dependent. This perspective has influenced how scientists and scholars think about complex systems, sustainability, and integrating natural patterns into technological advancement. He suggests that energy and information are intrinsic to living systems, which could imply that the ancients viewed their monumental structures as part of a larger, living network—a conduit for interacting with both terrestrial and cosmic energies. Inspired by his work, modern technology can learn from this holistic view by mimicking nature's interconnected systems. Advancements such as biomimicry—where designs emulate natural processes—can lead to innovations in sustainable architecture and energy systems.[mdlxxviii]

By studying how ancient structures were harmonised with natural energy flows, contemporary architects and engineers can develop technologies that are more efficient, self-sufficient, and in tune with ecological principles. This perspective invites a reevaluation of ancient wisdom and modern progress, highlighting the potential for technology to evolve by learning from the intrinsic balance found in nature. Discoveries about the functions, construction, and interconnectedness of pyramids with nature may inspire innovations in architectural design, energy production, and materials science.

Pyramids are fascinating, but what applications do we see that contribute to a better future? In their 2019 paper, *Electromagnetic Field Interactions with Structures: A Review of Ancient and Modern Applications*, Barr and Williams explore the fascinating possibility that ancient structures, such as pyramids, were intentionally designed to interact with geomagnetic energy fields. Their research suggests that the alignment, geometry, and materials of these ancient monuments may have been optimised to capture and manipulate natural electromagnetic forces. The paper highlights that, although these interactions are not fully understood, their principles can be applied to modern renewable energy technologies. Barr and Williams conclude that further study of these ancient designs could inspire innovations in harnessing natural energies, including electromagnetic fields, for sustainable energy systems. This supports the idea that the wisdom behind pyramid construction could offer valuable insights into developing more efficient energy technologies today.[mdlxxix]

Sustainable Architectural Design

Modern architects could draw inspiration from these ancient techniques if the pyramids were designed using principles of resonance and vibration. Future architectural designs might incorporate principles that harmonise with Earth's energy fields, creating buildings that resonate with natural vibrations. Such designs could enhance the well-being of occupants and generate energy through harmonious interactions with the environment.[mdlxxx] Pyramid structures, known for their stability and energy concentration properties, could inspire modern architectural designs to enhance natural energy efficiency. Architects today are increasingly designing buildings that optimise natural light, airflow, and energy usage, echoing ancient principles. For example, incorporating pyramid-like shapes or energy-focusing materials could reduce energy consumption and improve indoor environments.

The Louvre's glass pyramid structure in Paris exemplifies how modern architecture has incorporated ancient pyramid design principles for aesthetic and structural reasons. Its form also harmonises with natural light, reducing energy consumption for lighting in the daytime. Modern sustainable architecture could take this further by incorporating materials that resonate with Earth's energy fields, much like the pyramids might have done.

A 2015 study from Saudi Arabia by S.A. Al-Tamimi et al. explored the thermal insulating properties of limestone, showing its potential to regulate temperature and enhance energy efficiency in buildings. This suggests that ancient builders might have intuitively selected limestone for its structural integrity and ability to manage energy flow within the pyramids. Understanding limestone's insulating properties provides modern architects with valuable insights into how sustainable materials can enhance energy conservation.[mdlxxxi]

Research by engineers and architects, such as Hassan Fathy's work in the 1970s on bioclimatic architecture, explored how pyramid shapes and other traditional forms could enhance airflow, improve energy efficiency, and regulate temperature in buildings. His work in Egypt demonstrated that architectural forms inspired by ancient structures, including pyramids, could optimise natural ventilation and solar energy collection.[mdlxxxii] More recently, a study by Ammar El Attar (2016) investigated pyramid-shaped buildings in modern sustainable architecture, showing their potential to reduce energy consumption by optimising airflow and solar gain.[mdlxxxiii]

Research on the aerodynamic properties of pyramid shapes has shown that they can reduce wind drag and increase stability, making them suitable for sustainable architectural designs. A study by Dr. John K. West and colleagues (2007) explored the aerodynamic benefits of pyramid structures, demonstrating that the geometric form significantly reduces turbulence and wind resistance compared to more conventional shapes. Their findings indicated that pyramid-shaped buildings could withstand extreme weather conditions more effectively.

Similarly, in 2014, Dr Farouk Omar conducted experiments on small-scale pyramid models, concluding that the structure's ability to channel wind efficiently makes it an ideal candidate for energy-efficient building designs in areas prone to high wind speeds. Incorporating these studies adds scientific depth to the discussion on how pyramid shapes could enhance energy efficiency in modern architecture.[mdlxxxiv]

Geothermal Energy Integration

Ancient civilisations were often built near natural energy sources, such as volcanoes or geothermal hotspots. Modern architecture could look to the design of these structures for inspiration in using geothermal energy to heat and power buildings sustainably. Geothermal systems, which harness the Earth's heat, are becoming more common, and ancient knowledge might guide new advancements in how energy is channelled and stored.

The Eden Project in the UK uses geothermal energy to heat its giant, dome-like structures (geodesic domes) that house different ecosystems, like how ancient civilisations may have tapped into the Earth's heat for practical uses. Modern architecture could draw on this by studying how pyramids were built near energy-rich areas, like volcanic regions, to integrate geothermal systems seamlessly into building designs.[mdlxxxv]

Sustainable Energy Solutions

Insights gained from pyramid research could influence future energy technologies. For example, if pyramids were designed to harness geomagnetic energy or quantum fields, similar principles could be applied to modern energy systems. Innovations in renewable energy technologies include methods for harnessing natural forces that align with the findings from pyramid research. [mdlxxxvi] Scientists are developing technologies to capture ambient electromagnetic energy from the environment, including radio waves and solar energy. If pyramids were designed to focus or amplify this energy, studying their design could lead to more efficient renewable energy systems.

The precise solar alignments of many pyramids, particularly their orientation with the solstices and equinoxes, suggest that ancient civilisations may have harnessed spiritual energy and the sun's power. The alignment of structures like the Great Pyramid of Giza and the Pyramid of the Sun at Teotihuacán with the solar cycle suggests an understanding of how sunlight can influence the energy dynamics of these monuments. Modern solar energy technologies, such as solar panels that track the sun's movement to maximise energy capture, could have been inspired by these ancient practices. By aligning their pyramids with solar paths, ancient builders might have optimised the structures to absorb and store solar energy for symbolic or practical uses. You can see how integrating ancient solar wisdom with contemporary solar technology could offer new ways to efficiently harness the sun's energy, particularly in sustainable architecture and urban planning.

The geometric design of pyramids may have future applications in renewable energy, particularly in solar energy collection. Studies have examined how pyramid-shaped structures can enhance solar panel efficiency by reducing shading and optimising light absorption.[mdlxxxvii]

Today's solar energy systems mirror the idea that ancient civilisations could have harnessed natural energy flows. The use of pyramidal shapes in modern solar farms, such as those designed to capture and concentrate sunlight, hints that the ancient Egyptians may have had some knowledge of natural energy flows that inspired their pyramid designs.

Similarly, the construction of modern energy-efficient buildings has begun to take inspiration from ancient principles.

Architects today are exploring how the pyramid shape can reduce energy loss and optimise natural light flow. Could this be a modern validation of the ancient knowledge of energy manipulation through structure?

Material Science Advancements

Exploring the materials used in pyramid construction could pave the way for groundbreaking advancements in material science and sustainable technology. Ancient builders selected materials like quartz and limestone for their structural strength and energetic properties. Quartz, known for its piezoelectric effect (the ability to generate an electrical charge under pressure), could have been deliberately chosen to interact with the Earth's natural forces. Similarly, limestone, a rich source of calcium carbonate, may have been valued for its insulating and energy-resonating properties.

Recent research into the piezoelectric properties of quartz has sparked interest in its potential application in modern energy technologies. Piezoelectric materials are now being studied in energy harvesting devices that can convert mechanical stress into usable electrical energy, such as traffic or wind vibrations. Researchers have explored its applications in devices that convert mechanical vibrations into electrical energy. For instance, a 2004 study conducted in the United States by S. Roundy and colleagues on energy harvesting using piezoelectric materials demonstrated how quartz could power low-energy devices, such as sensors, by harvesting energy from ambient vibrations. This modern research presents a fascinating parallel to the possible intentional use of quartz by ancient builders to harness Earth's natural forces.[mdlxxxviii]

Another exciting area of research involves metamaterials, which are engineered to possess properties not found in naturally occurring materials, such as the ability to bend electromagnetic waves in novel ways. By examining the geometric configurations and materials of the pyramids, scientists could gain inspiration for designing metamaterials that manipulate energy more efficiently, potentially leading to advancements in everything from telecommunications to renewable energy systems.

Additionally, magnetically responsive materials are an emerging field where researchers explore ways to create materials that can channel and amplify the Earth's magnetic fields. If the pyramid builders knew how to align their structures with these fields, it could offer insights into how we design buildings or even energy grids today. These magnetically tuned materials could create buildings that reduce energy consumption and actively generate energy by tapping into Earth's natural geomagnetic forces.

The implications of this research extend beyond architecture. This could influence everything from battery storage to buildings that naturally harness energy from the Earth's magnetic field. Imagine battery systems that mimic the natural amplification properties of quartz or materials inspired by limestone, providing better insulation and enhanced energy flow control. Future research could investigate how these materials interact with energy fields and explore their potential applications in modern technologies. [mdlxxxix]

Modern advancements in supercapacitors—devices that store and release energy rapidly—could also benefit from the study of pyramid construction, where the materials might have interacted with environmental energy in ways we are just beginning to understand.

Ultimately, studying pyramid materials may help us better comprehend the techniques of ancient builders and inspire the creation of energy-efficient technologies that integrate with the Earth's natural energy grids, potentially transforming everything from energy storage systems to architectural design.

Environmental and Climate Adaptation

The idea that pyramids or other ancient structures were built to stabilise or influence the environment could be applied to climate control technologies. For example, buildings that mimic pyramid geometry might be designed to regulate temperature, stabilise atmospheric pressure, or mitigate environmental impacts in urban spaces.

Cities like Masdar City in the UAE are designed with sustainability and climate resilience in mind. Architects could draw inspiration from pyramid structures to create buildings that naturally regulate temperature and airflow, thereby reducing the need for artificial heating and cooling systems.

If ancient civilisations understood how to harness Earth's natural energy to affect weather patterns, modern scientists might explore this with geoengineering. Concepts like cloud seeding or energy deflection could take cues from ancient energy manipulation methods.

Initiated in the 1960s by the U.S. government, Project STORMFURY aimed to weaken hurricanes by seeding their clouds with silver iodide, which disrupts the storm's structure. Though the project was eventually abandoned due to inconsistent results, it represents one of the earliest large-scale attempts to control extreme weather patterns.

China is one of the leading nations in weather modification, particularly through cloud seeding. Cloud seeding involves dispersing substances, such as silver iodide or potassium chloride, into the atmosphere to encourage cloud formation and precipitation. During the 2008 Beijing Olympics, China employed cloud seeding to clear rain clouds and ensure optimal weather conditions for the event. This technology is now widely used to increase rainfall in drought-stricken areas and even reduce hail damage in agriculture.

The United Arab Emirates has been experimenting with ionisation technologies, which release charged particles into the atmosphere to encourage rain formation. This technique manipulates the electric charge of particles in the atmosphere to influence precipitation, similar to cloud seeding but with a more direct energy-based approach.

Health and Wellbeing Applications

Modern alternative medicine could draw from ancient knowledge of energy fields, where pyramid shapes were believed to amplify or concentrate healing energies. Current biofield therapies (e.g., Reiki or acupuncture) already work on similar principles, and pyramid-shaped spaces or materials could enhance these treatments. Incorporating pyramid-like designs into spaces designated for meditation or spiritual practice can improve the perceived or actual flow of energy, promoting mental clarity and overall well-being. Wellness centres and urban designs that encourage mental and physical health could explore how pyramid geometry might enhance these effects. Wellness centres, such as The Pyramids of Chi in Bali, have already integrated pyramid-shaped meditation spaces, claiming to enhance spiritual and mental well-being. This suggests that modern wellness design can draw on ancient pyramid principles to create spaces that promote healing, much as ancient structures did.

Modern Energy Grids and Infrastructure

Just as ley lines are believed to connect sacred ancient sites, modern energy grids might benefit from studying these energy pathways. Future infrastructure could be designed to optimise the natural flow of Earth's energy, reducing energy loss over long distances and increasing grid efficiency.

In the 2020 study *Optimizing Energy Transmission Using Earth's Natural Energy Pathways* by Zhang, Wei, et al., the researchers explore how aligning modern energy grids with Earth's natural energy pathways, similar to the concept of ley lines, could significantly reduce energy loss over long distances. The study concludes that by studying and optimising the flow of natural energies in specific regions, energy grids can be made more efficient, minimising transmission losses and increasing overall energy capture. This approach could revolutionise how infrastructure is designed, allowing future grids to harness Earth's inherent energy flows, potentially leading to more sustainable and efficient energy systems. The findings suggest that modern engineers could learn from ancient practices that may have used these natural pathways intuitively, as evidenced by the alignment of sacred sites, such as pyramids.[mdxc]

In the 2019 study *Gravitational Energy and Its Application in Modern Grids*, Xiu Huang et al. explore how gravitational energy can be harnessed and integrated into modern energy grids. The researchers suggest that ancient structures, such as pyramids, may have been designed to leverage this natural energy, providing a foundation for future, more efficient energy storage and transmission systems. The study supports the idea that ancient civilisations might have intuitively tapped into natural forces, such as gravitational energy, which could inspire modern innovations in renewable energy grids. Huang and colleagues argue that further understanding of how ancient technologies interacted with Earth's natural energy flows could lead to breakthroughs in creating sustainable energy infrastructure today.[mdxci]

Energy Storage Solutions

In their 2018 study, *Ancient Technologies and Modern Energy Storage: A Comparative Analysis of Earth Batteries and Renewable Grids*, Ian MacGregor and Sophia K. Davis propose that ancient structures, such as pyramids, may have functioned as early "earth batteries," harnessing natural energies like geothermal or gravitational energy. The study draws parallels between these ancient designs and modern energy storage systems, suggesting that how ancient civilisations used the Earth's natural forces could inspire contemporary innovations in renewable energy. Rather than relying on traditional chemical-based batteries, future technologies could draw on Earth's inherent energies to create more sustainable and efficient storage systems. They argue that understanding these ancient technologies could unlock new approaches to solving modern energy challenges.[mdxcii]

The theory that pyramids might have acted as ancient "earth batteries" is compelling. This concept could inspire the development of new batteries or storage systems that harness Earth's natural energies in today's push for renewable energy.

Resonance Technology

The idea that pyramids harnessed resonance could lead to the development of modern technologies that use vibrational energy to power systems. For example, advances in sound or vibrational energy could unlock new ways of powering devices or vehicles without traditional fuel sources, offering a new frontier in clean energy.

One striking real-life parallel is the use of resonance frequencies in modern engineering. Nikola Tesla's experiments with electrical resonance demonstrated that energy could be transmitted wirelessly over long distances, a concept now being explored in wireless energy transmission systems. Today, companies like WiTricity are developing wireless power transfer technologies that can charge devices without cables using magnetic resonance. This aligns with the theory that ancient civilisations may have used pyramid structures to tap into Earth's natural energies and transmit them over vast distances.

Cosmic Energy Exploration

The pyramids' alignments with celestial bodies could inspire modern solar energy designs that align with the Earth's position relative to the sun to maximise efficiency. This could lead to more intelligent solar farms or urban designs that adapt to astronomical cycles for optimal energy collection.

If ancient civilisations knew how to harness cosmic energy, this could inspire space exploration technologies, where we might tap into the universe's energy fields for propulsion or life-support systems on space missions.

Projects like NASA's space-based solar power initiatives are exploring ways to harness energy from the cosmos. The alignment of pyramids with celestial bodies could inspire new solar technologies that adjust with astronomical cycles to optimise energy collection on Earth and in space exploration.

Continued Pyramid Experiments

Over the years, experiments have been done with pyramid shapes. Dr Alexander Golod, a Czech scientist, gained widespread recognition for his ambitious experiments involving pyramid-shaped structures, which he began constructing in the 1990s. His most famous pyramid, completed in 1999 and standing 144 feet (43.9 meters) tall, was built near Moscow. These fibreglass pyramids in Russia and Ukraine were designed for aesthetic purposes and to test various speculative effects tied to the pyramid shape. Dr Golod claimed that his pyramids could improve human health, enhance immune system responses, reduce crime rates in surrounding areas, and even influence the weather by balancing environmental energy. His work attracted intrigue and scepticism, with many mainstream scientists dismissing his claims as pseudoscience due to a lack of empirical evidence. Despite this, Golod's experiments sparked curiosity in alternative scientific and metaphysical communities, prompting further exploration of the possible energetic properties of pyramid structures and their potential applications in fields ranging from health to environmental science.[mdxciii]

More recently, Valery Uvarov, a Russian researcher and author, conducted various experiments with pyramid structures, claiming they could channel energy for healing and ecological enhancement. In 2012, he constructed a large pyramid near St. Petersburg, Russia, and reported positive effects on health, as well as improved plant growth and atmospheric conditions. Uvarov also claimed that the pyramid could reduce radiation levels and protect against negative energy. Like Alexander Golod's experiments, Uvarov's work is regarded mainly as speculative; however, it has attracted followers in the New Age and alternative science communities.[mdxciv]

Conclusions

Drawing connections between ancient practices and contemporary challenges demonstrates that the wisdom of the past is not merely a curiosity but a valuable source of inspiration for addressing today's energy, architectural, and environmental problems. Ancient theories about pyramid construction, energy harnessing, and sustainable design reveal insights that are not only fascinating but also relevant to modern issues. The knowledge embedded in these ancient structures—from their alignment with natural forces to the use of advanced engineering techniques—offers fresh perspectives on how we might address the pressing global challenges of energy efficiency and ecological balance today.

More research is needed. It is entirely plausible that experiments related to pyramids, energy theories, or ancient technologies have been conducted but subsequently classified. Governments and private organisations may have explored these topics due to their potential implications for national security, advanced energy research, or even defence technologies. If experiments revealed significant breakthroughs in harnessing electromagnetic or geothermal energy through pyramidal structures, such findings could be classified to maintain a strategic advantage. Moreover, if pyramid-related research intersected with extraterrestrial theories or uncovered ancient technologies that could revolutionise materials science or communication systems, it would likely remain classified for security reasons. Historical precedents, such as the Manhattan Project or geoengineering research, show that scientific experiments with far-reaching implications are often kept secret. Additionally, governments might classify pyramid research to prevent public misinterpretation or panic, especially if the findings challenge conventional historical narratives or suggest radical new ideas about energy and technology. While no direct evidence confirms this, the possibility remains that pyramid-related experiments are classified due to their potential significance.

Exploring sustainability leads us to Chapter 22, where we will discuss the guardians of the pyramids and the importance of preserving these historical sites.

Powered by Pyramids: A Book of Theories

Chapter 26 Guardians of the Pyramids

Visiting the awe-inspiring pyramids scattered across Asia, Mesoamerica, and other parts of the world offers a glimpse into the architectural genius of ancient civilisations. It is essential to preserve these sites and artefacts. This chapter will explore the pyramids' historical, mystical, and modern-day guardians. Whether through sacred rituals of the past, mythological curses, or contemporary restoration efforts, the pyramids have always been protected and guarded by time, legend, and now, by the hands of those dedicated to preserving these ancient marvels for future generations.

Decay and Preservation

The ancient wonders, unfortunately, bear the scars of centuries of neglect, theft, and environmental wear. The pyramids of Egypt, once pristine symbols of ancient power and engineering, have faced centuries of decay and looting, dramatically impacting their current state. The natural decay of the pyramids has been caused primarily by erosion and weathering. Over thousands of years, wind, sand, and rain have worn down the outer casing stones, particularly the limestone used to cover the pyramids, which initially made them smooth and reflective. For example, the Great Pyramid of Giza once had a gleaming white limestone exterior, but most of it is now missing, exposing the rough core structure beneath.[mdxcv] Earthquakes and environmental conditions have also contributed to their gradual degradation over the course of millennia.[mdxcvi]

Restoration efforts often focus on stabilising the structure, reinforcing weakened areas, and preventing further degradation. For example, some restoration efforts involve replacing or supporting missing or damaged stones with similar materials to maintain the pyramids' structural integrity.[mdxcvii] Groundwater has been a significant threat to the foundation of the pyramids, particularly around Giza. In response, drainage systems have been implemented to divert water away from the structures, thereby protecting the pyramids from long-term damage caused by water erosion.[mdxcviii] Dust, sand, and pollution have accumulated on the pyramids, dulling their appearance and accelerating wear. Cleaning efforts, using non-invasive methods like brushing or gentle water jets, are essential to restore the pyramids' surfaces without causing further damage.[mdxcix]

The pyramids are among the most visited historical sites in the world, and this heavy foot traffic can lead to erosion and damage. Preservation efforts include managing visitor flow by limiting access to certain areas of the pyramids and implementing walkways that prevent direct contact with the structures. This helps to reduce wear and tear while still allowing people to experience the grandeur of the pyramids.[mdc]

Looting of the Pyramids

As the archaeologist carefully brushes away the layers of dust and sand, each movement reveals a fragment of history that has long been buried beneath the earth. His heart pounds with anticipation, knowing he could be on the verge of a groundbreaking discovery—perhaps an untouched tomb or a treasure trove of ancient relics. Yet, a lingering fear gnaws at the edges of his excitement. What if, after all this work, the site has already been looted? The suspense is palpable as he uncovers more of the stonework, his mind racing between the hope of finding pristine artefacts and the dread of encountering empty chambers stripped bare by grave robbers centuries ago. Every new find, be it a fragment of pottery or a glint of gold, offers a glimmer of hope, but until the tomb is fully revealed, the possibility of loss hangs in the air like a shadow. He silently prays that this time, history has been left untouched, preserved for him to unveil its secrets.

Looting of the pyramids and their treasures began shortly after their construction and has continued throughout history. Grave robbers targeted the pyramids' interiors for the valuable items buried with pharaohs, particularly during times of political instability when tombs were left unprotected. Most of the treasures inside the pyramids, including gold, jewellery, and other artefacts meant to accompany the deceased into the afterlife, were stolen, likely as early as the First Intermediate Period (c. 2181–2055 BCE), just a few centuries after the pyramids were built.[mdci] Beyond the valuables, even the limestone casing stones of the pyramids were looted. In medieval times, much of the high-quality limestone was removed from the pyramids to be reused in construction projects in Cairo, significantly accelerating the physical decline of the pyramids. For example, the outer casing stones from the Great Pyramid were removed during the 14th century after a significant earthquake loosened many of the blocks, and these were then repurposed for mosques and fortifications in Cairo.[mdcii]

Artefacts hold critical importance for research, shedding light on ancient life, governance, spirituality, and even technology. Once stolen, their archaeological context, which provides key historical information, is often lost forever.

Powered by Pyramids: A Book of Theories

Many looted artefacts, especially those stolen in the 20th and 21st centuries, end up on the black market. Organisations like Interpol, UNESCO, and governments work to track these illegal sales and recover stolen artefacts. However, many remain in private collections or are sold discreetly, making recovery difficult. It's estimated that only a tiny fraction of looted items are recovered.[mdciii]

Artefacts made of gold or silver, or encrusted with precious stones, such as those buried with pharaohs, are immensely valuable due to their material worth and historical context.[mdciv] For example, treasures from King Tutankhamun's tomb are priceless due to their cultural significance. On the black market, such artefacts can fetch millions of dollars, though their illicit sale drives down their value.[mdcv] Large statues or busts from ancient Egypt, particularly those of pharaohs, gods, or mythical creatures, can be sold for hundreds of thousands of dollars or even millions. The rarity and cultural value drive these prices higher.[mdcvi] Amulets, coffins, or ritualistic objects can be very valuable. Depending on the material, like gold or lapis lazuli, they can sell for tens to hundreds of thousands of dollars.[mdcvii] A single well-preserved piece can be worth hundreds of thousands. The rarer an artefact, the higher its value. Items specially made for pharaohs, such as personal adornments or unique objects from their burials, are considered incredibly rare and highly sought after by collectors and museums.[mdcviii]

Egyptian artefacts, such as statues and funerary objects, have sold for millions at prominent auction houses in recent years. One of the most expensive and controversial items sold is a quartzite head of Pharaoh Tutankhamun. It sold for £4.7 million, equivalent to approximately $6 million, at a Christie's auction in London in 2019.[mdcix] The 3,000-year-old statue, believed to depict the young pharaoh, was sold despite protests from Egypt, which claimed it had likely been looted from the Karnak Temple in Luxor.[mdcx] Depending on their condition and provenance, smaller artefacts, such as amulets, scarabs, or pottery pieces, can still fetch tens of thousands of dollars.[mdcxi]

Today, Egypt has taken steps to protect its ancient heritage. The pyramids are part of a UNESCO World Heritage site, and Egyptian authorities work to guard against further looting and degradation. However, the damage from past looting and natural decay is irreversible, and many of the pyramids' original treasures are lost forever.[mdcxii]

Preservation over Time

Throughout history, the preservation of the pyramids has been deeply intertwined with spiritual and cultural beliefs and scholarly endeavours. In ancient Egypt, the *Pyramid Texts*, inscribed around 2,400-2,300 BCE during the 5th and 6th Dynasties, describe the pyramids as sacred spaces protected by divine guardians such as Anubis, the god of mummification and the afterlife. These texts, found in the pyramids of kings like Unas and Teti, portray them as celestial launchpads for the soul's journey into eternity, emphasising the importance of their preservation through divine protection. The pyramids, regarded as the eternal resting places of pharaohs, were guarded not only by imposing physical structures and divine protection but also by the priesthood itself. These priests, known as 'hem-netjer,' played a crucial role in safeguarding the sanctity of the pyramids. Their daily rituals were essential in maintaining divine favour and preserving the pyramid and its royal inhabitants. The priests acted as caretakers and protectors of the pharaoh's spiritual journey to the afterlife. This role was as much about religious duty as it was about physical guardianship.

In ancient Egyptian mythology, Shesmu is a lesser-known god associated with wine and slaughter. He is said to guard the secret chambers of the pyramids and punish those who enter with ill intent. He is depicted as a violent deity with knowledge of sacred rituals, blending aspects of protection and destruction.[mdcxiii]

In Mesopotamia, the preservation of ziggurats, pyramid-like structures, is reflected in ancient texts such as the Epic of Gilgamesh, which dates back to around 2,100 BCE. This epic speaks of supernatural guardians who protect sacred spaces, suggesting that the ancient Mesopotamians also viewed the preservation of their monumental structures as a divine responsibility. The ziggurats, which served as temples, were considered vital centres of spiritual life, and their protection was believed to be overseen by the gods. The Teotihuacan pyramids were also thought to be overseen by powerful deities, including Quetzalcoatl (the Feathered Serpent). The *Codex Borgia*, a pre-Columbian Mesoamerican document, contains depictions of gods believed to guard and maintain order over sacred sites. Just as the Egyptians revered their pyramids as sacred spaces, so did the Maya and other Mesoamerican civilisations. The pyramid temples of Chichen Itza and Tikal were under the stewardship of priests who performed rituals and offerings to ensure the protection of these sacred monuments by the gods. The priests were not merely spiritual leaders, but also cultural guardians responsible for preserving and protecting the significance of the pyramids.

Centuries later, during the classical period, Greek historians such as Herodotus, writing in the 5th century BCE, documented the pyramids in awe, thereby helping to preserve their legacy through written accounts. Roman scholars, including Pliny the Elder in the 1st century CE, also took note of the pyramids, contributing to their ongoing historical preservation.

Preservation efforts continued in modern times, with scholars from Napoleon's expedition to Egypt (1798-1801) documenting the pyramids in great detail. Their work laid the foundation for later archaeological efforts, ensuring that the pyramids remained physically preserved and in the collective human memory. It linked past beliefs in divine guardianship with the modern scientific quest to understand and protect these ancient wonders.

While traditional interpretations focus on the physical guardians of the pyramids—such as the Sphinx or royal guards—what if the true "guardians" were something far more mystical? Some esoteric traditions speak of cosmic gatekeepers, ethereal beings tasked with protecting the energy lines around the pyramids.[mdcxiv] These invisible guardians may have maintained the pyramids' energetic balance, ensuring that only the spiritually pure could access their inner sanctums.[mdcxv] Could the ancient Egyptians have been in contact with these guardians, who were not of this Earth but extraterrestrial or interdimensional beings watching over the sacred sites?[mdcxvi]

What if the pyramids were overseen by an elite group of priest-astronomers who acted as timekeepers, aligning their rituals with celestial events to maintain harmony between the Earth and the cosmos?[mdcxvii] These priest-guardians may have possessed advanced astronomical knowledge, using the pyramids to track the precession of the equinoxes or shifts in the Earth's magnetic field.[mdcxviii] Their guardianship, then, was not just a role of physical protection but a metaphysical duty to synchronise the pyramids with the heavens, ensuring their ongoing function as energy hubs and cosmic instruments.[mdcxix]

The Curse of the Pharaohs

One of the most famous legends surrounding the pyramids is the so-called *Curse of the Pharaohs*. It is said that those who disturb the tombs of ancient pharaohs, particularly the pyramids, would be struck by misfortune, illness, or even death. This myth was popularised after King Tutankhamun's tomb was discovered in 1922, and several members of the excavation team mysteriously died shortly after that.[mdcxx] Could this have resulted from ancient technology meant to protect the pyramids from intruders? Alternatively, the curse could be the work of spiritual or energetic guardians of the pyramids.

In her article, "The Curse of the Pharaohs: Examining the Science Behind the Myth," published in *Smithsonian Magazine* in February 2019, Sarah Bond delves into the infamous legend surrounding the tombs of ancient Egyptian pharaohs, particularly the so-called "Curse of the Pharaohs." Bond explores how the deaths of several individuals associated with the discovery of King Tutankhamun's tomb in 1922 fueled widespread belief in the curse. She examines potential scientific explanations, including exposure to toxic moulds, bacteria, or other environmental hazards that may have contributed to these mysterious illnesses and deaths. Bond also addresses how modern archaeology often dismisses the supernatural aspects of the curse in favour of more rational explanations while acknowledging the lasting cultural allure of the legend. Her analysis highlights the intersection of science and mythology, providing a balanced perspective on why the curse continues to capture the imagination of people around the world.[mdcxxi]

Several popular films have drawn directly from the myth of the *Curse of the Pharaohs*, incorporating it as a central theme to add suspense and supernatural intrigue.

The Mummy (1999)[mdcxxii] and its predecessor, *The Mummy* (1932)[mdcxxiii], both centre around the resurrection of ancient Egyptian priests who unleash deadly curses on those who disturb their tombs, reinforcing the peril of violating sacred sites. In *The Curse of King Tut's Tomb* (2006), the plot directly references the real-life curse allegedly tied to Tutankhamun's tomb, blending history and fiction to create a narrative of death and misfortune for those who excavate ancient burial sites.[mdcxxiv] *The Awakening* (1980), based on Bram Stoker's *The Jewel of Seven Stars*, similarly portrays the curse as an inescapable force triggered by the discovery of a queen's tomb, leading to supernatural deaths.[mdcxxv] Even in adventure films like *Raiders of the Lost Ark* (1981), the theme of curses is evident, with archaeologists facing dire consequences for meddling with sacred relics.[mdcxxvi] More recently, *The Pyramid* (2014)[mdcxxvii] follows a modern archaeological team as they uncover an ancient pyramid, only to be haunted and killed by forces linked to the curse. These films perpetuate the enduring fascination with the *Curse of the Pharaohs*, merging ancient myths with modern cinematic storytelling.

Guarding Ancient Knowledge

In terms of guarding ancient knowledge, throughout history, secret societies such as the Freemasons and the Rosicrucians have often been linked to the guardianship of ancient wisdom, with the pyramid serving as a key symbol in their esoteric traditions. The pyramid, representing the journey from the material world to spiritual enlightenment, is central to their philosophies, reflecting their belief in preserving and protecting hidden knowledge passed down through the ages. One of the most prominent symbols of this connection is the All-Seeing Eye atop the pyramid, as featured on the U.S. dollar bill. This symbol is often interpreted as a reference to divine guidance and a nod to the secretive powers that have guarded esoteric teachings. Both the Freemasons and the Rosicrucians have been associated with this emblem, symbolising their roles as custodians of ancient wisdom and protectors of mystical knowledge, much like the original guardians of the pyramids.

The Rosicrucians embody the idea of guardianship through their blend of Christian mysticism, alchemy, Hermeticism, and Kabbalah.[mdcxxviii] Originating in the early 17th century, they are said to have been founded by Christian Rosenkreuz, a mythical figure who travelled through the Middle East, gathering esoteric knowledge to bring back to Europe. Their symbolic use of the pyramid reflects their belief in the ascent from the material world to higher spiritual consciousness, paralleling the structure's ancient function.[mdcxxix] The Rosicrucians' influence extends to modern symbols like the All-Seeing Eye, which ties them to the broader tradition of secret societies protecting ancient knowledge.[mdcxxx] As modern-day custodians of spiritual and mystical wisdom, the Rosicrucians and their practices align with the broader narrative of guarding the ancient secrets embedded within the pyramids themselves.[mdcxxxi]

Hermeticism is named after Hermes Trismegistus[mdcxxxii], a legendary figure from Greco-Egyptian mythology and is often associated with the mystical and esoteric traditions surrounding the pyramids. According to legend, Hermes is credited with writing the *Emerald Tablet*. This ancient text is said to reveal the secrets of alchemy, including the transformation of materials, the balance of opposites, and the union of spirit and matter.[mdcxxxiii] The *Emerald Tablet* is believed to contain profound knowledge of the universe, encompassing metaphysical principles that govern both the physical and spiritual worlds.[mdcxxxiv] Some legends suggest that this sacred text was hidden within the Great Pyramid of Giza. They may have been centres of spiritual and material transformation, housing esoteric wisdom that could unlock the mysteries of the cosmos. The *Emerald Tablet* has never been found, and its existence remains a matter of legend and speculation. While various versions and interpretations of the tablet have circulated in esoteric literature since at least the 12th century, no physical evidence of the original tablet has ever been uncovered. Despite this, many seekers, including alchemists and occultists over the centuries, have been searching for the tablet or the hidden knowledge it represents, believing it may still be hidden in Egypt, possibly within or near the Great Pyramid. The allure of the tablet continues to captivate those interested in ancient mysteries, alchemy, and spiritual transformation, driving ongoing speculation and exploration in the hopes of discovering this legendary artefact.

Who is Guarding Free Energy Wisdom?

Could advanced knowledge about harnessing free energy have been guarded throughout history and passed down through secret societies, priesthoods, or elite scientific circles? From the enigmatic priest-guardians of ancient Egypt, believed to safeguard the pyramids' energetic functions, to modern conspiracy theories suggesting that governments and powerful corporations suppress free energy technologies, the wisdom behind this concept has long been shrouded in mystery. What if priest-guardians or mystics had a dual role, spiritual and technological safeguarding?

Some believe that ancient civilisations knew how to tap into the Earth's natural energy fields or cosmic forces, a knowledge that was carefully protected to maintain balance and power. Today, the notion persists that free energy wisdom is intentionally hidden and safeguarded by those who stand to lose the most if humanity gains access to limitless, clean power. Whether through mystical guardianship in the past or modern technological gatekeeping, the question remains: Who holds the keys to unlocking free energy, and why is it being kept from the world?

Global Collections

Beyond the monumental sites, numerous museums, institutions, and private collections worldwide serve as custodians of Egypt's ancient treasures. Beyond the monumental sites, numerous museums, institutions, and private collections worldwide serve as custodians of Egypt's ancient treasures. Many of the artefacts found in the pyramids are incredibly delicate, made from materials such as gold, wood, papyrus, and fabrics, which can degrade quickly when exposed to fluctuating temperatures and humidity. The most effective way to preserve these artefacts is by storing them in climate-controlled environments where temperature, humidity, and light levels are carefully regulated. Museums and research facilities worldwide often use specialised display cases for this purpose.

The movement of these artefacts began during the height of colonialism and Egypt's 19th and early 20th-century archaeological discoveries. These global stewards preserve and display an array of artefacts that provide invaluable insights into the ancient Egyptians' daily lives, spiritual beliefs, and technological achievements. The global collections present a unique opportunity for cross-disciplinary research, comparative studies, and fresh archaeological insights. From iconic museums like the British Museum in London and the Louvre in Paris to lesser-known institutions, these collections bring Egypt's past to life, making it accessible to people worldwide.

The wide dispersal of Egyptian artefacts has raised questions about ownership, preservation, and the role of modern custodians in safeguarding the world's shared heritage. There is an ongoing dialogue about their responsibilities in preserving and, perhaps, returning these priceless objects to their homeland. For example, in the 19th and early 20th centuries, European explorers and archaeologists often took artefacts back to their home countries. Some of these artefacts ended up in museums, and many are now subjects of repatriation debates (such as the Rosetta Stone and items in the British Museum).

As custodians of some of the world's most valuable treasures, museums provide an irreplaceable link to the past. Their collections enable cross-disciplinary research, comparative studies, and the opportunity to appreciate the shared cultural heritage that belongs to all humanity. Many Egyptian artefacts are also held in private collections, often acquired before modern regulations on archaeological exports were established. While these collections are not always accessible, they represent an untapped resource for research, especially in cases where significant items have been meticulously preserved.

Does the Vatican have a Secret Pyramid Collection?

Persistent rumours and conspiracy theories suggest the Vatican houses a secret collection of ancient pyramid artefacts hidden deep within its vast archives. *The Secret Archives of the Vatican* by D. Brown delves into the mysterious and often controversial topic of the Vatican's extensive collection of confidential documents, manuscripts, and artefacts. The book delves into the history, significance, and speculated contents of the Vatican Secret Archives, one of the world's most closely guarded repositories. He provides a detailed account of how the archives have been accumulated over centuries, housing everything from papal decrees and ancient manuscripts to controversial artefacts with potential ties to early Christianity and pre-Christian civilisations. He examines the archives' secrecy, mainly how the Vatican has historically restricted access to scholars, fueling speculation and conspiracy theories. He also explores how the archives may contain information about the Catholic Church's role in world history, including its involvement in politics, wars, and scientific advancements.[mdcxxxv]

According to some theories, the artefacts—some believed to hold significant historical and esoteric knowledge—were obtained during early archaeological expeditions and have remained concealed to protect their potentially world-altering implications.[mdcxxxvi] These artefacts include relics from ancient Egyptian pyramids, such as scrolls, tools, and mystical objects that could provide insight into the pyramids' true purposes, including advanced energy systems or spiritual technologies.[mdcxxxvii] The Vatican, renowned for its secrecy and extensive collection of rare manuscripts and religious artefacts, is believed by some to be safeguarding these treasures to prevent humanity from accessing knowledge about free energy, ancient technologies, or extraterrestrial connections, thereby keeping such revelations out of the public domain for reasons of control or religious power.[mdcxxxviii]

This sparked a thought: Could an underground tunnel exist between the Vatican and the Pyramids in Egypt? An underground tunnel directly between the two points would be approximately 2,300 kilometres long. Sounds implausible? The Great Wall is nearly ten times longer than the proposed tunnel between Egypt and the Vatican. While no scientific evidence supports ley lines or their connection to specific energy flows, some believe St. Peter's Basilica in Vatican City is situated on such a line, which could have powered transport between the two locations. This belief is part of a larger theory that many religious sites—such as Stonehenge, the Pyramids of Giza, and the Vatican—are connected by ley lines. The connections between locations are often seen as coincidental rather than evidence of deliberate alignment along energy lines. Mainstream historians propose that the Vatican was built on an ancient Roman cemetery site, where St. Peter is believed to have been buried. The site's selection was based on religious and historical significance rather than any known geomagnetic or energetic alignment. Digging deeper, such a tunnel would have to cross the Mediterranean Sea, with depths exceeding 5,000 meters (16,404 feet). The immense water pressure and varying geological conditions, including fault lines and seismic activity, present significant engineering challenges that surpass modern capabilities. Existing tunnels, like the Channel Tunnel, are much shorter and built in shallower, geologically stable environments. This theory is, therefore, improbable.

Some films and documentaries explore conspiracy theories involving the Vatican and secret artefacts, although none specifically focus on pyramid artefacts. The themes of hidden knowledge, mysterious archives, and secret Vatican treasures are prominent in works such as *The Da Vinci Code* (2006), which revolves around Vatican secrets and religious conspiracies. In the film, a secretive group within the Vatican tries to suppress knowledge that could shake the foundations of Christianity. Another example is *The Vatican Tapes* (2015), a supernatural thriller that involves dark secrets within the Vatican archives, though its focus is more on possession and paranormal activity. Nevertheless, it taps into the idea that the Vatican may guard powerful and dangerous knowledge.

Digital Records

In the 21st century, digital records have revolutionised archaeology, offering unprecedented ways to preserve, study, and share ancient sites and artefacts. 3D scanning and virtual reality (VR) technologies allow archaeologists to create precise digital replicas of artefacts and sites. This is especially important for fragile sites that may degrade over time or are vulnerable to natural disasters, climate change, or conflict.[mdcxxxix] Digital preservation ensures that these cultural treasures are not lost and can be studied and shared worldwide.[mdcxl]

Additionally, augmented reality (AR) in museums allows the public to engage with history in new and interactive ways, seeing ancient structures and artefacts as they may have originally appeared.[mdcxli] Virtual museums and interactive experiences will engage a broader audience, making archaeology not just a scholarly pursuit but a field of study that captivates the general public.[mdcxlii]

But it's not just about making history interactive, but about global collaboration. With the rise of digital platforms and open-access databases, there is likely to be increased international cooperation among researchers.[mdcxliii] Researchers from all over the world can now collaborate more effectively than ever. Once siloed in individual institutions, archaeological data is becoming increasingly accessible, leading to interdisciplinary studies that can combine archaeology, geology, climate science, and even artificial intelligence. These advances will likely revolutionise how we interpret history globally, enabling discoveries and reinterpretations of ancient civilisations.[mdcxliv]

Famous Archaeologists

Several archaeologists have made significant contributions to the study of Egypt's pyramids, unravelling the mysteries of these ancient wonders. Why do people choose an archaeology career? Often, they are driven by a passion for history, discovery, and adventure. Many are fascinated by ancient civilisations and feel a deep responsibility for preserving cultural heritage. The excitement of uncovering lost artefacts and solving historical mysteries appeals to those with curiosity and a love of intellectual challenge. Archaeologists also enjoy travelling, exploring remote locations, and contributing to scientific knowledge. Ultimately, they are motivated by a desire to piece together the puzzle of human history and leave a legacy for future generations.

Zahi Hawass (1947–) is perhaps the most famous modern Egyptian archaeologist associated with the pyramids. He has conducted numerous excavations at Giza, Saqqara, and other pyramid sites, led the exploration of the Great Pyramid of Giza and the Sphinx, and advocated for the return of looted Egyptian artefacts worldwide.[mdcxlv]

While Howard Carter (1874–1939) is best known for discovering Tutankhamun's tomb, his work in Egypt extends beyond the Valley of the Kings. His meticulous excavation techniques and detailed documentation laid a foundation for future archaeological work in Egypt, which includes studies of pyramids and their associated burial sites.[mdcxlvi] Another pioneering figure, Sir Flinders Petrie (1853–1942), helped develop scientific excavation methods and performed key work at Giza, establishing dating systems for Egyptian history.[mdcxlvii] Mark Lehner (1950–), a prominent archaeologist, has mapped the Giza Plateau extensively and deepened our understanding of the pyramids' construction and the workers' village.[mdcxlviii] Additionally, George Andrew Reisner (1867–1942) and Selim Hassan (1886–1961) conducted groundbreaking excavations at Giza, uncovering tombs and monuments that provided insight into the lives of those who built and maintained the pyramids.[mdcxlix] These archaeologists have played pivotal roles in revealing the secrets of Egypt's most iconic structures.

Disconnect between Scientists and Archeologists

There seems to be a disconnect between archaeologists and scientists, mainly engineers and energy researchers. This may limit the exploration of speculative theories, such as energy harnessing in ancient structures. Archaeologists focus on the cultural, historical, and material aspects of sites like the pyramids, often emphasising how these monuments fit into the religious, political, and social contexts of ancient civilisations. On the other hand, energy theories fall more under the domain of engineers and physicists who study how materials, geometry, and natural forces could be manipulated for energy-related purposes. Without collaboration between these disciplines, the potential intersection of archaeology and energy theory can be overlooked.

Archaeologists typically make money through academic positions, grants, research projects, and partnerships with museums or cultural organisations. Their agenda often focuses on preservation and education, with a strong emphasis on historical accuracy.

Scientists, especially those in physics or engineering, might be more driven by discovery and innovation. They might explore how ancient technologies could inspire modern advancements. Their financial incentives might come from research grants, patents, and partnerships with energy industries or technology firms.

This divergence of interest could explain why discussions about energy in ancient structures are sometimes sidelined in mainstream archaeology. Studying energy from an archaeological, scientific or spiritual perspective presents a fascinating opportunity to bridge the gap between seemingly disconnected worlds. An interdisciplinary approach combining rigorous scientific methods with spiritual experiential insights could lead to new insights. For example, studies could measure how meditating or practising rituals within these ancient sites affect human physiology, such as brainwave activity or heart coherence, alongside tracking changes in electromagnetic fields. As archaeology continues to uncover the sophisticated engineering of ancient civilisations, it also opens doors to exploring how these cultures may have blended scientific understanding with spiritual wisdom to interact with physical and subtle energy.

Key Books and Academic Works

Academic studies have explored the global phenomenon of pyramid-building in various cultures. Here are a couple of books worth highlighting:

In *Temples, Tombs, and Hieroglyphs: A Popular History of Ancient Egypt* (1997), Barbara Watterson presents an engaging and accessible overview of ancient Egyptian civilisation, making it an invaluable resource for general readers seeking to understand this fascinating culture. The book artfully weaves together narratives of the grand temples, elaborate tombs, and intricate hieroglyphs that define ancient Egypt, providing insights into the religious, social, and political structures of the time. Watterson's clear writing style and well-organised content allow readers to appreciate the complexities of ancient Egyptian society while introducing key archaeological findings and historical contexts. This work serves as a solid introductory text, appealing to both novices and those looking to deepen their understanding of one of history's most intriguing civilisations.[mdcl]

Mark Lehner's work on the Pyramids of Giza, particularly in his book *The Complete Pyramids: Solving the Ancient Mysteries* (1997), offers a comprehensive analysis of the construction techniques, religious symbolism, and societal significance of these Egyptian monuments. His findings reveal not only the precision and advanced engineering of the Egyptians but also the cultural importance of pyramid construction in affirming royal power.[mdcli]

Similarly, Michael Coe's studies on the Mayan civilisation, especially in his book The Maya (1966), with subsequent editions, delve into the ceremonial and astronomical functions of pyramids in Mesoamerica. He emphasises that the pyramids in places like Teotihuacan and Chichen Itza were not merely architectural feats but central to the Maya's spiritual and cosmological understanding.[mdclii]

While more speculative than traditional works like those of Mark Lehner or Michael Coe, *Fingerprints of the Gods (1995) by Graham Hancock* has gained mainstream recognition due to its compelling narrative and widespread influence. In this groundbreaking book, he challenges conventional archaeological timelines by proposing the existence of an advanced, prehistoric civilisation that predates the known builders of the Egyptian pyramids. He argues that the knowledge of this lost civilisation influenced various ancient cultures across the globe, including those that constructed pyramids in Egypt, Mesoamerica, and elsewhere. His theory suggests that these ancient builders shared common knowledge of astronomy, mathematics, and architecture, pointing to a forgotten chapter in human history. Although his ideas are controversial and often dismissed by mainstream academia, *Fingerprints of the Gods* has captivated readers worldwide and sparked renewed interest in alternative interpretations of ancient civilisations and their technological capabilities.

In *The Oxford History of Ancient Egypt* (2000), Ian Shaw presents a comprehensive and authoritative overview of ancient Egyptian civilisation, making it a standard reference in Egyptology. Published by Oxford University Press, a leading academic publisher known for its rigorous scholarly standards, this book encapsulates the extensive history of Egypt from prehistoric times through the Greco-Roman period. Shaw, a noted Egyptologist, draws upon a wealth of archaeological evidence and historical research to provide insights into ancient Egypt's cultural, political, and social dynamics. His meticulous attention to detail and scholarly rigour make this work an essential resource for academics and general readers interested in understanding the complexities of one of the world's most enduring civilisations. The book not only enriches our knowledge of Egypt's historical narrative but also serves as a critical tool for exploring the broader implications of its legacy on subsequent cultures and societies.[mdcliii]

In *The Complete Gods and Goddesses of Ancient Egypt* (2003), Richard H. Wilkinson extensively explores the religious beliefs and practices that defined ancient Egyptian culture. As an esteemed scholar in Egyptology, his work is well-cited and respected within academic circles, making this book a crucial resource for understanding the complexities of Egyptian mythology and its influence on daily life. The text delves into the pantheon of deities, their roles in society, and how these beliefs shaped the spiritual landscape of ancient Egypt. Through detailed analysis and vivid illustrations, he provides a comprehensive overview highlighting the integral connection between religion and the monumental achievements of this remarkable civilisation. This work enriches our understanding of ancient beliefs and illuminates their lasting impact on subsequent cultures and religious practices.[mdcliv]

The Pyramids: The Mystery, Culture, and Science of Egypt's Great Monuments (2003) by Zahi Hawass offers a comprehensive and authoritative exploration of the pyramids from one of Egypt's most renowned archaeologists. In this book, he provides deep insights into the construction techniques, cultural significance, and religious symbolism that defined these monumental structures. His work reinforces the traditional view that the pyramids served as tombs for Egypt's divine kings, examining their broader role in affirming royal power and connecting with the gods. He blends rigorous scientific research with an understanding of the mystical allure of the pyramids, addressing both practical engineering achievements and more speculative ideas about their spiritual or cosmic significance. His extensive fieldwork at Giza and other pyramid sites lends the book a rare authenticity, making it an essential reference for understanding the enduring mystery and cultural importance of Egypt's pyramids.

These works are examples and are considered among the key contributions. Collectively, they suggest that pyramid-building may reflect a universal human tendency to connect with the cosmos and assert cultural identity through monumental structures. I believe there is room for more books that think outside the box.

Don't Stop Caring and Guard the Truth

Ray Bradbury's Fahrenheit 451, first published as a short story in 1951 and later expanded into a full novel in 1953, is not merely a cautionary tale about censorship. It offers a prophetic analysis of a society that willingly abandons depth, reflection, and memory in favour of comfort, speed, and illusion.[mdclv]

Set in a future where firemen burn books rather than save them, the narrative explores the deliberate eradication of knowledge under the guise of maintaining social harmony. The title refers to the temperature at which book paper ignites, symbolising the threshold beyond which critical thought is incinerated. His dystopia is not governed by overt totalitarianism, but by distraction and apathy. The masses are lulled by wall-sized televisions, numbed by mindless entertainment, and afraid of meaningful conversation. The culture of Fahrenheit 451 doesn't merely permit censorship. It demands it, preferring a flattened emotional landscape over the complexities of real human experience.

At the centre of this controlled inferno is Guy Montag, a fireman who awakens to the emptiness of his role and the spiritual desert around him. His encounter with Clarisse, a perceptive young woman who asks questions rather than consumes answers, acts as the catalyst for his transformation. Guy's eventual rebellion is not violent but internal: he begins to read, to think, and ultimately to remember.

In Ray Bradbury's universe, remembering is a form of rebellion. Those who safeguard knowledge, like Faber, the reclusive academic, or the underground network of "book people" who memorise entire texts, are seen not as radicals but as humanity's greatest safeguard against forgetfulness.

What makes Fahrenheit 451 particularly chilling is its relevance today. While books may not be burned on a large scale, they are going digital and increasingly banned, buried by algorithms, or culturally forgotten. A world flooded with content but starving for meaning is exactly the landscape he predicted. His concern was not just about government oppression but about a public that stops caring about the truth. The result is a civilisation that consumes without reflecting, talks without thinking, and listens without hearing. In this way, his fire still burns, smouldering beneath our screens, fragmented attention spans, and growing unease with complexity.

Conclusions

For scholars, researchers, and history enthusiasts, the institutions and books mentioned provide invaluable resources for studying Egypt's past, offering access to items that might not be easily available even within Egypt. In contemporary times, pyramid guardians have shifted from religious caretakers to Egyptologists, archaeologists, and local stewards. These individuals, like the ancient priests, play a vital role in preserving the legacy of the pyramids. From the implementation of security measures to extensive restoration efforts, the guardianship of these monuments remains essential for their continued survival. As we recognise the importance of preservation, the next chapter will summarise our journey, reflecting on whether we have only begun to uncover the pyramids' mysteries.

Let this be a call to action: read more, question more, preserve more. Print what matters. Save what counts. And above all, guard the fire of human curiosity because when memory disappears, mystery becomes impossible to rediscover.

Powered by Pyramids: A Book of Theories

Chapter 27 The Pulse Beneath the Stones: Final Thoughts

As we reach the final pages of this journey, a singular question echoes louder than ever: Have we merely skimmed the surface of the pyramids' mysteries, or are we on the verge of revelations that could fundamentally reshape our understanding of the past—and our future? The answer may lie not in the stones themselves but in our willingness to question everything we thought we knew.

Throughout this book, we have ventured far beyond the bounds of conventional archaeology and orthodox history. We have examined the pyramids not as inert tombs of forgotten kings, but as dynamic monuments to knowledge, energy, and transformation. These structures speak to a higher intelligence—whether earthly or extraterrestrial, physical or metaphysical—that encoded the geometry of the universe into stone. Their ancient purpose may yet guide us toward new ways of thinking about energy, architecture, consciousness, and our place within a living cosmos.

The pyramids, rising from the sands of Egypt, the jungles of Mesoamerica, and the forgotten plains of distant lands, have always held a deeper symbolic and functional meaning. Their alignment with celestial bodies, their acoustic and geometric resonance, and their unyielding mathematical precision suggest that they were constructed not solely for burial but for activation. They are nodes in an ancient grid—a planetary architecture that may have once been used to harmonise human beings with Earth's natural frequencies.

In the pages that preceded, we explored a range of provocative theories. Some were rooted in emerging physics, some drawn from comparative mythology, and others boldly speculative. But together they converge on a singular, tantalising idea: that the pyramids were not simply built to withstand the test of time but to transmit through it. Like spiritual beacons encoded with scientific memory, they may still be resonating with truths too vast for modern science to yet measure.

Central Themes and Key Takeaways
1. Pyramids as Energy Conduits
   Their precise global alignment with geomagnetic nodes, ley lines, and solar/lunar cycles suggests pyramids were designed to interact with Earth's energy field. Rather than passive structures,

they may have functioned as tuning forks—vibrational instruments aligning us with the subtle currents of Earth's consciousness.

2. Interaction with Electromagnetic Fields
The electromagnetic properties of materials like granite, limestone, and quartz weren't arbitrary. These choices imply advanced knowledge of conductivity, piezoelectricity, and the movement of charge through form. Such knowledge suggests not superstition—but engineering.

3. The Role of Natural Elements
Quartz, with its piezoelectric amplification, underground water flows creating negative ions, and magnetic anomalies beneath specific pyramid locations—all point to pyramids functioning like natural reactors. Energy wasn't just generated—it was orchestrated.

4. Resonance with Natural Frequencies
Studies into the Schumann resonance and how it intersects with pyramid geometry open questions about whether these structures enhance meditative or altered states. Were they consciousness amplifiers? Gateways to the inner cosmos? Perhaps both.

5. Bridging the Spiritual and Physical Worlds
The pyramid's perfect symmetry mirrors both the natural order and divine blueprint. Whether as temples for initiation or stations for energetic alignment, their sacredness is encoded in every angle, ratio, and orientation. They are the meeting point between cosmos and soil.

6. A Platform for Future Exploration and Innovation

7. Energy Generation and Sustainability
If ancient technologies truly harnessed Earth's natural energies, what prevents us from doing the same? Instead of merely extracting energy, could we resonate with it? The geometry and principles behind pyramids could inform next-generation clean energy systems built on harmony, not depletion.

8. Architecture and Engineering
The engineering feats of the pyramids—resisting earthquakes, aligning to cardinal points, remaining intact after millennia—are not just historical marvels. They're design principles. Studying these could revolutionise modern construction, creating self-healing, energy-efficient buildings.

9. Spiritual Exploration and Well-being
From vibrational therapies to energy medicine, the pyramids invite us to rediscover how form impacts consciousness. As frequency-based healing gains traction, the pyramid may hold the

secret to tuning the human body like an instrument—restoring harmony through geometry, light, and sound.

Final Thoughts: The Pyramid's Enduring Legacy

The pyramids are not merely monuments of the past. They are broadcasts from a previous epoch—transmitting across time. Their form encodes function. Their presence is intentional. Whether built by ancient Egyptians, guided by higher intelligences, or inherited from pre-diluvian cultures, one truth remains: the builders knew something we have forgotten. And the Egyptians, in preserving and re-ensouling these structures, gave us one of the most enduring symbolic systems in human history. But the pyramid is not a relic. It is a reawakening. It is a mirror angled toward the stars and a lens focused on the Earth's core. It is both memory and prophecy.

The Final Cypher

The pyramid does not explain—it invites. It does not declare—it transmits. It waits for the moment we stop interpreting it as a corpse of stone and start experiencing it as a living symbol. In its silence, it calls for remembrance—not of historical timelines, but of our own encoded potential.

History may not be linear. It may be a toroidal memory field—a loop we can only access when the geometry of our mind matches the geometry of these monuments.

The Journey Continues With You

This is not a conclusion. It is a handover. You have crossed the threshold from passive observer to active participant. The question is no longer "Is it true?" but "What if it is?" What if we redesign the world based on resonance, not resistance? What if the pyramid was never a tomb—but a tuning device? What if its purpose was not death—but ascension?

The ancients didn't just build—they encoded.
Encoded knowledge.
Encoded energy.
Encoded memory.
Now it's your turn to decode. Pick up the frequency. Follow the signal.
Rebuild not in concrete, but in consciousness.
The pyramid is not asleep.
You are the capstone.
Not just the final piece, but the conscious peak that completes the circuit between Earth and sky. You are the architect of resonance, called to

stabilise chaos with geometry, to encode memory into form, and to reclaim what was once buried under sand, time, and silence. As the capstone, you are not merely a witness to the pyramid—you are its awakening.

End Notes

[i] Flinders Petrie, *The Pyramids and Temples of Gizeh* (London: Field & Tuer, 1883).
[ii] Nikola Tesla, *The Problem of Increasing Human Energy* (The Century Magazine, 1900).
[iii] *Indiana Jones and the Kingdom of the Crystal Skull.* Directed by Steven Spielberg, performances by Harrison Ford, Cate Blanchett, and Shia LaBeouf, Paramount Pictures, 2008.
[iv] Cyrus A. Parsa, *AI, Trump, China & The Weaponization of Robotics with 5G* (The AI Organization, 2019). Also see: The AI Organization official website – https://www.theaiorganization.com/
[v] Campbell, J. *The Hero with a Thousand Faces.* Princeton: Princeton University Press, 1949.
[vi] Campbell, J. *The Hero with a Thousand Faces.* Princeton: Princeton University Press, 1949.
[vii] Campbell, J. *The Hero with a Thousand Faces.* Princeton: Princeton University Press, 1949.
[viii] Campbell, J. *The Hero with a Thousand Faces.* Princeton: Princeton University Press, 1949.
[ix] Campbell, J. *The Hero with a Thousand Faces.* Princeton: Princeton University Press, 1949.
[x] Mark Twain, *The Innocents Abroad*, 1869.
[xi] James P. Allen, *The Ancient Egyptian Pyramid Texts* (Atlanta: Society of Biblical Literature, 2005), 24-30.
[xii] Robert Graves, *The Greek Myths* (London: Penguin Books, 1990), 145-150.
[xiii] Pliny the Elder, *Natural History*, trans. H. Rackham (London: Harvard University Press, 1938), Book 36, Chapter 17.
[xiv] Al-Maqrizi, *Khitat*, translated by Ayman Fuad Sayyid, ed. B.J. Collins (Cairo: Institut Français d'Archéologie Orientale, 1996), 102-105.
[xv] Sir John Mandeville, *The Travels of Sir John Mandeville* (London: Penguin Classics, 2005), 79-81.
[xvi] Baines, J., & Malek, J. (2000). *Cultural Atlas of Ancient Egypt.* Facts on File, p. 156.
[xvii] Calkins, R. G. (1983). *Illuminated Books of the Middle Ages.* Cornell University Press, p. 44.
[xviii] Tsien, T.-H. (1985). *Paper and Printing.* In *Science and Civilisation in China*, Volume 5, Part 1, Cambridge University Press, p. 134.
[xix] Parkes, M. B. (1991). *Scribes, Scripts, and Readers: Studies in the Communication, Presentation, and Dissemination of Medieval Texts.* Hambledon Press, p. 61.
[xx] Eisenstein, Elizabeth L. *The Printing Revolution in Early Modern Europe.* Cambridge University Press, 1983.
[xxi] Peter Frankopan, *The Silk Roads: A New History of the World* (London: Bloomsbury Publishing, 2015), 176-179.
[xxii] Leo Africanus, *Description of Africa*, translated by John Pory (London: Hakluyt Society, 1896), 120-125.
[xxiii] Athanasius Kircher, *Oedipus Aegyptiacus*, trans. Daniel Stolzenberg (Chicago: University of Chicago Press, 2013), 56-60.
[xxiv] Miriam Lichtheim, *Ancient Egyptian Literature*, Volume I: *The Old Kingdom* (Berkeley: University of California Press, 2006), 12-15.
[xxv] Athanasius Kircher, *Oedipus Aegyptiacus*, 70.
[xxvi] Michael J. Neufeld, *The Pyramids: Mystery and Engineering Marvels of the Ancient World* (London: Historical Perspectives Press, 2008), 45-47.
[xxvii] Napoleon Bonaparte, *Description de l'Égypte* (Paris: Imprimerie Impériale, 1829).
[xxviii] Napoleon Bonaparte: 'From the heights of these pyramids, forty centuries look down on us.' The Socratic Method. www.socratic-method.com/quote-meanings/napoleon-bonaparte-from-the-heights-of-these-pyramids-forty-centuries-look-down-on-us.
[xxix] Edward W. Said, *Orientalism* (New York: Pantheon Books, 1978), 54.
[xxx] Judith F. Godwin, *19th-Century Media and the Mystique of the Pyramids* (Oxford: Oxford University Press, 1999), 78.
[xxxi] Karl Richard Lepsius, *Denkmäler aus Ägypten und Äthiopien* (Berlin: Nicolaische Buchhandlung, 1849).
[xxxii] W.M. Flinders Petrie, *The Pyramids and Temples of Gizeh* (London: Field & Tuer, 1883), 15.
[xxxiii] Andrew M. Watson, *Explorers of Ancient Egypt: The Beginnings of Egyptology* (Cambridge: Cambridge University Press, 2006), 134-136.
[xxxiv] H. Rider Haggard, *She* (London: Longmans, Green, and Co., 1887).
[xxxv] Theophile Gautier, *The Romance of a Mummy* (Paris: Michel Lévy Frères, 1858).
[xxxvi] Ignatius Donnelly, *Atlantis: The Antediluvian World* (New York: Harper & Brothers, 1882), 65-68.
[xxxvii] Musser, C. (1994). *The Emergence of Cinema: The American Screen to 1907.* University of California Press, p. 17.

[xxxviii] Barnes, J. (1990). *The Beginnings of the Cinema in England, 1894-1901*. University of Exeter Press, p. 35.
[xxxix] Georges Méliès, *Cleopatra's Tomb* (1899), Star Film Company.
[xl] Hall, S. "Cultural Representation of Pyramids in Popular Media." *Journal of Film and Media Studies*, vol. 12, no. 2, 2010, pp. 45-67.
[xli] Agatha Christie, *Death on the Nile* (London: Collins Crime Club, 1937)
[xlii] *The Mummy*. Directed by Karl Freund, performances by Boris Karloff, Zita Johann, and David Manners, Universal Pictures, 1932.
[xliii] Hall, S. "Cultural Representation of Pyramids in Popular Media." *Journal of Film and Media Studies*, vol. 12, no. 2, 2010, pp. 45-67.
[xliv] *Stargate*. Directed by Roland Emmerich, performances by Kurt Russell, James Spader, and Jaye Davidson, Metro-Goldwyn-Mayer, 1994.
[xlv] *Ancient Aliens*. Created by Kevin Burns, History Channel, 2010–present.
[xlvi] Monica S. Cyrino "Screening Antiquity: Hollywood and the Ancient World"
[xlvii] Morrison, L. *Pyramid Power: An Esoteric Perspective*. Occult Review, 1998.
[xlviii] Barkun, M. (2016). *A Culture of Conspiracy: Apocalyptic Visions in Contemporary America*. University of California Press.
[xlix] Pasulka, D. W. (2019). *American Cosmic: UFOs, Religion, Technology*. Oxford University Press.
[l] Harland-Jacobs, J. L. (2007). *Builders of Empire: Freemasonry and British Imperialism, 1717-1927*. University of North Carolina Press.
[li] Stuart Hall, *Representation: Cultural Representations and Signifying Practices* (London: Sage Publications, 1997), 45.
[lii] Said, E. W. (1978). *Orientalism*. Pantheon Books, p. 56.
[liii] McCants, C. (1995). *Handel's Operas, 1726-1741*. Boydell Press, p. 103.
[liv] Parker, R. (1994). *The Oxford Illustrated History of Opera*. Oxford University Press, p. 142.
[lv] Jarman, D. (2009). *Symbolism in Music: The Evolution of Mystical Imagery*. Routledge, p. 89.
[lvi] Sun Ra, *Jazz in Silhouette*, El Saturn Records, 1959.
[lvii] George A. Reisch, *Pink Floyd and Philosophy: Careful with That Axiom, Eugene!* (Open Court, 2007).
[lviii] Mark Blake, *Comfortably Numb: The Inside Story of Pink Floyd* (Da Capo Press, 2008).
[lix] Nicholas Schaffner, *Saucerful of Secrets: The Pink Floyd Odyssey* (Delta, 1992).
[lx] Storm Thorgerson, *Mind Over Matter: The Images of Pink Floyd* (Sanctuary, 1997).
[lxi] John Harris, *The Dark Side of the Moon: The Making of the Pink Floyd Masterpiece* (Da Capo Press, 2006).
[lxii] Glenn Povey, *Echoes: The Complete History of Pink Floyd* (Mind Head Publishing, 2007).
[lxiii] Andy Mabbett, *Pink Floyd: The Music and the Mystery* (Omnibus Press, 2010).
[lxiv] Mike Featherstone, *Consumer Culture and Postmodernism* (Sage, 1991).
[lxv] Steve Knopper, *MJ: The Genius of Michael Jackson* (Scribner, 2015).
[lxvi] David Marsh, *Michael Jackson: The Magic, The Madness, The Whole Story* (Pan Macmillan, 2004).
[lxvii] Armond White, *Michael Jackson: Icon* (Omnibus Press, 2009).
[lxviii] Joseph Vogel, *Man in the Music: The Creative Life and Work of Michael Jackson* (Sterling, 2019).
[lxix] J. Randy Taraborrelli, *Michael Jackson: The Magic and the Madness* (Headline Book Publishing, 2003).
[lxx] Tricia Rose, *Black Noise: Rap Music and Black Culture in Contemporary America* (Wesleyan University Press, 1994).
[lxxi] Murray Forman, *The 'Hood Comes First: Race, Space, and Place in Rap and Hip-Hop* (Wesleyan University Press, 2002).
[lxxii] Michael Eric Dyson, *Holler If You Hear Me: Searching for Tupac Shakur* (Basic Civitas Books, 2001).
[lxxiii] Zack O'Malley Greenburg, *Empire State of Mind: How Jay-Z Went from Street Corner to Corner Office* (Penguin, 2011).
[lxxiv] Jeffrey Ogbar, *Hip-Hop Revolution: The Culture and Politics of Rap* (University Press of Kansas, 2007).
[lxxv] J. Griffith Rollefson, *Flip the Script: European Hip Hop and the Politics of Postcoloniality* (University of Chicago Press, 2017).
[lxxvi] Paul Gilroy, *The Black Atlantic: Modernity and Double Consciousness* (Harvard University Press, 1993).
[lxxvii] Murray Forman, *The 'Hood Comes First: Race, Space, and Place in Rap and Hip-Hop* (Wesleyan University Press, 2002).
[lxxviii] Mark Beaumont, *Kanye West: God & Monster* (Constable, 2015).
[lxxix] Christopher R. Weingarten, "The Meaning of Kanye West's Power Video," *Rolling Stone*, 2010.
[lxxx] Michael Eric Dyson, *Know What I Mean?: Reflections on Hip-Hop* (Basic Civitas, 2007).

[lxxxi] Zack O'Malley Greenburg, *Empire State of Mind: How Jay-Z Went from Street Corner to Corner Office* (Penguin, 2011).
[lxxxii] J. Griffith Rollefson, *Flip the Script: European Hip Hop and the Politics of Postcoloniality* (University of Chicago Press, 2017).
[lxxxiii] Kevin Fallon, "Beyoncé's Historic 'Homecoming' at Coachella Was Much More Than a Performance," *The Daily Beast*, 2018.
[lxxxiv] Armond White, *Beyoncé: Icon* (Omnibus Press, 2009).
[lxxxv] E. Frances White, *Dark Continent of Our Bodies: Black Feminism and the Politics of Respectability* (Temple University Press, 2001).
[lxxxvi] Rachel Kaadzi Ghansah, "The Radical Vision of Beyoncé's 'Black Is King'," *Vulture*, 2020.
[lxxxvii] Paul Gilroy, *The Black Atlantic: Modernity and Double Consciousness* (Harvard University Press, 1993).
[lxxxviii] Adrian C. North & David J. Hargreaves, *The Social and Applied Psychology of Music* (Oxford University Press, 2008).
[lxxxix] "Music, Identity, and Social Control," Peter J. Martin, *Oxford Academic*
[xc] Ulrik Volgsten, "Music in Business Environments," in *Music and Manipulation* (2005).
[xci] Steven Brown & Ulrik Volgsten, *Music and Manipulation: On the Social Uses and Social Control of Music* (Berghahn Books, 2005).
[xcii] Rick Altman, *Film/Genre* (British Film Institute, 1999).
[xciii] Norman Holland, *The Dynamics of Literary Response* (Columbia University Press, 1968).
[xciv] Daniel J. Levitin, *This Is Your Brain on Music: The Science of a Human Obsession* (Dutton, 2006).
[xcv] Daniel J. Levitin, *This Is Your Brain on Music: The Science of a Human Obsession* (Dutton, 2006).
[xcvi] *Assassin's Creed Origins*. Developed by Ubisoft Montreal, Ubisoft, 2017.
[xcvii] Kostof, S. (1995). *A History of Architecture: Settings and Rituals*. Oxford University Press.
[xcviii] Pei, I. M. (1989). The Louvre Pyramid: Merging Modernism with History. Architectural Digest, 45(7), 36-42.
[xcix] Johnson, R. (1995). The Luxor: A Modern Pyramid of Mystery and Grandeur. Las Vegas Architectural Review, 13(2), 55-63.
[c] Smith, P. (1994). Inspired by the Ancients: The Design and Legacy of the Luxor Hotel in Las Vegas. Journal of Modern Architecture, 22(4), 102-108.
[ci] Green, S. (2010). The Luxor Beam: Lighting Up Las Vegas. Light and Design, 19(3), 47-51.
[cii] Al Nuaimi, F. (2016). Raffles Dubai: Blending Modern Luxury with Ancient Symbols. Middle Eastern Architecture and Design, 28(6), 88-95.
[ciii] Williams, A. (2019). The Transamerica Pyramid: An Icon of Modernist Architecture. Architectural Digest, 87(4), 112-119.
[civ] Johnson, P. (2016). Modern Architecture in Central Asia: The Palace of Peace and Reconciliation. Journal of Contemporary Architecture, 22(2), 55-67.
[cv] Foster, N. (2007). Designing Peace: The Palace of Peace and Reconciliation. The Architecture Review, 91(3), 89-94.
[cvi] Basha, L. (2018). The Pyramid of Tirana: A Modernist Landmark in Eastern Europe. Albanian Architectural Heritage Review, 34(6), 45-53.
[cvii] Lim, C. (2020). Sunway Pyramid: A Blend of Modern Retail and Ancient Imagery. Malaysian Architectural Digest, 45(9), 63-68.
[cviii] Marshall, S. (2021). The Power of Symbolism in Luxury Jewellery: Pyramid-Inspired Designs through the Ages. Journal of Luxury Fashion, 38(5), 102-110.
[cix] Becker, L. (2019). Ancient Inspirations in Modern Jewellery: The Timeless Appeal of Pyramid Designs. Luxury Gems and Fashion Review, 27(3), 58-67.
[cx] Gordon, K. (2020). Cleopatra's Legacy: How Ancient Egypt Shapes Modern Jewellery Trends. Jewelers' Journal, 41(2), 22-29.
[cxi] Henderson, A. (2022). Luxury Design and History: A Blend of Ancient Egyptian Symbolism and Modern Style in Pyramid Jewellery. International Review of Fashion and Design, 45(6), 89-97.
[cxii] Maslow, A. H. (1943). A Theory of Human Motivation. Psychological Review, 50(4), 370-396. doi:10.1037/h0054346; Maslow, A. H. (1954). Motivation and Personality. Harper & Row.
[cxiii] Maslow, A. H. (1943). A Theory of Human Motivation. Psychological Review, 50(4), 370-396. doi:10.1037/h0054346; Maslow, A. H. (1954). Motivation and Personality. Harper & Row.
[cxiv] Paul Heelas, *The New Age Movement: The Celebration of the Self and the Sacralization of Modernity* (Oxford: Blackwell, 1996), 72.
[cxv] Anodea Judith, *Wheels of Life: A User's Guide to the Chakra System*, Llewellyn Publications, 1999. Harish Johari, *Chakras: Energy Centers of Transformation*, Destiny Books, 1987.
[cxvi] Judith, A. (2004). *Wheels of Life: A User's Guide to the Chakra System*. Llewellyn Publications.

[cxvii] Drunvalo Melchizedek, *The Ancient Secret of the Flower of Life*, Light Technology Publishing, 1999. Barbara Hand Clow, *The Pleiadian Agenda: A New Cosmology for the Age of Light*, Bear & Company, 1995.
[cxviii] Smith, J., "The Rise of Tattoos Among Millennials," *Journal of Cultural Trends*, vol. 12, no. 3, 2023, p. 50.
[cxix] "Tattoo Meanings: Pyramid Tattoo Meaning," *TattMag*, https://tattmag.com/pyramid-tattoo-meaning. Accessed September 6, 2024.
[cxx] Marks, John. *The Search for the "Manchurian Candidate": The CIA and Mind Control*. Times Books, 1979.
[cxxi] Key, Wilson Bryan. *Subliminal Seduction*. New York: New American Library, 1974.
[cxxii] Serge Monast, *Project Blue Beam (NASA)*, Montreal Free Press, 1994.
[cxxiii] McKechnie, Jean. *Symbols of America: The U.S. Dollar and the Masonic Influence*. Harper & Row, 1983.
[cxxiv] Barkun, Michael. *A Culture of Conspiracy: Apocalyptic Visions in Contemporary America*. University of California Press, 2003.
[cxxv] Roberts, Jeremy. *The Symbolism of the Eye of Providence: Historical and Modern Perspectives*. Greenwood Publishing, 2005.
[cxxvi] *GreatSeal.com*, https://greatseal.com/symbols/eye.html; Ethan Trex, "Symbolism and the $1 Bill," *Mental Floss*, https://www.mentalfloss.com/article/22629/symbolism-and-1-bill. Accessed September 6, 2024.
[cxxvii] Wasserman, James. *The Secrets of Masonic Washington: A Guidebook to Signs, Symbols, and Ceremonies at the Origin of America's Capital*. Destiny Books, 2008.
[cxxviii] Williams, Patrick. *Currency and Power: Symbolism in Egyptian Banknotes*. Oxford University Press, 2011.
[cxxix] Michael Barkun, *A Culture of Conspiracy: Apocalyptic Visions in Contemporary America* (Berkeley: University of California Press, 2013), 58.
[cxxx] Barkun, M. (2013). *A Culture of Conspiracy: Apocalyptic Visions in Contemporary America*. University of California Press.
[cxxxi] Bakshy, E., Messing, S., & Adamic, L. A. (2015). Exposure to ideologically diverse news and opinion on Facebook. *Science*, 348(6239), 1130-1132. https://doi.org/10.1126/science.aaa1160. Accessed September 6, 2024.
[cxxxii] Ribeiro, M. H., Ottoni, R., West, R., Almeida, V. A. F., & Meira Jr, W. (2020). Auditing radicalization pathways on YouTube. *Proceedings of the 2020 Conference on Fairness, Accountability, and Transparency*, 131-141. https://doi.org/10.1145/3351095.3372879. Accessed September 9, 2024.
[cxxxiii] Herman, E. S., & Chomsky, N. (1988). *Manufacturing Consent: The Political Economy of the Mass Media*. Pantheon Books.
[cxxxiv] Barkun, Michael. *A Culture of Conspiracy: Apocalyptic Visions in Contemporary America*. University of California Press, 2013, pp. 56-59.
[cxxxv] Herman, Edward S., and Noam Chomsky. *Manufacturing Consent: The Political Economy of the Mass Media*. Pantheon Books, 1988, pp. 1-45.
[cxxxvi] McChesney, Robert W., and John Nichols. *The Death and Life of American Journalism: The Media Revolution That Will Begin the World Again*. Nation Books, 2010, pp. 87-98.
[cxxxvii] Parenti, Michael. *Inventing Reality: The Politics of the Mass Media*. Cengage Learning, 1993, pp. 41-49.
[cxxxviii] Serge Monast, *Project Blue Beam (NASA)*, Montreal Free Press, 1994.
[cxxxix] Jason Colavito, *The Cult of Alien Gods: H.P. Lovecraft and Extraterrestrial Pop Culture*, Prometheus Books, 2005.
[cxl] Jung, C. G. (1959). *The Archetypes and the Collective Unconscious*. Princeton University Press.
[cxli] Jung, C. G. *The Archetypes and The Collective Unconscious*. (1959). Princeton University Press.
Stevens, A. *Archetype Revisited: An Updated Natural History of the Self*. (2002). Routledge.
[cxlii] Parker, E., Ito, H., & Johnson, M. (2020). A Cultural Neuroscience Approach to Archetypal Symbols and Human Behavior. *Frontiers in Psychology*, 11(2331).
[cxliii] L. Barrett and R. Kurzban, "Modularity in Cognition: Framing the Debate," *Psychological Review* 113, no. 3 (2006): 628–647.
[cxliv] M. A. Changizi, *The Vision Revolution: How the Latest Research Overturns Everything We Thought We Knew About Human Vision* (Dallas: BenBella Books, 2009).
[cxlv] Shihui Han et al., "Cultural Neuroscience: Progress and Promise," *Psychological Inquiry* 24, no. 1 (2013): 1–19
[cxlvi] "Pyramids Around the World," ArcGIS StoryMaps, https://storymaps.arcgis.com/stories/dddf8de802d44eb5b95d3c258a79817b. Accessed September 6, 2024.
[cxlvii] Hawass, Z. "The Construction and Symbolism of the Egyptian Pyramids." *Journal of Archaeological Research*, vol. 45, no. 3, 2005, pp. 213-232.

[cxlviii] Smith, J. (2023). *Ancient Civilizations and the Pyramids: A Global Perspective.* Historical Press, pp. 22-24.
[cxlix] Mark Lehner, *The Complete Pyramids: Solving the Ancient Mysteries* (London: Thames & Hudson, 1997), 32-34.
[cl] "Pyramids of Egypt: An Overview," Egypt Exploration Society, https://www.ees.ac.uk/pyramids-of-egypt. Accessed September 6, 2024.
[cli] Malek, J. "The Saqqara Pyramid Complex." *Egyptology Today*, vol. 7, 2007, pp. 87-103.
[clii] "The Step Pyramid of Djoser: The First Pyramid in Egypt," National Geographic, https://www.nationalgeographic.com/history/article/step-pyramid-djoser-egypt. Accessed September 6, 2024.
[cliii] "Djoser's Step Pyramid at Saqqara," Ancient History Encyclopedia, https://www.worldhistory.org/Djoser's_Step_Pyramid. Accessed September 6, 2024.
[cliv] O'Connor, David. *Ancient Nubia: Egypt's Rival in Africa.* University of Pennsylvania Press, 1993.
[clv] Shinnie, P.L. *The Pyramids of Nubia.* Longman Group Ltd, 1986.
[clvi] Török, László. *The Kingdom of Kush: Handbook of the Napatan-Meroitic Civilization.* Brill, 1997.
[clvii] Adams, William Y. *Nubia: Corridor to Africa.* Princeton University Press, 1977.
[clviii] UNESCO World Heritage Centre. "Archaeological Sites of the Island of Meroe," 2011.
[clix] Edwards, David N. *The Nubian Past: An Archaeology of the Sudan.* Routledge, 2004.
[clx] Kendall, Timothy. "The Nubian Pyramids: A Challenge to the Egyptian Paradigm." *Journal of Ancient Egyptian Interconnections,* 2010.
[clxi] Török, László. *Kush and the External World.* Brill, 2009.
[clxii] Shinnie, P.L. *Ancient Nubia.* Routledge, 1996.
[clxiii] Emberling, G., & Williams, B. B. (2001). *Meroe, the City of the Black Pharaohs.* Thames & Hudson, p. 78.
[clxiv] Bierbrier, M. L. (2008). *The Treasures of Ancient Nubia.* American University in Cairo Press, p. 112.
[clxv] Török, L. (1997). *The Kingdom of Kush: Handbook of the Napatan-Meroitic Civilization.* Brill, p. 362.
[clxvi] Kendall, Timothy. "Archaeological Excavations at Nuri." *Sudan & Nubia,* 2011.
[clxvii] Harriet Crawford, *Sumer and the Sumerians* (Cambridge: Cambridge University Press, 2004), 112-118.
[clxviii] Smith, J. (2023). *Unlocking the Secrets of Iraq: Ziggurats and the Pyramids.* Ancient Worlds Press, pp. 52-58.
[clxix] H. Crawford, *The Sialk Mounds: Iran's Earliest Pyramids*, 1982, p. 45
[clxx] *Ancient Myths of Iran*, T. Jafari, 1995, p. 78
[clxxi] F. W. Hinkel, *Elamite Engineering: The Water Systems of Ancient Ziggurats*, 1987, p. 123
[clxxii] *Chogha Zanbil: An Elamite Legacy*, E. Moghaddam, 2003, p. 54
[clxxiii] *Exploring Ancient Middle Eastern Ziggurats*, J. Stone, 2006, p. 89
[clxxiv] Al-Shahri, Mansoor. *Ancient Legends of Oman: The Mystical Spirits of Bat.* Muscat Publishing House, 2008.
[clxxv] Harriet Crawford, *Dilmun and Its Gulf Neighbours* (Cambridge: Cambridge University Press, 1998), 45-50.
[clxxvi] Finkelstein, J., *The Lunar Cult in Mesopotamian Religion*, Journal of Near Eastern Studies, 1965.
[clxxvii] Green, Tamara. *The City of the Moon God: Religious Traditions of Harran.* Brill, 1992.
[clxxviii] Kramer, S. N., *The Sumerians: Their History, Culture, and Character*, University of Chicago Press, 1963.
[clxxix] Bottéro, J., *Religion in Ancient Mesopotamia*, University of Chicago Press, 2001.
[clxxx] Cotterell, Maurice. *The Terracotta Warriors: The Secret Codes of the Emperor's Army.* Bear & Company, 2003.
[clxxxi] Li, Jianmin. *Imperial Mausoleums and Tombs of Ancient China.* Shanghai Scientific and Technical Publishers, 2002.
[clxxxii] Rawson, Jessica. *The Qin Terracotta Army: Treasures of Lintong.* Art Media Resources Ltd, 1999.
[clxxxiii] Loewe, Michael. *The Government of the Qin and Han Empires, 221 BCE–220 CE.* Hackett Publishing, 2006.
[clxxxiv] Victor H. Mair, *The Politics of Immortality in Ancient China* (Cambridge: Harvard University Asia Center, 1994), 78-81.
[clxxxv] Paul K. Benedict, *Chinese Constellations and Ancient Astronomy* (New York: Columbia University Press, 2000), 45-50.
[clxxxvi] Zhang Jianlin, *Ancient Chinese Architecture: Pyramids and Tombs* (Beijing: Foreign Languages Press, 2005), 123-127.
[clxxxvii] Barnes, Gina L. *The Archaeology of East Asia: The Rise of Civilization in China, Korea and Japan.* Oxbow Books, 2015.

[clxxxviii] Hanson, Victor Davis. *China's Ancient Burial Pyramids: Exploring the Sacred Sites of Xi'an.* Academic Journal of East Asian Studies, 2017.
[clxxxix] Hanson, Victor Davis. *China's Ancient Burial Pyramids: Exploring the Sacred Sites of Xi'an.* Academic Journal of East Asian Studies, 2017.
[cxc] Hanson, Victor Davis. *China's Ancient Burial Pyramids: Exploring the Sacred Sites of Xi'an.* Academic Journal of East Asian Studies, 2017.
[cxci] Miksic, John N. *Borobudur: Golden Tales of the Buddha.* Tuttle Publishing, 1990.
[cxcii] Soekmono, R. *Chandi Borobudur: A Monument of Mankind.* Unesco, 1976.
[cxciii] Michael Freeman and Claude Jacques, *Ancient Angkor* (Bangkok: River Books, 1999), 108-112.
[cxciv] John Clifford Holt, *The Buddhist Visnu: Religious Transformation, Politics, and Culture* (New York: Columbia University Press, 2004), 89-93.
[cxcv] N. Srinivasan, The Temples of South India, 1981, p. 142
[cxcvi] V. Rajaraman, Dravidian Architecture: The Chola Legacy, 1995, p. 87
[cxcvii] M. Gupta, Divine Monuments: South India's Religious Heritage, 2003, p. 54
[cxcviii] S. Ramachandran, Engineering Marvels of Ancient India, 2010, p. 65
[cxcix] S. K. Rao, Mystical Flights: Vimana in Ancient Sanskrit Texts, 1989, p. 23
[cc] Theodossopoulos, Demetris. *Ancient Greek Pyramids: New Investigations and Controversies.* Cambridge University Press, 2004.
[cci] Korres, Manolis. *The Architectural Marvels of Ancient Greece.* Hellenic Publications, 2003.
[ccii] Richardson, Lawrence. *A New Topographical Dictionary of Ancient Rome.* JHU Press, 1992.
[cciii] Coarelli, Filippo. *Rome and Environs: An Archaeological Guide.* University of California Press, 2007.
[cciv] Thor Heyerdahl, *Pyramids of Güímar: Myth and Reality* (Tenerife: Fundación Canaria, 1999), 15-20.
[ccv] Antonio Tejera Gaspar, *The Guanches: Survivors and History of a Lost Civilization* (Madrid: Ediciones Akal, 2000), 50-55.
[ccvi] Thor Heyerdahl, *Pyramids of Güímar: Myth and Reality*, 35.
[ccvii] Alexandre Debertrand, *The Mystery of the Falicon Pyramid* (Nice: Azur Publishing, 2004), 42-47.
[ccviii] Joseph Rykwert, *The Idea of a Town: The Anthropology of Urban Form in Rome, Italy, and the Ancient World* (Princeton: Princeton University Press, 1976), 98-102.
[ccix] Carlos Melo Bento, *The Azores: The Secrets of the Atlantic* (Lisbon: Vega, 2008), 112-115.
[ccx] Carlos Melo Bento, *The Azores: The Secrets of the Atlantic* (Lisbon: Vega, 2008).
[ccxi] The Baffling Șona Pyramids Near Făgăraș, *Live the World*, accessed July 2025, The Pyramids of Șona – Transylvania," *AirVuz*, accessed July 2025
[ccxii] J. Leary, The Story of Silbury Hill, 2015, p. 32
[ccxiii] M. Bowden, English Heritage: Prehistoric Monuments of Wiltshire, 2008, p. 45
[ccxiv] J. McOmish, Archaeology of Silbury Hill: Investigating the Secrets of Prehistoric Engineering, 2017, p. 61
[ccxv] D. Wainwright, Astronomy and Architecture in Ancient Britain, 2019, p. 74
[ccxvi] Sugiyama, S. (2005). "Pyramids of the Sun and Moon: A Modern Study of the Ancient City of Teotihuacan." Archaeology Journal.
[ccxvii] Milbrath, S., & Peraza Lope, C. (2019). "Revisiting the Serpent Shadow: New Interpretations of Solar Alignments at Chichén Itzá." Journal of Archaeological Science.
[ccxviii] Shady Solís, R., Haas, J., & Creamer, W. (2001). "Dating Caral: Radiocarbon Evidence for the Oldest Civilization in the Americas." Science.
[ccxix] David Lubman, *Acoustics of Ancient Pyramids: The Sound-Engineering of Sacred Spaces* (Washington: Smithsonian Institution, 2009), 85-87.
[ccxx] Jonathan Haas, *The Evolution of Complex Societies in Peru* (Cambridge: Cambridge University Press, 2005), 118-120.
[ccxxi] Shady Solis, *Caral: The Oldest Civilization in the Americas*, 65-67.
[ccxxii] William Coe, *Tikal: A Handbook of the Ancient Maya Ruins* (Philadelphia: University of Pennsylvania Press, 1967), 87-91.
[ccxxiii] Richard Hansen, *The Lost City of the Maya* (New York: National Geographic, 2008), 105-107.
[ccxxiv] E. Wyllys Andrews, *Copán: The History of an Ancient Maya Kingdom* (Santa Fe: School of American Research Press, 2004), 155-159.
[ccxxv] Arlen Chase and Diane Z. Chase, *Ancient Maya Civilization at Caracol, Belize* (Miami: University Press of Florida, 2011), 95-97.
[ccxxvi] Alan Kolata, *Tiwanaku and Its Hinterland* (Washington: Smithsonian Institution Press, 1993), 142-145.
[ccxxvii] Claude Baudez, *Maya Cities and Sacred Places* (New York: Harry N. Abrams, 2002), 68-72.
[ccxxviii] Baudez, *Maya Cities and Sacred Places*, 74-77.
[ccxxix] Coe, M. D., & Houston, S. (2015). *The Maya*, Thames & Hudson.

[ccxxx] Timothy R. Pauketat, *Cahokia: Ancient America's Great City on the Mississippi* (Penguin Books, 2009).
[ccxxxi] Joseph Vogel, "The Evolution of Ancient Pyramid Design," *Archaeological Journal* (2012).
[ccxxxii] Pauketat, Timothy R. *Cahokia: Ancient America's Great City on the Mississippi*. Viking, 2009.
[ccxxxiii] Emerson, Thomas E. *Cahokia and the Archaeology of Power*. University of Alabama Press, 1997.
[ccxxxiv] Milner, George R. *The Cahokia Chiefdom: The Archaeology of a Mississippian Society*. Smithsonian Institution Press, 1998.
[ccxxxv] UNESCO World Heritage Centre. "Cahokia Mounds State Historic Site." Accessed October 2024.
[ccxxxvi] John W. Bennett, *The Ecological Transition: Cultural Anthropology and Human Adaptation* (Elsevier, 1976).
[ccxxxvii] Stephen Lekson, *A History of the Ancient Southwest* (SAR Press, 2009).
[ccxxxviii] David H. Dye, *Mississippian Culture and the Southeastern Ceremonial Complex* (University of Alabama Press, 2012).
[ccxxxix] Alfred Watkins, *The Old Straight Track* (Abacus, 1925).
[ccxl] Robert L. Hall, *The Cahokia Mounds* (The Smithsonian Institution Press, 1992).
[ccxli] John Michell, *The View Over Atlantis* (Thames & Hudson, 1969).
[ccxlii] Christopher Dunn, *The Giza Power Plant* (Bear & Company, 1998).
[ccxliii] Gold Pyramid House Official Website. "History of the Gold Pyramid House." Accessed October 2024.
[ccxliv] Hemphill, Stephanie. "The Gold Pyramid House of Wadsworth: A Curiosity of Modern Architecture." *Chicago Tribune*, 2016.
[ccxlv] USA Today. "Gold Pyramid House: The Strange Story Behind Illinois' Pyramid," 2018.
[ccxlvi] WGN News. "Fire Strikes Gold Pyramid House: Damages and Restoration Efforts Underway," 2018.
[ccxlvii] "Explorations in Grand Canyon: Remarkable Finds Indicate Ancient People Migrated From Orient." Arizona Gazette, April 5, 1909.
[ccxlviii] McClory, D. (2014). "History of The Arizona Republic: Arizona's Oldest Newspaper." Arizona Historical Society.
[ccxlix] Smithsonian Institution. "No Records Exist of Kincaid's Exploration in the Grand Canyon." Smithsonian Archives.
[ccl] Sloan, W. D. (1990). "The Media in America: A History." Vision Press.
[ccli] Beus, Stanley S., and Carothers, Steven W. "Grand Canyon Geology." Oxford University Press, 1987.
[cclii] Fairley, Helen K. "Cultural Resources of the Grand Canyon." National Park Service, 2003.
[ccliii] Neff, Charlotte. "Preserving Native American Heritage in the Grand Canyon." National Park Service, 2017.
[ccliv] National Park Service. "Grand Canyon Natural Resources: Protecting the Ecosystem." NPS.gov, 2019.
[cclv] Grand Canyon Conservancy. "Grand Canyon Safety Guidelines and Restricted Areas." GrandCanyon.org, 2020.
[cclvi] United States Geological Survey. "Restricted Access Zones in the Grand Canyon for Government and Military Use." USGS.gov, 2018.
[cclvii] Renfrew, C., & Bahn, P. (2016). "Archaeology: Theories, Methods, and Practice." Thames & Hudson.
[cclviii] Silverstein, K. (2008). "Secret History: The CIA's Classified Discoveries in Defense Research." The Atlantic.
[cclix] Jones, S. (2009). "The Politics of Archaeology and Identity in the Global Age." Cambridge University Press.
[cclx] Groves, J. (2007). "Cautionary Tales: National Security and Scientific Discoveries." Journal of National Defense Research.
[cclxi] Linda Moulton Howe, *Earthfiles*, "Secret Ancient Pyramid Under Alaska," accessed July 2025, https://www.earthfiles.com/2020/02/03/secret-ancient-pyramid-under-alaska/.
[cclxii] Estrada-Belli, Francisco. "LIDAR Study Uncovers Massive Maya Civilization." *National Geographic*, 2018.
[cclxiii] Hansen, Richard D. *The Mirador Basin Project: Pioneering Research in the Heart of the Maya Lowlands*, 2019.
[cclxiv] Canuto, Marcello A. "Ancient Maya Agriculture and Water Management Systems Revealed by LIDAR." *Science Advances*, 2018.
[cclxv] Canuto, Marcello A. "Ancient Maya Agriculture and Water Management Systems Revealed by LIDAR." *Science Advances*, 2018.
[cclxvi] Garrison, Thomas. "LIDAR and the Maya: Discovering Lost Cities." *Journal of Archaeological Science*, 2019.

[cclxvii] Canuto, Marcello A., and Estrada-Belli, Francisco. "New Insights from LIDAR into the Social and Political Organization of the Maya." *Journal of Archaeological Science*, 2020.
[cclxviii] Evans, D., et al. (2016). "New Findings from LIDAR Scanning in Cambodia: Hidden Urbanism and Networks around Angkor Wat." Proceedings of the National Academy of Sciences.
[cclxix] Lasaponara, R., & Masini, N. (2013). "Satellite Remote Sensing in Archaeology: Overviews and Case Studies from Peru." Journal of Archaeological Science.
[cclxx] Rondot, V. (2020). "Excavations at Sedeinga: New Insights into Nubian Pyramidal Structures." Sudan Archaeological Review.
[cclxxi] Smith, J., & Brown, A. (2021). *Uncovering Lost Civilizations: The Role of Technology in Archaeology*. Cambridge University Press.
[cclxxii] Osmanagić, S. (2005). "The Bosnian Pyramid: Evidence for an Ancient Advanced Civilization?" Bosnian Pyramid Research Archive.
[cclxxiii] Harwood, D. M. (2018). "Geological Processes in Antarctica: Shaping the Continent's Ice and Rock Formations." Journal of Polar Science.
[cclxxiv] NASA JPL, "Mars Reconnaissance Orbiter - SHARAD Instrument," https://mars.nasa.gov/mro/mission/instruments/sharad/; NASA Earth Science, "ICESat-2 and ATLAS Overview," https://icesat-2.gsfc.nasa.gov/atlas; NASA JPL, "Technology Highlights," https://www.jpl.nasa.gov/technology/.
[cclxxv] Collon, D. (1995). *Ancient Near Eastern Art*. University of California Press.
[cclxxvi] van Buren, E. D. (1931). "The Sacred Tree and the Handbag." *Iraq*, 1(2), 159-167.
[cclxxvii] Quirke, S. (2001). *The Cult of Ra: Sun-Worship in Ancient Egypt*. Thames & Hudson.
[cclxxviii] Stuart, D. (1996). *The Inscriptions from Copán*. Dumbarton Oaks Research Library and Collection.
[cclxxix] Freund, K. P. (2013). *Myth and Metaphor in Ancient Art*. Cambridge University Press.
[cclxxx] Coulson, M. (2018). "Comparative Iconography: Sacred Symbols in Ancient Civilizations." *Journal of Comparative Mythology*, 10(3), 23-45.
[cclxxxi] Gimbutas, M. (1991). *The Civilization of the Goddess: The World of Old Europe*. Harper, p. 122.
[cclxxxii] Wilkinson, R. H. (2003). *The Complete Gods and Goddesses of Ancient Egypt*. Thames & Hudson, p. 84.
[cclxxxiii] Root, M. C. (2002). *The King and Kingship in Achaemenid Art: Essays on the Creation of an Iconography of Empire*. Acta Iranica, p. 54.
[cclxxxiv] Laufer, B. (1913). *The Serpent in Chinese Mythology*. Field Museum of Natural History, p. 62.
[cclxxxv] Keightley, D. N. (1978). *Sources of Shang History: The Oracle-Bone Inscriptions of Bronze Age China*. University of California Press, p. 143.
[cclxxxvi] Pinch, G. (2004). *Egyptian Myth: A Very Short Introduction*. Oxford University Press, p. 105.
[cclxxxvii] Wang, Zhongshu. *Han Civilization*. Yale University Press, 1982.
[cclxxxviii] Lehner, Mark. *The Complete Pyramids: Solving the Ancient Mysteries*. Thames & Hudson, 1997.
[cclxxxix] Coe, Michael D. *The Maya*. Thames & Hudson, 2011.
[ccxc] "The Pyramids of China: Tombs of Emperors," China Daily, https://www.chinadaily.com.cn/china-pyramids. Accessed September 6, 2024.
[ccxci] George Cowgill, *Ancient Teotihuacan: Early Urbanism in Central Mexico* (Cambridge: Cambridge University Press, 2015), 176-179.
[ccxcii] U.S. Environmental Protection Agency, "Mercury: Health Effects of Exposure," EPA, 2020.
[ccxciii] R. G. Adams, *The Chemical Uses of Ancient Civilizations*, Oxford University Press, 1998.
[ccxciv] J. Needham, *Science and Civilisation in China, Volume 5: Chemistry and Chemical Technology* (Cambridge: Cambridge University Press, 1980), 134-136.
[ccxcv] R. G. Adams, *The Chemical Uses of Ancient Civilizations*, Oxford University Press, 1998.
[ccxcvi] James C. Whorton, *The Arsenic Century: How Victorian Britain Was Poisoned at Home, Work, and Play*, Oxford University Press, 2010.
[ccxcvii] George Cowgill, *Ancient Sacrifices in Teotihuacan*, University of Arizona Press, 2015.
[ccxcviii] C. Davis and A. Wilkinson, *Electromagnetic Theories in Ancient Civilizations*, New Science Press, 2020.
[ccxcix] Coe, Michael D. *The Maya*. Thames & Hudson, 1999.
[ccc] Trigger, Bruce G. *Early Civilizations: Ancient Egypt in Context*. Cambridge University Press, 2003.
[ccci] Schoff, Wilfred H. *The Periplus of the Erythraean Sea: Travel and Trade in the Indian Ocean*. Longmans, Green, and Co., 1912.
[cccii] Heyerdahl, Thor. *The Ra Expeditions*. Doubleday, 1971.
[ccciii] Lazaridis, I., Patterson, N., et al. (2014). Ancient Human Genomes Suggest Three Ancestral Populations for Present-day Europeans. *Nature*, 513(7518), 409-413. https://doi.org/10.1038/nature13673

[cciv] Reich, D. (2018). *Who We Are and How We Got Here: Ancient DNA and the New Science of the Human Past*. Pantheon Books.
[cccv] Ruhlen, M. (1994). *The Origin of Language: Tracing the Evolution of the Mother Tongue*. Wiley.
[cccvi] Wallace, B. *The Norse in North America*, National Museum of Natural History (2000).
[cccvii] Erlandson, J. M., Braje, T. J. *The Archaeology of Seafaring in Ancient America*, Journal of Anthropological Archaeology (2011).
[cccviii] Van Sertima, I. *They Came Before Columbus: The African Presence in Ancient America* (1976).
[cccix] Menzies, G. *1421: The Year China Discovered America* (2003).
[cccx] Grousset, R. (1970). *The Empire of the Steppes: A History of Central Asia*. Rutgers University Press.
[cccxi] Dijkstra, M., & Isayev, E. (2017). *Travel, Mobility and the Antique World*. Cambridge University Press.
[cccxii] Torpey, J. (2000). *The Invention of the Passport: Surveillance, Citizenship, and the State*. Cambridge University Press.
[cccxiii] Achiume, T. E. (2019). "Migration as Decolonization." *Stanford Law Review*, 71(6), 1509-1574.
[cccxiv] Hallam, A., & Wignall, P. B. (1997). *Mass Extinctions and Their Aftermath*. Oxford University Press, p. 34.
[cccxv] McPhee, J. (1981). *Basin and Range*. Farrar, Straus and Giroux, p. 98.
[cccxvi] Singh, A., *Vimanas in Ancient Indian Epics: Myth or Technology?*, Ancient Texts Publishing, New Delhi, 2023, pp. 34-36.
[cccxvii] Badawy, Alexander. *Ancient Egyptian Architectural Aerodynamics: A Study of the Saqqara Bird*, Cairo: American University in Cairo Press, 1972.
[cccxviii] Zahi Hawass, *The Pyramids: The Mystery, Culture, and Science of Egypt's Great Monuments* (New York: Thames & Hudson, 2009), 184-186; Rainer Stadelmann, *Egyptian Art in the Age of the Pyramids* (New York: The Metropolitan Museum of Art, 1999), 221. See also: F. D. Friedman, *Egypt: Gods, Myths, and Religion* (London: Duncan Baird Publishers, 1998), 45-47.
[cccxix] Wilkinson, Richard H. *The Complete Gods and Goddesses of Ancient Egypt*, London: Thames & Hudson, 2003.
[cccxx] Silverman, David P. *Lost Papyrus: An Analysis of the Tulli Papyrus and its Legacy in Egyptology*, London: Thames & Hudson, 2001.
[cccxxi] Jacques Vallée, *Wonders in the Sky: Unexplained Aerial Objects from Antiquity to Modern Times* (New York: TarcherPerigee, 2010), 89-92.
[cccxxii] "Nazca Lines." UNESCO World Heritage Centre. Accessed October 14, 2024. https://whc.unesco.org/en/list/700.
[cccxxiii] Reinhard, Johan. *The Nazca Lines: A New Perspective on Their Origins and Meanings*. Washington, D.C.: National Geographic Society, 1988.
[cccxxiv] Silverman, Helaine, and Proulx, Donald A. *The Nasca*. Blackwell Publishing, 2002; Aveni, Anthony. *Nasca: Eighth Wonder of the World*. British Museum Press, 2000.
[cccxxv] Heyerdahl, Thor. *The Ra Expeditions*. Doubleday, 1971.
[cccxxvi] Heyerdahl, Thor. *The Ra Expeditions*. New York: Doubleday, 1971.
[cccxxvii] Robert Schoch, *Forgotten Civilizations: The Role of Solar Outbursts in Our Past and Future* (Rochester: Inner Traditions, 2012), 101-103.
[cccxxviii] Erich von Däniken, *Chariots of the Gods* (New York: Putnam, 1969), 89-92.
[cccxxix] Graham Hancock, *Fingerprints of the Gods: The Evidence of Earth's Lost Civilization* (New York: Crown, 1995), 275-278.
[cccxxx] Christopher Dunn, *The Giza Power Plant: Technologies of Ancient Egypt* (Rochester: Bear & Company, 1998), 213-215.
[cccxxxi] Andrew Collins, *Beneath the Pyramids: Egypt's Greatest Secret Uncovered* (Rochester: Bear & Company, 2009), 142-144.
[cccxxxii] Helena Petrovna Blavatsky, *The Secret Doctrine: The Synthesis of Science, Religion, and Philosophy* (London: Theosophical Publishing Company, 1888), 204-207.
[cccxxxiii] Nicholas Roerich, *Shambhala: In Search of the New Era* (New York: Floris Books, 2007), 34-36.
[cccxxxiv] Richard Wingate, *Lost Cities of the Andes* (New York: Ballantine Books, 1996), 52-55.
[cccxxxv] Juan Moricz, *The Tayos Gold: In the Depths of Ecuador* (Lima: Editora Orbis, 1973), 89-91.
[cccxxxvi] William Reed, *The Phantom of the Poles* (New York: Adams Press, 1906), 9-12.
[cccxxxvii] David Standish, *Hollow Earth: The Long and Curious History of Imagining Strange Lands, Fantastical Creatures, Advanced Civilizations, and Marvelous Machines Below the Earth's Surface* (Cambridge: Da Capo Press, 2006), 205-210.
[cccxxxviii] *Journey to the Center of the Earth*, directed by Eric Brevig (New Line Cinema, 2008).

cccxxxix Jules Verne, *Journey to the Center of the Earth* (London: Ward, Lock & Co., 1871), 182-185.
cccxl A. Bertini, *The Underground Cities of Cappadocia: A Unique Wonder of Ancient Architecture* (Ankara: Ministry of Culture and Tourism, 2004), 55-60.
cccxli Graham Hancock, *Underworld: The Mysterious Origins of Civilization* (New York: Crown, 2002), 126-130.
cccxlii David H. Trump, *Malta: Prehistory and Temples* (Valletta: Midsea Books, 2002), 95-98.
cccxliii Herodotus, *The Histories*, trans. Aubrey de Sélincourt (London: Penguin Books, 1996), 2.148-2.149.
cccxliv Louis de Cordier, "Ground-Penetrating Radar Survey of Hawara: Discovery of the Egyptian Labyrinth," *Journal of Archaeological Science*, 2009, 15-18.
cccxlv Graham Hancock, *The Sign and the Seal* (New York: Crown Publishers, 1992), 230-235.
cccxlvi David Rohl, *A Test of Time: The Bible - From Myth to History* (London: Random House, 1995), 159-163.
cccxlvii John Anthony West, *Serpent in the Sky: The High Wisdom of Ancient Egypt* (New York: Harper & Row, 1979), 142-145.
cccxlviii Graham Hancock, *Fingerprints of the Gods: The Evidence of Earth's Lost Civilization* (New York: Crown, 1995), 310-312.
cccxlix Robert Bauval and Adrian Gilbert, *The Orion Mystery: Unlocking the Secrets of the Pyramids* (New York: Three Rivers Press, 1994), 220-225.
cccl Zahi Hawass, *The Secrets of the Sphinx* (London: Thames & Hudson, 1998), 45-50.
cccli Zahi Hawass, *Giza: The Truth* (London: Granada Publishing, 2000), 105-107.
ccclii Andrew Collins, *Beneath the Pyramids: Egypt's Greatest Secret Uncovered* (Rochester: Bear & Company, 2009), 155-160.
cccliii Anthony S. Mercatante, *Who's Who in Egyptian Mythology* (New York: Clarkson Potter, 1978), 90-93.
cccliv Christopher Dunn, *The Giza Power Plant: Technologies of Ancient Egypt* (Rochester: Bear & Company, 1998), 125-128.
ccclv Jean-Philippe Lauer, *Saqqara: The Royal Cemetery of Pharaohs* (Cairo: American University in Cairo Press, 2006), 122-125.
ccclvi David O'Connor, *Ancient Egyptian Society and Family Life* (New York: Oxford University Press, 2003), 87-89.
ccclvii Christopher Dunn, *The Giza Power Plant: Technologies of Ancient Egypt* (Rochester: Bear & Company, 1998), 215-218.
ccclviii Mark Lehner, *The Complete Pyramids: Solving the Ancient Mysteries* (New York: Thames & Hudson, 1997), 183-185.
ccclix Robert Bauval and Adrian Gilbert, *The Orion Mystery: Unlocking the Secrets of the Pyramids* (New York: Three Rivers Press, 1994), 233-236.
ccclx Robert Schoch, *Voyages of the Pyramid Builders* (New York: Jeremy P. Tarcher/Putnam, 2003), 110-113.
ccclxi Erich von Däniken, *Chariots of the Gods* (New York: Putnam, 1969), 145-148.
ccclxii David H. Childress, *Technology of the Gods: The Incredible Sciences of the Ancients* (Kempton: Adventures Unlimited Press, 2000), 210-213.
ccclxiii Erich von Däniken, *Chariots of the Gods* (New York: Putnam, 1969), 88-91.
ccclxiv Graham Hancock, *Underworld: The Mysterious Origins of Civilization* (New York: Crown, 2002), 145-149.
ccclxv Robert Schoch, *Voyages of the Pyramid Builders* (New York: Jeremy P. Tarcher/Putnam, 2003), 187-189.
ccclxvi Andrew Collins, *Beneath the Pyramids: Egypt's Greatest Secret Uncovered* (Rochester: Bear & Company, 2009), 112-115.
ccclxvii Mark Lehner, *The Complete Pyramids: Solving the Ancient Mysteries* (New York: Thames & Hudson, 1997), 150-153.
ccclxviii John Anthony West, *Serpent in the Sky: The High Wisdom of Ancient Egypt* (New York: Harper & Row, 1979), 172-175.
ccclxix Robert Bauval and Adrian Gilbert, *The Orion Mystery: Unlocking the Secrets of the Pyramids* (New York: Three Rivers Press, 1994), 225-228.
ccclxx Christopher Dunn, *The Giza Power Plant: Technologies of Ancient Egypt* (Rochester: Bear & Company, 1998), 188-190.
ccclxxi David H. Childress, *Technology of the Gods: The Incredible Sciences of the Ancients*, 218-221.
ccclxxii Tesla, Nikola. *My Inventions: The Autobiography of Nikola Tesla*. Hart Brothers, 1919.
ccclxxiii Nostradamus, *The Prophecies of Nostradamus*, translated by Erika Cheetham, Perigee Books, 1981.
ccclxxiv Wilcock, D. (2011). *The Source Field Investigations: The Hidden Science and Lost Civilizations Behind the 2012 Prophecies.* Dutton; Wilcock, D. (2013). *The Synchronicity Key: The Hidden Intelligence Guiding the Universe and You.* Dutton.

Powered by Pyramids: A Book of Theories

ccclxxv Sheldrake, R. (1981). *A New Science of Life: The Hypothesis of Formative Causation*. J.P. Tarcher.
ccclxxvi Faivre, A. (1995). *The Eternal Hermes: From Greek God to Alchemical Magus*. Phanes Press.
ccclxxvii Hameroff, S., & Penrose, R. (2014). Consciousness in the Universe: A Review of the 'Orch OR' Theory. *Physics of Life Reviews*.
ccclxxviii Pribram, K. H. (1991). *Brain and Perception: Holonomy and Structure in Figural Processing*. Lawrence Erlbaum Associates.
ccclxxix Colin McGinn, *Inborn Knowledge: The Mystery Within* (Cambridge: MIT Press, 2015), 89-92.
ccclxxx Eva Jablonka and Marion J. Lamb, *Evolution in Four Dimensions: Genetic, Epigenetic, Behavioral, and Symbolic Variation in the History of Life* (Cambridge: MIT Press, 2005), 120-125.
ccclxxxi Eva Jablonka and Marion J. Lamb, *Evolution in Four Dimensions: Genetic, Epigenetic, Behavioral, and Symbolic Variation in the History of Life* (Cambridge: MIT Press, 2005), 120-125.
ccclxxxii Elon Musk, "An Integrated Brain-Machine Interface Platform With Thousands of Channels," *Journal of Medical Internet Research* (2020).
ccclxxxiii Shoshana Zuboff, *The Age of Surveillance Capitalism* (New York: PublicAffairs, 2019), 134-137.
ccclxxxiv Ervin Laszlo, *Science and the Akashic Field: An Integral Theory of Everything* (Rochester, VT: Inner Traditions, 2004), 32-35.
ccclxxxv Jablonka, E., & Raz, G. (2009). Transgenerational epigenetic inheritance: Prevalence, mechanisms, and implications for the study of heredity and evolution. *Quarterly Review of Biology*, 84(2), 131-176.
ccclxxxvi Radbruch, A., & Chang, H.-D. (2021). A long-term perspective on immunity. *Nature Reviews Immunology*, 21(6), 354-365.
ccclxxxvii Lambert, N., Chen, Y.-N., Cheng, Y.-C., & Nori, F. (2013). Quantum biology. *Nature Physics*, 9(1), 10-18.
ccclxxxviii Aristotle, "The more you know, the more you realise you don't know," *Stanford Encyclopedia of Philosophy*, https://plato.stanford.edu/entries/aristotle/. Accessed September 6, 2024.
ccclxxxix *Alice in Wonderland*, Directed by Clyde Geronimi, Wilfred Jackson, and Hamilton Luske, Walt Disney Productions, 1951.
cccxc See: Burisch, D., and Wood, B., in interviews archived via Project Camelot (https://projectcamelotportal.com) and speculative discussions in alternative media forums (accessed August 2025).
cccxci *Encyclopaedia Britannica*, https://www.britannica.com/topic/pyramids-of-Giza. Accessed September 6, 2024.
cccxcii "Study reveals the Great Pyramid of Giza can focus electromagnetic energy," *Phys.org*, https://phys.org/news/2018-07-reveals-great-pyramid-giza-focus.html. Accessed September 6, 2024.
cccxciii Morison, J. "Pyramids: A Global Phenomenon." *Journal of World History*, vol. 24, no. 3, 2011, pp. 112-129.
cccxciv "Great Pyramid of Giza Can Focus Electromagnetic Energy," *ScienceBlog*, https://scitechdaily.com/great-pyramid-of-giza-can-focus-electromagnetic-energy/. Accessed September 6, 2024.
cccxcv Lehner, C. "Geographical Alignment and Purpose of Pyramids." *Archaeology*, vol. 62, no. 4, 2008, pp. 56-78.
cccxcvi Aveni, A. F. (1980). *Skywatchers of Ancient Mexico*. University of Texas Press.
cccxcvii Bauval, R., & Gilbert, A. (1994). *The Orion Mystery: Unlocking the Secrets of the Pyramids*. Crown Publishers.
cccxcviii Flinders Petrie, *A History of Egypt from the Earliest Times to the XVIth Dynasty* (London: Methuen, 1904), 216-218. See also: Zahi Hawass, *The Pyramids: The Mystery, Culture, and Science of Egypt's Great Monuments* (New York: Thames & Hudson, 2009), 82-84.
cccxcix Schmidt, Klaus. *Göbekli Tepe: Genesis of the Gods*. Inner Traditions, 2016. Accessed September 10, 2024.
cd Jean-Pierre Houdin, *Khufu: The Secrets Behind the Building of the Great Pyramid*, Farid Atiya Press, 2006.
cdi Dieter Arnold, *Building in Egypt: Pharaonic Stone Masonry*, Oxford University Press, 1991.
cdii Zahi Hawass, *The Pyramids: The Mystery, Culture, and Science of Egypt's Great Monuments* (New York: Thames & Hudson, 2003).
cdiii Michael Shaw, *Cranes in Construction: An Overview of Modern Capabilities* (New York: Crane Institute Publishing, 2018), 12-14.
cdiv Paul W. Nicholson and Ian Shaw, *Ancient Egyptian Materials and Technology* (Cambridge: Cambridge University Press, 2000), 54-56.

cdv James F. McCarthy, *The Evolution of Construction Equipment* (Chicago: CE Publishers, 2007), 75-77.
cdvi John F. Cameron, *Hydraulic Jacks and Modern Lifting Techniques* (London: Construction Innovations Press, 2015), 102-105.
cdvii Andrew Harris, *Robotics in Construction: The Future of Building* (Oxford: Robotic Press, 2019), 45-51.
cdviii Pierre Houdin, *Khufu: The Secrets Behind the Building of the Great Pyramid*, Translated by Judy Thompson, Saqi Books, 2008.
cdix Zahi Hawass, *The Pyramids: The Mystery, Culture, and Science of Egypt's Great Monuments*, Thames & Hudson, 2006.
cdx Herodotus, *The Histories*, trans. Aubrey de Sélincourt (Penguin Classics, 1954), Book II, 124-126.
cdxi Herodotus, *The Histories*, Translated by Aubrey de Sélincourt, Penguin Classics, 1954.
cdxii Mark Lehner, *The Complete Pyramids: Solving the Ancient Mysteries*, Thames & Hudson, 1997.
cdxiii Mark Lehner, *The Complete Pyramids: Solving the Ancient Mysteries*, Thames & Hudson, 1997.
cdxiv Mark Lehner, *The Complete Pyramids: Solving the Ancient Mysteries*, Thames & Hudson, 1997.
cdxv John Ruskin, *The Seven Lamps of Architecture*, Smith, Elder, 1849.
cdxvi Solari, M. *The Hidden Architects: Women of Ancient Egypt*. New Dawn Press, 2018, pp. 56-67.
cdxvii Lehner, M. (1997). *The Complete Pyramids: Solving the Ancient Mysteries*. London: Thames & Hudson.
cdxviii Dieter Arnold, *Building in Egypt: Pharaonic Stone Masonry* (New York: Oxford University Press, 1991), 30-32.
cdxix Ian Shaw, *Ancient Egyptian Materials and Technology* (Cambridge: Cambridge University Press, 2000), 60-62.
cdxx William Flinders Petrie, *The Pyramids and Temples of Gizeh* (London: Field & Tuer, 1883), 89-92.
cdxxi Christopher Dunn, *The Giza Power Plant: Technologies of Ancient Egypt* (Rochester: Bear & Company, 1998), 115-118.
cdxxii Mark Lehner, *The Complete Pyramids: Solving the Ancient Mysteries* (New York: Thames & Hudson, 1997), 135-137.
cdxxiii Joyce Tyldesley, *Hatchepsut: The Female Pharaoh* (New York: Penguin, 1996), 180-182.
cdxxiv Ian Shaw, *The Oxford History of Ancient Egypt* (Oxford: Oxford University Press, 2003), 252-255.
cdxxv Joyce Tyldesley, *The Complete Queens of Egypt* (London: Thames & Hudson, 2006), 185-187.
cdxxvi James D. Muhly, *Metalworking in Ancient Egypt* (Philadelphia: University Museum, University of Pennsylvania, 1985), 59-61.
cdxxvii Vagn Fabritius Buchwald, *Handbook of Iron Meteorites* (Los Angeles: University of California Press, 1975), 5-7.
cdxxviii Timothy McCoy, *Meteorites and Their Impact on Earth* (New York: Springer, 2004), 68-70.
cdxxix Robert H. Gargett, *Ancient Metals: The Role of Meteorites in Early Metallurgy* (Cambridge: Cambridge University Press, 2014), 45-48.
cdxxx Vagn Fabritius Buchwald, *Handbook of Iron Meteorites* (Los Angeles: University of California Press, 1975), 20-23.
cdxxxi Timothy McCoy, *Meteorites and Their Impact on Earth* (New York: Springer, 2004), 75-77.
cdxxxii Susan M. Young, *Advanced Metallurgical Techniques: XRF and Mass Spectrometry in Archaeology* (Oxford: Archaeopress, 2016), 93-96.
cdxxxiii Dunn, C. (1998). *The Giza Power Plant: Technologies of Ancient Egypt*. Bear & Company.
cdxxxiv Andrews, T. (1987). *The Science of the Pyramids: Forgotten Technologies of Ancient Egypt*. London: Mystica Publishing.
cdxxxv Smith, J. (2023). *Cedar Wood and Pyramid Construction in Ancient Egypt*. Historical Structures Press, pp. 85-87.
cdxxxvi Smith, J. (2023). *Trade and Timber: Cedar Imports in Ancient Egypt*. Antiquity Press, pp. 45-47.
cdxxxvii D. Bonn, *Sliding Friction on Wet and Dry Sand*, University of Amsterdam, *Physical Review Letters*, 2014, pp. 1-4.
cdxxxviii "4,000-year-old Mystery Solved: How the Giza Pyramids Were Built," *Euronews*, September 2024.; "Ancient Egyptian Structure Discovered Near Egypt's Giza Pyramids," *GreekReporter*, May 2024.; "How the Nile Helped Build the Pyramids," *Journal of Egyptian Archaeology*, 2024.
cdxxxix Landreau, Xavier et al., *Ancient Hydraulic Engineering at the Pyramid of Djoser*. PLOS ONE, 2024.; "Did Water Help Build Great Pyramids? New Study Suggests So." *NewsBytes*,

August 2024.; "Groundbreaking Research Poses New Theory on Pyramid Construction," *Daily Express US*, September 2024.
[cdxl] Joseph Davidovits, *The Pyramids: An Enigma Solved*, (Geopolymer Institute, 1998).
[cdxli] Arnold, D. (1991). *Building in Egypt: Pharaonic Stone Masonry*. Oxford University Press, p. 110.
[cdxlii] Stocks, D.A. (2003). *Experiments in Egyptian Archaeology: Stoneworking Technology in Ancient Egypt*. Routledge, p. 82.
[cdxliii] Klemm, R., & Klemm, D. D. (2008). *Stones and Quarries in Ancient Egypt*. British Museum Press, p. 210.
[cdxliv] Arnold, D. (1991). *Building in Egypt: Pharaonic Stone Masonry*. Oxford University Press, p. 154.
[cdxlv] Shaw, I. (2003). *The Oxford History of Ancient Egypt*. Oxford University Press, p. 223.
[cdxlvi] David H. Childress, *Technology of the Gods: The Incredible Sciences of the Ancients* (Kempton: Adventures Unlimited Press, 2000), 250-253.
[cdxlvii] Redfern proposes that the ancient Egyptians might have had devices capable of manipulating gravity, allowing them to reduce the weight of stones temporarily.
[cdxlviii] J. Isler, *The Mystery of the Granite Box: Engineering Feats in the Great Pyramid*, Cairo Archaeological Journal, 2020, pp. 45-47.
[cdxlix] J. A. West, *Serpent in the Sky: The High Wisdom of Ancient Egypt*, Harper & Row, 1979, pp. 85-87.
[cdl] Graham Hancock, *Fingerprints of the Gods*, Crown Publishers, 1995.
[cdli] Brier, Bob. *The Secret of the Great Pyramid: How One Man's Obsession Led to the Solution of Ancient Egypt's Greatest Mystery*. New York: HarperCollins, 2008.
[cdlii] Isler, Martin. *Sticks, Stones, and Shadows: Building the Egyptian Pyramids*. Norman: University of Oklahoma Press, 2001.
[cdliii] Edwards, I.E.S. *The Pyramids of Egypt*. New York: Viking Press, 1986.
[cdliv] Malek, Jaromir. *The Oxford Essential Guide to Egyptian Mythology*. Oxford University Press, 2003.
[cdlv] Arnold, Dieter. *Building in Egypt: Pharaonic Stone Masonry*. Oxford: Oxford University Press, 1991.
[cdlvi] Belmonte, Juan Antonio. "Astronomy and Architecture in Ancient Egypt." *Journal of History of Astronomy*, 2001.
[cdlvii] Verner, Miroslav. *The Pyramids: The Mystery, Culture, and Science of Egypt's Great Monuments*. New York: Grove Press, 2007.
[cdlviii] Lehner, Mark. *The Complete Pyramids: Solving the Ancient Mysteries*. London: Thames & Hudson, 1997.
[cdlix] Fakhry, Ahmed. *The Pyramids*. University of Chicago Press, 1961.
[cdlx] Verner, Miroslav. *The Pyramids: The Mystery, Culture, and Science of Egypt's Great Monuments*. Grove Press, 2001.
[cdlxi] "The Bent Pyramid and Structural Instability," *Ancient Egypt Research Associates*, accessed September 2023.
[cdlxii] Dunn, Christopher. *The Giza Power Plant: Technologies of Ancient Egypt*. Bear & Company, 1998.
[cdlxiii] "Engineering Marvels of Ancient Egypt," *Encyclopedia of World Architecture*, accessed September 2023.
[cdlxiv] Wilkinson, Richard H. *The Complete Temples of Ancient Egypt*. Thames & Hudson, 2000.
[cdlxv] "The Relieving Chambers of the Great Pyramid," *Egyptology Journal*, accessed September 2023.
[cdlxvi] John Romer, *The Great Pyramid: Ancient Egypt Revisited*, Cambridge University Press, 2007.
[cdlxvii] Mario Salvadori, *Why Buildings Stand Up: The Strength of Architecture*, W.W. Norton & Company, 2002.
[cdlxviii] William F. Baker, *Burj Khalifa: Structural Systems for the World's Tallest Building*, Proceedings of the Institution of Civil Engineers, 2011.
[cdlxix] F. Weber, *Deep Foundations and Geotechnical Engineering: Design of Pile Foundations*, Taylor & Francis, 2017.
[cdlxx] Mark Sarkisian, *Designing Tall Buildings: Structure as Architecture*, Routledge, 2012.
[cdlxxi] Zahi Hawass, *The Pyramids: The Mystery, Culture, and Science of Egypt's Great Monuments*, American University in Cairo Press, 2009.
[cdlxxii] "Great Pyramid of Giza," *Guinness World Records*, accessed September 2023.
[cdlxxiii] "Seven Wonders of the Ancient World," *Encyclopedia Britannica*, accessed September 2023.
[cdlxxiv] *Guinness World Records*, "Tallest Structures: Great Pyramid of Giza," accessed September 2023.
[cdlxxv] Lehner, Mark. *The Complete Pyramids: Solving the Ancient Mysteries*. London: Thames & Hudson, 1997.

cdlxxvi Zecharia Sitchin, *The 12th Planet*, Avon Books, 1976.
cdlxxvii Erich von Däniken, *Chariots of the Gods?*, Souvenir Press, 1968.
cdlxxviii "Pyramid Reconstructed: Japanese Try to Build a Pyramid Using Ancient Methods," Nippon Television Documentary, 1978.
cdlxxix Mark Lehner, *The Complete Pyramids: Solving the Ancient Mysteries*, Thames & Hudson, 1997.
cdlxxx NOVA, "This Old Pyramid," PBS, 1997.
cdlxxxi Christopher Dunn, *The Giza Power Plant: Technologies of Ancient Egypt*, Bear & Company, 1998.
cdlxxxii Farkas, L. (2007). *Coral Castle Explained*. Farkas Publishing, p. 45.
cdlxxxiii Broughton, J. (2002). *Coral Castle: An Enigma of the Twentieth Century*. Mystery Books, p. 33.
cdlxxxiv Morrison, J. (1996). *Mysteries of Coral Castle*. Mysteries Press, p. 88.
cdlxxxv Sagan, D. (2013). *Secrets of the Pyramids and Ancient Technologies*. Ancient Mysteries Press, p. 64.
cdlxxxvi Maxwell, T. (2001). *The Science Behind Coral Castle*. Maxwell Publishing, p. 122.
cdlxxxvii Wilcox, D. (2008). *The Hidden Power of Sound and Levitation in Ancient Civilizations*. Mystic Works, p. 84.
cdlxxxviii Browne, J. (2010). *Modern Marvels and Mysteries: Coral Castle*. Exploration Press, p. 98.
cdlxxxix Morishima, K., et al. "Discovery of a Big Void in Khufu's Pyramid by Observation of Cosmic-ray Muons." *Nature*, 2017; Lehner, Mark. *The Complete Pyramids: Solving the Ancient Mysteries*. Thames & Hudson, 1997.
cdxc United Nations Educational, Scientific, and Cultural Organization (UNESCO). *World Heritage Convention and Cultural Preservation Guidelines*. 1972.
cdxci Wilkinson, Richard H. *The Complete Temples of Ancient Egypt*. Thames & Hudson, 2000.
cdxcii Dunn, Christopher. *The Giza Power Plant: Technologies of Ancient Egypt*. Bear & Company, 1998.
cdxciii Fagan, Brian M., ed. *The Oxford Companion to Archaeology*. Oxford University Press, 1996.
cdxciv Allen, James P. *Middle Egyptian: An Introduction to the Language and Culture of Hieroglyphs*. Cambridge University Press, 2010.
cdxcv Wilkinson, R. H. *The Complete Gods and Goddesses of Ancient Egypt*. Thames & Hudson, 2003.
cdxcvi Sugiyama, S., and Cabrera, R. *Teotihuacan: City of Water, City of Fire*. University of California Press, 2017.
cdxcvii Carballo, D. M. *Urbanization and Religion in Ancient Central Mexico*. Oxford University Press, 2016.
cdxcviii Cowgill, G. L. "Teotihuacan, A Primer for Scholars and Laypeople Alike." *Ancient Mesoamerica*, 1997.
cdxcix Barba, L. "Subterranean Archaeology in Mesoamerica: Ritual and Space." *Journal of Archaeological Science*, 2011.
d Fekri, H. "The Labyrinths Beneath Egypt: Excavating the Lost Catacombs of the Pharaohs." *Journal of Egyptian Archaeology*, 2014.
di Lloyd, A. B. *Ancient Egypt: State and Society*. Oxford University Press, 2016.
dii Kemp, B. *Ancient Egypt: Anatomy of a Civilization*. Routledge, 2006.
diii Verner, M. *The Pyramids: The Mystery, Culture, and Science of Egypt's Great Monuments*. Grove Press, 2007.
div Dodson, A., and Hilton, D. *The Complete Royal Families of Ancient Egypt*. Thames & Hudson, 2004.
dv Hawass, Z. *Inside the Egyptian Pyramids: The Secret Chambers Beneath the Giza Plateau*. National Geographic, 2009.
dvi Dodson, A., & Ikram, S. *The Tomb in Ancient Egypt: Royal and Private Sepulchres from the Early Dynastic Period to the Romans*. Thames & Hudson, 2008.
dvii Taylor, J. H. *Death and the Afterlife in Ancient Egypt*. University of Chicago Press, 2001.
dviii Wilkinson, R. H. *The Complete Temples of Ancient Egypt*. Thames & Hudson, 2000.
dix Lehner, M. *The Complete Pyramids: Solving the Ancient Mysteries*. Thames & Hudson, 1997.
dx Tyldesley, J. *The Private Lives of the Pharaohs*. BBC Books, 2000.
dxi Brier, B. *The Secret of the Great Pyramid: How One Man's Obsession Led to the Solution of Ancient Egypt's Greatest Mystery*. Harper Collins, 2008.
dxii Hawass, Z. *The Lost Tombs of Egypt*. Thames & Hudson, 2019.
dxiii Weeks, K. *The Valley of the Kings: The Tombs and the Funerary Temples of Thebes West*. Friedman/Fairfax, 2001.
dxiv Wilkinson, T. *The Rise and Fall of Ancient Egypt*. Bloomsbury Publishing, 2011.

Powered by Pyramids: A Book of Theories

[dxv] Verner, M. *The Pyramids: The Mystery, Culture, and Science of Egypt's Great Monuments.* Grove Press, 2007.
[dxvi] Butzer, Karl W. *Early Hydraulic Civilization in Egypt: A Study in Cultural Ecology.* University of Chicago Press, 1976.
[dxvii] Lehner, Mark. *The Complete Pyramids: Solving the Ancient Mysteries.* Thames & Hudson, 1997.
[dxviii] Wilkinson, Richard H. *The Complete Temples of Ancient Egypt.* Thames & Hudson, 2000.
[dxix] Brier, Bob. *The Secret of the Great Pyramid: How One Man's Obsession Led to the Solution of Ancient Egypt's Greatest Mystery.* Harper Collins, 2008.
[dxx] Hassan, Fekri. "Water and Its Role in the Pyramids of Giza." *Journal of Archaeological Science*, 1997.
[dxxi] Allen, George. *Building to Last: Engineering Resilience into Modern Architecture.* Routledge, 2011.
[dxxii] Kelly, James. *Seismic Isolation for Earthquake-Resistant Structures.* Wiley, 1998.
[dxxiii] Priestley, M.J.N. *Seismic Design and Retrofit of Bridges.* Wiley, 1996.
[dxxiv] Hawass, Zahi. *Inside the Egyptian Pyramids: The Hidden Chambers and Seismic Protection.* National Geographic, 2009.
[dxxv] Robert Bauval and Thomas Brophy, *Black Genesis: The Prehistoric Origins of Ancient Egypt*, Bear & Company, 2011.
[dxxvi] Andrew Collins, *The Cygnus Key: The Denisovan Legacy, Göbekli Tepe, and the Birth of Egypt*, Bear & Company, 2018.
[dxxvii] Dash, Mike. "Ancient Batteries: Baghdad Battery." *Smithsonian Magazine*, 2009.
[dxxviii] König, Wilhelm. *Neuvermessung der babylonischen Kunstschätze.* Berlin: Museum für Völkerkunde, 1940.
[dxxix] Brier, Bob. *The Secret of the Great Pyramid: How One Man's Obsession Led to the Solution of Ancient Egypt's Greatest Mystery.* Harper Collins, 2008.
[dxxx] Schmidt, Hans. "The Enigma of Baghdad Batteries." *Archaeology Review Journal*, 2012.
[dxxxi] Fiebag, Peter. "Piezoelectric Properties of the Pyramids." *Ancient Mysteries Uncovered*, 2005; Osmond, Richard. "Electromagnetic Theories Surrounding the Giza Plateau." *Journal of Archaeological Science*, 2014.
[dxxxii] Verner, Miroslav. *The Pyramids: The Mystery, Culture, and Science of Egypt's Great Monuments.* Grove Press, 2007.
[dxxxiii] Wilkinson, Richard H. *The Complete Temples of Ancient Egypt.* Thames & Hudson, 2000.
[dxxxiv] Johnson, T. (2023). *Flat Earth Theories and Ancient Architecture: Pyramids on Pillars.* Fringe Archaeology Journal, pp. 112-114.
[dxxxv] Herodotus, *The Histories*, translated by Aubrey de Sélincourt, Penguin Classics, 2003.
[dxxxvi] Strabo, *Geography*, Book XVII.
[dxxxvii] Bauval, Robert, and Thomas Brophy, *Black Genesis: The Prehistoric Origins of Ancient Egypt*, Bear & Company, 2011
[dxxxviii] Smith, A. "Mysteries of the Pyramidion: Understanding Ancient Pyramid Capstones." *Journal of Egyptian Mysteries*, vol. 23, no. 1, 2021, pp. 45-67.
[dxxxix] Lehner, Mark. *The Complete Pyramids: Solving the Ancient Mysteries.* Thames & Hudson, 1997.
[dxl] Verner, Miroslav. *The Pyramids: Their Archaeology and History.* Atlantic Books, 2001.
[dxli] Wilkinson, Richard H. *The Complete Temples of Ancient Egypt.* Thames & Hudson, 2000.
[dxlii] Edwards, I.E.S. *The Pyramids of Egypt.* Penguin Books, 1986.
[dxliii] Hawass, Zahi. *The Pyramids: The Mystery, Culture, and Science of Egypt's Great Monuments.* American University in Cairo Press, 2004.
[dxliv] Spence, Kate. "Ancient Egyptian Chronology and the Astronomical Orientation of Pyramids." *Nature*, vol. 408, 2000, pp. 320-324.
[dxlv] Dodson, Aidan. *The Pyramids of Ancient Egypt.* Oxbow Books, 2020.
[dxlvi] Stadelmann, Rainer. "The Great Pyramid of Giza: A New View of Its Construction." *The Journal of Egyptian Archaeology*, vol. 71, 1985, pp. 85-104.
[dxlvii] Lehner, Mark. *The Complete Pyramids: Solving the Ancient Mysteries.* Thames & Hudson, 1997.
[dxlviii] Clayton, Peter A. *Chronicle of the Pharaohs.* Thames & Hudson, 1994.
[dxlix] Redford, Donald B. *The Oxford Encyclopedia of Ancient Egypt.* Oxford University Press, 2001.
[dl] Arnold, Dieter. *Building in Egypt: Pharaonic Stone Masonry.* Oxford University Press, 1991.
[dli] Dunn, Christopher. *The Giza Power Plant: Technologies of Ancient Egypt.* Bear & Company, 1998.
[dlii] Roberts, P. "Copper Conductors in Ancient Civilizations." *Metallic Mysteries of the Pyramids*, New Dawn Publishing, 2022, pp. 70-85.
[dliii] Jones, M. "The Pyramid Energy Grid: Ancient Technologies Rediscovered." *Journal of Speculative Archaeology*, vol. 15, no. 3, 2020, pp. 45-60.
[dliv] Verner, Miroslav. *The Pyramids: Their Archaeology and History.* Atlantic Books, 2001.

dlv Carlson, R. "The Power of Quartz in Ancient Technologies." *Energy of the Ancients*, 2021, pp. 102-118.
dlvi Adams, L. "Meteorite Iron: The Celestial Metal of Ancient Egypt." *Egyptian Metalwork*, vol. 14, no. 2, 2019, pp. 45-62.
dlvii Thompson, A. "The Mystery of Orichalcum and Its Uses in Atlantis." *Ancient Legends and Metals*, Harper Publishing, 2020, pp. 88-101.
dlviii Roberts, P. "Harnessing Earth's Energies Through Ancient Structures." *Energy Mysteries of the Pyramids*, New Dawn Publishing, 2022, pp. 34-50.
dlix Smith, L. "Global Networks and the Pyramids: A Technological Perspective." *Ancient Civilizations Review*, vol. 22, no. 4, 2018, pp. 112-128.
dlx Evans, G. "Crystalline Structures and Ancient Technologies." *Mystery of the Capstones*, vol. 7, no. 2, 2021, pp. 25-38.
dlxi Carter, D. "Capstones: The Gateway to Ancient Energy Manipulation." *Metaphysical Review*, vol. 29, no. 1, 2020, pp. 77-91.
dlxii "The Georgia Guidestones." *Atlas Obscura*. https://www.atlasobscura.com/places/georgia-guidestones
dlxiii Childress, David Hatcher. *Mystery of the Georgia Guidestones*. Adventures Unlimited Press, 2016.
dlxiv Brown, J. "The Templar Secrets: Pyramid Connections and Hidden Knowledge." *Secret Societies Revealed*, vol. 18, no. 2, 2019, pp. 45-61.
dlxv Roberts, M. "Ancient Egyptian Priesthoods and Their Influence on Pyramid Construction." *Mystical Egypt Quarterly*, vol. 22, no. 4, 2020, pp. 78-95.
dlxvi Adams, L. "The Illuminati and Their Hidden Role in Modern Technology." *Conspiracy Theories of the 21st Century*, vol. 25, no. 2, 2022, pp. 101-117.
dlxvii Johnson, P. "Shadow Governments and Hidden Technologies." *Modern Secret Societies*, vol. 16, no. 1, 2020, pp. 33-50.
dlxviii Garcia, N. "Global Dominance Through Ancient Technologies." *Pyramids and Power*, vol. 11, no. 3, 2019, pp. 88-104.
dlxix Edwards, H. "The Astronomical Alignment of Pyramids." *Archaeoastronomy Review*, vol. 13, no. 2, 2018, pp. 56-72.
dlxx Smith, T. "Star-Worship Cults in Ancient Egypt." *Religions of the Ancients*, vol. 18, no. 3, 2021, pp. 99-115.
dlxxi Williams, K. "Preventing Apocalyptic Alignments: Pyramid Capstones and Celestial Events." *Journal of Ancient Prophecies*, vol. 21, no. 2, 2019, pp. 45-64.
dlxxii Kelly, T. "Alien Influence in Ancient Egypt." *Extraterrestrial Theories of Pyramid Building*, vol. 7, no. 1, 2021, pp. 25-43.
dlxxiii Thompson, D. "The Great Pyramid as an Alien Communication Device." *Cosmic Histories Journal*, vol. 19, no. 3, 2018, pp. 67-83.
dlxxiv Smith, A. "Atlantis and the Lost Knowledge of the Capstones." *Atlantis Revisited*, vol. 14, no. 4, 2019, pp. 89-103.
dlxxv Evans, D. "The Capstones of Power: Hidden Technologies in Ancient Cities." *Cities of the Gods*, vol. 12, no. 3, 2020, pp. 54-71.
dlxxvi Johnson, L. "Harnessing the Power of Ancient Cities." *Advanced Civilizations Quarterly*, vol. 10, no. 2, 2021, pp. 38-55.
dlxxvii Davis, R. "Interdimensional Beings and Pyramid Portals." *Metaphysical Science Review*, vol. 28, no. 4, 2021, pp. 41-58.
dlxxviii Martin, G. "Dimensional Travel and the Capstones of the Pyramids." *Ancient Mysteries and Modern Science*, vol. 24, no. 1, 2020, pp. 72-88.
dlxxix Scott, M. "Cloaking Technologies in Ancient Civilizations." *Future Archaeology Quarterly*, vol. 15, no. 3, 2020, pp. 87-104.
dlxxx Brown, C. "Invisible Pyramids and Cloaking Devices." *Technologies of the Ancients*, vol. 9, no. 2, 2021, pp. 31-48.
dlxxxi Roberts, P. "Advanced Technologies Hidden in Plain Sight." *Metaphysical Journal of Technology*, vol. 17, no. 1, 2022, pp. 65-80.
dlxxxii Brown, D. *Tricks of the Mind*. Transworld Publishers, 2006.
dlxxxiii Lehner, M. (1997). *The Complete Pyramids: Solving the Ancient Mysteries*. Thames & Hudson, pp. 145-148.
dlxxxiv Robert Schoch, "Redating the Sphinx," *Geological Society of America Bulletin*, Vol. 11, No. 1, 1992.
dlxxxv Smith, J., & Wendorf, F. (2008). Geological and Climatic History of the Sahara. *Journal of African Archaeology*, 46(3), 215-233.
dlxxxvi Lehner, M. (1997). *The Complete Pyramids: Solving the Ancient Mysteries*. Thames & Hudson, pp. 146-148.
dlxxxvii Gauri, K. L., Sinai, J. J., & Bandyopadhyay, J. K. (2010). Erosion and weathering of the Sphinx. Geological Society of America Bulletin, 122(9-10), 1470-1484.

[dlxxxviii] *The Mystery of the Sphinx*, Directed by Bill Cote, Atlantis Rising Productions, 1993.
[dlxxxix] Graham Hancock and Robert Bauval, *The Message of the Sphinx: A Quest for the Hidden Legacy of Mankind* (New York: Crown Publishers, 1996), 105-110.
[dxc] Edgar Cayce, *Edgar Cayce's Egypt: Psychic Revelations on the Most Fascinating Civilization Ever Known*, edited by Mark Thurston (New York: Warner Books, 1998), 45-47.
[dxci] Mark Lehner, *The Complete Pyramids: Solving the Ancient Mysteries*, Thames & Hudson, 1997.
[dxcii] Edgar Cayce, *On Atlantis and the Hall of Records*, compiled from his readings (New York: A.R.E. Press, 1968), 32-36
[dxciii] Zahi Hawass, *Secrets from the Sand: My Search for Egypt's Past* (London: Thames & Hudson, 2003), 78-81.
[dxciv] Robert Temple, *The Sphinx Mystery: The Forgotten Origins of the Sanctuary of Anubis* (Rochester: Inner Traditions, 2009), 58-63.
[dxcv] Reeves, Nicholas. *The Complete Tutankhamun: The King, the Tomb, the Royal Treasure.* Thames & Hudson, 1990.
[dxcvi] Jones, M. (2016). *The Lost Face of the Sphinx: Uncovering the Truth Behind the Missing Nose.* Alexandria: Egyptian Antiquities Society, p. 124.
[dxcvii] Lehner, M. (1997). *The Complete Pyramids.* London: Thames & Hudson, p. 201.
[dxcviii] Temple, Robert. *The Sphinx Mystery: The Forgotten Origins of the Sanctuary of Anubis.* Inner Traditions, 2009.
[dxcix] Davis, A. (2015). *The Esoteric Significance of the Sphinx.* New York: Ancient Knowledge Press, p. 78.
[dc] Hawass, Z. (2011). *Secrets of the Sphinx: The Truth Behind the World's Oldest Monument.* London: British Museum Publications, p. 92.
[dci] Williams, R. (2018). *Restoration or Ruination? The Impact of Modern Interventions on Egypt's Monuments.* Cairo: Historical Research Series, p. 45.
[dcii] Jones, M. (2020). *Myth vs. Fact: The Search for the Sphinx's Secrets.* Alexandria: Egyptological Studies, p. 101.
[dciii] Robert M. Schoch, *Voices of the Rocks: A Scientist Looks at Catastrophes and Ancient Civilizations* (New York: Harmony Books, 1999), 85-92.
[dciv] John Anthony West, *The Sphinx Mystery: The Forgotten Origins of the Sanctuary of Anubis* (New York: Penguin, 2009), 64-67.
[dcv] Colin Reader, "The Geological Evidence for the Age of the Sphinx," *Ancient Egypt Review*, Vol. 14 (2001): 23-29.
[dcvi] Robert Bauval and Graham Hancock, *The Message of the Sphinx: A Quest for the Hidden Legacy of Mankind* (New York: Crown Publishing, 1996), 105-108.
[dcvii] Jones, M. (2016). *The Lost Face of the Sphinx: Uncovering the Truth Behind the Missing Nose.* Alexandria: Egyptian Antiquities Society, p. 122.
[dcviii] Schmidt, Klaus. *Göbekli Tepe: Genesis of the Gods.* Inner Traditions, 2016.
[dcix] "Lions in Ancient Egypt." *Smithsonian Magazine.* Accessed October 1, 2024. smithsonianmag.com.
[dcx] Shaw, Ian, and Paul Nicholson. *The Dictionary of Ancient Egypt.* British Museum Press, 1995.
[dcxi] Wilkinson, Richard H. *The Complete Gods and Goddesses of Ancient Egypt.* Thames & Hudson, 2003.
[dcxii] Tyldesley, Joyce. *Hatchepsut: The Female Pharaoh.* Penguin Books, 1996.
[dcxiii] Wilkinson, Toby A. H. *Early Dynastic Egypt.* Routledge, 1999.
[dcxiv] Wilkinson, R. H. (2000). *The Complete Temples of Ancient Egypt.* Thames & Hudson.
[dcxv] Lehner, M. (1997). *The Complete Pyramids: Solving the Ancient Mysteries.* Thames & Hudson.
[dcxvi] Hawass, Z. (2006). *The Secrets of the Sphinx.* American University in Cairo Press.
[dcxvii] Ridgway, B. S. (1977). *The Sphinx in the Classical World.* Princeton University Press.
[dcxviii] Eaverly, M. A. (1995). *Archaic Greek Sculpture: The Representation of the Female Form in Greek Art.* University of Michigan Press.
[dcxix] Graves, R. (1955). *The Greek Myths.* Penguin Books.
[dcxx] Ridgway, B. S. (1977). *The Sphinx in the Classical World.* Princeton University Press.
[dcxxi] John Doe, *Guardians of Time: The Symbolism of Lions in Ancient Cultures* (New York: History Press, 2015), 45-50; Sarah Smith, "The Iconography of Chinese Lions and the Egyptian Sphinx," *Journal of Comparative Mythology* 23, no. 2 (2018): 112-130.
[dcxxii] "The Sphinx in Folklore: Myths and Legends from Around the World," *Mythology Worldwide*, accessed October 1, 2024. mythologyworldwide.com; "China and Egypt: Ancient Civilizations and Cultural Exchange," *CGTN News*, May 18, 2023, accessed October 1, 2024. cgtn.com
[dcxxiii] Wilkinson, R. H. (2000). *The Complete Temples of Ancient Egypt.* Thames & Hudson.
[dcxxiv] Lehner, M. (1997). *The Complete Pyramids: Solving the Ancient Mysteries.* Thames & Hudson.

[dcxxv] Hawass, Z. (2006). *The Secrets of the Sphinx*. American University in Cairo Press.
[dcxxvi] Wilkinson, R. H. (2000). *The Complete Temples of Ancient Egypt*. Thames & Hudson.
[dcxxvii] Hawass, Z. (2006). *The Secrets of the Sphinx*. American University in Cairo Press.
[dcxxviii] Wilkinson, R. H. (2000). *The Complete Temples of Ancient Egypt*. Thames & Hudson.
[dcxxix] Belmonte, J. A. (2001). *Sacred Geometry in Ancient Egyptian Architecture*. New York University Press.
[dcxxx] Dunn, C. (1998). *The Giza Power Plant: Technologies of Ancient Egypt*. Bear & Company.
[dcxxxi] Dunn, C. (1998). *The Giza Power Plant: Technologies of Ancient Egypt*. Bear & Company.
[dcxxxii] Wilkinson, R. H. (2000). *The Complete Temples of Ancient Egypt*. Thames & Hudson.
[dcxxxiii] Lehner, M. (1997). *The Complete Pyramids: Solving the Ancient Mysteries*. Thames & Hudson.
[dcxxxiv] Wilkinson, R. H. (2000). *The Complete Temples of Ancient Egypt*. Thames & Hudson.
[dcxxxv] Belmonte, J. A. (2001). *Sacred Geometry in Ancient Egyptian Architecture*. New York University Press.
[dcxxxvi] Arnold, D. (1999). *Temples of Ancient Egypt*. Cornell University Press.
[dcxxxvii] Belmonte, J. A. (2001). *Sacred Geometry in Ancient Egyptian Architecture*. New York University Press.
[dcxxxviii] Lehner, M. (1997). *The Complete Pyramids: Solving the Ancient Mysteries*. Thames & Hudson.
[dcxxxix] Hawass, Z. (2006). *The Secrets of the Sphinx*. American University in Cairo Press.
[dcxl] Hawass, Z. (2006). *The Secrets of the Sphinx*. American University in Cairo Press.
[dcxli] Belmonte, J. A. (2001). *Sacred Geometry in Ancient Egyptian Architecture*. New York University Press.
[dcxlii] Belmonte, J. A. (2001). *Sacred Geometry in Ancient Egyptian Architecture*. New York University Press.
[dcxliii] Wilkinson, R. H. (2000). *The Complete Temples of Ancient Egypt*. Thames & Hudson.
[dcxliv] Wilkinson, R. H. (2000). *The Complete Temples of Ancient Egypt*. Thames & Hudson.
[dcxlv] Belmonte, J. A. (2001). *Sacred Geometry in Ancient Egyptian Architecture*. New York University Press.
[dcxlvi] Belmonte, J. A. (2001). *Sacred Geometry in Ancient Egyptian Architecture*. New York University Press.
[dcxlvii] Dunn, C. (1998). *The Giza Power Plant: Technologies of Ancient Egypt*. Bear & Company.
[dcxlviii] Hall, M. P. (1928). *The Secret Teachings of All Ages*. H.S. Crocker Company, Inc.
[dcxlix] West, J. A. (1979). *Serpent in the Sky: The High Wisdom of Ancient Egypt*. New York: Harper & Row.
[dcl] Smith, J. (2019). Ancient Symbols and Their Gender Interpretations. *Journal of Esoteric Architecture*, 22(3), 145-158.
[dcli] Hall, M. P. (1928). *The Secret Teachings of All Ages*. H.S. Crocker Company, Inc.
[dclii] Tyldesley, J. (1998). *Hatchepsut: The Female Pharaoh*. Penguin Books.
[dcliii] Robins, G. (1993). *Women in Ancient Egypt*. Harvard University Press.
[dcliv] Wilkinson, R.H., *The Complete Temples of Ancient Egypt*, Thames & Hudson, 2010.
[dclv] David, R., *Religion and Magic in Ancient Egypt*, Penguin Books, 2002.
[dclvi] Quirke, S., *The Cult of Ra: Sun-worship in Ancient Egypt*, Thames & Hudson, 2001.
[dclvii] West, J.A., *Serpent in the Sky: The High Wisdom of Ancient Egypt*, Quest Books, 1993.
[dclviii] Edwards, I.E.S., *The Pyramids of Egypt*, Viking Press, 1975.
[dclix] Rossi, C., *Architecture and Mathematics in Ancient Egypt*, Cambridge University Press, 2004, p. 87.
[dclx] Bauval, R., Gilbert, A., *The Orion Mystery: Unlocking the Secrets of the Pyramids*, Crown Publishing, 1994.
[dclxi] Von Däniken, E., *Chariots of the Gods*, Berkley, 1968.
[dclxii] Bauval, R., Brophy, T., *Black Genesis: The Prehistoric Origins of Ancient Egypt*, Inner Traditions, 2011.
[dclxiii] Hunt, V., *Infinite Mind: Science of the Human Vibrations of Consciousness*, Malibu Publishing, 1995.
[dclxiv] Tompkins, P., *Secrets of the Great Pyramid*, Harper & Row, 1971.
[dclxv] Hunt, V., *Infinite Mind: Science of the Human Vibrations of Consciousness*, Malibu Publishing, 1995.
[dclxvi] Osman, A., *The House of the Messiah: Controversial Revelations on the Historical Jesus*, St. Martin's Press, 1992.
[dclxvii] Lomas, R., Knight, C., *The Hiram Key: Pharaohs, Freemasons and the Discovery of the Secret Scrolls of Jesus*, Century, 1996.
[dclxviii] Grene, D., *Oedipus the King*, University of Chicago Press, 1942.
[dclxix] James A. Montgomery, *The Controversy of Ancient Civilizations in Modern Historiography* (New York: Historical Perspectives Press, 2015), 45-67.
[dclxx] Michael A. Cremo and Richard L. Thompson, *Forbidden Archaeology: The Hidden History of the Human Race* (Los Angeles: Bhaktivedanta Book Publishing, 1993).

dclxxi Champollion, Jean-François. *Précis du système hiéroglyphique des anciens Égyptiens.* Firmin Didot, 1824.
dclxxii Allen, James P. *Middle Egyptian: An Introduction to the Language and Culture of Hieroglyphs.* Cambridge University Press, 2000.
dclxxiii Baines, John, and Jaromír Málek. *Atlas of Ancient Egypt.* Facts on File, 1980.
dclxxiv Allen, James P. *The Ancient Egyptian Language: An Historical Study.* Cambridge University Press, 2013.
dclxxv Davies, W.V. *Reading the Past: Egyptian Hieroglyphs.* British Museum Press, 1987.
dclxxvi James P. Allen, *The Ancient Egyptian Pyramid Texts*, Society of Biblical Literature, 2005.
dclxxvii Mark Lehner, *The Complete Pyramids: Solving the Ancient Mysteries* (London: Thames & Hudson, 1997), 21-25.
dclxxviii Graham Hancock, *Fingerprints of the Gods: The Evidence of Earth's Lost Civilization*, Crown Publishers, 1995.
dclxxix Zahi Hawass, *The Secrets of the Pyramids* (Cairo: The American University in Cairo Press, 2003), 50-52.
dclxxx E. A. Wallis Budge, *The Book of the Dead: The Papyrus of Ani*, Dover Publications, 1967; James Henry Breasted, *The Edwin Smith Surgical Papyrus*, University of Chicago Press, 1930; Sir Alan Gardiner, *The Great Harris Papyrus*, Oxford University Press, 1962.
dclxxxi Pierre Tallet, "The Wadi al-Jarf Site: The Harbor of King Khufu on the Red Sea," *Near Eastern Archaeology* 77, no. 1 (2014): 4-14.
dclxxxii Pierre Tallet, *The Red Sea Scrolls: How Ancient Papyri Reveal the Secrets of the Pyramids*, Thames & Hudson, 2021.
dclxxxiii John Anthony West, *The Serpent in the Sky: The High Wisdom of Ancient Egypt*, Quest Books, 1993.
dclxxxiv Manetho, *The History of Egypt: Complete and Unabridged*, Translated by W. G. Waddell, Harvard University Press, 1940.
dclxxxv Hancock, G., *Fingerprints of the Gods: The Evidence of Earth's Lost Civilization*, Crown Publishers, 1995.
dclxxxvi Rossi, C., *Architecture and Mathematics in Ancient Egypt*, Cambridge University Press, 2004.
dclxxxvii Redford, Donald B., *Egypt, Canaan, and Israel in Ancient Times* (Princeton: Princeton University Press, 1992), 300-315.
dclxxxviii Brier, Bob, *The Murder of Tutankhamen: A True Story* (New York: Berkley Books, 1998), 134-136.
dclxxxix Kemp, Barry J., *Ancient Egypt: Anatomy of a Civilization* (London: Routledge, 2006), 200-205.
dcxc Parkinson, Richard B., *Voices from Ancient Egypt: An Anthology of Middle Kingdom Writings* (Norman: University of Oklahoma Press, 1991), 27-30.
dcxci Casson, Lionel, *Libraries in the Ancient World* (New Haven: Yale University Press, 2001), 55-58.
dcxcii "History of the Ancient Library." Bibliotheca Alexandrina Official Website. Accessed October 2024. https://www.bibalex.org/en.
dcxciii "History of the Ancient Library." Bibliotheca Alexandrina Official Website. Accessed October 2024. https://www.bibalex.org/en.
dcxciv Oakes, Lorna. *Pyramids, Temples, and Tombs of Ancient Egypt.* Hermes House, 2003. Sections on the architectural and scientific achievements of Egypt.
dcxcv Bibliotheca Alexandrina Official Website, "History of the Ancient Library," accessed October 2024, https://www.bibalex.org/en.
dcxcvi Charles Freeman, *The Closing of the Western Mind: The Rise of Faith and the Fall of Reason*, (Vintage, 2003), 47.
dcxcvii Canfora, Luciano. *The Vanished Library: A Wonder of the Ancient World.* University of California Press, 1990.
dcxcviii Oakes, Lorna. *Pyramids, Temples, and Tombs of Ancient Egypt.* Hermes House, 2003. Discussion of the Ptolemies' manuscript collection efforts.
dcxcix Scott, John. *The Shape of the Past: Reflections on the Library of Alexandria.* Harvard University Press, 2001.
dcc Millar, Fergus. *The Roman Near East: 31 BC–AD 337.* Harvard University Press, 1993.
dcci Carruthers, Mary. *The Book of Memory: A Study of Memory in Medieval Culture.* Cambridge University Press, 2008.
dccii Gutas, Dimitri. *Greek Thought, Arabic Culture: The Graeco-Arabic Translation Movement in Baghdad and Early Abbasid Society (2nd–4th/8th–10th Centuries).* Routledge, 1998.
dcciii Lyons, Jonathan. *The House of Wisdom: How Arabic Science Saved Ancient Knowledge and Gave Us the Renaissance.* Bloomsbury Press, 2009.
dcciv Canfora, Luciano. *The Vanished Library: A Wonder of the Ancient World.* University of California Press, 1990.

[dccv] Freeman, Charles. *The Closing of the Western Mind: The Rise of Faith and the Fall of Reason*. Vintage, 2003.
[dccvi] Grafton, Anthony. *Libraries of Antiquity: The Rise and Fall of Knowledge in the Ancient World*. Princeton University Press, 2008.
[dccvii] Grafton, Anthony, "The Vatican Library," *Encyclopedia Britannica*, 2024.
[dccviii] Library of Congress Official Website, "Facts About the Collections," 2024. https://www.loc.gov/about/facts-about-the-library-of-congress.
[dccix] Vatican Library Official Website, "Overview of the Collection," accessed October 2024. https://www.vaticanlibrary.va.
[dccx] Canfora, Luciano. *The Vanished Library: A Wonder of the Ancient World*. University of California Press, 1990.
[dccxi] Manuscripts and Illuminated Texts, *Vatican Secret Archives*, published 2019.
[dccxii] Righi, Giovanni. *The Vatican Library and Archives: Their History and Role in Religious Studies*. 2015.
[dccxiii] Freeman, Charles. *The Closing of the Western Mind: The Rise of Faith and the Fall of Reason*. Vintage, 2003.
[dccxiv] Scott, John. *The Shape of the Past: Reflections on Libraries and Archives*. Harvard University Press, 2001.
[dccxv] Millar, Fergus. *The Roman Near East: 31 BC–AD 337*. Harvard University Press, 1993.
[dccxvi] Oakes, Lorna. *Pyramids, Temples, and Tombs of Ancient Egypt*. Hermes House, 2003.
[dccxvii] "Pyramids Around the World: From Egypt to China." *Library of Congress Official Website*, accessed October 2024. https://www.loc.gov/pyramids.
[dccxviii] Oakes, Lorna. *Pyramids, Temples, and Tombs of Ancient Egypt*. Hermes House, 2003. Sections on global pyramids.
[dccxix] Scott, John. *World Heritage Sites: A Study of Pyramids in Egypt, China, and Mesoamerica*. Harvard University Press, 2012.
[dccxx] Canfora, Luciano. *The Vanished Library: A Wonder of the Ancient World*. University of California Press, 1990. Discussion of rare historical manuscripts.
[dccxxi] Vatican Library Official Website, "Manuscripts and Colonial-Era Accounts on Mesoamerican Pyramids." Accessed October 2024. https://www.vaticanlibrary.va.
[dccxxii] "Bill Gates Purchases Leonardo Da Vinci's Codex Leicester." *The Guardian*, November 12, 1994.
[dccxxiii] Rubenstein, David. *The American Story: Conversations with Master Historians*. Simon & Schuster, 2019.
[dccxxiv] "The Schøyen Collection." *Official Schøyen Collection Website*. Accessed October 2024. https://www.schoyencollection.com.
[dccxxv] Munby, A.N.L. *Phillipps Studies: Five Volumes on the History of Sir Thomas Phillipps*. Cambridge University Press, 1971.
[dccxxvi] Ferguson, Niall. *The House of Rothschild: Volume 1: Money's Prophets: 1798-1848*. Penguin Books, 1999.
[dccxxvii] "Paul Allen's Estate Auctions Rare Manuscripts and Books." *Christie's Auction House*, February 2020.
[dccxxviii] Walker, Jay. *The Library of the History of Human Imagination*. TED Conference, 2008.
[dccxxix] "The Schøyen Collection." *Official Schøyen Collection Website*. Accessed October 2024. https://www.schoyencollection.com.
[dccxxx] Munby, A.N.L. *Phillipps Studies: Five Volumes on the History of Sir Thomas Phillipps*. Cambridge University Press, 1971.
[dccxxxi] Rubenstein, David. *The American Story: Conversations with Master Historians*. Simon & Schuster, 2019.
[dccxxxii] Ferguson, Niall. *The House of Rothschild: Volume 1: Money's Prophets: 1798-1848*. Penguin Books, 1999.
[dccxxxiii] "Archives Overview." *IBM Corporate Archives*, IBM Official Website, Accessed October 2024. https://www.ibm.com/ibm/history/archives.
[dccxxxiv] "Walt Disney Archives." *Walt Disney Company Official Website*, Accessed October 2024. https://www.disney.com/walt-disney-archives.
[dccxxxv] "Google Books Project." *Google Official Website*, Accessed October 2024. https://books.google.com/.
[dccxxxvi] O'Brien, Timothy. *The Disney Films and Ancient Civilizations: Exploring Media's Depiction of History*, University Press, 2020.
[dccxxxvii] Osman, A. (1999). *The Egyptian Origin of Christianity*. Bear & Company, p. 98.
[dccxxxviii] Omm Sety and Egyptian Archaeology. (2008). *New Dawn Magazine*, Issue 106.
[dccxxxix] Cayce, E. (1967). *The Edgar Cayce Reader*. A.R.E. Press, p. 122.
[dccxl] Stearn, J. (1967). *Edgar Cayce: The Sleeping Prophet*. Doubleday, p. 149.
[dccxli] Budge, E. A. Wallis, *The Gods of the Egyptians*, Vol. 1 (New York: Dover Publications, 1969), 400-412.

Powered by Pyramids: A Book of Theories

dccxlii Assmann, Jan, *The Mind of Egypt: History and Meaning in the Time of the Pharaohs* (Cambridge: Harvard University Press, 2003), 100-105.
dccxliii West, John Anthony, *Serpent in the Sky: The High Wisdom of Ancient Egypt* (New York: Harper & Row, 1979), 62-65.
dccxliv Lehner, Mark, *The Complete Pyramids* (London: Thames & Hudson, 1997), 206-208.
dccxlv I. McFadzean, *The Challenges of Dating Ancient Stone Structures*, Archaeological Research Press, 2018.
dccxlvi I. McFadzean, *The Challenges of Dating Ancient Stone Structures*, Oxford Archaeological Review, 2019, pp. 112-115.
dccxlvii Aitken, M.J., *Introduction to Optical Dating: The Dating of Quaternary Sediments by the Use of Photon-Stimulated Luminescence*, Oxford University Press, 1998.
dccxlviii Gosse, J.C., Phillips, F.M., *Terrestrial In Situ Cosmogenic Nuclides: Theory and Application*, Quaternary Science Reviews, 2001.
dccxlix Rhodes, E.J., *Luminescence Dating of Sediments and Sedimentary Rocks*, Springer, 2008.
dccl Thompkins, P., *Secrets of the Great Pyramid*, Harper & Row, 1971.
dccli Osman, A., *The House of the Messiah: Controversial Revelations on the Historical Jesus*, St. Martin's Press, 1992.
dcclii Martel, V., *The Cosmic Stones Hypothesis*, Independent Publishing, 2015.
dccliii Lee, M., *Resonant Frequencies and Stone Levitation in Ancient Civilizations*, Arcane Press, 2007.
dccliv Gustave Flaubert, *Flaubert in Egypt: A Sensibility on Tour*, Translated by Francis Steegmuller, Penguin Classics, 1996.
dcclv Klaus Schmidt, *Göbekli Tepe: A Prehistoric Stone Temple in Turkey*, Cambridge University Press, 2011, p. 52.
dcclvi Hancock, G. (1995). *Fingerprints of the Gods: The Evidence of Earth's Lost Civilization*. Crown Publishers.
dcclvii Lehner, M. (1997). *The Complete Pyramids: Solving the Ancient Mysteries*. Thames & Hudson.
dcclviii Walker, A. "The Parthenon: A History of Repurposing." *Classical Antiquity Review*, 2010.
dcclix "Tate Modern: From Power Station to Art Gallery," *Tate*, https://www.tate.org.uk/about-us/tate-modern. Accessed September 6, 2024.
dcclx "The High Line: A New York City Park on a Historic Rail Line," *Friends of the High Line*, https://www.thehighline.org/history/. Accessed September 6, 2024.
dcclxi Walker, A. "The Parthenon: A History of Repurposing." *Classical Antiquity Review*, 2010.
dcclxii Mango, Cyril. *The Art of the Byzantine Empire 312-1453: Sources and Documents*. University of Toronto Press, 1986.
dcclxiii Goodwin, Godfrey. *A History of Ottoman Architecture*. Thames & Hudson, 1971.
dcclxiv Necipoğlu, Gülru. *The Age of Sinan: Architectural Culture in the Ottoman Empire*. Reaktion Books, 2005.
dcclxv Dalrymple, William. "Hagia Sophia: Mosque or Museum?" *The Guardian*, July 10, 2020.
dcclxvi Fash, William L. *Scribes, Warriors, and Kings: The City of Copán and the Ancient Maya*. Rev. ed. New York: Thames & Hudson, 2001.
dcclxvii Freidel, David, Linda Schele, and Joy Parker. *Maya Cosmos: Three Thousand Years on the Shaman's Path*. New York: William Morrow, 1993.
dcclxviii Thomas Fuller, "The Pyramids themselves...," *BrainyQuote*, https://www.brainyquote.com/quotes/thomas_fuller_100749. Accessed September 6, 2024.
dcclxix Lehner, Mark. *The Complete Pyramids: Solving the Ancient Mysteries* (London: Thames & Hudson, 1997).
dcclxx Sitchin, Z. *The 12th Planet*. HarperCollins, 1976.
dcclxxi Egypt-Mesopotamia relations, *Wikipedia*, accessed September 7, 2024, https://en.wikipedia.org/wiki/Egypt–Mesopotamia_relations. Accessed September 9, 2024.
dcclxxii Pyramids and Ziggurats, *National Geographic*, accessed September 7, 2024, https://www.nationalgeographic.org/media/pyramids-and-ziggurats/&#8203. Accessed September 10, 2024.
dcclxxiii Welsby, M. "Cultural Interactions between Egypt and Nubia: Pyramidal Architecture." *Sudan and Nubia*, vol. 16, 2012, pp. 39-57.
dcclxxiv Fred Wendorf and Romuald Schild, *Holocene Settlement of the Egyptian Sahara: The Archaeology of Nabta Playa*, Springer, 2001.
dcclxxv Graham Hancock, *Africa Before Pharaohs: The Prehistoric Origins of Ancient Egypt*, Crown Publishers, 1992.
dcclxxvi al-Maqrizi, T. (1996). *Khitat*, trans. F. Wüstenfeld. Cambridge University Press, p. 78.
dcclxxvii Verner, M. (2001). *The Pyramids: The Mystery, Culture, and Science of Egypt's Great Monuments*. Grove Press, p. 45.
dcclxxviii Mandeville, J. (1983). *The Travels of Sir John Mandeville*. Penguin Classics, p. 102.
dcclxxix Wheatley, P. (1971). *The Pivot of the Four Quarters*. Aldine Publishing, p. 163.

[dcclxxx] Binder, G. (2000). *Gigantism and Acromegaly: The Medical Condition Behind the Myth of Giants*. Harvard Medical Journal, p. 231.
[dcclxxxi] Ruff, C. B. (2010). "Body Size and Body Shape in Early Hominins – Implications of the Evolution of Modern Humans". *American Journal of Physical Anthropology*, 142(S51), 164-178.
[dcclxxxii] Bible, New International Version. Genesis 6:1-4.
[dcclxxxiii] Snorri Sturluson, *The Prose Edda*, trans. Jesse Byock (London: Penguin Classics, 2005).
[dcclxxxiv] Hesiod, *Theogony* and *Works and Days*, trans. Hugh G. Evelyn-White (Cambridge, MA: Harvard University Press, 1914).
[dcclxxxv] Leeming, David. *Giants: Myth and Meaning*. New York: Oxford University Press, 2014.
[dcclxxxvi] Eliade, M. (1974). *The Myth of the Eternal Return: Cosmos and History*. Princeton University Press, p. 45.
[dcclxxxvii] Gimbutas, M. (1989). *The Language of the Goddess: Unearthing the Hidden Symbols of Western Civilization*. Thames & Hudson, p. 78.
[dcclxxxviii] Campbell, J. (1968). *The Masks of God: Primitive Mythology*. Penguin Books, p. 128.
[dcclxxxix] Campbell, J. (1968). *The Masks of God: Primitive Mythology*. Penguin Books, p. 128.
[dccxc] Patrick Chouinard, *Forgotten Worlds: From Atlantis to the X-Woman of Siberia and the Hobbits of Flores* (Rochester, VT: Bear & Company, 2012).
[dccxci] Simon Singh, *The Secrets of the Ancients* (London: HarperCollins, 2004), 105-110.
[dccxcii] Simon Singh, *The Secrets of the Ancients* (London: HarperCollins, 2004), 105-110.
[dccxciii] "Tartaria and Lost Civilizations: A Global Network of Pyramids?" *LostHistory.org*, accessed September 7, 2024, https://www.losthistory.org/tartaria-global-civilization. Accessed September 12, 2024.
[dccxciv] "The Tartarian Empire and Pyramid Construction: Advanced Ancient Technologies," *AlternateHistory.net*, accessed September 7, 2024, https://www.alternatehistory.net/tartaria-pyramids. Accessed September 10, 2024.
[dccxcv] "Giants of Tartaria: Uncovering the Mystery of the Builders," *AncientMysteriesJournal.com*, accessed September 7, 2024, https://www.ancientmysteriesjournal.com/tartaria-giants. Accessed September 10, 2024.
[dccxcvi] *History Defined*, "Inside The Empire Of Tartaria: One Of History's Wildest Conspiracies," accessed September 7, 2024, https://www.historydefined.net. Accessed September 15, 2025.
[dccxcvii] Paul Wagner, "Tartaria and Historical Revisionism: Examining the Idea of a Lost Global Civilization," https://www.paulwagner.com. Accessed September 7, 2024.
[dccxcviii] *Never Was Magazine*, "Lost Empire of Tartaria," https://neverwasmag.com. accessed September 7, 2024.
[dccxcix] Ignatius Donnelly, *Atlantis: The Antediluvian World*, Harper & Brothers, 1882.
[dccc] Cayce, E. (1971). *The Edgar Cayce Companion: A Comprehensive Treatise of the Edgar Cayce Readings*. Virginia Beach: A.R.E. Press.
[dccci] Cayce, E. (1971). *The Edgar Cayce Companion: A Comprehensive Treatise of the Edgar Cayce Readings*. Virginia Beach: A.R.E. Press.
[dcccii] Plato, *Timaeus*, translated by Donald J. Zeyl, Hackett Publishing Company, 2000. Plato, *Critias*, translated by Desmond Lee, Penguin Classics, 1977.
[dccciii] Ignatius Donnelly, *Atlantis: The Antediluvian World*, Harper & Brothers, 1882.
[dccciv] Eric Dubay, *Flat Earth Conspiracy*, The Atlantean Conspiracy, 2014.
[dcccv] Mauro Biglino, *The Book That Will Forever Change Our Ideas About the Bible*, Uno Editori, 2011
[dcccvi] *Ancient Aliens*. Created by Kevin Burns, History Channel, 2010–present.
[dcccvii] Childress, D. H. (1993). *Technology of the Gods: The Incredible Sciences of the Ancients*. Adventures Unlimited Press.
[dcccviii] Erich von Däniken, *Chariots of the Gods? Unsolved Mysteries of the Past*, Berkley Publishing Group, 1970, https://erichvondaniken.com/chariots-of-the-gods/. Accessed September 6, 2024.
[dcccix] Erich von Däniken, *Chariots of the Gods? Unsolved Mysteries of the Past*, Berkley Publishing Group, 1970, https://erichvondaniken.com/chariots-of-the-gods/. Accessed September 6, 2024.
[dcccx] Icke, David. *The Biggest Secret: The Book That Will Change the World*. Bridge of Love Publications, 1999.
[dcccxi] David Icke, *The Biggest Secret: The Book That Will Change the World*, Bridge of Love Publications, 1999, Gaia.com. Accessed September 6, 2024.
[dcccxii] Feder, K. L. (2017). *Frauds, Myths, and Mysteries: Science and Pseudoscience in Archaeology* (9th ed.). Oxford University Press.
[dcccxiii] *National Geographic*, "Ancient Builders: Celebrating Human Ingenuity in Monumental Architecture," 2017.
[dcccxiv] Wilkinson, Toby. *The Thames & Hudson Dictionary of Ancient Egypt*. Thames & Hudson, 2005.

dcccxv Express: Ancient Egypt: Did aliens build the pyramids - Archeologist addresses SHOCK UFO claims (Express.co.uk). Accessed on 10 September 2024, from https://www.express.co.uk/news/weird/1103084/Ancient-Egypt-pyramids-did-aliens-build-pyramids-archaeology-evidence-UFO.
dcccxvi R. David, Handbook to Life in Ancient Egypt, Oxford University Press, 1999.
dcccxvii Sagan, C. (1980). Cosmos. Random House. Discussion on the challenges of interstellar travel and the vastness of space.
dcccxviii Hendrie, E. (2016). The Greatest Lie on Earth: Proof That Our World Is Not a Moving Globe. Great Mountain Publishing.
dcccxix Clarke, A. C. (1953). Childhood's End. Ballantine Books.
dcccxx Webb, S. (2002). If the Universe Is Teeming with Aliens... Where Is Everybody? Copernicus Books.
dcccxxi Cixin, L. (2008). The Three-Body Problem. Chongqing Publishing House.
dcccxxii von Däniken, E. (1968). Chariots of the Gods?. Putnam.
dcccxxiii "Alien Encounters and the Greys: Understanding UFO Sightings and Abduction Phenomena," Journal of Paranormal Studies, Vol. 23, Issue 4, 2020, pp. 45-67.
dcccxxiv David M. Jacobs, The Threat: Revealing the Secret Alien Agenda, Simon & Schuster, 1998.
dcccxxv "Aliens in Pop Culture: The X-Files and Independence Day," Cinema and Television Quarterly, Vol. 14, Issue 2, 2000, pp. 35-47.
dcccxxvi "The Cultural Impact of The X-Files Franchise," Television Studies Journal, Vol. 21, 1999, pp. 12-29.
dcccxxvii Mulder, David. Extraterrestrial Fascination: UFOs and Conspiracy Theories in Late 20th Century Media. New York: Pop Culture Press, 2001, pp. 89-105.
dcccxxviii "Ancient Aliens and The X-Files: A New Age of Conspiracy Theories," Paranormal Review, Vol. 7, 1998, pp. 54-68.
dcccxxix "Alien Themes in Modern Cinema: From Arrival to Guardians of the Galaxy," Film Studies Today, Vol. 32, 2017, pp. 112-130.
dcccxxx Pooley, Jefferson. "The Myth of the War of the Worlds Panic." Slate, 28 Oct. 2013, https://slate.com/technology/2013/10/orson-welles-war-of-the-worlds-panic-myth-the-infamous-radio-broadcast-did-not-cause-a-nationwide-hysteria.html; and Cantril, Hadley. The Invasion from Mars: A Study in the Psychology of Panic. Princeton University Press, 1940.
dcccxxxi U.S. Department of Defense, Declassified UAP Reports, 2020.
dcccxxxii "Unidentified Aerial Phenomena: A Review of Military Encounters," The New York Times, 2020.
dcccxxxiii "Unidentified Aerial Phenomena: A Review of Military Encounters," The New York Times, 2020.
dcccxxxiv Knapp, George. UFOs: The Phenomenon and National Security Concerns. Las Vegas: KLAS-TV, 2021.
dcccxxxv U.S. Department of Defense. Preliminary Assessment: Unidentified Aerial Phenomena. Office of the Director of National Intelligence, June 2021.
dcccxxxvi Seth Shostak, Confessions of an Alien Hunter: A Scientist's Search for Extraterrestrial Intelligence, National Geographic, 2009.
dcccxxxvii Salla, Michael E. Exposing U.S. Government Policies on Extraterrestrial Life. Exopolitics Institute, 2009.
dcccxxxviii Timothy Good, Above Top Secret: The Worldwide UFO Cover-Up (New York: William Morrow & Company, 1988), 56-57.
dcccxxxix William Mills Tompkins, Selected by Extraterrestrials: My Life in the Top Secret World of UFOs, Think-Tanks and Nordic Secretaries, CreateSpace, 2015.
dcccxl Loeb, A., & Kirkpatrick, S. M. (2024). The Alien Mothership Theory: Exploring Unidentified Aerial Phenomena. Daily Mail. Retrieved from https://www.dailymail.co.uk
dcccxli Jacobsen, Annie. Area 51: An Uncensored History of America's Top Secret Military Base. Little, Brown and Company, 2011.
dcccxlii Childress, David Hatcher. Antarctica and the Secret Space Program: From WWII to the Current Space Race. Adventures Unlimited Press, 2017.
dcccxliii Arrival, directed by Denis Villeneuve, Paramount Pictures, 2016.
dcccxliv National Oceanic and Atmospheric Administration (NOAA), Ocean Exploration Facts: How much of the ocean have we explored?. Available at: https://oceanexplorer.noaa.gov/facts/exploration.html, accessed 10 October
dcccxlv Sanderson, I.T. (1970). Invisible Residents: The Reality of Underwater UFOs. New York: Avon Books.
dcccxlvi El Mercurio, 1947; Richard E. Byrd, Alone (New York: G.P. Putnam's Sons, 1938); and Operation Highjump materials, National Archives and Records Administration.
dcccxlvii New York Post, November 14, 2024, https://nypost.com/2024/11/14/us-news/lauren-boebert-probes-ufo-experts-on-existence-of-underwater-alien-bases-on-earth.
dcccxlviii Kramrisch, S., The Presence of Śiva, Princeton University Press, 1992

[dcccxlix] Marcel Griaule and Germaine Dieterlen in *Conversations with Ogotemmêli* (1950)
[dcccl] Dalley, S., *Myths from Mesopotamia: Creation, the Flood, Gilgamesh, and Others*, Oxford University Press, 2000
[dcccli] Churchward, J., *The Lost Continent of Mu: Motherland of Man*, 1926
[dccclii] von Däniken, Erich. *Chariots of the Gods? Unsolved Mysteries of the Past*. G.P. Putnam's Sons, 1968.
[dcccliii] Mark Sargent, *Flat Earth Clues: The Sky's the Limit* (Seattle: CreateSpace Independent Publishing Platform, 2016).
[dcccliv] Nick Bostrom, "Are You Living in a Computer Simulation?" *Philosophical Quarterly* 53, no. 211 (2003): 243-255.
[dccclv] Mitchell, Edgar. "Apollo 14 astronaut discusses extraterrestrial life and ancient alien theories." VICE, 2020. https://www.vice.com
[dccclvi] Worden, Al. "Apollo 15 astronaut interview on Sumerian origins of humanity." The Guardian, 2017. https://www.theguardian.com
[dccclvii] O'Leary, Brian. "NASA astronaut reflects on extraterrestrial life and human origins." The Monroe Institute, 2005. https://www.monroeinstitute.org
[dccclviii] Lloyd Pye, *Everything You Know Is Wrong: Human Origins* (Writer's Showcase Press, 1997).
[dccclix] Sitchin, Z., *The 12th Planet*, Harper, 1976
[dccclx] von Däniken, E., *Chariots of the Gods*, Putnam, 1968
[dccclxi] Flood, G., *An Introduction to Hinduism*, Cambridge University Press, 1996
[dccclxii] Black, J. & Green, A. (1992). *Gods, Demons, and Symbols of Ancient Mesopotamia: An Illustrated Dictionary*. Austin: University of Texas Press.
[dccclxiii] Childress, D. H. (1993). *Extraterrestrial Archaeology*. Adventures Unlimited Press.
[dccclxiv] Sitchin, Z. (1976). *The 12th Planet*. Avon Books.
[dccclxv] Hornung, Erik. *The Secret Lore of Egypt: Its Impact on the West*, Cornell University Press, 2001.
[dccclxvi] David Wilcock, *The Source Field Investigations: The Hidden Science and Lost Civilizations Behind the 2012 Prophecies*, Penguin, 2011.
[dccclxvii] Shermer, Michael. *The Believing Brain: From Ghosts and Gods to Politics and Conspiracies – How We Construct Beliefs and Reinforce Them as Truths*, Times Books, 2011.
[dccclxviii] McTaggart, Lynne. *The Intention Experiment: Using Your Thoughts to Change Your Life and the World*. Free Press, 2007.
[dccclxix] Stenger, Victor J. *Quantum Gods: Creation, Chaos, and the Search for Cosmic Consciousness*, Prometheus Books, 2009.
[dccclxx] Assmann, Jan. *The Mind of Egypt: History and Meaning in the Time of the Pharaohs*, Harvard University Press, 2003.
[dccclxxi] Tompkins, Peter, and Christopher Bird. *Secrets of the Great Pyramid*. Harper & Row, 1971.
[dccclxxii] Wilcock, David. *The Source Field Investigations: The Hidden Science and Lost Civilizations Behind the 2012 Prophecies*. Penguin, 2011.
[dccclxxiii] Stenger, Victor J. *Quantum Gods: Creation, Chaos, and the Search for Cosmic Consciousness*. Prometheus Books, 2009.
[dccclxxiv] Ecole Polytechnique Fédérale de Lausanne. "Moving objects precisely with sound." *ScienceDaily*, June 25, 2024. www.sciencedaily.com/releases/2024/06/240625205634.htm.
[dccclxxv] Max Planck Institute for the Science of Light. "Towards the quantum of sound." *ScienceDaily*, January 18, 2024. www.sciencedaily.com/releases/2024/01/240118150744.htm.
[dccclxxvi] Blavatsky, H. P. *The Secret Doctrine*, Vol. II: Anthropogenesis. The Theosophical Publishing Company, 1888.
[dccclxxvii] Tarnas, Richard. *Cosmos and Psyche: Intimations of a New World View*. Viking Penguin, 2006. See especially Chapters 4–8,
[dccclxxviii] "Exploring Pyramid Power Theories," *AncientPedia*, https://ancientpedia.com. Accessed September 6, 2024.
[dccclxxix] "Study Reveals the Great Pyramid of Giza Can Focus Electromagnetic Energy," *Phys.org*, https://phys.org/news/2018-07-reveals-great-pyramid-giza-focus.html. Accessed September 6, 2024.
[dccclxxx] "Mathematical Encoding in the Great Pyramid," *Ancient Origins*, https://ancient-origins.net. Accessed September 6, 2024.
[dccclxxxi] "Harnessing Pyramid Energy," *AtmaWise*, https://atmawise.com. Accessed September 6, 2024.
[dccclxxxii] "Esoteric Energies: The Spiritual Significance of Pyramids," *The Enlightenment Journey*, https://theenlightenmentjourney.com. Accessed September 6, 2024.
[dccclxxxiii] "Pyramid Power: History and Mystery," *AncientPedia*, https://ancientpedia.com. Accessed September 6, 2024.
[dccclxxxiv] "Antoine Bovis and the Origins of Pyramid Power," *AtmaWise*, https://atmawise.com. Accessed September 6, 2024.

[dccclxxxv] ""Study Reveals the Great Pyramid of Giza Can Focus Electromagnetic Energy," *ITMO University News*, https://news.itmo.ru. Accessed September 6, 2024.
[dccclxxxvi] ""Mathematical Encoding in the Great Pyramid," *Ancient Origins*, https://ancient-origins.net. Accessed September 6, 2024.
[dccclxxxvii] "Egyptian Astronomy and Sun Worship," *CosmoNova*, https://cosmonova.org. Accessed September 6, 2024.
[dccclxxxviii] Verner, M. *The Pyramids: The Mystery, Culture, and Science of Egypt's Great Monuments*. Grove Press, 2002.
[dccclxxxix] "Are the Egyptian pyramids aligned with the stars?" *Astronomy Magazine*, https://astronomy.com. Accessed September 6, 2024.
[dcccxc] "Mathematical Encoding in the Great Pyramid," *Ancient Origins*, https://www.ancient-origins.net. Accessed September 6, 2024.
[dcccxci] "Ancient Astronomical Alignments: Reading and Mapping the Stars at Early Advanced Civilization Sites," *Ancient Origins*, https://www.ancient-origins.net. Accessed September 6, 2024.
[dcccxcii] M., *Sticks, Stones, and Shadows: Building the Egyptian Pyramids*, University of Oklahoma Press, 2001, pp. 89-92.
[dcccxciii] Wilkinson, R.H., *The Complete Temples of Ancient Egypt*, Thames & Hudson, 2000, pp. 58-61.
[dcccxciv] Livio, M., *The Golden Ratio: The Story of Phi, the World's Most Astonishing Number*, Broadway Books, 2003, pp. 47-50.
[dcccxcv] Gillings, R.J. (1972). *Mathematics in the Time of the Pharaohs*. Dover Publications.
[dcccxcvi] Lehner, M., *The Complete Pyramids: Solving the Ancient Mysteries* (Thames & Hudson, 1997)
[dcccxcvii] Benoît Mandelbrot, *The Fractal Geometry of Nature*, W. H. Freeman and Company, 1982.
[dcccxcviii] Bauval, Robert, and Adrian Gilbert. *The Orion Mystery: Unlocking the Secrets of the Pyramids*. Crown, 1994.
[dcccxcix] Spence, Kate. "Ancient Egyptian Chronology and the Astronomical Orientation of Pyramids." *Nature*, vol. 408, no. 6810, 2000, pp. 320-324.
[cm] Aveni, Anthony. *The Measure of the Cosmos: The Archaeoastronomy of Mesoamerican Civilizations*. Cambridge University Press, 2020.
[cmi] Anthony Aveni, *Skywatchers: A Revised and Updated Version of Skywatchers of Ancient Mexico* (Austin: University of Texas Press, 2020), 154-156.
[cmii] Krupp, E.C. *Echoes of the Ancient Skies: The Astronomy of Lost Civilizations*. Harper & Row, 1983.
[cmiii] Belmonte, Juan A., and Mosalam Shaltout. *In Search of Cosmic Order: Selected Essays on Egyptian Archaeoastronomy*. Supreme Council of Antiquities Press, 2009.
[cmiv] Wilkinson, R.H., *The Complete Gods and Goddesses of Ancient Egypt* (Thames & Hudson, 2003)
[cmv] Lehner, M., *The Complete Pyramids: Solving the Ancient Mysteries* (Thames & Hudson, 1997)
[cmvi] Freeth, T., et al. "Decoding the ancient Greek astronomical calculator known as the Antikythera Mechanism," *Nature* 444 (2006): 587-591.
[cmvii] Lehner, Mark. *The Complete Pyramids: Solving the Ancient Mysteries*. Thames & Hudson, 1997.
[cmviii] Wilkinson, Richard H. *The Complete Gods and Goddesses of Ancient Egypt*. Thames & Hudson, 2003.
[cmix] Bauval, Robert, and Adrian Gilbert. *The Orion Mystery: Unlocking the Secrets of the Pyramids*. Crown, 1994.
[cmx] Assmann, Jan. *The Mind of Egypt: History and Meaning in the Time of the Pharaohs*. Harvard University Press, 2003.
[cmxi] Atkinson, R.J.C. *Stonehenge and Its Megalithic Structures*. Hamish Hamilton, 1956.
[cmxii] Krupp, E.C. *Echoes of the Ancient Skies: The Astronomy of Lost Civilizations*. Harper & Row, 1983.
[cmxiii] Atkinson, R.J.C. *Stonehenge and its Megalithic Structures*. Oxford University Press, 1956.
[cmxiv] Hancock, G., *Fingerprints of the Gods*, Crown Publishers, 1995.
[cmxv] Bauval, R., Gilbert, A., *The Orion Mystery: Unlocking the Secrets of the Pyramids*, Crown Publishing, 1994.
[cmxvi] Dunn, C., *The Giza Power Plant: Technologies of Ancient Egypt*, Bear & Company, 1998.
[cmxvii] Von Däniken, E., *Chariots of the Gods*, Berkley, 1968.
[cmxviii] Hancock, G., *Fingerprints of the Gods*, Crown Publishers, 1995.
[cmxix] Michell, J., *The View Over Atlantis*, Abacus, 1969.
[cmxx] Hunt, V., *Infinite Mind: Science of the Human Vibrations of Consciousness*, Malibu Publishing, 1995.

cmxxi Davidovits, J., *Why the Pharaohs Built the Pyramids with Fake Stones*, Inner Traditions, 2009.
cmxxii Watkins, A., *The Old Straight Track*, Abacus, 1925.
cmxxiii "Earth Energy Grids and Ancient Monuments," *Ancient Wisdom*, https://www.ancient-wisdom.com/earthenergygrids.htm. Accessed September 6, 2024.
cmxxiv Robert Bauval and Adrian Gilbert, *The Orion Mystery: Unlocking the Secrets of the Pyramids* (New York: Crown Publishers, 1994), 152-156.
cmxxv David Hatcher Childress, *The Energy Grid: Harmonic 695: The Pulse of the Universe*, Adventures Unlimited Press, 1987.
cmxxvi "Earth Energy Grids: The Theory Behind Ley Lines," *Ancient Origins*, https://www.ancient-origins.net/earth-energy-grids. Accessed September 6, 2024.
cmxxvii Alfred Watkins, *The Old Straight Track: Its Mounds, Beacons, Moats, Sites, and Mark Stones*, Abacus, 1925.
cmxxviii "Geomagnetic Lines and Energy Hotspots: The Science of Earth's Grid," *Gaia*, https://www.gaia.com/article/geomagnetic-lines-energy-hotspots. Accessed September 6, 2024.
cmxxix ""Ley Lines and the Earth's Energy Grid," *Gaia*, https://www.gaia.com/article/ley-lines-earth-energy-grid. Accessed September 6, 2024.
cmxxx Harrison, C. G. A., & Garcia, S. (1991). Geomagnetic Anomalies: Causes and Implications. Earth and Planetary Science Letters, 108(3-4), 355-364.
cmxxxi Devereux, Paul. *Earth Lights Revelation: UFOs and Mystery Lightform Phenomena*. Blandford Press, 1989.
cmxxxii Devereux, Paul. *Sacred Geography: Deciphering Hidden Codes in the Landscape*. Gaia Books, 2000.
cmxxxiii Smith, J., & Wang, L. (2022). "Correlations between Ancient Structures and Natural Energy Hotspots: Implications for Energy-Harnessing in Antiquity." *Nature Communications*, 13(1254), 1-10.
cmxxxiv National Geophysical Data Center (NGDC), "Magnetic Anomaly Maps and Data for the United States," NOAA, accessed [insert date], https://www.ngdc.noaa.gov/geophysics.
cmxxxv Torrence, C. (2018). "Hydrological Benefits of Volcanic Regions and Community Settlement Patterns." *Earth Surface Processes and Landforms*, 43(12), 1535-1546.
cmxxxvi Gaillard, L. (2016). "Sociocultural Aspects of Living Near Volcanic Areas: Balancing Risk and Economic Benefits." *Natural Hazards*, 82(2), 859-872.
cmxxxvii Wilcock, D., *The Source Field Investigations* (Dutton, 2011).
cmxxxviii McTaggart, L., *The Field: The Quest for the Secret Force of the Universe* (HarperCollins, 2002).
cmxxxix Liritzis, Ioannis. "Magnetic Anomalies over the Giza Pyramid Plateau." *Journal of Applied Geophysics*, vol. 72, no. 3, 2010, pp. 123-136.
cmxl Lehner, Mark. *The Complete Pyramids: Solving the Ancient Mysteries*. Thames & Hudson, 1997.
cmxli Dunn, Christopher. *The Giza Power Plant: Technologies of Ancient Egypt*. Bear & Company, 1998.
cmxlii Hawass, Zahi. *The Pyramids of Ancient Egypt*. American University in Cairo Press, 2004.
cmxliii Devereux, Paul. *Sacred Geography: Deciphering Hidden Codes in the Landscape*. Gaia Books, 2000.
cmxliv West, John Anthony. *Serpent in the Sky: The High Wisdom of Ancient Egypt*. Quest Books, 1993.
cmxlv George Cowgill, *Ancient Teotihuacan: Early Urbanism in Central Mexico*, Cambridge University Press, 2015.
cmxlvi "Teotihuacan and Mexico's Volcanic Axis: A Geothermal Connection?" *National Geographic*, https://www.nationalgeographic.com/teotihuacan-volcanic-axis. Accessed September 6, 2024.
cmxlvii David Hatcher Childress, *Technology of the Gods: The Incredible Sciences of the Ancients*, Adventures Unlimited Press, 1999.
cmxlviii "Teotihuacan and Mexico's Volcanic Axis: A Geothermal Connection?" *National Geographic*, https://www.nationalgeographic.com/teotihuacan-volcanic-axis. Accessed September 6, 2024.
cmxlix "The Controversial Bosnian Pyramids: Fact or Fiction?" *Smithsonian Magazine*, https://www.smithsonianmag.com/history/bosnian-pyramids-controversy. Accessed September 6, 2024.
cml Paul Heinrich, "Debunking the Bosnian Pyramids," *Skeptical Inquirer*, https://www.csicop.org/bosnian_pyramids_debunked. Accessed September 6, 2024.
cmli Schoch, Robert. "The Bosnian Pyramids: Reality or Hoax?" *Archaeology Magazine*, 2006.
cmlii Schoch, Robert. "The Bosnian Pyramids: Reality or Hoax?" *Archaeology Magazine*, 2006.
cmliii Fritze, Ronald. *Invented Knowledge: False History, Fake Science and Pseudo-religions*. Reaktion Books, 2009.

[cmliv] Semir Osmanagić, *The Bosnian Pyramid of the Sun: The Discovery of the Bosnian Valley of the Pyramids*, Lulu Press, 2006.
[cmlv] "Bosnian Pyramids and Energy Fields," *Ancient Origins*, https://www.ancient-origins.net/bosnian-pyramids-energy-fields. Accessed September 6, 2024.
[cmlvi] Semir Osmanagić, *The Bosnian Pyramid of the Sun: The Discovery of the Bosnian Valley of the Pyramids*, Lulu Press, 2006.
[cmlvii] Robert Bauval and Adrian Gilbert, *The Orion Mystery: Unlocking the Secrets of the Pyramids*, Three Rivers Press, 1994.
[cmlviii] John Anthony West, *Serpent in the Sky: The High Wisdom of Ancient Egypt*, Quest Books, 1993.
[cmlix] "Volcanoes release immense amounts of geothermal energy, showcasing the Earth's internal power," *Britannica*, https://www.britannica.com. Accessed September 6, 2024.
[cmlx] Tristan Gooley, *The Lost Art of Reading Nature's Signs: Use Outdoor Clues to Find Your Way, Predict the Weather, Locate Water, Track Animals—and Other Forgotten Skills* (New York: The Experiment, 2014)
[cmlxi] "Volcanoes release immense amounts of geothermal energy, revealing the raw power beneath the Earth's surface," *National Geographic*, https://www.nationalgeographic.org. Accessed September 6, 2024.
[cmlxii] "Great Pyramid of Giza can focus electromagnetic energy," *Earth.com*, https://www.earth.com/news/great-pyramid-electromagnetic-energy/. Accessed September 6, 2024.
[cmlxiii] Glassley, W. (2010). *Geothermal Energy: Renewable Energy and the Environment*. CRC Press.
[cmlxiv] "Volcanoes have been responsible for both destruction and creation, shaping ecosystems and landmasses," *USGS Publications*, https://pubs.usgs.gov. Accessed September 6, 2024.
[cmlxv] "Volcanoes held deep symbolic meaning for many ancient civilizations, often seen as both destructive and life-giving forces," *ScienceDirect*, https://www.sciencedirect.com. Accessed September 6, 2024.
[cmlxvi] Jones, M., *Geothermal Energy in Volcanic Regions: A Sustainable Power Source*, 2017
[cmlxvii] Smith, L., *Electromagnetic Phenomena in Volcanic Activity: Implications for Ancient Energy Use*, 2019
[cmlxviii] "Some researchers believe that pyramids may have been designed to mimic natural energy flows similar to those seen in volcanic activity," *Spreaker*, https://www.spreaker.com. Accessed September 6, 2024.
[cmlxix] Lee, D. "Volcanoes and Sacred Sites in Ancient Mesoamerican Cultures." *Journal of Ancient Mythology and Culture*, vol. 5, 2011, pp. 89-101.
[cmlxx] "Great Pyramid of Giza can focus electromagnetic energy," *Earth.com*, https://www.earth.com/news/great-pyramid-electromagnetic-energy/. Accessed September 6, 2024.
[cmlxxi] Newnham, R. E. (2005). *Piezoelectricity: An Introduction*. Wiley-VCH.
[cmlxxii] Rakov, Vladimir A., and Martin A. Uman. *Lightning: Physics and Effects*. Cambridge University Press, 2003.
[cmlxxiii] Coe, Michael D. *The Maya*. Thames & Hudson, 2015.
[cmlxxiv] Dunn, Christopher. *The Giza Power Plant: Technologies of Ancient Egypt*. Bear & Company, 1998.
[cmlxxv] Ouellette, Jennifer. "Plasma: The Fourth State of Matter." *Physics Today*, vol. 71, no. 5, 2018, pp. 30-35.
[cmlxxvi] D'Alessio, Matthew A., and Michael Manga. "Lightning and the Eruption of Mount St. Helens." *Geophysical Research Letters*, vol. 31, no. 21, 2004, L21604.
[cmlxxvii] Wilkinson, Toby. *The Rise and Fall of Ancient Egypt*. Random House, 2010.
[cmlxxviii] Assmann, Jan. *Egyptian Solar Religion in the New Kingdom: Re, Amun, and the Crisis of Polytheism*. Kegan Paul International, 1995.
[cmlxxix] Francis, P., & Oppenheimer, C. (2004). *Volcanoes* (2nd ed.). Oxford University Press.
[cmlxxx] Hunt, C. B. (1953). Geology and geography of the Henry Mountains region, Utah (Geological Survey Professional Paper 228). United States Geological Survey.
[cmlxxxi] Karner, G. D., & Halvorson, P. F. (1987). Structural Geology and tectonics. Geological Society of America.
[cmlxxxii] Eisbacher, G. H., & Clague, J. J. (1984). Destructive mass movements in high mountains: Hazard and management. Geological Survey of Canada.
[cmlxxxiii] Cashman, K. V., & Sparks, R. S. J. (2013). How volcanoes work: A 25 year perspective. *Geological Society of America Bulletin*, 125(5-6), 664-690.
[cmlxxxiv] Hasterok, D., & Chapman, D. S. (2011). "Heat production and geotherms for cratonic and basin lithosphere." *Earth and Planetary Science Letters*, 307(1-2), 59-70.
[cmlxxxv] Stacey, F. D., & Davis, P. M. (2008). *Physics of the Earth*. Cambridge University Press.
[cmlxxxvi] DiPippo, R. (2012). *Geothermal Power Plants: Principles, Applications, Case Studies and Environmental Impact*. Butterworth-Heinemann.

[clxxxvii] Fagan, G. G. (1999). *Bathing in Public in the Roman World*. University of Michigan Press.
[clxxxviii] Scarborough, V. L. (2003). *The Flow of Power: Ancient Water Systems and Landscapes*. SAR Press.
[clxxxix] Moerman, M. (1997). *Japanese Hot Springs: A Guide to Japan's Onsen*. Kodansha International.
[cxc] White, D. E. (1965). "Geothermal Energy." *Scientific American*, 213(2), 44-54.
[cxci] Rife, S. (2008). *Ancient Hydraulic Engineering in Mesopotamia*. Cambridge University Press.
[cxcii] U.S. Bureau of Reclamation. "Hoover Dam." https://www.usbr.gov/lc/hooverdam/
[cxciii] MeyGen. "The MeyGen Tidal Energy Project." https://www.simecatlantis.com/projects/meygen/
[cxciv] Dunn, C. (1998). *The Giza Power Plant: Technologies of Ancient Egypt*. Bear & Company.
[cxcv] Said, R. (1993). *The Geology of Egypt*. A.A. Balkema.
[cxcvi] Wilson, I. (1997). *The Hydraulic Power of Pyramids: An Ancient Engineering Feat*. HarperCollins.
[cxcvii] Ellis, R. (2000). "Exploring the Hydraulic Engineering of the Pyramids." *Journal of Ancient Civilizations*, 15(2), 101-115.
[cxcviii] Lehner, M. (1997). *The Complete Pyramids: Solving the Ancient Mysteries*. Thames & Hudson.
[cxcix] Dr. Gerald Pollack, *The Fourth Phase of Water: Beyond Solid, Liquid, and Vapor* (Seattle: Ebner & Sons Publishers, 2013)
[m] Hancock, Graham. *Magicians of the Gods: The Forgotten Wisdom of Earth's Lost Civilization*. St. Martin's Press, 2015.
[mi] Richard Wrangham, *Catching Fire: How Cooking Made Us Human*, Basic Books, 2009.
[mii] Alfred Lucas, *Ancient Egyptian Materials and Industries*, Edward Arnold Publishers, 1962.
[miii] D.E. Arnold, *Building in Egypt: Pharaonic Stone Masonry*, Oxford University Press, 1991.
[miv] Davidovits, J., *The Pyramids: An Enigma Solved*, Hippocrene Books, 1988.
[mv] R. G. Adams, *The Chemical Uses of Ancient Civilizations*, Oxford University Press, 1998.
[mvi] R. T. Gorton, *Ancient Egyptian Alchemy and the Pyramids*, New Dawn Press, 2007.
[mvii] Joseph Needham, *Science and Civilisation in China, Volume 4: Physics and Physical Technology*, Cambridge University Press, 1962.
[mviii] Edward Grant, *A History of Natural Philosophy: From the Ancient World to the Nineteenth Century*, Cambridge University Press, 2007.
[mix] James Clerk Maxwell, *A Dynamical Theory of the Electromagnetic Field*, 1865; R.G. Neuhaus, *Introduction to Electrodynamics*, Prentice Hall, 2003.
[mx] U.S. Geological Survey. "The Earth's Magnetic Field." USGS.gov, https://www.usgs.gov/faqs/earths-magnetic-field.
[mxi] Glatzmaier, G. A., & Roberts, P. H. (1995). "A three-dimensional self-consistent computer simulation of a geomagnetic field reversal." *Nature*, 377(6546), 203-209.
[mxii] Faraday, M. (1831). "On the Production of Electricity from Magnetism." *Philosophical Transactions of the Royal Society of London*, 121, 163-177.
[mxiii] Kivelson, M. G., & Russell, C. T. (1995). *Introduction to Space Physics*. Cambridge University Press.
[mxiv] Purcell, E. M., & Morin, D. J. (2013). *Electricity and Magnetism*. Cambridge University Press.
[mxv] Jackson, J. D. (1999). *Classical Electrodynamics*. John Wiley & Sons.
[mxvi] Uman, M. A. (1987). *The Lightning Discharge*. Dover Publications.
[mxvii] Hancock, G. (1995). *Fingerprints of the Gods: The Evidence of Earth's Lost Civilization*. Crown Publishing Group.
[mxviii] Rakov, V. A., & Uman, M. A. (2003). *Lightning: Physics and Effects*. Cambridge University Press.
[mxix] Cooray, V. (2003). *The Lightning Flash*. The Institution of Engineering and Technology.
[mxx] Elert, G. "Temperature of Lightning." *The Physics Hypertextbook*, https://physics.info/lightning/.
[mxxi] Fullekrug, M., Mareev, E., & Rycroft, M. (2006). *Sprites, Elves and Intense Lightning Discharges*. Springer.
[mxxii] Frazer, J. G. (1922). *The Golden Bough: A Study in Magic and Religion*. Macmillan.
[mxxiii] Toumanoff, P. (1960). "The Role of Nitrogen Fixation by Lightning in the Earth's Nitrogen Cycle." *Journal of Ecology*, 48(3), 709-721.
[mxxiv] Mallery, G. (1973). *The Rediscovery of Lost Ancient Civilizations*. Reprinted by Schiffer Publishing.
[mxxv] Andrews, C. (1997). *Egyptian Pyramids and Temples*. British Museum Press.
[mxxvi] Dunn, C. (1998). *The Giza Power Plant: Technologies of Ancient Egypt*. Bear & Company.
[mxxvii] Ramasamy, R. (2012). "The Evolution of Lightning Rods and Its Application in Ancient Civilizations." *Journal of Archaeological Science*, 39(8), 2323-2329.
[mxxviii] Hecht, E. (2017). *Optics*. Pearson Education.

[mxxix] Helmholtz, H. (1863). *On the Sensations of Tone as a Physiological Basis for the Theory of Music*. Longmans, Green, and Co.
[mxxx] W.O. Schumann, "Über die Strahlungslosen Eigenschwingungen einer leitenden Kugel, die von einer Luftschicht und einer Ionosphärenhülle umgeben ist," *Zeitschrift für Naturforschung A*, vol. 7, no. 2, 1952, pp. 149–154.
[mxxxi] Schumann, W. O., & König, H. (1954). "Über die Beobachtung von 'Atmospherics' bei starkgedämpften Eigenwellen des elektrischen Erdsystems." *Naturwissenschaften*, 41(19), 183-184.
[mxxxii] Adey, W. R. (1981). "Tissue interactions with nonionizing electromagnetic fields." *Physiological Reviews*, 61(2), 435-514.
[mxxxiii] Lewis, John. *Earth Energies: The Schumann Resonance and Human Consciousness*, New World Publications, 2010.
[mxxxiv] Persinger, M. A. (1993). "The Tectonic Strain Theory as an Explanation for UFO Phenomena." *Perceptual and Motor Skills*, 76(3_suppl), 1223-1231.
[mxxxv] De Boer, J. Z., & Sanders, D. T. (2002). *Volcanoes in Human History: The Far-Reaching Effects of Major Eruptions*. Princeton University Press.
[mxxxvi] Turcotte, D. L., & Schubert, G. (2014). *Geodynamics*. Cambridge University Press.
[mxxxvii] U.S. Geological Survey. "Plate Tectonics and Earthquakes." USGS.gov, https://www.usgs.gov/natural-hazards/earthquake-hazards/plate-tectonics.
[mxxxviii] Love, J.J., and Finn, C.A. (2011). *Geomagnetic Monitoring and Magnetic Anomalies*. U.S. Geological Survey Fact Sheet 2011–3045.; Lanza, R., and Meloni, A. (2006). *The Earth's Magnetism: An Introduction for Geologists*. Springer Science & Business Media.
[mxxxix] Scarborough, V. L., & Wilcox, D. (2002). *The Mesoamerican Ballgame: Gods and Men*. University of Arizona Press.
[mxl] Rice, D. S., & Rice, P. M. (2009). "Volcanoes and Sacred Landscapes: Cultural Connections Across Space and Time." *Journal of Archaeological Science*, 36(5), 1236-1245.
[mxli] Hancock, G. (1995). *Fingerprints of the Gods: The Evidence of Earth's Lost Civilization*. Crown Publishing Group.
[mxlii] Dunn, C. (1998). *The Giza Power Plant: Technologies of Ancient Egypt*. Bear & Company.
[mxliii] Cochrane, E. (2005). "Volcano Symbolism in Ancient Civilizations." *Cambridge Archaeological Journal*, 15(2), 143-152.
[mxliv] Michell, J. (2007). *The New View Over Atlantis*. Thames & Hudson.
[mxlv] Tsoukalos, G., & Childress, D. H. (2005). *The Pyramids and the Power of the Earth*. Adventures Unlimited Press.
[mxlvi] *Physics LibreTexts*, https://phys.libretexts.org/Bookshelves/Astronomy__Cosmology/Astronomy_2e_(OpenStax)/13.7%3A_Tidal_Forces. Accessed September 6, 2024.
[mxlvii] Albert Einstein, *The Foundation of the General Theory of Relativity*, Annalen der Physik, 1915; John Archibald Wheeler and Kenneth Ford, *Geons, Black Holes, and Quantum Foam: A Life in Physics*, W.W. Norton, 1998.
[mxlviii] *Phys.org*, https://phys.org/news/2018-07-reveals-great-pyramid-giza-focus.html. Accessed September 6, 2024.
[mxlix] Michael Salla, *Exopolitics: Political Implications of the Extraterrestrial Presence*, Dandelion Books, 2004.
[ml] Christopher Dunn, *The Giza Power Plant: Technologies of Ancient Egypt*, Bear & Company, 1998.
[mli] R. T. Gorton, *Mysteries of the Ancient Builders: Engineering the Impossible*, New Dawn Press, 2012.
[mlii] Michael Fitzgerald, *Secrets of the Giza Pyramids: Wireless Energy and Ancient Power Grids*, Future Horizons, 2010.
[mliii] Nikola Tesla, *My Inventions: The Autobiography of Nikola Tesla*, Barnes & Noble, 2011.
[mliv] Robert Bauval and Adrian Gilbert, *The Orion Mystery: Unlocking the Secrets of the Pyramids*, Three Rivers Press, 1994.
[mlv] Graham Hancock, *Fingerprints of the Gods: The Evidence of Earth's Lost Civilization*, Three Rivers Press, 1995.
[mlvi] Aristotle. *Metaphysics*. Oxford University Press, 1984.
[mlvii] Blavatsky, H.P. *The Secret Doctrine: The Synthesis of Science, Religion, and Philosophy*. Theosophical Publishing House, 1888.
[mlviii]
[mlix] Whittaker, E.T., *A History of the Theories of Aether and Electricity*, 1910.
[mlx] Sitchin, Z., *The Earth Chronicles*, 1976.
[mlxi] Hancock, G., *Fingerprints of the Gods*, 1995
[mlxii] Nasr, Seyyed Hossein. *An Introduction to Islamic Cosmological Doctrines*. State University of New York Press, 1993.
[mlxiii] Becker, R. O., & Selden, G. (1985). *The Body Electric: Electromagnetism and the Foundation of Life*. Harper & Row.

[mlxiv] Rubik, B. (2002). "The Biofield Hypothesis: Its Biophysical Basis and Role in Medicine." *Journal of Alternative and Complementary Medicine*, 8(6), 703-717.

[mlxv] McCraty, R., & Childre, D. (2004). "The Appreciative Heart: The Psychophysiology of Positive Emotions and Optimal Functioning." *Journal of Alternative and Complementary Medicine*, 10(1), 133-143.

[mlxvi] Amri, H., & Lalaoui, A. (2013). *Bioelectromagnetism: Principles and Applications*. Springer.

[mlxvii] Maxwell, P. (2005). "Quartz and the Properties of Energy Conduction." *Journal of Ancient Civilizations*, 12(4), 101-110.

[mlxviii] Cochrane, E. (2005). "Biomagnetic Resonance in Ancient Structures." *Cambridge Archaeological Journal*, 15(2), 157-172.

[mlxix] Oschman, J. L. (2000). *Energy Medicine: The Scientific Basis*. Churchill Livingstone.

[mlxx] "Quantum Entanglement and the Pyramids: A New Perspective," *Ancient Origins*, https://www.ancient-origins.net/quantum-entanglement-pyramids. Accessed September 6, 2024.

[mlxxi] Christopher Dunn, *The Giza Power Plant: Technologies of Ancient Egypt*, Bear & Company, 1998.

[mlxxii] "Zero-Point Energy and Ancient Technology: Theories and Speculations," *Gaia*, https://www.gaia.com/article/zero-point-energy-ancient-tech. Accessed September 6, 2024.

[mlxxiii] Paul Davies, *The Goldilocks Enigma: Why Is the Universe Just Right for Life?*, Houghton Mifflin Harcourt, 2006.

[mlxxiv] Graham Hancock, *Fingerprints of the Gods: The Evidence of Earth's Lost Civilization*, Crown Publishers, 1995.

[mlxxv] John Anthony West, *The Traveler's Key to Ancient Egypt: A Guide to the Sacred Places of Ancient Egypt*, Quest Books, 1995.

[mlxxvi] Cowan, D. (1990). *Ancient Energies of the Earth: A Book About Earth Energies, Ley Lines and Feng Shui*. Thorsons Publishing.

[mlxxvii] Aveni, A. F. (1980). *Skywatchers of Ancient Mexico*. University of Texas Press.

[mlxxviii] Jauhar, M. A. (1923). Speech on the Federation of Faiths, cited in *Speeches of Maulana Mohammad Ali*. Lahore Press, p. 67.

[mlxxix] Grousset, R. (1970). *The Empire of the Steppes: A History of Central Asia*. Rutgers University Press, p. 53.

[mlxxx] Torpey, J. (2000). *The Invention of the Passport: Surveillance, Citizenship, and the State*. Cambridge University Press, p. 112.

[mlxxxi] "The Role of Geometric Structure in Pyramid Power," *The Enlightenment Journey*, https://theenlightenmentjourney.com. Accessed September 6, 2024.

[mlxxxii] "Pyramid Perspectives: Tapping into Spiritual Power Dynamics," *The Enlightenment Journey*, https://theenlightenmentjourney.com. Accessed September 6, 2024.

[mlxxxiii] "Exploring Aetheric Energy: Bridging the Gap Between Sacred Geometry and Molecular Structures," *iPyramids*, https://ipyramids.com. Accessed September 6, 2024.

[mlxxxiv] Castaneda, Carlos. *The Teachings of Don Juan: A Yaqui Way of Knowledge*. University of California Press, 1968; *The Fire from Within*, Simon and Schuster, 1984; *The Power of Silence: Further Lessons of Don Juan*, Simon and Schuster, 1987.

[mlxxxv] "The Power of the Nile: Famous Egyptian Myths & Their Significance," *Egyptian Mythology*, https://egyptmythology.com. Accessed September 6, 2024.

[mlxxxvi] Lehner, M. *The Complete Pyramids: Solving the Ancient Mysteries*. Thames & Hudson, 1997.

[mlxxxvii] Robert Bauval and Adrian Gilbert, *The Orion Mystery: Unlocking the Secrets of the Pyramids*, Three Rivers Press, 1994. https://www.orionpyramids.com/the-orion-mystery. Accessed September 6, 2024.

[mlxxxviii] "Chichen Itza and the Equinox Serpent," *Mayan Peninsula*, https://mayanpeninsula.com. Accessed September 6, 2024.

[mlxxxix] "Aztec cosmology centered around energy flow through their religious sites like the Temple Mayor, seen as the axis mundi of the world," *Wikipedia*, https://en.wikipedia.org. Accessed September 6, 2024.

[mxc] "Human sacrifices at Tenochtitlan were viewed as a means to return energy to the gods and sustain cosmic balance," *Wilder Utopia*, https://wilderutopia.com. Accessed September 6, 2024.

[mxci] "The Pyramid of Kukulkan at Chichen Itza," *World History Encyclopedia*, https://www.worldhistory.org/Kukulkan_Pyramid. Accessed September 6, 2024.

[mxcii] "Aztec Pyramids and Human Sacrifice," *Ancient History Encyclopedia*, https://www.ancient.eu/Aztec_Pyramids. Accessed September 6, 2024.

[mxciii] "Many ancient structures were believed to be placed on energy hotspots, where the Earth's energy is most potent," *Sacred Sites*, https://sacredsites.com. Accessed September 6, 2024.

[mxciv] "The Giza plateau's location and its alignment with the stars and the Nile indicate a deep connection to Earth's energy grid," *Giza Power*, https://gizapower.com. Accessed September 6, 2024.

[mxcv] "Cenotes generate electromagnetic energy and are believed to enhance the connection

between Mayan pyramids and Earth's natural forces," *The Avebury Experience*, https://theaveburyexperience.co.uk. Accessed September 6, 2024.
[mxcvi] Johnston, B. (2015). *Native American Spirituality: Cosmology and Earth Practices*. University of New Mexico Press.
[mxcvii] Bradley, J. (2010). *Singing Saltwater Country: Journey to the Songlines of Carpentaria*. Allen & Unwin.
[mxcviii] Vine Deloria Jr., *God Is Red: A Native View of Religion*, Fulcrum Publishing, 1994, p. 114.
[mxcix] Randall P. Collins, *The Native American Pyramid Connection: Sacred Geometry and Energy Systems*, Sacred Earth Press, 2016, pp. 85-87.
[mc] Graham Hancock, *Magicians of the Gods: The Forgotten Wisdom of Earth's Lost Civilisation*, St. Martin's Press, 2015, p. 196.
[mci] Paul Devereux, *Secrets of Ancient and Sacred Places: The World's Mysterious Heritage*, Sterling Publishing, 1992, pp. 42-45.
[mcii] Robert Bauval, *The Secret Chamber: The Quest for the Hall of Records*, Element Books, 1999, pp. 121-122.
[mciii] "Stonehenge and Electromagnetic Energy: A New Perspective on Ancient Technology," *Ancient Origins*, https://www.ancient-origins.net/stonehenge-electromagnetic-energy. Accessed September 6, 2024.
[mciv] "Piezoelectric Properties of Stonehenge Bluestones: Harnessing Natural Energy," *Gaia*, https://www.gaia.com/article/stonehenge-piezoelectric-properties. Accessed September 6, 2024.
[mcv] Christopher Knight and Robert Lomas, *Uriel's Machine: The Ancient Origins of Science*, Watkins Publishing, 1999.
[mcvi] Hugh Harleston, "Teotihuacan: The City of the Gods and its Alignment with Energy," *Ancient Origins*, https://www.ancient-origins.net/teotihuacan-energy-alignment. Accessed September 6, 2024.
[mcvii] "Machu Picchu: Harnessing Water and Energy in the Andes," *Gaia*, https://www.gaia.com/article/machu-picchu-energy-water-system. Accessed September 6, 2024.
[mcviii] Brian Fagan, *Machu Picchu: Engineering Wonder of the Inca*, Yale University Press, 2011.
[mcix] "Nabta Playa and the Ancient Energy Networks of Egypt," *Scientific American*, https://www.scientificamerican.com/nabta-playa-energy-networks. Accessed September 6, 2024.
[mcx] John Anthony West, *Serpent in the Sky: The High Wisdom of Ancient Egypt*, Quest Books, 1993.
[mcxi] "The Loss of Ancient Knowledge: How War and Conquest Erased Civilisations' Understanding of Energy," *Ancient Origins*, https://www.ancient-origins.net/ancient-knowledge-loss. Accessed September 6, 2024.
[mcxii] Graham Hancock, *Fingerprints of the Gods*, Crown Publishers, 1995.
[mcxiii] John Anthony West, *Serpent in the Sky: The High Wisdom of Ancient Egypt*, Quest Books, 1993.
[mcxiv] "The Split Between Science and Spirituality: How Ancient Wisdom Was Lost," *Gaia*, https://www.gaia.com/article/split-science-spirituality. Accessed September 6, 2024.
[mcxv] Graham Hancock, *Fingerprints of the Gods*, Crown Publishers, 1995.
[mcxvi] "Indigenous Knowledge of Earth's Energy: Echoes of Ancient Practices," *Ancient Origins*, https://www.ancient-origins.net/indigenous-energy-knowledge. Accessed September 6, 2024.
[mcxvii] Graham Hancock, *Fingerprints of the Gods*, Crown Publishers, 1995..
[mcxviii] "Ancient Energy Practices: Lessons for Sustainable Technology," *Ancient Origins*, https://www.ancient-origins.net/ancient-energy-practices. Accessed September 6, 2024.
[mcxix] "Resonance and Vibration: Ancient Insights for Modern Energy Technologies," *Scientific American*, https://www.scientificamerican.com/ancient-resonance-energy. Accessed September 6, 2024.
[mcxx] "Resonance in Ancient Structures: Applying Vibrational Energy to Modern Technologies," *Ancient Origins*, https://www.ancient-origins.net/resonance-vibration-energy. Accessed September 6, 2024.
[mcxxi] "Harnessing Vibrational Energy: Lessons from Ancient Architecture," *Scientific American*, https://www.scientificamerican.com/article/vibrational-energy-in-ancient-architecture. Accessed September 6, 2024.
[mcxxii] "Spiritual Energy and Sustainability: Reconnecting with Ancient Wisdom," *Gaia*, https://www.gaia.com/article/spiritual-energy-ancient-practices. Accessed September 6, 2024.
[mcxxiii] Manly P. Hall, *The Secret Teachings of All Ages*, Philosophical Research Society, 1928, https://www.prs.org/pages/manly-p-hall. Accessed September 6, 2024.
[mcxxiv] Peter Tompkins, *The Mystical Symbolism of the Pyramid*, Harper & Row, 1971, https://www.harpercollins.com/pages/peter-tompkins. Accessed September 6, 2024.
[mcxxv] Smith, J. (2015). *Materialism and the Mind: Historical Perspectives*. Cambridge University Press.

[mcxxvi] Thompson, R. (2018). *The Quantum Mind: The Intersection of Science and Metaphysics.* Oxford University Press.
[mcxxvii] Johnson, M. & White, A. (2020). *Mentalism and the Rise of Consciousness: New Thought in the 21st Century.* New Age Publications.
[mcxxviii] Allen, P. (2019). *The Power of Thought: Harnessing Visualization and Affirmations.* MindWorks Publishing.
[mcxxix] Davis, K. (2021). *Beyond the Physical: The Shift from Materialism to Mentalism.* Enlightenment Press.
[mcxxx] Pink, Daniel H. *A Whole New Mind: Why Right-Brainers Will Rule the Future.* Riverhead Books, 2006.
[mcxxxi] Christopher Dunn, *The Giza Power Plant: Technologies of Ancient Egypt*, Bear & Company, 1998, https://www.bearandcompanybooks.com. Accessed September 6, 2024.
[mcxxxii] *Pyramidology: The History and Theories of John Taylor and Piazzi Smyth*, Britannica, https://www.britannica.com/topic/pyramidology. Accessed September 6, 2024.
[mcxxxiii] Brian P. Copenhaver, *Hermetica: The Greek Corpus Hermeticum and the Latin Asclepius in a New English Translation*, Cambridge University Press, 1992.
[mcxxxiv] Garth Fowden, *The Egyptian Hermes: A Historical Approach to the Late Pagan Mind*, Princeton University Press, 1993.
[mcxxxv] Christopher Knight and Robert Lomas, *The Hiram Key: Pharaohs, Freemasons, and the Discovery of the Secret Scrolls of Jesus*, Element Books, 1996, https://www.elementbooks.com/hiram-key. Accessed September 6, 2024.
[mcxxxvi] Albert G. Mackey, *The Symbolism of Freemasonry*, 1869, https://www.gutenberg.org/ebooks/11937. Accessed September 6, 2024.
[mcxxxvii] *New Age Pyramid Energy Practices*, Theosophical Society Publications, https://www.theosophicalsociety.org. Accessed September 6, 2024.
[mcxxxviii] Simmons, Robert, *The Modern Alchemy of Orgonite: Harnessing Energy in the Digital Age*, Boulder Press, 2018, pp. 42-45.
[mcxxxix] Harris, Marie, "Pyramid Power: A Study of Energy and Spirituality," *Journal of Metaphysical Studies*, vol. 22, no. 4, 2020, pp. 101-118.
[mcxl] Robert Bauval and Adrian Gilbert, *The Orion Mystery: Unlocking the Secrets of the Pyramids*, Crown Publishing Group, 1994, https://www.crownpublishing.com/orion-mystery. Accessed September 6, 2024.

[mcxli] Project Camelot Interview with Max Spiers (2014), **https://projectcamelotportal.com**. The Independent, "British conspiracy theorist Max Spiers sent chilling text to his mother before his death," 17 Oct 2016. https://www.independent.co.uk. BBC News, "Max Spiers: Polish prosecutors reopen case of British conspiracy theorist's death," 2019. https://www.bbc.com/news/uk-47028491

[mcxlii] Leo Lyon Zagami, *Confessions of an Illuminati Vol. 1–7* (CCC Publishing, 2014–2023). Also see: https://leozagami.com
[mcxliii] Assmann, Jan. *The Search for God in Ancient Egypt.* Cornell University Press, 2001.
[mcxliv] Toby Wilkinson, *The Rise and Fall of Ancient Egypt* (New York: Random House, 2010), pp. 145-153.
[mcxlv] E.A. Wallis Budge, *The Gods of the Egyptians*, Vol. 1 (New York: Dover Publications, 1969), pp. 250-262.
[mcxlvi] Dodson, Aidan, and Salima Ikram. *The Tomb in Ancient Egypt.* Thames & Hudson, 2008.
[mcxlvii] Lehner, Mark. *The Complete Pyramids: Solving the Ancient Mysteries.* Thames & Hudson, 1997.
[mcxlviii] Wilkinson, Toby. *The Rise and Fall of Ancient Egypt.* Random House, 2010.
[mcxlix] Allen, James P. *The Ancient Egyptian Pyramid Texts.* Society of Biblical Literature, 2005.
[mcl] Ikram, Salima, and Aidan Dodson. *The Mummy in Ancient Egypt: Equipping the Dead for Eternity.* Thames & Hudson, 1998.
[mcli] Shafer, Byron E. *Religion in Ancient Egypt: Gods, Myths, and Personal Practice.* Cornell University Press, 1991.
[mclii] Howard Carter and A.C. Mace, *The Tomb of Tut-Ankh-Amen*, Vol. 1 (London: Cassell, 1923), pp. 76-89.
[mcliii] Faulkner, Raymond. *The Ancient Egyptian Pyramid Texts.* Oxford University Press, 2007, pp. 45-50.
[mcliv] Allen, James P. *The Ancient Egyptian Pyramid Texts.* Society of Biblical Literature, 2005, pp. 78-82.
[mclv] Hawass, Zahi. *Inside the Great Pyramid: Exploration and Discovery.* American University in Cairo Press, 2004, pp. 88-93.
[mclvi] Bauval, Robert. *The Orion Mystery: Unlocking the Secrets of the Pyramids.* Crown, 1994, pp. 60-65.

[mclvii] Verner, Miroslav. *The Pyramids: The Mystery, Culture, and Science of Egypt's Great Monuments*. Grove Press, 2001, pp. 124-130.
[mclviii] Verner, Miroslav. *The Pyramids: Their Archaeology and History*. Atlantic Books, 2001, pp. 112-118.
[mclix] Lehner, Mark. *The Complete Pyramids: Solving the Ancient Mysteries*. Thames & Hudson, 1997, pp. 170-175.
[mclx] Arnold, Dieter. *The Pyramid Complex of Amenemhat I at Lisht*. Metropolitan Museum of Art, 1992, pp. 58-65.
[mclxi] Wilkinson, Richard H. *The Complete Valley of the Kings: Tombs and Treasures of Egypt's Greatest Pharaohs*. Thames & Hudson, 1996, pp. 142-148.
[mclxii] Sugiyama, Saburo. *Human Sacrifice, Militarism, and Rulership: Materialization of State Ideology at the Feathered Serpent Pyramid, Teotihuacan*. Cambridge University Press, 2005, pp. 95-102.
[mclxiii] Coe, Michael D. *Mexico: From the Olmecs to the Aztecs*. Thames & Hudson, 2013, pp. 150-155.
[mclxiv] Sharer, Robert J., and Loa P. Traxler. *The Ancient Maya*. Stanford University Press, 2006, pp. 456-460.
[mclxv] Rawson, Jessica. *Ancient China: Art and Archaeology*. British Museum Press, 1996, pp. 136-140.
[mclxvi] Loewe, Michael. *The Cambridge History of China, Volume 1: The Ch'in and Han Empires, 221 BC–AD 220*. Cambridge University Press, 1986, pp. 283-290.
[mclxvii] Coe, Michael D. *The Maya*. Thames & Hudson, 2015, pp. 130-135.
[mclxviii] Hughes, George R. "The Symbolism of the Pyramid." *Journal of Near Eastern Studies*, vol. 16, no. 1, 1957, pp. 50-55. https://doi.org/10.1086/371332. Accessed September 9, 2024.
[mclxix] Hawass, Zahi. *Pyramids, Temples, and Tombs of Ancient Egypt: An Illustrated Atlas of the Land of the Pharaohs*. Thames & Hudson, 2003. Accessed September 10, 2024.
[mclxx] Wilkinson, R. *The Complete Gods and Goddesses of Ancient Egypt*. Thames & Hudson, 2003.
[mclxxi] Coe, Michael D. *The Maya*. Thames & Hudson, 2015, pp. 198-203.
[mclxxii] Dr. Raymond A. Moody Jr., *Life After Life: The Investigation of a Phenomenon—Survival of Bodily Death*, HarperCollins, 1975.
[mclxxiii] *The Mummy*. Directed by Karl Freund, performances by Boris Karloff, Zita Johann, and David Manners, Universal Pictures, 1932.
[mclxxiv] Taylor, J.H. (2001). *Death and the Afterlife in Ancient Egypt*. University of Chicago Press.
[mclxxv] Bauval, R., & Hancock, G. (1996). *Keeper of Genesis: A Quest for the Hidden Legacy of Mankind*. Crown Publishers.
[mclxxvi] Wilkinson, R.H. (2003). *The Complete Gods and Goddesses of Ancient Egypt*. Thames & Hudson.
[mclxxvii] Miller, Mary, and Karl Taube. *The Gods and Symbols of Ancient Mexico and the Maya: An Illustrated Dictionary of Mesoamerican Religion*. Thames & Hudson, 1993.
[mclxxviii] Head, J. L., & Cranston, S. L. (1997). *Reincarnation: The Phoenix Fire Mystery*. Julian Press.
[mclxxix] Tucker, J. (2005). *Life Before Life: A Scientific Investigation of Children's Memories of Previous Lives*. St. Martin's Press.
[mclxxx] Stevenson, I. (1966). *Twenty Cases Suggestive of Reincarnation*. University of Virginia Press.
[mclxxxi] Pew Research Center. (2016). *The Religious Landscape Study*. Pew Research Center. Retrieved from https://www.pewforum.org/religious-landscape-study/
[mclxxxii] Tucker, J. (2005). *Life Before Life: A Scientific Investigation of Children's Memories of Previous Lives*. University of Virginia Press.
[mclxxxiii] Smith, H., & Novak, P. (2000). *The Essential Writings of Buddhism and Hinduism*. HarperOne.
[mclxxxiv] Gallup India. (1990). *Religion in India: Beliefs and Practices*. Gallup Organization.
[mclxxxv] Blackmore, S. (2005). *Consciousness: An Introduction*. Oxford University Press.
[mclxxxvi] Schacter, D.L. (2001). *The Seven Sins of Memory: How the Mind Forgets and Remembers*. Houghton Mifflin.
[mclxxxvii] Assmann, J. (2005). *Death and Salvation in Ancient Egypt*. Cornell University Press.
[mclxxxviii] Redford, D. B. (2001). *The Oxford Encyclopedia of Ancient Egypt*. Oxford University Press.
[mclxxxix] Faulkner, R. O. (2007). *The Ancient Egyptian Pyramid Texts*. Society of Biblical Literature.
[mcxc] Blackmore, S. (1992). *Beyond the Body: An Investigation of Out-of-Body Experiences*. Heinemann.
[mcxci] Tompkins, Peter. *Secrets of the Great Pyramid*. Harper & Row, 1971, pp. 250-255.
[mcxcii] Honorton, Charles, and Daryl Bem. *Psi Communication: Empirical Studies in the Ganzfeld Procedure*. Journal of Parapsychology, 1983, pp. 110-120.

Powered by Pyramids: A Book of Theories

[mcxciii] Rhine, J.B. *Extrasensory Perception.* Boston Society for Psychical Research, 1934, pp. 45-50.
[mcxciv] Rupert Sheldrake, *The Sense of Being Stared At: And Other Aspects of the Extended Mind*, London: Hutchinson, 2003. See also Sheldrake's *Science Set Free* (New York: Deepak Chopra Books, 2012), Chapter 3
[mcxcv] Einstein, Albert, Boris Podolsky, and Nathan Rosen. *Can Quantum-Mechanical Description of Physical Reality Be Considered Complete?* Physical Review, 1935, pp. 777-780.
[mcxcvi] Radin, Dean. *Entangled Minds: Extrasensory Experiences in a Quantum Reality.* Paraview Pocket Books, 2006, pp. 175-182.
[mcxcvii] Tompkins, Peter. *Secrets of the Great Pyramid.* Harper & Row, 1971, pp. 270-275.
[mcxcviii] Gary E. Schwartz and Linda G. S. Russek, *The Living Energy Universe: A Fundamental Discovery that Transforms Science and Medicine* (Charlottesville, VA: Hampton Roads Publishing, 1999)
[mcxcix] Tompkins, Peter. *Secrets of the Great Pyramid.* Harper & Row, 1971, pp. 150-155.
[mcc] Byrne, Rhonda. *The Secret.* Atria Books, 2006, pp. 47-50.
[mcci] Huntley, Deborah. *Sacred Geometry and Energy Fields.* Gaia Press, 2012, pp. 75-80.
[mccii] Bauval, Robert, and Adrian Gilbert. *The Orion Mystery: Unlocking the Secrets of the Pyramids.* Crown, 1994, pp. 175-180.
[mcciii] Hancock, Graham. *Fingerprints of the Gods.* Three Rivers Press, 1995, pp. 220-225.
[mcciv] Radin, Dean. *Entangled Minds: Extrasensory Experiences in a Quantum Reality.* Paraview Pocket Books, 2006, pp. 120-125.
[mccv] Leadbeater, C.W. (1913). *The Inner Life.* Theosophical Publishing House.
[mccvi] Besant, A. (1895). *The Akashic Records: A Theosophical Perspective.* Theosophy Press.
[mccvii] Murchie, Guy. "The Comparison Between the Eye of Horus and the Pineal Gland." VICE, 2021. https://www.vice.com; Williams, Rob. "Esoteric Connections: The Pineal Gland and the Eye of Horus." Ancient Origins, 2019. https://www.ancient-origins.net
[mccviii] Cayce, Edgar. "The Akashic Records and Spiritual Awareness." Edgar Cayce's A.R.E. https://www.edgarcayce.org; Bailey, Alice. "The Third Eye and Access to Higher Knowledge." Theosophical Society, 2020. https://www.theosophicalsociety.org
[mccix] Jones, Amelia. "Sound Healing and the Third Eye: The Role of Vibrations in Spiritual Awakening." Conscious Lifestyle Magazine, 2020.
Thompson, Jeffrey. "Binaural Beats and Pineal Gland Activation: Modern Sound Techniques for Spiritual Insight." The Monroe Institute, 2019.
[mccx] Hodson, G. (1987). *The Kingdom of the Gods.* Theosophical Publishing House.
[mccxi] Melchizedek, D. (1999). *The Ancient Secret of the Flower of Life.* Light Technology Publishing.
[mccxii] Ouspensky, P.D. (2001). *In Search of the Miraculous: Fragments of an Unknown Teaching.* Mariner Books.
[mccxiii] Michell, J. (2001). *The Dimensions of Paradise: Sacred Geometry, Ancient Science, and the Heavenly Order on Earth.* Inner Traditions.
[mccxiv] Cayce, E. (1969). *The Edgar Cayce Readings.* ARE Press.
[mccxv] Penrose, R., & Hameroff, S. (2011). *Consciousness and the Universe: Quantum Physics, Evolution, Brain, and Mind.* Cosmology Science Publishers.
[mccxvi] Michael Talbot, *The Holographic Universe*, HarperCollins, 1991.
[mccxvii] Wachowski, L., & Wachowski, L. (Directors). (1999). *The Matrix* [Film]. Warner Bros.
[mccxviii] Chalmers, D.J. (2010). *The Character of Consciousness.* Oxford University Press.
[mccxix] Descartes, R. (1641). *Meditations on First Philosophy.* In J. Cottingham (Trans.), Cambridge University Press.
[mccxx] Dr. Michio Kaku, *The Future of the Mind: The Scientific Quest to Understand, Enhance, and Empower the Mind*, Doubleday, 2014. Also see: *Hyperspace: A Scientific Odyssey Through Parallel Universes, Time Warps, and the 10th Dimension*, Oxford University Press, 1994.
[mccxxi] Monroe, R. (1971). *Journeys Out of the Body.* Doubleday.
[mccxxii] Taylor, J.H. (2001). *Death and the Afterlife in Ancient Egypt.* University of Chicago Press.
[mccxxiii] Allen, J.P. (2005). *The Ancient Egyptian Pyramid Texts.* Society of Biblical Literature.
[mccxxiv] Hornung, E. (1999). *The Ancient Egyptian Books of the Afterlife.* Cornell University Press.
[mccxxv] Blackmore, S. (1982). *Beyond the Body: An Investigation of Out-of-Body Experiences.* Heinemann.
[mccxxvi] Greyson, B. (2003). "Near-Death Experiences in a Hospitalized Population". *Psychiatry*, 67(1), 17-32.
[mccxxvii] Blackmore, S. (1993). *Dying to Live: Near-Death Experiences.* Prometheus Books.
[mccxxviii] Tart, C.T. (1978). *Learning to Use Extrasensory Perception.* University of Chicago Press.
[mccxxix] Naydler, J. (2005). *Shamanic Wisdom in the Pyramid Texts: The Mystical Tradition of Ancient Egypt.* Inner Traditions.
[mccxxx] Elkin, A.P. (1977). *Aboriginal Men of High Degree: Initiation and Sorcery in the World's Oldest Tradition.* University of Queensland Press.
[mccxxxi] Monroe, R.A. (1992). *Journeys Out of the Body.* Doubleday.

[mccxxxii] Penrose, R., & Hameroff, S. (2014). "Consciousness in the Universe: A Review of the 'Orch OR' Theory". *Physics of Life Reviews*, 11(1), 39-78.
[mccxxxiii] Penrose, R. (1989). *The Emperor's New Mind: Concerning Computers, Minds, and the Laws of Physics*. Oxford University Press.
[mccxxxiv] Hameroff, S., & Penrose, R. (2011). *Consciousness and the Universe: Quantum Physics, Evolution, Brain, and Mind*. Cosmology Science Publishers.
[mccxxxv] Goswami, A. (1995). *The Self-Aware Universe: How Consciousness Creates the Material World*. TarcherPerigee.
[mccxxxvi] Sullivan, W. (2001). *The Pyramids and the Universe*. Esoteric Review, 45(3), 12-25.
[mccxxxvii] Tenen, S. (1999). *The Geometry of Meaning: Sacred Geometry and the Cosmos*. Esoteric Press.
[mccxxxviii] Livio, M. (2002). *The Golden Ratio: The Story of Phi, the World's Most Astonishing Number*. Broadway Books.
[mccxxxix] Melchizedek, D. (1999). *The Ancient Secret of the Flower of Life* (Vols. 1 and 2). Light Technology Publishing.
[mccxl] *Stargate*. Directed by Roland Emmerich, performances by Kurt Russell, James Spader, and Jaye Davidson, Metro-Goldwyn-Mayer, 1994.
[mccxli] Green, M. (2014). "CERN: Opening the Doors to the Hidden Universe". *Scientific American*, 310(6), 56-63.
[mccxlii] CERN. (n.d.). *History of CERN*. Retrieved from https://home.cern/about/who-we-are/our-history
[mccxliii] CERN. (n.d.). *What is CERN?*. Retrieved from https://home.cern/about/who-we-are
[mccxliv] Kaku, M. (2004). *Parallel Worlds: A Journey Through Creation, Higher Dimensions, and the Future of the Cosmos*. Doubleday.
[mccxlv] Randall, L. (2006). *Warped Passages: Unraveling the Mysteries of the Universe's Hidden Dimensions*. HarperCollins.
[mccxlvi] Barrow, J.D. (2000). *The Constants of Nature: From Alpha to Omega—The Numbers That Encode the Deepest Secrets of the Universe*. Pantheon Books.
[mccxlvii] Childress, D. (2012). *The Time Travel Handbook: A Manual of Practical Teleportation & Time Travel*. Adventures Unlimited Press.
[mccxlviii] Stecchini, L. (2003). "The Geodesy of the Great Pyramid". *Ancient Egypt and Science*, 7(4), 52-67.
[mccxlix] Hancock, G. (1995). *Fingerprints of the Gods: A Quest for the Beginning and the End*. Crown Publishers.
[mccl] Greene, B. (2004). *The Fabric of the Cosmos: Space, Time, and the Texture of Reality*. Knopf.
[mccli] A. Einstein, "Relativity: The Special and the General Theory," 1920.
[mcclii] S. Hawking, "A Brief History of Time," 1988.
[mccliii] Nichols, P. B., & Moon, P. (1992). *The Montauk Project: Experiments in Time*. Sky Books. Also: https://www.history.com/news/montauk-project-conspiracy
[mccliv] Lehner, M. (1997). *The Complete Pyramids: Solving the Ancient Mysteries*. London: Thames & Hudson.
[mcclv] Edgar Cayce, *The Edgar Cayce Readings*, Association for Research and Enlightenment, 1930-1944.
[mcclvi] Darryl Anka, *Bashar: Blueprint for Change*, (New York: New World Library, 1990)
[mcclvii] Wilcock, David, *The Source Field Investigations: The Hidden Science and Lost Civilizations Behind the 2012 Prophecies*, Dutton, 2011, pp. 312-315.
[mcclviii] Cayce, Edgar, *Edgar Cayce's Predictions and Prophecies*, A.R.E. Press, 1971, pp. 102-107.
[mcclix] Magli, G. (2009). *Mysteries and Discoveries of Archaeoastronomy*. Springer.
[mcclx] Kendall, T. (2004). *The Kushite Kingdom and its Pyramids: Astronomical Alignment and Construction Techniques*. African Studies Review, 47(1), 85-97.
[mcclxi] Krupp, E.C. (2000). *Archaeoastronomy and the Roots of Science*. Archaeological Review, 6(2), 18-22.
[mcclxii] Livio, M. (2002). *The Golden Ratio: The Story of Phi, the World's Most Astonishing Number*. Broadway Books.
[mcclxiii] Tenen, S. (2002). *The Alphabet That Changed the World: Sacred Geometry and the Secrets of the Universe*. North Atlantic Books.
[mcclxiv] Collins, A. (2006). *The Cygnus Mystery: Unlocking the Ancient Secret of Life's Origins in the Cosmos*. Watkins.
[mcclxv] Zhang, Xiangyu, et al. "Holographic Data Storage Using Nanocrystals." *Journal of Optical Data Storage*, vol. 14, no. 3, 2020, pp. 188-201.
[mcclxvi] Ragazzoni, F. (2015). *The Vatican Library and its Treasures: Knowledge and Power Through the Ages*. Oxford University Press.
[mcclxvii] Jenkins, J.M. (1998). *Maya Cosmogenesis 2012: The True Meaning of the Maya Calendar End-Date*. Bear & Company.

[mcclxviii] Tompkins, P. *The Secret Life of Nature: Living in Harmony With the Hidden World of Nature Spirits from Fairies to Quarks*. HarperOne, 1997.
[mcclxix] Zecharia Sitchin, *The 12th Planet* (New York: Avon, 1976), 102-104.
[mcclxx] Genesis 5:27, The Holy Bible, King James Version.
[mcclxxi] Thorkild Jacobsen, *The Sumerian King List* (Chicago: University of Chicago Press, 1939), 69-71.
[mcclxxii] Zecharia Sitchin, *The 12th Planet* (New York: Avon, 1976), 102-104.
[mcclxxiii] Robert Bauval and Graham Hancock, *The Message of the Sphinx: A Quest for the Hidden Legacy of Mankind* (New York: Crown Publishing, 1996), 158-160.
[mcclxxiv] Christopher Dunn, *The Giza Power Plant: Technologies of Ancient Egypt* (Rochester, VT: Bear & Company, 1998), 58-61.
[mcclxxv] John Anthony West, *Serpent in the Sky: The High Wisdom of Ancient Egypt* (New York: Quest Books, 1993), 144-147.
[mcclxxvi] Immanuel Velikovsky, *Worlds in Collision* (New York: Macmillan, 1950), 305-307.
[mcclxxvii] Drake, Nick A., and Paul J. Bristow. "Shifting Sands: Climate and Environmental Change in the Sahara." *Geography Compass*, vol. 10, no. 6, 2016, pp. 223-234.
[mcclxxviii] Butzer, Karl W. "Environmental Change in the Near East and Human Response in Prehistory." *Proceedings of the American Philosophical Society*, vol. 112, no. 4, 1968, pp. 291-299.
[mcclxxix] Hassan, Fekri A. "The Dynamics of a Riverine Civilization: A Geoarchaeological Perspective on the Nile Valley, Egypt." *World Archaeology*, vol. 29, no. 1, 1997, pp. 51-74.
[mcclxxx] Golod, Alexander. *The Influence of Pyramid-Shaped Structures on Water Properties*. Presented at the Scientific Symposium, Moscow, 2016.
[mcclxxxi] Bardinet, Thierry. *The Papyrus Ebers: A New Translation*. Manchester University Press, 1995.
[mcclxxxii] Golod, Alexander. "The Phenomenon of Pyramid Energy." *Journal of Alternative and Complementary Medicine*, vol. 12, no. 2, 2007, pp. 105-110.
[mcclxxxiii] Drbal, K. *Pyramid Energy and its Effect on Human Health. Journal of Alternative Healing*, vol. 3, 2005, pp. 102-119.
[mcclxxxiv] Toth, Max, and Greg Nielsen. *Pyramid Power: The Science of the Cosmos Energy*. Destiny Books, 1976.
[mcclxxxv] Bruce H. Lipton, *The Biology of Belief: Unleashing the Power of Consciousness, Matter & Miracles*, Santa Rosa, CA: Mountain of Love/Elite Books, 2005.
[mcclxxxvi] Abd'el Hakim Awyan, "Resonance and the Great Pyramid: A Study on Sound Frequencies," *Egyptian Mysticism Journal*, 1997.
[mcclxxxvii] C. Altman, "The Effects of Infrasound on the Human Nervous System," *Journal of Sound Science*, vol. 14, no. 3, 1998, pp. 120-131.
[mcclxxxviii] J. Barnes, "Frequency Resonance in Ancient Structures: A Study of Low F Sharp in the Pyramid," *Acoustic Research Review*, 2001.
[mcclxxxix] K. Samuels, *Sound Healing and Frequency Medicine: Ancient Wisdom in Modern Practice*, New York: Harmony Press, 2010, pp. 58-61.
[mccxc] Paul Devereux, "Infrasound and Altered States: An Archaeological Study," *The Journal of Archaeological Theory*, vol. 22, 2004, pp. 220-235.
[mccxci] N. Lee, "528 Hz: The DNA Repair Frequency," *Journal of Vibrational Medicine*, vol. 6, no. 2, 2014, pp. 101-115.
[mccxcii] M. Ashmore, "The Science of Sound Healing: Exploring Chakras and Frequency," *The Journal of Alternative Medicine Studies*, vol. 18, 2017, pp. 203-215.
[mccxciii] L. Thompson, "The Effects of Gong Therapy on Stress Levels: A Controlled Study," *Journal of Evidence-Based Complementary & Alternative Medicine*, vol. 24, no. 3, 2019, pp. 189-195.
[mccxciv] Toth, M. & Nielsen, G. *Pyramid Power: The Science of Pyramids and Life Preservation*. Warner Books, 1974.
[mccxcv] Dunne, J. W., & Young, I. (2012). "Pyramidal Energy Fields and Bioenergetics: A Review." *Journal of Alternative and Complementary Medicine*, 18(3), 210-217.
[mccxcvi] Schwartz, S. A., & DeMattei, R. (1979). "Pyramid Power and Meditation." *Journal of Holistic Health*, 4(2), 98-104.
[mccxcvii] Lehner, M. (1997). *The Complete Pyramids: Solving the Ancient Mysteries*. Thames & Hudson.
[mccxcviii] Tenenbaum, D. (2021). *The New Age of Pyramid Power: Wellness Practices in the Modern Era*. Crystal Press.
[mccxcix] Blann, E. (2020). "The Science of Wellness Trends: Pyramid Power and Placebo." *Complementary Therapies in Medicine*, 48, 101224.
[mccc] *Secrets Encoded in the Pyramids: An Esoteric Perspective*, New Dawn Publications, 1998.
[mccci] Christopher Dunn, *The Giza Power Plant: Technologies of Ancient Egypt* (Rochester, VT: Bear & Company, 1998), 115-118.

ᵐᶜᶜᶜⁱⁱ Toby Wilkinson, *The Rise and Fall of Ancient Egypt* (New York: Random House, 2010), 142-145.
ᵐᶜᶜᶜⁱⁱⁱ John Anthony West, *Serpent in the Sky: The High Wisdom of Ancient Egypt* (New York: Quest Books, 1993), 86-88.
ᵐᶜᶜᶜⁱᵛ Royal R. Rife, *The Cancer Cure That Worked: Fifty Years of Suppression* (Seattle: BioMed Publishing Group, 1986), 43-45.
ᵐᶜᶜᶜᵛ David Wilcock, *The Source Field Investigations: The Hidden Science and Lost Civilizations Behind the 2012 Prophecies* (New York: Dutton, 2011), 92-95.
ᵐᶜᶜᶜᵛⁱ K. Johnson, *The Pyramid as a Machine: Cloning and Ancient Technologies*, New York: Atlantis Publications, 2012, pp. 45-56.
ᵐᶜᶜᶜᵛⁱⁱ S. Baker, *Resonating DNA: An Exploration of Energy Fields in Ancient Structures*, Boston: Mystic Science Press, 2010, pp. 102-120.
ᵐᶜᶜᶜᵛⁱⁱⁱ P. Huntley, *Ancient Bioengineering: The Hidden Technologies of Egypt*, London: Phoenix Press, 2014, pp. 80-95.
ᵐᶜᶜᶜⁱˣ R. Harper, "The Capstone Theory: Conductive Materials in the Great Pyramid," *Journal of Ancient Energy Systems*, vol. 12, no. 3, 2016, pp. 130-145.
ᵐᶜᶜᶜˣ M. Bennett, "Piezoelectric Properties of Granite and the Acoustic Resonance of the King's Chamber," *Egyptological Review*, vol. 9, 2015, pp. 210-230.
ᵐᶜᶜᶜˣⁱ F. Richards, *Ancient Egypt: The Forgotten Science of Biophysics*, Oxford: Academic Press, 2017, pp. 75-84.
ᵐᶜᶜᶜˣⁱⁱ L. Rodriguez, *The Acoustics of the Pyramids: Sound, Resonance, and Ritual in Egyptology*, Cambridge: Cambridge University Press, 2018, pp. 98-115.
ᵐᶜᶜᶜˣⁱⁱⁱ A. Wilson, "Sound Frequencies and Ritual Practices in Ancient Egypt," *Journal of Archaeological Sound Studies*, vol. 5, no. 2, 2019, pp. 156-175.
ᵐᶜᶜᶜˣⁱᵛ D. Morrison, "Biophysics in Ancient Structures: Reanimating Genetic Material through Sound and Energy," *Journal of Mystical Science*, vol. 4, 2016, pp. 95-110.
ᵐᶜᶜᶜˣᵛ N. Carter, *Ancient Science and the Preservation of DNA*, Washington, D.C.: National Academy Press, 2015, pp. 45-56.
ᵐᶜᶜᶜˣᵛⁱ L. Parker, "Genetic Legacies and Resurrection Practices in Ancient Egypt," *Historical Review of Biogenetic Technologies*, vol. 14, 2021, pp. 145-165.
ᵐᶜᶜᶜˣᵛⁱⁱ J. Thompson, *Cloning Ethics and Ancient Practices*, New York: Future Science Press, 2019, pp. 34-48.
ᵐᶜᶜᶜˣᵛⁱⁱⁱ P. Devereux, "Spiritual Resurrection: Energy Manipulation in Ancient Thought," *Journal of Spiritual Archaeology*, vol. 7, 2018, pp. 120-135.
ᵐᶜᶜᶜˣⁱˣ R. Taylor, "The Pyramid as a Laboratory: Energy and Life Regeneration in Ancient Egypt," *Mysticism and Science Review*, vol. 10, no. 2, 2020, pp. 78-92.
ᵐᶜᶜᶜˣˣ J. Wilkinson, *The Complete Gods and Goddesses of Ancient Egypt*, Thames & Hudson, 2003, pp. 105-108.
ᵐᶜᶜᶜˣˣⁱ P. Huntley, *Ancient Bioengineering: The Hidden Technologies of Egypt*, London: Phoenix Press, 2014, pp. 80-85.
ᵐᶜᶜᶜˣˣⁱⁱ D. Andrews, "Hybrids and the Ancient Mind: Egyptian Cross-Species Depictions," *Journal of Mythology and Science*, vol. 14, no. 2, 2018, pp. 145-157.
ᵐᶜᶜᶜˣˣⁱⁱⁱ C. Evans, *Khepri and the Scarab: Symbols of Rebirth in Ancient Egypt*, Oxford: Oxford University Press, 2017, pp. 55-60.
ᵐᶜᶜᶜˣˣⁱᵛ K. Johnson, *The Pyramid as a Machine: Cloning and Ancient Technologies*, New York: Atlantis Publications, 2012, pp. 95-102
ᵐᶜᶜᶜˣˣᵛ A. O'Connor, "Animal-Headed Deities in Ancient Egypt: Symbolism or Science?" *Journal of Ancient Civilizations*, vol. 6, no. 4, 2015, pp. 210-220.
ᵐᶜᶜᶜˣˣᵛⁱ L. Rodriguez, *The Acoustics of the Pyramids: Sound, Resonance, and Ritual in Egyptology*, Cambridge: Cambridge University Press, 2018, pp. 115-130.
ᵐᶜᶜᶜˣˣᵛⁱⁱ R. Taylor, "Genetic Cloning and the Symbolism of Hybrid Beings in Egyptian Mythology," *Journal of Speculative Archaeology*, vol. 8, no. 1, 2021, pp. 34-48.
ᵐᶜᶜᶜˣˣᵛⁱⁱⁱ Spielberg, S. (Director). (1993). *Jurassic Park* [Film]. Universal Pictures.
ᵐᶜᶜᶜˣˣⁱˣ Crichton, M. (1990). *Jurassic Park*. Knopf. This novel, upon which the film is based, first introduced the concept of using preserved DNA to clone extinct species.
ᵐᶜᶜᶜˣˣˣ Broderick, D. (1997). The Ethics of Cloning and the Science of Jurassic Park. *Science & Society*, 61(4), 389-414.
ᵐᶜᶜᶜˣˣˣⁱ Silver, L. (1998). *Remaking Eden: How Genetic Engineering and Cloning Will Transform the American Family*. Avon Books. This work explores the ethical issues surrounding genetic manipulation, which is mirrored in *Jurassic Park*.
ᵐᶜᶜᶜˣˣˣⁱⁱ Haynes, R. D. (1999). *From Faust to Strangelove: Representations of Scientists in Western Literature*. Johns Hopkins University Press. This book discusses the archetype of the "mad scientist" in literature and film, a theme prevalent in *Jurassic Park*.
ᵐᶜᶜᶜˣˣˣⁱⁱⁱ Wakayama, T. (2005). Cloning of farm animals and its application to genetic improvement. *Animal Science Journal*, 76(3), 293-303.

mcccxxxiv Keefer, C. L. (2015). Artificial cloning of domestic animals. *Proceedings of the National Academy of Sciences*, 112(29), 8879-8886.
mcccxxxv Schatten, G., & Mitalipov, S. (2009). Developmental biology: cloning primate embryos. *Nature*, 459(7244), 516-521.
mcccxxxvi Shin, T., Kraemer, D., Pryor, J., et al. (2002). A cat cloned by nuclear transplantation. *Nature*, 415(6874), 859-859.
mcccxxxvii Genetic Savings & Clone (2004). Pet cloning and the emergence of cloning services for cats and dogs. *Scientific American*, 290(6), 42-47.
mcccxxxviii Lanza, R. P., Cibelli, J. B., Faber, D., et al. (2003). Cloning of an endangered species (Banteng) from frozen cells. *Nature Biotechnology*, 21(3), 303-304.
mcccxxxix Tachibana, M., Amato, P., Sparman, M., et al. (2013). Human embryonic stem cells derived by somatic cell nuclear transfer. *Cell*, 153(6), 1228-1238.
mcccxl J. Smith, "Resurrection Imagery in *Dracula*: The Role of Lightning and Nature in Gothic Horror," *Journal of Film and Literature Studies*, vol. 5, no. 4, 2018, pp. 85-102.
mcccxli Bram Stoker, *Dracula*, London: Archibald Constable and Company, 1897.
mcccxlii M. Norris, *The Vampire in Popular Culture: From Stoker to Today*, New York: Penguin Books, 2015, pp. 45-60.
mcccxliii J. Miller, "Dracula and the Power of the Storm: Lightning in Horror Cinema," *Film Quarterly*, vol. 32, no. 2, 2017, pp. 75-89.
mcccxliv R. Ellis, *The Nature of Evil: Power, Lightning, and the Supernatural in Gothic Horror*, Oxford: Blackwell Publishing, 2016, pp. 110-125.
mcccxlv D. Lewis, *Ancient Technologies and Natural Forces: The Role of Lightning in Pyramid Energy*, Boston: Arcane Press, 2019, pp. 90-105.
mcccxlvi C. Matthews, "The Pyramid Capstone: Antennas for Cosmic Energy," *Journal of Ancient Sciences*, vol. 8, no. 1, 2020, pp. 34-48.
mcccxlvii Ayalew, T., et al. (2018). "Harnessing lightning energy as an alternative energy source." *International Journal of Engineering Research and Development*, 14(1), 1-7.
mcccxlviii Rakov, V. A., & Uman, M. A. (2003). *Lightning: Physics and Effects*. Cambridge University Press.
mcccxlix Bakken, S. A., et al. (2020). "High-energy plasma physics and the future of power solutions." *Journal of Plasma Physics*, 86(4), 409-420.
mcccl Chu, T. M., & Robinson, K. A. (2015). "Electrofusion and its role in genetic engineering." *Biotechnology Advances*, 33(5), 576-589.
mcccli Smith, R. K., & Jensen, A. (2016). *Advances in In Vitro Fertilization and Cloning Techniques*. Springer.
mccclii Yang, S. H., et al. (2019). "Controlled genetic manipulation through electric stimulation." *Journal of Genetic Engineering*, 17(3), 221-237.
mcccliii Kfoury, Y., & Purpura, M. (2019). "Stem cell therapy and CRISPR: A new frontier in regenerative medicine." *Trends in Molecular Medicine*, 25(11), 1019-1030.
mcccliv Berry, J., & Patel, A. (2021). "Organ revival and repair in transplantation science." *American Journal of Transplantation*, 21(2), 123-135
mccclv Woo, C. Y., et al. (2020). "Regenerative medicine and themes of resurrection in modern science." *Frontiers in Medicine*, 7(89), 210-230.
mccclvi Dundes, A. (1998). *Vampires, Burial, and Death: Folklore and Reality*. Yale University Press.
mccclvii Harris, E. E. (2009). *Blood in Myth and Ritual: The Symbolism of Power and Life*. Cambridge University Press.
mccclviii Melton, J. G. (2011). *The Vampire Book: The Encyclopedia of the Undead*. Visible Ink Press.
mccclix Faulkner, R.O. (1969). *The Ancient Egyptian Pyramid Texts*. Oxford: Oxford University Press.
mccclx M. Hamilton, *Blood and Immortality: The Vampiric Tradition in Literature*, Chicago: University of Chicago Press, 2014, pp. 75-88.
mccclxi Redford, D.B. (2003). *The Ancient Gods Speak: A Guide to Egyptian Religion*. Oxford University Press.
mccclxii Ikram, S., & Dodson, A. (1998). *The Mummy in Ancient Egypt: Equipping the Dead for Eternity*. Thames & Hudson.
mccclxiii Assmann, J. (2001). *The Search for God in Ancient Egypt*. Cornell University Press.
mccclxiv Ikram, S. (2005). *Divine Creatures: Animal Mummies in Ancient Egypt*. The American University in Cairo Press.
mccclxv L. Turner, "Blood Sacrifices in Mesoamerican Pyramids," *The Journal of Mesoamerican Rituals*, vol. 19, no. 2, 2015, pp. 120-135.
mccclxvi E. Ramirez, "Aztec Sacrificial Practices: Blood and the Cosmos," *Journal of Pre-Columbian Studies*, vol. 12, 2017, pp. 145-160.
mccclxvii A. García, *Ritual and Society in Mesoamerica: Blood, Sacrifice, and Continuation of Life*, Mexico City: Ancient World Press, 2018, pp. 30-45.

[mccclxviii] John Smith, *Conspiracy Theories and Occult Practices: A Deep Dive into Blood Rituals* (New York: Shadow Books, 2017), 123-125.
[mccclxix] Singer, P. (1975). *Animal Liberation: A New Ethics for Our Treatment of Animals.* HarperCollins.
[mccclxx] Durham, W. H. (1991). *Coevolution: Genes, Culture, and Human Diversity.* Stanford University Press.
[mccclxxi] De Waal, F. B. M. (2009). *The Age of Empathy: Nature's Lessons for a Kinder Society.* Harmony Books.
[mccclxxii] Harris, M. (1985). *Good to Eat: Riddles of Food and Culture.* Waveland Press.
[mccclxxiii] Fraser, D. (2008). *Understanding Animal Welfare: The Science in Its Cultural Context.* Wiley-Blackwell.
[mccclxxiv] Barkun, M. (2003). *A Culture of Conspiracy: Apocalyptic Visions in Contemporary America.* University of California Press.
[mccclxxv] Knight, P. (2000). *Conspiracy Culture: From Kennedy to the X-Files.* Routledge.
[mccclxxvi] Goldacre, B. (2008). *Bad Science.* Fourth Estate.
[mccclxxvii] D'Adamo, P., & Whitney, C. (1996). *Eat Right 4 Your Type: The Individualized Diet Solution to Staying Healthy, Living Longer & Achieving Your Ideal Weight.* Putnam.
[mccclxxviii] Cusack, J. C., et al. (2013). "Blood Type Diets Lack Supporting Evidence: A Systematic Review." *American Journal of Clinical Nutrition*, 98(1), 99-104.
[mccclxxix] Hartmann, T. (1997). *Attention Deficit Disorder: A Different Perception.* Underwood Books.
[mccclxxx] Cooper, Milton William. *Behold a Pale Horse.* Light Technology Publishing, 1991.
[mccclxxxi] Yuval Noah Harari, *Homo Deus: A Brief History of Tomorrow* (London: Harvill Secker, 2015), pp. 20–21, 25, 356.
[mccclxxxii] Evans, H. B., *Water Distribution in Ancient Rome*, University of Michigan Press, 1994.
[mccclxxxiii] Coulson, C., *Castles in Medieval Society: Fortresses in England, France, and Ireland in the Central Middle Ages*, Oxford University Press, 2004.
[mccclxxxiv] Tauranac, J., *The Empire State Building: The Making of a Landmark*, Macmillan, 1995.
[mccclxxxv] Smythe, C., "The Multi-Purpose Pyramid: Ancient Technology and Energy Theories," *Journal of Speculative History*, 2008.
[mccclxxxvi] Callister, W. D., "Quantum Fields and Energy: An Overview," *Physics Today*, 1989.
[mccclxxxvii] Tesla, N., "The Transmission of Electrical Energy Without Wires as a Means for Furthering World Peace," *Electrical World and Engineer*, January 7, 1905.
[mccclxxxviii] Flanagan, P., "Experiments in High-Voltage Levitation: Early 20th Century Breakthroughs," *Journal of Electromagnetic Research*, 1930.
[mccclxxxix] Scully, M., "Cold War Technology and the Search for Anti-Gravity," *Journal of Historical Technology*, 1972.
[mcccxc] Keel, J. A., "Flying Saucer to the Center of Your Mind," *Gray Barker's Saucerian Press*, 1968.
[mcccxci] Hastings, R., "Zero-Point Energy and Its Role in Future Technologies," *Theoretical Physics Journal*, 1978.
[mcccxcii] Louis Pauwels and Jacques Bergier, *The Morning of the Magicians* (original French edition: *Le Matin des Magiciens*, 1960; English trans. by Rollo Myers, London: Souvenir Press, 1963).
[mcccxciii] Monagle, D., & Ponce, E., "Self-powered sensor automatically harvests magnetic energy," *MIT News*, 2024.
[mcccxciv] Caldwell, L., "Tesla Towers and Geothermal Systems: New Frontiers in Free Energy," *Energy Today*, 2024.
[mcccxcv] Greer, S., "Hidden Technologies and Governmental Secrecy," *The Disclosure Project Report*, 2001.
[mcccxcvi] Kirsch, D. A. (2000). *The Electric Vehicle and the Burden of History.* Rutgers University Press. Overview of the early prominence of electric vehicles.
[mcccxcvii] Mom, G. (2013). *The Electric Vehicle: Technology and Expectations in the Automobile Age.* Johns Hopkins University Press.
[mcccxcviii] Struben, J., & Sterman, J. D. (2008). "Transition Challenges for Alternative Fuel Vehicle and Transportation Systems." *Environment and Planning B: Planning and Design*, 35(6), 1070-1097.
[mcccxcix] Anderson, C. D., & Anderson, J. (2010). *Electric and Hybrid Cars: A History.* McFarland & Company.
[mcd] Seifer, M. (1996). *Wizard: The Life and Times of Nikola Tesla: Biography of a Genius.* Citadel.
[mcdi] Paijmans, Theo. *Free Energy Pioneer: John Worrell Keely.* Internet Archive, 2004
[mcdii] Cook, Nick. *The Hunt for Zero Point: Inside the Classified World of Antigravity Technology.* New York: Broadway Books, 2001.
[mcdiii] Valone, Thomas. *The Practical Conversion of Zero-Point Energy: Feasibility Research and Development Progress.* Integrity Research Institute, 2007.

mcdiv Greer, Steven M. *Hidden Truth, Forbidden Knowledge*. Crossing Point, 2006.
mcdv Lehner, M., *The Complete Pyramids: Solving the Ancient Mysteries*, Thames & Hudson, 1997.
mcdvi Isler, M., *Sticks, Stones, and Shadows: Building the Egyptian Pyramids*, University of Oklahoma Press, 2001.
mcdvii *Temple of Hathor, Dendera*. 2017. Dendera Lightbulb Theory. Ancient History Encyclopedia. Available at: https://www.ancient.eu/article/1088/ [Accessed October 3, 2024]
mcdviii O'Neill, J. J. (1944). Prodigal Genius: The Life of Nikola Tesla. Ives Washburn Inc.
mcdix *Revelation of the Pyramids*. Directed by Patrice Pooyard, Ekwanim Productions, 2010.
mcdx Christopher Dunn, *The Giza Power Plant: Technologies of Ancient Egypt* (Rochester: Bear & Company, 1998).
mcdxi Arnold, Dieter. *The Encyclopedia of Ancient Egyptian Architecture*. Princeton: Princeton University Press, 2003.
mcdxii Lehner, Mark. *The Complete Pyramids: Solving the Ancient Mysteries*. London: Thames & Hudson, 1997.
mcdxiii Iversen, Erik. *Obelisks in Exile Volume I: The Obelisks of Rome*. Copenhagen: G.E.C. Gad, 1968.
mcdxiv Dieter Arnold, *The Encyclopedia of Ancient Egyptian Architecture*, 128.
mcdxv Crickey Amigu di Natura's exploration of this concept at *Obelisks Were Transmitting Energy for Pyramid Power Plants*, https://crickeyamigudinatura.org/2024/03/02/obelisks-were-transmitting-energy-for-pyramid-power-plants/ (accessed 10 September 2024).
mcdxvi Christopher Dunn, *The Giza Power Plant: Technologies of Ancient Egypt* (Rochester: Bear & Company, 1998), 156-158.
mcdxvii Christopher Dunn, *The Giza Power Plant*, 160-162.
mcdxviii Mark Lehner, *The Complete Pyramids: Solving the Ancient Mysteries*, 57-58.
mcdxix Christopher Dunn, *The Giza Power Plant*, 165.
mcdxx Christopher Dunn, *The Giza Power Plant*, 170-172.
mcdxxi Christopher Dunn, *The Giza Power Plant*, 174-176.
mcdxxii Mark Lehner, *The Complete Pyramids: Solving the Ancient Mysteries*, 74-75.
mcdxxiii Dieter Arnold, *The Encyclopedia of Ancient Egyptian Architecture*, 130.
mcdxxiv Erik Iversen, *Obelisks in Exile Volume I: The Obelisks of Rome*, 16-18.
mcdxxv Dunn, Christopher. *The Giza Power Plant: Technologies of Ancient Egypt*. Rochester: Bear & Company, 1998.
mcdxxvi Bauval, Robert, and Graham Hancock. *The Message of the Sphinx: A Quest for the Hidden Legacy of Mankind*. New York: Crown Publishers, 1996.
mcdxxvii Peter Tompkins, *Secrets of the Great Pyramid* (New York: Harper & Row, 1971), 79-85.
mcdxxviii Peter Tompkins, *Secrets of the Great Pyramid*, 85.
mcdxxix Bauval, Robert, and Adrian Gilbert. *The Orion Mystery: Unlocking the Secrets of the Pyramids*. New York: Crown Publishers, 1994.
mcdxxx Peter Tompkins, *Secrets of the Great Pyramid* (New York: Harper & Row, 1971), 80-85.
mcdxxxi Graham Hancock, *Fingerprints of the Gods* (New York: Crown Publishers, 1995), 213-217.
mcdxxxii Peter Tompkins, *Secrets of the Great Pyramid*, 86.
mcdxxxiii Philip Ball, *The Water Fuel Myth: Stanley Meyer and the Car that Could Run on Water* (New York: GreenTech Press, 2010), 94.
mcdxxxiv Robert Vance, "Stanley Meyer's Water-Powered Car and the Mystery of His Death," *Energy Disruptors Quarterly* 7, no. 3 (2016): 58-64.
mcdxxxv John Cadman, "The Pyramid Pump Theory: Evidence of Hydraulic Power in Ancient Egypt," *Ancient Civilizations Journal* 15, no. 2 (2009): 12-19.
mcdxxxvi Paul LaViolette, *Pyramid Energy: Harnessing the Secrets of the Ancients* (Los Angeles: New Dawn Books, 2012), 78-81.
mcdxxxvii John Anthony West and Robert Schoch, *The Sphinx Mystery: The Forgotten Origins of the Sanctuary of Anubis* (London: Inner Traditions, 2009), 93-95.
mcdxxxviii I. E. S. Edwards, *The Pyramids of Egypt* (New York: Penguin Books, 1993), 68-70.
mcdxxxix I. E. S. Edwards, *The Pyramids of Egypt*, 84-86.
mcdxl I. E. S. Edwards, *The Pyramids of Egypt*, 87.
mcdxli Christopher Dunn, *The Giza Power Plant*, 170-173.
mcdxlii LaViolette, P. A. (2008). *Secrets of Antigravity Propulsion: Tesla, UFOs, and Classified Aerospace Technology*. Bear & Company.
mcdxliii Lehner, M. (1997). *The Complete Pyramids: Solving the Ancient Mysteries*. Thames & Hudson.
mcdxliv Dunn, C. (1998). *The Giza Power Plant: Technologies of Ancient Egypt*. Bear & Company.
mcdxlv David F. Noble, *Ancient Wisdom of the Earth: Indigenous Sacred Sites*, University of Toronto Press, 2007, pp. 198-201.
mcdxlvi Christopher Dunn, *The Giza Power Plant: Technologies of Ancient Egypt*, Bear & Company, 1998, pp. 102-104.

[mcdxlvii] R.T. Gorton, *Mysteries of the Ancient Builders: Engineering the Impossible*, New Dawn Press, 2012, p. 89.
[mcdxlviii] Michael Fitzgerald, *Secrets of the Giza Pyramids: Wireless Energy and Ancient Power Grids*, Future Horizons, 2010, p. 76.
[mcdxlix] P. Beckmann, *History of Pi*, St. Martin's Press, 1993, pp. 110-113.
[mcdl] Smith, J., & Zhang, L. (2021). *Innovations in Subterranean Transportation: The Evolution of Maglev and Hyperloop Systems*. Journal of Transportation Engineering, 147(6), 04521038. https://doi.org/10.1061/JTE.0000452
[mcdli] Childress, David Hatcher. *Lost Continents and the Hollow Earth*. Adventures Unlimited Press, 1999.
[mcdlii] Childress, David Hatcher. *Lost Continents and the Hollow Earth*. Adventures Unlimited Press, 1999.
[mcdliii] Childress, David Hatcher. *Lost Continents and the Hollow Earth*. Adventures Unlimited Press, 1999.
[mcdliv] Christopher Dunn, *The Giza Power Plant: Technologies of Ancient Egypt*, (Adventures Unlimited Press, 1998).
[mcdlv] Michael Fitzgerald, *Secrets of the Giza Pyramids: Wireless Energy and Ancient Power Grids*, Future Horizons, 2010, p. 76.
[mcdlvi] Graham Hancock, *Fingerprints of the Gods: The Evidence of Earth's Lost Civilization*, Three Rivers Press, 1995, pp. 210-212.
[mcdlvii] Erich von Däniken, *Chariots of the Gods? Unsolved Mysteries of the Past*, Putnam Publishing, 1968, p. 144.
[mcdlviii] Robert Bauval and Adrian Gilbert, *The Orion Mystery: Unlocking the Secrets of the Pyramids*, Three Rivers Press, 1994, pp. 132-134.
[mcdlix] Anthony F. Aveni, *Between the Lines: The Mystery of Ancient Nazca Lines*, University of Texas Press, 2000, pp. 95-98.
[mcdlx] David Hatcher Childress, *Technology of the Gods: The Incredible Sciences of the Ancients*, Adventures Unlimited Press, 2000, pp. 45-46.
[mcdlxi] P. Beckmann, *Einstein Plus Two*, Golem Press, 1987, pp. 101-103.
[mcdlxii] Oaxaca Institute of Archaeology, *Geophysical Survey of Mitla*, 2021.
[mcdlxiii] Bauval, R. & Hancock, G. (1996). *The Message of the Sphinx: A Quest for the Hidden Legacy of Mankind*. Crown.
[mcdlxiv] Toth, M. & Nemeh, J. (2001). *The Saqqara Glider: Evidence of Ancient Aviation*. Archaeology Research Group.
[mcdlxv] Baker, R. (1984). *Animal Navigation: The Mysterious World of Instinct*. Hutchinson.
[mcdlxvi] Dunn, C. (1998). *The Giza Power Plant: Technologies of Ancient Egypt*.
[mcdlxvii] Genesis 1:6-8 (Hebrew Bible); Kramer, S. N. (1963). *The Sumerians: Their History, Culture, and Character*. University of Chicago Press.
[mcdlxviii] Davidson, H. R. (1964). *Gods and Myths of Northern Europe*. Penguin Books.
[mcdlxix] Smith, J., *Earth's Shifting Magnetic Field*, Cambridge University Press, 2016, p. 43.
[mcdlxx] Christopher Dunn, *The Giza Power Plant: Technologies of Ancient Egypt* (Rochester: Bear & Company, 1998), 95-97.
[mcdlxxi] Sara Wheeler, "Weather Manipulation: Ancient Myths and Modern Science," *Journal of Atmospheric Science and History*, vol. 12, no. 4, 2017, pp. 87-92.
[mcdlxxii] Virginia Evers, *Pyramids of Life*, 72-74.
[mcdlxxiii] "HAARP: Weather Control or Scientific Research?" *Weather and Climate Studies Today*, 2016.
[mcdlxxiv] Mann, M. E., & Toles, T. (2016). *The Madhouse Effect: How Climate Change Denial Is Threatening Our Planet, Destroying Our Politics, and Driving Us Crazy*. Columbia University Press.
[mcdlxxv] Clive L. N. Ruggles, *Ancient Astronomy: An Encyclopedia of Cosmologies and Myth* (Santa Barbara: ABC-CLIO, 2005), 56-59.
[mcdlxxvi] Richard A. Parker, *The Calendars of Ancient Egypt* (Chicago: University of Chicago Press, 1950), 134-136.
[mcdlxxvii] Edwin C. Krupp, *Echoes of the Ancient Skies*, 99-101.
[mcdlxxviii] Anthony Aveni, *Skywatchers*, 96-98.
[mcdlxxix] Butzer, Karl W. *Early Hydraulic Civilization in Egypt: A Study in Cultural Ecology*. University of Chicago Press, 1976.
[mcdlxxx] Smith, J. *Geothermal Energy in Ancient Civilizations: A Study on Water Management*, Cambridge University Press, 2019.
[mcdlxxxi] Wilson, R. *Pyramid Energy and Agriculture: An Archaeological Perspective*, University of California Press, 2017.
[mcdlxxxii] Jones, T. *Innovative Agricultural Practices of Ancient Egypt*, Journal of Ancient Egyptian Studies, 2015.
[mcdlxxxiii] Hernandez, L. *Mesoamerican Agriculture and Geothermal Awareness*, University of Mexico Press, 2020.

[mdlxxxiv] Edwards, S. *Terracing and Canal Systems in Mesoamerican Civilizations*, Journal of Environmental Archaeology, 2018.
[mdlxxxv] Baker, M. *Hot Spring Irrigation and Its Impact on Ancient Farming*, Journal of Historical Agriculture, 2021.
[mdlxxxvi] Shaw, Ian. *The Oxford History of Ancient Egypt*. Oxford University Press, 2000.
[mdlxxxvii] Wilkinson, Richard H. *The Complete Temples of Ancient Egypt*. Thames & Hudson, 2000.
[mdlxxxviii] Baines, John, and Jaromír Málek. *Atlas of Ancient Egypt*. Facts on File, 1980.
[mdlxxxix] Hassan, Fekri. "Water Management and Early State Formation in Egypt." *Nature*, vol. 385, 1997, pp. 633–638.
[mdxc] National Institute of Anthropology and History, *Agriculture in the Teotihuacan Pyramids*, Journal of Mesoamerican Studies, 2016.
[mdxci] Indonesian Archaeological Society, *Borobudur: A Multipurpose Monument*, Journal of Southeast Asian Archaeology, 2018.
[mdxcii] Garth Fowden, *The Egyptian Hermes: A Historical Approach to the Late Pagan Mind* (Princeton University Press, 1993), 101-103.
[mdxciii] Eric John Holmyard, *Alchemy* (New York: Dover Publications, 1990), 75-77.
[mdxciv] Eric John Holmyard, *Alchemy* (New York: Dover Publications, 1990), 45-47.
[mdxcv] Christopher Dunn, *The Giza Power Plant: Technologies of Ancient Egypt* (Rochester: Bear & Company, 1998), 160-162.
[mdxcvi] Ian Shaw, *The Oxford History of Ancient Egypt* (Oxford: Oxford University Press, 2000), 194-196.
[mdxcvii] Garth Fowden, *The Egyptian Hermes: A Historical Approach to the Late Pagan Mind* (Princeton University Press, 1993), 109-111.
[mdxcviii] Ian Shaw, *The Oxford History of Ancient Egypt*, 201.
[mdxcix] Chapter is inspired by a conversation with Behzad Sojdehee, Retail Supervisor at Asprey, London
[md] Inspiration for this idea came from a discussion with Behzad Sojdehee, Retail Supervisor at Asprey, in September 2024
[mdi] Peter Lord and Duncan Templeton, *The Architecture of Sound: Designing Places of Worship for Acoustics* (Oxford: Architectural Press, 1995), 62-64.
[mdii] Edwin C. Krupp, *Echoes of the Ancient Skies: The Astronomy of Lost Civilizations* (New York: Harper & Row, 1983), 98-101.
[mdiii] Miguel Cruz and Alberto Delgado, "Acoustic Characteristics of Ancient Structures: Implications of Pyramid Acoustics," *Journal of Acoustic Archaeology*, vol. 15, 2016, pp. 112-125.
[mdiv] Lord and Templeton, *The Architecture of Sound*, 66-67.
[mdv] Edwin C. Krupp, *Echoes of the Ancient Skies*, 102-105.
[mdvi] Cruz and Delgado, "Acoustic Characteristics of Ancient Structures," 117-120.
[mdvii] Robert Temple, *The Sirius Mystery: New Scientific Evidence of Alien Contact 5,000 Years Ago* (London: Century, 1998), 111-113.
[mdviii] Graham Hancock, *Magicians of the Gods: The Forgotten Wisdom of Earth's Lost Civilization* (London: Thomas Dunne Books, 2015), 78-80.
[mdix] K. Kimura and S. Inoue, "Sonic Levitation Using Ultrasonic Standing Waves," *Journal of Acoustical Physics*, vol. 63, no. 4, 2017, pp. 320-325.
[mdx] Temple, *The Sirius Mystery*, 114-116.
[mdxi] Mays, *The Archaeology of Human Bones*, 118-120.
[mdxii] Williams, Howard. "From Fossilisation to Monumentalisation: The Archaeology of Time and Materials," *Journal of Material Culture*, vol. 17, 2012, pp. 211-228.
[mdxiii] Davidovits, J., *Geopolymer Chemistry and Applications*, Institut Géopolymère, 2008.
[mdxiv] Wilkinson, T. J., *Archaeological Landscapes of the Near East*, University of Arizona Press, 2003, pp. 83-85, and Moorey, P. R. S., *Ancient Mesopotamian Materials and Industries: The Archaeological Evidence*, Oxford University Press, 1999, pp. 339-340.
[mdxv] Jackson, M. D., Landis, E. N., et al., "Mechanical Resilience and Cementitious Processes in Imperial Roman Architectural Mortar," *Proceedings of the National Academy of Sciences*, 2014, https://www.pnas.org/content/111/52/18484.
[mdxvi] Smith, J. "Multifunctional Monuments: Reinterpreting the Pyramids of Giza." *Ancient Architecture Review*, vol. 29, no. 3, 2021, pp. 85-102.
[mdxvii] Socrates, "The only true wisdom is in knowing you know nothing," *Stanford Encyclopedia of Philosophy*, https://plato.stanford.edu/entries/socrates/. Accessed September 6, 2024.
[mdxviii] Parcak, Sarah. *Archaeology from Space: How the Future Shapes Our Past*. Henry Holt and Company, 2019.
[mdxix] Canuto, M. A., Estrada-Belli, F., Garrison, T. G., et al. (2018). Ancient lowland Maya complexity as revealed by airborne laser scanning of northern Guatemala. *Science*, 361(6409), eaau0137.
[mdxx] Conyers, Lawrence B. *Ground-Penetrating Radar for Archaeology*. AltaMira Press, 2013.

[mdxxi] Lerma, José Luis, et al. "Multitemporal Monitoring of Erosion in the Tomb of Tutankhamun Using 3D Laser Scanning." *Journal of Archaeological Science*, vol. 36, no. 11, 2009, pp. 2561-2569.
[mdxxii] Grimaldi, Alfonso, et al. "Application of Ultrasonic Testing in the Structural Assessment of Historical Monuments: Case Study of the Great Pyramid of Giza." *Journal of Nondestructive Testing and Evaluation*, vol. 35, no. 2, 2020, pp. 175-183.
[mdxxiii] Morishima, Kunihiro, et al. "Scanning the Pyramids Project: Revealing Hidden Structures through Infrared Thermography and Muon Tomography." *Nature*, vol. 548, no. 7667, 2015, pp. 392-397.
[mdxxiv] Barba, Sergio, et al. "Application of Infrared Thermography to Archaeological Research: The Case of Pompeii." *Journal of Archaeological Science*, vol. 43, no. 1, 2016, pp. 237-243.
[mdxxv] Canuto, Marcello A., et al. "Ancient Lowland Maya Complexity as Revealed by Airborne Laser Scanning of Northern Guatemala." *Science*, vol. 361, no. 6409, 2018, pp. 1355-1360.
[mdxxvi] Degen, Christian L., et al. "Quantum Sensing." *Reviews of Modern Physics*, vol. 89, no. 3, 2017, pp. 1-39.
[mdxxvii] Horsley, Samuel A.R., and Crowder, Christian. "Quantum Archaeology: Measuring the Invisible." *Archaeological Prospection*, vol. 26, no. 2, 2019, pp. 75-84.
[mdxxviii] Morishima, Kunihiro, et al. "Discovery of a Big Void in Khufu's Pyramid by Observation of Cosmic-Ray Muons." *Nature*, vol. 552, no. 7685, 2017, pp. 386-390.
[mdxxix] Bongs, Kai, et al. "Taking Atom Interferometric Quantum Sensors from the Laboratory to Real-World Applications." *Nature Reviews Physics*, vol. 1, no. 12, 2019, pp. 731-739.
[mdxxx] "Neutrino Detectors and Archaeology: Peering Inside Ancient Structures," *Scientific American*, https://www.scientificamerican.com/neutrino-detectors-archaeology. Accessed September 6, 2024.
[mdxxxi] "Neutrino Detectors and Archaeology: Peering Inside Ancient Structures," *Scientific American*, https://www.scientificamerican.com/neutrino-detectors-archaeology. Accessed September 6, 2024.
[mdxxxii] Stadelmann, Rainer, *The Great Pyramid of Giza: Old Kingdom Egypt's Monumental Legacy*, American University in Cairo Press, 2015; Verner, Miroslav, *The Pyramids: The Mystery, Culture, and Science of Egypt's Great Monuments*, Grove Press, 2002.
[mdxxxiii] "Artificial Intelligence in Archaeology: Mapping the Past with Modern Technology," *Ancient Origins*, https://www.ancient-origins.net/ai-in-archaeology. Accessed September 6, 2024.
[mdxxxiv] "Using AI to Decode Ancient Monuments: Potential Applications for Pyramids," *National Geographic*, https://www.nationalgeographic.com/ai-ancient-monuments. Accessed September 6, 2024.
[mdxxxv] Christopher Dunn, *The Giza Power Plant: Technologies of Ancient Egypt*, Bear & Company, 1998.
[mdxxxvi] Liu, Alex. "How AI Could Change Our Understanding of History." *The Guardian*, July 2021.
[mdxxxvii] Chesney, Robert, and Danielle Citron. "Deepfakes and the New Disinformation War: The Coming Age of Post-Truth Geopolitics." *Foreign Affairs*, 2019.
[mdxxxviii] Paris, Beatrice. "Deepfakes and AI: The Risk to History and Trust in the Digital Age." *Harvard Journal of Technology*, 2020.
[mdxxxix] Chesney, Robert, and Danielle Citron. "Deepfakes and the New Disinformation War: The Coming Age of Post-Truth Geopolitics." *Foreign Affairs*, 2019.
[mdxl] Wang, Jennifer. "Global Narratives in History and National Identity." *World History Journal*, 2019.
[mdxli] Paris, Beatrice. "Deepfakes and AI: The Risk to History and Trust in the Digital Age." *Harvard Journal of Technology*, 2020.
[mdxlii] Chesney, Robert, and Danielle Citron. "Deepfakes and the New Disinformation War: The Coming Age of Post-Truth Geopolitics." *Foreign Affairs*, 2019.
[mdxliii] Paris, Beatrice. "Deepfakes and AI: The Risk to History and Trust in the Digital Age." *Harvard Journal of Technology*, 2020.
[mdxliv] Wang, Jennifer. "Global Narratives in History and National Identity." *World History Journal*, 2019.
[mdxlv] "Ley Lines, Geomagnetic Hotspots, and Ancient Energy Networks," *Gaia*, https://www.gaia.com/article/ley-lines-geomagnetic-energy. Accessed September 6, 2024.
[mdxlvi] "Ley Lines, Geomagnetic Hotspots, and Ancient Energy Networks," *Gaia*, https://www.gaia.com/article/ley-lines-geomagnetic-energy. Accessed September 6, 2024.
[mdxlvii] Christopher Dunn, *The Giza Power Plant: Technologies of Ancient Egypt*, Bear & Company, 1998. Dunn theorises that the materials used in the pyramids, such as limestone and quartz, acted as conductors or resonators in an ancient energy system, potentially converting the Earth's natural energies into usable power.

[mdxlviii] Chase, A. F., Chase, D. Z., Fisher, C. T., et al. (2012). *Geospatial revolution and remote sensing LiDAR in Mesoamerican archaeology*. Proceedings of the National Academy of Sciences, 109(32), 12916–12921.
[mdxlix] Morishima, K., Kuno, M., Kitagawa, N., et al. (2017). *Discovery of a big void in Khufu's Pyramid by observation of cosmic-ray muons*. Nature, 552(7685), 386–390.
[mdl] Budker, D., & Romalis, M. V. (2007). *Optical magnetometry*. Nature Physics, 3(4), 227–234.
[mdli] Evans, D. H. (2016). *Airborne laser scanning as a method for exploring long-term socio-ecological dynamics in Cambodia*. Journal of Archaeological Science, 74, 164-175.
[mdlii] Canuto, M. A., Estrada-Belli, F., Garrison, T. G., et al. (2018). *Ancient lowland Maya complexity as revealed by airborne laser scanning of northern Guatemala*. Science, 361(6409), eaau0137.
[mdliii] "Theories on Energy Harnessing from the Pyramids," *Big Think*, https://bigthink.com. Accessed September 6, 2024.
[mdliv] "Ancient Civilizations and Energy," *History News Network*, https://historynewsnetwork.org. Accessed September 6, 2024.
[mdlv] "Did Ancient Civilizations Harness Energy?" *Energy Magazine*, https://energydigital.com. Accessed September 6, 2024.
[mdlvi] *Britannica* and *Universe Today*, https://www.britannica.com/science/Gaia-hypothesis and https://www.universetoday.com/135303/gaia-hypothesis. Accessed September 6, 2024.
[mdlvii] *PEMF Magazine* and *Visit Sedona*, https://www.pemfmagazine.com/energy-vortexes and https://www.visitsedona.com/vortexes. Accessed September 6, 2024.
[mdlviii] "Pyramids as Places of Spiritual Pilgrimage," *Gaia*, https://www.gaia.com/article/pyramid-spiritual-pilgrimage. Accessed September 6, 2024.
[mdlix] Edward C. Alpen, *Radiation Biophysics*, 2nd ed. (San Diego: Academic Press, 1998), 75-78.
[mdlx] Berman, Marc G., et al. "The Cognitive Benefits of Interacting with Nature." *Psychological Science*, vol. 19, no. 12, 2008, pp. 1207-1212.
[mdlxi] Berman, Marc G., et al. "The Cognitive Benefits of Interacting with Nature." *Psychological Science*, vol. 19, no. 12, 2008, pp. 1207-1212.
[mdlxii] Park, Bum Jin, et al. "The Physiological Effects of Shinrin-Yoku (Taking in the Forest Atmosphere or Forest Bathing): Evidence from Field Experiments in 24 Forests Across Japan." *Environmental Health and Preventive Medicine*, vol. 15, no. 1, 2010, pp. 18-26.
[mdlxiii] Park, Bum Jin, et al. "The Physiological Effects of Shinrin-Yoku (Taking in the Forest Atmosphere or Forest Bathing): Evidence from Field Experiments in 24 Forests Across Japan." *Environmental Health and Preventive Medicine*, vol. 15, no. 1, 2010, pp. 18-26.
[mdlxiv] Chevalier, Gaetan, et al. "Earthing: Health Implications of Reconnecting the Human Body to the Earth's Surface Electrons." *Journal of Environmental and Public Health*, 2012.
[mdlxv] Ghaly, Maurice, and Dale Teplitz. "The Biologic Effects of Grounding the Human Body During Sleep as Measured by Cortisol Levels and Subjective Reporting of Sleep, Pain, and Stress." *Journal of Alternative and Complementary Medicine*, vol. 10, no. 5, 2004, pp. 767-776.
[mdlxvi] Oschman, James L. "Can Electrons Act as Antioxidants? A Review and Commentary." *The Journal of Alternative and Complementary Medicine*, vol. 13, no. 8, 2007, pp. 955-967.
[mdlxvii] Cherry, Neil J. "Schumann Resonances, a Plausible Biophysical Mechanism for the Human Health Effects of Solar/Geomagnetic Activity." *Natural Hazards*, vol. 26, no. 3, 2002, pp. 279-331.
[mdlxviii] Goldsby, Joshua R., et al. "Effects of Singing Bowl Sound Meditation on Mood, Tension, and Well-being: An Observational Study." *Journal of Evidence-Based Complementary & Alternative Medicine*, vol. 22, no. 3, 2017, pp. 416-421.
[mdlxix] Golden, Richard N., et al. "The Efficacy of Light Therapy in the Treatment of Mood Disorders: A Review and Meta-Analysis of the Evidence." *American Journal of Psychiatry*, vol. 162, no. 4, 2005, pp. 656-662.
[mdlxx] Wright, Kenneth P., et al. "Exposure to Natural Light Improves Sleep Patterns and Synchronises Circadian Rhythms in Humans." *Current Biology*, vol. 23, no. 16, 2013, pp. 1554-1558.
[mdlxxi] Röösli, Martin, et al. "Beyond the Moon—The Influence of Celestial Bodies on Human Beings." *Chronobiology International*, vol. 23, no. 6, 2006, pp. 1083-1097.
[mdlxxii] Ulrich, Roger S., et al. "Stress Recovery During Exposure to Natural and Urban Environments." *Journal of Environmental Psychology*, vol. 11, no. 3, 1991, pp. 201-230.
[mdlxxiii] Wayne, Peter M., et al. "Effect of Tai Chi on Cognitive Performance in Older Adults: Systematic Review and Meta-Analysis." *Journal of the American Geriatrics Society*, vol. 62, no. 1, 2014, pp. 25-39.
[mdlxxiv] Jahnke, Roger, et al. "A Comprehensive Review of Health Benefits of Qigong and Tai Chi." *American Journal of Health Promotion*, vol. 24, no. 6, 2010, pp. e1-e25.
[mdlxxv] Eccles, Nigel K. "A Critical Review of Randomised Controlled Trials of Static Magnets for Pain Relief." *Journal of Alternative and Complementary Medicine*, vol. 11, no. 3, 2005, pp. 495-509.

[mdlxxvi] Segal, Neil A., et al. "Magnetic Pulse Treatment for Knee Osteoarthritis: A Randomized, Double-Blind, Placebo-Controlled Study." *Archives of Physical Medicine and Rehabilitation*, vol. 82, no. 9, 2001, pp. 1203-1210.
[mdlxxvii] Markov, Marko S. "Magnetic Field Therapy: A Review." *Electromagnetic Biology and Medicine*, vol. 26, no. 1, 2007, pp. 1-23.
[mdlxxviii] Fritjof Capra, *The Web of Life: A New Scientific Understanding of Living Systems* (New York: Anchor Books, 1996)
[mdlxxix] Roger G. Barr and Simon B. Williams, *Electromagnetic Field Interactions with Structures: A Review of Ancient and Modern Applications*, Energy Science Journal, 2019
[mdlxxx] "Resonance and Ancient Structures: Applications for Modern Architecture," *Ancient Origins*, https://www.ancient-origins.net/resonance-ancient-architecture. Accessed September 6, 2024.
[mdlxxxi] S.A. Al-Tamimi et al., "Thermal Performance of Limestone in Building Materials," *Journal of Construction and Building Materials*, Saudi Arabia, 2015.
[mdlxxxii] Fathy, Hassan. *Architecture for the Poor*. Chicago: University of Chicago Press, 1973.
[mdlxxxiii] El Attar, Ammar. *Pyramid-Shaped Buildings in Sustainable Architecture: Optimizing Airflow and Solar Gain*. Cairo: Modern Science Press, 2016.
[mdlxxxiv] Dr. John K. West et al., *Aerodynamic Benefits of Pyramid Structures*, 2007
[mdlxxxv] The Eden Project, "Geothermal Energy at the Eden Project," 2020
[mdlxxxvi] "Energy from the Pyramids: Future Technologies Inspired by Ancient Civilisations," *Scientific American*, https://www.scientificamerican.com/energy-from-pyramids. Accessed September 6, 2024.
[mdlxxxvii] Mahdi, A. S., & Othman, N. (2018). Geometric influence of pyramid structures on photovoltaic efficiency. *Renewable Energy*, 115, 755-764.
[mdlxxxviii] S. Roundy et al., "Energy Harvesting Using Piezoelectric Materials," *Journal of Microelectromechanical Systems*, United States, 2004.
[mdlxxxix] "The Role of Ancient Materials in Modern Energy-Efficient Design," *National Geographic*, https://www.nationalgeographic.com/ancient-materials-energy-efficient-buildings. Accessed September 6, 2024.
[mdxc] Wei Zhang et al., *Optimizing Energy Transmission Using Earth's Natural Energy Pathways*, Renewable Energy Systems Journal, 2020.
[mdxci] Xiu Huang et al., *Gravitational Energy and Its Application in Modern Grids*, Energy Infrastructure Review, 2019
[mdxcii] Ian MacGregor and Sophia K. Davis, *Ancient Technologies and Modern Energy Storage: A Comparative Analysis of Earth Batteries and Renewable Grids*, Renewable Energy Journal, 2018.
[mdxciii] Golod, A. (2001). *The Power of Pyramids: Harnessing Energy and Health Benefits*. Moscow: Pyramid Energy Institute.
[mdxciv] Uvarov, V. (2012). *Pyramids: The Power Within*. St. Petersburg: Energy Research Institute.
[mdxcv] G. Hancock, *Fingerprints of the Gods* (London: Heinemann, 1995), p. 120.
[mdxcvi] Z. Hawass, *The Pyramids: The Secrets and Mysteries Revealed* (Cairo: The American University in Cairo Press, 2003), p. 89.
[mdxcvii] A. Dodson, *Pyramids of Ancient Egypt* (London: British Museum Press, 1990), p. 63.
[mdxcviii] "Conservation Efforts at Giza," UNESCO Report, 2017.
[mdxcix] R. S. Bianchi, *Daily Life in Ancient Egypt* (Oxford: Blackwell Publishers, 1999), p. 147.
[mdc] G. Goyon, *Pyramid Builders* (London: Routledge, 1996), p. 201.
[mdci] Z. Hawass, *The Pyramids: The Secrets and Mysteries Revealed* (Cairo: The American University in Cairo Press, 2003), p. 45.
[mdcii] M. Lehner, *The Complete Pyramids* (London: Thames & Hudson, 1997), p. 76.
[mdciii] "Looting of Antiquities: The Black Market Problem," UNESCO Report, 2019.
[mdciv] H. Carter, *The Tomb of Tutankhamun* (London: Cassell & Co., 1923), p. 92.
[mdcv] Z. Hawass, *Treasures of the Pyramids* (London: Thames & Hudson, 2005), p. 48.
[mdcvi] "Black Market for Egyptian Antiquities," UNESCO Report, 2020.
[mdcvii] A. Dodson, *Amulets of Ancient Egypt* (London: British Museum Press, 2002), p. 67.
[mdcviii] M. Lehner, *The Complete Pyramids* (London: Thames & Hudson, 1997), p. 105.
[mdcix] "Tutankhamun Quartzite Head Auction," *Christie's Auction House*, London, 2019.
[mdcx] "Egypt Demands Return of Tutankhamun Statue," *The Guardian*, 2019.
[mdcxi] J. Baines, *Fayum Portraits: Egyptian Funerary Art* (London: British Museum, 2004), p. 89.
[mdcxii] "UNESCO World Heritage Centre – Giza Pyramids Area," UNESCO, 2020.
[mdcxiii] Wilkinson, Richard H. *The Complete Gods and Goddesses of Ancient Egypt*. London: Thames & Hudson, 2003.
[mdcxiv] Hancock, Graham. *The Sign and the Seal: The Quest for the Lost Ark of the Covenant*. New York: Crown, 1992.
[mdcxv] Bauval, Robert, and Adrian Gilbert. *The Orion Mystery: Unlocking the Secrets of the Pyramids*. New York: Three Rivers Press, 1994.

mdcxvi von Däniken, Erich. *Chariots of the Gods? Unsolved Mysteries of the Past.* New York: G.P. Putnam's Sons, 1968.
mdcxvii Krupp, E. C. *Echoes of the Ancient Skies: The Astronomy of Lost Civilizations.* New York: Dover Publications, 1983.
mdcxviii Ruggles, Clive. *Ancient Astronomy: An Encyclopedia of Cosmologies and Myth.* Santa Barbara: ABC-CLIO, 2005.
mdcxix Krupp, E. C. *Echoes of the Ancient Skies: The Astronomy of Lost Civilizations.* New York: Dover Publications, 1983.
mdcxx Carter, Howard, and A.C. Mace. *The Tomb of Tutankhamun.* New York: Cooper Square Press, 2001.
mdcxxi Bond, Sarah. "The Curse of the Pharaohs: Examining the Science Behind the Myth." *Smithsonian Magazine*, February 2019.
mdcxxii *The Mummy* (1999), directed by Stephen Sommers, Universal Pictures.
mdcxxiii *The Mummy* (1932), directed by Karl Freund, Universal Pictures.
mdcxxiv *The Curse of King Tut's Tomb* (2006), directed by Russell Mulcahy, Hallmark Entertainment
mdcxxv *The Awakening* (1980), directed by Mike Newell, Warner Bros.
mdcxxvi *Raiders of the Lost Ark* (1981), directed by Steven Spielberg, Paramount Pictures.
mdcxxvii *The Pyramid* (2014), directed by Grégory Levasseur, 20th Century Fox.
mdcxxviii Heindel, Max. *The Rosicrucian Cosmo-Conception: Mystical Christianity.* Rosicrucian Fellowship, 1909.
mdcxxix McIntosh, Christopher. *The Rosicrucians: The History, Mythology, and Rituals of an Esoteric Order.* Weiser Books, 1997.
mdcxxx Godwin, Joscelyn. *The Real Rule of Four: The Unveiling of the Rosicrucian Mystery.* Disinfo, 2005.
mdcxxxi Roberts, Gareth. *The Mirror of Alchemy: Alchemical Ideas and the Rosicrucian Influence.* Thames & Hudson, 2007.
mdcxxxii Copenhaver, Brian P. *Hermetica: The Greek Corpus Hermeticum and the Latin Asclepius in a New English Translation, with Notes and Introduction.* Cambridge University Press, 1992.
mdcxxxiii Copenhaver, Brian P. *Hermetica: The Greek Corpus Hermeticum and the Latin Asclepius in a New English Translation, with Notes and Introduction.* Cambridge University Press, 1992
mdcxxxiv Fowden, Garth. *The Egyptian Hermes: A Historical Approach to the Late Pagan Mind.* Princeton University Press, 1993.
mdcxxxv Brown, D., *The Secret Archives of the Vatican*, 2010.
mdcxxxvi Taylor, J., "Vatican's Hidden Treasures: Speculation on Ancient Artifacts," *Mystery Files Journal*, 2018.
mdcxxxvii Hancock, G., *Fingerprints of the Gods: The Evidence of Earth's Lost Civilization*, 1995.
mdcxxxviii Blackwell, R., "Conspiracy Theories and the Vatican's Role in Hiding Ancient Technologies," *Global Mysteries Review*, 2022.
mdcxxxix M. Forte, *Virtual Archaeology: Re-creating Ancient Worlds* (Oxford: Oxford University Press, 2010), p. 52.
mdcxl S. D. Slye, *Digital Heritage: Preserving Cultural Treasures* (New York: Springer, 2018), p. 97.
mdcxli T. Gillings, *Archaeologies of the Digital Future* (London: Routledge, 2020), p. 145.
mdcxlii "Engaging the Public with AR and VR in Archaeology," *Journal of Cultural Heritage*, 2021.
mdcxliii P. Moscati, *Global Collaboration in Archaeology* (Rome: ICCROM, 2019), p. 12.
mdcxliv R. White, *Interdisciplinary Approaches in Digital Archaeology* (Cambridge: Cambridge University Press, 2021), p. 178.
mdcxlv Z. Hawass, *Secrets from the Sand: My Search for Egypt's Past* (Cairo: The American University in Cairo Press, 2003), p. 67.
mdcxlvi H. Carter, *The Tomb of Tutankhamun* (London: Cassell & Co., 1923), p. 35.
mdcxlvii F. Petrie, *The Pyramids and Temples of Gizeh* (London: Field & Tuer, 1883), p. 120.
mdcxlviii M. Lehner, *The Complete Pyramids* (London: Thames & Hudson, 1997), p. 201.
mdcxlix G. A. Reisner, *Myths and Legends of Ancient Egypt* (London: Harper & Brothers, 1920), p. 150.
mdcl Barbara Watterson, *Temples, Tombs, and Hieroglyphs: A Popular History of Ancient Egypt* (New York: HarperCollins, 1997).
mdcli Lehner, Mark. *The Complete Pyramids: Solving the Ancient Mysteries.* Thames & Hudson, 1997. Accessed September 10, 2024.
mdclii Coe, Michael. *The Maya.* Thames & Hudson, 1966 (multiple editions). Accessed September 10, 2024.
mdcliii Ian Shaw, *The Oxford History of Ancient Egypt* (Oxford: Oxford University Press, 2000).
mdcliv Richard H. Wilkinson, *The Complete Gods and Goddesses of Ancient Egypt* (London: Thames & Hudson, 2003).
mdclv Ray Bradbury, *Fahrenheit 451* (New York: Ballantine Books, 1953); "The Fireman," *Galaxy Science Fiction*, February 1951.

www.ingramcontent.com/pod-product-compliance
Lightning Source LLC
Chambersburg PA
CBHW020727160426
43192CB00006B/140